Library of
Davidson College

Publications of the Center for Hellenic Studies
Bernard M. W. Knox, General Editor

ONE AND MANY
IN PRESOCRATIC PHILOSOPHY

ONE AND MANY
IN PRESOCRATIC
PHILOSOPHY

Michael C. Stokes

Published by the Center for Hellenic Studies,
Washington, D.C.
Distributed by Harvard University Press,
Cambridge, Massachusetts
1971

© Copyright 1971 by the Trustees for Harvard University
The Center for Hellenic Studies, Washington, D.C.
All rights reserved
Distributed in Great Britain by Oxford University Press, London
Library of Congress Catalog Card Number 71-123570
SBN 674-63825-5
Printed in the United States of America

TO C.W.S.
IN MEMORIAM H.M.S.

PREFACE

The purposes of this book are explained in the first chapter, but a word is necessary about its scope. By "Presocratic" is meant no narrow chronological classification, for I have included Democritus, probably younger than Socrates but a continuator of the Presocratic tradition. By "philosophy" is meant the work of the "physicists," not excepting the denial of physics by the Eleatics. I have excluded from my purview—this work is long enough—the writings of Gorgias (with one short exception) and the other Sophists and have not discussed the famous argument that one thing, by virtue of possessing many attributes, is many things, an argument I am inclined to believe is sophistic in origin. I do not imply thus any definition of "philosophy," which is here merely the most convenient term to include both the Ionians and the Eleatics. The Pythagoreans are treated only so far as they seem to me relevant to the central themes of the book.

I do not claim to have read nearly all that other scholars have written on Presocratic philosophy; even if the spirit were willing, the flesh would not bear that burden. I hope (but hardly believe) that I have missed nothing of high importance prior to the autumn of 1967, since when I have made only minor additions to the bibliography. It may be observed that I have not mentioned in my notes everything I have read; nor, unfortunately, can I make the proud claim of A. E. Taylor ("with certain obvious exceptions") to have read from cover to cover every work to which I refer. My bibliography is designed solely to facilitate reference.

I take pleasure in gratefully acknowledging help from many sources. First, the University of Edinburgh not only for two grants towards the costs of preparation for publication, but also for giving me leave of absence in the year 1963–1964 to pursue my studies; second, the Center for Hellenic Studies for permitting me to do so in ideal surroundings. Also to several individual scholars: to Professor Gregory Vlastos for reading an early draft and giving me, then and since, much encouragement and constructive advice, and to Professor G. E. L. Owen for criticism given in several stimulating talks; to Mr. D. B. Robinson and Professor Richard Sorabji for reading drafts of the first chapter and saving me from an uncomfortably large number of obscurities and errors, and to Messrs. D. A. West and J. R. G. Wright for reading and helpfully criticizing other parts of the work; to Professor J. Herrero for help with an early draft and for much useful discussion, especially of Plato's *Parmenides*; to members of the Scottish and Northern English Associations for Ancient Philosophy for patiently listening to several papers and shedding light on mistakes in them. The Center's anonymous readers made several constructive suggestions, most of which I have thankfully adopted. For remaining errors, opacities, and heresies I bear sole responsibility. Since I have in many places expressed disagreement with my Cambridge teachers, I should like to take this opportunity of expressing my deep gratitude to them for their stimulating, thorough, and friendly teaching, which has been indeed the foundation of all my work. I only hope they will prove as understanding now as they did then.

Two more personal debts remain: the first, inadequately marked by my dedication, is to my parents, without whose indefatigable care and farsighted understanding I should never have begun this work; the second is to my wife, without whose manifold support I should never have finished it.

Edinburgh M.C.S.
February 1969

CONTENTS

I.	ARISTOTLE AND THE ANALYSIS OF UNITY AND PLURALITY	1
II.	THE MILESIANS	24
III.	XENOPHANES	66
IV.	HERACLITUS	86
V.	PARMENIDES AND MELISSUS	109
VI.	EMPEDOCLES	153
VII.	ZENO OF ELEA	175
VIII.	ONE-MANY PROBLEMS IN ATOMISM	218
IX.	MISCELLANEOUS PRESOCRATIC CONTEXTS	237
X.	CONCLUSION	249
	APPENDIX	253
	ABBREVIATIONS	258
	BIBLIOGRAPHY	259
	NOTES	267
	INDEX OF PASSAGES	341
	GENERAL INDEX	347

I

ARISTOTLE AND THE ANALYSIS OF UNITY AND PLURALITY

INTRODUCTORY

This work has two main themes: the precise place of the antithesis between "one" and "many" in early Greek (especially Ionian and Eleatic) thought, and the degree to which the early philosophers failed to recognize the distinctions between different kinds of unity and plurality. Both lead naturally to the examination of a number of fundamental doctrines and lines of argument, to see if they raise such questions as arise from one thing either being or becoming many and if they were affected by failure to perceive this particular kind of distinction. It would not be surprising if such a deficiency were the explanation of some mistakes of the Presocratics. It is not only the analytic school of the twentieth century which has accused its philosophical predecessors of ignoring important verbal distinctions; in this habit they were preceded by Plato and especially by Aristotle.

Aristotle indeed accuses some of his predecessors of making the particular kind of mistake which concerns us. In the second chapter of his *Physics* he digresses to deal with the Eleatic denial of the physical world and begins an argument (185b5ff) by asking in which of its many senses the Eleatics applied the term "one" to "what is." The implication is plain, that the Eleatics failed to make clear in what sense they were using the word. After examining various possible meanings of the Eleatic thesis, Aristotle rejects them all and passes on to "the later of the ancients," who he says[1] "were in a pother to avoid having the same thing at the same time one and many." The linguistic recommendations of these later thinkers were bizarre. Lycophron removed the word "is" from the language in its predicative use, aided by the Greek idiom which allows the omission of predicating "is" provided that the article is placed in a particular position. Some replaced such expressions as "is white" by other locutions such as "is-in-a-state-of-having-been-whitened" (λελεύκωται). These procedures, according to Aristotle, rested on the failure to realize that the words "one" or "is" had more than one sense. He proceeds (185b32ff) to point out two senses of the word "many" —obviously corresponding to two senses of "one." Finally he somewhat clouds the issue by importing his own favourite potential-actual distinction; a thing can be one potentially or actually, and (it is implied) if it is one potentially there is nothing to stop it being many in actuality. The most important point emerging from the whole account is that Aristotle believed some at least of his predecessors to have been misled by failure to see that "one" and "many" had more than one meaning. When he says they avoided making the same thing at the same time one and many, the reference to his own formulation of the law of contradiction is obvious: according to that law one cannot predicate of the same subject contraries at the same time *and in the same respect* (*Metaphysics* 1005b19f); this last qualification was ignored by the thinkers here discussed.

In this connection attention has recently been drawn to instances of a similar neglect by the Eleatics.[2] Zeno of Elea, for example, argues in support of the proposition that what is, is one, by attempting to refute the proposition that things are many. He nowhere, so far as I can see, specifies the kind of plurality or the sense of "many" with which he is concerned, but simply assumes that to call reality "many" is automatically to contradict someone who calls it "one." He makes the further tacit assumption that there is no possible middle way; not only can one not combine the views that Being is one and that Being is many, but one cannot evade the choice between them. As a general interpretation of Zeno this is highly controversial and would not appeal to all recent investigators.[3] But there is one particular place in his argumentation where Zeno has recently, and surely with justice, been convicted of arguing on the basis that plurality excludes unity. On the basis of infinite divisibility he suggests that nothing will be one; the reason is clearly that each "one" will be divisible, and therefore "many": plurality, Zeno assumes, excludes unity. It will be appropriate in a later chapter to support this explanation of Zeno in detail. A similar argument is used by Gorgias.[4] What needs emphasis here is merely that to treat "one" and "many" as simply incompatible if predicated of the same subject at the same time is either to be ignorant of the polysemy of these words, or to deny it, or to ignore its relevance to the argument. One must admit that to make a mistake in one argument is not necessarily to repeat it in others; but we are nevertheless justified in searching for other examples of it.

SOME SEMANTIC CONSIDERATIONS

These remarks presuppose an affirmative answer to questions which need to be brought into the open. Is it legitimate to talk of polysemy in general and, if so, are the words "one" and "many" genuine examples? This is not the place for a general discussion of the theory of meaning. But it is necessary to make clear to readers with even a passing interest in linguistics or in the philosophy of language exactly what is being attempted here.

A recent and distinguished contribution to semantics,[5] binding "meaning" more firmly than usual to context and treating various meaning-relations as fundamental, has an interesting corollary on polysemy, or multiple meaning. Difference in "sense" "will be attributable to a variety of things; sometimes to a clear difference of application, sometimes to a difference in the lexical subsystems to which the form in question belongs (though these subsystems may not be everywhere valid)." Such difference "is not a term that enters into the description of the language" but is convenient for talk about the native speaker's semantic intuitions. When native speakers hesitate about whether a given form has more than one "sense," their hesitation will be "grounded in their use of the form in a variety of different contexts."

Much of this seems eminently sound, though difference of lexical subsystem and of application may be hard to separate, but the example chosen to illustrate it requires brief examination. "One might suppose, for instance, that the native speaker of Classical Latin would have been in some doubt as to whether *altus* had one or two 'senses' (because of its two different antonyms)."[6] Certain conditions attaching to this kind of hesitation are relevant to the present discussion. The first is that before any native speaker hesitates over any such question, the question must first have occurred to him. This seems obvious, but it is none the less important. For to ask the question whether a word has more than one sense or not presupposes a fairly high degree of self-consciousness in the use of language. It presupposes a degree of reflection on linguistic phenomena which we would certainly not expect of the primitive and need not necessarily expect of the early Greeks, who retained, in spite of their extraordinarily rapid advance, many traces of primitive habits of mind. One of these was the supposition that one word designated, stood for, or was attached to one object. The application of the human reason to itself and its own tools appears (in Greece at least) to have developed only gradually. Another condition attaching to the asking of such a question is that the difference between the contexts in which a word is applied should also have occurred to the questioner. The example given above is a fairly easy one, which might be expected to occur to a not specially gifted questioner. But there are others which require considerable analytical gifts to ferret out and understand. Thus Plato (in the *Sophist*) appears to have been the first to point out two (at least) of the different types of context in which the locution "is not" can occur. It is not a rule but is nevertheless a frequent phenomenon that the more common and seemingly transparent an expression, the more difficult it is to appreciate the variety of its applications. When we speak of "a clear difference of application" we must be careful about the word "clear"; what is extremely obscure to the ordinary user of a language may become clear to a philosopher reflecting on arguments employing the term(s) concerned and may only subsequently pass into the common stock of educated linguistic thinking.

In such cases it is possible for a speaker ignorant (for chronological or other reason) of the philosopher's work to imagine that there is no difference between one kind of application and the other(s), and in consequence either to speak vaguely or to argue incorrectly. He might think that there was no doubt of his meaning in a given verbal context when further analysis showed that doubt was justified. An example would be the Eleatic statement to the effect that what is, is one, which Aristotelian analysis showed to be dangerously ambiguous. A speaker might, alternatively, make a mistaken assimilation of one type of application to another, being misled by the use of the same form in each, and produce in consequence an invalid argument. No theory of semantics is complete which does not allow for equivocation. An example of such an argument is not far to seek; it is well known that Plato's *Euthydemus* is a storehouse of them. One is to be found, for instance, in Dionysodorus' argument (283d); ἐπεὶ βούλεσθε αὐτὸν ὃς νῦν ἐστὶν μηκέτι εἶναι, βούλεσθε αὐτόν, ὡς ἔοικεν, ἀπολωλέναι. Here the premiss could mean either "you wish him no longer to be the kind of man he is" or "you wish him no longer to be who he now is" or "you wish him no longer to be a presently existing man"; the second and/or third meanings carry for Dionysodorus the implication that "you wish him to be destroyed," and Socrates is constrained to accept this implication; but Socrates is well aware that he (Socrates) meant the first construction to be put on his original words. In normal parlance the sentence of Socrates has three "meanings" or "senses," and Dionysodorus is "playing" or "equivocating" on this ambiguity. If one wishes to talk in terms of types of application or of context, one can explain this phenomenon very simply by saying that Dionysodorus assimilates one type of context in which Socrates' sentence could be used to another in which it would be intelligible, though (as it happens) foolish. One application of Socrates' words is assimilated illegitimately to another. For the interpretation of such arguments, whether like this one they are obvious frauds or whether they are more subtly wrong, it does not seem to matter very much whether the terminology of senses or of different types of application be used. Often, as Professor John Lyons implies, the term "sense" is convenient.

But there is a further complication. It is possible to think of arguments which appear to some readers at least to depend on verbal ambiguity of a kind different only in degree from the absurdities of a Dionysodorus but which their authors would argue were not genuine examples of equivocation. Such may be the well-known argument which brings to a close the first book of Plato's *Republic*.[7] Socrates there first convinces the moral sceptic Thrasymachus that the function of the soul is to live, that in living well it is fulfilling its ἀρετή, and that its ἀρετή is justice. He then goes on to argue that the just man will live well and *therefore* be happy and prosperous; to the modern reader the equivocation on two senses of "live well" seems intolerable. But Plato certainly believed that happiness was inevitable if one lived rightly, that to "live well" in the sense "lead a virtuous life" was in fact to "live well" in the sense of "enjoy happiness." Since he neither says nor denies that the argument is analytic, he might remain unmoved by the explanation that it rested on the synthetic truth (if it is a truth) which he had set out to prove. In the terms we shall be using here, Plato assimilates one use of the locution "live well" to another, not necessarily in ignorance that one kind of context is different from another, but possibly in the belief that the differences are not relevant. Not relevant, that is, in this particular case—for Plato knew full well the dangers of equivocation in many other cases, even if he never enunciated a general rule against it. In another convenient phrase, Plato did not see that there were here two "different senses" of "live well," because he was misled by his own belief that to live well in one sense was in fact to live well in the other; he therefore had no pressing need to distinguish the two senses which his opponents ought to have distinguished in order to refute him. This situation of Plato's should be carefully distinguished from that of someone insufficiently trained in reasoning to realize at all that the existence of two senses of an expression constitutes a pitfall.

It is not always clear what kind or degree of difference between two types of application can legitimately be said to suffice for the setting up of two or more different senses. Something must inevitably be left here to what Lyons calls the native speaker's intuition; something perhaps to an Englishman's intuitions concerning the word "sense." But we are not thrown back on this last resort immediately. If we can find a single definition of our word which is not falsified by any of its uses in any of the kinds of context in which it is used, then it is prima facie reasonable to suppose that we have to do with a single-sense or univocal word. But this is not ultimately *necessary*. A word may be of a very general kind, admit of a very general definition, and have a wide "central" meaning, and yet be applied in such widely differing contexts that it is easiest to speak in terms of "senses." "Central" meaning may be defined a little more sharply by contrasting it with "focal" meaning.

Some words may be used in ways which can only be defined *with reference to* one focal usage; as Aristotle, at some periods, thought that "being" could be studied, known, and eventually defined only with reference to the being of a substance;[8] the "being" of a quality was different from the being of a substance; the former was owed to the latter: where an individual substance could exist by itself, a quality cannot. An easier example is that of "medical," expounded in Aristotle's *Eudemian Ethics*.[9] Aristotle there distinguishes univocal words ($\kappa\alpha\theta$' $\ddot{\epsilon}\nu$) from species of a single genus on the one hand and simple homonymy on the other. "Medical," he says, can be applied to a mind, a body, a tool, and an operation. But the proper (or "focal") sense is the primary one, the one whose definition is implicit in the definition of each; a medical man is not defined with reference to an implicit definition of a medical instrument, but the medical instrument is defined with reference to the doctor. Aristotle continues with a warning about "friendship" which may be taken to imply that one should be careful not to exclude the instrument from the class of things to which "medical" is applicable on the grounds that when "medical" is so applied its definition is different from that of "medical" as applied to man.

Thus, where we have "*focal*" meaning we have logical priority on the one hand and logical dependence on the other. But in cases of "*central*" meaning the outlying senses are merely varieties of application of the central one; no single application is logically prior to all the others. In cases of "focal" meaning it is one *application* that domineers over all the others; in cases of "central" meaning the centre is occupied not by a particular application but by a general notion waiting to be applied.

Two senses may be postulated in at least two different kinds of case. In one, the different kinds of context in which the word is usable have nothing in common that can be fairly described by a single definition.[10] In the second, the definition is so general that different areas of application are best separated out as "senses." There are indeed cases where "in some sense" and "in some respect" are not usefully to be distinguished. A caveat may here be entered from the historian's point of view: it is possible for a thinker to say "in some respect," where we should prefer to say "in some sense," when he has not thought out all the distinctions elaborated here, and in particular without even having the notion of difference of "sense" at all; even if the thinker concerned has the notion of homonymy, he need not have dreamt that it was applicable to the word whose application he is considering.

Cases where "in some sense" and "in some respect" are not usefully distinguishable may be dealt with by a more overtly logical approach. But it is doubtful whether one can eliminate subjectivity altogether; it may be doubted whether this approach is any more objective in the final analysis than the strictly linguistic. Suppose, for instance, one determines to talk of two senses of an epithet E when (and only when) it is employed in two different types of context in such a way that, if the subject of which it is predicated in each kind of context were the same, it would be illegitimate to deduce from the truth of the sentence "S is E" in one context that it was also true in the other; and in such a way that, if a further proposition p followed from the premiss "S is E" in one type of context (with or without the addition of another constant premiss), it would be illegitimate to draw the same conclusion p from the truth of "S is E" in the other type of context: even here subjective judgement enters by the back door. Trouble might arise in precisely those cases which are likely to interest the philosopher, namely those in which he might disagree either with the layman or with his colleague. If either chooses to dispute the philosopher's claim to have detected equivocation, he will surely be compelled to fall back on his argument that there is a crucial difference between the kinds of context appropriate to the word in question; and, if it is denied that the difference is crucial, then there will be little that the philosopher can do except exercise his powers of persuasion to enforce his personal judgement.

ARISTOTELIAN ANALYSES

PRELIMINARIES

Semantic problems become more difficult when we are confronted with complicated words in an alien language. When the language is two and a half millennia old and survives only in a much altered form, and when the culture which used the old form is so different from our own as was that of early Greece, then our difficulties are multiplied. But we are fortunate in having available the analyses of unity and plurality in Aristotle. Aristotle at least spoke Greek and had therefore a native speaker's intuition for the contexts in which a Greek could use ἕν and related words. He was also in important respects an "ordinary language" philosopher.[11] The term "one" and its relations "unity," "unite," "unified," etc. have not, so far as I can discover, been subjected to such detailed study in modern times as they were by Aristotle, particularly in his *Metaphysics*. The modern English-speaking school of "ordinary language" philosophers has not attempted a full-scale analysis of "one" and "many." But there have been important advances,[12] and Aristotle's pioneering efforts must be used critically. There are places where his own philosophical habits led him astray. Aristotle's mistakes are nearly always in themselves illuminating, but the task of disentangling the specifically Aristotelian from the generally Greek or more generally occidental is a delicate one. We should bear in mind the probability that there was dispute even in the Platonic Academy over the analysis of unity.[13]

Aristotle had good philosophical reason to examine the use of the words "one" and "many" with some care. As a relatively young man he wrote a book entitled "Concerning Opposites," in which every opposition between terms was "reduced" in some way to the opposition between the terms "one" and "many."[14] Neither he nor any of his commentators tells us exactly how the contraries were reduced to this single opposition, but a hint is offered at *Metaphysics* 1054a29ff. Aristotle speaks there as if there were two columns, one headed by "one" and the other by "many"; in the "one" column were "the same," "similar," and "equal," while "the different" and "dissimilar" and "unequal" were in the "many" column. To this list Syrianos (*in Metaphysica* 61.12ff) adds "straight" for the "one" column and offers a value judgement of the superiority of the "one" column, a value judgement which may or may not go back to Aristotle himself.[15] At *Metaphysics* 1003b35ff, "same," "like," and others are (by implication) εἴδη τοῦ ἑνός. At *Metaphysics* 1004b27ff, rest is said to belong to unity, and movement (including change) to plurality. Aristotle himself adds an "etc." to the list, and Alexander speaks in this connection of "almost all the opposites." At *Metaphysics* 1061a10ff, likeness/unlikeness are associated with one/many as the primary differentiations of being, without pressing the point, and in any case, it is added, "one" and "being" are convertible. That "one," "the same," and "similar" were closely related for Aristotle could be deduced in any case from the parallelism between parts of the chapters devoted to these concepts in Aristotle's "dictionary" of the fifth book of the *Metaphysics*. Since opposition is for Aristotle a species of difference, and "different," being opposed to "same" and "similar," is associable with "many" as the opposite of "one," Aristotle plausibly held "one" and "many" to be logically prior to the other opposites.

UNITY AND BEING

There is another and more important reason why Aristotle should set much store by the analysis of unity. He often refers to the intimate connection of unity with being as a predicate predicable in each category. The same class of predicates includes "good" and "same." He maintains, for example, that what it is for a place to exist is different from what it is for a quality or substance to exist. "Lexicographers," as Owen writes,[16] "manage to resist the suggestion" that "good" and "same" have different senses; presumably they regard these as merely types of areas of application, without sufficient difference to warrant the setting up of separate senses. There is enough in common between these applications for lexicographers to find a "central" definition of, for example, "same" which will not exclude any of them. Indeed subjectivity envelops the question how far words so dependent on the context for their force can be called homonymous. Aristotle does not find acceptable an unrestricted number of senses of "being,"[17] even though an unrestricted number of things exist. He does not make clear why he limits himself to the particular categories chosen by him, and their number and nomenclature are alike elastic. Similar questions of limitation arise where "one" is concerned.

But before tackling these we must digress for a moment and mention a very important factor which Aristotle does not explicitly take into account, although he occasionally speaks as if he were half aware of it. We do not usually in English say that A, B, and C are "one" simpliciter: we say either (asserting identity or agreement) "A is one with B," or "A and B are one *something*"; as J. L. Austin put it,[18] "one" is a substantive-hungry word. For example, the British Motor Corporation manufactured in 1967 a series of types of car called the Austin, Morris, Wolseley, or Riley 1100, with broadly similar bodies and engines but differing in details such as the possession of single or twin carburettors, different shapes of radiator grille, and so forth. Under these circumstances we could reasonably say "All the BMC 1100 models are virtually one"— but we could not say this without supplying after "one" the nearest substantive. What we mean is that the BMC 1100 models are virtually one *model*. The saying would be clearer if the speaker were to supply his own substantive (using a synonym to avoid repetition): "All the BMC 1100 models are virtually one car." If, after saying that X and Y are "one," I then stop, you will rightly ask, in unfeigned ignorance, "One what?" If, however, I were to say "X and Y are a unity," this particular question could gain no foothold. "Unity," itself a substantive, is not substantive-hungry—at least not in the same way. When Heraclitus says of day and night that they are "one," we are correct in asking immediately "One what?" and in expecting a substantive as the answer. Furthermore, the production of the answer "One thing" does not help, since the word "thing" is as vague and homonymous as the word "one." But the availability in English of the more abstract "unity" raises other questions. If we render Heraclitus' remark about day and night, "for they are a unity," one impertinent question is silenced, but others spring up, to ask either "A unified what?" or "A unity in what sense, or of what type?" Whatever one thinks of it, this use of the abstract was not available to the ancient Greeks, who had only εἶς in its various forms. It is important to remember that Aristotle in his analyses is sometimes supplying answers to the question "What kind or sense of 'unity'?" and sometimes suggesting answers to the question "One what?" or at least to the question what classes there are of answers to the question "One what?" I know of no explicit remark enabling us to say for sure that Aristotle was fully conscious of such difference as there is between "What kind of unity?" and the two latter questions.[19]

Thus we habitually talk of one *something*. And here the same problems arise as in the limitation of the senses of "being." When we talk of "one man" we divide him off mentally from his surroundings in time or space by different criteria from those distinguishing one crab, or one colour, from another member of the same class. The same goes for plurality; for "one" is under suspicion of being what Austin termed a "trouser-word";[20] we normally use the word "one" to deny a plurality, and the sorts of plurality evidently have much say in the decision how many sorts of "one" there are. When we talk of men, many men, or several men, we distinguish them from each other by criteria different from those of a fisherman counting crabs, or of a child trying to count the colours in the rainbow. Again it is not clear why one should stop at distinctions of substance and quality and place and so forth, or why the number of such categories should be small. It seems that this division of senses of "one" in Aristotle is at least to some extent arbitrary and, though based on cool analysis of common language, would not necessarily meet the approval of other users of language. Philosophically it was important to Aristotle to investigate the class of trans-category predicates because their nature was the foundation, at least in Aristotle's early period, of several refutations of the Academy in metaphysics and ethics. The status of being and unity as predicates or "disjunctive sets of predicates"[21] is important in Aristotle's riposte to Plato's view of them as (in Aristotle's terminology) substances.

The analysis of being into different senses according to category was made by Aristotle into the scaffolding for an apparently contradictory account of being in the *Metaphysics*. In the earlier works, the dissection of senses is given as the reason for denying a single science of being. But the central books of the *Metaphysics* constitute an inquiry into "first philosophy," concerned with being as being. This is done by adopting the particular science of substance (universal because primary) as the general science of being.[22] The question arises, what then happens to the account of "one" as following "being" through all the categories? It appears that it too was maintained, in a form altered in much the same way. That is to say that there remains a unity in each category, but each is defined and known by reference to the unity in one particular category, possibly (though I believe Aristotle is not explicit) substance. Hence there can after all be a study of τὸ ἓν ᾗ ἕν, to be located perhaps in the study of unity of substance. This is not to reject the idea that τὸ ἓν πολλαχῶς λέγεται, but to build upon it. What it fails to do is to draw attention to the possibility of there being a single central meaning of "one," a single definition which will cover its uses in all categories. I do not believe that Aristotle ever fully realized this possibility. But there is at least one passage where he seems to begin saying something of the kind, without every carrying the suggestion through. Before settling down to a somewhat more consecutive treatment of Aristotle's analysis in the *Metaphysics*, in the midst of which this "central" meaning is for a moment adumbrated, it is worth while to see what Aristotle makes of it.

CENTRAL MEANING

We find Aristotle at *Metaphysics* 1052a34 summing up, and forging a transition to a new approach. λέγεται μὲν οὖν τὸ ἓν τοσαυταχῶς, he says, and after a list adds "but all these things are one in virtue of indivisibility either of movement or of thought or of definition." He then proceeds to explain himself as follows: δεῖ δὲ κατανοεῖν ὅτι οὐχ ὡσαύτως ληπτέον λέγεσθαι ποῖά τε ἓν λέγεται, καὶ τί ἐστι τὸ ἑνὶ εἶναι καὶ τίς αὐτοῦ λόγος. λέγεται μὲν γὰρ τὸ ἓν τοσαυταχῶς, καὶ ἕκαστον ἔσται ἓν [τούτων] ᾧ ἂν ὑπάρχῃ τις τούτων τῶν τρόπων· τὸ δὲ ἑνὶ εἶναι ὁτὲ μὲν τούτων τινὶ ἔσται, ὁτὲ δὲ ἄλλῳ ὃ καὶ μᾶλλον ἐγγὺς τῷ ὀνόματί ἐστι, τῇ δυνάμει δ' ἐκεῖνα, ὥσπερ καὶ περὶ . . . He then offers the example of the words "fire" and "element," pointing out that fire is in a sense an element (in Greek "an" is omitted), but in a sense not, for to be fire is not the same thing as to be (an) element. If we think, he says, of the facts and the nature of the case, fire *is* (an) element, but predication of the *word* "element" signifies, as predication of "fire" does not, that something *has* the subject for an ultimate ingredient. The result, as applied to the term "one," is summarized in the words τὸ ἑνὶ εἶναι τὸ ἀδιαιρέτῳ ἐστὶν εἶναι... Unity is indivisibility (1052b16).

As Ross says in commenting on this passage, Aristotle "introduces the distinction expressed in modern logic as that between extension and intension, or denotation and connotation." One might add "meaning and reference" to this list.[23] It appears on the face of it that there is an example here of a state of affairs envisaged in the preceding section of this chapter; for a number of different types of application Aristotle produces a single definition expressing a "central" meaning not falsified by any of those applications. Things are called "one" in species, genus, or simply in kind, just because one cannot divide or distinguish the kind of one from the kind of the other. Things are called one by continuity because one cannot use a gap, whether of absolute emptiness or merely of something different, to distinguish more than one thing in the whole. There are various ways in which things can be distinguished from each other; if two of them cannot in one way be distinguished, then so far as that way is concerned they are one thing. In many contexts in English, especially where a unity has more than one member, the word "indistinguishable" might replace the word "one." So far Aristotle's analysis is a characteristic "central meaning" analysis. But, even if it remained so throughout the passage and if it proved correct, we should still deem it a matter of subjective judgement whether the applications of the word "one" are sufficiently distinct to talk about "senses," and Aristotle himself still uses the expression πολλαχῶς λέγεται of the term "one."[24] Further, whether or not one should, strictly, talk about "senses" of "one," the possibility obviously arises of equivocation between two or more of its applications. If one argues or assumes that, because things are uniform, therefore they are one by continuity, he is evidently guilty of equivocation. In this context it is purely a matter of personal judgement and of convenience whether one continues to talk of "types of application" or of "senses." In this work I shall continue to talk about senses, without being unaware that there may be a single definition which covers them all.

But to the statement quoted above, τὸ ἑνὶ εἶναι τὸ ἀδιαιρέτῳ ἐστὶν εἶναι, Aristotle adds the following: ὅπερ τόδε ὄντι καὶ ἰδίᾳ χωριστῷ ἢ τόπῳ ἢ εἴδει ἢ διανοίᾳ, ἢ καὶ τὸ ὅλῳ καὶ ἀδιαιρέτῳ, μάλιστα δέ τὸ μέτρῳ εἶναι πρώτῳ ἑκάστου γένους καὶ κυριώτατα τοῦ ποσοῦ· ἐντεῦθεν γὰρ ἐπὶ τὰ ἄλλα ἐλήλυθεν. Here the essentially *focal* (as opposed to "central") mode of Aristotle's thought about unity is re-established. The meaning of "one," in cases where it signifies "individually separable" in place, form, or thought, is derivable from its use to denote the primary measure of each kind, and most properly of quantity. This appears to chime well with "focal" meaning, with the focus here on quantity.[25] (It should not be forgotten that in his "dictionary" Aristotle talks at 1016b17ff of the essence of "one" being ἀρχῇ τινὶ τοῦ ἀριθμοῦ εἶναι, which he explains as "being the first measure" of number.)

Aristotle explains the indivisible by equating it with the individual and that which can be marked off as a particular from other things[26] either in place, kind, or thought. Another kind of indivisibility, he goes on to explain, is that of something *whole* and indivisible. This seems repetitive and obscure; but it is worth recalling that one can speak *either* of a single thing as "one" *or* of a unity formed by (or subsisting between) more than one thing. Aristotle is perhaps alluding to this dual possibility: "one" is predicated of a single thing when it is indivisible in the sense that it is separate from other things, occupying its own place, or being of a different kind from its neighbours, or being distinguishable in thought from its neighbours (and when no separation of the kind concerned is possible within it); "one" is also predicated of many such singles when they form a whole in some sense or respect indivisible.

TYPES OF APPLICATION

We must stop generalizing and look at the two main treatments of "one" in the *Metaphysics*. The first in our order of the books, and probably also the earlier in composition,[27] is that of *Metaphysics Δ*, the later and more subtle is that of the tenth book, *Metaphysics I*. We need not confine ourselves to these two, for they can be eked out with many incidental discussions of varying length elsewhere in the Aristotelian corpus; but these are our major sources, and it is necessary to choose one of them to follow through, not without digressions. The more suitable is *I*, which, though less full, is better ordered and more explicit at some important points.

At the beginning of the first chapter of his tenth book, then, Aristotle states that "one" πολλαχῶς λέγεται. Of the many "ways" or "senses" he proposes to ignore the ways in which things can be one per accidens, and for the moment we may follow suit. Aristotle then picks out four main kinds of unity, namely unity of continuity, wholeness, number, and form, and subjoins a brief analysis to each. We may follow his order.

τό τε γὰρ συνεχὲς (Aristotle begins, 1052a19) ἢ ἁπλῶς ἢ μάλιστά γε τὸ φύσει καὶ μὴ ἁφῇ μηδὲ δεσμῷ (καὶ τούτων μᾶλλον ἓν καὶ πρότερον οὗ ἀδιαιρετωτέρα ἡ κίνησις καὶ μᾶλλον ἁπλῆ). A thing or things, Aristotle means, may be described as one thing if there is an absence of gaps between the parts or between the individual things. The most obviously deserving of the name of "one" is the continuous by nature; less truly or less clearly one are things continuous merely by accidental contact or because they are tied. This allows (with the caveat ἢ μάλιστά γε) the *possibility* of referring to the continuity of what is merely in contact or tied, saying only that this is at best a strained usage and not rejecting it outright. It therefore represents less strict doctrine than that of Δ (1015b36ff), where the ascription of "one" to things merely in contact or glued is expressly rejected. The example there given is that of two pieces of wood laid so as to be in contact. Of this Aristotle says flatly, "You will not call them one piece of wood, one body or a continuous anything else" (εἰ γὰρ θείης ἁπτόμενα ἀλλήλων ξύλα, οὐ φήσεις ταῦτα εἶναι ἓν οὔτε ξύλον οὔτε σῶμα οὔτ' ἄλλο συνεχὲς οὐδέν). It must be confessed that mere contact—whether temporary, as between foot and football, or more lasting, as between two books side by side on a shelf—is unlikely to entitle the two things to be called one in English, and I know of no example in ordinary Classical Greek where the word "one" is so applied. It would appear that mere contact, artificial and/or temporary, is normally insufficient to amount to unity for the English and the Greek alike.[28] It is at least plausible to suppose that Aristotle's early strictness is realistic analysis of ordinary language (as implied by his use of the generalizing second person singular φήσεις) and that his later laxness in this matter is due to a philosophical intuition that some kind of continuity, and therefore some degree of connection amounting to unity, *is* conferred by even casual contact. Strictly, the later view could be justified; but the earlier is more in accord with the normal everyday use of language.[29] The possibility needs to be borne in mind that Aristotle, for all his sharpness of expression in this sentence from *Metaphysics Δ*, was not sure just how far the word "one" could at a pinch be stretched by an unphilosophical Greek.

Aristotle's analysis of continuity is not always conducted on the same lines as in this passage of the *Metaphysics*, but it is doubtful if the better analysis at *Physics* E 3 produces any difference in his analysis of unity. The *Metaphysics* tends to define continuity in terms of unity of movement, but in this chapter of the *Physics* it is worked out by contrast and comparison with such notions as "together," "in contact," and so on. The continuous here, as is implied in *Metaphysics Δ*, is a species of that which is in contact; what distinguishes the continuous from the merely contiguous is the unity of the touching extremities. With this kind of definition in mind, Aristotle proceeds (*Physics* 227a14f) to say that, as the Oxford translators put it, " continuity belongs to things that naturally in virtue of their mutual contact form a unity." But while apparently excluding a unity of *mere* contact, Aristotle admits it by the back door; for in the very next sentence he admits that "in whatever way that which holds them together is one, so too will the whole be one, e.g., by a rivet or glue or *contact* or organic union" (Oxford translation, italics mine).

This clearly implies the acceptance of a kind of unity resulting from mere contact, without the touching extremities actually coinciding, and without the proviso that the contact must be natural and stable. Whether mere contact conferred unity and, if so, whether that unity was unity by continuity seem to have been doubtful points to a thoughtful Greek, however he chose to define continuity; but Aristotle leaves little doubt that mere contact confers unity in a more strained sense. Incidentally, if ἕν in Greek could be used where we in English are compelled to use the expression "a unity," one can see better why the analysis of *Metaphysics* Δ should not always have seemed as cast-iron as when it was written. For whereas two pieces of wood laid together are not "one" *anything*, except "one pair," they could perhaps be described momentarily as "a unity," being united by contiguity, and in any case possessed of some degree of uniformity. But such a locution in such a context remains dubious and difficult. Easier, as I think Aristotle would agree, is to call a river whose course is known throughout "one river," whereas one would not make a "unity" of two watercourses with no known link and an apparent gap between them.

Be it observed in passing that "continuous," like "one," cuts across the categories. We can describe a substance as a unity in this sense ("The Brahmaputra is one continuous river") or we can so describe a colour (". . . making the green one red")[30] or speak of one (continuous) period of residence in America, as opposed to two (with necessarily a *temporal* gap between them).

The second type or sense of unity to be considered is that of the whole.[31] As Aristotle puts it at *Metaphysics* I 1, in the sentence following that previously quoted (1052a22ff), ἔτι τοιοῦτον καὶ μᾶλλον τὸ ὅλον καὶ ἔχον τινὰ μορφὴν καὶ εἶδος, μάλιστα δ' εἴ τι φύσει τοιοῦτον καὶ μὴ βίᾳ, ὥσπερ ὅσα κόλλῃ ἢ γόμφῳ ἢ συνδέσμῳ, ἀλλὰ ἔχει ἐν αὑτῷ τὸ αἴτιον αὐτῷ τοῦ συνεχὲς εἶναι. He goes on to add: τοιοῦτον δὲ τῷ μίαν τὴν κίνησιν εἶναι καὶ ἀδιαίρετον τόπῳ καὶ χρόνῳ, ὥστε φανερόν, εἴ τι φύσει κινήσεως ἀρχὴν ἔχει τῆς πρώτης τὴν πρώτην, οἷον λέγω φορᾶς κυκλοφορίαν, ὅτι τοῦτο πρῶτον μέγεθος ἕν. This concept of the unity of a whole is clearly related to that by continuity, and Aristotle marks the two off together from the other pair mentioned in this chapter. But in *Metaphysics* Δ the remarks about "the whole" do not occur till much later in the discussion (1016b11ff): ἔτι δ' ἔστι μὲν ὡς ὁτιοῦν ἕν φαμεν εἶναι ἂν ᾖ ποσὸν καὶ συνεχές, ἔστι δ' ὡς οὔ, ἂν μή τι ὅλον ᾖ, τοῦτο δ' ἂν μὴ τὸ εἶδος ἔχῃ ἕν· οἷον οὐκ ἂν φαῖμεν ὁμοίως ἓν ἰδόντες ὁπωσοῦν τὰ μέρη συγκείμενα τοῦ ὑποδήματος, ἐὰν μὴ διὰ τὴν συνέχειαν, ἀλλ' ἐὰν οὕτως ὥστε ὑπόδημα εἶναι καὶ εἶδός τι ἔχειν ἤδη ἕν· διὸ καὶ ἡ τοῦ κύκλου μάλιστα μία τῶν γραμμῶν, ὅτι ὅλη καὶ τέλειός ἐστιν.

The doctrine of these passages, despite the differences of wording, is substantially the same. There is a sense of "one," as *Metaphysics I* has it, in which we refuse to call a thing "one" or "a unity" unless it has not mere spatial continuity to commend it but also a single (and definite) form. If we saw the parts of a shoe lying or even fastened together higgledy-piggledy, we should allow them only that degree of unity attributable to the continuous (here defined without reference to coincident extremities), but, if they were so arranged as to be a shoe and to have the single form of a shoe, then they could be called "a unity" in the sense of "a whole."[32] Not every continuum, therefore, constitutes a whole, and Aristotle accordingly makes the whole, with a certain shape and form, a higher and stricter type of unity than the merely continuous.

Here the substantive-hunger of "one" makes itself felt again; the random heap (σωρός) is to ordinary speakers as much "one heap" as the shoe is "one shoe." If he acknowledged that a heap could exist, Aristotle should accordingly have accepted this point (since "one," as Aristotle has it, *follows* "being"). But he did not accept it;[33] and, if presented with it, he might have replied[34] that a heap was not an οὐσία, since it was matter without form, and as its title to "being" was doubtful so was its claim to "one." One heap has the property of being analysable, or divisible by mere physical separation, into any number of heaps, but one man is not divisible into any plural number of men. This seems to have been what A. E. Taylor was driving at when he remarked, "we should find it much harder to decide whether what we perceive as a mere inorganic mass is one or many, and harder still to give reasons for our decision in a particular case."[35] If we insist despite this on recognizing with ordinary language that one heap can be accorded existence *qua* one heap, then we shall have to admit that Aristotle is here expounding what in English we should call "a unity" rather than "one."

Even less hesitation, one gathers, could attach to the labelling as "one" of a thing which was not merely a whole, but naturally so.[36] It may be doubted here whether Aristotle is being Aristotelian or is sticking to normal usage, and the doubt is not lessened by his continuation on unity of motion. I am not sure whether I should call a hedgehog more easily and more obviously "one" or "a unity" than a shoe, and the parts or organs of a body are in the long run as dissoluble as the parts of a shoe; but perhaps the common English use of the term "an organic whole" is a symptom of a general tendency to treat the natural whole as the paradigm of wholes in general. If we ask what constitutes a form of the sort which confers this kind of unity, we run into hot water, but clearly Aristotle's use of the term "form" is to some degree teleological. English also, as A. E. Taylor once pointed out,[37] tends to confer the name of "one object" on that which of itself suffices to fulfil a particular purpose;

though it is worth noting that the purpose concerned need not be anything more than analysis, as when one talks of a single molecule as "a whole" or "one molecule."

These two types of unity, continuity and wholeness, Aristotle summarizes before passing on (*Metaphysics I* 1052a29) to the next pair, the unities belonging to things the thought of which is one or indivisible. Of these the first is unity of form. Aristotle here does not bother to mention unity of genus or unity by analogy, which figured prominently (together with unity of definition) in *Metaphysics Δ*. He may have thought these distinctions of his own too technical and too dependent on his own philosophy of classification to be useful in a discussion of usage. The series of unities at *Metaphysics Δ* 1016b31ff is admittedly somewhat artificial but deserves a mention. Aristotle there constructs the order (1) one in number, (2) one in form or species, (3) one in genus, (4) one by analogy. Of this series he says it is in logical order, since (a) things that are one in number are necessarily one in form, but (b) the converse is not true, and things one in form are necessarily one in genus, but the converse is not true, and so on. This series is faulty, as Bonitz pointed out; for things which are one in genus are not one by analogy, since that kind of unity holds only between things not in the same genus.[38] Aristotle's construction has run away with him.

But philosophical or no, and artificial or no, Aristotle's construct receives partial justification in his earlier remark that the equilateral and isosceles triangle are one and the same shape, namely the triangle, but are not the same triangle.[39] If, to generalize, there are two classes A, B, such that A is contained in B and there is one name for each class, namely, a, b, respectively, then in Greek and English alike two members of A are not one (for they are two a's) but are, nevertheless, in some cases described as "one b," in others "one kind of b." In order for the description "one b" or "one kind of b" to apply to them, there must be something in common between the two b's in question, namely that they have in common the property defining A and belonging to all the a's. Thus the word "one" appears in the predicate assignable to the a's because they have something in common, and that something is the defining property of their class, A. Thus it is not simply perverse to speak of the a's as one in species.

But I find no such analysis in Aristotle, and it must regretfully be conceded that Aristotle may have been overassimilating the word "one" to the word "same"; things may have been for him "one in species" because they were identical in species. (It should not be forgotten that "the same" was for Aristotle a species of "one.") In the *Topics*, for example, Aristotle analyses sameness (or, as we should be more inclined to say, "identity") as numerical, specific, or generic (103a6ff). Numerical identity obtains when we have a plurality of expressions for one object; identity of species obtains between two members of a given species, and so on. Ordinary language, Aristotle appears to say (103a23f), is most commonly found using the word "identical" of the numerically one. We may turn this round and remark that, at least in English, we most often use the word "one" with or replacing the word "same" when absolute numerical identity is in question. We readily say, if we are Unitarians in the Homeric Question, that the author of the *Iliad* and the author of the *Odyssey* are one, or that they are one and the same. But we are less inclined to talk of the *Iliad* and *Odyssey* as being "one" because they both belong to the class of epic poems, and less inclined still to call them one in genus because they are both poems. Here English does sometimes use the idiom "one with," to mean "identical to," and this can be used more easily than plain "one" in cases where numerical identity is not in question. What is more, we should, I think, be prepared to allow that a set of similar objects—say a uniformly bound set of novels—had a unity, formed a unity, or was a unity. Uniformity (or "homogeneity") is a very important form of "unity," and the instinctive recognition of this, the realization that the sharing of a property between two objects constitutes in a sense a unity of them, is perhaps a factor in Aristotle's artificial hierarchy of ones in form, genus, and even by analogy. As Aristotle remarks, ὅμοια λέγεται ... ὧν ἡ ποιότης μία, and elsewhere he speaks of a ἓν κατὰ τὸ ποιόν.[40] Incidentally, it should not be forgotten that uniformity can subsist between the parts of a single object as well as between the members of a set of objects. The pages of a book can be uniform as well as an edition of an author.[41]

In this connection should be mentioned unity of substrate. This is not mentioned in *Metaphysics I* at all, but it does find a place in *Metaphysics Δ*(1016a17ff). There one of the examples Aristotle offers is that of water. Now water was said in the *Topics* (103a19ff) to be called "the same in form" because of a certain degree of likeness. In *Metaphysics Δ* the analysis goes further and is transferred to "one" from "same." "One is applied in another way," says Aristotle, "when the substrate is indistinguishable in form." As far as this goes, it rings true. Things are, in a sense, what they are made of. If, then, they are made of one thing, they can be said to be "all one thing" or "the same thing." In this sense there is a unity between objects whose matter is identical in kind. In this part of the *Metaphysics*, Aristotle apparently wants this unity extended to any things which are not *perceptibly* different in matter; "By 'indistinguishable' I refer to things whose form is not perceptibly divisible": ἀδιάφορον δ' ὧν ἀδιαίρετον τὸ εἶδος κατὰ τὴν αἴσθησιν. In this he is probably following common, if careless, usage. The fact that similarity gives rise to a respectable use of "one" may have been yet another factor in Aristotle's development of the notion of unity of form. But, however that may be, we have here another and clearer case where homogeneity can legitimately be called a type of unity and things homogeneous (whether parts of an object or members of a set) may be termed "one." That usage is not unfairly represented here may be divined from some pre-Aristotelian passages.[42]

To be associated with this notion of "homogeneity" is also Aristotle's conception of a unity by mixture. This is referred to once or twice in the *Metaphysics*, but the locus classicus is the tenth chapter of the first book of *De generatione et corruptione*. Aristotle rejects the notion that mixture either is indistinguishable from synthesis or involves total destruction of the ingredients, employing the distinction between the actual and potential existence of the ingredients: potential when mixed, actual when only laid side by side. The process of mixing things is described at the end of the chapter as the "unification of the possible ingredients resulting from their alteration,"[43] in Greek ἡ δὲ μῖξις τῶν μικτῶν ἀλλοιωθέντων ἕνωσις. Particularly interesting from our point of view is the doctrine that true mixture must result in a stuff with the same properties in the parts as in the whole. Ingredients are made one by a process which results in the disappearance of difference between them, and the production of a qualitatively homogeneous whole. Uniformity here is certainly regarded as a kind of unity.

A much easier subject is unity in number. Numerical unity is for Aristotle the same as numerical identity, and numerical identity is for him sameness par excellence (*Topics* 103a23ff). This is the strictest kind of unity or identity there is, being predicated, for example, of one thing for which there are two names; an example offered in this chapter of the *Topics* is that of "robe" or "cloak." Elsewhere, Aristotle makes it pretty clear that you are numerically identical with yourself. The numerically one is said to be the same as the individual, τὸ καθ' ἕκαστον (*Metaphysics* 999b33f). This kind of unity is also equivalent to unity of matter—not, this time, sharing the same *kind* of matter, but the same actual *piece* of matter (*Metaphysics* 1016b32f). This is a usage common enough in both Greek and English, and nothing more need be said about it here.

Here we may again desert the order of *Metaphysics I* and take a look at the senses in which, according to Aristotle, a thing or things may be called one per accidens. These are listed at the beginning of the chapter on unity in *Metaphysics Δ*. The uncertainties of the text hardly affect the main issues.[44] Examples of accidental unity include: an attribute and its subject, such as musical and Coriscus; two attributes attached to the same subject, such as musical and just and the subject to which they are attached; attribute plus subject is one with subject, as musical Coriscus with Coriscus; and one combination of subject and attribute is "one" with a combination of the same subject with another attribute, as musical Coriscus with just Coriscus; and these hold true if the subject is not an individual such as Coriscus but a species or genus, for example, man.

It may be doubted whether anyone would have quarrelled with the idea that an individual and his attributes constitute one thing altogether, except perhaps a Platonist determined to separate Forms from particulars as far as possible. But it is hardly to be believed that anyone in normal speech would ever find himself compelled to describe Coriscus and "musical" and "just" as one thing or attribute unity to them, though we might say that musicality and justice were "united" in Coriscus. We can be fairly sure that whatever Aristotle was driving at here was a philosophical point rather than a layman's usage. At least it is to be remarked that he carefully distinguishes such unities from those which of their own nature are called one. His words τρόπον τινά surely indicate awareness that he is stretching language (1015b23f). Perhaps we may suppose him to mean that things which are not unified in any other way may be parts of a single unity or included in a single unity, and derive a kind of accidental unity from that inclusion. A later remark (1016b6) leads us to suppose that the relation involved need not be such inclusion but could be a wide variety of different kinds of connection. Aristotle's words are: τὰ μὲν πλεῖστα ἓν λέγεται τῷ ἕτερόν τι ἢ ποιεῖν ἢ ἔχειν ἢ πάσχειν ἢ πρός τι εἶναι ἕν, τὰ δὲ πρώτως λεγόμενα ἓν ὧν ἡ οὐσία μία, μία δ' ἢ συνεχείᾳ ἢ εἴδει ἢ λόγῳ. This appears to extend "accidental" unity to any pair of things which do, have, suffer, or are related to another unity. Any relationship, it seems, to a single thing will ensure that one can attribute unity to the most diverse and otherwise unconnected things. It is hard to think of very plausible examples of this from ordinary speech, and it is not hard to think of counterexamples. My typewriter and my son are not one thing and do not constitute a unity merely because both are in their different ways related to me. Not, that is, in ordinary language; not in any language known to me. Certainly there is a connection between the pair in the example; but the connection is not such as normally to give rise to the predication of unity. Of course, the sum total of people and things in my house form a unity, a single household; but they do so because they form a single whole, a social and perhaps legal unit, and this wholeness is what entitles them to the predicate "a unity," not their relationship (as such) to me. Aristotle here is doing a rather special kind of philosophy, rather than analysing ordinary language, and we need not be on the look-out for such usage.

One particular relationship which Aristotle hardly examines, but which may be of some interest later in this inquiry, is that of sharing a common origin. Aristotle mentions in the *Topics* (103a14ff) a particular kind of sameness, which is predicated of things flowing from a common source. He points out that water from the same fountain is called the same water but thinks this is merely a special case, with a specially high degree of sameness, of the specifically same. Here Aristotle is certainly analysing normal usage, but one may suspect that he is analysing it wrongly; for the water from one fountain is called the same *water* or the same stream, whereas other things watery are said to be the same *stuff*: we are reminded of the distinction Aristotle himself draws between the unity of triangles which are the same triangle and the unity of those which are merely the same shape.[45] It does seem that this concerning the stream is a special usage, which it would be wrong to elevate into a whole category of unity or of sameness. We do not normally call two houses "one house" or "the same" because they emanate from the same builder and/or architect; we predicate these terms of them if they are precisely similar. I believe the same to be true of Greek usage. The origin of the predication of sameness to the water from the same fountain may not be so much the specific unity of the water as the continuity of the stream. But in any case we have here, in my opinion, an unusual extension of usage.[46]

In *Metaphysics I*, Aristotle points out,[47] as we have seen, that the unit is the measure of everything, and especially of quantities, and suggests that measurement by units originated in the case of quantity and was transferred to the other genera. It is odd that Aristotle regards the unit as indivisible, and odder still that he regards units of extension as indivisible, since they are obviously themselves continuous lengths and, being continuous, ought for Aristotle to be divisible. The notion that a foot is indivisible πρὸς τὴν αἴσθησιν is scarcely an easy way out. Number to Aristotle was a discrete series of integers, not a continuum; so, even if fractional remainders are allowed at a pinch for lengths, in number division by the unit is always exact. Aristotle points out that the unit in any genus need not be one in number; thus there were two different kinds of quarter-tone in use in measuring musical intervals. But into the ramifications of Aristotle's profoundly mistaken theory of number it is not necessary to delve here.

PLURALITY

It is time to say something about the various uses of "many." Aristotle is less comprehensive on these than on the senses of "one," perhaps partly because he failed (despite *Metaphysics* 1016b6–11)[48] to appreciate fully the importance of "one's" status, in Austin's terminology, as a "trouser-word," governed largely by the term to which in a given context it is opposed. If we take a lax view of the requirements for a unity, we shall take a strict view of the requirements of a plurality, and vice versa. For example, Aristotle in early maturity, probably adopting for the nonce from the First Hypothesis of Plato's *Parmenides* the doctrine that a unity must be strictly and absolutely indivisible, like a point, speaks of a body in contact with its neighbour at different places as ex hypothesi "in a sense, many"—presumably because it has parts not numerically identical. This is about the laxest possible requirement of a plurality, and Aristotle does well to add "in a sense." But the correspondence between senses of "one" and "many" emerges.

The correspondence is explicitly noted by Aristotle himself at least once.[49] There the senses given are plurality by discontinuity, by different sort of matter, and by definition. As Bonitz observed, these are merely given exempli gratia. The same is doubtless true of another list in the *Metaphysics* (1016b9ff), where continuity, form, and definition appear, and of a passage in the *Physics* (185b32) where things are many either by definition or by division, as in the case of whole and parts. It is surprising that Aristotle does not explicitly correlate unity of the whole with a corresponding plurality. But perhaps he thought that his analysis of "whole" as opposed to a mere heap sufficed; Aristotle sometimes contrasts a heap with a syllable.[50]

CONCLUSION

It is not easy to see what are the relations (in fact or in Aristotle's belief) between the three analyses of "one" mentioned in this chapter, namely by category and focal meaning, by central meaning, and by various types such as continuity. Aristotle mentions the analysis by category and by types in *Metaphysics Z* (1030b7ff), without stating any relation between them. It is not, I think, quite clear with what degree of awareness he perceived that the division by types cuts across that by categories, though he knew that "continuous" straddles some category boundaries. The notion that "one" has a focal meaning, in that its other uses are explicable with reference to its use as the "principle" of number, is not necessarily dependent on Aristotle's particular list of categories. The relation of central and focal meanings is a harder subject. What can be said with certainty is that the concept of a central meaning makes that of a focal meaning for the same word entirely unnecessary. I am not quite sure that the two are positively inconsistent but cannot think of any good example to show they are not; it may well be that they are.[51] One interesting distinction between the analysis by "types" and the other two is that it is only (I think) in this analysis that "one" fails to be, as "existent" is, a superfluous predicate. If we ascribe unity to the plot of the *Iliad*, as being a well-organized whole, we are saying something more than that the *Iliad* has a plot; "unified plot" says more than "plot" or "existent plot." Similarly, in normal circumstances "one library" says no more than "existent library"; but "This library is essentially one" might say, for example, that the collection of books in question is centred on a single subject, or that the books are in some other way homogeneous.

From time to time we shall inquire what answer the Presocratics, when they used the word "one," would have given to the question "One what?" But their wholesale overlooking of this question would make it tedious to repeat it every time. The analysis by categories is too disputable a construction to serve as the basis for agreement on cases of equivocation or confusion between one sense and another. For the purposes of this book the analysis by "types" is the most relevant and useful.

A word of warning. On occasions it is tempting to say that one or other of these senses is the "true" sense and suggest the inferiority of others. This is a temptation to which even Aristotle on occasion succumbed but which should nevertheless be resisted. It may be possible to talk of the "*strictly*" one, meaning either the totally indivisible or the absolutely identical, but no sense is *linguistically* prior to any other. Some Presocratics also probably yielded to the temptation to talk about "the truly one"; but this is only one of the least significant symptoms of their general inability to think their way through the polysemy of the words we are discussing.

II

THE MILESIANS

INTRODUCTORY: THE SOURCES

The investigation of our questions must begin where the history of Greek philosophy begins, in sixth-century Miletus, with Thales, Anaximander, and Anaximenes. The honest critic must admit that we know little about these men and in particular that the little we do know contains hardly any of their original words. We can therefore hardly discuss the question how they used the terms "one" and "many" without becoming academic in the worst sense. All we can do is to analyse what little evidence remains and inquire into the plausibility of ancient and modern attributions to these thinkers of the idea of the world's unity. Much dispute centres on the doctrine ascribed to them by the ancient historians of philosophy that water, "Boundless," or "air" was the ἀρχή or "principle" of everything. Since the influence of Aristotle and Theophrastus on subsequent doxography is agreed to have been profound, any assessment of the ancient evidence for the Milesians must start from an appraisal of these two ultimate authorities. This vexed question is here presented in a sharp form. Did the word ἀρχή form part of the earliest philosophical vocabulary, or was it foisted on early thinkers by Peripatetics to whom it was abundantly familiar? If the Milesians did use the word, what are they most likely to have meant by it? Whatever their vocabulary, what lay behind Aristotle's ascription to them of a belief in the unity of things? Before embarking on these discussions we may once more emphasize the severe limitations on our knowledge and even on our legitimate conjecture. If we would seek for fresh light on the Milesians, it is as likely in the last resort to come from the analysis of Eastern antecedents as from renewed perusal of the Greek authorities.

First, however, we must take a reasoned attitude to Aristotle's historical remarks and to Theophrastus' whole history of philosophy.[1] This involves us in complex problems, and nothing more than a few general considerations can be advanced here concerning either the standing of Aristotle as a historian or the degree of independence to be expected of Theophrastus.

These subjects have been dominated for a generation by the opinions of H. F. Cherniss.[2] Examining in detail the argument of each passage where Aristotle criticized his predecessors, Cherniss came to the conclusion that Aristotle's philosophical purposes often led him to distort their actual views. Setting up debates between them, to be resolved by his own theories, Aristotle was betrayed by a lack of interest in historical facts as such into putting questions to his predecessors which they had not put to themselves and into making them more articulate than they really were. To support the allegation of distortion Cherniss produced a massive array of Aristotelian self-contradictions,[3] as well as certain other statements that he deemed demonstrably unhistorical.[4] He took justifiable exception to the policy, still all too prevalent, of accepting Aristotle's interpretations when and only when they suit one's own book.[5] He insisted that the separation of the wheat from the chaff in Aristotle's historical passages should not be conducted on an instinctive basis, but demanded careful inspection of the context of argument surrounding the historical remarks, and a just appreciation of Aristotle's philosophical purposes in it.[6]

Certain facets of this argument have long come under attack, explicit or implicit. Discrepancies alleged by Cherniss have been reconciled by various means other than the postulation of distortion due to the structure of Aristotle's argument. If Aristotle ascribed to the Pythagoreans now the belief that things are numbers and now that things imitate numbers, that was perhaps because the Pythagoreans themselves were unable or unwilling to distinguish between these two doctrines or found no difficulty in holding them simultaneously.[7] Aristotle's differing accounts of Anaximander's "Boundless," as a mixture, and as a single stuff apart from the elements, were explained not on the supposition that at least one of them was wrong but on the theory that Anaximander had not in the brief space at his disposal made himself clear on the topic, since he was not so concerned with the question as Aristotle.[8] It was argued also that Aristotle, like a modern scholar, could be allowed an occasional change of mind. For some of Aristotle's opinions there might be found more justification in the original text than Cherniss would allow. Thus Empedocles' reference (B22.5) to some things being "made alike" by Aphrodite might make more understandable Aristotle's insistence on the alteration of Empedocles' unalterable "roots" and his treatment of Empedocles' sphere as a substrate. It must, however, be admitted that this explanation would leave us finding fault with Aristotle's judgement and still inclined to believe the origin of Aristotle's remarks to be more the exigencies of his own arguments than those of Empedocles' text.[9] Not all the misunderstandings of earlier doxographical pronouncements ascribed by Cherniss to Aristotle convince,[10] and the offence of translating earlier thought into his own philosophical terminology, even if sometimes misleading, is, as Cherniss himself remarked,[11] the most venial of the types of error attributed to Aristotle. Aristotle's tendency to assume Presocratic knowledge of his own theories is very difficult to assess, since it is often unclear whether Aristotle is not merely translating into his own terminology a theory known earlier.[12] At least it may be said of Aristotle that he sometimes gives his readers the opportunity to test his statements against the evidence, including a surprising number of quotations for a writer of his brevity, and that he is often careful to mark the status of his remarks, whether it be that of conjecture or certainty[13] and whether they constitute a statement of meaning or the drawing out of an implication.[14] Nor is Cherniss himself always so extreme in his views as some of his opponents tend to assume.[15] Thus he says,[16] "Here, too, when the purpose is understood, it is impossible to criticize Aristotle for misrepresentation or lack of 'the historical sense,'" even if he continues (with some justification) "but it is likewise impossible to use his groupings and representations of the affinity and relationship of various doctrines as historical evidence." Aristotle was often perceptibly better on individual philosophers than on groups and their interrelationships.

But, when all this is said, there remains a core of Aristotelian perversion, from one cause or another;[17] enough to give us pause in any one case and to suggest that we must treat Aristotle's historical remarks on their several merits, even if we should still require arguments of some force before we abandon Aristotle's ideas. Greatness in logic, in science, and in philosophy is no bar to historical myopia, and respect for one's predecessors does not guarantee understanding of them (for it is by no means necessary for such respect to be based on a true or even sympathetic interpretation). It is not sympathetic criticism that Aristotle needs—he would be the first to reject the idea—but detached criticism. It is not always reasonable to suppose that Aristotle's guesses are founded on evidence fuller in all respects than we have. His Ionian origin did not necessarily give him some mysterious advantage over modern historians of Ionian philosophy. Nor is it necessary to feel for one's philosophical views as an evangelist about his religion in order to overlook possible objections to them. Aristotle was a great man; but he was human.

Theophrastus is another question. Hardly anyone denies that Aristotle's account of the Presocratic principles has influenced his pupil's history of philosophy. The influence extends at times to verbal echoes of the most surprising kind.[18] But when we ask whether Theophrastus did nothing but copy Aristotle, then the answer comes sharply back in the negative; if for no other reason, then because Theophrastus' book covered a vastly wider field than Aristotle's remarks on his predecessors.[19] The two men lived next to each other for a generation, but Theophrastus did not lose all critical power through this constant association with a more powerful intellect.[20] Theophrastus certainly read the Presocratics, or such of them as he could find, and when he records some doctrine it is not *simply* because he found it in Aristotle's notes.[21] Recent writers have rightly drawn attention to some of Theophrastus' departures from or corrections of his master. But these corrections, while they serve to show that Theophrastus recognized that Aristotle could be misleading, do not show that Theophrastus was *always* on the look-out for his master's errors. Even if Theophrastus is sometimes demonstrably independent,[22] and the examples include some not wholly insignificant points on the Milesians, we still may find it easy to credit that Theophrastus should have his master's work so much in his head that he should on occasion fail to notice that the texts did not support his interpretations. Most of us have seen examples of pupils' work reflecting their teachers' in similar fashion, even in later life, and even where the pupil was not lacking either in scholarship or in critical power. We should be wary indeed of approaching Theophrastus with reverence, and wary of using him as an independent witness on Presocratic problems to support Aristotle's historical theses. More especially should we exercise care when the philosophical presuppositions which helped to mislead Aristotle were shared by Theophrastus.

It is true that, if Aristotle and Theophrastus' literary heirs were removed from our ken, our knowledge of Presocratic philosophy would shrink alarmingly. It is true that many of our remaining bits of Presocratic texts were preserved precisely because they were used to support Aristotelian or Theophrastean interpretations. It is also true that even our picture of Presocratic interests must be derived largely from the Peripatetics and that if the Peripatetics much mislead us there is little else to fall back on. But even admitting the possibility that Lyceum history was not all it should have been, we have still some support left. The fragments of the Presocratics are not so skimpy as to leave no scope for the interpretative art—thanks above all to Aristotle's Greek commentators: where the Peripatetics produce evidence which does not support them, it is legitimate to doubt their interpretation; and even where there are no original words to interpret, the evidence of other philosophers, or of external influences at work of which Aristotle knew nothing, may throw light on places left dark by Aristotle and Theophrastus. To say this is not to be unaware of the danger of replacing an ancient by a modern conjecture, an old dogmatism by a new one, no less shaky; it is merely to recognize the possibility that in some cases the balance of the evidence may be weighted, however slightly, against Aristotle and his pupil. The Milesians present, perhaps, an instance of this; and to them we must now return.

DID THE MILESIANS USE THE WORD ἀρχή?

This question seems somewhat less important than the amount of ink spilt on it would suggest, but it is not without interest. I take the view that Anaximander probably did use the word, though in what context he used it will remain unknown. It seems that Simplicius has one statement which is wholly unambiguous, to the effect that Anaximander was the first to name the substrate "ἀρχή."[23] This statement I see no reason whatever to disbelieve, even though Simplicius does not tell us his source for it; since it is a purely incidental remark, it could be derived either from Theophrastus or from Eudemus, or conceivably in the first instance from an earlier commentary on Aristotle's *Physics*.[24] The other statement which is sometimes interpreted to mean that Anaximander was the first to use the term ἀρχή seems to me to have, on the face of it, no relevance to the problem, and I am unable to see why scholars are so eager to peer behind that face.[25] There is no reason for forcing the two quite separate sentences to say the same thing or to talk about the same subject, and the best policy is to take both of them in the most natural sense. If we do this, then we find that Theophrastus attributed to Anaximander the first description of the principle of things as "unlimited" and that an unknown author ascribed to Anaximander the first use of the term ἀρχή to designate the primary substance of the world. There could be reason, but I do not think there is good reason, to doubt whether the word was used by Anaximander in the nominative; there is serious reason to doubt whether he used it in the same way as Aristotle and the post-Aristotelians; but that he used the word of his "unlimited" body seems to me not, admittedly, beyond all doubt, but beyond reasonable doubt.

This information is valuable, but we must be careful to define our continuing ignorance. We do not know whether Thales used the word in his pronouncements about water, but we do know that there was a tradition of uncertain provenance that he did not and that Anaximander was the first to use the term. We do not know that Anaximenes used it, though there is no reason why he should not have. It would be unsafe to draw conclusions about Anaximenes, and still more unsafe to draw conclusions about Thales, on the evidence concerning Anaximander's employment of the word ἀρχή. Furthermore, we do not know in what precise grammatical construction Anaximander used the word. Kirk has conjectured that Anaximander may have used it in phrases meaning "in the beginning" and so forth, but it is doubtful whether such a usage would have attracted doxographical attention.[26] Nor does our knowledge necessarily cover the total of what Anaximander meant by the word when he wrote it down. Here conjecture may be more fruitful, but it is not likely to be successful until a decision is reached on what the function of the Milesian ἀρχή in general was; not having a context to analyse, one must fall back on the general probabilities of the matter. The mere fact that Anaximander called the "unlimited" an ἀρχή, illuminating though it may be for the delineation of the course of Anaximander's argument at one key point, says little about the limits placed on the functions of the "unlimited" by its inventor. The principal scholarly quarrel over the Milesians concerns the question whether water, "unlimited," and "air" were merely beginnings, or were also the stuff of which things were made, or were "the permanent ground of being" for things, as one recent writer has it.[27] The use of the term ἀρχή can tell us that the Milesians, if Anaximander was typical, regarded their primary substances as "beginnings" but cannot tell us whether or not they regarded them as anything more. The limits to be set by conjecture on Anaximander's sense of ἀρχή depend on the limits set to his theory, and not the other way about.

But, before we turn to the general question of the function of the ἀρχή in Milesian naturalism, there is a clue to Aristotle's historical habits, as well as to Anaximander's line of thought, which should not be neglected. C. H. Kahn has shown that the arguments of Aristotle's *Physics* 203b3–15 form a unity and may confidently be attributed in substance to Anaximander.[28] The argument here, Kahn observes, "forms a valid syllogism only if ἀρχή and πέρας are taken as identical or co-extensive in meaning." Actually, as close inspection shows, the argument is valid if an ἀρχή is merely a kind of πέρας.[29] But the point that Kahn goes on to make remains true. "Although Aristotle is quite familiar with this concrete use of ἀρχή, he normally employs the term to indicate a universal 'principle' or 'first cause' ... and it is the latter sense of ἀρχή that we naturally expect here. But in that case the desired conclusion does not follow; and the ancient commentators were accordingly obliged to defend Aristotle against a charge of παραλογισμός." Here, then, we have an argument almost certainly attributable to Anaximander, in which the word ἀρχή is involved in a sense which Kahn well calls "concrete," a sense in which it is a kind of limit. Aristotle reports that argument with what Kahn has shown to be a high degree of fidelity. And yet Aristotle has evidently assimilated Anaximander's ἀρχή to his own kind of ἀρχή, and does not notice the difference between them, or at least does not think it worth while to point out the difference to his audience or readers. It is worth the trouble to delimit precisely what this proves. It shows that Aristotle was capable of ignoring a difference between his own philosophical usage and that of an earlier thinker. It does not prove that he habitually did this, but it must inevitably weaken our confidence in his attribution to other early thinkers of a view containing the word concerned in his own sense. It shows that though (naturally enough) good at summarizing an argument he was liable (but not necessarily habitually inclined) to take for granted that early thinkers used philosophical terms in the same way as he did himself. It cannot be said that this improves the chances that Aristotle's attribution to some Milesians[30] of the doctrine of a single "principle" and "element" is fully correct. But at the same time, it must be admitted that one swallow does not make a summer and that the argument cited above fails to *prove* that Anaximander made his ἀρχή only a beginning and not a "principle." The resolution of this problem, if it is to be resolved at all, must still depend partly at least on the function of the primary substance in Milesian thinking, as it can be gathered from the available evidence.

THE FUNCTION OF THE MILESIANS' PRIMARY SUBSTANCE

ANAXIMANDER'S ἄπειρον IS MORE THAN A "BEGINNING"

Still for the moment sticking to Anaximander, we may make some further deductions from the passage of Aristotle's *Physics* discussed in the previous paragraph. Aristotle's summary of Anaximander's conclusions contains the statement that the "unlimited" "encompasses all things and steers all things." The first half of this is confirmed by Hippolytus, doubtless reproducing the substance of Theophrastus, and there is no reason to doubt its correctness; it is simply the spatial counterpart of the temporally limiting function of the ἀρχή deduced in the Anaximandrean argument. The second half of the statement is perhaps a little more dubious, for there is no obvious connection between this and the preceding argument, and the presence of this or similar phrases in other early writers and philosophers affords ample material for Aristotelian conflation or confusion as well as (on the other side) the possibility that Anaximander expressed himself similarly. There is little doubt, however, that Aristotle meant to attribute this phrase also to the Milesian "school," since his ascription to "those who have not other causes beside the unlimited, such as Mind or Love" rules out everyone else except the Atomists, and they are ruled out by the substance of the doctrine concerned.[31] Which of the Milesians Aristotle here had particularly in mind is not of immediate importance to us: but in any case the probability that the whole context goes back to Anaximander tips the balance of probability in favour of ascribing this particular phrase also to the same philosopher.[32]

From these two phrases we may gather that Anaximander's ἀρχή was not without functions in the visible world after the cosmogonic period was over.[33] Though not found a place within the world—the whole point is that it was not one of the great masses that make up the visible universe[34]—the unlimited stuff is still active. It certainly surrounds the world and probably "steers" or "governs" it. Of one at least of the Milesians it may be said that his primary stuff "steers" or "governs" the universe. The way in which the primary substance fulfilled this function will remain obscure, but the fact is hard to deny. One can, unfortunately, only speculate on the closeness of this conception to the notion of a "permanent ground of being." The fact that the "unlimited" or other Milesian ἀρχή steered or governed would not make it a "ground of being" in our logic, and there is nothing to show that anything in Milesian logic made it so. To "steer" or govern might be to constitute a ground of becoming, to be the arbiter or sustainer of change—though this would leave the functions of Time and the "unlimited" a little confused in our scanty evidence.[35] But one thing is clear: in no system of logic is it reasonable to regard the doctrine that X is the governor of the universe as equivalent to or as implying the further doctrine that X is either the stuff of which the universe and all in it are made, or the reality which sustains their being. No supporting evidence yet appears for the Peripatetic ascription to the "unlimited" of the function of "element." What is forthcoming is a reason why the Peripatetics should be inclined to make the "unlimited" more than just the "source" or "beginning" of things; it probably was indeed more, and as κυβερνήτης could well be dignified as a "cause" of movement.

THE HISTORY OF GREEK THOUGHT ABOUT COMING-TO-BE

It is time to examine the actual passages in which the Peripatetics offer this ascription and see the form which it takes. The best known of them is part of Aristotle's account of earlier theories of causation in *Metaphysics A*. Aristotle is here avowedly (at 983a33ff) looking through his predecessors to find what causes and principles they talk about and to add persuasiveness to his doctrine of the four causes in the event of his finding no other principle or cause in what they say. In the paragraph immediately following this statement of purpose, it is Aristotle's thesis that most of the earliest philosophers thought only of material causes. The way in which Aristotle expresses this thesis (983b6ff) is of some interest and importance for the argument:

τῶν δὴ πρώτων φιλοσοφησάντων οἱ πλεῖστοι τὰς ἐν ὕλης εἴδει μόνας ᾠήθησαν ἀρχὰς εἶναι πάντων· ἐξ οὗ γὰρ ἔστιν ἅπαντα τὰ ὄντα καὶ ἐξ οὗ γίγνεται πρῶτου καὶ εἰς ὃ φθείρεται τελευταῖον, τῆς μὲν οὐσίας ὑπομενούσης τοῖς δὲ πάθεσι μεταβαλλούσης, τοῦτο στοιχεῖον καὶ ταύτην ἀρχήν φασιν εἶναι τῶν ὄντων, καὶ διὰ τοῦτο οὔτε γίγνεσθαι οὐθὲν οἴονται οὔτε ἀπόλλυσθαι, ὡς τῆς τοιαύτης φύσεως ἀεὶ σωζομένης, ὥσπερ οὐδὲ τὸν Σωκράτην φαμὲν οὔτε γίγνεσθαι ἁπλῶς ὅταν γίγνηται καλὸς ἢ μουσικὸς οὔτε ἀπόλλυσθαι ὅταν ἀποβάλλῃ ταύτας τὰς ἕξεις, διὰ τὸ ὑπομένειν τὸ ὑποκείμενον τὸν Σωκράτην αὐτόν, οὕτως οὐδὲ τῶν ἄλλων οὐδέν· ἀεὶ γὰρ εἶναί τινα φύσιν ἢ μίαν ἢ πλείους μιᾶς ἐξ ὧν γίγνεται τἆλλα σωζομένης ἐκείνης. τὸ μέντοι πλῆθος καὶ τὸ εἶδος τῆς τοιαύτης ἀρχῆς οὐ τὸ αὐτὸ πάντες λέγουσιν, ἀλλὰ Θαλῆς μέν . . .

As it stands, this description cannot possibly be historical. No one believes the Milesians to have used the word στοιχεῖον or "element," and it is difficult to believe them to have had a general word such as πάθος for "quality."[36] Nor is it at all probable that the Milesians—or indeed any Presocratics—would have been able to understand the full distinction between subject and property involved in Aristotle's illustration of Socrates. If such understanding had been available to the Greeks at anything like the date of the Milesian philosophers, then the history of Greek thought would have been very different in many respects. To take but one example, it would be hard to understand why Lycophron should take the trouble to avoid having one thing be many by eliminating the copula, if the distinction between the one subject and its many attributes were already familiar to him from more than a hundred years of philosophizing. The distinction between various senses of "one" and "many" is necessary for the complete answer to Lycophron, but the distinction between subject and attribute would go a long way towards rendering him harmless.

This basic point about Aristotle's account of the first philosophers has been established for a long time and should not any longer be in doubt.

But it does not, as some scholars seem to think, settle the main issue of this discussion.[37] The possibility arises—to be cautious—that Aristotle was not so much reading back into the Milesians a conception entirely his own as overgeneralizing a theory they had expressed in more concrete and particular terms. We are here presented with an especially difficult form of the perennial problem just how much distortion has been caused by Aristotle's translation of earlier views into his own philosophical jargon. It is no longer enough simply to point to the presence of distortion; one must investigate its precise degree. In this case investigation is complicated by the possibility that the early Naturalists believed that everything was *made of* (for example) water—a notion that they would have been as capable of expressing as they were of saying that a house was made of wood or a helmet of bronze. They could have said, without straining the resources of vocabulary available to them, that rocks were heavy, dense, dark, hard water, whereas fire was bright, rare, light, and unusually mobile water. It is not shown that this kind of conception was impossible for them when it is proved that they had no words for "subject" and "attribute." Nor is it shown by the suggestion that "the hot," "the hard," and "the dense" were just as much separate substances to these thinkers as were water, fire, or earth. For it was open to them to say that the "hot" was made of, e.g., water, just as they could say that fire was; one cannot argue, I think, that "the hot" could not have been for them equivalent to, say, hot water. The line of argument here opposed, while it is thoroughly convincing as an example of Aristotelian distortion by making a doctrine more abstract and general than it was in the mouths of its originators, does not of itself prove that the term "element" or "principle" is not, within limits, an accurate generalized description of what the Milesians may legitimately be said to have meant.

Much more difficult to answer, and worth more extended discussion, is the question whether the Milesians' view as described by Aristotle constitutes an unacceptable anticipation of Eleatic arguments. Cherniss,[38] following W. A. Heidel,[39] believed Aristotle to have assumed that "the Ionians were aware of the logical implications of identity," and that this made the Eleatic position "inexplicable." Cherniss added that "the effect of this historical conception comes vividly to light in his interpretation of Parmenides' identity of Being as an identity of contraries." Leaving this last point for the moment, we may start by seeing how, according to Aristotle himself, the Eleatic position was to be construed as an advance on Milesian thinking. For if we find this advance plausible, Cherniss' argument is robbed of force. The passage is all the more important since in it Aristotle has the Eleatics carry their predecessors' theories to their logical conclusion, and that is what in several different ways modern scholars have often believed the Eleatics to have been doing.[40] What Aristotle says at 984a27ff[41] is this:

οἱ μὲν οὖν πάμπαν ἐξ ἀρχῆς ἁψάμενοι τῆς μεθόδου τῆς τοιαύτης καὶ ἓν φάσκοντες εἶναι τὸ ὑποκείμενον οὐθὲν ἐδυσχέραναν ἑαυτοῖς, ἀλλ' ἔνιοί γε τῶν ἓν λεγόντων, ὥσπερ ἡττηθέντες ὑπὸ ταύτης τῆς ζητήσεως, τὸ ἓν ἀκίνητόν φασιν εἶναι καὶ τὴν φύσιν ὅλην οὐ μόνον κατὰ γένεσιν καὶ φθοράν (τοῦτο μὲν γὰρ ἀρχαῖόν τε καὶ πάντες ὡμολόγησαν) ἀλλὰ καὶ κατὰ τὴν ἄλλην μεταβολὴν πᾶσαν· καὶ τοῦτο αὐτῶν ἴδιόν ἐστιν.

Aristotle thus maintains that the early monists had believed in the unity of things in the sense that their one substance remained the same through change, without coming-to-be or passing-away; and that the Eleatics merely extended the earlier veto on coming-to-be and passing-away to all possible kinds of change including locomotion.[42] Is this a plausible theory of the development of Parmenides' arguments? It would be hard, I believe, to deny its *possibility*. Detailed analysis of Parmenides' argument must await a later chapter, but it may be said in anticipation that Parmenides starts from the assumption of the possibility of discourse and goes on to deduce that the subject of discourse must exist. Granted the impossibility of its non-existence, certain further deductions are made. The first is that it cannot come to be or pass away; the second is that it is continuous; and the third is that it is ἀκίνητον, by which Parmenides meant that it was unchanging and unmoving. Thus Parmenides' proof that coming-to-be and passing-away are impossible precedes (and is separate from) his argument that change and movement are impossible. If one cares to, one can imagine on this basis that Parmenides first proved what his predecessors had believed without proof, and then added, as Aristotle would have us believe, arguments against other kinds of change including locomotion. But in order to believe this it is necessary to credit that Parmenides would spend many lines on an elaborate argument proving what was already believed in philosophical circles which he was ex hypothesi addressing. It is necessary to believe, moreover, that he was so unaware of what he was doing as to make his goddess pass from genesis and destruction to change and movement without drawing attention at all to the fact that this was the novel and important part of her message. It is actually necessary to believe that the goddess of Parmenides' poem deduces the impossibility of change of quality from the principle of invariance (symbolized by "limit"), without observing that some of the "mortal" victims of her invective had anticipated her principle and had merely failed to effect this necessary deduction from it. It is possible, I think, to believe all these things, and I do not hold that we have here disproof of the development as described by Aristotle; but I can only express my conviction that, if Aristotle is right here, then Parmenides for much of his poem is making much ado about surprisingly little. Certainly I have never met the reader to whom Parmenides' ringing denunciation of becoming and destruction gave the impression on the first reading of being old hat.

The probabilities of this matter may also be affected by another consideration. That is that the view attributed to the Milesians by Aristotle is very like some of the answers to Parmenides excogitated in the latter half of the fifth century. None of these was a good, let alone a perfect, answer; for none of their authors understood the central question bothering the Eleatics. But nevertheless some very important compromises were developed between Eleatic logic on the one hand and the demands of common sense on the other. These all had in common the rejection of coming-to-be and destruction, and the admission of motion. Some of them explained the apparent qualitative changes by changes of arrangement, in defiance of Eleatic arguments against motion;[43] others (for example, Empedocles and Anaxagoras) explained them by differences in the proportions in which the basic realities were mixed, thus defying not only the arguments against motion but also the arguments in favour of complete homogeneity and against difference. To the Eleatic there is no doubt that all these theories are simply false, since one and all ignore the point that what is other than an/the existent cannot exist, and that change or motion and difference involve something other than what exists. It is difficult to see, in face of the complete logical failure of these systems to tackle the fundamental problem of Eleaticism, why Diogenes of Apollonia, who adopted a standpoint similar to the Peripatetic interpretation of the Milesians, should have been singled out (with Hippo) as talking "as if Parmenides had never lived."[44] Diogenes held, as the Milesians are commonly believed to have held, that the multitudinous things of this world are differentiations of one substance. Diogenes Laertius attributes to his Apolloniate namesake the denial of coming-to-be and of destruction, and the fragments reveal that he held that all things are the same thing.[45] Elsewhere Diogenes says that all things partake of air, but not in the same way; air can be hotter or colder, drier or wetter, more stable or in more rapid motion.[46] Diogenes accepted for reasons of his own[47] the Eleatic denial of differentiation in the real, only to allow differentiation in by the back door. This is a characteristic late-fifth-century compromise between Eleaticism and common sense. But it is also the view attributed by the Peripatetics to the Milesians. We have to face the question whether it is plausible to find in a sixth-century group of thinkers a system which makes an answer to Parmenides as good as, or rather no worse than, those of his immediate successors. Once again it is possible, but once again a trace of suspicion remains. Such a curious irony of the history of philosophy necessitates a very careful look at the motives alleged by scholars for the appearance in the sixth century of an answer to Parmenides not unplausible by the standards of the fifth century.[48]

MOTIVES FOR SIXTH-CENTURY MATERIAL MONISM?

No one pretends to *know* what were the reasons which prompted Thales to choose water or Anaximenes to choose air as the primary stuff, even if we do know at least part of the reasons which directed Anaximander's choice elsewhere.[49] Theophrastus, if Simplicius does him no injustice, thought he knew why Thales chose water for the ἀρχή and gives certain reasons (*Physicorum Opin.* frag. 1, apud Simplicium *in Physica* 23.21ff); but Aristotle, when giving reasons which include all of Theophrastus' except one, is careful to mark his ideas as conjecture.[50] It is at least doubtful whether Theophrastus (let alone Simplicius) had any better evidence than Aristotle had; whence the dispute in antiquity even on the basic question whether Thales published any book.[51] We must take the reasons alleged by the Peripatetics in the case of Thales as pure guesswork. It is also doubtful whether Aristotle was in any much better position to speculate soundly on this than we are, and indeed the possibility must be remembered that his speculation may have been guided partly by remarks in fifth-century monists by whom we cannot be misled since we can no longer read them.[52] But that is no good reason for being arbitrary or high-handed in the substitution of new guesses for old, and we should proceed with caution.

It will no longer suffice, for example, to follow Burnet and denounce the reasons given by Aristotle as physiological and therefore unsuited to an age concerned principally with meteorology.[53] An interest in certain basic elements of physiology such as sex and the difference between the living body and the dead has proved absorbing from time immemorial, as anthropology has amply shown. This is a specimen of the type of arbitrariness that we should reject. But there are other reasons why we should be cautious before accepting Aristotelian or Theophrastean guesses. We should try to look, in as cold blood as possible, at Thales' supposed line of thought and see if it is such as could reasonably be pursued by an intelligent Milesian in the sixth century B.C. This is bound to be a tricky question, and almost bound to have a subjective answer; but it nevertheless repays attention. Thales, as is well known,[54] inherited from Near Eastern sources the notions that the earth and everything else in the universe rose up from water (or the sea, or something similar) and that the water is still under the floating earth. If Aristotle and Theophrastus are right, Thales made a very important addition to these doctrines. This addition consisted in making water not merely the starting-point of creation, the origin of all things, but actually the stuff of which things are made, the only real stuff of which all things visible are merely modifications. Why should he have made this particular momentous addition to the stock of human ideas? It seems to me that we are given but dusty answers to this question if we search either in the Peripatetics or in modern publications.

To take Aristotle first. It is not clear whether Aristotle was in fact trying to answer my question, for he gives the following prelude to his conjectured motives for Thales (*Metaphysics* 983b18ff): τὸ μέντοι πλῆθος καὶ τὸ εἶδος τῆς τοιαύτης ἀρχῆς οὐ τὸ αὐτὸ πάντες λέγουσιν, ἀλλὰ Θαλῆς μὲν ὁ τῆς τοιαύτης ἀρχηγὸς φιλοσοφίας ὕδωρ εἶναί φησιν (διὸ καὶ τήν γῆν ἐφ' ὕδατος ἀπεφαίνετο εἶναι), λαβὼν ἴσως τὴν ὑπόληψιν ταύτην ἐκ κτλ. "The number and kind of such a principle was not agreed by all [the physicists], but Thales at any rate, the founder of this type of philosophy, says that the principle is water (for which reason also he declared that the earth floats on water), perhaps basing his opinion on..." It is not absolutely clear whether Aristotle thought he was suggesting answers to the question why Thales chose *water* as the principle or to the quite different question why Thales made water the *principle*. But on the face of it, it is more likely that Aristotle intended to answer the first question, why Thales chose water in particular; for he seems to take for granted the type of philosophy concerned. And, indeed, Aristotle's questions are highly intelligent guesses at the answer to his question. According to the guesses Thales saw (a) that the nourishment of all things is moist, (b) that the hot itself comes to be from the moist and lives by it, and (c) that the seeds of all things are moist: the coping-stone is set on this edifice of argument by the remark that "water is the cause (ἀρχή) of the nature of moist things."

These arguments might seem to make it plausible, given that there is one sole constituent of things, to suppose that water is that constituent. For all our food is moist, in some degree however slight, and the clouds are drawn up from the sea towards the hotter part of the universe as the Greeks saw it, and plant and animal seed alike depend on a moist environment for survival. All these facts were such as to be known to Thales, even if we may be inclined to doubt whether he would have been quite as ready as Aristotle to accept the reference of the second to the continuing life of the heavenly bodies and the bright sky. But it cannot be said that this list of arguments contains any that are likely to make anyone think for the first time of the idea that everything in the world is made of one stuff. Water is palpably not the only constituent of food; the relation between fire and water as cosmic masses is not such as to suggest to an unbiased observer that one of them is the sole constituent of the other, let alone that water, rather than fire, is the one to select as constituent; and, if animal seed might give the impression that life starts with the sole aid of moisture, plant seed would rapidly disabuse one of the idea. In short, though arguments of some force if deployed in favour of the hypothesis that water is the principle, these are not even plausible as arguments that there is such a thing in the first place as a single "principle and element." We may remind ourselves that here at least we are not going against or beyond Aristotle's evidence, for Aristotle most probably did not mean them to be arguments in favour of the assertion that "there is a single principle (namely water)."

Much the same is probably to be said of Theophrastus' only addition to the Aristotelian list of arguments to be attributed to Thales in this connection. Theophrastus adds, probably just as conjecturally as Aristotle, that Thales was struck by the fact that dead bodies dry up, that the living body soon loses its liquids in death or in some cases shortly before death.[55] This again is a presentable argument in favour of the fundamental importance of water, and might add persuasiveness to an argument for choosing water as the principle; but it is hardly calculated to convince an unbeliever that the postulation of a single principle is inevitable in the first place.

The Peripatetics, and therefore the other Greeks, tell us of no sound reason why it was that Thales allegedly "founded this kind of philosophy." Nor can it be said that more recent writers supply any more definite reason why the great step of postulating a single constituent for the material universe should have been taken in the early sixth century B.C. The search for such a reason is usually fobbed off with generalities.[56] A common line of approach is to stress the close kinship between material monism and the scientific outlook. The one, like the other, appears to aim at a simplification of the universe around us; where science tries to unify many phenomena under one hypothesis, material monism sought to unify all things in one substance. Where science tends to look for something permanent underlying the many individuals and many changes of the observable world, material monism supplied a single permanent stuff unchanging in itself through all the changes of the visible appearances. All this is true and not without importance; but it entirely fails to do what we are at present asking of it, which is to supply a reason why we should put the birth of material monism in the sixth century rather than the fifth. It fails to show why in particular it should be the sixth century which gave birth to this extreme form of simplification. In this context the suggestion[57] that "there seems to be a deep-rooted tendency in the human mind to seek ... something that persists through change" should be received cautiously; the suggestion is that this deep-rooted tendency in the human mind sprang suddenly above the surface in the sixth century B.C. to produce a dazzling flower, and no explanation is forthcoming either for its long dormancy or for this precipitate efflorescence. We are sometimes, in effect, asked to credit the Greeks with a mind more scientific than their predecessors or neighbours, so that on its first contact with Eastern myth it transformed the myth into a scientific hypothesis, or at least a hypothesis resembling a basic postulate of science. If this belief ever had anything to commend it, it has nothing now, when anthropology has been allowed to shed light on Greek irrationalities; and the Milesians are in any case not the first recorded Greeks to have demonstrable points of contact with Eastern myths.

To speak, then, of deep-rooted tendencies is to prove too much; but there is another line of approach which, though illuminating in itself, proves too little to help us in our present quandary. It seems to be a tenet of Marxist historians that the rise of Milesian merchant classes led to an attack on the prestige of the aristocratic gods of Homer.[58] This led, it is suggested, to the rise of the scientific outlook in sixth-century Ionia. This is but a bald outline of what is in essence an extremely persuasive viewpoint. It is not necessary to be a Marxist to appreciate the importance of economic and social factors in the history of ideas, and there is no reason to exempt Ionia from their operation. The whole theory, though it remains just a theory, has an air of great plausibility. The great seminal cosmogonic myths of the East would on this hypothesis have fallen in Ionia on fertile soil; and their growth, probably with the initial support of Hesiod,[59] into a system without personal and arbitrarily interfering deities would have followed an inevitable course. Here, if anywhere, lies the germ of an explanation for the rise of a scientific outlook in the earliest Ionian monists. But for our purposes this theory, even if true up to the hilt, proves too little. It accounts well for the abolition of personal and arbitrary divine intervention in natural processes; but it would not even begin to suggest a reason why that abolition should be accompanied by the postulation of a single material for everything and by the commencement of an argument as to which material should be selected.

It does not take a long survey of this field to find that it is empty. There simply has been suggested in print no good reason for so strange a beginning to Greek philosophy. Nor does common sense afford any suggestion to alleviate its strangeness; the world around us has nothing obviously suggesting a single material. Why this departure from common sense in men probably distinguished for the faculty? It will not even do to suggest that the early thinkers tended to generalize on a most inadequate basis. The suggestion is true, as witness the extraordinary generalizations of a Heraclitus.[60] But it is still no explanation of a generalization on no basis whatever, which is what is normally since Aristotle attributed to the Milesian "school" of philosophers.

For suggestion of a motive more substantial than any hitherto seen in print I am indebted to Gregory Vlastos,[61] who kindly suggested to me by letter that early Greek writers tend to feel justified, given "all the X's *come from* Y and Z," in saying "all the X's *are* Y and Z." Thus Xenophanes, at B29, says γῆ καὶ ὕδωρ πάντ' ἐσθ' ὅσα γίνοντ(αι) ἠδὲ φύονται, "earth and water are all things that come into being and grow," where, given the origin of all things that come into being and grow, Xenophanes feels justified in speaking of that origin as if it were the material of which they are made. Vlastos also referred to Heraclitus' remark that the world *is* fire (B30), given the fact that "all things come from ('are an exchange of') fire" (B90), and to his further saying that "half of the sea *is* earth, the other half '*prester*'" (B31) on the strength of the fact that half of the sea comes from earth and the other half from fire. Vlastos noted further that this is a very old pattern of thought. "Where X comes from Y, or Y from X, Homer will talk as though X is Y or vice versa: *Od.* 20.110, barley and wheat-meal are 'the marrow of men.'" The suggestion is that the Greeks were accustomed to speak of an "originative substance" as if it were also the stuff of which things are made in their finished state. If this were so, the argument runs, it would be dangerous to distinguish too sharply between "originative stuff" and "constituent stuff." The early Greeks would talk naturally in terms of both when they talked of either.

In the whole literature on Milesian monism, so far as I can claim to have read it, I have found no argument in favour of the Peripatetic interpretation with a tithe of the force of this one. On this view of the matter, the Milesian thinkers would have slipped almost by accident, as a natural consequence of a tendency in the language which they spoke, into thinking of the "beginning" as the stuff of which things were made. Thinking of things as arising out of water and of air, they could naturally fall into the habit of speaking of things as *being* water or air. This habit would then impress itself naturally on the Peripatetic historians of thought, perhaps first on their sources. The Peripatetic interpretation would be justified, and a motive for the specifically Greek transformation of origin into element would be visible.

But we should still walk warily in this matter. To take Xenophanes, for example, it is not clear that the *only* basis for the pronouncement that all things were made of earth and water was the supposition that all things arise out of earth and water. Xenophanes makes both pronouncements, that we come from earth and water and that all things are earth and water; there is nothing to show that the one type of pronouncement is sufficient support for the other. Nor, in this context, is the "old pattern of thought" one-sided; when Menelaus in the *Iliad* curses the Achaeans with "May you all become earth and water," the implication is that within this type of belief it was clear to the average man that he arose from earth and water and might return to them but that he was not, in his normal living state, earth and water (but rather flesh and blood).[62] If he might say in a high-flown moment that he *was* earth and water, then it would be as a *façon de parler*, a figure of speech not to be taken literally. Nor will we be convinced by the retort that primitive thought did not distinguish between the figurative and the literal. Of course the primitive thinker has no such terms as "literal" and "figurative" at his disposal; but he *can* say (for example) that the Muses sometimes speak the truth, and sometimes lies resembling the truth (Hesiod *Theogony* 27–28). It would be a way of depreciating a part of the body to say it is merely barley, when it comes from barley; it is a way of appreciating barley to say that it is, or is the material of, part of the body when the hard literal truth is that it was the original state of the stuff from which the relevant organ was formed. No Homeric hero or poet ever believed that he could recover barley if he could get at his own marrow. Now, what is attributed to the Milesians is a cold sober, for the most part prosaic suggestion that the world was in its normal state made of some one thing; as a figure of speech it might have been found in the mouths of one or more of them, but as a sober scientific doctrine it is much less plausible. I fail to see that its plausibility as a scientific doctrine is enhanced by the existence of the figure of speech we have been discussing.

Heraclitus also, to be dealt with more fully below, does not in my view substantiate this reason why the Milesians should have cloven to a single world-material. When Heraclitus says that the world is a fire, he also says that it is being kindled in measures and extinguished in measures. That which is extinguished we have no good reason to suppose was itself fire, though it might be looked on as part of *a* fire. If half of the sea is "prester," and half earth, that also may not be because of their origins. What Heraclitus is talking about is probably not in any case what things are, but their τροπαί, what they turn into; but, even if he could say that half of the sea was earth on the grounds that it was going to turn into earth, then we should bear in mind his predilection for paradox and graphic statement. Such a way of thought in more precise moments need by no means be attributed to his contemporaries on this basis.

If, however, we turn to the fifth century B.C., we find without the slightest difficulty a perfectly adequate explanation for the rise of the philosophical doctrine that all things are modifications of one stuff. The early cosmogonies all started from the presumption that in the beginning things were less separate than they are now. The myth of the initial separation of the earth and the sky is world-wide and was certainly known to the Greeks. The first philosophical cosmogonists took over from the myths the belief in an original undifferentiated state of the world; it is immaterial for present purposes that some of them gave it the name of "water," some "air," and one "the unlimited." The important point is that the age-old belief in a single beginning for the manifold world was taken over by the Milesians even when they succeeded in emancipating themselves from the direct intervention of personal deities.[63] (It is, after all, only a limited amount of originality that is accorded to each generation.) Then came the temporarily overwhelming shock of Parmenides' argument. The change of one substance into another was forbidden. Nothing could arise from anything else without paying the penalty of total unreality. Under these conditions no single substance could possibly give rise to a manifold world. It was not (if we may anticipate) that Parmenides argued that the single could not give rise to the multiple; he had no need to. All he needed to do, to demolish the old cosmogony, was to prove that one substance could not change into another. Granted this impossibility, a single substance could only give rise to the same single substance—if indeed one could talk about "giving rise" at all. It is a plausible explanation of material monism of the type evident from the fragments of Diogenes of Apollonia that it originates from the simple acceptance of this point. If the universe arose from air, then it must still be air; for nothing comes to be or is destroyed. True, the fragments do not say that this is what Diogenes is doing. But in answer to this we need hardly even invoke the incompleteness of the fragments; in any case Diogenes had to defend his views not only against Eleatic viewpoints but especially against those who took the other possible path and declared that, since there were many different things now, there must always have been many things.[64] Whence he could not defend himself simply on the lines here suggested as the origin of his theory. But we *are* told that he denied coming-to-be and passing-away, and we are also told enough about sixth- and fifth-century cosmogonies to make clear the large dependence of the later on the earlier.[65] Such an origin for the notion that the world is at present constituted of one stuff is easy to understand and removes at once the motiveless quality pervading its alleged introduction in the sixth century.

We have therefore found three different, but closely related, considerations to throw doubt on the Peripatetic ascription to the Milesians of the notion that everything is made of a single stuff: the impression of originality given by the Parmenidean argument against destruction and coming-to-be; the difficulty of accounting for material monism in the sixth century as opposed to the ease of explaining it as a fifth-century phenomenon; the fact that it presents an answer to Parmenides, of standard fifth-century type, before Parmenides had ever spoken. None of these constitutes by itself a decisive point against the authority of Aristotle, but taken together they constitute a case against Peripatetic interpretations which is worth at least further investigation. It may be that the case will disappear under further examination; the proof that one of the sixth-century systems had by its very nature to be monistic, the citation of pre-Aristotelian evidence for sixth-century monism—either of these, let alone both, would save the authority of Aristotle. Furthermore, to be convincing the view argued in the preceding paragraphs needs to be bolstered with some detailed exposition of how Aristotle and Theophrastus both came to make this particular mistake. It remains also to be seen if there is any pre-Aristotelian evidence telling against his interpretation of the Milesians.

MONISM AND CONDENSATION-RAREFACTION

Let us take first the strongest argument against the case we have erected. This argument is based on the philosophy of Anaximenes, as reported by the unanimous (if sparse) testimony of antiquity. Anaximenes had thought of a process whereby the originative substance was converted into at least some of the things of this world.[66] This process, Anaximenes' main claim to fame, was condensation and rarefaction. The importance of that fact in the present context is that condensation and rarefaction are processes which, to all appearances, must leave the substance concerned the same substance as it was before. If Anaximenes' air underwent condensation, it ought, if we follow our own common sense, to have been at the end of the process condensed air, and not some other substance. Similarly with rarefaction; these processes evidently (to our way of thinking) alter not the substance concerned but the amount of it present in a given volume. If Anaximenes, then, employed (as he undoubtedly did), rarefaction and condensation to generate the world from his primary substance, then it seems common sense that he held that air was the sole constituent of things. This would not wholly disprove the arguments against an early form of material monism given above; it would leave untouched at least one argument against Thales' and Anaximander's material monism, namely the absence of any good reason for their having held such a view. But it would mean that there was *a material monism*, *a* belief in the substantial unity of things in the sixth century B.C.

It would seem to be the most transparent common sense to take this view of Anaximenes, and brash recklessness to cast doubt on it. But it is equally dangerous to suppose that what is common sense to us is common sense to others widely separated from us in time and space. Let the question, then, be raised whether Anaximenes, in talking of his condensation and rarefaction, would necessarily have seen the implications of it as easily as we can. Was the result of condensing air condensed air, or was it something wholly different from air? To raise this question is at once to see that we have available singularly little evidence with which to answer it.[67] But the following considerations may be relevant.[68]

There was a good deal of confusion, as it seems to me, about the implications of condensation and rarefaction in the Classical period of Greek thought. Some thinkers appear to have spotted the obvious implication that such changes by their very nature are quantitative, not qualitative; others, even after the implication had been pointed out to them, refused to accept it. Aristotle, as we shall see, was as difficult to follow on this topic as anybody. But we may first inspect the remarks of thinkers who were quite definite about this. Melissus, for example, immediately following a denial of emptiness or void (and consequently of motion), points out (B7.8) that "(what is) could not be dense and rare; for the rare cannot be as full as the dense, but by its very nature the rare is emptier than the dense." Enough said. The Pythagorean Xuthus, of uncertain date but probably post-Parmenidean, declared, Aristotle tells us (*Physics* 216b22ff), that the universe will bulge whenever anything moves if compression and "felting" are not possible. Little is known of Xuthus, but he may have been one of those, mentioned earlier in Aristotle's chapter, who used the argument from compression in favour of the existence of void. The Atomists, if the report of Alexander (*Quaestiones* 2.23, DK 68A165) is to be trusted, also accepted that things rare and dense took on these qualities by virtue of the amount of void they contained. Alexander records their doctrine that iron and stone were composed of similar atoms (except for the fineness of the stone ones) but that iron was rarer and had more void in it (ἀραιοτέραν τε καὶ πολυκενωτέραν ... εἶναι). Such a doctrine would naturally help to ease the formidable task facing Atomism of finding different shapes of atom for every substance. So far we need have no doubt that the Presocratics understood the common-sense implications of condensation and rarefaction.[69] Plato also evidently implies the existence of void and associates it with variation in density, even if he is less than transparent at *Timaeus*

59b, in saying that copper was πυκνότητι δὲ τῇ μὲν χρυσοῦ πυκνότερον ... τῷ δὲ μεγάλα ἐντὸς αὐτοῦ διαλείμματα ἔχειν͵ κουφότερον.

Some remarks of Parmenides, however, must first give us pause. Even in the "Opinions of Mortals" Parmenides seems to avoid the supposition that emptiness exists. Thus he declares[70] that all things are named light and night and that there is nothing in which neither has a share (*or* which has a share in neither). If this is not a denial of emptiness, it is difficult to see what it is; and yet Parmenides can talk of night as a thick and heavy body, using for "thick" the same word used by most Greek philosophers for "dense"; whether he also used the word for "rare" or meant the same thing is more doubtful.[71] It may be urged that Parmenides was not concerned to avoid contradictions in the "Opinions of Mortals"; I should not subscribe to such a view without reservations, but it is well that we have less ambivalent evidence.

Anaxagoras talks of "rare" and "dense" without ambiguity but does not explain in any extant fragment how to reconcile this with the denial of void attributed to him by our authorities.[72] Nor does he make clear the relationship between "rare" and "dense" and the other powers named side by side with this pair twice in the fragments (DK59B12 and B15). Anaxagoras gives no indication that this was in any way a peculiar kind of opposite pair. Quite possibly he had not observed the difference between one sort and another, that one involved quantitative, the other qualitative, difference; or that change from one pole to the other was effected in one case by movement, in the other case by a change of character. If Anaxagoras had possessed the insight to see that density and rarity meant merely compressed and decompressed states of the same kind of matter, then it would be surprising if he did not see the difficulties into which that would lead him. The difficulties are pointed out by Simplicius at *in Physica* 174.30ff. Simplicius' purpose there is to foist the Aristotelian notion of ἀλλοίωσις on Anaxagoras, but his argument is worth heeding. How, he asks, could so much vapour be separated out of a small ladle of water without ἀλλοίωσις? To ask this is to question how Anaxagoras could envisage the extraction of larger quantities from smaller if he would neither accept the void nor accept the doctrine of one and the same matter taking on now the quality "dense" and now the quality "rare." The question is an eminently reasonable one to ask; and indeed, without assimilating dense and rare to other qualities, it is hard to see what Anaxagoras' answer could have been. But such assimilation supplies an answer which Simplicius had not seen and which is more likely than an Anaxagorean anticipation of the Aristotelian system of alteration. This answer is that Anaxagoras looked on the rare and the dense, as on the hot and the cold, as two different stuffs. In vapour there would then be more of the rare than the dense; in the liquid the reverse is true. Anaxagoras would thus resemble Aristotle in assimilating change of density to normal qualitative change but would differ (as is generally agreed) in thinking of qualities as things. The change from dense to rare would thus mean for Anaxagoras the substitution of one thing for another; he would then be led to ignore the spatial relations involved. I cannot see why one should doubt this, unless on the basis of sheer reluctance to accept a radical difference between early and modern modes of thought.[73] I cannot see how else to make sense of Anaxagoras at this point;[74] and Anaxagoras is a thinker of sufficient subtlety to be given the benefit of the doubt.

The question may also be raised how Empedocles accounted for condensation and rarefaction, while maintaining the denial of void. Empedocles seems to have used the terms "rare" and "dense," but we have no very clear context and no detailed account of his own reconciliation of this usage with the absence of emptiness. It is not certain whether he predicated these terms of substances or of arrangements of them,[75] but this problem makes little, if any, difference to the question how he reconciled any notion of dense and rare with the abolition of void. Empedocles, indeed, may have seen no problem here.

Aristotle could see a problem, but left no clear solution. His denial of the existence of the void is well known, and in the course of his argument against it in *Physics* Δ he brings up the argument from condensation and rarefaction only to knock it down. It is difficult to see the force of Aristotle's reasoning. He appears to reject (*Physics* 216b30) the possibility of a separate void and hence of any kind of rarefaction based on it. The alternative of a rarefaction involving the postulation of a void, but not a separable void, he condescendingly says is less impossible (whatever that may mean!) but is still, for various reasons, to be rejected (216b33ff). Aristotle's subsequent arguments are not concerned with the *existence* of a void, but deal with the void *as a cause of motion*. Thus the final argument of his paragraph (217a8–10) points out that, if a higher degree of rarity means less void and entails upward motion, then, if there were absolute void, its speed would be infinite. Aristotle here answers his opponents, as often, simply by assuming his own general theory of cosmology to be true. He does this again in the following paragraph. There he answers those who say that there will not be movement without condensation and rarefaction unless either the universe bulges or one change is invariably counteracted by another equal and opposite change. His answer is to confront such a view with his own theory of alteration; condensation and rarefaction are evidently to be defended, without admitting void, by the hypothesis of a matter underlying each pair of opposites and by the description of change in terms of the actualization of the potential. To defend his position thus is to assimilate density and rarity to the other physical opposites and extinguish any decisive difference. But this appears to quarrel with the doctrine of the *Categories*;[76] for in that early treatise the rare and the dense are linked with the rough and the smooth as being distinct from other qualities, even ἀλλότρια ... τῆς περὶ τὸ ποιὸν διαιρέσεως. Aristotle in this youthful work properly remarked that each of the two pairs of opposites thus linked represented a positioning of the parts of the body possessing these qualities. Density he goes on to describe as due to the nearness of the parts to one another, and rarity to their mutual distance; but he does not explain (for this is logic, not physics) how one substance can be denser than another without void. In the *Physics*, however, all that he is concerned to say is that dense is opposed to rare and that change from one to the other follows the normal Aristotelian pattern of the inherence in one and the same matter of first one opposite and then the other.

This conflict between Aristotelian logic and physics shows that even Aristotle was not fully clear about the nature of the rarefaction process. It also shows, however, that it was possible to conceive of condensation and rarefaction without a void and yet not be wholly ignorant of the difference between dense-rare and other oppositions. But he would be a rash man who would deduce from this the possibility that earlier thinkers who deemed a void unnecessary for rarefaction were as clear-headed as the youthful Aristotle, seeing as well as he did the essential difference between dense-rare and other pairs of opposites. If Anaxagoras puts the rare and the dense alongside the hot and the cold, this is more likely to be because he saw no fundamental difference.

If Anaxagoras thought of condensation as the substitution of "the dense" for "the rare," then Anaximenes is not prima facie likely to have achieved greater insight, at least by a deliberate process of reasoning. If the Ionian Anaximenes (rather than an Eleatic like Melissus) had pointed out the fundamental difference between rarefaction and, say, heating, then it is not probable that Anaxagoras would have ignored the problem as Simplicius implies that he did. Anaxagoras' debt to Milesian thinking is obvious and needs no new emphasis.[77] Eleatic argument could be, and indeed had to be, partly ignored by the fifth-century pluralists, but the Ionian scientists seldom ignore each other. Naturally, however, it remains *possible* that Anaximenes had, in his instinctive habits of thought, advanced beyond the stage reached by Anaxagoras to the insight shown by Melissus. It remains possible that he had advanced to the notion of rarefaction as distinct from other kinds of change and, in the consciousness of that distinctiveness, made it the basic type on which all other kinds depended. Not being, like Anaxagoras and Aristotle, obliged for other reasons expressly to reject the void, Anaximenes may possibly have conceived of rarefaction and condensation as being due to the presence and absence of empty space. But it is hard to see that this is likely. Once again we should have to stand the history of philosophy on its head, this time to envisage a retrograde process in Ionian science from understanding to misunderstanding. Such retrogressions are possible; but I doubt if it can honestly be said that they are probable. What Anaxagoras and Aristotle either did not see or passed over as insignificant is not likely to have struck Anaximenes with blinding clarity, or even to have been in his mind. It is doubtful whether Anaximenes bothered to ask himself what was involved in the physics of condensation and rarefaction and whether, if he had, he would have arrived at the right answer. Certainly the point should not be assumed without further proof, as it often is. It was sufficient advance on previous views when Anaximenes brought philosophy down to brass tacks by naming a process easily discernible on a cosmic scale by which the original substance gave rise to the manifold world. There is no need to attribute to him the further step of a complete understanding of this process. It is at least as likely that Anaximenes considered the result of condensing as applied to air to be not, as we should say, condensed air, but simply water, earth, or any other appropriate substance. It is at least as likely that he posed the questions "What did the world arise from, and how?" as it is that he posed the (for his time) peculiar question, "What is the one stuff of which the world is made?" We can hardly *know*, in the prevailing shortage of evidence, how Anaximenes conceived his process of condensation and rarefaction, but it should require more than merely that process to convince us of his anticipation of Melissus in understanding it and his anticipation of Parmenides in banishing genesis and destruction from the real world.

SOME NON-PERIPATETIC EVIDENCE

[HIPPOCRATES] DE NATURA HOMINIS I

Pre-Aristotelian support for the doctrine that the Milesians believed in a single world-constituent is often sought in the first chapter of an early Hippocratic treatise, the *De natura hominis*:

φασί τε γὰρ ἕν τι εἶναι ὅτι ἔστι καὶ τοῦτ' εἶναι τὸ ἕν τε καὶ τὸ πᾶν, κατὰ δὲ τὰ ὀνόματα οὐχ ὁμολογέουσιν· λέγει δ' αὐτῶν ὁ μέν τις φάσκων ἠέρα τοῦτο εἶναι τὸ ἕν τε καὶ τὸ πᾶν, ὁ δὲ πῦρ, ὁ δὲ ὕδωρ, ὁ δὲ γῆν κτλ.

This passage was used by authorities as reputable as John Burnet and G. S. Kirk as evidence prior to Aristotle for the material monism of the early Milesians.[78] The first, so far as I know, to urge some degree of caution in the matter was Guthrie,[79] who pointed out that "the writer gives the impression that he is speaking of contemporary thinkers." It is indeed more than a mere impression; as Guthrie points out, the author starts by talking of "whoever is accustomed to hearing them speak..." and goes on to say that "anyone would know who... was present to hear their contradictions." Further reasons for doubt may be briefly expounded.

The author of this medical treatise is roundly and indiscriminately condemning all the a priori accounts of the world hindering the advance of science. The author of such a round of condemnation would be doing his cause little service if he attacked thinkers who lived a century or more before his time. One would expect him in the first instance to attack his contemporaries, perhaps his older contemporaries. It is indeed these that in the first instance he does attack. It is possible to argue that reference in the main to his contemporaries fails to exclude a passing reference to his predecessors of remoter date. But the question to be asked is surely not "What right have we to suppose that he was *not* referring to writings at least a century old?" but rather "Have we any evidence that he was?" The burden of proof rests squarely on those wishing to use this passage as evidence for the early Milesians. Without any other pre-Aristotelian evidence for material monism in Miletus, it would be rash to rely on this single sweeping remark.

The identification of the thinkers concerned is a subject on which too much time can easily be wasted. Does one always expect a man uttering so dashing a condemnation to stop and make sure of the accuracy of his remarks? Need we look for a proponent of every single view here mentioned? Surely not, any more (perhaps less) than we expect every Aristotelian generalization to be universally true. If we do look for such proponents, it behoves us to remember our desperate ignorance of the physical speculation of the late fifth century apart from the Atomists and Diogenes; the argument that "if any known thinker called earth the sole $\dot{\alpha}\rho\chi\dot{\eta}$, it can only have been Xenophanes" carries its defects on its face, for the possibility of a minor unknown thinker having held that view is by no means remote. Aristotle's generalization to the effect that none of the physicists made earth the $\dot{\alpha}\rho\chi\dot{\eta}$ is proved false[80] by the instance of Xenophanes and might well find other minor exceptions. The other thinkers concerned are easier of identification anyway. Diogenes (to say nothing of Idaeus)[81] will do for air, Hippo for water,[82] and we know of at least one so-called Heraclitean, named Antisthenes,[83] who might have held that fire was, as the post-Parmenidean "eclectics" would no doubt have put it, the thing comprising the "one" and "the all." If anyone were to object that I have not proved that this passage *cannot* refer to the Milesians, I should merely accept the point. The possibilities raised here for the Hippocratic references are in some cases no more than possibilities, in others only probabilities. But it should be stressed once more that the onus of proof does not rest on one who believes the author to be mentioning his contemporaries, perhaps his older contemporaries; the author himself indicates this as plain as a pikestaff. The proof would need to be given with the utmost clarity, and has not been given at all, that "Hippocrates" is doing anything other than, or in addition to, what he thus appears on the surface to be doing.

PLATO, SOPHIST 242 d-e

Extant pre-Aristotelian evidence for the Peripatetic interpretation of Milesian thought there is none. But there is a pre-Aristotelian passage which, if taken seriously and investigated closely, tells against the Aristotelian version of the history of early thought. This is the well-known passage of Plato's *Sophist* where the Eleatic Stranger offers some remarks on previous theories about reality.[84] These remarks have been the subject of innumerable notes already; but they have not always been sensible notes. What follows may not be sensible either but attempts at least to be consistent both with itself and with the facts of Platonic usage. What it does not claim is exhaustiveness.

ΞΕΝΟΣ. Εὐκόλως μοι δοκεῖ Παρμενίδης ἡμῖν διειλέχθαι καὶ πᾶς ὅστις πώποτε ἐπὶ κρίσιν ὥρμησε τοῦ τὰ ὄντα διορίσασθαι πόσα τε καὶ ποῖά ἐστιν.
ΘΕΑΙΤΗΤΟΣ. Πῇ;
ΞΕ. Μῦθόν τινα ἕκαστος φαίνεταί μοι διηγεῖσθαι παισὶν ὡς οὖσιν ἡμῖν, ὁ μὲν ὡς τρία τὰ ὄντα, πολεμεῖ δὲ ἀλλήλοις ἐνίοτε αὐτῶν ἄττα πῃ, τότε δὲ καὶ φίλα γιγνόμενα γάμους τε καὶ τόκους καὶ τροφὰς τῶν ἐκγόνων παρέχεται· δύο δὲ ἕτερος εἰπών, ὑγρὸν καὶ ξηρὸν ἢ θερμὸν καὶ ψυχρόν, συνοικίζει τε αὐτὰ καὶ ἐκδίδωσι· τὸ δὲ παρ' ἡμῖν Ἐλεατικὸν ἔθνος, ἀπὸ Ξενοφάνους τε καὶ ἔτι πρόσθεν ἀρξάμενον, ὡς ἑνὸς ὄντος τῶν πάντων καλουμένων οὕτω διεξέρχεται τοῖς μύθοις. Ἰάδες δὲ καὶ Σικελικαί τινες ὕστερον Μοῦσαι συνενόησαν ὅτι συμπλέκειν ἀσφαλέστερον ἀμφότερα, καὶ λέγειν ὡς τὸ ὂν πολλά τε καὶ ἕν ἐστιν ...

Much controversy has been provoked in particular by the second half of the Stranger's tale, concerning Heraclitus. But most scholars now accept Plato's account of Heraclitus as substantially true, despite its poetic expression, and many use the passage against the theory of an ecpyrosis in Heraclitus.[85] Doubts may be raised concerning the precision of Plato's interpretation of Eleaticism itself, on the grounds that what Parmenides said in the Way of Truth had little or nothing to do with "all things" but rather concerned "what is" or "what can be talked and thought about."[86] These strictures at least seem well founded, and we must bear in mind the possibility of some distortion of previous views in this passage. Well founded also, in my belief, are the doubts of those who question whether Xenophanes really anticipated Eleaticism in any significant way.[87] It is difficult to see what is significant for the Eleatics in Xenophanes' talk about god(s) or about the universe (in so far as he talked about the universe). Certainly Xenophanes had no stricter a notion of unity or of reality than his Ionian predecessors. If Xenophanes' epistemology influenced the Eleatics, that is hardly relevant to the Eleatic Stranger's history of the theory of Being. The allegation of anticipation of Eleaticism by Xenophanes put into the Stranger's mouth is an example of the perennial Greek tendency to thrust one's views back into the past as far as possible in order to give them greater authority. One may suspect that Plato has had the Stranger put into Eleatic mouths views that the Eleatics did not genuinely hold, partly in order to bring them closer to Xenophanes and partly in order to bring them closer to Heraclitus; the latter is unlikely to have talked about "reality"[88] but might have been considered with more plausibility to have talked about "all things." The reference to Xenophanes should not in this case be taken at face value. As Campbell remarked in his edition of the *Sophist*,[89] the words "from Xenophanes downwards, and even before Xenophanes" are "conceived in the same spirit as the attempt in the *Theaetetus* to refer the Heraclitean dogma to an unknown antiquity." It is difficult to imagine Plato's reference at *Theaetetus* 179e being taken seriously by anybody nowadays; Homer may have influenced Thales, but his anticipation of Heraclitus is hardly even specious, and the extension of the anticipation to thinkers "even older" is without factual basis of any sort known to Plato. This is not an accusation of bad faith; Plato just did not mean this extension to be taken seriously. No more need one take the whole of what Plato says in the *Sophist* passage with a straight face. Xenophanes is not necessarily there because Plato seriously thought he belonged there. It may be instructive to consider alternative reasons, conscious or unconscious, for his presence.

The whole passage represents a miniature dialogue by unnamed Presocratic thinkers concerning the number of real things. The first views mentioned are varieties of pluralism. Of these one holds that there are three, the second that there are two realities. This is contradicted by the Eleatics, who propound a monistic doctrine, and there follows a pair of compromises between monism and pluralism, compromises associated with Heraclitus and Empedocles. For this dialogue to have the appearance of a dialogue and not of a mere catalogue, it was necessary to make sure that the forms of pluralism were earlier, and the compromises later, than the first named monist. Plato probably intended to make the later date of the compromises clear with the word "later," though the precise application of the word has been disputed.[90] But Heraclitus did not in fact take Parmenides' views into account, since (evidently) he did not know of them. Therefore, if historical sense was to be made at all, a monist earlier than Heraclitus had to be found. The nearest Plato could think of to pre-Eleatic monism was apparently Xenophanes' theory of the greatest god. In effect Plato is departing somewhat from historical exactitude to avoid a more serious departure. But if the Milesians had held that all things were one, then the perversion (and indeed the mention) of Xenophanes would have been unnecessary.

But we have not yet squeezed the last drop of evidence from the *Sophist*. If Plato is talking chronological sense, and as much genuine history as that allows, it ought to be possible (given a little luck) to fix on the believers in three realities and in two realities. The most obvious believer in a triad is Ion of Chios, but there is no sound reason to suppose that Plato is deserting correct chronology so far as to name Ion first in such a "dialogue."[91] More likely is Pherecydes, with his initial trio of Zas, Time, and Earth (DK 7B1). If Plato or the Eleatic Stranger thought these were the sole realities rather than merely the three initial powers, then they were wrong. But the mistake would be a plausible one for an Eleatic or one imbued with Eleatic ideas to make. (It is to Plato's credit that he evidently did not make a similar mistake with respect to Thales.) A similar mistake could perhaps have been made concerning Hesiod, whose cosmogony starts with the triad of Chaos, Earth, and Eros (*Theogony* 116ff). So far we have no reason to doubt Plato's chronology, though we might feel a little doubtful of his status as an interpreter where he stands in need of a particular illustration of his general thesis. We come then to the Stranger's dualists. For this position there are two main candidates. Alcmaeon is one, and the Milesians are the other. But there are grave doubts about Alcmaeon's chronology,[92] and he is hardly early enough to meet Plato's chronological requirements—given that Plato had any. Alcmaeon suffers also from the defect, from the point of view of the interpreter of the Eleatic Stranger, that the evidence for his special interest in, and accordance of priority to, the particular opposites hot/cold and wet/dry is of the thinnest.[93] This last point rules out the Pythagorean school as well; to represent them as interested in marrying off hot and cold, wet and dry, would be sorry history. The only plausible candidates for the position of the Stranger's dualist(s) are the Milesians. I see no need to suppose that the Stranger is talking in vague and general terms about the Ionian Presocratics. Nor is there any need to suppose that Plato converted the Milesians into dualists from the necessity of forcing a dualism into the scheme somehow. For, first, Plato needed only to talk of thinkers believing in a plurality of real things and had no need of the specific number two; and, second, if he felt it improved the symmetry of his scheme to have a dualist faction, there was nothing to prevent him from alluding to the earliest Pythagoreans. The most reasonable interpretation of the evidence is that Plato did not think of the Milesians as monists, but as dualists.[94] His opinion is entitled to some respect. It should certainly not be dismissed as it was by Cornford in his later years "as superficial and misrepresenting the facts."[95]

But can we talk in this context of "the Milesians" as a group? The Eleatic Stranger's singular subjects are no bar,[96] but it is not possible to be very sure about the chronology of the relevant thinkers. If Anaximenes is "active about the middle of the sixth century"[97] and Xenophanes' life runs hardly earlier than 570–470,[98] then chronology gives no reason against including all the Milesians in Plato's dualists. But the only one to whom our sources ascribe a theory giving primacy to hot, cold, wet, and dry is Anaximander; hot and cold seem in Anaximenes' thought to have been somewhat subordinated to the rare and the dense. This is not, in my opinion, sufficient to exclude Anaximenes from the Eleatic Stranger's purview (it is a long way from the type of view attributed by Aristotle to Alcmaeon), though it does mean that one cannot *prove* him to have been in Plato's mind as one of the dualists.

Since the foregoing account of Plato's manner of constructing his historical paragraph is necessarily somewhat conjectural, it will be well to consider one alternative explanation of Plato's pressing of Xenophanes into service as an Eleatic. The obvious explanation might seem to be that Plato was *merely* following the well-known Greek tendency to push theories as far back into the past as possible to lend them respectability. If the Stranger attributes to Xenophanes "and thinkers even earlier" the doctrine that all things are one, this may be due merely to the attaching of greater authority to old beliefs. If this is the explanation, then it is worth noting that the logical consequences of this are the same for our purposes as those of the previously analysed hypothesis. The consequence is that the Milesian philosophers are still not regarded by Plato as monists. It might be thought that the phrase "and even earlier" implies some definite thinkers in Plato's mind; Steinhart[99] even suggested Orpheus. But in reality this phrase indicates, on the hypothesis here under discussion, that Plato knew of *nobody* relevant before Xenophanes, that he did *not* attribute monism to at least the early Milesians. If he had, he would have mentioned such monist(s) by name. This is evidence, not that he had somebody other than Xenophanes in mind, but that he had nobody else in mind.[100] On this hypothesis also we are driven to the conclusion that Plato either knew nothing of the alleged Milesian monists or believed them not to be monists.

The possibility must be reckoned with that Plato had simply not heard about the philosophical activities of the Milesians, though he had heard of certain activities of Thales.[101] Here, apart from the general probabilities of the case, it is necessary to digress in order to draw on the results of an article (often cited but until recently little discussed) by Bruno Snell.[102] Snell reminded us[103] that Aristotle's remark that Thales held the "principle" to be water was not based on Thales' own writings. Noting the pre-Aristotelian connection of Thales with earlier "theologians" implied at *Metaphysics* 983b27ff, Snell suspected (surely correctly) that this connection at least was not handed down in oral tradition alone but was more likely to have originated in a written work. Be that as it may, Snell went on to observe that readers of the *Metaphysics* are usually referred to Plato's *Cratylus* 402b and *Theaetetus* 152e and 180c–d.[104] These passages, he pointed out, do not mention Thales. But they are indeed connected with the Aristotelian account of Thales' antecedents; both share the mention of Homer on Oceanus, and if one were asked to put names to Aristotle's παμπαλαίους καὶ πρώτους θεολογήσαντας the obvious and indeed (except perhaps for Musaeus) the only ones (Homer being pre-empted) are Hesiod and Orpheus, whom Plato cites.[105] If Aristotle, however, had Plato in mind at all, he was not Aristotle's principal source, because Plato does not mention Thales or water in this connection. One could not therefore cite Plato, as Aristotle cites his τινές, for the resemblance between the myths and Thales. The question arises whether the connection of the myths with Thales was post-Platonic or pre-Platonic. To this question also Snell returns indubitably the right answer. We need not use the argument that Plato is merely joking—for some scholars have declared Aristotle capable of misunderstanding a joke—but can rely on other considerations. Snell observed that Plato's context consists mostly of etymologies but that the citations do not; dealing not with language but with facts, they are to that extent alien to Plato's context. More pertinently still, as illustrations—even joking illustrations—of a doctrine of perpetual flux, the passages cited by Plato are feeble. Only the Orphic epithet καλλίρροος provides any reference to flux whatever; but all the passages cited by either Plato or Aristotle suggest, without exception, that the beginning of things was, as Thales doubtless thought, water. Each and every one of the citations shows a close resemblance to the doctrine that things began with water; only one of them shows, in an incidental epithet, that connection with flux which would associate the passage naturally with Heraclitus. One may cheerfully agree that it is remotely conceivable that Heraclitus was the original thinker to whom these passages were attached; it would be difficult to argue that it was probable. It is much more probable that Plato jocularly misapplied an historical statement afterwards, and rightly, taken seriously by Aristotle. The identity of Aristotle's and Plato's joint source is a matter at present of small importance;[106] but it is established beyond reasonable doubt by Snell's brilliant argument that there was such a common source.

To make this important point clear, let us consider what is entailed by the conceivable alternatives. It *could* be an accident that the passages of Plato and Aristotle resemble one another so closely; it *could* be that Plato's joke was taken up by Aristotle. But the hypothesis of accident has not, so far as I am aware, been entertained explicitly for a very long time. It would take a devout believer in the goddess Chance to swallow this; we have against it not merely the choice of the same Homeric passage and the same rare word παμπαλαίους but also the probability that Hesiod and Orpheus are in Aristotle's mind as in Plato's. I only mention this alternative for the sake of logical completeness and need not mention it again. The other possibility, that Plato's joke on Heraclitus was seen to be more appropriate, if taken fairly seriously, to Thales, is apparently believed by a number of scholars,[107] but none of them has publicly scrutinized Snell's argument. Since τινές in Aristotle can hardly mean himself, especially when he is ironical at their expense, we are driven to suppose that between Plato's *Cratylus* and Aristotle's *Metaphysics A* there stands a source which preceded Aristotle in taking Plato's joke seriously (more seriously even than Aristotle, if one may take Aristotle's οἴονται at face value). Not only must this source be supposed to have taken Plato's joke with a straight face, but Aristotle was presumably aware, since the source is unlikely to have been unconnected with the Academy, that this was the origin of its view. We have to presuppose a high incidence of humourlessness in the Academy. Even this desperate series of hypotheses still ignores the coincidence that Thales is much more appropriate than Heraclitus to be illustrated by the poetic passages cited. To put the inappropriate before the appropriate in the way demanded by the hypothesis that Plato originated this set of poetic quotations is a sure way in general to be wrong. Chance must indeed be given a field-day by those who cling to the notion that Aristotle is here borrowing directly or indirectly from Plato.

It follows that among the sources Aristotle and Plato had read on the subject of early philosophy was one which attributed to Thales the doctrine of the primacy of water, stating the resemblance of this doctrine to some expressions of the ancient poets. It remains, on return from what may seem a digression, to point out that this has a bearing on Plato's account of the history of theories of "Being," put into the mouth of the Stranger from Elea. Its most obvious bearing is on the question whether Plato had heard of Milesian philosophical activities. In fact it enables us to answer in the affirmative the question whether Plato had heard of a doctrine of Thales concerning water; for it shows that at least one of the sources for Aristotle's remarks on Thales was known to Plato and that this one pointed out the resemblance between Thales' doctrine and the Homeric statement that Ocean is the origin of all. We can therefore say with some confidence that, if Plato's mention of Xenophanes is motivated by the desire to secure ancient authority for monism, then either he dated Xenophanes before Thales—another remotely conceivable alternative without supporting evidence or antecedent probability —or he did not interpret this statement about Thales' water doctrine in a monistic sense. At least Plato's implied rejection of the belief that Thales was a monist was not due to ignorance of his water doctrine. Indeed, for whichever reason we suppose the reference to Xenophanes to have been inserted, it implies a genuine rejection of the monistic interpretation of at least one version of Thales' water doctrine.

ARISTOTLE'S SOURCE(S) FOR THALES' WATER DOCTRINE

Some sceptics do not pay sufficient attention to the fact that Aristotle refers to previous tradition for his statement of Thales' views about water. If Aristotle is genuinely reproducing the sense of what these sources, or even one of them, actually said, then that source would be pre-Aristotelian and not open to the suspicion of having invented Thales' water monism in order to fit Peripatetic doctrine or argument. The suggestion that Hippo, seeking authority for his own views, was responsible,[108] at best a plausible conjecture, fails to account for the Platonic rejection of Hippo's hypothetical remarks in favour of another tradition not making Thales a monist like Hippo. The question arises, and must be discussed with some care, whether Aristotle's own remarks give any indication of what he found in his source(s). All avenues of approach must be utilized in order to see whether we should trust Plato's interpretation of his sources (which for all we know may have included Hippo) or Aristotle's version of the evidence available to the Lyceum. If we are going to argue that a passage of Plato, admittedly poetical in tone,[109] and admittedly not sound at all points, deserves credit before a professedly historical statement of Aristotle's, then we should neither do so, nor ask anyone else to do so, without exploring all the extant evidence with the greatest thoroughness. Did Aristotle's source(s) say the same as Plato's appear to have said, or something different?

The key to this question is to be found in Aristotle's own text. It lies in the very sentence in which Aristotle first records the doctrine that water for Thales is the ἀρχή of all things: Θαλῆς μὲν ὁ τῆς τοιαύτης ἀρχηγὸς φιλοσοφίας ὕδωρ φησὶν εἶναι [sc. τὴν τοιαύτην ἀρχήν] (διὸ καὶ τὴν γῆν ἐφ᾽ ὕδατος ἀπεφήνατο εἶναι) . . . (983b20–22). The word διό, "wherefore," by which Aristotle links the doctrines that water is the ἀρχή and that the earth floats on water, has caused some disagreement. This διό can signify two things, and two things only. It can signify that Aristotle found attributed to Thales the argument that, because water is the ἀρχή of all things, therefore the earth floats on it; or it can signify that Aristotle found attributed to Thales the doctrine that the earth floats on water, and himself deduced from it the further doctrine that water was the ἀρχή of all things. There is no other alternative signification for the word διό in such a context in Aristotelian or indeed in any normal Greek. We have to choose between these alternatives and cannot escape the choice. Cherniss,[110] seeing this point, suspected that Aristotle himself deduced Thales' belief in the doctrine of water as ἀρχή from the doctrine that the earth floats on water. By so doing on grounds merely of suspicion of Aristotle's methods in general, without adducing specific argument, he earned a rebuke from Guthrie.[111] One cannot indeed rely solely on one's general estimate of Aristotle, unless one is prepared to put him completely outside the pale; for Aristotle remarks a few lines below (984a2) that "Thales *is said to have* declared himself thus about the first cause"; unless Aristotle was referring simply and solely to his own "saying" a few lines before, which would put him indeed beyond the pale, he has obtained the doctrine that water is the ἀρχή not by his own deduction from any other doctrine but from tradition (or at least from his interpretation of tradition). We are left with the only other possibility, which is that Aristotle found—or thought he found—in his sources the argument that because water is the ἀρχή of all things, therefore the earth floats on it. The peculiarity of this argument has not escaped scholarly notice; Cherniss was probably impelled by its oddness to take the path that he did, and Snell[112] in a German paraphrase of the sentence writes, as well he might, an exclamation mark after the word *deswegen*. But Cherniss' way of escape from the peculiarity is not the right way, as we have seen, and another must be found; no one can seriously entertain the possibility that Thales or anyone else in the whole history of serious argument defended the view that water is what holds the earth up on the grounds that water was the sole constituent of things, the "ground of being," or an ἀρχή such as Aristotle has just described. Premiss and conclusion would manifestly have nothing to do with each other. What, then, was Thales said in the tradition to have argued?

To ask this question is to see at once that the argument, from being thus nonsensical, becomes sensible, immediately we suppose that the argument attributed to Thales ran as follows: Everything began from water (a premiss derived from Eastern myths); therefore the earth rests on water.[113] This argument is—though not sound—at least worth putting forward. If the initial state of things was a mass of water, and the earth, as the Egyptians believed, rose out of the water, then it is reasonable (though not a common Egyptian belief) to suppose that what is underneath the earth supporting it is still the water out of which it rose. It is of course possible even on this hypothesis that the earth is supported by further earth, continuing down indefinitely below the water and constituting also the water's bed or support. It is a legitimate question that Aristotle asks: What supports the water? But, to one who believed the original state to have been water, the question what held up the water could very naturally fail to arise; it cannot have been held up in the beginning by anything else, since there was, in the beginning, nothing else to hold it up. Why should it need support now? Thales makes very good sense if we believe him to have reasoned (perhaps for the first time) on these lines, and one can well understand why an authority reputable enough to be used by Aristotle should attribute the argument to him.

This suggestion makes, it seems, better sense of the tradition concerning Thales than any other yet put forward, and we may use it at least as a working hypothesis. It would follow that Aristotle makes a mistake in his account of the argument, and it is necessary to examine the nature of the mistake. On our hypothesis Aristotle has got the premiss of the argument wrong; he has implied clearly that Thales' premiss in this line of thought was that water is "such an ἀρχή," meaning something that persists as a substrate through change; this is, as we have seen, wholly irrelevant to Thales' alleged conclusion. What is relevant is the proposition that water was the beginning of things. Now, even if Thales did not use the word ἀρχή, and there was a persistent tradition implying that he did not,[114] the word could well have been used by a historian writing after Anaximander's use of the word, and it may have been this word which misled Aristotle. Of this we cannot be certain; but what at least makes sense of Aristotle's report of the tradition is the supposition that Aristotle has mistaken a statement of origin for a statement of constituent, in a context wherein Aristotle (whatever his source's vocabulary) uses the word ἀρχή. It is precisely this kind of mistake that we found him making in describing the course of Anaximander's argument,[115] so that surprise is hardly in order.

There are indeed some slighter indications in Aristotle's text that this is what he has done. These indications rest, however, on an implied argument from silence, and, though not negligible, would not be completely convincing by themselves. When Aristotle (983b27ff) cites from his τινές illustrations from the poets as possible anticipations of Thales' doctrine, not one of them tells in favour of the supposition that water is the substrate of all change, the stuff of which all things are made. The citation of Homer's 'Ωκεανὸς γένεσις πάντων is clearly a support for the supposition that Homer anticipated the doctrine that things began with water; it is no support for Homeric thinking about a substrate, element, or sole constituent. The same is true of the citation of Hesiod on the Styx; it is especially illuminating to observe here how Aristotle goes out of his way to argue that the object sworn by is the most highly honoured *and therefore the oldest*. This additional step in the argument is necessary for the proof that Hesiod's world (like Thales') began with water, but it is surely unnecessary for a proof that Hesiod anticipated Thales in the alleged doctrine that water is the sole constituent of things. For this allegation the object sworn by could be simply the "most honoured" thing, and thence the most real. The failure to take this path is the more striking since in early poetry there are (as we should expect) no direct and straightforward statements that water is the material of things; if poetic statements are to be interpreted symbolically as anticipations of Thales, it is at this point that such interpretation is particularly needed, rather than for the point about water as the origin of things. This argument may serve, incidentally, as a counter to the otherwise possible suggestion that the failure of Aristotle (and also of Plato)[116] to cite poetic anticipations of the substrate doctrine is due to the fact that there were none to cite; for it is clear that they and their source were not restricted to literal interpretation. The argument stands: all the citations in the relevant passages of Plato and Aristotle point or are made to point to a doctrine that water was the initial state of the world, and none of them is made to point to the doctrine that water is the material of the world, even where it would have been easy to make them point to this latter doctrine. This also looks as if Aristotle has taken over for his purposes an argument originally designed for others.

The explanation of the facts of Aristotle's text given above, that Aristotle's source(s) talked about beginnings, whereas Aristotle himself was constrained to talk about substrates and constituents, seems more reasonable than any other explanation put forward for those same facts —where, that is, the facts have not hitherto escaped notice. It results that this is the most plausible explanation of Aristotle's statements and observations in the very passage on which scholars have relied for the teaching that Thales believed water to be a sole constituent, a substrate of change, or a "ground of being." It results therefore that the most plausible available basis for modern beliefs in Thales' doctrine of the world's unity in water suggests rather that Aristotle did not find anything about substrates (or the like) in the traditions available to him. The most plausible explanation of the texts is that Aristotle misinterpreted the tradition and misapplied the arguments contained in it and that Plato (in the *Sophist*) interpreted it rightly. But, before we finally make up our minds, it is worth asking one more question.

WHY SHOULD THE PERIPATETICS HAVE MADE THIS KIND OF MISTAKE?

To follow Plato and ignore Aristotle's and Theophrastus' reading of the tradition requires courage, even on the basis of some facts of Aristotle's text which have found otherwise no satisfactory explanation. It behoves us to find a reason why the Peripatetics should make this kind of mistake and why Theophrastus could with a quiet conscience follow his friend and master in an erroneous interpretation. It is not enough to argue the general carelessness of Aristotle or the general dependence of Theophrastus on Aristotle; both these doctrines are currently under fire and need modification. Some more specific explanation of the Peripatetic misinterpretation needs to be found. There are two sources of light on this topic, one much brighter than the other. One is the Aristotelian doctrine of causation, and the other is the language available to the Milesians. Let us use the second, less clear, source first.

Necessarily, the subject is even more than usually speculative, but some suggestions can be made. We have seen that Milesian talk about an ἀρχή in the sense of "beginning," or traditions using the word, could have misled Aristotle. It is also conceivable—one cannot put it higher on the scale of probability—that the Milesians used another kind of expression to describe an initial state of the world which could very easily have been misunderstood by somebody on the look-out for a constituent. They could, and for all we know did, use the preposition ἐκ with the genitive case to describe the relation between things and the initial state; this expression, as Aristotle remarks (*Metaphysics* 1023a26ff), is used in more ways than one. First of the ways listed by Aristotle is to say that X is made of Y, as the statue is made of bronze, ὡς ἐκ χαλκοῦ ὁ ἀνδριάς.[117] Last, as it happens, on Aristotle's list is the use of ἐκ to denote temporal succession, either where X changes into Y or where Y merely follows X in time. The examples given for "X changes into Y" are all pairs of opposites, or virtual opposites, but that of course is due to Aristotle's tendency to regard all change as between opposites. The Milesians might easily have meant this sense when they said that things arose "from" their primal substance, and have been misunderstood by Aristotle and Theophrastus to mean the first sense, implying a material cause.

The Peripatetics would be all the more prone to make this error in their discussion of causes since they did not recognize as a cause that which preceded something in time, or was the state from which it arose, except in so far as the pre-existent bronze would be the material cause for the statue. Night, for example, is not in Aristotelian philosophy a cause of day, yet it is quite legitimate in Aristotelian Greek to say that day comes from night: the only way by which, e.g., Anaximander's "unlimited" could be fitted into the Aristotelian system of causation was as the material cause. It showed no signs of being the final or formal cause and could not well be the motive cause since it was also, in the first instance, the thing moved and Aristotle had, he thought, abolished self-motion (*Physics* 257a33ff). If the "unlimited" was to fit, and if any Milesian ἀρχή was to fit, into the Aristotelian system of causes, it had to be as the material cause, as the bronze which was there before the statue. Theophrastus does not differ materially from his master in his doctrine of causation, so far as we know, and would be exposed to the same temptation. The existence of a temptation is clear. Aristotle, with his own theory of the four causes already established and firmly in mind,[118] is going through previous philosophies to see if they had in mind any but his own four causes. Faced with the Milesian originative substance, if it fitted none of his four causes, he had the choice of adapting it to the nearest one or of saying that it was not a cause at all. To add another cause for originative substances would have been an odd extension of the meaning of "cause." Eased perhaps by the linguistic points we have suggested, the choice of adaptation was only natural and will have been virtually unconscious.[119] The assumption that his Milesian predecessors must have been talking about causes would be at most a semi-conscious one, and from that to the assimilation of their primary substance to his own matter was a short step, easily taken by a man in a hurry—and who, seeing Aristotle's colossal achievement, doubts that he was in a hurry?[120] We have to remember that Aristotle elsewhere reads back into a Presocratic his own notion of alteration by inherence of successive opposites in the same matter.[121]

We may further observe that Theophrastus, as in the case of Thales' alleged reasons for the choice of water as the ἀρχή, is without the hesitations and expressions of caution which characterize the Aristotelian pronouncements about Anaximander's belief in the material cause. Theophrastus goes further than Aristotle here, and in a scarcely acceptable way. Aristotle conspicuously omits Anaximander's name from the list of early thinkers concerned with material causes in the first book of the *Metaphysics*. We need not believe with Cherniss[122] that this is because Aristotle's thesis was that all the early thinkers thought of none but the material cause; for Aristotle himself remarks that [not all but] "*most* of the early philosophers thought that material kinds of principle were the principles of things."[123] Either, therefore, Aristotle was not overconcerned with completeness or he found Anaximander's "unlimited" even more awkward to assimilate to his substrate than the other Milesian "principles." Any doubts Aristotle had might be justified, if there is anything in Aristotle's distinction at *Physics* 187a12ff between the alteration used by the other Milesians and the separation process of Anaximander. When Aristotle attributes to Anaximander the notion of a substrate, it is either in a cautious note briefly inserted in the middle of an argument, a note whose original intention is disputable, or in a bold generalization not necessarily composed with Anaximander in mind throughout.[124] This is neither the nature nor the tone of the extant versions of Theophrastus on this subject. Theophrastus, though perhaps still distinguishing between separation and condensation-rarefaction, blandly and simply remarks that Anaximander's ἄπειρον was the "principle and element."[125] This statement is hardly defended today by even the most ardent supporters of the general Peripatetic interpretation of early Greek philosophy. No one believes that Anaximander thought the world was *made of* "unlimited"; but that is quite clearly what Theophrastus meant, if we have indeed the words of Theophrastus. In this context at least, to use Theophrastus as a check on Aristotle is more than difficult. What we see here is not Theophrastus correcting Aristotle but Theophrastus evincing a tendency easily understandable in a Peripatetic, and precisely that tendency of which we have been accusing Aristotle. The tendency to assimilate to an element or substrate that which was not similar in all relevant respects is here apparent, and not all Theophrastus' study of the text was sufficient to prevent it from taking effect. Indeed, Theophrastus lacks both Aristotle's caution and his excuse of compression and has probably taken an Aristotelian generalization too deeply to heart.[126]

CONCLUSION

We are not, it must be repeated, dealing with certainties. Such conclusions as can be drawn from the complex and often ambivalent evidence at our disposal are merely probabilities. Not all readers will necessarily agree with the present estimate of the balance of probability. But let that estimate at least be clear. We are confronted with the evidence of Aristotle and Theophrastus for a certain theory held by some at least of the early Milesian philosophers. This theory is historically unmotivated as a prosaic theory, if placed in the sixth century B.C., and constitutes there an extraordinary anticipation of a type of answer to Parmenides not uncommon in the fifth century. In the fifth century it is motivated very clearly as an answer to Parmenides on the manifold world and on the impossibility of coming-to-be and passing-away. Examination of the Peripatetic evidence shows that it is understandable without difficulty and without special pleading that they should be wrong in this question; there is detectable in both Aristotle and Theophrastus a tendency to read back into others of their predecessors views similar to those attributed by them to the Milesians, and we can see why they might make such a mistake in the case of the Milesians also. The Peripatetic interpretation is not supported by any earlier evidence and is contradicted by a passage of Plato—admittedly a passage hard to interpret with any assurance. On the whole, the balance of probability would already seem to be against the Peripatetic view; when we recall finally that in his main statement of the alleged theory Aristotle shows clear signs of having misinterpreted his source(s) and misapplied the arguments it/they contained (misapplying them indeed in the direction of just such a "reading back" as has been found elsewhere), then we should not hesitate overlong to abandon the Peripatetic judgement.

Assuming this judgement of the probabilities to be correct, there follow certain consequences for the subject of this book. For the history of problems involving the antithesis of the one and the many, there are two separate aspects to be considered. The first is that, if the Milesians did not believe in a single substance underlying all change, in the Aristotelian sense or in any sense put forward by recent writers, then there is no reason to associate with them the view that all things were one, or that one thing was many things, or any similar doctrine. The substantial homogeneity of matter on which the predication of unity could readily be based has, if our conclusions are sound, no place in the Milesian outlook. Nor is there any need to suppose that these early thinkers had any other compelling reason to talk about the unity of things, whether of all things or many things. For though, according to Aristotle,[127] one can attribute unity to things linked (in practically any way) to one further thing, and a common origin could not be excluded from the list of unities, yet this is a technically philosophical rather than a common-language analysis. Aristotle gives no hint that ordinary usage predicated unity of two or more things with a common origin. Nor is there known to me any Greek example of such a use of language. It follows that, always on the assumption that our analysis of Milesian naturalism is sound, there is no need whatever to suppose the Milesians to have believed in the unity of all things or of "the many." It would follow that there is no good reason to suppose that any attack on the belief in the unity of all or of many things could be launched in the direction of the Milesian philosophers. If theirs were the only such doctrine for Parmenides to attack, and if he did attack such a doctrine, he could have saved his breath. Once we accept the probabilities as they are here estimated, the historical sequence of Milesian belief in the unity of all or many things, and Eleatic assault on that belief, vanishes into a limbo of improbability.

It is somewhat otherwise with the problem—if problem it was—of one thing becoming many, or of many things arising out of the one. One can say with good reason that the Milesians may have described their cosmogonies in terms of one and many. They could describe their originative stuffs as unities, and the manifold world as manifold in its variety. They could have explicitly declared that the many things of this world arose from one initial thing. There is nothing against the supposition that they did so, nothing in either the facts of Greek linguistic usage or the history of thought. It remains possible that they did so express themselves. But, if they did, it can safely be said that we shall never know it. Practically any statement concerning Milesian linguistic usage is based on nothing but conjecture. Attention would obviously be directed by the Eleatics to the antithesis between one and many, in that they argued for the unity of reality against its plurality; no statement that is made after the Eleatics concerning earlier thinkers and imputing to them the one-many antithesis can ever be entirely free from suspicion of infection by Eleatic habits of thought. It is against such a background that one should look even at poetic statements such as the famous lines of Euripides,[128] put into the mouth of Melanippe:

> κοὐκ ἐμὸς ὁ μῦθος, ἀλλ' ἐμῆς μητρὸς πάρα,
> ὡς οὐρανός τε γαῖά τ' ἦν μορφὴ μία·
> ἐπεὶ δ' ἐχωρίσθησαν ἀλλήλων δίχα
> τίκτουσι πάντα κἀνέδωκαν εἰς φάος κτλ.

Did Melanippe's mother speak, or was she likely to have spoken, in terms such as these? Or would she have spoken rather in terms merely of a gap arising between earth and heaven? We do not know; but we observe that, if she did, she used the word "one" with more emphasis on contiguity than on the homogeneity more appropriate to the Milesian ἀρχή; and, since

Euripides had doubtless read his Parmenides as well as his Anaxagoras, we should do well to avoid conjecture. No extant Greek text earlier than the Milesians speaks in terms of one and many in the subject of cosmogony; neither do oriental cosmogonies normally emphasize this aspect.

Suspicious readers may think that the remainder of this argument will rest on the assumption that, because there is no evidence for Milesian usage of the terms "one" and "many" in cosmogonical context, therefore the Milesians did not use them so. But to do so would be to go beyond the evidence just as much as to argue on the contrary hypothesis would be. Where we are ignorant, we must admit it. There is, however, currently somewhat more danger of an argument's being founded, consciously or unconsciously, on the alleged likelihood of Milesian use of such terms in such contexts; it perhaps needs saying that the temptation to do this should be resisted. In this connection it is not the Milesian usage that is decisive one way or the other: it is Parmenides who needs examination. But first we must inspect the doctrines of some others of Parmenides' predecessors.

III

XENOPHANES

Xenophanes is one of the most vexed of the early Greek thinkers, and any attempt to explain even what he was talking about, let alone what he had to say, must inevitably be controversial. There is no need to shrink from controversy; but, since the bibliography of the subject has fairly recently been established in great detail by C. Corbato and M. Untersteiner,[1] it will be possible to dispense with some of the apparatus of modern scholarship that would otherwise have been necessary. It will be more profitable to discuss (without pretensions to great originality) ancient evidence for Xenophanes' belief in the unity of things, of the world, or of his god. The thesis maintained in this book, that no one before Parmenides can be proved to have advanced the theory of the unity of reality, is bound to come up against the ancient statements about Xenophanes; for Plato, possibly Aristotle, and certainly Theophrastus taught that Xenophanes did believe in the unity of the world. But the possibilities that Plato was not serious, and that Aristotle's ambiguity misled Theophrastus into misinterpreting Xenophanes' words, are alive enough to warrant closer examination of the evidence.

THEOPHRASTUS' REPORT

It is not an easy matter to discover exactly what Theophrastus reported about Xenophanes. One might turn to the passage where Simplicius cites Theophrastus and mentions him by name; but unfortunately the extent of Simplicius' quotation and paraphrase of Theophrastus cannot be taken for granted in this instance. Simplicius was apparently in some confusion here,[2] and we need to try by comparison of other doxographers to arrive at a recension of Theophrastus on Xenophanes. This recension will be assisted by the accompanying table (pages 68–69).[3]

That Theophrastus admitted the unity of the world to his account of Xenophanes is, on inspection of this table, obvious. On this point are agreed Hippolytus, Cicero (in the *Academica*), Simplicius, Pseudo-Galen, Sextus Empiricus, and Theodoret (probably deriving from Aëtius[4]). The form taken by the ascription of unity to Xenophanes' world is a subordinate question but is nevertheless worth discussion for the light the argument may throw on the assessment of the sources descended from Theophrastus. We should like to know if possible whether Theophrastus connected the god with the one world, and, if so, how; whether the sentence connecting or equating god and world had "god" for subject or predicate; whether it was τὸ πᾶν or τὰ πάντα that Theophrastus declared to be one in Xenophanes' thought. These questions concerning Theophrastus do not decide what Xenophanes actually thought, but they do offer a chance of evaluating Theophrastus' account. It is well to find out as much as the evidence can teach us about Theophrastus on Xenophanes before deciding whether to believe him.

To take the third of these questions first, the singular τὸ πᾶν is used in the relevant context by Hippolytus, Simplicius, Theodoret (probably representing Aëtius), and Pseudo-Plutarch. This list is formidable, but Sextus wavers,[5] speaking first of the singular τὸ πᾶν and then making the god συμφυῆ τοῖς πᾶσιν; and Cicero (in the *Academica*) and Pseudo-Galen are ranged on the other side. These supporters of the plural might normally be found lacking either in number or in weight, but there are some special factors to be considered. Plurals occur in Cicero's Academic doxography in earlier contexts and might have influenced the account there of Xenophanes; one plural occurs immediately before the relevant passage of Pseudo-Galen and may (though this is less plausible) have influenced this writer also in his version of Xenophanes. But this does not settle our question. On the opposite side may be urged that Xenophanes was regarded by the tradition as an Eleatic, and the temptation to assimilate his doctrine in such details to one (involving the singular τὸ πᾶν) often ascribed to Parmenides[6] may have proved too strong for a number of excerptors. The passage of Cicero probably derives from Theophrastean excerpts (made by Clitomachus?)[7] and may thus be nearer to Theophrastus' own work than any of our other doxographical sources, with the possible exception of Simplicius. It may be interesting first to compare this agreement between Cicero and Pseudo-Galen with another, and then to indicate an agreement in a third detail between Cicero, Simplicius, and (less exactly) Theodoret and the *MXG*.

Unfortunately, the further agreement between Cicero and Pseudo-Galen is also open to more than one explanation. Cicero has *et id esse deum* at exactly the point in the argument where Pseudo-Galen has καὶ

Author	Limited/Unlimited	Moved/Unmoved	Spherical
Plato *Soph*. 242c–d	—	—	—
Aristotle *Metaphys*. 986b18ff	both or neither (implied)	—	?
Ps.-Aristotle *MXG* §§3–4 (A28)	neither	neither	σφαιροειδῆ (because πάντῃ ὁμοῖον)
Simplicius *in Phys*. 22.22ff (A31)	neither	neither	probably unmentioned (see Diels's app. crit. at 23.19)
Nicolaus Damascenus Περὶ θεῶν (ap. Simpl. 23.14ff)	ἄπειρον	ἀκίνητον	—
Alexander (ap. Simpl. 23.16ff)	πεπερασμένον	—	σφαιροειδές (prob.)
Pseudo-Galen *Hist. Philos.* 7 (A35)	πεπερασμένον	—	—
Cicero *Acad.* 2.118 (A4 and A34)	—	—	*conglobata figura*
Cicero *De nat. deor.* 1.28 (A34)	*infinitum*	—	—
Hippolytus *Ref.* 6.14.2ff (A33)	πεπερασμένον τὴν γῆν ἄπειρον (no ἀήρ)	οὐδὲν ... κινεῖται	σφαιροειδῆ
Ps.-Plutarch *Strom.* 4 (A32)	τὴν γῆν ἄπειρον (no ἀήρ). (Cf. Aristot. et al. at A47)	—	—
Sextus Empiricus *Pyrrh. Hyp.* 1.224 (A35)	—	—	σφαιροειδῆ
Aëtius (Diels, *Dox.*, p. 332) (A37)	—	—	—
Theodoret 4.5 (A36)	πεπερασμένον	πάμπαν ἀκίνητον	σφαιροειδές
Diogenes Laertius 9.19 (A1)	κόσμους ἀπείρους	—	οὐσίαν θεοῦ σφαιροειδῆ μηδὲν ὁμοῖον ἔχουσαν ἀνθρώπῳ·

DOXOGRAPHY

πάντῃ ὁμοῖον	One	Subject	Eternal
—	ὡς ἑνὸς ὄντος	τῶν πάντων καλουμένων	—
—	τὸ ἓν εἶναί φησι	τὸν θεόν	—
ὁμοῖον... παντη, ὁρῶντα... πάντῃ (otherwise one part would be superior to another)	τὸν θεόν... ἕνα (3.11); cf. 3.3 and 3.9, τὸ δὴ τοιοῦτον ἕν	ὃν τὸν θεὸν εἶναι λέγει (τὸ ἕν at 3.11)	3.1–2: ἀγένητον (in effect) and therefore ἀΐδιον
—	μίαν δὲ ἕν / τὸ γὰρ ἕν	τὴν ἀρχὴν ἤτοι τὸ ὂν καὶ πᾶν... τοῦτο καὶ πᾶν τὸν θεὸν ἔλεγεν	23.4: ἀγένητον καὶ ἀΐδιον
—	—	τὴν ἀρχήν	—
διὰ τὸ πανταχόθεν ὁμοῖον	—	perhaps neuter: see 23.16 αὐτό	—
—	ἕν	εἶναι πάντα καὶ τοῦτο ὑπάρχειν θεόν... ἀμετάβλητον	—
—	unum esse	omnia neque id esse mutabile et id esse deum	...neque natum unquam ac sempiternum
—	—	omne praeterea quod esset... deum voluit esse	—
ὁμοῖον πάντῃ... καὶ πᾶσι τοῖς μορίοις αἰσθητικόν	ἕν	τὸν θεὸν εἶναι... ...ἕνα / τὸ πᾶν	ἀΐδιον / οὐδὲν γίνεται οὐδὲ φθείρεται
—	implies one using an resembling	god, argument that of MXG	?
—	ἓν εἶναι	τὸ πᾶν καὶ τὸν θεὸν συμφυῆ τοῖς πᾶσιν... ἀμετάβλητον...	—
—	—	τὸν κόσμον	ἀγένητον καὶ ἀΐδιον καὶ ἄφθαρτον τὸν κόσμον
—	ἓν εἶναι	τὸ πᾶν	οὐ γενητὸν ἀλλ' ἀΐδιον
ὅλον δὲ ὁρᾶν κτλ.	—	σύμπαντα δὲ εἶναι νοῦν καὶ φρόνησιν καὶ	ἀΐδιον

τοῦτο εἶναι θεόν. The precise coincidence here in wording and actually of order[8] argues either that this was Theophrastus' own phraseology or that Pseudo-Galen was excerpting the same intermediate source as Cicero. The second hypothesis is reinforced by the fact that only Pseudo-Galen and Sextus of the Greek sources have ἀμετάβλητον to correspond with Cicero's *neque id esse mutabile*, perhaps supported further by Diogenes' οὐ παραλλακτούς of the κόσμοι. That Pseudo-Galen here drew on an Academic source, perhaps Clitomachus, is not to be ruled out; the Sceptic Sextus may have drawn on the same tradition (despite his philosophical disagreement with Clitomachus at *Adversus mathematicos* 9.1), and Clitomachus' name actually appears (wrongly) in Pseudo-Galen's manuscripts as the last of the Eristics—this last perhaps an odd coincidence.[9] After all this it is very doubtful indeed whether Cicero's plural *omnia* is confirmed properly and independently by Pseudo-Galen and Sextus.

That Cicero is near to the wording of Theophrastus in this passage is, however, strongly suggested by another close similarity of structure, this time with Simplicius. Cicero's *neque natum unquam ac sempiternum* was justly turned by Diels[10] into ἀγένητον καὶ ἀΐδιον—exactly the wording of Simplicius *in Physica* 23.4. Nor could Diels be accused of simply recollecting the words of Simplicius: the resemblance is there for all to see. But again we have two possibilities. Simplicius is here, not without confusion, conflating Theophrastus with the *MXG*, both having perhaps been cited by his predecessor Alexander. The first possibility is that the phrase and the order ἀγένητον καὶ ἀΐδιον came to both Cicero and Simplicius via the *MXG*. For Pseudo-Aristotle has an argument at 3.1–2 to the effect that the existent (that is, the god) cannot come to be and is *therefore* eternal: ἀΐδιον μὲν οὖν διὰ ταῦτα εἶναι τὸν θεόν. Thus Cicero and Simplicius *could* represent either Theophrastus or an abridgement of the *MXG*.

This doubt, however, is settled by Aëtius, whose compilers have (1) ἀγένητον καὶ ἀΐδιον καὶ ἄφθαρτον τὸν κόσμον of Xenophanes alone (Pseudo-Plutarch *Epitome*), (2) the same of Xenophanes, Parmenides, and Melissus (Stobaeus), (3) οὐ γένητον ἀλλ' ἀΐδιον... of Xenophanes alone (Theodoret). This additional doxographical evidence makes it on the whole more probable that Cicero's wording goes back to Theophrastus. This in turn should make it easier (though still not necessary) to accept Cicero's wording in other parts of the same sentence, even down to the plural *omnia*. It is germane that if Theophrastus wrote the plural here he was in the company of Plato.[11]

Was the god the subject or the predicate of the relevant sentence? Cicero (twice) and Pseudo-Galen agree in making θεόν a predicate, and they are joined (in part) by the *MXG*,[12] to say nothing of Simplicius' τὸ γὰρ ἓν τοῦτο καὶ πᾶν τὸν θεόν ἔλεγεν. On the side of god as subject are to be found Hippolytus, Sextus, and Diogenes Laertius, all demonstrably tending in this passage to rather loose paraphrase. Probably, then, Theophrastus made the god the predicate in the sentence equating world with god. In this also Theophrastus was not the first; on the most natural interpretation he is here preceded by Aristotle (for whom see below). We have just about as much evidence for the god being the predicate in this sentence of Theophrastus as we have for the existence of such a sentence in the first instance.[13]

It is not clear whether the sentence having "god" as its predicate had "the one thing" as its subject, or whether the subject was otherwise characterized, limited, or amplified. Whatever Theophrastus may have said here, however, it is certain at least that he intended to equate world with god. It is not likely that *Xenophanes* spoke of "the one," for Parmenides did not do so (or Simplicius would hardly have omitted the passage) and such self-conscious allusion belongs rather to the consolidatory phase of Eleaticism, being first extant at Melissus B8. But had Theophrastus any right to equate world and god? The inquiry demands the investigation of the properties of the world and the god(s) in the fragments and tradition of Xenophanes. The next step must be the analysis of the whole Theophrastean description of god and world. What attributes did Aristotle's successor apply to Xenophanes' world besides unity?

The first item in Theophrastus' report falling now to be considered is his statement about the motion, or lack of it, of the god and/or world. Did he say that Xenophanes' god was moved, unmoved, or neither? The doxographical statements admit of a clear answer to this question at least. Hippolytus in his free paraphrase says that nothing is moved, and Theodoret and Nicolaus of Damascus (cited by Simplicius) agree that the god (Simplicius has Nicolaus say the ἀρχή, probably by accommodation to Simplicius' context) is unmoved. In the absence of any contrary opinion, this would be on the face of it incontrovertible evidence that Theophrastus made Xenophanes' god unmoved. But in the *MXG* we have a statement that Xenophanes' "Being" (as the author sometimes calls the god) was neither moved nor unmoved, and a similar statement is apparently attributed by Simplicius to Theophrastus. Now it is difficult to see how or why, if such a statement did appear in Theophrastus' account, it should be corrupted apparently independently by Hippolytus, Theodoret, and Nicolaus: Diels[14] accordingly deduced that Simplicius wrote without having Theophrastus' text in front of him and contaminated his second-hand quotation from Theophrastus with material directly or indirectly from the *MXG*. If we ask where the *MXG* got this strange doctrine and the odd arguments given for it, the answer can only be, out of the head of the author of the *MXG*. The temptation came upon him to make this heading symmetrical with that concerning limit and unlimited, and he yielded. A conceivable loophole needs to be mentioned only to be blocked; Theophrastus' account could have been ambiguous or have contained a statement of Xenophanes' ambiguity on the point; but the unanimity of the doxographers (apart from Simplicius and the *MXG*) virtually rules this out. Simplicius produces no evidence but a neo-Platonic interpretation, drastically forced, of a perfectly clear passage; on that passage Theophrastus could not possibly have relied to establish ambiguity. Theophrastus, then, said that Xenophanes' world was unmoved. In what sense he meant this and what relation the statement bears to the fragments are questions awaiting later investigation.

Did Theophrastus say that Xenophanes' god was limited, unlimited, or neither? This is a most obscure point on which the evidence is confusing. Apart from the *MXG* and Simplicius, who alone say "neither,"[15] the word "unlimited" appears three times in the doxographical tradition in contexts other than descriptions of natural phenomena. Diogenes Laertius' report of Xenophanes is evidently confused, and it is perhaps not vital that he ascribes to Xenophanes "infinite worlds"; but, since he makes the worlds "unchanging" as some other doxographers make the "whole" or "god," it may reasonably be supposed that in his source the epithet "unlimited" also was applied to the god. More satisfactory authorities are Cicero (in the *De natura deorum*) and Nicolaus of Damascus. In support of the epithet "limited" are lined up Alexander of Aphrodisias, Hippolytus, Pseudo-Galen, and Theodoret. It is hard to see what the origin of this divergence is. On the face of it, Nicolaus of Damascus for one is hard to set aside, since he was right according to Theophrastus on the question of movement; and yet the agreement of Alexander, Hippolytus, Pseudo-Galen, and Theodoret is formidable indeed.[16] The most plausible explanation of the differences of opinion thus laid before us is surely that the post-Theophrastean writers found no straightforward statement on this matter in Theophrastus.[17] Alexander, at least, probably *argued* that Xenophanes' god was limited, and Simplicius rebuts him by quoting what he (at least in part erroneously) thinks to be Theophrastus. It is perhaps from the production elsewhere of similar arguments to Alexander's that the Xenophanean dialectic of the *MXG* takes its rise. Be that as it may, if there was argument between post-Theophrastean scholars on the question whether Xenophanes' god was limited or unlimited, then several possibilities must be examined. Either Xenophanes was himself unclear or self-contradictory in statement or implication, or Theophrastus, with or without some justification in the shape of a misleading remark of Aristotle's, was either hesitant or unclear or self-contradictory. The evidence on this point must be considered as a whole, not necessarily in chronological order.

Xenophanes himself wrote that the earth has one limit at our feet but that below them it ἐς ἄπειρον ἱκνεῖται. Many historians in recent years have denied implicitly or explictly that this can mean either that Xenophanes' earth was strictly infinite or that his universe (in consequence) was infinite.[18] The common tendency is to assume that the Atomists were the first to envisage anything strictly infinite. But this tendency is based on inadequate evidence. Early epic indeed uses the word ἄπειρον to mean merely "indefinitely large," and the philosophical sense of "infinite" is a new departure. But it is unclear why the Atomists should be credited with this particular innovation, and there are strong arguments for the view that this passage of Xenophanes refers to something which the non-mathematical at least may recognize as infinite. Xenophanes is otherwise inept and difficult to understand. The earth, he says, has a limit (πέρας) at our feet where it meets the air; in the other direction it goes on ἐς ἄπειρον. The saying that the earth is limited, comes to an end, on one side but on the other extends for an indefinitely large distance (in the Homeric sense) gives an intolerably weak antithesis; the word ἄπειρον must here mean what it says, "without limit."[19] A piece of alleged Empedoclean polemic supports this view. Aristotle in the *De caelo* (294a21ff) quotes a polemic of Empedocles against the theory that the depths of earth or Aether are ἀπείρονα. It is not necessary to suppose that Empedocles was polemizing against Xenophanes in particular, though it is highly probable that Xenophanes was among the intended victims. The existence of such a polemic implies pre-Empedoclean, and therefore pre-Atomistic, holders of the view that the earth is infinite. Not, of course, that the earth was immensely deep; to that Empedocles could have assented. The view he had in mind was obviously that the earth continues downwards without end. This removes any historical scruples about taking Xenophanes to mean what he so clearly says.[20] In any event, Theophrastus (from whom derive Pseudo-Plutarch and Hippolytus) held that Xenophanes' earth was not surrounded by "air" and perhaps (Hippolytus alone) added that it was not surrounded by the οὐρανός—whatever exactly the word means here.[21] Whether or not Theophrastus was here misled by Aristotle or was making deductions from our passage of Xenophanes with no further warrant in the original text, it is still the case that Theophrastus believed the Xenophanean earth to stretch downwards to infinity. I find no reason to doubt that he was right in that belief.[22]

Xenophanes' earth, then, being infinite, his universe, or "whole," ought to have been infinite also. But this simple state of affairs would make it difficult to follow certain remarks of Aristotle in the light of Theophrastus. For Theophrastus certainly equated Xenophanes' world and his god, whatever the meaning of Aristotle's studiedly cautious language on this point, and this means that Theophrastus at any rate ought to have made Xenophanes' god infinite too. But if things were as simple as this, then Aristotle becomes even harder to understand. Aristotle states that "Xenophanes, the first of these partisans of the One (for Parmenides is said to have been his pupil) gave no clear statement, nor does he seem to have grasped the nature of either of these causes, but with an eye to the whole material universe he says that the One is God."[23] It is clear that, as the Oxford translator suggests,[24] Xenophanes did not show clearly whether or not he was talking about a material or a formal cause; but, since Parmenides and Melissus made it clear to Aristotle which they were severally talking about by using the expressions "limted" and "unlimited" respectively of the thing identified by Aristotle as nearest to a cause in their philosophy, it follows that Xenophanes did not state clearly whether the thing most like a cause in his philosophy was finite or infinite. From this it follows either that Xenophanes did not use the terms "finite" and "infinite" of such a subject at all, or that his remarks were either explicitly or implicitly self-contradictory. It follows that, if Aristotle is not here being obtuse, the whole matter is less simple than the meteorological sections of the doxography would make it appear. Either Aristotle did not notice in the *Metaphysics* the statement of the earth's infinite extent and its implications for the universe and therefore meant that Xenophanes said nothing at all about the finitude or infinitude of the universe, or he found somewhere else in Xenophanes a passage implying or stating that the universe was finite, and meant that Xenophanes was self-contradictory. If another passage of Xenophanes was responsible for Aristotle's uncertainty, then we do not know whether it referred to the god or the world. If Aristotle's rebuke was due to a statement of the world's infinity and another of the god's finitude, then we should have to abandon the equation of god and world in Xenophanes forthwith; but this is only one of several possibilities, and the evidence does not permit us to choose between them with any sureness.

A similar verdict of "non liquet" must be returned on the question of the sphericity of Xenophanes' god. The evidence is overwhelming that the world-god was described as spherical by Theophrastus. Since, however, Xenophanes' earth extended infinitely downwards his universe cannot without inconsistency have been a sphere.[25] One must, unless one is prepared to impute that inconsistency to Xenophanes, either abandon the Theophrastean epithet "spherical" for Xenophanes' god and world or relinquish the equation of god and world. Again the evidence is inadequate to determine our choice, but one point is clear: either Xenophanes was inconsistent or Theophrastus was wrong somewhere. If Theophrastus was wrong, it would be in the direction of over-Eleaticizing Xenophanes, and the tradition contains enough examples of this process to make us wary. It would not have been difficult for a historian to deduce the sphericity of the god from his being the same everywhere, and his being the same from his ability to see, hear, and perceive as a whole.[26] This last Xenophanes certainly proclaimed in a verse still extant, but the rest could be Peripatetic deduction, facilitated by assimilation to Parmenides. The possibility of Theophrastean error of some kind should certainly be borne in mind in assessing Xenophanes.

With this warning we may reopen the question of movement of or in Xenophanes' world. Now, if Hippolytus was right in thinking that Xenophanes allowed no movement of any kind, then all the meteorological ideas of Xenophanes are mere make-believe, of a kind extremely unlikely in so unsophisticated a thinker. We may therefore confidently ignore this possibility. What Theophrastus said must have been simply that the god-world was unmoving. But, if the world was unmoved, in what sense? The answer of some students is that the universe did not have to move about as a whole from place to place, in order to find food like the gods of epic.[27] If the god could properly be regarded as unmoved only in this sense, it would be in order still for god and universe to be equated. But it may be questioned whether this is in fact the case. A statement of the god's immovability is extant, and takes the following form:

αἰεὶ δ' ἐν ταὐτῷ μίμνει κινούμενος οὐδέν
οὐδὲ μετέρχεσθαί μιν ἐπιπρέπει ἄλλοτε ἄλλῃ.

If the god is to be equated with the whole universe, then everything in the world is divine. Accordingly, every part of the universe should be unlike the Homeric gods in being immovable. If it is not proper for a god to move, it is surely not proper for a part of a god to move. Further, the god's mode of action is described in the following line thus: ἀλλ' ἀπάνευθε πόνοιο νόου φρενὶ πάντα κραδαίνει. This means that, when the god moves all things by shaking them, he is, if we equate god and world, shaking himself. It is hard to see how this can be seemly for a god who has to remain motionless. Defensible this may be, but it seems odd.[28] It is also peculiar that movement of the god's own members should be described as νόου φρενί and ἀπάνευθε πόνοιο. This problem also would disappear immediately if we dissociated god and world; by itself it might not lead us to reject Theophrastus' equation, but as a point additional to the difficulty about Xenophanes' god's sphericity it may add to the doubts already raised. It is possible (to put it no stronger) that Theophrastus was mistaken.

THE "MONOTHEISTIC" FRAGMENT

We have seen that all is not necessarily well with Theophrastus on Xenophanes' god and world. It is now advisable to consider the fragment on which most discussion of Xenophanes' alleged monotheism is based. The fragment, B23, has been a headache indeed to modern scholars. It has been held to prove Xenophanes a polytheist, a monotheist, and a polytheist trying to develop a monotheism, and it has been held to prove none of these things. But there is no need for despair.

The first task is, as ever, to examine afresh the fragment's meaning. The precise implications of the plural θεοῖσι in the line εἷς θεὸς ἔν τε θεοῖσι καὶ ἀνθρώποισι μέγιστος are a good starting-point for inquiry. In strict grammar, this plural does not necessarily imply the existence of gods other than the one supreme god. "Polar" expressions of this antithetical type could be used in Greek even where one-half of the antithesis did not make logical sense. The issue has been befogged by the fact that Burnet selected,[29] from among the numerous parallels available, a fragment of Heraclitus which is not, as Guthrie recently emphasized,[30] an exact parallel. What Heraclitus says at his B30 is that neither god nor man made this cosmos, and this makes perfect sense if taken literally; the lack of Greek belief that a man made the world does not make the negative proposition "no man made the world" any less meaningful or less acceptable as Heraclitean. The half of this antithesis which offended Burnet is thus not nonsensical, merely less deserving of emphasis than the other half. But Wilamowitz[31] long ago cited other parallels less easily disposed of: Sophocles *Antigone* 1109, Antiphon *Tetralogy* 2β6, and Euripides *Heracles* 1106 seem to prove that a good writer could use a polar expression when (a) one of the poles made unacceptable sense and (b) the sentence was not negative, as in Heraclitus B30, but positive, as in Xenophanes. Nevertheless, this does not prove the fragment of Xenophanes easy to reconcile with a pure monotheism. One may reasonably follow J. Freudenthal[32] in doubting whether a convinced monotheist in an unreceptive polytheistic society would cloud the issue by a mention of plural gods which is at best ambiguous, in the very context where he is firmly stating his revolutionary view.

The second point about the meaning of the whole sentence is the syntactical connection of the crucial word εἷς. Clement of Alexandria, in citing the verse, introduces it as a declaration that God is one and incorporeal, and Diels and others[33] accordingly punctuate with a comma after θεός, making the first two words say that there is one god, or that God is one. But nobody supposes that Clement was right in making Xenophanes' god incorporeal, and it may legitimately be doubted also whether there is in Xenophanes any statement that god is one, or that there is one god.

Xenophanes' couplet is at first glance open to several interpretations. First, it is not quite clear whether it forms a complete sentence; it is conceivable, for example, that it was followed immediately by B24 οὖλος ὁρᾷ ... οὖλος δέ τ' ἀκούει ... or by some similar statement, in which case there would have been no need to take B23 as a nominal sentence.[34] Secondly, if one is to treat the couplet as a complete sentence in itself, one has a choice of places where, in translating, to insert the copula; one can insert it between εἷς θεός and μέγιστος or between the first line and the second. The resulting renderings are: "One god is greatest..." and "The one greatest god among gods and men is unlike..." Finally the possibility arises, at least in early Greek, of "understanding" ἔστι in the sense "exists"; "There is one god."

Now, a common Greek idiom uses εἷς to reinforce a superlative, and the idiom was probably known already to Homer, who at M 243 has εἷς οἰωνὸς ἄριστος ἀμύνεσθαι περὶ πάτρης. There are a substantial number of other examples, from prose and poetry, from Attic and non-Attic writers. The idiom is well established.[35] Since in Xenophanes we have in one and the same line the word εἷς and the superlative, it is arbitrary and unlikely to be right to separate the two by a comma. Anyone suggesting that εἷς and μέγιστος should be taken separately should first be required to show good cause, and this no one appears to have done. Adopting therefore as a working hypothesis the view that εἷς θεὸς ... μέγιστος means "the one greatest god," we shall accordingly rule out as unsupported by the Greek language the versions "one god, the greatest ..." and "There is one god, the greatest" and "God is one, the greatest." There are left the more plausible renderings "The one greatest god among gods and men is unlike mortals in form and thought" and "The one greatest god among gods and men, unlike mortals in form and thought, is..." These two renderings both presuppose that Xenophanes' greatest god is being contrasted with something, being singled out. It is possible that this contrast is with the gods of mythology in general or with Zeus in particular. No one is likely now ever to know which Xenophanes intended, as either would make reasonable sense. Our working hypothesis is therefore not found wanting on detailed exploration and should be regarded, prima facie, as offering the plain meaning of Xenophanes' words. When A. Lumpe duly suggested this interpretation, W. Pötscher replied that it ignores the data of fragment 24. But I can see nothing against Lumpe's view in this fragment. It passes my comprehension why Xenophanes should not believe in a single *highest* god, and at the same time say that that god heard, saw, and perceived as a whole. Pötscher added that no less an authority than Aristotle took the fragment to mean "God is one," but to one looking for confirmation of Aristotle in Xenophanes' text this is unhelpful.[36] It has recently been argued, in favour of "God is one," that εἶς, from its position in the sentence, must be emphatic.[37] This simply ignores the Homeric εἶς οἰωνὸς ἄριστος ἀμύνεσθαι περὶ πάτρης, where "The omen is one" is nonsensical, and "There is one omen" improbable.

Understanding "There exists..." we shall also find improbable the sense "There exists one greatest god among gods and men, unlike mortals..." This remains grammatically possible, but puts the emphasis firmly in the wrong place. There was nothing original or striking in Xenophanes' day in the *existence* of one greatest god among gods and men—Zeus was well enough known. What needed stressing was the attack on anthropomorphism.

The truth of the matter seems to be that nobody with a mind unaffected by preconceived ideas of Xenophanes' thought would combine (1) the reading of this sentence, including its mention of plural gods, as saying that there was only one god, with (2) the destruction of the obvious, natural, and idiomatic syntactical connection of εἶς with the superlative μέγιστος. Leaving aside for the moment the question of Aristotle's preconceptions, we may note that Xenophanes is not usually inept or ambiguous in the expression of his key views, and it is arbitrary to suppose that he was wilfully obscure in this, allegedly one of his most important pronouncements.

In a sense Heidel[38] and Joel[39] were right to compare Hebrew ideas with Xenophanean and allege a "preliminary stage" of monotheism in the latter; for the Hebrews thought of Yahweh as the greatest of gods before they thought of him as the only God. But such a comparison is misleading if it be accompanied by the implication that Xenophanes represents a significant step towards an eventual Greek monotheism: there was, to all intents and purposes, no Classical Greek monotheism.[40] Indeed, there was in Classical Greek philosophy hardly any discussion of the problem worth calling a discussion, and hardly anybody seems to have been interested in the subject; this argument from silence, although sometimes glossed over, seems alone virtually decisive against a true monotheism in Xenophanes. Nor does it really seem likely that the Ionian enlightenment of the sixth and fifth centuries had a higher religious consciousness than the fourth century; the continued existence of popular religious belief and practice side by side with profound philosophical doctrine is a phenomenon of both periods, and the fourth-century philosophers were certainly no less profound than their predecessors either in metaphysical or in religious insight. There is no evidence that the question "monotheism or polytheism?" was raised in fifth-century Greece, and we shall therefore join Guido Calogero[41] in looking to Eleatic metaphysical speculation for the origins of the monotheism of the *MXG* rather than finding in Xenophanes' religious thought the origin of the Eleatic opposition of one and many.

OTHER RELEVANT FRAGMENTS

It would follow from this assessment of the crucial evidence that passages where Xenophanes uses "god" in the singular or in the plural are to be interpreted in accordance with normal Greek literary usage[42] as not significant for either polytheism or monotheism. In any case, it is doubtful whether any of them is decisive. Even the first fragment, which offers the most help to those who support the polytheist interpretation of Xenophanes, is not wholly decisive. Corbato[43] indeed has applied to line 24 essentially the same argument as to B23, that the use of the plural in a passage where it is virtually synonymous with the previous singular at line 13, is unlikely if Xenophanes is a convinced monotheist. But, apart from the fact that we simply cannot tell how Xenophanes' thought may have developed from one poem to another and the inference that B1 strictly proves very little for the interpretation of B23, there remains a difficulty for Corbato's argument: the point at which Xenophanes is correcting popular belief in B1 is the tendency to ascribe immoral acts to the gods and is certainly not the number of deities; it is therefore much more plausible that he should have spoken in the plural of gods in this passage, as a concession to popular terminology and ways of thought, than it is to suppose such a concession in B23 while interpreting B23 as monotheist. The plural in B1 could be motivated at least in part by the plurals of Centaurs, Titans, and so forth which precede it.

Other occurrences of plural gods in Xenophanes' own words are much more liable than B23 to be concessional.[44] B11 admittedly represents in indirect speech the thoughts of Homer and Hesiod, as apparently does B12. B14 explicitly negatives a general opinion of mortals, and B15.4 is making fun of human practices. B18 has been held purely Xenophanean, but it also is strictly a denial of a common view; the denial that "the gods" showed all techniques to human beings in the beginning of things does not constitute an assertion that there is a plurality of gods. The singular θεός in B38 is hardly significant for the question of monotheism or polytheism. B34 is more difficult, even though the problems of epistemology raised in it are not our present concern. The general drift of the first sentence is that no man knows or will know the clear truth about (the) gods or on all the subjects Xenophanes talks about. Here too, however, Xenophanes could be using the language of concession and speaking of "gods" in general as a subject of discourse or object of knowledge without committing himself to a plurality of gods. It is not necessarily implied that Xenophanes talks about gods in the plural when offering his own opinions. None of Xenophanes' extant statements outside B23 is decisive one way or the other,[45] and we are thrown back on B23 and on arguments derivable from ancient testimonies to Xenophanes' doctrine.

The polytheist interpretation of Xenophanes can be supported further, perhaps not decisively, from Pseudo-Plutarch.[46] Pseudo-Plutarch reports an argument to the effect that there is no leadership among the gods, for it is not right that one god should be the master of another. The passage continues with the assertion that none of the gods stands in need of anything whatsoever. Now, as has often been remarked, this argument is closely paralleled by Euripides, at *Heracles* 1341ff, where the tragedian puts into Heracles' mouth the refusal to believe the gods adulterous (cf. Xenophanes B11 and B12) or captors of one another and adds a refusal to credit the mastery of one god over another on the grounds that a god who is in need of anything is no true god. The resemblance to Xenophanes (as expounded by Pseudo-Plutarch) is here striking, and it is confirmed, as Reinhardt pointed out,[47] by the final remark that "these are the unhappy tales of poets"; one is reminded of the Xenophanean attack (B11) on Homer and Hesiod. It is not possible to show that Euripides was wholly dependent on Xenophanes in writing these lines; but they certainly bear a striking resemblance to Pseudo-Plutarch's argument and help to confirm this version of the argument, a polytheistic one, against the version of *MXG*. *MXG* 3.3 makes the argument read "If the god is the most powerful thing of all ... then he must be one. For if there were two or more, then he would no longer be the most powerful and the best of all. For each god of the many would be of the same kind for the same reasons. For this is divine[48] and the quality of a god, to rule and not be ruled and to be the strongest of all things. If, then, there were more gods than one and they were of unequal strength, they would not be gods; for it is the nature of the divine not to be ruled. If they were equal, they would not possess the nature of a god, which is necessarily to rule, whereas equal things are neither better nor worse than one another. So if there were a god, and moreover a god of this kind, the god must be one alone." Now, if Xenophanes used *this* form of the argument, then clearly he was a monotheist, and no argument from silence elsewhere would have any weight. But we have already found the *MXG* prone to Eleaticization, and that is quite likely to have happened here also; on the other hand, Euripides was writing for polytheists, and Pseudo-Plutarch is not the most reliable transcriber of an argument.

The *MXG* form of the argument raises indeed awkward questions for a supporter of the polytheist interpretation of Xenophanes. If there were many gods in the Xenophanean pantheon then evidently they were not simply the gods of myth, who were guilty of the sins attacked in Xenophanes' fragments. But, if it is easy to say what the many gods were not, it is harder to say what they were. The relationship between the many gods and the one who is greatest among them raises these difficulties: if they are inferior, as one would naturally expect, then they could be regarded as lacking something compared with the greatest god; but this may have been inconsistent with their divinity; Euripides *may* mean to connect precisely the absence of divine need with the impropriety of mastership over a god, and Pseudo-Plutarch, like Euripides, juxtaposes the two points. If this were so, it would be scarcely relevant what sense is borne in Pseudo-Plutarch and Euripides by the word δεσπότης and its derivatives; for, even if the relationship between superior and inferior god were something less harsh than δεσπόζεσθαι in the full sense, it would still be such as to leave unsatisfied Xenophanes' other stipulation about deity, that gods must have no lack. If, on the other hand, we conceive Xenophanes' gods as being equal in power and full divinity, then again we run into difficulties: in what sense is the "one god" "greatest"? I can find no way out of these problems which is convincing philosophically as a likely solution for the obviously keen-witted Xenophanes and must rest content with the supposition either that the connection between inferiority and need does not go back to Xenophanes (a fairly unlikely hypothesis) or that Xenophanes was not particularly concerned with the relations between gods except to show the negative points that they were not the immoral relations depicted in the epic and were not arranged in a hierarchy of power. If he was not especially interested in the question whether there was one god or a plurality of gods, then this further lack of methodical investigation of the positive consequences of a plurality may be more understandable, if no more excusable.[49] In a somewhat similar problem he may not have specified the shape of his god(s), though he certainly described it negatively as unlike that of mortals (B14, B23).

The upshot of this section is that Xenophanes can hardly be proved either polytheist or monotheist from the fragments other than B23 and (to be cautious to the point of austerity) that ancient testimonies raise too many problems to be altogether safe support for either view. It may be that some vital passage, known to Aristotle and Plato, but not extant, gave the clue to the obscurities of Xenophanes and caused them to describe him as a believer in one reality or one god. But this must remain mere speculation, and nothing survives to compel belief in it. What we do have is a passage, B23, which, though bearing most naturally a sense making it imply belief in many gods, does contain the superficially monotheistic-looking phrase εἷς θεός. We need therefore only show that those ancient thinkers and historians who ascribed monotheism to Xenophanes were predisposed to accept this monotheistic-looking phrase at its face value, and thus to anticipate Clement's error of interpretation. We shall then have a viable alternative to the acceptance of that ascription. Demonstrable that alternative may not be; but it is probably the best way of explaining the apparent discrepancy between the plain meaning of Xenophanes' words and the plain purport of much ancient testimony to his doctrine.

ANCIENT TESTIMONIES TO XENOPHANES' PANTHEISTIC MONOTHEISM

This tale may be told fairly briefly. It begins with the "historical" passage of Plato's *Sophist* already discussed.[50] There Plato, we recall, was constrained for his peculiar constructive purposes to find somewhere a name of a thinker preceding Heraclitus (and incidentally Empedocles) who could with some plausibility be named as an anticipator of Parmenides in the belief in one real thing. Since no name sprang immediately with the blinding force of truth to Plato's mind, he would no doubt cast a rapid mental glance over the early thinkers he knew about. Xenophanes was probably prominent among these, for his moralizing theology could hardly fail to appeal to the author of the *Republic*. Xenophanes presented some features making a comparison with Parmenides not wholly frivolous. Xenophanes singled out one god, applying to him in the process the word εἷς. Parmenides taught that what is, the subject of discourse, is ἕν. Xenophanes' god (his B26) was always in the same place, unmoved; Parmenides' subject was described in similar terms (precisely *how* similar is uncertain) at Parmenides B8.29.[51] With Xenophanes' highest deity was connected νοῦς, in a special way (his B24 and B25): Parmenides' subject was also specially connected with νοῦς (Parmenides' B8.34).[52] Xenophanes says of his god (B24) that he sees, thinks, and hears as a whole: Parmenides' subject is also a uniform whole (especially Parmenides' B8.4 and B8.36–38).[53] Both thinkers adopted views violently opposed to the common outlook of their contemporaries (and also of Plato's). I do not think that it is a slander on Plato's historical conscience to suppose him capable of assimilating such a pair of thinkers in a minor stylistic emergency, even if Xenophanes did not write a statement (unknown to us) equating god, world, and ἕν. There can be no proof in such matters: the reader must make up his own mind whether such an assimilation is possible for Plato or not. One must bear in mind that in this very passage of the *Sophist* Plato shows himself historically acute in his interpretation of the painfully difficult Heraclitus; but one must also recall that Plato was capable elsewhere of singling out one doctrine (for example, Heraclitus' theory of flux) and giving it an importance more fundamental than it had originally. This may well be what he has done with Xenophanes: the phrases εἷς θεός and ἐν ταὐτῷ μίμνει have been, as it were, lifted from context and given an importance they do not deserve. The alleged misinterpretation of Xenophanes is admittedly more striking than that of Heraclitus; but I find nothing implausible about it. It seems more plausible at any rate than the linguistically improbable supposition that Xenophanes wrote εἷς θεός ... μέγιστος meaning unidiomatically "There is one god ..."

Once given this Platonic assimilation of Xenophanes to Eleaticism one may readily suppose Aristotle to have been predisposed to find Eleaticism in Xenophanes. Aristotle is no more exempt from the influence of Plato on historical questions than on matters philosophical. Capable of revolt of course Aristotle was; but he is an unusual pupil who rebels all the time.[54] It is by no means difficult to believe, as many have done, that Aristotle was predisposed by the Platonic view of Xenophanes to look for a "one" in his thought. Such a predisposition might easily have led Aristotle, as it has led many of the moderns, to pounce on the εἷς θεός of B23 and interpret it as referring to a single unique god. Once again, I would sooner believe in such a mistake than commit myself to the proposition that Xenophanes' Greek does not bear its plain, ordinary meaning.

Aristotle himself perhaps felt some puzzlement about the Platonic rapprochement between Xenophanes and the Eleatics. For at *Metaphysics* A 5.986b2 he begins by calling Xenophanes the first of them to be a monist but continues with the cautious parenthesis that Parmenides *is said* to have been Xenophanes' pupil[55] before going on to lament Xenophanes' lack of clarity on the point interesting to Aristotle. He then does *not* say that Xenophanes equated god and "one" with the world or even with the "heaven." He says, with obviously studied caution, that Xenophanes "looked to" the whole heaven and "said" the one was god.[56] The latter part of this is clearly unhistorical: Xenophanes may have said that (the) god was one but is scarcely likely to have made "the one" the subject of any sentence whatever; the definite article would have been meaningless. Aristotle is clearly (and doubtless involuntarily) Eleaticizing Xenophanes here. But his involuntary Eleaticization does not proceed so far as to credit Xenophanes explicitly with the view attributed to Parmenides in antiquity, and particularly by Plato, namely that all things (meaning the world) are one.[57] What Aristotle does is to *suggest* Xenophanes' adherence to this with the words εἰς τὸν ὅλον οὐρανὸν ἀποβλέψας without actually stating it. His reluctance to state it is perhaps evidence that he was unconsciously unhappy about it. Certainly Aristotle's cautious wording, if it is evidence at all, is evidence rather against than for the supposition that Xenophanes equated god and cosmic unity.[58]

From Aristotle to Theophrastus (and thence to the doxographical tradition) is but a short step. Whatever may be the current standing of Plato's influence on Aristotle, the closeness of Theophrastus' historical judgements to Aristotle's is common knowledge among students of ancient philosophy;[59] and we are accustomed to find in sources deriving from Theophrastus a lack of the caution which marks many of Aristotle's historical pronouncements. Both Aristotle and Theophrastus were in any case brought up in the Academy, and historical views expressed there are as liable to recur in one as in the other. It is not therefore difficult to feel sceptical about their attribution of monotheism or monism to Xenophanes.

THE "ONE-BECOMING-MANY" PROBLEM

There is no suggestion in Xenophanes' extant words, and should probably have been none in the tradition, that Parmenides' alleged predecessor equated one and many or described the many things of this world as one. But the question might still be raised whether the doctrine of earth at B27 states the coming-to-be of the many out of the one. ἐκ γαίης γὰρ πάντα, καὶ εἰς γῆν πάντα τελευτᾷ, said Xenophanes according to Sextus, and Aëtius says much the same. The authenticity of the line has been disputed, but not, I think, cogently.[60] However that may be, if the line does belong to Xenophanes, it still does not show that everything for Xenophanes was made of earth and of that one thing alone; but it might tend to show that Xenophanes believed in the one thing becoming, or giving rise to, many things. But one-and-many language is not to be found in this context, and it is far from clear whether Xenophanes was thinking in formally cosmogonical terms at all or using the word πάντα literally. Of course Xenophanes, if pressed with the question "Do you believe that one thing, the earth, was the origin of many other things?" would (supposing the line his) have replied in the affirmative. But there is no evidence that he thought in this way, and I have seen no concrete evidence that anyone in antiquity interpreted him in such a way. Certainly Parmenides, as we shall see, shows no clear sign of an attack on a Xenophanean view that what was one could become, or give rise to, a plurality. The time of philosophical prominence for the one-many antithesis, outside the philosophy of mathematics, is not yet.

IV

HERACLITUS

INTRODUCTORY

In turning next to Heraclitus we shall follow the path of least resistance, for the majority of recent students have believed Heraclitus prior (and indeed known) to Parmenides.[1] But this order of approach is adopted here as a matter of convenience rather than of conviction, in the belief that the evidence both internal and external is insufficient to prove that Parmenides knew the work of Heraclitus or that his argument was affected in any way by Heraclitus' thought. What it does prove conclusively is that Heraclitus did not, despite Karl Reinhardt's old arguments,[2] take up Parmenides' problems: for the Heraclitean theory of "constancy in change" ("Konstanz in Wechsel") is so constructed as to make it clear that Heraclitus did not know of the Eleatic arguments against genesis and destruction. In default of decisive evidence to the contrary, it seems best to treat Heraclitus and Parmenides as wholly independent thinkers, with related backgrounds but separate lines of argument; though it should not prove very difficult for those who disagree with this view to modify the conclusions here reached in accordance with their chronology.

A recent and valuable book had for the heading of its chapter on Heraclitus and Parmenides "Einheit und Vielheit";[3] and it is indeed in these thinkers that the antithesis first acquires anything like that prominence which it has in the doxographical tradition. In Heraclitus' extant fragments the notions of unity and plurality appear in several different types of context, showing that, whether Heraclitus discovered it or whether he found it in any other source, it certainly ran in his head. Its occurrence in ethical, epistemological, theological, and physical fragments has long been noted; it remains to set out the texts in coherent order and examine the interrelationships between these contexts, and the meaning of "one" and "many" in each.

The contrast between singularity and plurality was implicit in the old "Priamel," and it is indeed excellently suited to such a statement of an ethical ideal. Many things seem to others good (Tyrtaeus, fragment 9 Diehl) or beautiful (Sappho, fragment 16 Lobel–Page) but to the poet only one thing is good/beautiful, and according to the ancient priamel formula that one thing is finally expressed. But in none of the priamels with which Archaic Greek literature abounds is the contrast between one and many more than implicit; though the poet may list many things before offering his single choice, he does not yet possess self-consciousness enough to state in these terms what he is doing. In Heraclitus, on the other hand, we have no extant priamel; but we have an explicit formulation of the choice of a single ideal from many possible ends of life; B29 says that the best men choose one thing in exchange for all things, their choice being eternal glory instead of mortal things. This remark couples with the one-many antithesis, strengthened by the juxtaposition ἓν ἀντὶ ἁπάντων, the antithesis between eternal and transitory, eternal glory being pointedly contrasted with mere mortal things.[4] It is not merely "all things" that appear in this fragment of Heraclitus; in the second sentence οἱ πολλοί are also mentioned, in opposition to the "best." This antithesis is also found in B49, εἷς ἐμοὶ μύριοι, ἐὰν ἄριστος ᾖ, but it is not certain whether B49 is ethical, political, or epistemological in meaning.[5] Certainly epistemological is the attack on the "many" in B2, B17, B57, and B104.[6] The many (B2) live as if they had their own private wisdom: ζώουσιν οἱ πολλοὶ ὡς ἰδίαν ἔχοντες φρόνησιν. In B17, many people do not take thought of the things that they come across, and, though they learn them, they have no insight into them but only think they have. An even more violent attack on the many is B104; τίς γὰρ αὐτῶν νόος ἢ φρήν; δήμων ἀοιδοῖσι πείθονται καὶ διδασκάλῳ χρείωνται ὁμίλῳ οὐκ εἰδότες ὅτι «οἱ πολλοὶ κακοὶ ὀλίγοι δὲ ἀγαθοί.» It is evident that "good" and "bad" in this context have not an ethical but a practical or almost epistemological sense; the many are not good for anything, and in particular are bad teachers. It does not matter that the saying quoted by Heraclitus may originally have had a very different kind of sense.

Hecataeus' book began with the statement: Ἑκαταῖος Μιλήσιος ὧδε μυθεῖται· τάδε γράφω, ὥς μοι δοκεῖ ἀληθέα εἶναι· οἱ γὰρ Ἑλλήνων λόγοι πολλοί τε καί γελοῖοι, ὡς ἐμοὶ φαίνονται, εἰσίν.[7] Here it is the absurdity of the tales which is linked with their number and contrasted with what the writer says himself; Heraclitus' own rebukes of the stupidity of his fellow men are similar, but Heraclitus emphasizes less the number of opinions than the number of men and does not seem to have followed the idea that the many mutually contradictory opinions of men must therefore be false, the idea which seems to lie behind the proem of Hecataeus.

B57 is specially significant in this context: διδάσκαλος δὲ πλείστων Ἡσίοδος· τοῦτον ἐπίστανται πλεῖστα εἰδέναι, ὅστις ἡμέρην καὶ εὐφρόνην οὐκ ἐγίνωσκεν· ἔστι γὰρ ἕν. In this fragment Heraclitus condemns the many for their unthinking reliance on a poet lacking in Heraclitus' fundamental insight; but what they thought distinguished that poet, the knowledge of many things, was of no avail. There is a contrast implied here not only between the many who are ignorant and Heraclitus himself who has insight, but also between the knowing of many (or most) things and the single insight which is necessary in Heraclitus' eyes for the understanding of the world. There is no suggestion that the many things that Hesiod knew were all false; but some of them were false in that they contradicted Heraclitus' main thesis, and they were collectively of little importance when compared with that thesis. This point is brought more into the open at B40: πολυμαθίη νόον οὐ διδάσκει· Ἡσίοδον γὰρ ἂν ἐδίδαξε καὶ Πυθαγόρην αὖτίς τε Ξενοφάνεά τε καὶ Ἑκαταῖον. This fragment is followed in Diogenes Laertius by B41: ἓν τὸ σοφόν· ἐπίστασθαι γνώμην ὅκη κυβερνᾶται πάντα διὰ πάντων. As Kirk has written, "The contrast of πολυμαθίη and ἓν τὸ σοφόν does not appear to be accidental: the learning of many things (practised by Hesiod, Pythagoras, etc.) does not teach sense; true wisdom is one (and of one thing)."[8] The one being who has wisdom in B32 is parallel with the one object of wisdom, given in B41; one may note what at least on the surface looks like a similar parallel, between B22 and the above-quoted 104. B22 draws a contrast between the much earth dug by gold-diggers and the little gold they find, and if, as seems likely, this was epistemological in import,[9] the few people who are good at acquiring genuine knowledge are aptly paralleled by the small amount of knowledge they can acquire, just as the many people who do not acquire knowledge are parallel to the large number of comparatively useless facts they learn without acquiring knowledge.

It would be interesting to know more of the history of these ideas than we do; we have only occasional glimpses of conceptions similar to Heraclitus' and probably, but not certainly, related. The first of these is Archilochus' line (fragment 103 Diehl): πόλλ' οἶδ' ἀλώπηξ, ἀλλ' ἐχῖνος ἓν μέγα. This line may, as Bowra suggested,[10] be connected with a fable about a hedgehog and a fox, but we cannot tell for certain whether "Aesop" had the contrast between the manifold knowledge of the fox and the one important trick of the hedgehog. What is interesting here is the recognition by a poet known to Heraclitus, in a context perhaps almost proverbial, of the point that knowledge of many things can be less significant than one "big" trick.[11] What appears from our limited evidence to be new in Heraclitus is the contrast between mere "learning" and "insight" (νόος), together with the philosophical depth attached to the latter in Heracliteanism. A similar idea appears in a fragment of Aeschylus (fragment 390 Nauck): ὁ χρήσιμ' εἰδώς, οὐχ ὁ πόλλ' εἰδὼς σοφός. Aeschylus is more likely on the whole, whatever the chronology of the play concerned or of Heraclitus, to have drawn here on the proverbial than on the philosophical, and this fragment lends further colour to the suggestion that Heraclitus was deliberately applying and deepening a piece of popular wisdom. The probability that a well-known idea was being combated in their different ways by both Heraclitus and Aeschylus is increased by the verbal coincidence between Aeschylus' ὁ πόλλ' εἰδώς, Archilochus' πόλλ' οἶδ', and Pindar's σοφὸς ὁ πόλλ' εἰδὼς φυᾷ (*Olympian* 2.86); Pindar is best interpreted as having added φυᾷ in an unexpected stroke to a common, perhaps almost proverbial, opinion.

We need not linger over the senses of the words "one" and "many" in these fragments and other passages, for in all of them the sense is purely numerical, and we are not concerned with the question of what distinguished one piece of knowledge from another. But when we come to the more difficult questions of Heraclitus' physics the question of meaning becomes acute. In some sense at least, Heraclitus believed that all things are one thing; B50 says: οὐκ ἐμοῦ ἀλλὰ τοῦ λόγου ἀκούσαντας ὁμολογεῖν σοφόν ἐστιν ἓν πάντα εἶναι. But in what sense he meant this bizarre statement and how he arrived at it are questions needing careful study. The subjects especially relevant are the Heraclitean relationship of one member of a pair of opposites to the other and the relationship of opposites to the Logos and to fire, the stuff nearest in Heraclitus' thought to the primary stuff of the Milesians. This will also involve a brief discussion of Heraclitus' theology.

THE UNITY OF OPPOSITES

The unity of opposites was known to Philo as the principal doctrine of Heraclitus; the Jewish philosopher himself drew from Scripture the lesson that opposites were common in Nature, in fact infinite in number, and that in each case the two opposites together form a unity. οὐ τοῦτ' ἐστίν, he asks,[12] ὅ φασιν Ἕλληνες τὸν μέγαν καὶ ἀοίδιμον παρ' αὐτοῖς Ἡράκλειτον κεφάλαιον τῆς αὐτοῦ προστησάμενον φιλοσοφίας αὐχεῖν ὡς ἐφ' εὑρέσει καινῇ; Heraclitus never, indeed, in the extant fragments boasts specifically that no one before him has discovered the unity of opposites, but his general tone is very much that of a man announcing a new idea, and nothing even suggests that this tone is deceptive. Adopting from the Milesians and perhaps also the Pythagoreans the thesis of the cosmic importance of opposites, Heraclitus said that despite appearances they were unities. That this was an essential part of his doctrine is clear from the considerable proportion of the fragments dealing with the topic—a fact even more significant in view of the almost total neglect of this side of his philosophy in extant Hellenistic writings.

It is possible that the number of such fragments has sometimes been exaggerated,[13] and the difficulties of interpreting Heraclitus' often metaphorical, pregnant, and allusive style are not lessened by the fragmentary state of the remains. Doubt attaches in almost every case to the reliability of the context of a quotation from Heraclitus as a guide to its context in the original book. But, when we have made every allowance for problems of this kind, there is a residue of sentences exemplifying the unity of opposites with sufficient clarity to enable us to see what for Heraclitus constituted unity, as applied to opposites. The relevant types of relationship have been listed several times in recent years;[14] but it is necessary to list them yet again to make the following discussion intelligible. The question may for the moment be left open whether Heraclitus would have seen any significance in the following analysis.

We may take the easiest kind of unity first: Heraclitus may imply that two opposites are the same because, in a particular instance, they are logically indistinguishable. The only example of this that I can find is B103, which says: ξυνὸν γὰρ ἀρχὴ καὶ πέρας ἐπὶ κύκλου ("Beginning and end are common on the circle"). Acceptance of the likelihood that this fragment is an instance of the unity of opposites need not necessarily imply that "common" directly describes the relationship between this pair; as Olof Gigon has remarked,[15] the natural word for that would be rather "the same." To say that beginning and end are "common" should mean, in Heraclitus' normal terminology, that they are omnipresent. It follows, however, if both beginning and end are omnipresent on the circle, that beginning and end coincide; whatever point one chooses on a circle's circumference can be described both as beginning and as end of the circle. Beginning and end are in this special case logically indistinguishable.[16]

Closely related to this is the kind of case in which the two opposites concerned are to be attributed to one and the same physical entity. There are two clear examples of this in extant sayings: first, the famous remark that the way up and the way down are one and the same (B60), ὁδὸς ἄνω κάτω μία καὶ ὠυτή.[17] Here the road is physically the same road, whether one goes up it or down it, or whichever way one goes along it. The statement therefore that the way up and down is the same is physically true—even a truism. But it does not logically imply to modern ways of thinking what it apparently did for Heraclitus, that up and down are the same. The gap in Heraclitus' reasoning becomes more intelligible when we recall that the distinction which comes so easily to us between the subject and the predicate(s) inhering in it was not available to Heraclitus; if the way up and the way down were the same, it followed, in the absence of such a distinction, that, in this case at least, up and down are themselves the same. Another example of this kind of unity between opposites is to be found in the statement (B59) "Of the carding-roller the straight and crooked way is one and the same."[18] Here one wants to interpret by supposing that the "qualities" of curvature and straightness inhere in the same "object," the path of the roller; but Heraclitus knew nothing of "qualities" as opposed to objects, and the word "inhere" is a hopeless anachronism. Again it follows, given that the roller takes at once a straight and crooked path, that the straight path and the crooked path are in this special case one and the same, and without a distinction between quality and object it would be difficult to persuade Heraclitus that this did not involve the further inference that straight and crooked were the same. One might paraphrase Heraclitus' point here, in terms whose Heraclitean basis will be examined below, by saying that "straight" and "crooked" are, since they appear in the one process of carding, connected. What connects them is the path of the roller, for it is in the special case of carding that this pair of opposites is united, appearing simultaneously and in the same place.

Similar to this, though appearing to the moderns less objective, is the kind of assertion exemplified by B61. θάλασσα, writes Heraclitus, ὕδωρ καθαρώτατον καὶ μιαρώτατον, ἰχθύσι μὲν πότιμον καὶ σωτήριον, ἀνθρώποις δὲ ἄποτον καὶ ὀλέθριον. Here we have two pairs of opposite qualities, which in our language "inhere" in the "object" sea with respect to the two animate creatures man and fish. But of course Heraclitus could not think in these terms; apart from the distinction between "qualities" and "objects," this account would necessitate the germ of a distinction between absolute and relative terms, a distinction made much later. Equally obscure to Heraclitus would be the distinction between subjective and objective. For Heraclitus it seemed evident that "purest" and "foulest" coincide in sea-water; the opposition is enhanced by the double use of the superlative, and the unity is nevertheless illustrated by the appearance in the same place of both opposites at the same time; both must (we may explain) be present at the same time, since nothing happens to sea between its support to the fish and its unpleasant effects on mankind.

The type of opposition and connection to which we turn next is less immediately obvious, even in Heraclitean terms; or so it would appear, for Heraclitus probably took the trouble (most unusually for him) to point out to his readers the basis of his assertion of unity. This assertion, fundamental for the understanding of Heraclitus' thought, is contained in B88.[19] ταὐτό τ' ἔνι ζῶν καὶ τεθνηκὸς καὶ τὸ ἐγρηγορὸς καὶ τὸ καθεῦδον καὶ νέον καὶ γεραιόν· τάδε γὰρ μεταπεσόντα ἐκεῖνά ἐστι κἀκεῖνα μεταπεσόντα ταῦτα. The second sentence of this pronouncement clearly implies that the mutual and constant succession of opposites is one of the sufficient conditions for their unity. It is clear that Heraclitus believed that in some sense living and dead constantly succeed each other without a temporal break. The same is apparently true of the other opposites in this fragment. The meaning of this mutual succession in the case of living and dead, and again in the case of young and old, is highly obscure and would take us too deeply into Heraclitus' interpretation of Man.[20] But the succession of sleeping and waking is easier to understand. It should probably be linked with Heraclitus' rebuke to Hesiod for failing to observe the unity of day and night, the rebuke to be found in B57 (quoted above). In the case of day and night, in Mediterranean lands their mutual succession without sizable temporal interval is particularly conspicuous, and the same poet Hesiod had indeed expressed it in mythical terms in a famous passage of the *Theogony*, where Night and Day pass one another on the threshold of their joint abode, one on the way out, the other going home.[21] But this example is a good deal easier to follow in detail than the paradoxes of B88. Heraclitus may have intended the terms "sleeping" and "waking" metaphorically, as perhaps elsewhere in his writings.[22] What seems indisputable is that mutual and unvarying succession was an adequate basis for the Heraclitean assertion of unity between opposites. Another such statement, in terms somewhat easier to follow, concerns the hot and the cold, the wet and the dry. B126 reads: τὰ ψυχρὰ θέρεται, θερμὸν ψύχεται, ὑγρὸν αὐαίνεται, καρφαλέον νοτίζεται.[23] Behind Heraclitus' highly poetic vocabulary here,[24] an effect virtually impossible to render in English, we find the prosaic but important thought that hot and cold change into one another and wet and dry do the same. No theory of four "elements" is here implied,[25] and no way of integrating cosmic masses with the opposites. Here is a statement that one of a pair of opposites changes into the other, a sentence difficult, in view of B88 (to say nothing of Heraclitus' general theory), to dissociate from the belief that the pairs of opposites here mentioned are each "one," a unity. Again mutual succession appears to imply unity, and it is reasonable to suppose that Heraclitus believed this mutual succession, like that of night and day, to be unvarying. He probably thought that what was hot could only change, if change it must, into something cold—and vice versa.²⁶ Since he certainly believed in the inevitability of change, we have again an unvarying mutual succession. Now one sense of the word "one" that we have found in Greek is "continuous," and we have observed that the terms are not confined either in philosophical or in non-philosophical Greek to the category of space. If Sophocles²⁷ could use the word "one" to denote "temporally continuous," "without a temporal gap in it," there is no reason why Heraclitus should not be allowed to do the same. There would not in fact be anything wrong or even specially paradoxical about the statement that "Day and Night are parts of a temporal continuum"; and there would be nothing paradoxical in saying that "Day and Night are one, in that they are temporally continuous." What begins to sound odd and even paradoxical is the statement that "day and night are one thing" simpliciter; for this could be read (and was probably meant to be) as a statement of *identity*. Without some such qualification as we should add—and Heraclitus does not appear to have added any such qualification—one is liable to land in paradox. These problems may, however, be postponed for the moment. We may here content ourselves with one further remark: it is tempting to label the continuum which links hot and cold "temperature," and the continuum linking wet and dry would on the same basis be a scale of humidity; but this does not seem on the face of it a very likely answer to the problems raised by the relevant fragment. The Greeks in Heraclitus' time had no scale of temperature in the sense in which we have several, and they would have been aghast at the suggestion that one could measure humidity on a numerical continuous scale as one measures distance or height. Some notion of degrees of hot and cold they had, of course; and of course some things felt wetter to them than others. But the notion of one continuous scale seems a sophisticated one, and one that should not be imagined thus early without good evidence for it, and evidence of any sort is lacking. One has, on the other hand, very good evidence from Heraclitus' own words that he considered mutual succession a guarantee of unity; the burden of proof would appear to rest firmly on those who hold that Heraclitus had anything else than mutual succession in mind when he postulated the unity of hot and cold and of wet and dry.²⁸

Last²⁹ on the list of different ways in which things seemed to Heraclitus to be one is what may be called mutual validation. A possible example of this is the difficult B23.³⁰ More certain is B111: νοῦσος ὑγιείην ἐποίησεν ἡδὺ καὶ ἀγαθόν, λιμὸς κόρον, κάματος ἀνάπαυσιν. One cannot fully experience rest without knowing what weariness is like nor appreciate the benefits of a full stomach without having gone hungry; these might sound like the banalities of a mediocre preacher but are much more likely to have been the foundation of a way of unifying yet another pair of apparent opposites. One is tempted to say that the impossibility of experiencing one member of these pairs of opposites without experience of the other connects them indissolubly.

The English "connection" is indeed a tempting word for anyone analysing the relationship between opposites of the same pair in Heraclitus. Fortunately the temptation need not be resisted, for Heraclitus uses a very similar word himself.

The word concerned is ἁρμονία, whose meaning it is important to seize at the outset; and to do this we may start with B51. οὐ ξυνιᾶσιν ὅκως διαφερόμενον ἑωυτῷ ξυμφέρεται· παλίντονος ἁρμονίη ὅκωσπερ τόξου καὶ λύρης ("They do not understand how being borne apart it is being borne together with itself; a backward-stretching 'harmonia' as of bow and lyre"). The reading παλίντονος, "backward-stretching," is not the only one given by the ancient sources. Some have instead παλίντροπος, "backward-turning," a word found also in a context of Parmenides[31] where many have found other grounds for supposing a reference to Heraclitus. Most scholars seem now to be agreed on "backward-stretching," and against Vlastos,[32] who has recently defended the other view, Kirk brings cogent arguments.[33] If one is to take the harmony of bow and lyre (which cannot of course be a musical harmony) as backward-*turning*, one has to envisage the "harmonia" as an "adjustment" of the instruments. Kirk here argues that the return of string to former position after plucking or drawing "cannot be described as an adjustment in any kind of Greek." With this argument one may feel much sympathy; but the question seems to be one not only of Greek but of logic. In an adjustment something is adjusted to something else, but here (if one follows Vlastos) nothing is being adjusted *to* anything: all that happens is that the string returns to its former position. This one might conceivably refer to in English—if one were determined to import the idea of adjustment—as a readjustment, but it is not in any language an adjustment *tout court*. Nor does it help matters to call the adjustment backward-turning, since this does not have the same connotations as the (loosely used) English "readjustment": it does not imply merely a return to a previously occupied position but continues to imply that something is being adjusted to something else, in a backward-turning fashion. ἁρμόζω means, as Vlastos says, "fit, adapt, accommodate."[34] But, apart from the fact that language does not always work with such symmetry between verb and noun as Vlastos would wish, one should not deduce from this that ἁρμονίη means "adjustment" without going deeper into the connotations of the verb. The action denoted by ἁρμόζω can vary fairly widely, but the connotations emerging from examination of usage are principally two: on the one hand, contact, continuity, or connection resulting from the action; on the other, the appropriateness of this result. In some passages one connotation is clearly more prominent than the other, sometimes not. Neither ἁρμόζω nor ἁρμονίη is particularly common, and one cannot therefore expect that the order of appearance of their various senses will necessarily coincide with the historical order of their development.

Consider first the Homeric usage of ἁρμόζω. At ε 162, ἀλλ' ἄγε δούρατα μακρὰ ταμὼν ἁρμόζεο χαλκῷ / εὐρεῖαν σχεδίην, the goddess certainly means Odysseus to bring the elements of a raft together and fasten them with metal fastenings; but the raft would not last long unless this were done in such a way that the timbers fitted close and were fastened in appropriate positions. Similarly at ε 247, τέτρηνεν δ' ἄρα πάντα καὶ ἥρμοσεν ἀλλήλοισιν, both connotations are present, for similar reasons: the holes in one timber must be opposite the holes in another. Again at P 210 both connotations are felt, but that of suitability probably predominates, Κρονίων / Ἕκτορι δ' ἥρμοσε τεύχε' ἐπὶ χροΐ. At this point in Homer's narrative Hector has Achilles' armour on, but since it belonged to the mighty Achilles it hangs loose. What Zeus does about this is to establish contact between the armour and the relevant parts of Hector's body, the idea being that the armour then fits as armour should. Likewise at Γ 333, perhaps interpolated, ἁρμόζω (probably intransitive here) means "to fit close." One may compare with this Pindar *Pythian* 4.80, where again the verb is intransitive and means "to fit close," this time of the inner layer of clothing as opposed to the outer layer. Nor is this the only similarity between epic and lyric usages. *Pythian* 3.114 has the word of poets in their capacity as τέκτονες ἐπέων: poets have not merely to join words together, but to do so appropriately. Somewhat similar is Solon's use at fragment 24.19 (Diehl): εὐθεῖαν εἰς ἕκαστον ἁρμόσας δίκην ... Here the main point is that straight, not crooked, justice will be brought to bear; the connotation of suitability is contained already in the epithet εὐθεῖαν, but there can be little doubt that it at least influenced Solon's choice of verb. Pindar again at *Isthmian* 6 (7).39 writes ἀείσομαι χαίταν στεφάνοισιν ἁρμόζων; here it is evident that he will bring garland to hair and only secondarily produce a fitting result. A like example is *Nemean* 7.98, where the sense is again "bring near" or "give." Similar cases occur in tragedy; Sophocles at *Oedipus Coloneus* 198 has βάσει βάσιν ἅρμοσαι, Euripides *Troades* 763 has στόμ' ἅρμοσον of a kiss. Relations between man and woman are several times described with the aid of ἁρμόζω: from physical contact to sexual union is a natural enough step, and one may compare the English "What God hath *joined* let no man put asunder." Intercourse, wedlock, and betrothal are all occasions of which ἁρμόζω can be used—see Pindar *Pythian* 9.117, *Pythian* 9.13, and Sophocles

Antigone 570. The further transfer of ἁρμόζω to mean "lead," of an army or similar body, is more difficult to account for. Found in Alcman 95b (Page) with the sense "regulate," and similarly at Sophocles *Oedipus Coloneus* 908 and Aristophanes *Equites* 1236, ἁρμόζω is used of a military leader by Pindar at *Nemean* 8.11; the nouns ἁρμοστής and ἁρμόστωρ (Aeschylus *Eumenides* 456) are equivalent to "leader." Here, no doubt, the Greeks remembered that an army has to be brought and kept together, but they would also have associated fitness with order, and an army has to be orderly. The connotation of "appropriateness" is uppermost here. For Ionic prose of a date not long after Heraclitus we can do no better than refer to Herodotus: he uses the verb ἁρμόζω of betrothal[35] and of stones fitted closely and appropriately (λίθου ... ἁρμοσμένου τὰ μάλιστα, 2.124.5, cf. 2.148.7).

So much for the verb. When we look into the noun ἁρμονίη (remembering that it need not behave precisely similarly), we find in fact a corresponding state of things. The sense of "mode of connection" or "means of maintaining connection" is found at ε 248, ε 361, and Herodotus 2.96.2. As a goddess, Harmonia is associated with Aphrodite in Hesiod (*Theogony* 937) and in the *Homeric Hymn to Apollo* (195), as daughter and attendant respectively. ἁρμονιάων at X 255 means "agreement," "treaty"—a metaphorical use deriving, like "betrothal," from the sense of appropriate contact—much as in English we might speak of "the bringing together" of the parties to a treaty. At *Pythian* 8.68 the sense of "agreement" recurs.[36] In the sense related to the use of ἁρμόζω meaning "order," ἁρμονία is found to my knowledge but once, at Aeschylus *Prometheus Vinctus* 551 τὰν Διὸς ἁρμονίαν.[37] The medical use to mean "suture"[38] is naturally to be associated with the establishment of fitting contact. Perhaps the most interesting passage to compare with Heraclitus B51 is Sophocles *Thamyras* fragment 244 (Jebb–Pearson): ῥηγνὺς χρυσόδετον κέρας, ῥηγνὺς ἁρμονίαν χορδοτόνου λύρας. The meaning of ἁρμονία here cannot be determined for certain: Sophocles does not shrink from bold metaphor, and the object "broken" in the second line may be the musical scale playable on the whole lyre. But I think it is not mere prejudice which inclines me to the belief that the ἁρμονία is the set of strings; the strings are a more obvious object for the verb "break," offer a closer parallel to the obviously concrete κέρας, and are certainly not ruled out by the first half of the compound χορδοτόνου. If this second interpretation of the fragment is right, we have an example of ἁρμονία referring to the string of a lyre to support the likeliest explanation of Heraclitus B51.

Now, the word "adjustment" in English carries some of the connotations of the Greek ἁρμονία, in that it can indicate the establishment of contact in an appropriate manner. But it can be entirely divorced from the notion of contact, in a way not common for ἁρμόζω and very rare indeed for the noun ἁρμονία. The examples analysed above give no hint whatever that ἁρμονίη could be used to denote the return of something to an original position; in cases where the meaning of ἁρμονίη and ἁρμόζω has spatial content, they refer not to the mere taking up of a position but to the establishment of a connection; and the return of a bowstring or lyre-string to its original position after drawing or plucking, though it has spatial significance, is not the establishment of a connection. The upshot is that "adjustment" is a possible translation for ἁρμονίη in Heraclitus B51, but not in the sense in which Vlastos wants that English word to bear; and "connection" is a much safer translation, less likely to mislead. There is no need to doubt that Heraclitus considered the result of the ἁρμονίη fitting. We arrive, then, at the conclusion that, on the assumption that the second half of B51, like the first half, deals with the relationship between opposites, Heraclitus would have agreed that this relationship was a connection, that each pair of opposites being connected by a connection was in that way a continuous whole.[39] We may add that at this point Heraclitus could justly claim that he had ample reason for using the word "one" of his pairs of opposites, even if he meant his public to take "one" in another or in an additional sense. That B51 does in fact describe the relation between opposites has been made probable by Kirk.[40]

One should perhaps insert here a well-worn caveat, that practically any analysis in modern English of the connection between the opposites is likely to be overexplicit and to introduce terms which Heraclitus would not have understood. One is liable to be either too precise to suit Heraclitus' taste for ambiguity or too abstract for Heraclitus to have understood. One is also liable to misunderstand Heraclitus by taking his metaphors as literal statements, and vice versa. A particularly delicate example is the fragment with which we are next concerned.

The text and purely verbal problems of B26 have vexed a generation of scholars, and the despair voiced in public by Gigon[41] has probably been vented in private by many more. The interpretation here offered (largely Uvo Hölscher's)[42] is given only after much hesitation and with strong misgivings. What I believe with Hölscher to be the correct text is this: ἄνθρωπος ἐν εὐφρόνῃ φάος ἅπτεται [ἑαυτῷ ἀποθανὼν] ἀποσβεσθεὶς ὄψεις, ζῶν δὲ ἅπτεται τεθνεῶτος εὕδων, [ἀποσβεσθεὶς ὄψεις], ἐγρηγορὼς ἅπτεται εὕδοντος.[43] The reason for discussing the fragment here at all is that it seems to assert a contact between living and dead and between sleeping and waking, and it is a contact or connection between opposites that Heraclitus seemed to suggest in B51. What I believe Heraclitus to be saying in B26 is something like this: when a man's eyes are quenched (in sleep) he kindles a light (in dreams); when asleep a man is in contact with (or next to) the dead, even in life; when men are awake they are in their stupidity next best thing to (next to) asleep. Whatever the text and interpretation of the first clause, the second and third are, as Reinhardt observed,[44] a proportional statement; waking is to sleeping as sleeping to dead. But they are obviously more than that. Living and dead, awake and asleep, are opposites, one pair of which has its unity stressed elsewhere by Heraclitus. The word ἅπτεται expressed a type of unity, Aristotle's unity ἁφῇ,[45] and it seems probable that the proportional statement is here combined with a statement of the unity of these pairs of opposites. It is particularly interesting that the contact form of unity is here used. One might perhaps argue that this particular metaphor did not come of itself to Heraclitus' mind to express the unity of opposites but was intended primarily to complete the pun on the two senses of ἅπτεται, thus supplying in the Archaic manner the necessary verbal connection between his first two clauses. But if there has been accommodation to the pun, and verbal connection, it seems to have been the other way; for the verb is not found in the middle voice meaning "kindle," if LSJ is to be trusted, between this passage and Callimachus' *Hymn to Artemis*. Heraclitus, therefore, evidently had the second and third clauses in mind when he was writing the first; so that the notion of contact was already present to his mind when he penned the first ἅπτεται. Though this does not *exclude* the hypothesis that his metaphor of contact was owed entirely to his metaphor of kindling, it at least makes it much less likely. It may plausibly be alleged, accordingly, that Heraclitus envisaged the unity between living and dead, and likewise between asleep and awake, as not only substantiated by their mutual succession but cemented by actual resemblance, which he chose to indicate by the metaphor of close contact. His choice of metaphor, in view of the most probable meaning of ἁρμονίη, is unlikely to have been haphazard and adds a further indication that he was thinking of the unity of the opposites partly as unity by contact. An interesting point, if the foregoing argument be found acceptable, is that Heraclitus can have seen no inconsistency in the supposition that living and dead are both in contact and linked by mutual succession, and he need not have been aware that there was any difference between these as modes of unity.[46]

But, though Heraclitus certainly inferred unity in some cases primarily from temporal continuity, he speaks only this once of continuity between a particular pair of opposites and does not seem particularly concerned in the extant fragments to develop a proof that a given pair of opposites is continuous. This is understandable; for, if he had told his contemporaries simply that, for example, day and night were continuous, then they would have been justified in retorting that they knew this already, and so what? A continuity between death and life, or a resemblance amounting to continuity between sleeping and waking: that was new, and interesting; but a mere temporal continuity between hot and cold or night and day? If it needed a philosopher to point that out, then Anaximander would do: what did Heraclitus have to add? The answer to this last question must be that Heraclitus had added, at least by implication, the actual identity of the opposites whose continuity he detected. There are extant actual assertions of identity for the road up and the road down (B60), and probably for the straight and crooked way of a roller (B59).[47] There is further, to supplement and explain the apparent banality of the remarks on these two topics, the assertion in B88 that living and dead, awake and asleep, and young and old are in us as "the same." Unless one includes the difficult B103, these are the only actual statements of identity of opposites to be found in all the remains of Heraclitus' book. But from them two very important things become clear. The first is that we need not suppose Heraclitus' sole point to have been in all cases the banality that appears on the surface of his remarks; we need not suppose that the sole point of, for example, B126 was that hot things become cold, cold hot, wet dry, and dry wet. It becomes clear that Heraclitus had a point which was not merely not banal but was striking and bizarre, and it is reasonable to suppose that this striking doctrine, the identity of opposites, was at the back of his apparent banalities. This much is generally accepted. The second point is that Heraclitus apparently believed that, in illustrating alike the opposites' logical and physical indistinguishability, their mutual succession, or their continuity, he was arguing for their identity. It looks as though, as indeed we should expect at this early date, the distinction between unity of continuity and unity of absolute identity was not available to him. If it had been available, then Heraclitus ought to have seen that his paradoxes in so far as they were identity statements were mere puns, and his contemporaries ought to have seen in his paradoxical identity statements a series of equivocations.

But did Heraclitus perhaps, with an insight in advance of his time, deliberately *use* the paradoxical nature of the statement that X and Y (being opposites) are identical to draw attention to other kinds of unity which his contemporaries had not imagined to subsist between opposites in general or in any case had not associated with unity?[48] Certainly the constant alternation between certain opposites was a prominent feature of Anaximander's thought; and certainly we have no good evidence to suggest that this constant alternation was in any way linked to a statement of the unity of the opposites in particular or of the world in general. Heraclitus' originality, therefore, *could* consist merely in drawing attention by paradox to the implication of unity he found in Anaximander, and in extending the whole idea to other pairs of opposites. But, though theoretically possible, this development seems unlikely. Such a use of *suggestio falsi* in order to draw attention to a truth seems much too sophisticated for a thinker of Heraclitus' epoch. I do not doubt that Heraclitus was deliberately paradoxical but believe that he fully accepted his own paradoxes.

Even granted that Heraclitus failed to penetrate the difference between one kind of unity and another, he cannot be denied considerable importance. At least he saw that in the then state of logic and in the then state of understanding of the term "one" and related words, it followed, if two things were continuous, in time or in space, that they were identical; and by this paradoxical result he may well have helped to bring ambiguities to the surface which were hidden altogether before he wrote. It may be noted also that Heraclitus does not, in the fragments known to us, use the words "one" or "the same" in the series of fragments often called "relativistic," in which animate creatures find opposed properties in a single object. This may be mere coincidence—but it may indicate a reluctance to press the term "one" beyond all bounds. Furthermore, he did not attempt, even while declaring the identity of opposites, to avoid admitting some opposition between them; strife between opposites is even more fundamental in Heraclitean cosmology than in the Milesian.[49] So Heraclitus did not give vent to his paradoxes in total naïveté, without knowing their paradoxicality at all. But, if he knew their paradoxicality, then he was only a step from knowing that there was something wrong somewhere with the argument; only he could not lay his finger on the flaw and continued to proclaim the paradoxes with his unique vigour. One may credit Heraclitus with paving the way by his genius for much more than he knew, not only in the matter of incorporeality, as has been admitted,[50] but also in the elucidation of the ambiguities of "one" and "many." But, with all his ingenuity and half-insights, Heraclitus is surely still a child of his time in that a word like "one" has for him a rigidity which it did not have for a thinker like Aristotle who could analyse the various senses of such words.[51]

THE UNITY OF ALL THINGS

Heraclitus' transition from the unity of pairs of opposites to the unity of all things is sudden and to modern readers unexpected. The temptation here is to throw all talk of logic overboard. But, nevertheless, the fact must be observed that this is how Heraclitus' mind worked, and the best place to observe it is in the text of B10, which reads as follows:

συλλάψιες ὅλα καὶ οὐχ ὅλα, συμφερόμενον διαφερόμενον, συνᾷδον διᾷδον· ἐκ πάντων ἓν καὶ ἐξ ἑνὸς πάντα.[52] "Things taken together are wholes and not wholes, what is in agreement differs, what is in tune is out of tune, and from all things one thing and from one thing all things." Here Snell has shown that "things taken together" is the subject, not the predicate, and that "wholes and not wholes" and the rest are not normal Heraclitean pairs of opposites but alternative descriptions of "things taken together."[53] The "things taken together" are doubtless, to judge from the rest of Heraclitus' remains, primarily the opposites, and it is most likely that the pairs of relationships in which they stand are not successive states but simultaneous; thus opposites (compare B51) are both being pulled apart and straining together and are both in tune and at the same time out of tune.

Attention may rest for a moment on the phrase "wholes and not wholes"; we have seen that one possible sense for the Greek word ἕν was "whole," and Heraclitus appears in this fragment to treat unity and plurality as parallel in some way to wholeness and the lack of it. It seems either that a pair of opposites was both a whole and not a whole *or* that each single opposite was both a whole, distinct from its counterpart, *and* not a whole without its counterpart. The second alternative is easier to understand in logic, but either could be got out of the Greek, and neither can be dismissed. What is important is that unity by continuity such as usually obtains between Heraclitean opposites is not here sharply distinguished from wholeness; *either* a pair of opposites is regarded as one continuous whole and simultaneously discontinuous and therefore not a whole, *or* a single opposite is *both* a whole in itself *and* simultaneously a mere part of a connected whole. It would be mistaken at this point to speak of a confusion in Heraclitus' mind between wholeness and continuity; for continuity might very plausibly be regarded as an element in wholeness,[54] though strictly absence of gaps is not a necessary condition of wholeness. It is merely worth noting in passing that Heraclitus shows no sign of having made any distinction between connection and wholeness as different senses of the word "one," though he cannot be proved to have confused this particular pair of senses.

To resume: in the first half of B10 we have a statement of the simultaneous unity and diversity of opposites, and in the second half we have a statement of the simultaneous unity and plurality of all things. It appears that we have here a transition such as we were looking for between the unity of opposites and the unity of the world. I do not believe that "all things," in the neuter, refers to συλλάψιες rather than to things in general; a neuter such as ἐκ πάντων ἕν referring back to a feminine is harder to follow (and to parallel) than a neuter predicate such as ὅλα καὶ οὐχ ὅλα. There is no indication in B50 that it is the unity of opposites and of nothing else that is referred to in that fragment; so that, even if the transition from all opposites to all things is not to be seen in full in B10, it is reasonable to suppose that the generalized statement ἐκ πάντων ἓν καὶ ἐξ ἑνὸς πάντα was taken up direct into the similar phrase ἓν πάντα εἶναι in B50. In one fragment or the other (or between) the transition takes place. The fact of such a transition makes it likely that Heraclitus thought of the unity of all things in the same kind of context and with the same senses in his mind as for the unity of opposites. The identity of the objects of the world would therefore have been in his mind; but in his zeal on behalf of Strife Heraclitus is unlikely to have rested content with a simple statement of complete identity. We should think of all things as being identical but not identical; identical because "one" (in the sense of "connected," "continuous") and not identical, because Heraclitus was not devoid of common sense.

FIRE AS SUBSTRATUM?

It is apparent from B50 that the unity of all things is the principal content of the Logos[55] and that the Logos is closely related to Fire and Strife; it is therefore necessary to offer a brief discussion of these entities and the relations between them, the more so as the Heraclitean Fire has been considered by many as in effect a substratum, and even those who eschew such an interpretation are inclined to use words and phrases in English reminiscent of it. Cherniss and others[56] have argued convincingly that Fire was not a substratum, despite remarks of Aristotle's such as *De caelo* 298b29ff ... ἓν δέ τι μόνον ὑπομένειν, ἐξ οὗ ταῦτα πάντα μετασχηματίζεσθαι (referred to Heraclitus) or *Metaphysics* 984a7, making Heraclitus' doctrine parallel to the Milesians'. In principle it was, as we have seen already, unlikely that anyone in ignorance of Parmenides, and without having to get round his arguments, should have thought of all things as made of one substance. But it must be admitted that, if anyone could have held such a view in ignorance of Parmenides, it is most likely to have been Heraclitus, who already had views on the world's unity, and the subject accordingly deserves more discussion. First, we may discount the remarks of Aristotle, who has clearly failed on more than one occasion to distinguish adequately between the Heraclitean and the Milesian world-views. Since the possibility therefore arises that any statement of Aristotle's regarding a substratum in Heraclitus is tainted with Aristotle's misinterpretation of Milesian thought, the evidence for the "substratum" interpretation, if any, must come from the extant fragments of Heraclitus' own work.

Such evidence could perhaps best be sought in B31. Clement of Alexandria, who cites the fragment, interprets it on Stoicizing lines as cosmogonical, but this is not likely to be right.[57] Taking it rather as cosmological, we have the statement that πυρὸς τροπαί· πρῶτον θάλασσα, θαλάσσης δὲ τὸ μὲν ἥμισυ γῆ τὸ δὲ ἥμισυ πρηστήρ followed, not necessarily immediately, by θάλασσα διαχέεται, καὶ μετρέεται εἰς τὸν αὐτὸν λόγον ὁκοῖος πρόσθεν ἦν ἢ γενέσθαι [γῆ].[58] "The turnings (or changes) of Fire; first sea, and of sea half earth and half 'prester.'" "Sea is dispersed, and is measured in the same proportion as it was before it came to be." To this Clement adds: "Likewise the same is true for the other elements." The details of the changes involved need not be our concern; attention may be focussed on the constitution of the cosmic masses other than fire. First, like Heraclitus, we may examine "sea."

In the first half of B31 there are two ways of taking Heraclitus' Greek. He may be saying that sea *is* half earth and half "prester," or he may be saying that the sea *turns* half *to* earth and half *to* "prester." The theory that he both says and means that sea *is* half earth and half "prester," being thus a fifty-fifty mixture of earth and fire, has recently been revived by Cherniss;[59] but it is no more plausible now than when Teichmüller rebutted a similar view by pointing out that this would mean the abolition of sea-water as such.[60] It would, in any case, be a highly implausible doctrine, neither necessary in logic nor imposed on Heraclitus by any evidence. It is also completely irrelevant to what remains of Heraclitus' context, which is about the change of things, not about their constitution. It is relevant that even if the sea *were* half fire and half earth, that would not make Fire a substratum. It is not, however, certain whether the fragment merely *means* that sea turns to earth and "prester" or whether it actually *says* it.[61] But in either case the fragment is dubious evidence for anything resembling a substratum interpretation of Heraclitus' fire. For a statement about what fire changes into is no evidence that fire, when changed, in some sense remains fire. It might be tempting to believe that sea and earth are variant forms of fire, or variants of fire, or that there are higher and lower forms of fire. But one may ask how and why Heraclitus, any more than (say) Anaximenes, would have distinguished between variant forms and different substances, and (more pertinently still) whether there is any evidence that he did so. Such evidence cannot, of course, be found in the Greek word τροπαί: that fire when changed or turned gives rise to sea does not prove by any means that the result is a form or variant of fire or is describable by any similar phrase; sea is the end-result of a process undergone by fire, and we have no ground at all for supposing that this result is a form of fire.[62] Fire in Heraclitus persists *amid* change, but this fragment does nothing to show that it persists *through* change, in the sense of "provides an unchanging substratum."

Nor is there any proof to be found in B30: κόσμον τόνδε [τὸν αὐτὸν ἁπάντων] οὔτε τις θεῶν οὔτε ἀνθρώπων ἐποίησεν, ἀλλ' ἦν ἀεὶ καὶ ἔστιν καὶ ἔσται· πῦρ ἀείζωον, ἁπτόμενον μέτρα καὶ σβεννύμενον μέτρα. This is most probably to be interpreted as by Kirk,[63] the "measures" of the second half being not temporal but spatial, and the whole being not therefore a statement of the ecpyrosis doctrine but a depiction of the alternate kindling and rekindling of fire in the one eternal cosmos. But that the cosmos is a fire does not show that everything, every individual thing in the world, is a piece of fire or is fiery. Kirk has well used the simile of a bonfire in this connection. In a bonfire a twig need not be on fire itself to be part of the fire, to belong to it, or to be in it; so in Heraclitus' cosmos—whether this means "world" or "world order"—water and earth need not themselves be on fire or be fire to be part of the fire which is the cosmos. Further, he would be a bold man indeed who, dealing with this early stage of thought and of style, suggested that when Heraclitus wrote that fire was extinguished and rekindled he actually meant that the parts which were extinguished were still really or "essentially" fire. The word σβεννύμενον must have its full meaning to give the word ἁπτόμενον any meaning at all; and, if they both have full force, then the substratum interpretation can be ruled out at once. What has been extinguished is no longer fire.

Nor is the substratum theory any better off when confronted with B90: πυρός τε ἀνταμοιβὴ τὰ πάντα καὶ πῦρ ἁπάντων ὅκωσπερ χρυσοῦ χρήματα καὶ χρημάτων χρυσός. In this simile the relationship between all things and fire is made, one would suppose, tolerably clear. Money and goods, though one may be exchanged for the other, cannot be reduced physically to one another, and neither can be described as a variant form of the other; nor can goods be said to be "essentially" money—and it is at least doubtful whether money is "essentially" goods, supposing that such a statement were relevant in the present context when it is obviously fire which is represented by the singular "money." Heraclitus' comparison need not be exact; but, if these elementary deductions cannot be made from it, then one may wonder what it was intended to illustrate, and how.[64] The idea behind the fragment may well be that every thing has an equivalent in fire, as Cherniss has suggested; but one may doubt his further suggestion that this is the reason for the *unity* of all things.[65] What has this got to do with unity? How far would Heraclitus have to stretch the normal usage of the word to establish a unity between things which have equivalents in the same substance? Why should one associate unity, for example, with the goods of the simile?

Nor is there any reason why one should associate Heraclitus' unity of all things with a common origin; neither predication of more than one thing of a single subject nor mutual succession affords a precise parallel, and it may accordingly be wondered whether Kirk is right in saying that "The *cosmological* aspect of the connection of all things is that they are all πυρὸς τροπαί."[66] For one thing, we cannot be sure that "all things" *are* πυρὸς τροπαί; there is no mention of all things in B31.[67] The interpretation of B99 as showing that day and night are brought about by the same cause, namely the sun, and are for that reason also be to regarded as one is admittedly precarious.[68] It is possible, however, that it is in virtue of mutual succession that fire expresses the unity of all things, as Kirk seems to suggest in the following: "Fire always turns into sea, and indirectly to earth, earth and sea turn back into fire; *therefore* sea and earth are 'the same' as fire."[69] For the exchange of fire and all things, likened in B90 to the exchange of money and goods, could well be looked on as a kind of mutual succession; and I see no reason why indirect exchange also should not be allowed to count, in view of the opposition of all things to fire in B90, as succession.

Fire is closely associated with the Logos in Heraclitus' thought, and, the principal content of the Logos being the unity of all things, one would naturally expect Fire also to be bound up with that unity. It is, after all, Fire which steers all things, and they happen according to the Logos; there cannot be a radical dissension or even a clear fundamental distinction between the two entities; one may therefore with the more confidence suppose mutual succession to be the way in which Fire plays this prominent part in the unity of all things. This suggestion adumbrates, incidentally, a method of integrating the discussion of all things with that of the opposites; for, just as opposites are often connected and therefore unified by mutual succession, so the complex of fire and all things is united in the same way.

UNITY AND DEITY

Another way in which things may have been unified is in the deity mentioned in B67. Here several different pairs of opposites—doubtless chosen merely as representing all the opposites, as Hippolytus perhaps saw[70]—are predicated together of "the god." This need not conflict in Heraclitus' thinking with B102, which says that to god all things are just even if men find some things just and some unjust; there is no conflict even if the meaning of B102 is that all opposites are, from the divine standpoint, indistinguishable. B102 says, in effect, that of the two views about opposites the synthetic is the more important, and from the viewpoint of the god the only significant one.[71] The situation concerning the relation between the Logos and the god is admirably expressed by Kirk: "The Logos could certainly be identified with 'day night, winter summer, war peace, satiety hunger'; but if this Logos can correctly be described as divine there can be little objection to a saying which associates these same opposites (or any others) with ὁ θεός."[72] For the detailed argument in favour of the thesis that B67 states a unity between different pairs of opposites, rather than between the two members of a single pair, the reader may again be referred to Kirk's discussion.[73] The god, then, is (in a sense) the opposites, and there is no difference which he does not underlie, and in him they are all unified as Heraclitus elsewhere says that they are unified in the Logos. The Logos is described as "common," and so the type of unity here represented may most plausibly be analysed as dependent on the possession of something in common. This means (at Heraclitus' date) having a common ingredient, and it looks as if we may have to fall back again on the substratum theory. But it may still be doubted whether that was Heraclitus' intention. The content of the Logos is the unity of all things, and naturally all things are united in and by it; but the association of Logos and Fire is an association and not an equation, so that the omnipresence of the Logos does not imply the omnipresence of Fire. In any case, one common ingredient is not necessarily the sole constituent. The world in its totality, rather than individual things in it, is to be equated with the Fire.

It must be admitted that Heraclitus' doctrine of the god as expressed in B67 looks suspiciously like monotheism, and it has been for that reason compared with the doctrine of Xenophanes.[74] But we have seen that Xenophanes' doctrine of deity is hardly to be accepted as conscious monotheism deliberately opposed to polytheism, and there is equally no need to interpret Heraclitus in that sense. The use of the singular θεός certainly does not prove monotheism. Heraclitus evidently disapproved of certain cult practices of his day, perhaps as not being spiritual enough; to wash off the stain of blood with more sacrificial blood he likened (at B5) to washing off mud with mud, and praying to statues he compared with talking to walls. In this he takes an attitude consistent with the highest religious thought of his day; Xenophanes had also shown up crude anthropomorphism for what it is. But there is a wide gulf set between such disapproval and the avowal of monotheistic doctrine, and there is insufficient evidence that Heraclitus crossed this gulf any more than Xenophanes. His references to "the one wise thing" probably refer to the Logos or Fire; the statement (at B32) that one thing, the wise alone, is both willing and unwilling to be called by the name of Zeus can very plausibly be interpreted to mean that Fire or Logos is supreme (like the traditional Zeus) but that it lacks personal attributes attaching to the Zeus of myth and of cult.[75] This represents a real and significant step towards an attitude to divinity which we tend to associate with monotheism, but it is not equivalent to a statement that there is only one divine being. Heraclitus' denial of an external "daemon" in the statement that character is man's daemon, despite its enlightened appearance, also represents something short of formal monotheism. There is no good evidence that the Greeks of the Archaic period, even in Ionia, were occupied with the question whether there was one god or many.

B114 of Heraclitus also does not contain any explicit or implicit monotheism. Stating that all human laws are nourished by one divine law, the fragment places in contrast "one" and "all" as well as "human" and "divine." But there is no more suggestion of one single unique deity here than there is in Aristotle's *Rhetoric*[76] when he distinguishes between the common unwritten law and the individual written one. How original Heraclitus' statement was, and what precisely he intended to indicate with the metaphor of nourishing, are matters which must remain obscure. We certainly have here a plurality nourished by a single entity; but that should not encourage loose talk about "the One" being somehow related to "the Many." There is no need to look for any analogue of the many human laws in Heraclitus' physics, however tempting it is to associate or even equate the single divine law with the Logos.[77] Nor does the metaphor of nourishing represent a serious attempt to come to grips with any metaphysical problem of the relationship of a One and a Many.

ONE BECOMING MANY?

So much for problems connected with the question of one thing being many; the problems of one thing becoming many are not to be found in Heraclitus, for he had no cosmogony and believed in no final destruction of the world into one substance. It is true that reputable students of Heraclitus, from Aristotle to Mondolfo, have held to the contrary; but we are not obliged to follow them in their assimilation of Heraclitus to the Milesians.[78] If Aristotle had any particular evidence in mind when postulating the reabsorption of the world into fire, it is quite likely to have been B90, and there is no good reason for following this argument, however superficially attractive. At all events, the ancients had almost certainly no more evidence for the conflagration and for the supposed cosmogony than we have. The evidence of Plato, often cited as decisive *against* ecpyrosis, is perhaps not so strong as some have believed, and Plato is not always reliable as an authority for fifth-century thought. The crucial questions here concern not so much the later reports of Heraclitus' thinking as the interpretation of Heraclitus' own words, and these are, it seems to me, decisive against the ecpyrosis. Strife must always continue, or the world would come to an end; it is not enough in reply to this to suggest that war and peace are united in the god of B67, for the unity of such opposites does not exclude their difference in practice, and in this particular instance the rebuke administered for a prayer for the end of strife would be rendered nugatory by the belief that war and peace were completely identifiable. It is difficult to see how cosmic strife can continue without opposites to strive, and it is difficult to see how the opposites (among them "hot" and "cold": see B126) could meaningfully be said to persist in a total cosmic conflagration. Neither B30 nor B31 supplies good evidence for an ecpyrosis, and B66 has rightly been eliminated from this question by Marcovich.[79] The Great Year, often connected with the ecpyrosis, need not be so connected, and probably was not, except by the Stoics.[80] The ecpyrosis may safely be excluded from our consideration of Heraclitus.

There is only one remaining obstacle to the removal of any suggestion that Heraclitus postulated a world in which on a cosmic scale unity is succeeded by plurality: that is the second half of B10, ἐκ πάντων ἓν καὶ ἐξ ἑνὸς πάντα ("From all things one thing, from one thing all things"). Taken in isolation this might seem to suggest that "all things" and "one thing" succeed one another in a way reminiscent (according to Gigon,[81] for example) of Milesian philosophies. But Kirk is surely right in arguing that, with συλλάψιες as subject, the second part of the fragment must refer to a static condition of affairs and not to successive states of the world.[82] Details of the correct interpretation may be arguable;[83] but we cannot at all events find here, any more than we find elsewhere in Heraclitus, a doctrine that what was one became many.

V

PARMENIDES AND MELISSUS

RELATIVE CHRONOLOGY OF PARMENIDES AND HERACLITUS

EXTERNAL EVIDENCE

Most of what is needful to say on this subject has been said recently with exemplary clarity by M. Marcovich.[1] Once the workings of the mind of the Hellenistic chronological versifier Apollodorus are understood, the ancient external evidence for the date of Heraclitus is seen to be mere fabrication, with no visible foundation in fact. It follows that it cannot be used to date Heraclitus before Parmenides, any more than it can be used to date Heraclitus absolutely. The date of Heraclitus must rest purely on conjecture, and his relative chronology must rest on internal evidence, for whatever such evidence may turn out to be worth. Few oddities in the history of scholarship have so piquant an irony as the still all-too-frequent reliance on the external evidence to date Parmenides after Heraclitus.

Apollodorus dated Heraclitus in the sixty-ninth Olympiad, placing his ἀκμή at that time. Evidence for this is to be found in Diogenes Laertius, the *Suda*, and (possibly with less accuracy) in Eusebius' *Canon*.[2] The form it takes in the *Suda* has apparently been responsible for some unwary theorizing. The *Suda* says, after giving Heraclitus' Olympiad, that this was in the time of Darius the son of Hystaspes. So far as I can see, it is on this basis and on no other that Jacoby, discussing this part of Apollodorus, supposed the chronologer to have derived Heraclitus' date not only from a well-known synchronism with Parmenides but also from good evidence that connected Heraclitus with this particular king of Persia. Jacoby supposed that Apollodorus for this reason fixed Heraclitus in the middle of Darius' reign. All this is baseless. No one has ever shown that any tradition of Heraclitus' connection with Darius ever existed before the forged Letters of Heraclitus or that these Letters rested on a genuine tradition of such a connection. Jacoby apparently relied upon a passage of Clement of Alexandria[3] to show the existence of such an independent tradition, but there is no reason, chronological or other, to doubt that the very learned Clement had access to the Letters or to some intermediary source. What the *Suda*'s source was, we can only guess, but there is no need to postulate one earlier than, or independent of, the Letters. The Letters themselves could easily be explained as reflecting not a tradition but a forger's romantic notion, the choice of Persian king being based on—of course, the Apollodoran chronology of Heraclitus and (doubtless) of Darius the Great. The Hellenistic age sometimes (not unnaturally) expected its philosophers to be so unworldly as to refuse royal invitations and readily projected its notions into the past; the biographies of the philosophers are full of romances of this sort.

This being so, there is no shadow of a reason for supposing Apollodorus to have been motivated in his dating of Heraclitus by anything but the above-mentioned synchronism with Parmenides. Placing Xenophanes' floruit at the foundation date of Elea, Apollodorus no doubt recognized not only Parmenides but also Heraclitus as pupils of Xenophanes[4] and therefore placed the birth of each in the year of their master's floruit, giving them a floruit forty years later. Heraclitus was sometimes regarded as a pupil of Xenophanes, and the interval between them is duly ten Olympiads, if the majority of our sources have the correct numbering. There is no good reason to doubt that such was Apollodorus' motivation: it would be entirely consistent with what else we know of his work.

But the majority of scholars now cast doubt, and rightly so, on the Apollodoran dating of Parmenides.[5] The evidence of Plato's *Parmenides* shows pretty conclusively that, in the fourth century at least, Parmenides was thought to have been born about a generation later than Apollodorus reckoned; Kirk and Raven plausibly suggest a date of birth for Parmenides of "about 515–510."[6] The normal acceptance of this doctrine shows how little value is normally placed on the constructions of Apollodorus.

Yet it is still that same chronology of Apollodorus that is invoked to place Heraclitus before Parmenides. We are confronted with the ironic truth that a dating originally designed with the purpose of making these two philosophers contemporaries is now used to put one many years before the other. It has not been sufficiently observed that, if Apollodorus could be wrong by twenty-five years on Parmenides, he could be equally wrong on Heraclitus. It has not been sufficiently observed that references by Heraclitus to other writers do not serve to date him exactly and certainly do not allow us to choose between (say) 490 and (say) 485 for the composition or first dissemination of his work.[7] Nor is there any good evidence to show at what time of his life Parmenides first wrote or recited his poem.[8] For this also we cannot tell whether (say) 485 or (say) 480 is the date on which it would be safest to bet. Scholarly guessing in this particular case is worthless. So far as the external evidence goes, we do not know, and should freely admit that we do not know, whether Heraclitus wrote before Parmenides and, if he did, whether it was sufficiently before Parmenides' composition to have had any effect on him. If we are to be told these things, it will have to be on the basis of internal evidence alone.

Furthermore, that internal evidence will have to be taken from the extant remains of Parmenides and Heraclitus themselves, and of them alone. The references to Heraclitus by other writers and the imitations of Parmenides by later thinkers offer us no useful dating for the philosophical activity of either. Epicharmus? If we knew the date of the plays in question, were sure that the fragments were authentic, and also knew how long it would take Heraclitus' work to become known in Sicily and Italy, we should be able to use the evidence of Epicharmus; but we are sure of none of these things, and, if we were, we should still have to show that Epicharmus' jokes were not sufficiently comprehensible without any reference to Heraclitus—a point on which the learned differ and will no doubt continue to differ.[9] All in all, it will be more profitable to discuss the actual argument of Parmenides and see if at any point it clearly reflects a knowledge of Heraclitus' work or doctrine.[10]

INTERNAL EVIDENCE

Many scholars still believe that Parmenides' knowledge of Heraclitus' work—and hence his deliberate reaction against it—can be proved from internal evidence.[11] Others maintain that, whatever the truth about an anti-Heraclitean reaction, Parmenides included in his poem no detectable references to Heraclitus.[12] Such disagreement invites inquiry. The obvious place to begin would be with detailed criticism of the numerous supposed allusions to Heraclitus collected by Alois Patin in his *Parmenides in Kampfe gegen Heraklit*;[13] scholars supporting his thesis have adduced linguistic resemblances selected according to individual judgement from the long list of verbal similarities provided by Patin but have not normally gone outside that list.[14] To examine the whole collection would be a tedious task; fortunately we are relieved of it by the existence of a brilliant review of Paul Shorey's excoriating Patin's approach[15] and by the steady diminution (though unfortunately not the annihilation) of scholarly readiness to see an allusion in every verbal resemblance.[16] Dead issues are best left to bury their dead: there are enough live ones to occupy our attention.

Chief among these is the interpretation of Parmenides B6, for it is in this fragment that some even of the most acute and cautious students detect a reference of some kind to Heraclitus:

> χρὴ τὸ λέγειν τε νοεῖν τ' ἐὸν ἔμμεναι· ἔστι γὰρ εἶναι,
> μηδὲν δ' οὐκ ἔστιν· τά σ' ἐγὼ φράζεσθαι ἄνωγα.
> πρώτης γάρ σ' ἀφ' ὁδοῦ ταύτης διζήσιος ⟨εἴργω⟩,
> αὐτὰρ ἔπειτ' ἀπὸ τῆς, ἣν δὴ βροτοὶ εἰδότες οὐδέν
> πλάττονται δίκρανοι· ἀμηχανίη γὰρ ἐν αὐτῶν
> στήθεσιν ἰθύνει πλακτὸν νόον· οἱ δὲ φοροῦνται
> κωφοὶ ὁμῶς τυφλοί τε, τεθηπότες, ἄκριτα φῦλα,
> οἷς τὸ πέλειν τε καὶ οὐκ εἶναι ταὐτὸν νενόμισται
> κοὐ ταὐτόν· πάντων δὲ παλίντροπός ἐστι κέλευθος.

Parmenides' goddess here appears to reject two ways of inquiry, one at line 3, and one at line 4 and in the succeeding lines. One of these is not referred to any particular person or persons; the second is attributed to "mortals knowing nothing . . ." The first is usually held to be the παναπευθὴς ἀταρπός of B2, the way of not-Being, while the second is assigned either to mankind in general or to Heraclitus and/or his followers.[17] Recent years have seen questions raised concerning both ways, and each way in turn is discussed here.

The First Way: A Textual Problem

There are two questions concerning the first rejected way. What is the way? How can the obvious answer to the first query be reconciled with the existing text? One would expect the first rejected way to be the way of not-Being, and so, in common with most students of Parmenides, I believe it to be. This way of negation is then normally sought, since the demonstrative ταύτης more often refers back to a preceding antecedent, in the preceding couplet. But Leonardo Tarán has recently argued strongly that it cannot be found there.[18] The only plausible place in the preceding couplet for it to be found is at μηδὲν δ' οὐκ ἔστιν; but that is not a statement of the false way at all but is a denial of the false way of B2. Parmenides' goddess orders him to bear in mind the denial, but she probably also asks him to keep in mind the true statement "it is possible for the subject to exist."[19] Now, the denial of the false way is, at B2.3, part of the statement of the way of truth, which reads ἔστιν τε καὶ ... οὐκ ἔστι μὴ εἶναι: this makes it all the less probable that the demonstrative ταύτης in B6.3 has as its antecedent the way denied in B6.2. The result would be hopelessly and needlessly obscure: it is highly artificial to separate and sharply distinguish μηδὲν δ' οὐκ ἔστιν from ἔστι γὰρ εἶναι; and to call the resulting construct "ad sensum"[20] does not seem to me to help.

Thus far Tarán convinces. But he is less happy in his solution of the problem thus created. He supposes that whatever verb is to be supplied at the end of B6.3 was qualified by some such word as "now," to be found in a gap in Parmenides' text after our line 3, so as to make the "abandonment" expressed in line 3 merely temporary. The demonstrative of line 3 would still then refer back, and the way abandoned in line 3 would be the way of truth, dropped by the goddess for the time being only, while she discusses other matters. To this theory there is one fatal objection: since line 4 contains no main verb and no qualification of the verb (ἔπειτα is a particle), both verb and qualification (if any) would continue to operate in line 4. So either the two abandonments are both temporary or they are both absolute. But it is highly unlikely that the goddess would detail two ways (at least one of them repetitively) merely in order to say "We'll talk about them later." It is surely improbable that she would heap the abuse of lines 4–9 on a way which she is abandoning only temporarily. Tarán's alleged gap can hardly have contained anything to exempt these lines from the supposed qualification, for αὐτάρ is most probably the first word in its clause.[21] The conclusion must be that previous scholars were right in thinking that Parmenides intended to abandon both ways for good. But then we run up against Tarán's initial problem: how can ταύτης refer to anything in lines 1–2?

We could solve this problem, or rather evade it, if we adopted Mrs. Rosamond Kent Sprague's re-arrangement of Parmenides' text.[22] Mrs. Sprague inserts after B6.3 the line B7.1; she further believes either that B7.2 was invented by Plato on the basis of B6.3 (surely a high-handed treatment of Plato) or that the whole couplet B7.1–2 should be inserted before B6.3 (surely a most improbably repetitious collocation). There is no good reason for separating B7.1–2 from the rest of that fragment.[23] If a simpler and less arbitrary solution than this should offer itself, then we should not be reluctant to give up this one.

In fact a solution more economical of hypothesis does present itself. To show this it is necessary to distinguish two questions, namely, that of a lacuna or lacunae in the manuscripts of Simplicius where he cites B6 and that of a gap in Simplicius' own original report of Parmenides' text.

To consider the question of Simplicius' manuscripts: there is almost certainly at least one lacuna in them, for at the end of line 3 Parmenides is cut off in mid-line and mid-sentence, and there is high probability that Simplicius would not have left Parmenides without a verb to complete his sentence. Some such verb as Diels's ⟨εἴργω⟩ is therefore a virtually certain supplement to the text of Simplicius as well as that of Parmenides. Further, Simplicius' sentence begins in his manuscripts εἰπὼν γὰρ ὅτι... and then continues to the end of his quotation of Parmenides without ever achieving a main verb. Emendation to εἶπεν... would serve, but it is more sparing in copyists' errors and, I believe, more in accordance with Simplicius' usage to postulate the omission of some such verb as ἐπάγει after the omitted εἴργω at the end of line 3.[24] If we thus accept Diels's two supplements, we have not only two words familiar to the vocabulary of the two authors concerned but also a ready-made explanation of the single corruption in Simplicius, by haplography due to the repetition of the syllable ει in εἴργω and ἐπάγει. If there is simply a lacuna in Simplicius' text including a more substantial part of Parmenides' poem, then again the most economical place to put it is after the end of line 3 where we already have a lacuna.

If Simplicius himself reported Parmenides incompletely, then the location of the gap is a more complicated question. If, in our search for an antecedent to ταύτης which makes sense, we take this alternative, we may locate the gap either before or after line 3. Against putting the missing lines before line 3 is the resulting oddness of the γάρ in line 3. It is difficult to imagine a context in which one would enunciate the way of not-Being and then say "For from this way I hold you back." One would be writing strangely indeed if one said "This is the way of not-Being; it is wrong, *for* I hold you back from it." If Parmenides' goddess said "This is the way of not being; you must not go along it, *for* I hold you back from it," she would at least have been talking sense; but she would not really have been likely to say (as this last hypothesis makes her) "You must not go along way X, for I hold you back both from way X and from way Y, which is the one ignorant mortals travel..." and so on for six more lines; the sentence loses thus all proportion. It is more natural to suppose that Parmenides made his goddess say "You must keep in mind the true way for which I have just argued, for the first alternative way, the one that says οὐκ ἔστιν, is barred as well as the illegitimate confusion between the two." The γάρ is clearer, and the structure of the whole fragment more perspicuous, if we suppose that B6.1–2 contain an argument for the proposition that the subject ἔστιν, and that this argument is buttressed—whence the γάρ—by the exclusion of the two alternatives. For the γάρ ought surely to connect with what precedes not merely the first half of the sentence but also the second half, which goes with it so closely in logic and syntax. If we place the lacuna *after* line 3 and suppose given in it a statement of the way of not-Being to serve as antecedent to ταύτης, this is indeed the function of γάρ; the justification of the way of truth is then supported by a denial of the two possible alternatives.[25] An argument by elimination is, after all, what Parmenides has clearly carried through by the time he comes to the beginning of B8; μοῦνος δ' ἔτι μῦθος ὁδοῖο / λείπεται ὡς ἔστιν.

If the gap in Parmenides *is* due to Simplicius rather than to the latter's scribes, then we have to account for Simplicius' omission. This also is easiest on the assumption that the gap occurred after line 3 rather than before it. Simplicius, when quoting B6.8–9 at *in Physica* 78.2, appears to hold that Parmenides rejects two ways, that of τὸ μὴ ὄν and the combination τὸ ὄν καὶ τὸ μὴ ὄν, and he there assigns αὐτὰρ ἔπειτ᾽ . . . (or at least lines 8–9) to the combination. This means that he did not believe that the way of mortals in B6 (whatever he may have thought about B7) was the way of not-Being. Now, in his main citation of the fragment at 117.2, Simplicius probably meant to distinguish two statements, one marked by εἰπὼν γὰρ ὅτι and the other, beginning at line 3, by some such verb as Diels's ἐπάγει. Since the second statement was of the way of mortals and not the way of not-Being, the first statement, at least in Simplicius' opinion, must have been either the way of truth or the way of undiluted not-Being. But it is improbable that Simplicius thought this first statement was of the way of truth, for if he had he would have stopped at ἄνωγα and not included the εἴργω sentence at all; he cannot seriously have believed that Parmenides rejects the way of truth.[26] Therefore he must have anticipated many moderns in holding that μηδὲν δ' οὐκ ἔστιν was somehow referred to by the ταύτης in line 3: he is unlikely to have done this unless he saw line 3 following in his text immediately after line 2. If his text had indeed lines 2 and 3 consecutively, then his mistake is easily accounted for: it is admittedly commoner for οὗτος to refer backward than forward. It is this grammatical fact which accounts also for the modern failure to consider the possibility that ταύτης refers to an enunciation of the way of not-Being following line 3. But a glance at examples shows that this possibility does not deserve such neglect.[27]

The upshot is that, whether Simplicius or his scribes are to be held responsible for the omission in the extant text of Parmenides B6, the most economical and probable place for the omitted description of the way of not-Being is after line 3. On this assumption we may account easily for the omission; we may also accept Tarán's valid argument against the previously accepted interpretation, without being forced to abandon the view that Parmenides' goddess here absolutely rejects two ways she considers false.

The Second Rejected Way: The Gender of πάντων

Fortified in this belief, we may next examine the syntax and meaning of the following lines. The principal question here is the gender of πάντων. A whole generation of scholars virtually ignored the possibility that it was masculine, and it is a legacy of this period that even now the possibility finds expression in footnotes to translations rather than in translations themselves.[28] In a previous paper I argued that, if we took πάντων as neuter and made its clause into part of the beliefs of mortals, we ended up with syntactical difficulties.[29] The dative οἷς has then two functions, as the dative of the agent with νενόμισται and as the "ethic" dative with the πάντων ... clause. Furthermore, I could find no parallel for the dative used to indicate the person who held an opinion on a matter of fact rather than on a matter of value.[30] No one has yet produced a parallel that convinces me, and the zeugma, though slight, seems still awkward. But I would not now argue that these syntactical roughnesses were actually impossible for an author struggling like Parmenides with intractable material. Rather I should argue that it is more charitable to Parmenides, and more likely to be right in any given instance, if we take the simplest and most straightforward way of construing his sentences, rather than making needless difficulties. It must be admitted that, if πάντων be taken as masculine, all the features which have made this a difficult piece of Greek simply disappear. It seems unreasonable not to do this.

There is a further argument in favour of the masculine gender of πάντων which has not had the currency it deserves since Shorey first propounded it.[31] In Parmenides' context the words "the path of all is backward-turning" are most naturally understood of the path taken by all men. κέλευθος is for Parmenides a synonym of ὁδός, as can be seen from the comparison of B2.4 with B2.2. Parmenides has been talking of ways, roads, or paths of thought taken by thinkers, both in B2 and in B6 itself, and there is no reason whatever why his readers should suspect a change to the subject of a physical path taken by physical entities. By B7, be it noted, the ὁδός is again a mental path. Even if B6.8–9 did contain a reference to Heraclitus' philosophy, this would still be true; Heraclitus cannot be shown to have used the word "backward-turning" to describe the path taken by things,[32] and there is no obvious reference in Parmenides B6.8–9 to the types of physical entity which Heraclitus referred to (if Theophrastus was right) in his remark about the way up and down.[33] The normal reader coming to this passage for the first time would naturally take the κέλευθος to be a mental rather than a physical path. It is hard to see why scholars should in this matter continue to prefer the difficult to the easy, the complex to the simple, and the farfetched to the obvious.

Kirk and Raven took the masculine gender of πάντων in their first impression to be "possible" and in the second to be "attractive."[34] This still seems to me too weak a statement, but it would be unkind to quibble further on this topic. They then infer that, granted the masculine gender, πάντων would have to refer to all men—which weakens the plausibility of any reference to Heraclitus. To this it has recently been replied that, if πάντων is masculine, it is parallel to the pronoun οἱ δέ in line 6 and that these are not all men, but merely those εἰδότες οὐδέν ... οἷς τὸ πέλειν τε καὶ οὐκ εἶναι ταὐτὸν νενόμισται κοὐ ταὐτόν.[35] But both βροτοί and οἱ δέ can perfectly well refer to all men, and to take them otherwise raises some awkward questions. How could Parmenides expect his readers to recognize, when his goddess refers *de haut en bas* to "ignorant mortals who ...," that she really means "*some* ignorant mortals who"? Since their humanity would be all too obvious, why not say τινές instead of βροτοί to make her point clear? Why should Parmenides single out one man, or at best a small group of mortals, and then bother to stress that they were *all* guilty of a certain confusion? (It would add to the abusive effect of these lines to hear that their *opinions* were all wrong, but it does not add to the abusive effect to hear that all the thinkers were mistaken.) When the reader got to B8.39, what was there in the syntax or context to bring to his attention a change in the application of the term "mortals"? Of course it is *possible* to give these questions some sort of answer; of course it is *possible* that Parmenides was needlessly obscure; but the possibility is comparatively remote and affords no good reason for assailing the inference that, if πάντων is masculine, then it most naturally refers to all men and that this weakens the plausibility of any reference to Heraclitus.

The Second Rejected Way: Philosophical Interpretation

Guthrie concedes wisely that "Parmenides' language ... makes it clear that the stricture is directed against all and sundry, not confined to a particular philosopher. It can only be a question of whether Heraclitus was in his mind as an outstanding representative of the 'hordes with no judgment.'"[36] It is important to notice that, if one accepts that Parmenides refers in the first instance to all men, then there can be no philosophical proof that Heraclitus was in his mind. For, having accepted the application of the lines to all men, one is compelled to interpret the philosophy of these lines as intelligible with reference to common sense; and, if it is intelligible with reference to common sense, then there can be no philosophical reason for bringing in Heracliteanism.

There is in fact no good philosophical reason for supposing that these lines refer to Heraclitus. If Parmenides had known of Heraclitus' work, he might have had him uppermost in his mind in his description of mortal belief; but there is no good evidence that he did know him in the first place. It is admitted that, if we had reason to think that Parmenides was referring to Heraclitus, we should not be startled by the form of doctrine which Parmenides would then be assigning to him. But that is not the same as saying that the doctrine is such that it could on Parmenidean lines be assigned *only* to Heraclitus.

One cannot discuss this problem without asking whether Parmenides was giving a literal statement of what his "mortals" believe or putting into their mouth his own deductions from their views. It is not unheard of for doubters of any reference to mankind at large in this passage to assume that Parmenides was putting into someone's mouth the *explicit* view that Being and not-Being are the same and not the same.[37] But this view sits uneasily on the lips of those who attribute the philosophy in question to Heraclitus, since it is highly unlikely that Heraclitus would have been so interested in abstract ontology as to commit himself to the identity of Being and not-Being—or even formally to express their difference. The request to opt for a reference to Heraclitus in order to be able to take Parmenides literally, followed by the necessity to hold that Parmenides is "interpreting" Heraclitus, justifies a certain scepticism.

On a different plane is the doctrine that the allusion is specifically to Heraclitus' theory of the identity of opposites. Thus Tarán has this to say; "The expression 'Being and non-Being are the same and not the same' is . . . the exact characterization of the doctrine of the identity of contraries, although Heraclitus did not express this in the words, Being and non-Being."[38] Further, "It is intelligible that for Parmenides, who reduced all opposition to that of Being and non-Being, the doctrine of Heraclitus, who asserted that contraries are one and yet different, was tantamount to the assertion that Being and non-Being are the same and yet not the same.[39] Since he would call one of Heraclitus' opposites Being, the other would automatically become its contrary, i.e., absolute non-Being; and since Heraclitus said that both are one thing and yet are different, all this to Parmenides meant that ἄκριτα φῦλα regarded τὸ πέλειν τε καὶ οὐκ εἶναι ταὐτὸν κοὐ ταὐτόν." It is indeed intelligible that Parmenides should think in this way. But the question is not whether it is intelligible but whether we have good evidence that Parmenides actually did think in this way. We have to judge whether it is substantially more difficult to interpret Parmenides' words by postulating a Parmenidean interpretation of common sense than it is by supposing him to have here interpreted the views of Heraclitus. It will be seen from the ensuing discussion that is is indeed somewhat more difficult; but it demands only one more step in the deduction, and that not a difficult one. It may accordingly be doubted whether enough is gained by regarding the passage as anti-Heraclitean to make such a view of it necessary.

It is not only opposites that could be represented in Parmenides by "not-Being" and "Being." Any pair of different things can be thus represented. For, if we accord to either one of them the title of "existent thing," then the other will be for Parmenides non-existent. Since the general run of men believe in a large number of different things, and believe in their existence, they would be held by Parmenides to call non-existent things existent; in fact, if we keep to Sextus' arrangement of the lines,[40] that is exactly what Parmenides makes them say at B7.1–2. But to make the range of non-existent things virtually coextensive with that of existent things is for practical purposes to treat Being and non-Being as one and the same. This is one step further removed from what mortals explicitly say than is Tarán's version from what Heraclitus actually said. But it is only a short step, namely, from saying that non-existent things exist to saying that existence and non-existence are indistinguishable. As for the other half of the total statement of Parmenides' mortals, embodied in the phrase κοὐ ταὐτόν, it is as evident that mankind (when it thinks about it) distinguishes existence from non-existence as it is that Heraclitus regarded opposites as being not only one but different. On the whole, if we are once prepared to allow Parmenides to express other people's views in his own terms before denouncing them, it is not significantly more difficult to understand his remarks as applied to ordinary men than as applied to Heraclitus.

The Second Rejected Way: The Position of B.7.1–2, and the subject of ἔστι

It is relevant here to enlarge on the import of B7.1–2, mentioned briefly above. The view there attributed to mankind or to common sense is that things which are not, are. Now this is pretty clearly not as it stands a commonsense view, nor one that the general run of mankind ever held explicitly when relying on their senses. This shows without more ado that Parmenides was perfectly capable of stating other people's views in his own terms preparatory to denunciation. Further, the relation of this statement to the wrong ways of B2 and B6 repays inspection. Between the two wrong ways of B6 there must be an essential ontological distinction, but between εἶναι μὴ ἐόντα and τὸ πέλειν τε καὶ οὐκ εἶναι ταὐτὸν κοὐ ταὐτόν there is hardly the essential difference required; for to believe in the Being of non-being things is at once (as we have seen) to confuse Being and non-Being in thought and to distinguish them in language. Therefore εἶναι μὴ ἐόντα can hardly be the first false way of

B6. Furthermore, there is no good reason for refusing to identify the second false way of B6 (lines 8–9) with the views denounced at B7.1–2.[41] It was evidently open to Parmenides to interpret the deduced belief εἶναι μὴ ἐόντα as implying the identity of the things that are with those that are not. There is no reason why he should not have identified by the confusion alone in B7 the combination of distinction and confusion denounced in B6, since neither ordinary men nor Parmenides himself ever doubted the distinction and it is not the distinction which characterizes ordinary belief as opposed to Eleaticism. On the other hand, it is much more difficult to identify the first false way of B6 (presumably also the false way of B2) with the view damned at B7.1–2. To identify ὅπως οὐκ ἔστι καὶ ὡς χρεών ἐστι μὴ εἶναι with εἶναι μὴ ἐόντα is possible, so far as I can see, only on one condition; namely, that the subject of οὐκ ἔστιν, in the proposition denied at B2, is τὸ ἐόν. (Of course, in Parmenidean terms, there would be no difference between ἔστι μὴ ἐόντα and τὸ ἐὸν οὐκ ἔστιν.) But this is unlikely unless the subject of ἔστιν is also τὸ ἐόν, and this, despite the impressive scholarly support for it, remains in my view improbable.

It is not possible to give a full discussion of this last point here; little more can be said than that discussion subsequent to G. E. L. Owen's well-known article "Eleatic Questions" has not convinced me that he is wrong in essentials.[42] Tarán argues against the subject being "what can be talked or thought about": first, that there is nothing in the text of B2 to suggest that this is the subject, and that "this premiss cannot be inferred... from the fact that the impossibility of οὐκ ἔστιν is due to οὔτε γὰρ ἂν γνοίης τό γε μὴ ἐόν... οὔτε φράσαις (fr. II. 7–8), for these words assert the *impossibility* of uttering or thinking non-Being and the converse of this proposition for Parmenides would be the *necessity* of saying and thinking Being, not Owen's 'what can be thought or spoken of exists.'" Secondly, Tarán urges the grammatical impossibility of interpreting B6 to mean "That which can be thought and spoken of..."; and, thirdly, he attributes Owen's view partly to "his desire to find a demonstration for the premiss of line 3 and that of line 5, which in itself is unnecessary." These arguments are of varying force. The last is simply erroneous, for it is difficult to say what lines 6–8 of B2 are if they are not an argument against (or a brief dismissal of)[43] the second way, and hence an argument in favour of the first. Owen does not have to seek a demonstration: it is there in the text. In any case, it is dangerous to damn a view by attacking its supposed motive. As for the grammar of B6.1–2, this is a complex and debatable subject; but it should be stressed that the grammatically unexampled and the grammatically impossible are by no means the same thing.[44] Tarán's argument about the converse of the impossibility of uttering or thinking non-Being seems to backfire; what Owen actually wrote[45] was not what Tarán puts between inverted commas but "what can be spoken and thought of must exist," which seems a reasonable "converse" to the argument that (you cannot learn that it does not exist, for) it is impossible to think or talk about what does not exist. The necessity of "saying and thinking Being"—if one is to speak or think at all—is precisely what Owen rightly makes Parmenides stress. Tarán's first argument, however, deserves more attention. It is true that, when Parmenides' first readers came to B2.3 and 5, they had probably no reason to give the verbs ἔστιν and οὐκ ἔστιν any particular subject. In fact, there is reason to suppose them as mystified for the moment as modern scholars have often been. But, as they read on, they will have found that the exclusion of not-Being is grounded on the impossibility of conceiving or expressing it. The exclusion of the non-existence of the subject, on the grounds that the subject could not in that case be conceived or expressed, should have given them to understand that only a subject which could be conceived or expressed could be the subject of a true statement of existence. The minimum definition of the subject of Parmenides' ἔστιν is therefore "the legitimate subject of thought or expression." With this to guide them they would have been confirmed by the first line of B6 in the belief that this minimal degree of definition was sufficient. Owen occasionally makes Parmenides' writing appear simpler, and his reasoning more clear-cut, that it really was;[46] but in essentials he is right. If one can sympathize to a certain extent with those who maintain that there is no subject of ἔστιν, it is nevertheless only true to say that it has no definite subject at its first appearance;[47] the subject is progressively defined as the argument proceeds, and is defined in such a way as to make plain that Parmenides' real starting-point is not existence but the possibility of rational discourse.

Owen's central argument against the rival theory that the subject is "Being" or "what is," apart from the point that it is not made clear that this is the subject, is that Parmenides *argues* for his ἔστιν and that he would not have argued for a tautology. To this point no critic has yet returned a satisfying reply. À propos of a different question, Tarán makes the point that Parmenides "accepts" the tautology that "Being exists" at B8.36–37.[48] The point is well taken, but it is necessary in examining it to distinguish four grades of tautology in philosophical discourse: (1) the implied acceptance of a truism as true; (2) the inclusion of a truism in an argument as one horn of a dilemma; (3) the plain open affirmation of a tautology for its own sake; and (4) the support of a tautology by argument. Tarán produces an example of (1): it is possible to produce a Parmenidean example of (2), namely at B8.46, οὔτε γὰρ οὐκ ἐόν ἐστι. But these examples do nothing whatever to show that Parmenides could or would have used either of the two more extreme grades of tautology. It is not particularly helpful to cite examples of the necessity that occasionally arises in philosophy for the emphatic affirmation of tautologies;[49] for Parmenides does not once unambiguously and emphatically affirm that Being exists, unless we believe him to have done so at B6.1–2, where the resulting treble tautology "It is necessary to say and think that what exists exists; for existence exists, and the non-existent does not exist" is too much for my stomach and has been too much for most recent students to accept as Parmenidean.[50] There is no reason whatever to suppose that Parmenides would have thought it necessary to argue for a tautology; and argue he certainly does for his ἔστιν, even if only through an argument by elimination.[51] However vague the reader may find Parmenides' subject at the first appearance of his two chief ways, we may rest content with the belief that what Parmenides had in mind, and intended his readers to understand, was "what can be talked and thought about."

This being so, it is hardly possible to identify the false way of B2.5 with the view denounced at B7.1–2. We therefore have to find a place in the Parmenidean analysis for the latter denunciation; on the face of it, the view concerned is a contradiction which it is best to assign to the same people as the other contradictory way of Parmenides, namely the way of the ignorant mortals of B6. The ignorant mortals will then have been following habit and the senses; and they can therefore hardly have been Heracliteans.

The Second Rejected Way: The Contradictions in Relation to B8.53ff and to Heraclitus' Paradoxes

In support of the Heraclitean interpretation of B6.8–9 scholars have urged that the views there put into mortal mouths contradict, or at least differ from, the views ascribed to mortals at B8.53ff.[52] It is sometimes argued that the two groups of mortals cannot be the same, which would give us a motive for refusing to admit that all mankind share in the views of B6.8–9. On this it should not be necessary to expend much ink. At B8.52–53 mortal opinions are described as deceptive, and at B8.54 mortals themselves are called wanderers. Both descriptions are consistent with B6, and the second is perhaps reminiscent of it. Parmenides then offers an account of how mortals started from a conventional assumption of the reality of different things and how any phenomenon may be traced back to this initial mistake.[53] Neither of the two assumed realities (namely, night and fire) ought to have been accepted, because neither measures up to the requirements of Being: neither is immovable and all-embracing, and neither is simply Being, so that for Parmenides both are not-Being.[54] The opposed bodies are apparently self-identical, but distinguished from each other. If one interprets B6.8–9 of the opposites, then indeed B8 has only half the doctrine of B6, and that the undistinctive half, namely the difference between the opposites. To this one answers that (a) nothing in the B8 passage *contradicts* B6; and (b) if Parmenides is in one passage extracting a contradictory ontology from human belief and in the other showing the minimum mistake from which all human belief springs, it is hardly shocking if he stresses in the first passage the paradoxical consequences of treating non-existent things as existent, and in the second the difference between the different existents men assume (since the presence of difference is the most fundamental distinction between the sensible world and the Truth). It is hard to understand why it should come as a surprise that Parmenides does not attack human belief always on precisely the same grounds or maintain always the tone of vehement denunciation heard in B6.[55]

Finally, the objection that B6.8–9 is formally reminiscent of Heraclitean paradoxes has but little weight.[56] If Heraclitus was (for whatever reason) fond of paradox and Parmenides is deliberately extracting paradox from human belief, it is not a remarkable coincidence that Parmenides should hit on one of the forms of paradox favoured by Heraclitus. Since the form concerned is neat, but by no means recherché, we may congratulate the two writers without any suspicion on this ground of any direct contact between them.[57]

The Second Rejected Way: Its Relation to Common Sense

To establish more solidly the theory that Parmenides expounds at B6.8–9 his own interpretation of common sense, it would be well to discuss in more detail the question how Parmenides extracted his paradoxes from normal human belief. On this subject there is a distressing lack of unanimity among the theory's exponents, and few even show signs of awareness that there is any disagreement. Owen,[58] arguing correctly against the fragmentation of the views expressed at B6.8–9, dismissed F. M. Cornford's version of the theory that mortals are mistaken in talking about the same thing being existent at one time and non-existent at another time; but he by no means refuted the theory itself and did not analyse the various respectable alternatives. Some of these are accordingly discussed below.

The general view taken by Cornford found an earlier representative in Heinrich Gomperz, who wrote as follows: "Indem nun die Menschen zwar von Seiendem reden, diesem Seienden aber Entstehen und Vergehen beilegen, machen sie das Seiende zu einem Nichtseienden, verwischen jeden Unterschied zwischen Sein und Nichtsein, setzen Sein und Nichtsein einander gleich. Dabei aber reden sie doch wieder davon, dass eines ist, ein anderes nicht ist, so also, als wäre zwischen Sein und Nichtsein doch wieder ein Unterschied."[59] Similar, in that he takes the equation of Being and not-Being to be derived from a belief in the reality of change, is Jaeger, who characterized the third way as that which "takes for granted that both Being and not-Being possess real existence" and continued: "But there are men who . . . hope to perform a reconciliation by regarding the same thing first as existent and then as non-existent, and who suppose they can go first the one way and then return and go the other."[60] This serves to connect coming-to-be and passing-away, inherent for Parmenides in all change, with the ontology implied in B6 and B7; it also allows a natural interpretation of B8.15ff, where the necessity of choice between "it is" and "it is not" is hammered home as part of an argument against coming-to-be and passing-away. These scholars and some others appear to suppose that it is at least mainly, if not only, distinctions caused by the passage of time which Parmenides at B6 accuses mortals of allowing, with paradoxical results.

Reinhardt, on the other hand, was prepared to sustain a more general interpretation of the paradoxes.[61] He wrote of "jede stoffliche wie zeitliche Unterscheidung" and continued: "Setze man hier ein Seiendes und dort ein Seiendes, so war beide durch Raum oder Zeit getrennt und unterschieden, und doch ihren Wesen nach dasselbe, also ταὐτὸν κοὐ ταὐτόν." The further details of Reinhardt's interpretation are difficult to follow and, in so far as I understand them, appear to end in that fragmentation of the paradoxes against which Owen has rightly protested.[62] But Reinhardt seems to be right in implicitly denying any distinction in Parmenides' argument between differences of time and of space. If Parmenides gives a hint at B8.15ff that he wants men to decide on ἔστι in order to abandon changes consequent on the passage of time, he offers a pretty clear hint in other parts of his work that mortals are wrong also in postulating distinctions between one part of space and another. Apart from the stress laid in the way of truth on the continuity and "wholeness" of the subject, the opening lines of the "Opinions of Mortals" indicate clearly enough that mortals are also mistaken in postulating two bodies which are different from one another and that each is a different *part* of what mortals believe to be real. Parmenides is as concerned with differences between parts as with those between states of affairs at different moments, and for fundamentally the same reasons.[63] There is no reason whatever for supposing his indictment of normal human beliefs to be concerned more with one type of difference than with another.

An even broader view has recently been taken by Owen.[64] "Ordinary men want to keep *both* εἶναι and οὐκ εἶναι in use: horses exist, mermaids do not; there is sandy soil here but not there; there are dodos at one time, not at another. It is this qualified answer [to ἔστιν ἢ οὐκ ἔστιν;] that Parmenides denounces ... and his first and fundamental argument against it is that it treats existence and non-existence as different and yet identical ... Ordinary men and cosmologists alike try to distinguish existence by saying, for instance, that lions do exist and mermaids do not; yet in distinguishing them they identify them, for (by the argument already brought against the first wrong road in B2) if non-existent mermaids could be talked about they would be existent."

Apart from its picturesque expression, there are two chief differences between this type of interpretation and the preceding ones. First, there is added to the differences produced by space and time the suggestion that mortals talk about things wholly fictitious. But did they, in the first half of the fifth century B.C.? It seems likely that, at that period, if people talked about things, it was in the belief that they existed. Had they talked about mermaids, it was because they believed in their existence; and it is doubtful whether Parmenides would have been any more bothered by talk (if any) about mermaids than by talk about (say) bricks. There were, of course, things in whose existence early-fifth-century Greeks did not believe: Achilles' tenth daughter, Priam's only son. But then they never talked about these things. Of course, if a traveller returned with tall stories, the audience might express disbelief in the things he spoke of; but it is doubtful whether Parmenides was a sophisticated enough logician to excogitate such a class of propositions or to be particularly exercised by it if he had. But I am willing to admit an element of subjectivity in my argument here and turn with rather more confidence to the second point at issue. Owen believes apparently that the subject of the ἔστιν and οὐκ ἔστιν of human belief to which Parmenides refers is not necessarily one, that the two verbs may have different subjects. He is still able to extract a contradiction between "This thing exists" and "That thing does not exist" only by dint of saying that, since men talk about the non-existent, they imply its existence, for only what exists can (according to Parmenides) be talked about. But there are some difficulties in this device. What it does is to bring the two false ways dangerously close together. Suppose someone to enter on the first false way, the wrong path of B2. Such a person will say that whatever he is talking about does not exist; but by talking about it he implies its existence: and he is therefore saying (if Owen's device is Parmenidean) both that it exists and that it does not exist, which lays him open to the charge of confusing existence and non-existence. But at the same time he is obviously distinguishing between the existent and the non-existent, for to say that something does not exist is to distinguish between Parmenides' alternatives and choose one of them. The result of this is that to enter on the first false way is to enter also on the second, and the distinction between the two evaporates. The conclusion must be that Parmenides was thinking of mortals as using both "is" and "is not" of the same subject, rather than of different ones. But in so far as Owen, like Reinhardt, recommends us to take Parmenides as referring in his disagreement with common sense to distinctions resulting from distance either of time or of space, he is right.

In that Parmenides was endeavouring to obliterate variation in both time and space, he inevitably came into conflict on these two fronts with customary human belief. We can easily understand how he could reject both facets of common sense because they at once led to the being of what is not and thus not only distinguished Being from not-Being but also confused the two. There is accordingly no need to introduce into the interpretation of B6 any attack on Heraclitus. In view of the lack of any external evidence that Heraclitus influenced Parmenides at all, or was even available to be read by him, the most extreme caution should be used in postulating interaction between the two thinkers.

The Second Rejected Way: Conclusion

It is just this circumspection which is often abandoned. One can say, for example, that if Heraclitus' work were known to Parmenides, then it would be possible, perhaps even probable, that Parmenides had the Ephesian in mind as a principal representative of some of the views he rejects. But the extreme opposition between their attitudes is not in itself evidence of any connection between them. We are left with a few verbal "reminiscences"; the effect of these, if they have any, must of course be considered as cumulative. If scholars choose to regard their cumulative effect as decisive, little or nothing can be done to change their minds. But the cumulative effect of nothings is nothing, and it may legitimately be doubted whether any of the alleged reminiscences have any effect at all; it would be exceedingly hard to specify any single passage of Parmenides which needs the postulation of a reference to Heraclitus to make it either intelligible or pointed. If Parmenides and Heraclitus have certain elements of vocabulary in common, that in itself proves nothing; they were both Greeks, both writing at least mainly in Ionic, and they were near contemporaries. I can find no reason whatever to suppose that either of them was known to the other and shall treat them throughout as independent thinkers. Such practice is justifiable even if Parmenides did know of Heraclitus, at least until it is shown (as it has never been) that Parmenides would have written even so much as a single syllable differently if Heraclitus had never opened his mouth or set pen to papyrus.

PARMENIDES' ARGUMENT

Having decided to treat of Parmenides separately from Heraclitus, we must turn to consider the role of unity, and of the one-many antithesis, in Parmenides' thought, and the kind(s) of unity and plurality that he had in mind. We must also consider whether a question of "what is one" being or becoming many arises in Parmenides' argument. It seems clear that the function of the one-many antithesis in this, the first extant European piece of consecutive metaphysical reasoning, has been greatly exaggerated in some quarters; though the exaggeration has been somewhat diminished in successive works of recent years,[65] it still remains an obstacle to the understanding and appreciation of a great philosopher and needs therefore still to be pointed out and criticized. If any single antithesis occupied a high place in Parmenides' thought, it was that between Being and not-Being. The word "one" appears in only two extant places in Parmenides' poem, and the phrase "the one" appears in Melissus apparently for the first time, in conscious reference back to that Being which has been *proved* to be one; the phrase "the One Being," beloved alike of Cornford and of the Neoplatonist Simplicius, is not to be found in the extant remains of Presocratic Eleaticism. Once more the questions at issue can be decided only on the basis of close textual analysis; and again we have to deal with a thinker recognized even by the ancients as obscure.[66]

PARMENIDES' PROGRAMME FOR THE WAY OF TRUTH

Opening the Way of Truth after rejecting possible alternatives, Parmenides has his goddess announce the many signposts along this remaining Way. These signposts amount to a statement of what the goddess intends to prove in the whole Way of Truth. The properties she intends to assign by irrefutable logic to her subject are, according to the best ancient texts, the following:

$$\text{ὡς ἀγένητον ἐὸν καὶ ἀνώλεθρόν ἐστιν}$$
$$\text{οὖλον, μουνογενές τε καὶ ἀτρεμὲς ἠδ' ἀτέλεστον.}$$

Some emendation of the last phrase seems to be necessary and modern proposals include ἠδὲ τελεστόν, ἠδὲ τελεῖον and οὐδ' ἀτέλεστον.[67] Brandis' οὐδ'... is clearly inelegant, and palaeographically Owen's ἠδὲ τελεῖον is unconvincing. Tarán's ἠδε τελεστόν, though it introduces a rare word, is probably the best available, though I admit to uncertainty as to what Parmenides wrote. But in any case the meaning is clear. Redundancy excludes the sense "everlasting";[68] and the perfection of Being, its completeness, its need of no additions from outside, needs stressing as much as its wholeness in the sense of the absence of gaps in it (whether composed of void or merely of something different).

The subsequent lines are also, if the majority of interpreters are right, part of the statement of the σήματα. If we are to follow Simplicius *in Physica* 78.5ff, the whole of B8 to line 14 gives the principal σήματα; but this obviously goes too far, and most of the moderns start the proof of the total demonstration with τίνα γὰρ γένναν διζήσεαι αὐτοῦ; (including in the statement of the σήματα the sentence οὐδέ ποτ' ἦν οὐδ' ἔσται ἐπεὶ νῦν ἔστιν ὁμοῦ πᾶν). This, as Guthrie has remarked, makes ἕν, συνεχές seem to duplicate μουνογενές and οὖλον respectively in what is otherwise a compressed statement. Further it makes the demonstrand include a demonstration; for ἐπεί must mark the beginning of an argument, if the word is to have any meaning here whatever.[69] Now it *may* be that Parmenides was guilty of this offence against the canons of good writing, and of this neglect of the rules for the presentation of a proof; for he may have been a bad writer and was not brought up on Euclidean rules of presentation. But we are not, surely, entitled to believe that so great a man expounded his argument with such clumsiness until we can prove that he did. But this no one has seriously attempted to do.

One can imagine a pair of arguments which might be advanced for the inclusion of these lines in the σήματα. The first is that it is strange to begin a demonstration with οὐδέ: one expects either a γάρ (as at τίνα γὰρ...) or some similar particle, or else total asyndeton. In answer to this argument one may suggest that the first οὐδέ is to be taken adverbially (it even did not ever exist); the combination οὐδέ... οὐδέ cannot be ruled out.[70] If we take the particles in either of these ways we are left with a normal asyndeton at the commencement of an explanation or argument. The second argument is that οὐδέ ποτ' ἦν οὐδ' ἔσται introduces a new predicate, namely the timelessness of Being as opposed to its mere eternity. But if we ask what evidence there is for this interpretation of the lines, then there appears, as Tarán has argued in detail, no satisfying answer.

The first to oppose this "timelessness" interpretation was Hermann Fränkel. He did so on two grounds: first, that ποτέ, clearly to be taken with both οὐδέ's, implies that "er spricht ... nicht von *der* sondern von *einem* gewissen Zeitstrecke"; second, that Parmenides' use of the verb μένειν implies a duration and even in the present tense ought therefore to have been avoided in speaking of a timeless Being. This note of Fränkel's has aroused considerable controversy.[71] Owen showed the use of μένειν to be inconclusive, pointing out that Parmenides was in something of a dilemma: "The very proof which rules out all variation in time and space has to use language which implies temporal and spatial distinctions." Guthrie added against Fränkel's use of ποτέ that "in particular the addition of ποτέ in v. 5 seems rather to emphasize the negation of past and future than to qualify it in any way." That ποτέ emphasizes the denial of ἦν and of ἔσται may be accepted, but it does not seem to show that Parmenides was denying the applicability of time to his Being. More fundamental—or perhaps simply more explicit—is Owen's further argument concerning the whole phrase οὐδέ ποτ' ἦν οὐδ' ἔσται. Claiming that ποτέ means ∃t, and therefore οὔ ποτε must mean ∼ (∃t), Owen declines accordingly to accept "It is not true that it once was (and is not now), nor that it will be (but is not now)" as a paraphrase of οὐδέ ποτ' ἦν οὐδ' ἔσται.[72] He further employs, in an ingenious attempted reductio ad absurdum, the suggestion that οὐδέποτ' ἦν οὐδὲ ἔσομαι κλέπτης could not mean "I have not yet given up, nor started, thieving." But this also is less than conclusive. Utterances cannot be interpreted out of context, and ἐπεὶ νῦν ἔστιν ... supplies a very important part of the context of Parmenides' οὐδέ ποτ' ἦν οὐδ' ἔσται. Suppose that our thief were to say οὐδέποτ' ἦν οὐδ' ἔσομαι κλέπτης ἐπεὶ νῦν εἰμὶ κλέπτης. Faced with the interpretation of this, we should suppose him to be saying in his subordinate clause something which conflicted with the contradictory of his main clause. If someone says not-p because q, we conclude that p and q are incompatible. We therefore look for an interpretation of his words which will make p incompatible with q. We deduce that by "I never was a thief" he must mean that it was never true to say "I was a thief," using "I was" in the same way as the Romans used the perfect in such phrases as *vixerunt* (meaning "they are no longer alive"). If we suppose a reader (like Parmenides' contemporaries) who had never heard of "timeless presents" nor dreamt that there existed such strange animals, then this is how he must have been constrained to take Parmenides' Greek. To put the matter algebraically, he must have believed Parmenides to be saying οὔ (ποτ' ἦν)—using ποτ' ἦν in a sense excluding νῦν ἔστιν ... —rather than (οὔ ποτ') ἦν. A question arises, of course: Why should such a reader not leap to the conclusion that Parmenides meant to describe the "timelessness" of Being? The answer is surely quite clear: νῦν is a time word. Owen wants Parmenides to have seen that "The subject exists" is a timeless truth, on a par (whether or not Parmenides saw this parity) with "Twice two is four." But if Parmenides saw that it is nonsense to say (for example) "Twice two will be four to-morrow" or "Twice two was four yesterday," then it is surely quite impossible to suppose that he was ignorant of the equal absurdity of saying "Twice two is four now." If it was because he was removing Being from time altogether that he said οὐδέ ποτ' ἦν οὐδ' ἔσται, then it made not merely nonsense, but obvious nonsense, to use such a time expression as νῦν with his ἔστιν. Owen has Plato in the *Timaeus* remove νῦν from the timeless present;[73] but it is clear that it can never have belonged there and that the credit for discovery of the class of timelessly true propositions belongs to later thinkers than Parmenides.

If we ask the further question why Parmenides wrote in such riddling fashion, then we are in deep waters. Human motivation is a tricky subject. But we may reflect that the very subject of Parmenides' ἔστι is never announced, is wholly obscure at the first appearance of ἔστι in the poem, and only becomes clear by a mental effort on the reader's part as he proceeds. Certainly one would rather have Parmenides a trifle obscure than have him commit so evident a blunder as "now" attached to a statement of timelessness.

The whole sentence needs, as Tarán has rightly stressed, to be taken together, down to and including ἕν, συνεχές.[74] Past (but not present) being and future (but not present) being are excluded because it cannot be true to say of any part of Being that it is not now (it is ὁμοῦ πᾶν)—or to say that there is anything apart from Being which does not exist now but could either in past or in future be added to the tally of existents; this since (a) Being is the only thing, μουνογενές or ἕν, and (b) there is no gap (either of void or of the merely different) in Being which could at any time have been filled (but not now) or will be filled (but is not now), since it is συνεχές, continuous.[75]

It will be noticed at once that, on any straightforward interpretation of B8.5–6, the oneness (that is, uniqueness) of Being and its continuity are premisses of the argument *at this point*. But Parmenides has already placed them (or rather their equivalents, μουνογενές, οὖλον) among the things to be proved, and proved they will eventually be. But, in the meantime, in order to prove that one cannot say either that Being was (but is not now) or that it will be (but is not now), he shows that destruction of what once exists is impossible, as is also the coming-to-be of what is not already now in existence. This argument depends on the uniqueness of Being: if one allowed anything other than Being, and/or outside it, this would be not-Being, and Parmenides' argument would collapse.

Strictly, the uniqueness of Being consists in the absence of not-Being, and on its uniqueness in this sense depends the subsequent argument. This kind of uniqueness, as Parmenides points out, has been decided on before the argument of B8 began (κέκριται δ' οὖν . . .). Uniqueness and homogeneity (qualitative/quantitative) are alike consequences of the impossibility of not-Being. Parmenides may have used ἕν only in the numerical sense meaning "unique," and συνεχές for homogeneity; there is certainly nothing to show that he separated "unique" and "homogeneous" *as meanings of "one."*

PARMENIDES' ARGUMENT IN THE WAY OF TRUTH

Parmenides, having thus at B8.5–6 summarized the essential point of the succeeding argument, begins with the question, designed to disprove γένεσις, "What origin of it [that is, Being] will you seek?" Clearly the argument ought to indicate the alternative possibilities and then demolish each of them. As the text stands in the manuscripts it does not; for both at 8.7 and at 8.12 they have the same possibility; ἐκ μὴ ἐόντος. The possibility that the text is wrong occurred to scholars long ago; since the first μὴ ἐόντος at line 7 is guaranteed by μηδενός in line 10, and indeed by the whole tenor of lines 9–10, it is the second one that has to be emended.[76] The best emendation seems to be ἐκ τοῦ ἐόντος.[77] Negatives are a frequent source of scribal error.[78]

Having expounded the objections[79] to allowing Being to come from not-Being, Parmenides asserts that the subject must either wholly be or wholly not-be: it cannot be said of any subject that it "is not," in any sense or in any degree. Nor, the goddess goes on, will the force of belief allow anything besides Being to come into being from what is. Parmenides offers no argument to prove this point here, and we are therefore driven to other texts to look for his reason(s). We shall not have to look far; for we have already been told that one reason for rejecting the existence of Being in the future or past (not not now) is that it is single. Now, evidently, if the subject were to give rise to some other existent thing, it would no longer be single; there would then be two conceivable subjects, neither of which would be unique. If we ask why it must be single, then the answer comes back at once: because anything apart from, or other than, what exists does not exist and cannot be talked about. And, sure enough, after concluding that genesis and destruction (the coming-to-be of Being and the coming-to-be of something else out of Being) are now disallowed, we are informed that the decision in this whole matter depends on our answer to the question whether it (the subject) exists or not, and that this question has already been decided—

as indeed it has, at B2 and B6. The whole argument is then summed up and reinforced in three vehement lines (19–22). Retaining the reading of the manuscripts, which there is no good reason to alter,[80] the argument goes: "How then could what exists be in future? How would it come to be? For if it came to be, the subject is not, nor (is it) if it is at any time going to be. Thus genesis is quenched, and unheard-of destruction too." Here it is clear that the arrangement of the first two lines is chiastic: the possibilities of future being and of becoming are mentioned first in that order and then reversed. The reason why the subject is not (now) if it is going to be in the future is obvious; but it is very far from evident why past becoming should exclude being. In fact, if the subject of οὐκ ἔστι is still "Being," or "what is," the argument is only intelligible, as Tarán says,[81] if we take ἔγεντ' to mean, or to include in its meaning, "it was." But this, in Parmenides of all writers, is intolerable. Parmenides cannot have used γίγνεσθαι as the equivalent of, or as including, εἶναι in the Way of Truth, where the whole burden of his argument is the total dissociation of γίγνεσθαι from τὸ ἐόν. The explanation is the same as that of lines 7–8; namely, that the subject of οὐκ ἔστι is "the subject" and not, primarily at least, "Being." The point is that, if Being had come to be, it would have to be true at some stage that a subject, something you can talk about, does not exist. But you cannot have a non-existent subject; οὐ γὰρ φατὸν οὐδὲ νοητόν ἐστιν ὅπως οὐκ ἔστι, as Parmenides has said.[82]

The upshot of Parmenides' argument here is evidently that coming-to-be is extinguished. But where is the argument for the extinction of destruction? Parmenides claims to have proved this by his refutation of future being, and of becoming in general, and he claims to have refuted it by the middle of line 13. Yet no separate argument is visible. This riddle has received many answers. But only one seems at all reasonable:[83] that Parmenides regarded the argument against the possibility that anything besides Being should arise from Being as an argument against destruction. For, in Parmenides' terms, destruction must indeed be the turning of what is into something besides Being, that is, into what is not.[84]

It remains to sort out the structure of the whole paragraph down to B8.21. The goddess begins (B8.5–6) by summarizing her following argument: future and past being, which are inconsistent with present being, are alike ruled out because of the logical impossibility of even talking about what is not; that is, because Being is single and continuous, with no gaps of the different or of nothingness. The goddess then (B8.6–15) elaborates the details of this line of thought. She will not allow coming-to-be from what is not, since that necessitates the proposition that some subject of discourse is not, and, even if this were not a necessary implication and one could somehow talk about non-Being, there is nothing which could cause it to produce Being. Thus, what is must be completely, with no not-being whatever. On the other hand, the force of conviction forbids coming-to-be from what is, since that necessitates the postulation of something apart from what is, which is impossible (since what is, is single and unique). Coming-to-be is thus eliminated by the demolition of the two logically conceivable alternative ways of imagining it. The elimination of the second alternative also eliminates destruction (B8.13–14). Having thus completed this phase of her argument, the goddess says she has completed it (B8.13–15), states once again the fundamental choice (B8.15–18) on which it is based, and then summarizes it again (B8.19–21) in such a way as to illustrate its dependence on this choice. This concluding summary is at once more vehement with its rhetorical questions, more picturesque with the metaphor ἀπέσβεσται, and more abstract with the nouns γένεσις and ὄλεθρος than the opening summary of B8.5–6. But the two summaries resemble one another closely and should not be considered apart.[85] The simplest way of taking the second is to have it eliminate future (without present) being and also eliminate "it came to be." Both involve the conception of the inconceivable, of a subject of which at some time it can be said "it does not exist." Lines 19–20 eliminate both past and future coming-to-be, and in eliminating coming-to-be they also (in a way we have already seen) abolish destruction.

Line 20 could, I suppose, be rendered so as to say, in effect, that, if "The subject exists" (on a par with "Twice two is four") even *came to be* true, then it is not timelessly true, and therefore (since it belongs to the timeless class of propositions) not true; and that, if it makes sense to say "'The subject exists' (on a par with 'Twice two is four') is going to be true some day," then again the proposition concerned is not timelessly true and therefore (since it belongs to the class of timeless propositions) is not true. But this complex interpretation would merely throw into still sharper relief the intrusion of νῦν in the earlier passage. If not only the prospective truth of "The subject exists" but also the suggestion that it came to be true (*without any mention of its being now untrue*) is *in itself* incompatible with its truth, then one wonders still more (if possible) how on earth it happened that Parmenides added the word "now" to his ex hypothesi timeless proposition. Timelessness mixes ill with Parmenides' text.

The structure thus outlined may appear repetitive, and indeed it is, in that the goddess first says how her argument will develop, then develops it, and finally says how it has developed. But that is not a valid objection to the above interpretation, since Parmenides is thus made to teach not only according to the normal canons of oral literature but also according to the best rules of pedagogy; anyone who has been taught by a British Army N.C.O. will recognize the technique immediately.

In a sense, the oneness of Being, in that it is unique of its kind (numerically one?) and continuous, is the premiss of this argument. But it is not a premiss taken over from Parmenides' predecessors and used unthinkingly as the basis on which any argument about reality must be raised. It is a premiss itself deduced by Parmenides from the assumptions merely that discourse is possible and that neither speech nor thought can have the non-existent for object.

Parmenides has now shown, according to his lights, that what is, the proper subject of discourse, cannot come to be or pass away, since there is no second thing, other than or different from Being, into which it could pass away or out of which it could come to be. But he has not yet elaborated the formal proof that Being has no gaps of non-existent or different within it, or that his subject must be unique: it is these points that he now proceeds to establish. The first, that it is οὖλον or συνεχές, is argued at B8.22–25; the argument's structure is not so transparent as it might be and has led to a number of interpretations which cannot all be discussed here.

But let analysis here precede controversy.

οὐδὲ διαιρετόν ἐστιν, ἐπεὶ πᾶν ἔστιν ὁμοῖον·
οὐδέ τι τῇ μᾶλλον, τό κεν εἴργοι μιν συνέχεσθαι,
οὐδέ τι χειρότερον, πᾶν δ' ἔμπλεόν ἐστιν ἐόντος.
τῷ ξυνεχὲς πᾶν ἐστιν· ἐὸν γὰρ ἐόντι πελάζει.

The conclusion of this argument is ξυνεχὲς πᾶν ἐστιν, or (an alternative formulation) οὐδὲ διαιρετόν ἐστιν; Parmenides states his demonstrand, demonstrates it, and finally (ἐὸν γὰρ ... πελάζει) explains why it is that πᾶν ἔμπλεόν ἐστιν ἐόντος leads to the conclusion.[86] The continuity of the subject is the same, for Parmenides, as its indivisibility. "Continuous" in Greek can bear at least two senses, namely, "without gaps of emptiness" and "without gaps of something different." Since, however, anything different from Being is for Parmenides not-Being (that is, nothing), the two kinds of continuity amount for him to the same thing: there need be no doubt that he meant both, without feeling any need to make the point clear.[87] To say that a thing is indivisible is also an ambiguity: it is to imply either that it cannot be physically taken to pieces or that its parts cannot be distinguished by the mind. If we ask which Parmenides meant here, the answer must surely be that he is referring to mental distinctions.[88] For as a reason for his statement of the subject's indivisibility Parmenides says *not* that you cannot cut into it or that you cannot create gaps where there were none before, nor anything like that; but that it all alike *is*,[89] i.e., that in respect of being there is no distinction between the parts (which makes it difficult to talk about parts at all, and Parmenides sedulously avoids doing so).

But, since bare being is all that can be asserted of the subject (for anything else, being other than Being, is not-Being), there is thus no distinction of any kind. The drift of Parmenides' argument is that, since every part of the subject *is*, there is no difference between the parts. He goes on to add that it is not the case that one part in one place has a higher degree of existence (or a lower degree, stigmatized by the value word χειρότερον) than the rest. This, he says, would prevent its continuity (τό κεν εἴργοι μιν συνέχεσθαι). If the presence of different degrees of being would infringe its continuity, clearly "continuity" cannot merely mean "absence of emptiness"; but emptiness might appear to be specially in point when the remark is offered that "it is all *full* of being." Appearances, however, in this case again deceive; for the important thing is that the subject is all full of *Being*, pure and simple, and of nothing else—not even different degrees of being. The rejection of emptiness is of course *included* in the rejection of difference, but it is not the only or even the most fundamental point being made.[90] The conclusion is, as we have seen, that the subject is continuous throughout, and this conclusion is explained further by the statement that what is draws (is)[91] near to what is—that is to say that between any two bits of Being there is no gap of emptiness or of anything other than Being: that is what the continuity of Being means, and that is what has been argued in the previous lines, culminating in πᾶν δ' ἔμπλεόν ἐστιν ἐόντος.

But is this continuity spatial or temporal? Are the forbidden gaps, in which something other than Being might be supposed to exist (if it could exist at all), gaps of space or of time? Is this argument a mere corollary of the abolition of genesis and destruction, or is it an independent argument? Since πάμπαν could be used of time at 8.11, there would be no linguistic objection to taking πᾶν in 8.22 also of time—the "whole of Being" would mean "Being, throughout its existence." Similarly with the τι, the πᾶν ἔμπλεον, the continuity, and the nearness in ἐὸν γὰρ ἐόντι πελάζει. There is but one serious linguistic obstacle, and that is the τῇ of line 23. In support of temporal continuity Owen wants this (a) to mean "in one respect," as at Empedocles B26.10, but (b) to retain some of the spatial metaphor.[92] But this is doubtful, for τῇ in the Empedocles passage means "in one way," not "in one respect," being an adverb of manner, and it must be admitted that (a) is a little hard to understand in Parmenides' context; "Nor is it in one respect/way in a higher degree, nor is it worse [in another respect/way]." If Parmenides meant this by τῇ, it is hard to see in what respect he can have meant to contrast the respect/manner of the forbidden higher degree with that of the forbidden lower degree. It is of course *possible* (Owen says "plausible")[93] that Stein was right in emending to πῇ. But I do not deem the ellipse of a second τῇ of place impossible Greek where the contrast is pointed by the repeated οὐδέ τι and the different adverbs and feel reluctance to emend except where it is essential to do so for reasons of sense or language. Linguistic considerations do not here seem decisive, and Owen does not seem to show that emendation is philosophically essential. His first and main philosophical point is that "the premiss of the continuity-argument at its first occurrence is taken from the refutations of γένεσις and ὄλεθρος that precedes it, and consequently must carry a temporal sense." But this argument presupposes that πᾶν ἔστιν ὁμοῖον is a repetition or restatement of πάμπαν πελέναι χρεών ἐστιν ἢ οὐχί from 8.11, and this is not a certain presupposition.[94] For the goddess has already said that the decision in the case of γένεσις and ὄλεθρος depends on the answer to the question ἔστιν ἢ οὐκ ἔστιν;, and the premiss πᾶν ἔστιν ὁμοῖον can be as easily derived from this as it can from the more remote line 11—in which case there is no good reason for it to be taken temporally, and we may with some relief take the spatial terms at 8.22–25 literally.[95] It is true that the rest of the argument down to 8.33 is temporal, but this is not odd; the bulk of Parmenides' programme deals indeed with temporal distinction: he *says* that the basis of his argument that there cannot be any process is the abolition of differences in the present, οὐδέ ποτ' ἦν οὐδ' ἔσται, ἐπεὶ νῦν ἔστι ὁμοῦ πᾶν, / ἕν, συνεχές. Having shown on these lines that there is no genesis or destruction, it is not unreasonable for him to show next more explicitly that difference is impossible, before proceeding to draw any corollaries from his demolition of genesis and destruction. Owen's final argument is that B8.34–41 is a summary of what precedes and that the conclusions stated at 40–41 are only temporal ones. But the basis of Parmenides' argument here is that (8.36–38) the subject not only will be, but *is now* unique (οὐδὲν γὰρ ⟨ἢ⟩ ἔστιν ἢ ἔσται / ἄλλο πάρεξ τοῦ ἐόντος); for Fate has bound it to be not only unchanged (and unmoved, ἀκίνητον) but also οὖλον, complete, with no gaps in it (whether of emptiness or of the merely different is again immaterial). If this is not a denial of differentiation in the present in addition to differentiation created by process, (and hence an elimination of all difference) it is hard to see what it can be. The alleged summary of what precedes therefore contains a denial of differentiation at the present moment as well as a denial of differentiation arising by process. The things denied in the final lines of the paragraph ending at B8.41 are mainly temporal (except perhaps for εἶναί τε καὶ οὐχί) simply because that is the direction in which Parmenides has consistently been arguing: from the denial of difference to that of process. In these circumstances it is not surprising that the denial of differentiation irrespective of process should find a place at 22ff in the centre of the argument against differences engendered by the passage of time.

The possibility must be admitted that Owen is right in making the argument of B8.22ff temporal; but it cannot be called a high probability. It involves, as we have seen, the metaphorical interpretation of several words and phrases which could otherwise be taken literally, and/or a modification of the traditional text. This it does for philosophical reasons which are insufficient if not misleading. It must be added that the result produced is less than satisfactory. Parmenides is made to draw two corollaries from the conclusion that the subject has neither beginning nor end in time. The first corollary is that there can be no succession of separate entities, the second that there can be no internal change in any one entity. The corollaries are alleged to be drawn at 8.22 and 8.23–24 respectively. Now, even if one accepts Owen's version here of the conclusions of 8.21, the need to draw the first corollary is surely imaginary; if one cannot have a single beginning and end in time, then it scarcely needs emphasis that one cannot have a succession of beginnings and endings in time. The second corollary, in so far as it is not proved by the disproof of coming-to-be in the paragraph down to 8.21, is proved under the head of κίνησις at 8.26ff; and, in any case, it is exceedingly hard to extract from the lines about degrees of being at 8.23–24. On the whole, the spatial interpretation of B8.22ff seems to stand up best to examination.

But one trouble with Parmenides is that any interpretation of any part of the poem must be worked through and shown to be compatible with the whole. That is the justification for the continued examination here of the rest of the Way of Truth, even though it may not be itself immediately germane to my principal line of argument. It seems better on this occasion to sacrifice elegance of form than to leave the argument incomplete; the more so since several allusions to the rest of the Way of Truth have already been necessary.

After showing explicitly the absence of differentiation within the subject, Parmenides moves on to deny κίνησις to it. The first reason why the subject is bereft of κίνησις (best left untranslated for the moment) without beginning or end is given clearly enough: it is simply that γένεσις and ὄλεθρος have been exploded.[96] We are thus clearly intended to suppose that the eternal existence of the subject without κίνησις is to be explained by the demolition of coming-to-be and passing-away. This argument is to be understood only if κίνησις is a subordinate kind of γένεσις / ὄλεθρος—as of course it is: arguments of what we should call an ontological nature could be brought against motion and/or change of quality precisely similar to those urged against coming-to-be and passing-away; the denial of difference makes it as impossible to conceive any change of place or of quality as it is to conceive of absolute coming-to-be. In fact, as Owen points out,[97] the issue is not affected by the distinction between qualitative and absolute coming-to-be. If, therefore, we have abandoned γένεσις and ὄλεθρος, we have abandoned at the same time coming-to-be white or black or any other quality, and also coming-to-be in any place where the subject was not before. No *state of affairs* may either come to be or pass away.[98]

Having thus argued that his subject is ἀκίνητον, Parmenides then concludes that it remains ταὐτόν τ' ἐν ταὐτῷ τε μένον, and that it καθ' ἑαυτὸ κεῖται, and remains (? will remain) firmly in place. Evidently this is not intended as a summary of the whole argument to date or even of B8.22–28, but of the results of denying κίνησις. Each other section of the argument has in just this way been given its proper conclusion in its rightful place. Here we have apparently the conclusion of an argument which began, as usual with Parmenides, with a statement of what is to be proved, namely, that the subject is ἀκίνητον. The inclusion, in the results, of the point that the subject remains the same, and not only in the same place, makes it clear beyond reasonable doubt that change of quality and change of place are both, for Parmenides, included in κίνησις. This conclusion is supported by the argument at B8.36–38, where the point is that there neither *is* anything other than Being (given that Being is οὖλον) nor *will* be (since Being is ἀκίνητον). The rejection of κίνησις there excludes the future existence of anything other than Being, and in that argument κίνησις must therefore refer primarily to (qualitative) change.[99]

The exact structure of the argument B8.29–33 depends on the text we adopt. But Simplicius' is generally the best text of Parmenides, and there is no reason to forsake him here.[100] If we were to follow Proclus and read ταὐτὸν δ' ἐν ταὐτῷ μίμνει, καθ' ἑαυτό τε κεῖται, κτλ., then the various predicates of the subject in this passage would all be co-ordinate. But following Simplicius we would have the attribution of καθ' ἑαυτό and "remaining firm where it is" dependent on the statement that it remains the same and in the same place. The argument is then that, being the same and remaining in one place, the subject is καθ' ἑαυτό and will remain firm on the spot.[101] What καθ' ἑαυτό means is not perhaps immediately clear, and the frequent translation of it by the ambiguous English "by itself" does not help matters. "Alone" is perhaps not a good rendering of the Greek, and "independently," though suitable to Parmenides' subject, is not very suitable to a context dealing with κίνησις. καθ' ἑαυτό might mean, as in Plato's Theory of Forms, "pure," "homogeneous," or "without admixture of anything else"; or it might mean, on the analogy of κατὰ τὸ ἴσον in the Peripatetic accounts of Zeno's Flying Arrow, "occupying its own place."[102] Since the second of these two suggestions would tend to make καθ' ἑαυτό ... μενεῖ unduly repetitive and there is no reason to suppose this usage Eleatic, it should probably be abandoned. The first offers more acceptable sense, that the subject is (in that it remains the same) unadulterated by anything other than itself. Since ταὐτὸν ... μένον is thus equivalent to καθ' ἑαυτὸ κείμενον, and since the statement that it remains in the same place corresponds neatly to the statement that it stays (or will stay) on the spot (αὖθι), the whole has thus a pleasing and (more important) a readily intelligible symmetry.[103]

But Parmenides has not finished arguing against κίνησις. The reason given at once for the predicates just enumerated is "the bonds of Ἀνάγκη" —the usual metaphor in Parmenides for the force of logic.[104] The reason why the force of logic prevents infringement by the subject of the law against κίνησις is that the subject must be perfect and in need of nothing. That is to say that there can be nothing else outside it or different from it of which it could stand in need for completeness, and no place which it does not occupy and to which it can need to go. Therefore it cannot turn into anything else (for there is nothing else) and cannot move to any other place. The all-embracing nature of the subject is what prevents change: it is the denial of difference which prohibits alteration. It is in fact the singleness of the subject which prevents difference from arising.

Then follows a recapitulation (B.8.34ff), first of the argument of B2-3, second of the conclusion drawn from that argument. Thinking, says Parmenides, is the same as thinking that the subject is. For without what is, ἐν ᾧ πεφατισμένον ἐστίν, you will not find thought. For there is and will be nothing apart from what is, since fate has bound it to be whole and "unmoved" (ἀκίνητον). Here the argument is not easy to follow, the less so since the syntax of the phrase not translated above is obscure.[105] But evidently Parmenides means (1) (B8.34) that no thought is possible except of the subject's existence; (2) that if anything different from the existent is included in a thought it is not a thought but a nonsense; (3) that the reason why to think about anything other than the existent is nonsensical is that there is not (and never will be) anything else to think about. But the argument does not stop here, as one might expect: there is a reason given for (3), namely that (4) logic constrains the existent to be οὖλον and ἀκίνητον. Now, evidently Parmenides should not be supposed to have argued circularly that because there is no change or motion there is no difference: he has argued at B8.26ff that there is no change or motion because there is no γένεσις—which he excluded because there is no difference. The lack of change and of motion does, however, serve to prove that there never *will be* any state of affairs different from the present. The assertion that the subject is οὖλον must therefore (by elimination) constitute a denial of *present* differentiation. That is to say it must constitute a reference back to the conclusion of B8.22–26.[106] οὖλον in fact must represent for Parmenides the same property as συνεχές.[107] Now, the conclusions of 22–26 and of 26–33 depend on the original κρίσις of B2, restated in 8.15ff, ἔστιν ἢ οὐκ ἔστιν, and the consequent rejection of not-Being; so that the conclusion of 8.34 also depends, indirectly, on this κρίσις. In B2 the κρίσις between ἔστιν and οὐκ ἔστιν is made on the grounds that not-Being is not to be thought of or spoken of. This makes it appear that (even without the attachment of B3 to B2)[108] the train of thought in 8.34ff is such as to create a circle of argument when placed beside B2. Not-Being is excluded because you cannot think of not-Being because (ultimately) you cannot think of it. This should not surprise an attentive reader; Parmenides himself says at B2.7, οὔτε γὰρ ἂν γνοίης τό γε μὴ ἐόν (οὐ γὰρ ἀνυστόν). You cannot use your mind on something that does not exist—because it is impossible.

After brief rejection (as mere verbiage) of beliefs in coming-to-be and destruction, difference,[109] and change of place or property, Parmenides concludes the Way of Truth with the simile of the sphere. Being is likened to the body of a well-rounded sphere. The reason for its likeness is then given. There have been many suggestions as to the point of this likeness. Some think it a literal statement of the subject's shape.[110] But how Parmenides could have reconciled himself to a finite spherical Being without asking what lay beyond it is not clear to me. We are not dealing with a bungler, but with one of Greece's greatest thinkers, and his thought should not be deformed in this way without the utmost necessity. Further, supposing the spatial words of 43ff *are* to be taken as referring to a sphere, then Parmenides had in fact considered the possibility of a chunk of not-Being interrupting the uniformity of the sphere's shape οὔτε γὰρ οὐκ ἐὸν ἔστι, τό κεν παύοι μιν ἱκνεῖσθαι / εἰς ὁμόν . . .), only to reject it. It would then be extraordinary for him to forget, once he had got his sphere, about this possibility of something else. Furthermore, the denial of degrees of being at 47–48 is beside the point if what stands to be disproved is a shape other than spherical.[111] This denial only becomes logically appropriate if the Sphere is an image for the uniformity of Being.

But why this image so repetitive? Why say here what has been said already at 8.22–26? Since Owen's flat denial of the possibility of such pure repetition and his consequent attempt to distinguish the meanings of the two passages, I have seen three attempts to explain the similarity between them. There are two obvious lines of approach. One is to say that a new characteristic of Being is here being proved, namely, its spherical shape or its likeness to a sphere. But (a) this is intrinsically improbable, and (b) even if we take only likeness to a sphere as the point we have still to ask why Parmenides omits this new point from the original programme at B8.3-4.[112] Nobody, I hope, will allege that we have here an afterthought—the poem is too carefully put together (even if composed orally, as it may in the first instance have been) for that kind of solution to carry weight. The second line of approach, used by Tarán, is that, far from adding a new predicate to Parmenides' conception of Being, this is merely, at least in the culminating line 49, the "most complete formulation" of the self-identity of Being.[113] This more complete assertion is convenient for the immediately following description of the mortal mistake of not postulating a single uniform reality and shows the impression made on Parmenides by the uniformity of Being. All this may be true: impressing on his readers or on himself the uniformity of his subject is indeed convenient just before a description of mortal error. But there may also be truth in Cornford's remark that "the final paragraph [of the Truth] describes the character of the Real in positive terms."[114] Parmenides has given little but negative qualifications of his subject and has just rejected finally, as not belonging to it, all the attributes of variety associated by mankind with reality. He understandably ends with an attempt to show what his subject is really like. But this is in the nature of things difficult, since it can have no property except existence, for there *is* nothing other than the existent. Parmenides therefore is thrown back on imagery and, in the attempt to explain his image, is reduced once again to negation, until the last statement of self-identity at 8.49. Indeed, the only positive thing that can be said about Being is that it is self-identical.

Having pursued Parmenides' argument to the end, we may now pause to consider the function within it of the predicate ἕν applied to Being at the opening of the argument. We have observed that it is not a predicate that is formally announced as requiring proof. The nearest Parmenides comes to putting this predicate in the programme is to say that (8.4) the subject is μουνογενές, unique of its kind, or (quite simply) unique, single. But he nowhere devotes a separate paragraph to the proof of its μουνογενής nature alone. So much there is to be said for Cornford's assertion that Parmenides does not prove his Being to be one.[115] Where Parmenides does, however, prove it is in the middle of a paragraph (8.34ff) ostensibly aimed at proving that the only thought is the thought of the subject's existence, and it is the immediate premiss from which that conclusion is deduced. The subject's singleness is proved from another predicate (οὖλον) in its turn derivable from the original decision to speak or think of nothing save one thing, namely, what is. The assertion that Being is one is for Parmenides the statement that it is alone and single. This statement he bases on the assumption that one can think of nothing else, which in turn is based on the assertion that there is nothing else there to be thought of. Parmenides recognizes that the oneness of Being in this sense is an intermediate stage in his argument when he summarizes the thought of his opening denial of becoming by saying that "it was once" and "it will be" are inapplicable, *since* it is now all together, *one* and continuous, and when he goes on to argue at 8.22ff, as a necessary supplement to the argument against becoming, that it is indivisible and continuous. That Being is single follows from the fact that it is οὖλον and συνεχές, that there is nothing else. That it will remain single and unique is the result of its being unchanging and unmoving; but it must be unchanging and unmoving because there is nothing else for it to change into and no other place for it to move to. The singleness of Being is central to the argument and depends in its turn directly on the original disjunction ἔστιν ἢ οὐκ ἔστιν. It depends on the doctrine that you cannot talk or think about the non-existent and therefore cannot discourse about anything other than the existent. The only place where the impossibility of anything other than the existent is explicit is at 8.36ff, but it is nevertheless an important, indeed a cardinal, point.

Nowhere in the poem does Parmenides start from "what is one" and deduce anything about its nature; he appears to be doing so in the opening demolition of becoming and perishing, but this is illusory, in that Being's singleness is dependent in turn on the negation of non-existence. Further, Parmenides has nothing to say about "plurality" arising from unity. He would agree (or indeed argue) that his subject is one and cannot become many, but it is not in virtue of its unity that it cannot become many. It cannot become many, he would agree, because there never will be more than one thing; and there never will be more than one thing because that would infringe the rule that only Being can be thought of, and nothing else, either now or at any other time. Even if at B8.22 the denial of divisibility were a denial that the subject can become many, the reason given is not that it is one but that it *is*, all in a like degree. To say this is not to state that Parmenides would have agreed that what is one can become many—he would have excluded this or any other kind of becoming. It needs still to be said that Parmenides is concerned with becoming in general and that there is no reason in his text to suppose that the specific kind of becoming in which a unity gives rise to a plurality ever entered his head. Previous thought *might* have given him the idea, but his poem shows, and in logic need show, no trace of it whatever.

Nor does Parmenides show that what is one cannot *be* many.[116] For again, if οὖλον, συνεχές, ἕν, μουνογενές, οὐ διαιρετόν, ταὐτόν, and so forth constitute a denial of plurality, as they do, it is still not in virtue of its initial unity that Parmenides' subject has these predicates hung on it but in virtue of its own existence, as being the only thing that can be talked or thought about. It is not so much that what is one cannot be many (though Parmenides would certainly have agreed, if pressed, that it cannot) as that what *is* must be one, single, continuous whole. Again, Parmenides does not start from unity. As long as in πᾶν ἐστιν ὁμοῖον the word ὁμοῖον was taken adjectivally, there was some sort of case for supposing that line to infer the negation of plurality from the assertion of unity. But the case even then was not strong; for, though ὁμοῖον is in Aristotle a kind of ἕν, the two words are not interchangeable in Presocratic thought. Further, if ὁμοῖον *be* adjectival *and* equivalent here in Parmenides' mind to ἕν, one would still have to search for the argument that led Parmenides to postulate the unity (in this sense) of his subject. Parmenides would then be found guilty of proceeding from the proposition that the subject all *is* (πάμπαν line 11) to the statement that it is all alike. The basis for this *could* of course be the original κρίσις; the abolition of difference being equated with the abolition of not-Being. But this interpretation, apart from ignoring the stylistic difficulties of taking ὁμοῖον adjectivally, would have the philosophical disadvantage of making Parmenides less explicit and harder to follow. And, even if one followed it, one would still, it seems, be compelled to admit that unity was not an assumption for Parmenides but something he thought he had proved. One would also have to admit that Parmenides was not specially concerned to prove that what was one in general could not be many but was rather seeking to show that his subject in particular, since it was one, could not be many. There should therefore be no more heard of the hypothesis that Parmenides *proved* that what was one (in the sense of being homogeneous) could not have gaps in it and thus be many. It will be observed in subsequent chapters that, if Parmenides' successors did find such a proof in his text, at any rate they ignored it.[117]

It is important in this context to notice that Parmenides did not have to prove in particular that what was one could not become many, or that homogeneity could not give rise to a varied multiplicity, in order to invalidate cosmogonies of the type produced by his Ionian predecessors. There is no reason to suppose that he had them specially in mind; but, even if he had, his general argument refutes them along with the rest of mankind. For, to make a varied world arise from a substantially homogeneous beginning, clearly something must change, or homogeneity will be the only result. So that, quite apart from the Parmenidean wholesale rejection of the world perceived by the senses, a cosmogony of the Ionian kind was impossible. If becoming and perishing went, this sort of cosmogony went with them. Parmenides, even if he were specially concerned with his Milesian predecessors, and even if they had enunciated the principle that one thing could be or become many things, did not have to oppose them on that particular ground.

So much for the Truth. But before we leave Parmenides there remains the "Opinions of Mortals" to be dealt with, and in particular the introduction to them, which contains the most disputed use of the word "one" in Parmenides.

To the already long history of the debate over these lines have recently been added three important contributions, by Tarán, Guthrie, and Mansfeld.[118] But several questions still await a decisive answer. (1) Is τῶν μίαν οὐ χρεών ἐστιν part of mortal belief, and condemned as such in the clause ἐν ᾧ πεπλανημένοι εἰσίν, or are both relative clauses parts of the criticism of the postulation of two forms (in line 53)? (2) Does τῶν μίαν οὐ... mean (a) "a unity formed from the two... not..."[119] or (b) "not one of which"[120] or (c) "one of which (and not the other)"?[121] It is to be observed that (c) may be taken to imply either (ci) (Diels) that one of them may be named (that is, equated or associated with Being) and the other must not, or (cii)[122] that one of them cannot be named without the other.

It is difficult to answer question (1) without an answer to (2), since syntax and word-order offer no reason to doubt that ἐν ᾧ could refer either to 53–54 or only to the first half of 54.[123] Alternative (ci) was very probably what Aristotle believed Parmenides to have meant, when he stated at *Metaphysics* 986b27–987a2 that Parmenides ranged Fire under Being, and "Earth" (!) under not-Being. But it is difficult to see any good reason for Parmenides to think that Fire was real, or more real than anything else; neither possible symbolism in his proem nor his avowedly erroneous account of human knowledge in B16 supplies such a good reason, though they may have encouraged Aristotle in his error.[124] As Tarán and Guthrie say,[125] (cii) requires one to supply rather awkwardly some part of μόνος; but see Herodotus 5.86.1. Both (ci) and (cii), one would have thought, would require ἑτέρην rather than μίαν, which appears only to be used meaning "one of two" in contexts like those of LSJ s.v. εἷς 3.[126] One may concede with Guthrie that Parmenides sometimes uses odd expressions,[127] but one should take his Greek at face value whenever possible, and it is certainly possible to make much less heavy weather than this of his language here. Tarán, and others adopting (a), offer no parallels for the use of τῶν μίαν to mean "a unity made of which" or (more literally) "one form made of which." The meaning of the genitive dependent on substantive (or substantivized adjective) is extremely varied, and it is not possible to say that such Greek is impossible—particularly for Parmenides.[128] But to follow these rough paths seems unreasonable when there exists the possibility of taking the line according to well-established Greek usage and making at the same time eminently Parmenidean sense of it. This is the effect of (b) above. Guthrie cites only Aristophanes *Thesmophoriazusae* 549 as an example of εἷς followed by the negative and says that (b) (in Cornford's variant) "would more naturally be represented by οὐδὲ μίαν." But LSJ s.v. εἷς 1.d. cite Xenophon *Anabasis* 5.6.12 for εἷς μή, and for εἷς οὐ Raven[129] adds Demosthenes 30.33, and Kühner-Gerth[130] cite Herodotus 8.119, making the point that other compounds of οὐ behave similarly. In all these passages a strong negative is evidently intended. Van Leeuwen on *Thesmophoriazusae* 549 cites Herodotus 3.6, where we have ἐν . . . ἀριθμῷ . . . οὐκ ἔστιν. It is interesting to note the existence of τριήκοντα . . . οὐκ, Herodotus 5.89, and ὀλίγης . . . οὐ at Theognis 253. Anyone definitely plumping for one particular interpretation of this passage should admit (as Guthrie modestly does) that he may be mistaken; but, since Parmenides should logically have believed that neither of the two forms exists—and that is exactly what well-attested Greek idiom (not confined to Attic) makes him say—one may provisionally accept this interpretation.

Mansfeld objects to Cornford that his interpretation would require μίαν οὐ to mean οὐδετέρην, and that *this* is impossible.[131] In reply no precise parallel can be offered; but, if there was no established idiom ἕτερος οὐκ, Parmenides could of course easily slip into the well-known one with εἷς followed by a negative; particularly easily after the numerical δύο. The idiom appears to have been confined to numerical and quantitative expressions, of which in Greek ἕτερος is hardly one. It must be admitted in all candour that at (for example) Herodotus 8.73.1 ἐν . . . οὐχ . . . means "one . . . did not . . ." and that the expression εἷς οὐκ is therefore to be regarded as ambiguous; but I do not think this is fatal to the view that a good Greek idiom has Parmenides here say what he ought to say, namely, that neither of mortals' two forms is real.

Guthrie prefers H. Fränkel's rendering, making Parmenides say that "of two forms one should not be named";[132] this in the sense not that one of the forms is rightly named but simply that mortals ought to name one form (namely Being) but in fact name two forms (neither of which is Being). This results in practically the same sense as Cornford's rendering but seems to me to be harder to extract from the Greek; for on

Fränkel's interpretation the word τῶν must mean "of forms in general," whereas the antecedent of τῶν is not "forms in general" but the two particular forms which mortals have decided to name.

Several scholars have either explicitly[133] or by judicious use of italics[134] endeavoured to claim that their rendering alone does justice to the antithesis of δύο and μίαν. I cannot see that any of these claims is justified specially, for all the renderings submitted appear to give the antithesis considerable force. In any case, the diversity of the translations on whose behalf this argument is invoked suggests that it is subjective and hence inconclusive.

The upshot of the discussion is that my question (2) may be provisionally answered in favour of alternative (b); Parmenides' goddess says in all probability that mortals were entirely wrong in believing in the existence of either fire or night. Neither fire nor night has for Parmenides any claim on reality at all. Parmenides does not, on my rendering of the Greek, state in the passage under discussion any reason why to believe in either fire or night is wrong, and a reason must be supplied, if at all, by conjecture. The reason is not far to seek; neither night nor fire is all-embracing or unchanging, and each is therefore different from the Being of the Way of Truth. Therefore both are non-existent. It is perhaps true that one cannot be thought of without the other;[135] but Parmenides nowhere mentions this or any other analogous point, and we are not obliged to believe that it occurred to him.

This transitional passage cannot be considered fully interpreted without discussion of one further linguistic point. It is surprisingly often argued that οὐ χρεών cannot mean "one must not" and must mean "one need not"; it is surprisingly often alleged that οὐ χρεών must say in Greek that there is an absence of positive obligation and cannot say that there is present an actively negative obligation.[136] It must be stressed that this is simply false. Expressions such as οὐ δεῖ and οὐ χρεών are unfortunately ambiguous; they can mean either "one must not" or "one need not."[137] We have only to look at Parmenides' context, as interpreted above, to see which is intended by Parmenides here. It would be feeble to say merely that the different things postulated by mortals are unnecessary, in contrast to the strength of the pronouncement that both are definitely wrong. Of course, if the words are used by mortals, then they must have the weaker sense; but there is no good reason to suppose that they are spoken by mortals. We need have no qualms about supposing Parmenides' goddess here to say that neither one of the forms postulated of necessity by mortals in order to sustain a plurality is truly existent.

The transitional passage has been held to be an attack on the supposition "that there could be a transition in nature from the intellectual world of mathematical form to the world of physical bodies and change, and that both worlds are on the same level of reality."[138] To this it suffices to reply that both these worlds, that of mathematics and that of physics, are evidently for Parmenides on the same level of reality, or rather of unreality, for neither excludes plurality or difference.[139] There is not the slightest reason to suppose that reflection on a mathematical conception of physics led Parmenides to reject both mathematics and physics. It is clear that Parmenides reflected on possible objects of reflection—for which see B2. Parmenides does not argue that "from unity nothing can be derived"; he argues more comprehensively that any talk of derivation at all is nonsense. This argument of his, if it cannot be proved wrong, would be fatal to any cosmos or cosmogony; but Parmenides' successors, while seizing some of the point, either did not appreciate, or felt compelled to ignore, this central objection, despite their inability to disprove its premisses or to expose its fallaciousness. On no interpretation of Parmenides' literal meaning is it necessary to suppose that he is attacking an alleged contradiction between "a world containing many different things" and the theory that "this plurality arose from a single arché." Parmenides' argument is more fundamental; he argues rather that the notions of difference and of "arising" are each, separately, inconceivable.

To account for the appearance of difference and change one must, according to Parmenides, postulate some fundamental violation by appearances of the laws against difference and change. The more fundamental of the two laws is that against difference, from which the law forbidding change is derived. Parmenides accordingly says that mankind postulate two forms—that is, they postulate a difference. It is here that they go wrong; and, once they have gone wrong here, there is nothing to stop them infringing other requirements of logic. Parmenides then shows how, once this original breach is made in the dyke of his logic, the whole flood of human sensations pours in and the whole world is accounted for. It looks, however, as if, in accounting for the physical world in this way, Parmenides avoided the initial infringement of more of his rules than was absolutely necessary. He has his mortals posit only two forms, not more, and he seems to have stressed this fact, if not at 8.53-54, then at 57-58; each of the two forms is different from the other, but is, like the subject of the Way of Truth, the same as itself. The reason put into the goddess' mouth for giving this account is apparently to be found in B8.61, "Thus no mortal will ever outstrip you in intelligence." I take this—but here subjectivity is inevitable—to mean that no mortal will ever give an account of appearance which presents fewer violations of the laws of Truth. The Δόξα is the best that can be done for appearances. Whether this prophecy of the goddess was fulfilled is another question.

MELISSUS' ARGUMENT

Melissus' argument is essentially derivative, based on Parmenides but occasionally amplifying, rendering more explicit, or presenting a different side of the same problem. Uses of the words "one" and "many" in Melissus betray this dependence, and add but little to arguments already adduced. While the greater explicitness of Melissus makes it easier to see in him some of the points already made about Parmenides' arguments, the lack of novelty in the disciple's thought will excuse the brevity of the present survey.

On Melissus, as on Parmenides, it has been suggested that unity is a premiss of his argument.[140] But this is no more true—and no less true—of Melissus than of Parmenides. Arguments are to be found in 30B5, and almost certainly B6, proving that Being is one on the basis of its infinity, and no attempt to interpret these as arguments for infinity on the basis of unity can succeed. But, like Parmenides, Melissus does use the unity he has proved as a premiss for further argument. Unity is for both Parmenides and Melissus an important station on the line to more remote places. The route by which Melissus arrives at unity is not always, in the extant fragments, the same as Parmenides' extant route; but after this point their ways, even in extant arguments, converge.

Take for example 30B7, "Thus then," reads the opening sentence, "it is eternal and unlimited and one and all alike." The unity of Being and the indistinguishability of any parts within it have been "proved" in preceding arguments—that is the force of οὕτως οὖν.[141] But these conclusions, as in Parmenides, are used as premisses on which to found the denial of process. Several kinds of process are denied in the very next sentence, οὔτ' ἂν ἀπόλοιτο οὔτε μεῖζον γίγνοιτο οὔτε μετακοσμέοιτο οὔτε ἀλγεῖ οὔτε ἀνιᾶται, and the reason for this is that any process of the kind would infringe the unity of Being; εἰ γάρ τι τούτων πάσχοι, οὐκ ἂν ἔτι ἓν εἴη. The manner of this infringement is then elaborated as follows: εἰ γὰρ ἑτεροιοῦται, ἀνάγκη τὸ ἐὸν μὴ ὁμοῖον εἶναι, ἀλλὰ ἀπόλλυσθαι τὸ πρόσθεν ἐόν, τὸ δὲ οὐκ ἐὸν γίγνεσθαι. It is simply that change prohibits Being from being alike, ὁμοῖον. What prevents it from being ὁμοῖον under these circumstances is that Being is destroyed and not-Being comes to be. Clearly this infringement of the homogeneity and the uniqueness of Being is due to the requirement of not-Being to explain change. The oneness of Being for Melissus, as for Parmenides, would be broken by the possibility of the existence of anything other than Being. The rejection of differentiation thus carries with it the abolition of process. The central argument is that the uniqueness of Being and its homogeneity (both due to the non-existence of the non-existent) prove the impossibility of destruction, creation, and change. The rest of the fragment is mainly an enlargement of this theme. It matters not, says Melissus, that the change is only at snail's pace; if we admit any change it will eventually be complete.[142] It is not only creation, destruction, and change of property that are ruled out; change of arrangement also succumbs to the argument, since any arrangement which "is not" cannot come to be. Pain is excluded on three grounds, of which only one is relevant here, namely, that pain is caused by the addition or withdrawal of something; and, if Being were subject to these processes, it would no longer be ὁμοῖον—presumably since the added or subtracted thing would have to be or become other than Being.[143] Void is denounced explicitly as nothing—and nothing does not exist. Motion is ruled out by the absence of void—but be it observed that motion has already been dismissed by the argument against re-arrangement. We are here, I think, dealing with a set of subordinate arguments. Dense and rare are abolished next, because they too imply a void.[144]

A subsidiary argument, explicitly marked as such, is mounted in B8 for the unity of Being. This is a reductio ad absurdum of some ingenuity. To postulate the existence of more than one thing is to postulate, in accordance with Eleatic logic, their eternity. But the senses do not show us an eternal, but a changing, plurality of things. So the logical consequences of accepting the senses' existential data contradict the evidence of the senses. The senses, therefore (being self-contradictory) are not to be believed.[145] The trouble with this argument is that the Eleatic argument against change was based on the denial of difference and plurality, so this argument of Melissus' is open to the charge of *petitio principii*. At any rate, here we may note that at the end of the fragment the impossibility of becoming and destruction are based on the abolition of not-Being. That is why ἢν δὲ μεταπέσῃ, τὸ μὲν ἐὸν ἀπώλετο, τὸ δὲ οὐκ ἐὸν γέγονεν.

The place of the unity of Being in the development of Melissus' line of argument is thus established. The next fragment to be considered may be merely further evidence for the same point, or it may be a sign that Melissus confused different senses of "one" and "many." B9 begins with what looks like a recapitulation of the argument that existence is unique: εἰ μὲν ὂν (οὖν Diels) εἴη, δεῖ αὐτὸ ἓν εἶναι. Though strict certainty on the point is not perhaps attainable, I am convinced that that is indeed what this sentence represents.[146] There follows a deduction from the unity of Being, namely that as a unity it can have no body;

ἓν δ' ἐὸν δεῖ αὐτὸ σῶμα ἔχειν. Then comes the explanation: εἰ δὲ ἔχοι πάχος, ἔχοι ἂν μόρια καὶ οὐκέτι ἓν εἴη. The unity of Being (or indeed of anything else) would be infringed by the possession of parts; if it had parts, it could no longer be one. Nothing is said to indicate that these parts are to be different in quality from one another; it is only required by the argument that the parts shall be somehow distinguishable, the minimum distinction being (one supposes) that they occupy different places. Melissus may (on the supposition that he is talking about Being in this fragment) have meant that to occupy different places was impossible, since the laws of being rule out difference of any kind. He may have intended to argue that Being cannot be in more than one place, any more than it can move from one place to another; the same grounds would lie behind both denials. This is perhaps the most charitable interpretation of B9 but is not necessarily the right one. It is possible that Melissus proceeded more directly from the possession of parts to the lack of *any* unity. To us such an argument seems immediately absurd: a man is not any the less one man, nor any the less one unified whole, nor any the less continuous, simply because he has four limbs and a number of other parts. But to a thinker not educated in the different senses of "one" and their relevance to such difficulties the argument suggested for Melissus could make very good sense. What may tip the balance of probability in favour of this second interpretation of Melissus' B9 is the existence of similar arguments in other Eleatic contexts. Zeno appears to have argued that the possession of size and divisibility excluded the attribution of unity; and Plato's Parmenides argues that the possession of parts in itself, without intermediate step, suffices to abolish unity.[147] It may be observed, for what the point is worth, that the Platonic argument appears in a Melissan context, in that it is succeeded, after the derivation of the notions of beginning, middle, and end from that of parts, by the argument (compare B2 and B3) that, having no beginning and end, Being is unlimited. Certainty cannot be reached here, and one would not like to rest a whole case on this one argument of Melissus'. But it is clear that this argument is at least compatible with the thesis here being developed, that the Presocratics did not understand the implications of the ambiguity of the terms "one" and "many."

Certainty is also out of our reach at B7.2. There change rules out the unity of Being, in that it excludes the continued ὁμοῖον nature of Being. But ὁμοῖον here stands for the abolition of all difference, whether internal or due to the presence of something else outside Being. It is not, therefore, clear that Melissus was arguing directly from lack of homogeneity to lack of unity simpliciter, since ὁμοῖον here may include something more than internal homogeneity.[148]

There are admittedly two reports which would suggest that Melissus did in fact suppose being ὁμοῖον to be a *necessary* consequence of unity, but neither is of impeccable provenance. Simplicius at *in Physica* 103.31ff has this point in the middle of a more general argument: if one, Being is unmoved; for what is one is always like itself. But what is ὁμοῖον could not be destroyed, undergo rearrangement, or grow, or suffer pain, without ceasing to be one. This argument of Simplicius', however, is clearly a paraphrase of part of B7, which we can interpret for ourselves; it would seem that Simplicius has been inexact in committing Melissus to the view that unity implies homogeneity. Then, the *MXG* at 947a12ff has an argument specifically aimed at proving that, to be one, Being must be ὁμοῖον. The argument is that, if it is not ὁμοῖον, then Being will be not one but many. If indeed Melissus argued thus we should initially be inclined to accept that he was advanced enough to see that to be one is not immediately and necessarily, without further argument, to be ὁμοῖον. But this good impression is spoilt by the argument's being little more than an assertion. Any kind of plurality is apparently sufficient after all to exclude all unity of whatsoever kind. In any case, Melissus may never have argued in this fashion: the author of *MXG* is certainly not above invention or careless misunderstanding.[149] I should not like to press this passage on either side of the question whether the Eleatics understood the ambiguities of "one" and "many."

It is, therefore, not wholly clear from the study of his own extant words how far Melissus distinguished the different senses of "one" and "many." It can, however, be stated with assurance that the unity of Being, in whatever sense(s) he intended it, was an important conclusion for Melissus and at the same time a signpost on the road to further conclusions. It was not an initial unproved assumption for Melissus any more than for Parmenides. Nor is there any suggestion in the ancient testimonies that, because Melissus' Being was one, for that reason it could not become many. Divisibility is mentioned in the very difficult B10, but it is unclear what the argument behind that fragment is. Simplicius quotes it in the form: εἰ γὰρ διῄρηται τὸ ἐόν, κινεῖται· κινούμενον δ' οὐκ ἂν εἴη. If the divisibility here mentioned is the logical, static kind, then it is difficult to see the logic of the assertion that the state of being so divided implies motion; if the divisibility here mentioned is the process of splitting up, then we have indeed a prohibition on Being's becoming many, but it is unclear how Melissus argued for this prohibition. With the rendering of Kranz, "Wenn es sich aber bewegt, dann hört sein Sein auf," the point is that the *being* of Being, not its unity, is the reason for denying motion and hence divisibility. If one were (with somewhat less likelihood) to suppose κινούμενον ... εἴη to mean "But it could not be a moving object," then one must look elsewhere for the argument prohibiting motion. Now, in so far as the being of Being and the non-being of not-Being are responsible ultimately for the whole of Melissus' negative conclusions, one may accept that in this case also it is ultimately the acceptance of Being which necessitates the abandonment of motion. It is only in a limited sense that the unity or uniqueness of Being can be held responsible for the abolition of motion (and hence of divisibility), in that the uniqueness of Being results in the impossibility of different arrangements of Being and in the inconceivability of void. It would be seriously stretching a point to say on this evidence that the reason why Melissus' Being could not become many was that it was one. It may not have been expressly forbidden to become many; and if it was, and if that prohibition was not linked directly to its being, then at any rate unity is neither the immediate nor the ultimate reason for the prohibition. To derive from this evidence an Eleatic belief that what was one could not, for that reason, become many would be a serious error. The antithesis of "one" and "many" plays but a minimal part here.

It cannot be shown beyond doubt, probable though it is, that Melissus believed that what was one could not *be* many, that no unity could survive any touch of plurality. There is no argument certainly his which proves the point and none which *certainly* assumes it. In so far as the point is probably assumed, it is apparently as a truism incapable of proof —though here also we are not on firm ground. The antithesis of "one" and "many" here too plays a small part indeed in our sources. With arguments to show, according to his lights, that what is cannot be many and that what is cannot be subject to any kind of becoming, Melissus assuredly had no need for great emphasis on the logic of unity as such.

VI

EMPEDOCLES

THE CYCLE

The importance of unity and plurality in Empedocles' thought is obvious from the most superficial study of the texts. Not once but repeatedly Empedocles speaks of a one giving rise to a many and vice versa. But, though the meaning of this repeated statement has never been thoroughly investigated, there is at present sharp disagreement on its reference. Recent discussion of Empedocles' doctrine of the cycle (or single oscillation) from Strife to Love and back again makes it necessary at least to state a position on the major questions involved.[1] Without such a statement the discussion of the transitions from unity to plurality and back would have little meaning. The position taken up here will probably please neither side in the controversy but need not be the worse for that. It represents an attempt to extract what is sound from the often overstated arguments of each side.

The first point at issue has already been adumbrated. Did Empedocles conceive of the universe as oscillating once from the complete triumph of Strife to the absolute reign of Love and back, or did he believe in a never-ending cycle of alternating reigns? To find the answer to this question the ancient historians of philosophy have been ransacked; but, like most doxographical evidence, their pronouncements on this topic can be explained away by sufficiently determined expositors. It is all the more credit to Denis O'Brien[2] that he has recently produced a statement from Empedocles himself which is extremely hard to interpret except on the assumption of a continuing cycle and had indeed been needlessly emended by those who reject such a cycle.[3]

But that does not necessarily solve all the questions concerned. It does not, for instance, decide whether in Empedocles' mind or in his poem (not necessarily the same thing) the two halves of the cycle are completely symmetrical. Strictly, I suppose, a conscientious judge should enter the verdict "non liquet"; but there are indications which may lead us to a less austere conclusion. Leaving the doxographers aside for the moment, two passages or groups of passages are usually invoked in defence of a zoogony in each half of the cycle. These I now discuss in turn, bearing in mind that one of them constitutes an almost formulaic reference to unity and plurality and that the zoogony and Empedocles' conception of unity throw light on each other.

The first indication of an entirely symmetrical cycle, with a zoogony in each half-turn of the wheel, is to be found at the outset of Empedocles' main statement of his cosmology, in B17:

δίπλ' ἐρέω· τότε μὲν γὰρ ἓν ηὐξήθη μόνον εἶναι
ἐκ πλεόνων, τότε δ' αὖ διέφυ πλέον' ἐξ ἑνὸς εἶναι.
δοίη δὲ θνητῶν γένεσις, δοίη δ' ἀπόλειψις,
τὴν μὲν γὰρ πάντων σύνοδος τίκτει τ' ὀλέκει τε,
ἡ δὲ πάλιν διαφυομένων θρεφθεῖσα διέπτη.
καὶ ταῦτ' ἀλλάσσοντα διαμπερὲς οὐδαμὰ λήγει κτλ.

There are in print three ways (at least) of taking the crucial lines following the statement "Twofold is the coming-to-be of mortal things and twofold their destruction." The first, offered perhaps by Burnet and recently described as "the usual view,"[4] is to take τὴν μέν as a "concrete" or external accusative with γένεσις as antecedent, and ἡ δέ, also with γένεσις as antecedent, as correspondingly external subject of the passive verbs. This, it seems to me, is evidently wrong: there is no reason whatever why γένεσις should be the antecedent to the total exclusion of ἀπόλειψις; there is no justification for taking γένεσις as a concrete noun when in the context it is clearly a verbal noun; the symmetry of language in this highly rhetorical passage is all against such awkwardnesses. The second interpretation, from the pen of Uvo Hölscher,[5] is to the effect that τὴν μέν is an internal or cognate accusative, with γένεσις for antecedent, while ἡ δέ is again internal in sense, with ἀπόλειψις for antecedent. This is much more plausible and offends less against the linguistic symmetry of a highly-wrought passage, but it is none the less in the last analysis difficult to believe: Hölscher wants his cognate τήν (=γένεσιν) to be governed normally by τίκτει and then paradoxically by ὀλέκει, the whole of line 4 being then an expression of the doctrine that genesis and destruction are inseparably linked, in that the mixture of the elements to form one thing can only proceed if the elements are being, or have been, separated out of another thing. "Paradoxical" is indeed not a strong enough expression for this supposed contortion of the Greek language. It is hard to believe that the normal reader would take ὀλέκει as thus strangely governing γένεσιν as an internal accusative, particularly when the more obviously appropriate object ἀπόλειψις appears in the context. Less difficult, and no less in keeping with the symmetry of the whole passage, is the interpretation propounded by Guthrie;[6] this takes both τὴν μέν and ἡ δέ as internal, but regards one pair of γένεσις and ἀπόλειψις as the antecedent of each. The sense is then that one destruction and one genesis are the result of σύνοδος, and another pair of genesis and destruction was the work of the separation of the elements. This necessitates the acceptance of Panzerbieter's conjecture θρεφθεῖσα, in place of the manuscripts' θρυφθεῖσα, but that would probably have been necessary anyway.[7] This interpretation seems the only one to give a proper account of the correspondence of the pairs γένεσις and ἀπόλειψις and τίκτει τ' ὀλέκει τε (and probably also θρεφθεῖσα διέπτη). This it does at the small expense of having Empedocles use the singulars τὴν μέν and ἡ δέ where plurals or duals would do. Either singular or plural would be ambiguous, and Empedocles doubtless imagined that he had made his meaning clear by repeating in the verbs τίκτει τ' ὀλέκει τε the notions of the nouns γένεσις and ἀπόλειψις.

But we have still not answered the question whether these lines give voice to the theory of complete symmetry in the cosmic cycle. It must be asked whether they imply a complete genesis of all things animate and inanimate both in the course of the growth to one and in the course of the separation into a plurality. Some have supposed Empedocles more concerned with the microcosm, with the view that the coming-together of all the elements in one thing is connected with their separation from another thing.[8] The elements may indeed come together in either a given perishable object or the Sphere. But if the whole passage be taken as referring to individual sensible objects the sense of the whole is difficult to follow. For, in that case, the effect of the coming-together of the elements is to create one object and to destroy others, and the effect of their dissolution is to destroy one object and create others (since inevitably mixtures with different proportions result). This makes good sense of lines 4–5 in isolation but leaves the reader with a feeling of dissatisfaction about lines 1–3. There we are told that genesis and destruction are each twofold; this doubleness can hardly fail to have something to do with the doubleness of Empedocles' tale at the opening of the fragment. In fact, the one duality ought to correspond closely with the other. Now, the twofold tale, whatever it is about, talks of opposite processes happening at different times to the same things, and not to different things at the same time. It seems to follow that the corresponding double genesis and destruction must also happen at different times to the same things. But on Hölscher's explanation that cannot be the case. If the whole refers to the microcosm, it is simply not true that the coming-together of all the elements *first* creates and *then* destroys the same thing; the function of destruction belongs to Strife. On Hölscher's view the genesis of one thing is *simultaneous* with the destruction of others. On this interpretation, therefore, the doubleness of the processes must be quite different from the doubleness of Empedocles' tale, and the whole passage must be regarded as devoid of structural unity. Such carelessness of writing is hardly credible, let alone probable, in a passage so thoroughly worked up.[9] It results that the best interpretation of these lines is cosmological, in reference to the elements' concourse in the Sphere and separation in the reign of Strife. Incidentally, it seems hard to reconcile the aorists and presents of the fragment except on the assumption that both are used of repeated action; it would follow that the cosmological processes involved are repeated. Here also Empedocles is hard to interpret if he is not referring to a cosmic cycle. This cosmic cycle is, moreover, endowed at this, probably its first, appearance with a genesis and destruction of mortal things in each half of the cycle. There should really be no doubt that that is what Empedocles both says and means.

But from the symmetry of the Empedoclean cycle in theory it is a long, and not an inevitable, step to the symmetry of his narrative. Walther Kranz long ago suggested that the symmetry in theory was not backed by a necessarily repetitive double narrative.[10] and Solmsen has recently brought some formal and general grounds against the usual version of the supposition that Empedocles narrated the whole story twice.[11] We are, further, told by Aristotle (*De caelo* 301a15) that Empedocles neglected to offer a cosmogony in the period of Love's increase and Strife's decline. This statement should certainly not be simply dismissed.[12] It is interesting that in the lines we possess dealing with the transition from Strife to Love there is no cosmogony, but simply a plunge into zoogony. One must admit that some kinds of repetition are characteristic of Empedocles' style and that this need not have been the only account of the transition. But Aristotle is supported by sound reason,[13] since there is little to be narrated on the cosmic scale between the (supposed) situation at Strife's climax and the present distribution of the bulk of the "elements." Nor do I see any reason whatever why Aristotle should be mistaken on such a matter; misunderstanding is one thing, elementary error of fact is surely another.

But to deal with this whole question adequately necessitates the examination of the evidence for Empedocles' zoogony. A major obstacle to the belief that Empedocles narrated the whole series of events only once, the cosmogony under Strife and the zoogony—including the anthropogony—under Love, is the detection by many scholars[14] of two distinct tendencies in the zoogonical sequence recorded by Aëtius and supported in part by the fragments, as well as by some remarks in Aristotle and his commentators. Aëtius, here represented only by Pseudo-Plutarch, gives a single zoogony in four stages. (1) The formation of single limbs, supported by B57 and the Empedoclean parts of B58, and also by Aristotle and Simplicius.[15] (2) The chance "minglings" of the limbs to form monsters of mingled species and sex, resembling in some respects, as has often been noted,[16] the monsters of myth. These creatures are reported by Aristotle and Simplicius and appear in B60 and B61. (3) The ὁλοφυῆ, clearly mentioned and provided with an origin at B62. (4) Men and women and other creatures, able to reproduce themselves without having to be formed direct from the elements. The problem arises from a number of arguments advanced to show that the first two of these stages belong to the increase of Love, but the second pair to Strife's increase. But the arguments are inconclusive.

The first of two major arguments is that at B62 the Fire which brings up the οὐλοφυεῖς τύποι from the earth is being separated, κρινόμενον, and is also desirous of attaining to its like, θέλον πρὸς ὁμοῖον ἱκέσθαι.[17] It is argued that here Strife must be active, whereas in the formation of monsters from limbs Love was clearly active. But, notwithstanding the parallel between Fire's desire to reach Fire and the elements' behaviour under Love at B35.6 (οὐκ ἄφαρ, ἀλλὰ θελημὰ συνιστάμεν' ἄλλοθεν ἄλλα) this first argument fails to convince. Both powers are of course active in each world, and at least there is no reason why the same scholars who hold that Love is actively forming compounds and creatures in the present world (allegedly under Strife) should deny the possibility of Strife playing a part in the world of Love's increase. The second argument is that the process of conversion from οὐλοφυεῖς τύποι to male and female is one of differentiation and that this is also more appropriate to Strife's increase than to Love's.[18] This again is a subjective argument. It is hard to find an objective criterion for deciding whether to rule out the growth of sexuality from the world of Strife's increase or to rule out differentiation from the world of Love.[19] Love's function, as we shall see, is not only to assimilate but to produce a complete whole, and Empedocles could without difficulty be supposed to have considered animals imperfect without sexuality. The case would perhaps be a little harder to argue on behalf of Love's world as the venue for stages (3) and (4), if it were clear beyond all doubt that the process of transition was one of simple splitting of the οὐλοφυεῖς τύποι, but it is not clear at all; the passage from Simplicius usually invoked proves nothing of the sort.[20] Nor does

Aristotle's teleological argument in the *Physics* rule out the intervention of the οὐλοφυεῖς τύποι between the monsters and the full-fledged male and female creatures.[21] We should surely demand stronger reasons than these before rejecting a perfectly intelligible statement of a doxographic source.[22]

Before dismembering this passage of Aëtius, one should inspect it for signs of internal unity. These it duly displays. In Pseudo-Plutarch the whole zoogony begins by declaring expressly the first animals and plants μηδαμῶς ὁλοκλήρους γενέσθαι, ἀσυμφυέσι δὲ τοῖς μορίοις διεζευγμένας. The contrast with the ὁλοφυῆ of Aëtius' stage (3) is pointed, and pretty clearly intended. I see no reason to doubt either its Theophrastean origin or its correctness. If it is correct, then Empedocles, as Aëtius has him, meant the word ὁλοφυής to contrast not with the creatures that followed, but with those that preceded, the stage represented by B62. This is indeed a plausible supposition.

But it raises the problem what the word οὐλοφυεῖς meant to Empedocles, a problem with no obviously certain answer. On Aëtius' view the word apparently implied that the ὁλοφυῆ were the first complete and self-sufficient organisms.[23] This would be a perfectly plausible sense (etymologically speaking) for οὐλοφυής and would make perfectly good sense of Empedocles and Aëtius. But it is admittedly not the meaning ὁλοφυής has at Aristotle *De partibus animalium* 693a24–26. There we have the statement "The under and upper sides of the body (i.e., of what is called the trunk in quadrupeds) are in birds one uninterrupted whole" (.... οὗτος ὁ τόπος ὁλοφυὴς ἐπὶ τῶν ὀρνίθων ἐστιν);[24] the word ὁλοφυής appears to mean "continuous," referring to the lack of protrusions; the wings are folded back to give a smooth surface, whereas in the quadrupeds the forelegs stick out. But I do not think it follows that Empedocles was alluding to the shape of his τύποι when he calls them οὐλοφυεῖς—even though it is an odd coincidence that Empedocles' "whole-natured forms," like Aristotle's birds, have no limbs to interrupt the continuity of their shape. Whereas Aristotle makes explicit in his succeeding sentence the connection between the lack of limbs and the adjective "whole-natured," Empedocles does not, and the two factors may be independent of each other.[25] ὅλος is not a simple word in Greek, and there is no need to hold even a rare compound of it to a single meaning. I see, therefore, no reason to disbelieve either the Theophrastean derivation or the essential rightness of the sense given to ὁλοφυής by Pseudo-Plutarch, with its consequences for the unity of Aëtius' version of Empedocles' zoogony.

No support, it is plain, is derivable from the zoogony for the theory that Empedocles wearied his readers with the whole of his double tale.[26] It is worth adding that, on the hypothesis that Empedocles described the growth of the cosmos under Strife and the zoogony under Love, it is possible to account quite satisfactorily for two groups of Aristotelian passages. The first is those that describe the present cosmos as that of Strife;[27] for the hypothesis supposes that the cosmos of separated elements was formed by Strife, that nothing further was said about a backwards cosmic transition to the (certainly strikingly similar) present state of affairs before the plunge into the zoogony of Love, which would most naturally end in the creatures now in existence. The *cosmos*, then, which is broadly that now in existence was formed by Strife.[28] At the same time, we can offer a rational explanation of the passages referring to the rise of monsters as happening in the beginning and giving way to the present complete and unified living creatures by the law of the failure of the unfit to survive. If this is not what Empedocles meant, then we have to believe that Aristotle and Simplicius, in referring to the monsters as occurring ἐξ ἀρχῆς, meant "in the beginning of another world than this" —which borders, to me as to Hölscher, on the absurd: we have also to set the "mythical" monsters, so far as this world is concerned, not in the past, but the future![29] On no other hypothesis, it appears, than that of successive reigns of Strife and Love in a single world history can both sets of statements be so neatly accounted for.[30]

One more facet of the cosmic cycle must be examined in this preliminary survey. This is the postulated existence and placing within the cycle of any period(s) of rest. As the last section on the cycle was written to clear the ground for the analysis of the functions of Love and Strife, so this is composed in order to exhibit briefly and (mostly) derivatively the relation in Empedocles between rest and motion on the one hand and unity and plurality on the other. Once again we have to consider both the fragments and the secondary sources, and for once it will be convenient to take the latter first.

At the beginning of *Physics* Θ Aristotle, in a much-discussed passage,[31] declares that Empedocles believed in alternate rest and motion; in motion when Love is unifying and when Strife is forming a plurality, but in rest ἐν τοῖς μεταξὺ χρόνοις. Aristotle then cites the following lines from B26:

> οὕτως ᾗ μὲν ἓν ἐκ πλεόνων μεμάθηκε φύεσθαι,
> ἠδὲ πάλιν διαφύντος ἑνὸς πλέον' ἐκτελέθουσιν,
> τῇ μὲν γίγνονταί τε καὶ οὔ σφισιν ἔμπεδος αἰών·
> ᾗ δὲ τάδ' ἀλλάσσοντα διαμπερὲς οὐδαμὰ λήγει,
> ταύτῃ δ' αἰὲν ἔασιν ἀκίνητοι κατὰ κύκλον.

This is Aristotle's evidence for the supposition that Empedocles envisaged a period or periods of rest during the cycle. But, in fact, as has often been observed, the lines do not contain the required statement. How, then, did Aristotle take the lines in question, and was he simply mistaken? Most readers have supposed that he took the epithet ἀκίνητοι in the last line to mean that in the intervals between the movements of Love and Strife the elements were at rest.[32] But G. A. Seeck has recently shown that the crucial words for Aristotle were ᾗ δὲ τάδ' ἀλλάσσοντα, and that Aristotle (a) extracted from them and the two first lines of his quotation the theory that Empedocles' process was reversible rectilinear rather than circular and (b) deduced according to his own principles the periods of rest at each extremity. If, on the other hand, as O'Brien has recently been suggesting, the first two lines were alone sufficient to prove for Aristotle *both* that there was a passage from unity to plurality (and back) *and* that there was a period or periods of rest, then there was no need whatever for him to continue his quotation for three lines further; nobody can bring in evidence an Aristotelian habit of quoting to the end merely for the sake of completeness. In any case, there is no solid ground for crediting Aristotle with the supposition that unity entails rest, or plurality motion, even if the two are somehow connected.[33] Aristotle in some sense reduced the opposites to unity and plurality, but that is not to say that unity and plurality *entailed* the other pairs, and still less that Aristotle could assume that his readers or hearers would make the deduction for themselves without the slightest hint. Aristotle's "evidence," then, for the period(s) of rest between the cyclic movements was inadequate. There is thus no reason why we should believe him, unless we can prove from other evidence either that this was a theory that Aristotle was not likely to invent or that Empedocles' own words state or imply themselves the doctrine of rest between periods of motion. The first can certainly not be proved; rather the reverse.[34] The second is undemonstrable. No description of the reign of Strife (if it was different from our cosmos) has survived.[35] The Sphere of Love is described in terms which could conceivably indicate a period of rest, but none of these is inexplicable on other hypotheses of equal plausibility. The Sphere rejoices at B27 and B28 in its surrounding μονίη; but, though the meaning of this could possibly be "motionlessness," it is surely more likely in context to refer to the Sphere's property of being ἓν μόνον.[36] The description of the Sphere at B27 contains also the word ἐστήρικται, "it is fixed"—but this could easily be metaphorical and need no more imply a definite theory of motionless stability than the other metaphors of glue, bond, or nails used to illustrate the functions of Love. When at B31 Empedocles declares that the god's limbs shook in turn, this does not necessarily imply a period of rest, prior to the shaking, but could equally be true of a momentary Sphere. Proof is lacking, and we must avoid building an edifice of conjecture. There is no good reason to believe that rest was associated by Empedocles particularly with the Sphere and its unity.[37] It may be the case that there was a period of rest at the climax either of Love's growth or of Strife's; but, if so, it is surprising that Aristotle, Eudemus, and the moderns can produce no better evidence for it.[38]

THE FUNCTIONS OF LOVE AND STRIFE

Empedocles' "double tale" tells of the alternate growth of one thing from many and dissipation of one thing into many: unity under Love and plurality under Strife. The question obviously arises, What kinds of unity and plurality? It is unwise to look for explanations of Empedocles' doctrine, whether historical or other, until we are sure what that doctrine is—the more so since even a cursory investigation shows that the question just broached has no simple answer.[39] We may lead off with a brief survey of the kind of vocabulary used to describe the actions and effects of Love and Strife, and follow this with an analysis of these effects with a view to determining which of Aristotle's kinds or senses of unity is/are most helpful in the elucidation of Empedocles' thinking.

The fragments contain a large variety of compound verbs employed of the movements caused by Love and Strife. For Love they are compounded with συν-, and for Strife with δια-. Thus, we have at B17.7 and B35.5 συνέρχομαι, with the verbal noun σύνοδος at B17.4, at B71.4 συναρμοσθέντα, at B95 ξὺμ πρῶτ᾽ ἐφύοντο, at B35.6 συνιστάμενα, at B59.2 συμπίπτεσκον, and σὺν δ᾽ ἔβη at B21.8, all in descriptions of Love. Of Strife we have διέφυ at B17.2 (cf. B17.5, 10), διέπτη (probable reading) at B17.5, διατμηθέντα at B20.4, and the compound adjective διάμορφα at B21.7. Probably, therefore, οὐ διείδεται at B27, a negatived δια-compound, is used of the result of Love, as the negatived συν-compound συγγίνεσθαι ἀήθεα is used of Strife's effect at B22.8-9. But, unfortunately, these compounds are not helpful for our immediate purpose, since they are equally appropriate, on the whole, for unities by wholeness, continuity, or mixture, or to the dissolution of these kinds.

Similarly inconclusive are the various metaphors used of the effect of Love on the elements or the compounds. Longing (ποθεῖται B21.8) and affection (ἔστερκται B22.5) are merely verbal forms of Love and help not at all. The metaphors of binding (B32 and B33), of nailing (B33 and B87), and of gluing (B96.4 and in a simile at B34) are more obviously appropriate to a unity by continuity—that degree of continuity conferred by artificial or external means.[40] But, illuminating though it would be if we could at once convict Empedocles of thinking in terms appropriate to a unity by continuity when he should have been thinking in terms of mixture or of homogeneity, these expressions will not serve that purpose. They can be regarded with perfect equanimity as metaphors. Empedocles, perhaps an indifferent philosopher, was a great poet. One cannot help admiring his poetry and rejoicing that at least some lines of it remain to enrich the world's literature; but to interpret his elegant metaphors as exact philosophy would be misplaced enthusiasm.

It is not in such writers' tricks as these that we shall find the precise notions of unity and plurality that we are seeking. Nor shall we find them in the adverbs δίχα and ἄνδιχα used of the elements sundered by Strife, nor in the terms Love and Strife themselves. What we must do is to see what actually is the difference between the world of Strife and the Sphere and thus attempt to find what lies behind Empedocles' figures of speech.

One thing, evidently, which happens to the elements in the Sphere, and generally under the influence of Love, is their mixing. Here again we may expect unclarity, since the word μίγνυσθαι can in Archaic Greek be used to mean "draw near to," as well as "mingle with"; but there is sufficient evidence to indicate that mixture is specially in point in Empedocles. The notion of mixing appears in a simile, presumably illustrating the work of Love, at B23[41] and is explicitly associated with Love's effects at B71.3 (κιρναμένων). It is pretty clearly indicated by the state of the Sphere, in which individual elements cannot be distinguished. Does this mean that Empedocles anticipated Aristotle's theory of unity by mixture? In detail clearly not: Aristotle was justly proud of the theory of mixture clarified for the first time at *De generatione et corruptione A* 10. Nothing so sophisticated as this should be attributed to Empedocles, whether or not we subscribe to the common view that he held explicitly a particulate theory of matter.[42] Was there any kind of unity by mixture known to common speech, before Aristotle used the term in his own technical sense? At least one passage suggests that there was. The Hippocratic treatise *On the Ancient Medicine* contains in its sixteenth chapter (Littré I pp. 607–608) the statement that, when you mix certain powers (opposite ones) together, they are no longer φανερά and cause no harm. But, when they are unmixed, separated off, and on their own, they cause harm. When a man feeds on good plain food he comes to no harm because the food is "neither unmixed nor strong, but a whole both one and simple." This means that thorough mixture of things with different powers produces a simple whole, whose effect and power is neutral and homogeneous throughout. The Hippocratic writer was scarcely troubled with the ontology of his "powers," still less with the logical difficulties in the notion of mixture as expounded and solved by Aristotle in the *De generatione et corruptione*. But he has a practical notion of what it is to mix two things together to produce, in effect, one. There is no reason why the same sort of plain common-sense notion of unifying mixture should not have been known to Empedocles. It is plausible to believe, even though Empedocles did not associate his elements with opposites as carefully and exactly as did Philistion,[43] that he could readily accept that thorough mixture would cause them all to cancel each other out, so far as perception was concerned. It would, in fact, produce a species of what Aristotle would have called unity of kind, and what we have labelled homogeneity.

There is not in the Sphere strict material homogeneity, such as Aristotle could apparently associate with mixture by using the distinction between actual and potential. All four elements are quite simply present in it. The elements are designated or described at B7 as $\dot{\alpha}\gamma\acute{\epsilon}\nu\eta\tau\alpha$, and at B11 and B12 Empedocles follows Parmenides in denying roundly both that anything can come to be from what is not and that what is can be destroyed. The elements persist in an endless round of mixture and dissolution (B8–9), in the macrocosm certainly no less than in the microcosm. It is inconceivable for Empedocles that any part of any element should become anything but a part of that element, except in what he expressly says (at B9) is a non-philosophical sense of "become." If Empedocles held not only the milder position that an observer of normal human perception could not distinguish the elements in the Sphere but also the severer doctrine that no observer in principle could ever, however hawk-eyed, distinguish the elements, then he would run up against divisibility problems. But it is not likely that Empedocles thought the matter through that far, in his ignorance of Zenonian arguments. Strictly speaking, it might appear that the Sphere is no more a homogeneity than the reign of Strife, however that climax be conceived. Yet it is not only apparent homogeneity that has been achieved by the mixing process. The world is in a sense more genuinely homogeneous than it was under the separating force of Strife, in that no sizeable part of the Sphere is of different composition from any other sizeable part.[44] Under Strife, it is after all true, the whole is further from being one by homogeneity than it is under the complete sway of Love. Under Strife there are undoubtedly large masses of pure or virtually pure fire, air, earth, and water, each substantially different from the others, with more or less well-defined breaks between them; under Love there is no such differentiation.

The situation is somewhat similar with regard to unity of continuity. The denial of void by Empedocles, at B17.33 and at B13–14, following Parmenides' denial of not-Being, is unequivocal. So there are no fewer gaps of emptiness in the Sphere than out of it; there are no gaps of this sort at any time. But again it is fair to say that there is a higher degree of continuity in the Sphere than in the reign of Strife. Nowhere in the Sphere is there any clearly marked or delimited difference between the matter on one side and that on the other. (I assume again that Empedocles ignored problems of divisibility in this connection.) So the Sphere is in a sense more continuous than the realm of Strife. But the higher degree of continuity obtains only because the higher degree of homogeneity obtains. This is continuity as homogeneity.

Altogether more complicated is the question how far Love tends to produce a unity in the sense of a whole. Clearly, in the microcosm this is precisely what Love does, and the point is elaborated below. But in the Sphere? It would seem at first sight that in the Sphere we have one whole, and that, as Strife grows, we have a progressive tendency to the production of four discrete wholes. Nor is this only true in the sense that the Sphere obliterates perceptible lines of distinction: the Sphere is a single organism, and a single divine being,[45] and might therefore, despite Empedocles' metaphorical nails and glue, rank as a whole $\phi\acute{v}\sigma\epsilon\iota$. Four wholes to the one organic whole might well be termed a unification. And yet there is a sense in which the Sphere is less aptly called a whole than the reign of Strife. In the Sphere there is the utmost possible disorder of the "elements"; in the reign of Strife there is order, and the more complete we imagine that reign, the more complete the order becomes. The $\kappa\acute{o}\sigma\mu\sigma\varsigma$ appears, in the sense that everything is separated out of the higgledy-piggledy Sphere into proper discrete parts, each in its own clear position. The Sphere might well be described more in terms of Aristotle's heap than as a proper whole of parts, whereas the reign of Strife, though "harmonious" would be a misnomer, evidently results precisely in a whole of discrete parts arrayed in some order. If Aristotle is to be believed—and he and Simplicius quote plausibly in this context[46]—the order under Strife is a chance order, not produced by anything which Aristotle would recognize as a natural motion. But, nevertheless, the notion of a whole of parts can scarcely be excluded on this ground from the description of Strife's climax. As we have seen, Empedocles probably gave no account of the return (if any) from the reign of Strife to the present world, fit to receive living creatures at the hands of Love. There is probably little, if any, substantial difference between Strife's climax and the world we see around us, except that it has now received living creatures. It is not easy to believe that, as a disciple and admirer of Pythagoras, Empedocles looked on such a world as a disorderly heap.[47]

But if we turn to the microcosm our point of view changes. Love is innate in men's bodies and causes them to $\phi\acute{\iota}\lambda\alpha$ $\phi\rho\sigma\nu\epsilon\hat{\iota}\nu$ (B17.23) and ἄρθμια ἔργα τελεῖν. Since Love has among her titles Aphrodite (in this as in other contexts) and is ἔμφυτος ἄρθροις, it would appear that we have here a reference to sexual love.[48] The sexes in Greek "mingle," just as Empedocles' elements did in the macrocosm.[49] Possibly heterosexuality was the source of Empedocles' idea of Love operating between different things. But Love has in the fragments other functions among mortal things, the most important of which is to make them ordered wholes. The passages concerned deserve examination, and nearly all are highly controversial.

The first is B20:

> τοῦτο μὲν ἂν βροτέων μελέων ἀριδείκετον ὄγκον·
> ἄλλοτε μὲν Φιλότητι συνερχόμεν' εἰς ἓν ἅπαντα
> γυῖα, τὰ σῶμα λέλογχε, βίου θαλέθοντος ἐν ἀκμῇ·
> ἄλλοτε δ' αὖτε κακῇσι διατμηθέντ' Ἐρίδεσσι
> πλάζεται ἄνδιχ' ἕκαστα περὶ ῥηγμῖνι βίοιο.
> ὣς δ' αὔτως θάμνοισι καὶ ἰχθύσιν ὑδρομελάθροις
> θηρσί τ' ὀρειλεχέεσσιν ἰδὲ πτεροβάμοσι κύμβαις.

The beauty of these lines should not blind us to their difficulty. The most diverse interpretations have been put upon them, and we seem no nearer to agreement than at the rise of modern philology. Within this century the lines have been interpreted as referring to sexual intercourse, to youth and old age, or death, to the formation of creatures from isolated limbs in zoogony, to the health and sickness of the individual.[50] Such diversity as this among reputable scholars might seem to be cause for despair. But inspection shows, I believe, that only one of these views is strictly tenable.

Empedocles is illustrating something. He says "This" (whatever "this" may be)[51] "is conspicuous in the mass of mortal limbs." It follows that the succeeding lines are unlikely to refer to a special doctrine of Empedocles' own, since such a doctrine would not supply an acceptable illustration for his readers. One might, I suppose, imagine as a let-out that Empedocles has already expounded the doctrine (say) of the growth of limbs into bodies under Love's influence. But what feature of his more general doctrine will have been so obscure that it needs illustration from this detail? Can it be that Empedocles gives a general statement of the doctrine of the growing together of limbs and then says that this is what happens to mortals? I doubt it; for the word ἀριδείκετον would be inappropriate. It would be understandable for Empedocles to give a general statement and then say "That is what happens to mortals, and likewise to fish, plants, etc.," but it is not likely that he would say, with an air of proving his point, "you can see that, it is *conspicuous* in the cases of mortals, plants, and fishes." This hypothesis offends probability further by making little sense of the contrast between βίου θαλέθοντος ἐν ἀκμῇ and περὶ ῥηγμῖνι βίοιο. βίου θαλέθοντος ἐν ἀκμῇ surely cannot be anything but a reference to a time of life. It certainly cannot mean "when Life (note the capital letter) is flourishing and the creation of animals is at its height." Nor, meaning "in the prime of life," does it make a good contrast with the expression περὶ ῥηγμῖνι βίοιο, if that expression refers to the life of the species rather than of the individual. If Empedocles meant this, he was intolerably obscure, not only to us but also to his intended reader(s). "Possible, but hardly probable," must be the verdict on this interpretation. At least any view removing the need to postulate such obscurity will be welcome.[52]

I see no reason to bring health and sickness into the discussion, nor sexual intercourse; neither seems to make good sense of the contrast between the prime of life and its shores or outer extremities. One can be unhealthy, or quarrel with one's wife, in one's prime.[53] But a reference to the orderly and perfect wholeness of the normal body in its prime, and its dissolution in and around life's end into what is relatively a mere heap, seems to me entirely fitting. A recent objection is that πλάζεται is an unsuitable word for such dissolution,[54] and it is probably this word which gave rise to the evolutionary interpretation.[55] Yet it is worth considering whether Empedocles was incapable of using such a metaphor in a passage rich already in imagery. If one squarely puts this question, the answer must surely be "No." If Love not only binds but also glues and nails, surely Strife, which already "cuts apart," can hardly be denied the power to make things "wander" in separation. One must simply get used to treating Empedocles as a poet, and not merely as a philosopher.

The second passage on which some ground needs to be cleared is B26.3–7:

αὐτὰ γὰρ ἔστιν ταῦτα, δι' ἀλλήλων δὲ θέοντα
γίνοντ(αι) ἄνθρωποί τε καὶ ἄλλων ἔθνεα θηρῶν
ἄλλοτε μὲν Φιλότητι συνερχόμεν' εἰς ἕνα κόσμον
ἄλλοτε δ' αὖ δίχ' ἕκαστα φορούμενα Νείκεος ἔχθει,
εἰσόκεν ἓν συμφύντα τὸ πᾶν ὑπένερθε γένηται.

The interpretation of this passage hinges on the meaning assigned to line 7. If, as is usual, we understand this whole passage to speak of the cosmic alternation, we are faced with Hölscher's point that it is ridiculous to think of one and many alternating until unity be attained.[56] No more complete unity than the Sphere can have been possible for Empedocles, so we are left with the statement that Sphere and Strife alternate until the Sphere is reached—a statement of singular absurdity. The only hope of rescuing this approach is to transpose lines 6 and 7; but the transposition is needless and would be intolerably arbitrary. Nevertheless I admit I do not find Hölscher's own explanation convincing, as it goes against the run of the syntax. Taking ἓν συμφύντα to mean "the things that have grown to be one," he understands this of mortals which are then destroyed. In isolation such omission of the article is possible, but this line is far from isolated. The subject of the sentence is αὐτὰ ταῦτα, and the main verb of the group of clauses from δι' ἀλλήλων to γένηται is γίνοντ(αι) in line 4. Attached to that main verb are three successive participles, θέοντα, συνερχόμενα, φορούμενα, qualifying that subject, and hence with full verbal force and without article. The further participle συμφύντα without article in a temporal clause is most naturally and smoothly taken as also qualifying that subject, which is then also the subject of γένηται. The poet offers no signpost of a change of subject. I am entirely in agreement with Heinz Munding[57] that the "unity" of line 7 is different from that of line 5 and that it is marked as such by the adverbial τὸ πᾶν. The line may be translated "until having grown together to be entirely one they are submerged." The sense is that the elements go on giving rise to various creatures under the growing sway of Love, but being dissolved in turn by the (waning) power of Strife, until in the end (of this dispensation at least) the power of Strife declines to vanishing point and the complete unity of the Sphere is reached, when the elements are no longer discernible.

What Love does in the microcosm in the two fragments just discussed is to create a unity of wholeness on each occasion. By mixing the elements together in the right proportions for the right parts of the body and by fashioning the body from these limbs, Love acts as a craftsman.[58] Whence the descriptions of Cypris' activities at B73, B75, and B86: in the creation of eyes, of boned creatures, of "forms" in general, Love is represented as doing a creative craftsman's job, and in the similes of B34 and B23 her functions are compared with those of particular crafts. This impression is reinforced by the use of such words and phrases (not in themselves probative) as πεπήγασιν ἁρμοσθέντα and κολλῇσιν ἀρηρότα—not to speak of the name 'Ἁρμονίη, clearly here with the idea of fitness at least as prominent as that of mere attachment. All this may be further strengthened by the use of ἕνα κόσμον at B26.5 of the result of Love's action. When Love acts on the elements, and they form animals and men, they make one cosmos, on each occasion one single ordered whole. They receive, as Aristotle would have put it, a definite form (see especially B73 εἴδεα ποιπνύουσα). Of course, a certain degree of homogeneity among the parts is a necessary condition of this form. But it is not this homogeneity which of itself constitutes them a "cosmos," but rather the form itself, their appropriateness for their respective positions. Love is no mere mixer, but a good workman. Here, moreover, in the microcosm, the question of Strife forming a whole does not arise. In the microcosm, apart from the symmetrical statement of B17.1–5, it is the function of Strife to destroy, and not, with one odd exception,[59] to create. So, for example, at B9 εὖτε δ' ἀποκρινθῶσι, τὸ δ' αὖ δυσδαίμονα πότμον (sc. λέγουσι). What mortals call ill-fated death occurs when the elements are dispersed. The same point is clearly implied at B20.4–5. A whole generation of creatures may, it is true, be destroyed by the action of Love on a cosmic scale in the cycle; but Love is nowhere said to destroy an individual, an action appropriate rather to Strife. There is here a slight but understandable discrepancy between microcosm and macrocosm, of which Empedocles may have been aware; for he makes the point explicitly at B26.7 that after a series of what mortals would call creations and destructions there is a total destruction of lesser organisms, destruction due to the unifying force which produces the divine Sphere.

Evidently, Empedocles would not have added τὸ πᾶν at B26.7 if he had not thought the Sphere's unity more complete than the unity of the individual creatures. He may have had in mind a greater (perhaps more organic) degree of wholeness or of homogeneity; he may have thought some homogeneity necessary for the wholeness of animals, and have had both in mind: βουγενῆ ἀνδρόπρωρα could plausibly be thought lacking in homogeneity as well as in the unity of a perfect whole. The Sphere may be completely one either because it possesses a kind or kinds of unity that creatures of the microcosm do not or because it possesses a higher degree of the same kind(s). In either case, no confusion in Empedocles' thought on the subject is yet demonstrable; but, on the other hand, there is nothing to show that he had thought the subject through and clearly distinguished the different types of unity concerned.

DIFFICULTIES IN B22

B22 is not so easy to sort out. I reproduce the text of Diels and Kranz:

ἄρθμια μὲν γὰρ ταῦτα ἑαυτῶν πάντα μέρεσσιν,
ἠλέκτωρ τε χθών τε καὶ οὐρανὸς ἠδὲ θάλασσα,
ὅσσα φιν ἐν θνητοῖσιν ἀποπλαχθέντα πέφυκεν.
ὡς δ' αὔτως ὅσα κρῆσιν ἐπαρκέα μᾶλλον ἔασιν
5 ἀλλήλοις ἔστερκται ὁμοιωθέντ' Ἀφροδίτῃ.
ἐχθρὰ <δ' ἃ> πλεῖστον ἀπ' ἀλλήλων διέχουσι μάλιστα

γέννῃ τε κρήσει τε καὶ εἴδεσιν ἐκμάκτοισι,
πάντῃ συγγίνεσθαι ἀήθεα καὶ μάλα λυγρά
Νείκεος ἐννεσίῃσιν, ὅτι σφίσι γένναν ἔοργεν (?).

The fragment opens with the assertion that the main masses of the elements have an attraction for their respective parts scattered among mortal creatures. Similarly, Empedocles continues, those things which are more helpful in mixture are loved by each other, after having been made similar by Love.[60] On the other hand, there is hostility between the things that differ most from each other in race, mixture, and moulded form; these are altogether unaccustomed to come together and are very baneful, on the instructions of Strife which (if the emendations of Diels and Panzerbieter are anywhere near the truth) created them. With this the fragment comes tantalizingly to an end.

A major difficulty is that it is not normally Love's function to make X like Y but rather to produce a mixture X plus Y which is internally alike. Another is that it would appear that the attraction mentioned in the opening lines between the elements and their parts is implied to be the work of Love, whereas normally Strife attracts like to like, in so far as this function belongs to either cosmic force. There is no great difficulty in the "like-to-like" idea itself.[61] The difficulty lies rather in the clear implication that it is the work of Love as opposed to Strife, in the implication that the elements are ἄρθμια to their own parts in a sense closely analogous to that of ἔστερκται.[62] Further, Strife should be the force which drives apart what is different, acting on dissimilars to force or keep them apart; it should not be Strife which makes things different in the first place. Love and Strife are normally different phases of the relationship between dissimilars and never elsewhere act on similars.

Such complications have called forth various explanations. One possibility, at least, has rightly been rejected since Bignone,[63] namely that ἑαυτῶν in the first line meant ἀλλήλων, as in some other fifth-century writers. If ἑαυτῶν does mean ἀλλήλων here, then the things more helpful in mixture, which love each other when made alike by Love, behave in the same way as the elements. The elements are, of course, dissimilars, though they could no doubt be made in a certain sense ὁμοῖα by Aphrodite. The ἐπαρκέα κρῆσιν must, however, be compounds similar to each other, because ἐχθρά (in contrast to the ἐπαρκέα) are things unlike each other in mixture (among other respects). So we have Unlikes being compared (ὡς δ' αὔτως ...) with Likes and contrasted with Unlikes—which is not impossible, but seems uncharacteristically clumsy. To accept it would be not only tasteless but also against the odds, for ἑαυτούς is comparatively infrequently equivalent to ἀλλήλους.

An explanation of how similars can be attracted is offered by Guthrie,[64] who expounds the whole passage as referring to the doctrine of pores. Substances whose pores do not fit readily into one another are hard to mix, according to Empedocles, and Guthrie aptly cites B91, οἴνῳ ... μᾶλλον ἐνάρθμιον, αὐτὰρ ἐλαίῳ / οὐκ ἐθέλει. Applied to B22, which in language it resembles, this makes, at first glance, acceptable sense. B22.4–5 can be understood as referring to mixtures with pores which fit, and the ἐχθρά are mixtures whose pores do not fit; this Guthrie tops off by referring B22.1–2 to Empedocles' alleged particulate theory of matter and adding "Hence the attraction of like to like." But there are difficulties even in this undeniably attractive interpretation. It would seem that though the mixture and even the origin of compounds are relevant to this kind of context, the εἴδεα ἔκμακτα, "moulded forms," are quite irrelevant. What has the shape of a compound to do with its pores? I do not think that we have here a mere metaphor, to be dismissed as poetical embellishment; it is the third member of a list couched in plain straightforward Greek. If ἐκμάκτοισι (a ἅπαξ λεγόμενον) has the poetical function of adding an attractive and doubtless original epithet to εἴδεσιν, it has the prosaically expository function of making doubly clear which sense of εἶδος Empedocles was using. "Shapes" must be the sense—and yet on Guthrie's interpretation shapes are irrelevant. There is a further objection. The things in the universe which are most unalterably unlike each other are the elements; if things unlike are unable to fit together, then how are the mixtures of lines 4ff formed in the first instance? It is hard to deny pores to the elements. We thus remove one inconsistency from B22 only to throw new emphasis on another, and throw it, as we have seen, in peculiar language.

Another attempt is that of Munding.[65] He holds that the subject of B22 is the limbs which wander about in the initial stages of zoogony. Just as the elements are attracted to their own parts, these limbs, when made by Love into shapes sufficiently alike to fit together into a body, do indeed fit together. But the limbs not alike are rejected and the monsters fall apart. This ingenious theory is weakened by the air the whole fragment has of being a general statement. It accounts most elegantly for the triad γέννῃ τε κρήσει τε καὶ εἴδεσιν ἐκμάκτοισι but fails to show why the general statement about the elements and their parts should not be followed by another general statement about mixtures. That the parts of the elements should be referred to in the most general terms by ὅσσα in line 3 makes it difficult to believe that the relative pronouns of lines 4 and (probably) 6 have a more restricted reference.

C. W. Müller's explanation is no less ingenious.[66] He suggests that Love, from her nature, should subsist equally between Likes and Unlikes.

Any attraction at all is to be put down to Love, any repulsion to Strife. It just so happens that nothing can hate its like, whereas friendship can exist between likes or unlikes. Müller goes so far as to suggest that in the Sphere *all* things are one, and not only Unlikes. He suggests that in the Sphere "zwischen *gleich* und *ungleich*, zwischen Feuer- Luft- Wasser- und Erdartigen nicht mehr unterschieden wird."[67] But such an abolition of the distinction between like and unlike is nowhere suggested by Empedocles or his reporters, and it is only in a limited sense that the distinction between the elements vanishes. The attraction of like to like tends in Empedocles, as a rule, to produce not unity but plurality, at best a differentiated whole, whose wholeness is inexplicit. It is the reverse side of the same coin whose obverse is Strife between the different elements, and Empedocles was contradicting himself if he put it down to Love. It needs to be added that, if like-to-like has a venerable ancestry in epic, so does Strife between Likes; κεραμεὺς κεραμεῖ κοτέει (Hesiod *Erga* 25) is hardly less well known than ὡς αἰεὶ τὸν ὁμοῖον ἄγει θεὸς εἰς τὸν ὁμοῖον (Homer *Odyssey* 17.218). The notion of repulsion between likes is as old as the notion of their attraction. Why does Empedocles not put the former down to Strife, instead of having Love attract the Unlikes? It seems to me that Müller would not find it easy to answer this question. I suggest that the creative power of heterosexual passion had something to do with it, but that would not suit Müller's explanation of B22 at all.

In view of what seem to me the difficulties besetting these various attacks on the problem, I suggest another. The suggestion is tentative, hypothetical, and doubtless rash. I put it forward (let my critics remember) with the utmost diffidence, after long hesitation and frequent doubt. But I put it before the world of scholarship nevertheless as a serious hypothesis for consideration.

Suppose similars to be attracted to each other. They may then form a unified whole, where before the attraction there was a plurality of discrete wholes. So far as the process of forming one whole is concerned, Love can have the same effect on similars as on things that differ. Indeed, in one pertinent case Love is more successful with things to some extent similar than with things different. This case is that of the limbs, where the fundamental similarities between the limbs of the complete organism represent one of the factors responsible for its relatively stable organic wholeness. The case of the limbs need not be the only one. The same point might apply to less complex mixtures or even to the elements. A number of parts of the same element very readily form, when brought together, a single whole, in a way they do not when scattered abroad; they are, when brought together, more apt to have what Aristotle would have called a definite form. In this sense an element could be, under the sway of a force attracting each to its own parts, united, made more of a unified whole, and, by the same token, in a sense more continuous. The formula about the unifying effect of Love is one of which Empedocles never tires: it is not difficult to believe that he could be seduced by the word "one" into letting Love produce unity of wholeness between similars, and not only between dissimilars.

If similars are mixed—the usual effect, in physical terms, of Empedocles' Love—the effect on them is somewhat different from the effect on dissimilars. When dissimilars are mixed, as we have seen, a measure of homogeneity is produced above what was present before. But, when similars are mixed, the resulting progress towards homogeneity is the less, the more similar are the ingredients to start with. The more similar the similars, the less the difference in homogeneity between the first state and the last. When similars are mixed, the production of unity of homogeneity is, outside the Sphere, hardly in point. It is, however, in point when the normal action of Love between the dissimilars (especially the several elements) takes place. If Empedocles had clearly seen this difference between the kinds of unity at stake in the two cases, he would, I think, have been less willing to conflate the two. He would have been just that much more arbitrary in his decision to have Love act between similars in B22. The decision was to some extent arbitrary anyhow; but on the assumption, plausible on general historical grounds, that he had no clear analysis of unity at his disposal or in his head, then it becomes one degree less arbitrary. It may be retorted that Empedocles was something of a muddle-head anyway, and the charge would not be altogether easy to rebut. And a poet can be forgiven for an occasional peculiar use of his favourite symbols. But the analysis of B22 seems slightly to favour the already plausible supposition that in talking about unity and plurality Empedocles did not know what he was talking about.

It may be anticlimactic, but there is still the awkward phrase ὁμοιωθέντ' Ἀφροδίτῃ to be accounted for. It is not certain whether the things more helpful in mixture are made alike by Love before they embrace each other or as part of the process. But, in any case, what seems to be meant is that Love produces relative homogeneity and that out of the relatively homogeneous a whole is formed more easily and stably than out of things widely differing in composition or (on occasion) shape. Strife, on the other hand, though often producing through the combination of similars a higher degree of homogeneity in a given space, will be regarded as opposed to mixture, and hence as producing a lower degree of homogeneity; and the results of its work will be harder to put together into a whole—though not, of course, impossible. This particular expression of Empedocles' will not of itself help us to find a completely decisive answer to the question whether Empedocles knew about different kinds of unity.[68]

ONE AND MANY

Parmenides, we may recall, is sometimes alleged to have insisted or argued that what was strictly one could not become many.[69] Another version of this thesis is that he argued that a unity which was "ultimate" or "original" could not give rise to a plurality. Empedocles (the story goes) invented an ultimate plurality in answer to this argument.[70] In fact, however, Empedocles supplies one of the strongest reasons against the first version of this thesis and is barely compatible with the second. He not only once, but repeatedly, asserts precisely that what was one becomes many and vice versa. Not only in the world at large but also in living creatures, a unity is formed from a plurality, and the unity dissolves again into a plurality. Parmenides, on the first version, is supposed to argue against all becoming, but especially against one particular kind of becoming, namely, against a unity giving rise to a plurality. Yet Empedocles accepts that becoming is to be ruled out, and spoken of only in concession to popular usage: it is only and specifically the growth of a unity from a plurality (and vice versa) that he will allow (without mentioning that a special concession to popular usage is necessary for this). The specific acceptance by Empedocles of the very kind of becoming which Parmenides is supposed on this theory to have specially forbidden is striking. Coming hard on the heels of doubts about the passage of Parmenides where this alleged argument is supposed to be found, this should go far to complete the destruction of confidence in it. One thing at least is certain: it was not in obedience to an argument denying that unity could give rise to plurality that Empedocles postulated a plural number of existing things. If there was such an argument known to him, then Empedocles repeatedly contradicted it.

It is not certain how seriously one is meant to take the second version of the argument, since its authors are not quite consistent in their application of it.[71] But it may be remarked that certainly an ultimate unity could not give rise to a plurality after Parmenides. What concerns us is whether that point was due to the *ultimateness* of the unity forbidding *becoming* or to the *unity* specifically inhibiting the development of a *plurality*. Here the answer appears to be that it was not the unity of the ultimate unity which forbade the rise of plurality; in Parmenides there is, as we have seen, no place where such an argument is reasonably to be found; and Empedocles admits that a unity (admittedly not ultimate, if that means "real") can and does become a plurality. What is more, as has already been observed, neither the second version of the alleged argument nor the first is necessary to the understanding of the development of fifth-century thought about the world. A veto on becoming was in itself sufficient to rule out the development of a variety of things from a single stuff.

If a reason be sought why post-Parmenidean thinkers turned to a pluralistic explanation of the world's origins, it is to be sought in terms of reconciling with Eleatic logic not merely the data of common sense, but also the traditional type of cosmogony.[72] Cosmogony had it that the world began with a single stuff. The Parmenidean arguments against becoming made it impossible to start with a single stuff and end up with a variety. So one had to have a plurality of different stuffs to start with. These stuffs, of course, had to persist into the world as we see it; they could not perish, for their reality prohibited it. So the number and nature of the original stuffs now depended on one's analysis of the number and nature of the substances needed to account for the variety of present phenomena. Empedocles evidently thought that the present distribution of the major cosmic masses necessitated the postulation of four different "roots" as opposed to Parmenides' apparent assumption (in the account of mortal opinions) that two substances would serve as a minimum. That is all. Neither Empedocles nor (as we shall see) any other later Presocratic except the Atomists betrayed the slightest embarrassment at a unity turning into a plurality. There is no evidence outside Atomism that this particular kind of becoming was crucial in scientific development in the post-Parmenidean period.

The "problem" of one thing *being* many also appears to have failed, so far as our evidence goes, to embarrass Empedocles. The Sphere, though undeniably "one," is strictly composed of four things. No word of any prohibition of (strict) heterogeneity in the composition of something called "one" appears to have troubled Empedocles' ears. Of course he is concerned to play down as far as possible the strict heterogeneity of the Sphere, in order to bring his cosmogony that much nearer to the traditional development of varied world from single stuff. That may well be the historical origin of the statement that the elements cannot be discerned in the Sphere—the motif recurs in Anaxagoras. There is no need to believe that he was affected by any prohibition of the combination of unity and plurality. Further, he talks of Love as bringing the elements together in the microcosm into one ordered whole, and there also he shows no signs of inhibitions on combining one and many. Each one ordered whole has many parts and many ingredients, but Empedocles displays no perturbation at this obvious fact. However much such problems might trouble later quibblers, they do not appear to have entered Empedocles' head in the generation after Parmenides.

VII

ZENO OF ELEA

Present terms of reference would, if taken strictly, include Zeno's arguments against plurality and exclude those against motion. Indeed, the most detailed treatment is reserved for the arguments against plurality. But the total separation of the two sets of arguments is inadvisable, for three reasons. "The apparent fact of motion," writes Sir David Ross,[1] "involving the occupation of different places at different times, is a *prima facie* evidence of plurality"; one must reckon with the possibility that "Zeno tried to deprive pluralism of this apparent support by proving the non-existence of motion; and this he proved by means of the absurd consequences which he held to follow if motion be assumed to exist." Further, the opinion is current that Zeno's arguments against motion constitute a dilemma whose horns are alternative ways of analysing the plurality of the sensible world; some have supposed even that the arguments against motion are linked with those against plurality in a complex chain of argument driving the supporters of plurality from one position to another. Finally, there is ancient authority for the suggestion that Zeno used one line of argument in particular, namely, that from dichotomy, to attack directly both plurality and motion.

It is not quite certain whether the two groups of arguments, one preserved in Aristotle,[2] the other mainly by Simplicius,[3] come from the same original book of Zeno's. Most of our information on the nature of Zeno's writings derives from Plato's *Parmenides*,[4] and it is hard to set limits to Plato's powers of fantasy or irony. But Plato would imply that Zeno, by the dramatic date of the dialogue, had written only one book, and that directed against the assumption of a plurality. If Zeno did indeed throughout his life write only this one book, then it is necessary to assume that Plato represents both Socrates and Zeno as assenting to the proposition cited above from Ross; not that there is any difficulty in this assumption. If Zeno wrote more than one book, then he may well have been unusual among Presocratic philosophers—though not unique. The titles of other books of his handed down by the Alexandrians are unconvincing.[5] The proper verdict here is "non liquet"; if the theory that all the arguments together form a connected whole must start in this respect from slippery ground, the same is true of the assumption that the two main groups of arguments are strictly separate. Our ignorance does not stop here; we do not know the order of Zeno's arguments in his original text and can deduce but little from the order in which Aristotle and others mention them.[6] If the order in our sources is significant at all, that significance can only be proved by the inner structure and economy of the arguments themselves.

ZENO AND THE PYTHAGOREANS

Many scholars have held the structure of the arguments to be evidence that Zeno's attack was directed solely against the Pythagoreans. It would be tedious to repeat here the arguments adduced by other scholars, from Zeller onwards,[7] against this interpretation, and for the most part it will be ignored. There is virtually no evidence for it either in the recorded nature of Zeno's arguments or in our scanty records of the early development of Pythagoreanism. The theory could hardly be convincing until Pythagoreanism has been satisfactorily reconstructed without the help of Zeno's arguments in such a way as to make Zeno relevant to Pythagorean views and irrelevant to common views; and this prior condition has not been fulfilled. Only one piece of evidence will here be mentioned, namely, the relevant fragment of Eudemus (37a Wehrli; Lee, *Zeno*, no. 5). Zeno is there alleged to have stated that, *if* anyone could tell him what the one was, Zeno would be able to talk about existing things in the plural. From this account it is often inferred that "the polemic of Zeno is clearly directed in the first instance against a certain view of the unit."[8] But closer inspection shows that, if Zeno directed his arguments against one particular view of the unit, then he would not be entitled to say, in effect, that *no one* could produce a theory, immune from his arguments, of the units forming a plurality. So far from confirming the anti-Pythagorean view of Zeno's argument, this passage, in so far as it is valid evidence at all and not mere hearsay,[9] represents Zeno as arguing the impossibility of *any* view of the unit. All that this statement of Zeno's would require his opponents to believe is the common or garden supposition that a plurality must be made up of a plural number of individuals. It implies no special view concerning the nature of these individuals. The same goes for Alexander's paraphrase quoted by Simplicius at *in Physica* 99.12ff.

There may still be felt a temptation to concede that Zeno's paradoxes, though valid against the plurality of common sense, and intended to be so valid, were also valid especially against the Pythagoreans and directed especially against them. This view of the arguments, whether in whole or in part, has been adopted by some distinguished Hellenists[10] and has not been accorded, to my knowledge, the distinct criticism it deserves. It looks at first sight like a possible middle way, and indeed it remains, at least concerning some of Zeno's lines of thought, possible. But it is no less conjectural than the other view, shares with it some disadvantages, and adds some further drawbacks.

J. E. Raven, for example, finding a special anti-Pythagorean significance in the arguments, argues that to suppose it merely accidental is to do an injustice to Zeno. He adds that "wishing to give them as wide an interest and applicability as possible, he couched them in the most general terms, and so left his various pluralist opponents to read into them as much or as little significance as they in fact possessed against their particular variety of pluralism."[11] Now, the procedure thus attributed to Zeno is a curious and implausible one for an undoubtedly acute thinker. Ex hypothesi his arguments are valid against only (say) one school of opponents. From this it follows that they are not valid when expressed in general terms. But, nevertheless, Zeno proceeds to couch them in general terms, a course resulting in invalid logic and calculated to confuse the issues and/or to deceive the common reader: this in full cognizance of what he is doing. If Zeno on purpose put a valid argument in terms that made it invalid, then truly οὗτος θεωρεῖ φορτικῶς. The only obvious way out of this difficulty is to suppose that Zeno's arguments were valid not only against the Pythagoreans but also against the general popular conception of a plurality. It has, however, been insufficiently noted that, in that case, not only is there no evidence but there could in principle be no evidence within the arguments themselves for their anti-Pythagorean "significance." The crux of this matter is that the arguments are either valid against the supposed popular position or not—there is no middle way here. If the arguments are thus valid, then there is no need to import Pythagoreanism into the discussion; if the arguments are not so valid, then Zeno was being certainly foolish and perhaps dishonest in couching them in such terms as to make it look as though he was demolishing the general conception. The alleged procedure could only leave a hole gaping in the arguments—unless it served to deceive. A further prop to be knocked away is the argument that "only so [that is, on Raven's view], it seems, can we satisfactorily explain the diversity of interpretation that these arguments have been shown to admit."[12] This argument would seem to presuppose an unusual infallibility in Zeno's interpreters.

Restatement of Raven's theory in a more immediately appetizing form does not make it in the end more palatable. One could, for example, rephrase it thus; "The Pythagorean position was regarded by Zeno as one particular statement of the popular view of plurality, perhaps the only explicit statement available; this being so, he would be justified in putting in general terms an argument directed against the Pythagorean view." But in the end this is as hard to swallow as Raven's own statement. There is no good reason to suppose that Zeno was concerned with any explicit analysis of plurality, rather than with the vague unanalysed belief that more than one thing exists. What is more, we are faced once again with a choice between two equally unpleasant alternatives; either the vague popular belief amounted to the same as the Pythagorean view, or it did not. If Pythagorean and popular beliefs did not amount to the same, then Zeno was being either foolish or dishonest in representing the general conception as demolished by arguments relevant only to the Pythagorean theory. If the two conceptions amounted to the same thing, then there could be in principle no internal evidence for Zeno's concern with one as well as with the other.

There seems to be a lingering impression that it is remarkable, and a coincidence worth following up, that a common interpretation of Pythagorean doctrine makes it the same as one of the hypotheses lying behind a Zenonian argument. This coincidence, however, whatever the truth of the interpretations of Pythagoreans or of Zeno which are concerned in it, is entirely unremarkable and should mislead nobody. The Pythagoreans are alleged to have confused the indivisibles of which an infinite number (according to Cantor) can make a finite magnitude, with those of which only a finite number make up a finite magnitude: they confuse, it is alleged, that which has no extension with that which is extended. In short, they are supposed to confuse the point and the atom (and, for good measure, the unit). But there are only three ways of dividing a finite magnitude which are not either absurd (such as an infinite number of divisible magnitudes with finite extension) or non-problematic (such as a finite number of divisible finite extensions). These three are as follows: (1) an infinite number of unextended indivisibles, (2) an infinite number of extended indivisibles, (3) a finite number of extended indivisibles.[13] Inspection shows that, apart from the single combination of (2) and (3), if any pair of arguments is based on divisibility assumptions one of the arguments will assume one member, and the other argument the second member, of each of the two pairs extended/unextended and divisible/indivisible. It is these two pairs of terms which the Pythagoreans are accused of confounding. So, if one were to suppose that Zeno did, oddly, attack a confusion by reducing each item to absurdity instead of by reducing the whole to contradiction, then any pair but one of divisibility arguments which he could produce based on different divisibility assumptions would do the trick. To show from internal evidence that he intended his particular combination to fulfil this purpose in this way is therefore in principle scarcely possible; for the coincidence between his arguments and the Pythagorean views could easily be nothing but coincidence. There are not many different types of view to choose from.

External evidence for anti-Pythagorean emphasis in Zeno's arguments is thin indeed; there is not the slightest reason to suppose that only Pythagoreans rather than ordinary people criticized Parmenides and made fun of him—even if Plato's account (*Parmenides* 128c–d) is historical: if our Zeno wrote a work later entitled "Against the Philosophers," that would neither prove that whoever bestowed the title (perhaps a Sceptic?) meant Pythagorean philosophers in particular nor even suggest that any of the extant arguments were taken from this work or section of a work.

Some of these considerations, though evidently not all, apply whenever particular arguments are assigned a special anti-Pythagorean force. A popular choice, supported by no less an authority than R. Mondolfo,[14] is to take the four arguments against motion and form of them a dilemma, in which the first horn directly attacks the Pythagorean conception of plurality as a collection of spatially extended and discrete units, and the second aims a blow at the alternative possibility that plural material objects are infinitely divisible. One reason why this is a specially enticing form of the anti-Pythagorean interpretation is that these four arguments have been interpreted as a dilemma by several scholars who did not accept their anti-Pythagorean intention.[15] But, though tempting, it is not yet fully convincing; for there is little evidence that Pythagoreans of so early a date held such views on the nature of a plurality as to reject any continuum. A further objection is similar to others already advanced against similar theories. If Zeno's alleged dilemma is indeed a true dilemma, in that one half or the other must be accepted, then the form of the argument could not be shown to have been influenced by contemporary Pythagoreanism, for it would remain a true dilemma whether or not one half of it were accepted explicitly by a contemporary group of thinkers. In this case the argument itself cannot supply internal evidence for its association with Pythagoreanism. If the dilemma is not a true one, and if either the alternatives are not mutually exclusive or they are not exhaustive, then the special association of one horn of the dilemma with a particular school such as the Pythagoreans will not remedy this situation; nor is there any obvious reason why it should seem to Zeno to remedy it. On neither of these two hypotheses can the anti-Pythagorean import, if any, be shown to have any impact on the form of the argument.

In any case, the dilemma interpretation of Zeno's arguments against motion rests, as is beginning to be recognized, on a shaky foundation. That both Racecourse and Achilles presuppose a continuous and infinitely divisible space for motion is fairly clear, whether or not Aristotle's other criticisms are justifiable. But it is much less clear that the last two arguments in Aristotle's account reduce to absurdity the presupposition that the plurality of material things is composed of indivisible and discrete *minima*. It is convenient to take the Flying Arrow first, before the Stadium.[16]

In the Flying Arrow, then, Zeno argues that when the arrow occupies a space equal to itself, it is at rest. It occupies a space equal to itself at any moment (literally "in the now"); thus, at any and every moment of its flight it is at rest. From this Zeno apparently deduces that, despite appearances, the arrow does not move at all but is at rest throughout its flight. The surface simplicity of this argument belies its extreme complexity. There is much disagreement between students of Zeno on the exact presuppositions underlying Zeno's inferences. To take two interpreters of high quality; Tannery, since he believed[17] that "each instant corresponds (in this argument) ... to a single determinate position of the arrow," presumably regarded the presupposed view of time to be that it is made up of *durationless instants*, which are limits of periods, and not infinitesimal periods; Max Black,[18] though uncertain what Aristotle intended, is himself inclined to think that Zeno referred to *moments* (small intervals), not to *instants* (unextended boundaries). It should not surprise us unduly that, whereas Tannery wanted to make of the Arrow and Stadium a pair of arguments from *alternative* premisses, Black, in support (I suppose) of his inclination to think that Zeno meant extended but indivisible moments, draws attention to the alleged attack on the *same* premiss in the Stadium and refers to the two arguments together as taking for granted that space, time, or motion consists of indivisible *parts*. The third possibility must be borne in mind, that, as N. B. Booth has put it, "Zeno's 'now' was quite vague; he just had not thought out whether his 'now' was an indivisible small period or a point of time."[19] But there has recently recurred the opinion that Zeno spoke himself of indivisible and extended moments. One hesitant expression of this view, by Black himself, is not, I think, backed by argument.[20] But a second one is, arguing that Aristotle himself believed Zeno to have been talking about extended moments. G. Vlastos has argued unabbreviably as follows: "I think we may infer from the context (239B1–4) that the 'indivisible nows' which Aristotle believes (*ibid.* 8–9; 31–33) are being 'assumed' by Zeno's argument are atomic stretches, not extensionless instants (i.e. that he is using the νῦν in the second of the two senses in which he employs the term: cf. n. 13 above). For since he says that there is neither motion nor rest in a 'now' in 239B1–4, where he is using 'now' in the sense of *instant*, the assumption that time consists of instants would have warranted in his view the conclusion that the Flying Arrow *is neither moving nor resting*. But he says (*ibid.* 30–32) that the assumption warrants the conclusion that the arrow *is resting*. So unless he is being very careless, he must be thinking of the 'nows' of the supposed assumption not as instants, but as atomic durations."[21] This is a powerful and subtle argument, but I do not find it wholly persuasive, because I do not find Aristotle's language by any means incredibly careless if he did say that "the assumption warrants the conclusion that the arrow is resting." Aristotle could easily, I think, have thought there were *two* mistakes in Zeno's argument: (1) that he treats time as made up of instants and (2) that he treats motion and rest as alike predicable of a body at an instant. In that case his error at 239b31 is merely to use παρά, meaning "*just* because of," when he should have used a word meaning nothing more than "because of." This particular carelessness seems to me much less incredible than that Aristotle should (a) without warning have used the word νῦν in two consecutive sentences (239a35–b4 and 239b5–9) in two very different senses and (b) failed to observe the point beautifully expressed by D. J. Furley, "These moments cannot have any magnitude at all without destroying the plausibility of the arrow's being stationary."[22] But if Aristotle's understanding is (for once) disputable, it seems to me that Zeno's own meaning is clear beyond reasonable doubt.

In answer to this point of view it could perhaps be urged that there are certain conditions under which it is at least not wholly implausible to believe an arrow stationary, or "occupying a place equal to itself," for a minute period of time. Black, for example, writes as follows: "In order to be in two or more places, the arrow would have to be in one place during part of the moment and in another during another part of the moment. But you maintain (and I agree for the sake of argument) that a moment is indivisible, i.e., that there cannot be such a thing as a part of a moment."[23] At this point, however, Zeno's opponent could interrupt with the suggestion that, if space also were made up of indivisible extensions, then one could cross such an extended indivisible space in an extended indivisible time. Why should we (the opponent could continue) suppose the arrow to be in one place and then in another during part of the moment? Surely the arrow is at one place at the beginning and is at another place at the end. If there are spatial as well as temporal indivisibles, then it can after all move from one place to the next. But it is never at any instant between at any point between; for there are no points or instants between—if there were, they would delimit parts of an indivisible. It may be that under these conditions the arrow should be thought of as stationary rather than moving, but this is a proposition needing argument, and not one that is ready-made. It may be that during such a moment the arrow occupies a space equal to itself, but again the proposition is far from evident. The occupation of different places at the two limits of the moment makes it just as plausible to regard the arrow as occupying a space *greater* than itself in Aristotle's sense. For the second limit of the moment may as plausibly be said to belong to the moment as not, and the answer to *this* conundrum, if there is an answer, could only emerge after lengthy debate.

Zeno could alternatively escape from this kind of argument by doubling back on his tracks. He could have it both ways: he could say that in crossing an extended indivisible space the arrow had not crossed a space at all—for no space is extended but indivisible. But this is scarcely plausible against any but stupid opponents, who are prepared to accept the right assumption at the right point of the argument. To suppose an argument constructed on these lines is to suppose a nonsense.

Or Zeno could here be arguing on the basis that there are indivisibles in time, but not in space. But then the statement that the arrow is occupying a space equal to itself becomes implausible, since during a time, however small, some part of space will be covered and in Aristotle's terminology the arrow will occupy a space longer than itself.

Suppose Zeno to have been arguing on the assumption that time, but not space, is infinitely divisible, and we deprive of bite another part of the argument as given by Aristotle. For then it is not true that in *every* extended moment the arrow occupies a space equal to itself. It is only true that the arrow occupies a space equal to itself in every moment during which, at the speed at which it happens to be flying, the space travelled is so short that a space would be covered (suppose such a thing possible) less than the supposed spatial minimum extension. It is a hard thing to make τὸ νῦν mean such a moment as this; and, if τὸ νῦν does have such a meaning, then ἔστι δ' ἀεὶ τὸ φερόμενον ἐν τῷ νῦν is difficult to understand and on the face of it less plausible than one would expect from Zeno.

Whatever the philosophical position one wishes to take up oneself on the outcome of the Flying Arrow, it appears that the argument can hardly stand in anything resembling at all closely the form it takes in Aristotle's text if it is understood as referring to the arrow's remaining stationary for a period, however stiflingly small. To this we may add the reluctance of the man in the street (supposing him to have been in Zeno's mind at all) to accept that a moving arrow is not moving during any part, however stiflingly small, of its flying time.

It deserves mention that, of the alternatives here laid out to the assumption that Zeno was speaking about instants rather than periods, only Black's avoids implications unfortunate for the symmetry of the whole chain of argument. For on the others, even supposing that the Stadium refers to divisibility problems and is directed against the supposition that both space and time are composed of extended indivisibles, the resulting symmetry is hardly exciting. For the second pair of arguments would then share one hypothesis (the finite divisibility of time *or* of space) but would employ different assumptions in the matter of the continuum, assumptions left untouched by the shared hypothesis. This would lead one to expect, by symmetry, that the first two arguments, the Achilles and the Dichotomy or Racecourse, would be so constructed as to test two similarly distinct hypotheses. But this is not in fact the case. It is doubtful whether either of the first pair of arguments involves any assumption whatever about the divisibility of time; but, if they do, then it is absolutely clear that the assumption must be the same in each case. In consequence, we are left with, at best, an uneasy and asymmetrical pattern in which the first two arguments deal with the same assumptions and the next two deal with suppositions different not only from the first two but from each other. It is difficult to comprehend why such "evidence" as this from "symmetry" should ever have helped to persuade a generation of scholars that Aristotle's account of the fourth paradox was fundamentally mistaken or why it should now persuade us that the way in which Aristotle most probably understood the third paradox was not correct.

But, if the Flying Arrow argument rests, as Aristotle appears to imply, on the hypothesis of instants indivisible because they are without duration, then the question needs to be raised whether this hypothesis is a genuine alternative to the infinite divisibility of space presupposed in the first two paradoxes. We have to ask two questions: whether there is anything in the first two paradoxes that would exclude the notion of a point or an instant, and whether there is anything in the Flying Arrow to exclude the infinite divisibility of space or time. The answer to each of these two questions is in the negative. The infinite divisibility of space (or of time) precludes the possibility of an extended minimum in either dimension (or set of dimensions); but it does not preclude the notion of a null extension in either medium, and any null extension is of course indivisible. In fact, Zeno may even need the notion of a point to set up the first two paradoxes; we have to put the beginning of the Racecourse at a point, and we have to put Achilles and his intended victim at two points. In both paradoxes the would-be travellers pass through a series of points,[24] each of which is carefully specified, in the attempt to complete their allotted journey. Nor is the case different with the Flying Arrow. The proposition that at an instant the arrow is at a point would imply neither that time and/or space are infinitely divisible nor that time and/or space are not infinitely divisible. The plain logical truth is that the existence of points/instants is not in the least threatened by the supposition that one cannot ever reach a point/instant in any process of division. It is true that Zeno is with some justice[25] accused of treating instants in the Arrow as if they were moments with extension; but he is accused of doing this only in so far as he needs the word "rest" in a sense appropriate to rest during a moment, whereas he can only obtain the arrow's rest in a sense appropriate to an instant. Unless it was Zeno's purpose to show that his opponents made this illogical pun, relying on the word "rest" in two senses, then the argument does not touch on the distinction between instants and periods. And no one has yet suggested that Zeno's Flying Arrow was aimed at elucidating the two senses of "rest"; if it were so directed, it would be an intolerably roundabout approach to a semantic problem not likely to have troubled the fifth-century philosophers.[26]

If this argument be accepted, then the most probable interpretation of the Flying Arrow, the interpretation adopted by Aristotle and by most writers since Aristotle,[27] makes it rest on a hypothesis which is no fit alternative to the assumptions presupposed in the first two paradoxes on motion. This means that the whole group of paradoxes against motion cannot, at least in the way Tannery thought,[28] consist of a series of attacks driving the enemy from one position to another. It also means that the second pair of arguments do not together analyse a position alternative to that brought under fire in the first pair. In this case, there remains no sufficient reason for regarding the group of four as made up of two pairs attacking alternative positions; the only alternative to the presuppositions of the first two arguments would have to be supplied by the fourth paradox alone. This may serve to cast already some doubt on the reinterpretation of the fourth paradox to give us the required alternative, since we have now removed the alleged pattern of the four arguments on which that reinterpretation was largely based. But before discussion of the Aristotelian and principal modern interpretations of the Stadium it is in the interests of clarity to summarize as briefly as possible and without detailed controversy what Aristotle tells us.[29]

The apparatus needed for the argument consists of three parallel rows of four objects each, all the objects being equal in size. Of these one, the A's, is kept stationary. The second, the B's, moves in one direction parallel to the A's, the Cs in the opposite sense, both motions being of the same velocity. Then, accepting with gratitude much of Furley's recent restoration and interpretation of the text,[30] we suppose that the leading C and the leading B arrive simultaneously at opposite ends of the row of A's, each of the two having started from the middle of their row: my diagram shows the initial position.

$$A\ A\ A\ A$$

$$B\ B\ B\ B \rightarrow$$

$$\leftarrow C\ C\ C\ C$$

At the second stage the leading C has passed all the B's, while the B has passed only half the A's. Since each B and C spends an equal time opposite an A, the time taken by the B is half that taken by the C. Between the premiss and conclusion mentioned in my last sentence there needs to be inserted the additional step that a C must spend the same time opposite a B as a B opposite an A; this step, not explicit at this point of Aristotle's exposition, contains the basic fallacy. The "second half" of the argument examines the fortunes of the B's.[31] The B's have passed all the C's. Leading B and leading C arrive simultaneously at opposite ends of each other's row. The text of the next sentence is uncertain,[32] but the drift of the argument must be that, since a B and a C spend the same time opposite an A, they must spend the same time opposite each other. It may be observed again that this step is fallacious. It is not true that, because a B spends the same time as a C opposite the same A, therefore the B spends the same time opposite the C as opposite the A. To suppose that it does is, as Aristotle says, to ignore the fact that the B is passing a stationary A but a moving C; to put the point more succinctly, it ignores the distinction between relative and absolute motion.

In the belief that this was too elementary a fallacy for one of Zeno's undoubted intelligence to commit, the moderns from Tannery onwards have in general refused to believe that Aristotle's version of the argument is correct. With few exceptions they have preferred to construct an argument using (normally) the same conclusions as the argument given by Aristotle (that "twice the time equals half the time") but have made of Aristotle's "objects" indivisibles, either with or without extension, and either finite or infinite in number for a finite length. The point then is that when, for example, one of the B's has passed one of the C's it has passed only half an A; but ex hypothesi (on this interpretation) there is no such thing as half an A, since A's, B's, and C's are all indivisible.

It is clear that rewriting Aristotle in this fashion is not without its hazards. One of the hazards is that the evidence on which the rewriting is based is subject to revision, and this particular effort has been considerably undermined in recent years. One of the most persuasive arguments for going against Aristotle on the Stadium has been that, rewritten in Tannery's manner, the paradox is based on the hypothesis of extended indivisibles and that this makes the argument an acceptable member of a group forming a dilemma on the subject of divisibility. We have seen that the first three arguments do not, on the most probable view, offer such a dilemma, and we shall return to the point later. For the present, in the belief that that particular prop can be blown away, we may survey some of the other undermining operations recently conducted.

Tannery supported his thesis by supposing the word ὄγκοι, rendered in the above paraphrase as "objects," to refer to indivisibles, supposing also that the thesis to be demolished maintained that the ultimate elements of matter possessed a certain mass. Against translation of ὄγκοι by anything implying finite size, Tannery urged the use of this word by fourth-century Pythagorizing thinkers like Xenocrates and Heraclides of Pontus.[33] But this evidence cannot be called good. There is virtually no evidence for *explicit* atomism before Zeno's day among the Pythagorean school, and the Atomist philosophy of Ionia most probably drew on Zeno's arguments.[34] If Zeno used the word ὄγκοι at all, which is far from being proved by its occurrence here in Aristotle, he is not prima facie likely to have restricted it to indivisibles. Naturally, Aristotle himself was abundantly familiar with the terminology of fourth-century atomists, whether Pythagorean or other, and might therefore slip into their usage. But there is no reason for suspecting such a slip here, and Aristotle uses the word ὄγκος himself often enough to denote an object of finite bulk. If Aristotle did go wrong on this particular point, by missing a reference to indivisibles when he had it in front of him, this seems an odd place in the *Physics* for him to make such a mistake. For the whole context of these four paradoxes in the sixth book of the *Physics* is concerned with divisibility problems. Vlastos has rightly insisted on the point that Aristotle has employed earlier in this very book of the *Physics* the "logical twin" of the argument here foisted by the anti-Aristotelian party on Zeno.[35] It would be more than surprising for Aristotle to fail to understand an argument which he was fully capable of creating and thinking through; and to impute to Aristotle mere jealousy of his predecessor would be to pass the bounds of reasonable discussion. There remains a curious argument, if it was meant as an argument, recently produced in passing by

G. E. L. Owen;[36] it may be noted that Owen commits himself very cautiously, if at all, to the anti-Aristotelian view of the Stadium. He says, however: "So the move which takes t also takes $2t$; this is the alleged puzzle, and plainly it depends on disregarding the relative motions of the bodies. The Cs are moving, the As are not. That is Aristotle's sole comment on the argument, and it is generally felt that if it is refuted by such a comment it was not worth the considerable space he gave it." Two points may be put here. The first is that much of the "considerable space" is devoted to setting up the somewhat complex apparatus of the argument and to the attempt to make its precise form clear. The second, and more conclusive, is that, whatever we may think today, the fact remains that Aristotle thought the paradox could be despatched by this comment; and Aristotle himself nevertheless held that, despite the ease with which he eventually disposed of it, the argument was worth the space devoted to it in the *Physics*. Aristotle was under no compulsion other than his own judgement, and modern judgements are irrelevant. Aristotle also held, and this is important, that an argument which depended on the fallacy he attributes to Zeno here could cause trouble even in Aristotle's day (*Physics* 239b10f).

The question needs to be examined afresh whether Zeno was being quite so unbelievably stupid as the moderns tend to think in committing the fallacy alleged by Aristotle. Dogmatic denial is as fruitless as dogmatic assertion here; but it would seem relevant to ask those who deny the possibility of Zeno's committing the alleged fallacy whether there are any arguments of demonstrated fifth-century origin which display a clear knowledge of the necessary distinction between absolute and relative motion; also whether, when Plato was pointing out as late as the *Theaetetus* the distinction between the κίνησις of spatial movement and that of qualitative change, one can reasonably expect from Zeno nearly a century earlier a clear understanding of the much more subtle distinction between relative and absolute motion. It would not, I think, have satisfied Zeno to be presented with Aristotle's statement that it took a different time to pass a moving and a stationary object of the same size; Zeno might well have said, in effect: "Yes, I know; that is the whole point of the argument, and that is why it is found among my arguments against motion. But can you tell me why this is so and why the consequences are not as paradoxical as I think they are?" To answer these questions would very probably have been beyond most of Zeno's contemporaries and might well have been beyond Zeno himself. For Zeno's critical powers were almost certainly greater than his constructive ability, and Booth has done well to remind scholars that he accepted Eleatic doctrine with all its weaknesses.[37]

In this situation the opinion is clearly at least tenable that Aristotle was right in his account of the Stadium paradox. Yet one cannot yet dismiss the temptation to believe that the arguments against motion form a coherent pattern and that the Stadium may therefore belong to it despite the authority of Aristotle. We have still to consider the possibility of a pattern somewhat looser than any analysed up to this point. The possibility remains untouched that the Flying Arrow in its original form did not answer the question whether or not the "nows" had extension but specified merely that they were indivisible. If Zeno treated the Flying Arrow in this fashion and did not answer for himself or his readers this important question, then it becomes credible once more that the first two arguments attack the hypothesis of infinite divisibility, and the third, with perhaps the fourth, lays siege to the apparently alternative hypothesis of indivisibles. On this theory, the Flying Arrow would not have to attack a genuine alternative to the victim of the first pair of arguments but could be aimed at a vague notion which looked something like such an alternative.

The possibility of this view can hardly be denied. But it is hard to see that its probability is high. It requires the abandonment of a statement by Aristotle, who was evidently one of the few people in the ancient world to see Zeno's work and who was keenly interested in Zeno's arguments; and it requires it on a most slender basis of evidence. It exacts the belief that, because Aristotle gives a group of four arguments of which the first two involve infinite divisibility and the next one accepts a form of indivisibles, therefore one should reject Aristotle's account of the fourth and suppose it too to deal with indivisibles. Yet the vital word "indivisible" occurs only in Aristotle's criticism of the argument, not in his exposition, and we have to accept *this* from Aristotle as Zenonian, if the supposed point (however vague) is to be clear in Zeno's text. The belief is, moreover, imposed that the arguments form as a whole a dilemma, when Aristotle does not even suggest at any point that the arguments are linked in any way or are anything but the independent paradoxes that they appear on the surface of the Aristotelian account to be. The belief is imposed that Aristotle had completely missed the point, not only of an argument which he himself uses elsewhere, but also of a whole series of arguments which attracted his interest and which he admits still gave trouble—and therefore aroused general philosophic interest—in his own day. All this even though Aristotle paid such attention to the Flying Arrow that, as Owen has recently shown, it affected the fundamentals of his physics.[38] It is difficult to see why such theories should attain any wide acceptance, particularly at a time when Aristotle's evidence is ceasing to be dismissed out of hand as of little value. Judgement of arguments from pattern is obviously subjective; to a detached observer the amount of pattern in the three arguments whose interpretation is more or less agreed is not great. It is questionable indeed whether on the fourth it should outweigh the not inconsiderable authority of Aristotle. For all its ingenuity the dilemma interpretation of the four paradoxes on motion fails to convince.

It cannot therefore be used to buttress the already weakened view that Zeno's arguments were aimed especially at a Pythagorean target.

ZENO'S ARGUMENTS AS A MULTIPLE DILEMMA

A recent interpretation of Zeno,[39] while emphatically rejecting the connection of Zeno's arguments with Pythagoreanism, holds that not only the arguments against motion but also the arguments against plurality conjointly form a super-dilemma in which the pluralist opponent is driven from one analysis of his plurality to another until all possible analyses are exhausted and he is compelled to admit the untenability of the pluralist hypothesis in any form. Owen, believing Zeno, as is well attested, to have held that only one thing exists, rightly infers that a modern would indeed expect Zeno to take all possible ways—or all ways known to him—of satisfying the conditions for a plurality and show that each in turn is impossible. It is exactly this which, according to Owen, Zeno has done for the ways open to him of distinguishing spatially or temporally between the elements of a plurality. Worked out with both thoroughness and caution, this interpretation presents one of the most coherent accounts of Zeno's paradoxes ever to have appeared. But there are some details which are not satisfactorily tied up, as well as a number of general considerations which might be held to give grounds for doubt. We may approach certain details first.

So far, in the present account, the Achilles and the Racecourse (or Dichotomy) have been treated as depending on the same assumption; it is thus implied that, if the arguments are to be understood as the reduction to absurdity not of motion in general, but each of a different account of a plurality, then these two arguments must reduce the same account to absurdity. Owen tries to avoid this duplication by supposing that the Racecourse, "a closely associated paradox," argues: "Before reaching your destination you must reach half-way, but before reaching that you must reach half-way to it; and so back. So in this series there is no first move, and you cannot get started."[40] This differentiates the argument from the Achilles, which "takes care of" the assumption that there is no *last* move, whereas in Owen's version of the Racecourse there is no *first* move. Owen's version, however, as he well knows, is not the only one; it is conceivable that Zeno meant his hypothetical runner to arrive at the mid-point of the course, then at the mid-point of the remainder, then at the mid-point of what is left, and so on ad infinitum. If this is the correct version, this argument also assumes that there can be no last move in an infinite series. The grounds for preferring the second interpretation to Owen's are given by Vlastos;[41] to his reasons could perhaps be added that Aristotle speaks at least three times of the impossibility, according to this argument, of traversing either the racecourse or some distance unspecified; the two occasions where the result of the argument is that no motion can take place at all evaporate on closer inspection.[42] The Achilles and the Racecourse therefore do not examine alternative assumptions at all.

Nor is there satisfactory evidence that the Stadium (or Moving Rows) can be brought into Owen's scheme. We have seen that it is unlikely that Aristotle's evidence on this argument is false, and Aristotle does not associate this paradox with divisibility problems. Owen's own aside in support of its concern with infinitesimals has already been found wanting. But Owen does produce the very strong argument *against* the infinitesimals interpretation that it was wholly ignored by Plato; it is possible that other philosophers went the same way as Plato in this matter.[43] We have here, then, not merely a duplication of effort by Zeno but a definite gap in his programme; and yet the impression is strong that if Zeno was clever enough and had sufficient clarity of logic to think through Owen's programme he had enough grasp of the problems involved to think this one out too.

Finally, there are certain arguments very plausibly regarded as Zeno's which Owen does not take into account, because they will not fit into the scheme. The most certainly Zenonian of these is the argument against place, attributed by Aristotle to Zeno at *Physics* 209a23. If this argument has anything to do with the kind of problem discussed by Owen, it offers another duplication. The argument runs, in Aristotle's paraphrase: "Moreover, if place is one of the things that exist, where is it? For Zeno's problem demands an explanation; for if every thing that exists is in a place, obviously there will be a place of place, and so on ad infinitum." If this argument is about limits or edges disguised as "place" in which a body is situated,[44] then clearly it commits the same fallacy as the one alleged by Owen for the argument of B3; it assumes that limits are on a par with the things which they limit. But there is no *need* to interpret the argument in this way at all.

Owen does not mention the Millet Seed either; yet this is assigned to Zeno by Aristotle (*Physics* 250a19ff, Lee no. 37), and, whether or not

Simplicius' interpretation of the argument comes from a dialogue not by Zeno, there is no reason whatever to suppose that *Aristotle* was relying here (any more than elsewhere) on anything but Zeno's own writing(s). What Aristotle says here is this: "On this account Zeno's statement is not true, that any fraction of a grain of millet [or any grain of millet] makes a noise." Aristotle here accuses Zeno of ignoring the example of the ship which a single man cannot move and perhaps of ignoring the Aristotelian distinction of potential and actual: the grain of millet for Aristotle has only the potency of causing movement in the whole bushel; by itself it has no power. Zeno can hardly be blamed (but should not be overpraised) for not ignoring friction as Aristotle does here and may have been raising a divisibility problem, whether deliberately or not. If Zeno raised such problems deliberately, then it is not clear what assumption he was attacking here; the argument could conceivably be the missing attack on infinitesimal physical entities, but, if so, then (1) we have to reckon with its immediate pretermission by the Atomists and (2) it does not proceed along the lines laid down by Owen for Zeno's other attacks, for it does not seem on the surface probable that this argument assumed the existence of infinitesimals and then reduced the assumption to absurdity. (A millet seed is not an infinitesimal.) But there is no reason to suppose that all Zeno's arguments turned on questions of divisibility.

Apart from this obscure millet-seed argument, Owen's thesis of a grand design in Zeno's paradoxes has been shown to display at least one duplication, at least one major gap, and inability to take satisfactory account of one further argument, which may present a further duplication or may have to be left out altogether. We are not told, moreover, what happened in the arguments, perhaps numerous,[45] which we do not possess. Either they must be irrelevant to the scheme, in which case it is a curious coincidence that antiquity, without noticing the scheme, preserved so high a proportion of the right choice of arguments; or they are relevant, in which case it would seem probable that there was more duplication than we have detected in the extant paradoxes—unless Owen is inclined to admit that his scheme is drastically incomplete, in which case the argument from design folds up. The point at which an argument from design becomes convincing, or at which it ceases to convince, is a subjective issue—or at least an issue with subjective ramifications. No more can therefore be said here than that, in view of the general arguments which follow, the writer of this book finds the defects in Owen's scheme damaging.

A major consideration in any interpretation of Zeno must be the view taken of the Eleatic Palamedes by his contemporaries and near contemporaries. None of these apparently understood Zeno to have driven them successively from one position to another. There is no trace of any evidence that they so understood him, and it is more plausible to suppose that they did not.

The two most important ancient interpreters of Zeno are Plato and Aristotle. It will here be convenient to review Aristotle first, and it will be best, after the unfavourable account in the preceding section, to do the best we can for the dilemma theory. Let us for the moment, then, concede that Aristotle's authority as a source of information on his predecessors is not wholly unimpeachable and that it is rare in the history of philosophy for a great original thinker to present his predecessors' views with strict detachment and absolute historical fidelity. Let us concede that Aristotle was more interested in his own problems than in those of his predecessors and that the two, though naturally often connected, do not always coincide. In Zeno's case, Aristotle had long outgrown the belief in the unreality of things plural and moving, and had reasons for impatience with Eleatic arguments whether directly or indirectly supporting that fundamental Eleatic tenet. Let us even concede the possibility that Aristotle *may* have been so careless as to misrepresent the whole tenor of an argument likely to be of much interest to him. But let us remember at the same time that Zeno touched off some problems concerning the nature of continuity which worried Aristotle deeply and that the arguments preceding the reply to Zeno look as if designed to lead up to that reply as to a climax.

If we look once more at the text, we find Aristotle answering the Achilles and the Racecourse (or Dichotomy) in *Physics* Z by pointing out that time is as infinitely divisible as space, so that the antinomy between infinite space and finite time is not available to Zeno. In *Physics* Θ (263a4ff) he returns to these particular arguments and admits that this is not an answer to all the problems they raise; he replies then that what is potentially divisible ad infinitum is not actually so divided, and so Achilles does not have to run through an infinite number of positions, but only through a potentially infinite number. The Flying Arrow Aristotle dismisses in *Physics* Z with the curt comment that it depends on the composition of time from indivisible "nows," which he claims to have shown is not tenable. The Stadium (or Moving Rows) Aristotle claims to have solved by pointing out that the relative speed of two bodies passing each other differs from the speed of each relative to its environment.

Now, on the most favourable view this series of replies could, *conceivably*, be understood as an answer to an alleged Zenonian dilemma concerning the nature of space and even as a reply to a dilemma concerned with plurality and composed solely of the arguments against motion. For, though it might seem surprising that Aristotle should focus on each argument in turn to the exclusion of the others if they were the horns of a dilemma, his procedure is nevertheless, at a pinch, logical; for, since he himself accepts the horn of infinite divisibility, he can reply to the arguments proving the impossibility of this and then (having elsewhere proved to his own satisfaction the necessity of infinite divisibility) show that the arguments on the other horn of the dilemma involve the rejection of the now established view of the matter. But, though the form of Aristotle's arguments is thus compatible with a dilemma concerning the nature of space, it offers no support for this interpretation; it is equally compatible with the supposition (a) that Zeno's premiss was intended to be in each argument simply that motion exists and (b) that each of the four arguments against motion was meant as a reduction to absurdity of that single premiss.

The theory that Zeno included the arguments against plurality in the same many-horned dilemma with the arguments against motion is also just compatible with Aristotle's evidence. Aristotle does not even consider these further arguments in his discussion nor give any hint that he considered them relevant to the consideration of the arguments against motion; but he could *conceivably* have thought the arguments against plurality irrelevant to the theme of motion in space and time which occupies most of *Physics Z*. If he so thought, then he was careless; but he was forgivably careless, for Owen can claim that no one between Aristotle and himself saw this carelessness for what it was. And yet it must be remembered even on this lenient view that Aristotle offers no hint of any kind that Owen's view is right; he treats the arguments against motion not as parts of a dilemma nor as parts of a single wider super-dilemma, but each as a separate line of thought to be refuted by itself, and he offers no suggestion that they were, as a whole, connected with the arguments against plurality.

What would make Aristotle's silence more surprising—if he has indeed been thus silent—is that there is no *point* in driving your opponent from one position to another if you do not make it clear both from what position he has been driven to which inner bastion of defence and finally that you have exhausted all the possibilities for a rear-guard action. If Zeno did in fact point out these things, then his successors' silence becomes deafening. If he did not, then his intellectual labour was likely to go largely to waste; it may be thought that he was hardly the man not to press home an argument with all possible force.

NEGATIVE EVIDENCE FROM PLATO

The evidence of Plato is of an even more controversial kind; but nevertheless it seems likely that, whatever Plato's own processes of thought, he represents Zeno's methods as being other than those described by Owen. The dialogue concerned, the *Parmenides*, has called forth almost as many explanations of its purport as there have been Platonists; but the issues which the dialogue raises for Plato's later thought may largely be neglected here. All that is at present required is to discover what, precisely, Plato represents Zeno as having done. At 135dff Parmenides is made to state that the model for the "gymnastic" argument he is about to conduct is the manner of argument used by Zeno in his treatise. It follows that the argument pursued with the young Aristoteles by Parmenides is similar in structure to the argument of Zeno's book. It must be admitted that there are two substantial differences between the argument of Zeno's book and the argument conducted by Parmenides in the dialogue. Plato himself (*Parmenides* 135d–136a) makes the point that, whereas Zeno did not extend his argument to Forms (or, as we should put it in this context, to universals), Parmenides intends to do so; and instead of working out the consequences of a single proposition Parmenides will consider also the consequences of its contradictory—including the consequences to things other than the subject of the proposition. There may be added a further difference not mentioned by Plato, namely that, whereas we have no evidence that Zeno wrote in dialogue form, Plato maintains the convention of dialogue, transparent though it is,[46] throughout the second half of the work. This last difference, however, has virtually no effect on the course of the argument and does not encourage the belief that Plato's enumeration of the differences was so incomplete as to make his remarks untrustworthy. Indeed, the relation between Zenonian and Platonic arguments deserves closer attention than it has often received. Zeno is more often used to illuminate Plato than vice versa. But, though both problems are difficult, at least we have Plato's complete text and his own introduction.

The distinction needs reiterating between Plato's fictional context and Plato's own thought. What Parmenides does in Plato's fictional context[47] is presumably the kind of thing Plato thought Zeno did. What Plato intended his readers within or without the Academy to *deduce* from what Parmenides does in the dialogue is altogether a different matter. If Plato intended his readers to see that Parmenides in the dialogue makes logical errors and to learn from them, it by no means follows that Zeno intended his readers to learn that his logical errors or imported extra premisses were what they were. More particularly, when Plato makes Parmenides deduce a consequence from the proposition "one thing is" that follows only from one sense of the words and is not a necessary consequence of all senses, it may be that Plato is intending thus to define a sense of the words so that he may develop an argument from the definition. But it is idle to pretend that this gives us any right to suppose Zeno, when deducing from a proposition consequences following only from one sense of it as if they were necessary consequences of the proposition, to have intended thus to define his terms for the particular argument. If we find Parmenides in Plato's dialogue treating his propositions as if they had only one sense, Plato may have intended to indicate to his readers the pitfalls of ambiguity; but the conclusion cannot be drawn that Zeno meant to do the same. What one must rather conclude is that, in Plato's judgement, Zeno drew conclusions from one sense of a proposition which followed only from that sense and treated them as if they followed from that proposition *tout court*. One need not, of course, necessarily accept Plato's judgement; for it is hard to delimit Plato's irony and he is not infallible on his predecessors. But it is at least worthwhile to examine the fragments of Zeno's arguments to see whether or not they bear out what seems to have been Plato's judgement.

In the above argument the percipient reader will have noticed a gap. It could no doubt be argued that, if it can be supposed without absurdity that Plato, in having his Parmenides deduce, meant his readers to realize that here were definitions, then it *is* plausible to suppose that Zeno also meant his readers to take the first few steps of his deductions as definitions or as specifications of what he proposed to talk about. This hole is easily plugged. For Plato was writing imaginative dialogue, and Zeno was not. It is a reasonable proceeding for Plato to use his Parmenides' deductions to draw his readers' attention to definitions; but it is not a reasonable proceeding for Zeno, writing a treatise, to conceal definitions in the guise of deductions. What Plato's purpose was in writing the *Parmenides* remains a matter of legitimate dispute, even though we have the whole text. But it is not reasonable to suppose that Zeno's full text would set us the same kind of conundrum as the dialogue. If Zeno couched his definitions in the form of deductions, then the mystification was pointless, and his readers could understandably protest. It is also unlikely that Zeno's readers about or before the middle of the fifth century would have had anything like the degree of literary sophistication required for understanding such a device. Plato could fairly claim to have educated his own public away from the literal interpretation of discourse on one level only; but Zeno could certainly make no such claim. It is after all *not* plausible that Zeno should have forestalled Plato in the way required by this objection.

As a preliminary to examination of the fragments, we may bring out certain points concerning Parmenides' procedure in his fictional discussion with the youthful Aristoteles. It has often been supposed (for example by Cornford) that the first few steps in each of the Hypotheses of the second part of the *Parmenides* represent a definition of the terms "one," "being," and so on, for the purposes of that particular argument. It could be supposed that these definitions are sufficiently different to warrant a description of Plato's procedure as driving his opponents from one definition (proved absurd by the argument based on it) to another. Such a view of Plato's purpose would have much plausibility—though there are certain objections to it. But it does not follow, even if this interpretation of Plato be adopted, that this was the procedure adopted in Plato's opinion by Zeno. For even Cornford had to admit that the definitions which he claimed to find are concealed definitions, and that the form of the argument throughout is purely deductive.[48] Plato does not represent Parmenides as arguing that from such and such a definition of the terms "one" and "being" there follow, on the assumption, for example, that "one thing is," consequences too absurd for that definition to be retained. It is quite undeniable that Parmenides in the dialogue argues in each case on the assumption only that the relevant Hypothesis is true. The sets of propositions taken by Cornford to be definitions are, at the opening of each Hypothesis, ostensibly deduced from the Hypothesis itself. That is to say that Parmenides deduces them from it in the text before our eyes—as Cornford himself well knew and did not forget.

This thesis may be illustrated from any of the Hypotheses. Take the first (137cff):

> *Parm.* If one thing is, surely the one thing would not be many? *Ar.* How could it? *Parm.* There must, therefore, be no part of it, and it must not be a whole. *Ar.* Why is that? *Parm.* Surely a part is a part of a whole. *Ar.* Yes. *Parm.* And what is a whole? Would not that of which no part is absent be a whole? *Ar.* Yes indeed. *Parm.* In both cases, therefore, the one would be composed of parts, both as a whole and as having parts. *Ar.* It would have to be. *Parm.* In both cases, therefore, the one would thus be many and not one. *Ar.* True. *Parm.* But it must be one and not many. *Ar.* It must. *Parm.* Therefore it will neither be a whole nor have parts, if the one is going to be one. *Ar.* Certainly not. *Parm.* Now, if it has no part, it would have neither beginning nor end nor middle; for such things would already be parts of it. *Ar.* That's right.

At this point what Cornford called "the deduction proper" is already under way,[49] and Cornford specified that the deduction proper follows the "definition" without break and without change of form. Parmenides is not here represented in Plato's fictional context as defining; he is clearly represented as arguing and deducing. The point is clear in this and in most other instances; but a few further examples are worth mentioning, or need some discussion. At 157b6, after introducing the subject of "the others," Parmenides asks "Shall we consider, then, what ought to be true of the others if one thing is?" and Aristoteles assents. The word "ought" is here highly significant: Parmenides here does not propose to find out the consequences to "the others" *if* they or the "one" are defined in a certain way; he proposes to investigate the *necessary* consequences, to any "others," of the statement that "one thing exists." He deduces then that the others are parts of a unity; whatever Plato himself may have intended his readers to do with the deductions, whether to treat them as a definition or whatever, Parmenides in the dialogue does nothing but deduce, after saying that he will deduce. A similarly significant "must" is found in a similar context at the beginning of Hypothesis VIII, at 165e.

Possible arguments against this view of what Plato makes Parmenides do could be based on the transition from the first Hypothesis to the second, and again on the openings of the fifth and sixth. The end of the first Hypothesis finds Parmenides having deduced that the one thing cannot logically be named, talked about, or thought about and can have nothing predicated of it in any way, not even existence. At the end of a devastating list of negative statements about the one thing, Parmenides asks Aristoteles "Now can this possibly be the case with the One?"[50] Aristoteles meekly (but not surprisingly) replies in the negative. Parmenides then offers to go back once more to the beginning and see if, as they go over the argument again, any different conclusion emerges. Aristoteles accepts the suggestion, and Parmenides resumes with the words: "'If a one is,' we say, we have to agree what sort of consequences follow concerning it." The process of deduction then begins again. Now, this looks at first sight like a rejection of the first Hypothesis as leading to an absurd conclusion, and the substitution for it of a more accurate piece of reasoning which will lead to less absurd consequences. It looks in fact as if Parmenides is driving Aristoteles from one argument to another, having shown the first to be impossible. If one supposes, as is plausible, that the root of the matter lies in the first few steps in the argument and miscalls these a definition, then one may declare Parmenides to drive Aristoteles from one definition to another, from one meaning of the proposition "One thing exists" to another meaning. It may indeed be the case that Plato intended his readers to grasp that the argument of the first Hypothesis was inadequate in some way, but it certainly does not follow that Parmenides is represented as intending Aristoteles to grasp this inadequacy. If Parmenides rejects the first Hypothesis, then it is odd that, when the time comes to sum up the results of the positive Hypotheses, he asserts not that *either* the conclusions of Hypothesis I are true *or* the conclusions of Hypothesis II are true but that the conclusions of *both* Hypotheses are true (see 160b2). If Parmenides had framed Hypotheses I and II as a dilemma, then it was totally illogical of him to suggest that the two horns of the dilemma result in conclusions simultaneously true. But, on the other hand, if Parmenides intended the argument of the first two Hypotheses as an antinomy, then the conclusion to the first four Hypotheses states this, and the apparent rejection of the first Hypothesis falls into place as a superfluous, but not illogical, piece of byplay. For, if you are presenting your opponent with an antinomy, there is no harm whatever in showing not only that his proposition gives rise to contradictory conclusions but also that one (or more) of those conclusions is absurd. Further, if the total effect of Hypotheses I and II is a dilemma, then it would be expected that the total effect of the two corresponding Hypotheses about the Others (numbers III and IV) should be similar. But this is not the case; for the deductions of Hypothesis IV are at the outset presented as an addition to those of Hypothesis III, not as an alternative. This is clear from the opening question of Hypothesis IV at 159b3, which runs as follows: "What then if we were to pass over these consequences as obvious, and consider again the consequences if one thing is, and whether we must *also* deny these statements about the others than the one, or whether the affirmation *alone* is right?" It would also be expected that a Parmenides who was driving his opponent from one position to another would continue to do so throughout the whole discussion, and would explicitly reject each Hypothesis in turn; but in fact Parmenides does nothing of the kind, and at the conclusion of the whole dialogue he asserts not that *either* the positive *or* the negative conclusions must be sound but that the conclusions of both positive and negative Hypotheses have been demonstrated. I doubt if Plato believed this; but he offers no hint that Parmenides in his fiction doubts this particular point.[51]

It is time to turn to the opening sentences of the fifth and sixth Hypotheses and see precisely what Parmenides does there. He certainly mentions the meaning of the proposition hypothesized, but that does not mean that he takes one sense of the words, disposes of that sense, and then turns to an alternative; it turns out that he is made to do nothing of the sort. The fifth Hypothesis begins at 160b5 with Parmenides asking: "Well, must we not next consider what are the necessary consequences if the one thing is not?" Aristoteles assents. Parmenides goes on: "What then would this hypothesis be, if one thing is not? Does it differ from this hypothesis, namely if a non-one thing is not? *Ar.* It differs indeed. *Parm.*

Does it only differ, or is it actually quite the opposite thing, saying 'if a non-one thing is not,' to saying 'if one thing is not'?" Aristoteles agrees that it is quite the opposite, but in case he is the least bit unconvinced Parmenides illustrates the point from some other propositions of a similar logical structure but with predicates other than "one." He comes back to the hypothesis fortified in the belief that to talk about a non-existent one is different from talking about a non-existent non-one. It is in fact to talk about something knowable and different from other things; these are, according to Parmenides here, consequences[52] of talking about a "one" that does not exist (as opposed to a non-existent non-one). Having *established* this point, according to his lights, Parmenides now asks once again, at 160d3, what *must* happen to the non-existent one. And he refers to the doctrine of its knowability (just established) as a *necessary* consequence of the supposition that one thing is not, unless the supposition is to be meaningless. The process of deduction of course continues, but there is no need now to consider it further. It is already clear that Parmenides here suggests not a possible alternative meaning for the hypothesis but the meaning which it *must* bear to have any meaning at all; it is also clear that the consequences he deduces from the hypothesis in that meaning are regarded not as being merely conditional on that meaning but as certain consequences drawn by inexorable logic.

This situation is duplicated at the opening of the sixth Hypothesis. Here Parmenides suggests that they go back to the beginning, to see if the same or different consequences follow—without a trace of any rejection of the argument just completed. Here again, at 163c1, Parmenides speaks of determining the necessary consequences of the hypothesis. Here again he insists that one of the terms ("not-being" this time) *must* bear a certain meaning. Here again he proceeds to deduce *necessary* consequences from the hypothesis, in the sense he has just established as the right and necessary sense. Again there is not the least suggestion that the meaning of the hypothesis from which these consequences are deduced is a mere alternative; it is clearly represented as necessary. This pair of Hypotheses presents not a dilemma but an antinomy. Plato may have intended to suggest to his readers some dilemma; but he does not portray Parmenides as propounding anything but an antinomy or show him driving his interlocutor from one position to another.

Indeed, the conclusion of the whole dialogue is sufficient by itself to show that the Hypotheses form, in Parmenides' mouth, not so much a super-dilemma but rather a pair of super-antinomies; the consequences of Hypotheses V and VI are included in the summing-up of 166c. In that summary there are only two alternatives, namely whether the one is or is not. Hypotheses I–IV are thus alternatives to V–VIII; in that sense Parmenides presents a dilemma. But under each of these alternatives he presents a super-antinomy. To have Parmenides do this is to make him flout the rules of logic as we know it, and probably as Plato knew it; but that does not make it in any way probable that the historical Parmenides and Zeno would have found anything objectionable in the procedure. Until we find certain evidence to the contrary, it will be as well to use as a working hypothesis the assumption that Plato's avowed portrayal of Zeno's methods is the correct one. If we do this, we find in Plato strong evidence against the theory that Zeno drove his opponents from one definition of plurality to another.

NEGATIVE EVIDENCE FROM ZENO'S ARGUMENTS AIMED DIRECTLY AT PLURALITY

When we turn to the fragments of Zeno's own writings, we find their procedure a good deal harder to analyse than that of the argument conducted in Plato's *Parmenides*. Here we do not have the contexts of the arguments, and there is no interlocutor to whom the argument has to be made clear as it proceeds. But Zeno's language is at certain points highly suggestive, and what it suggests is not that Zeno is constructing out of several arguments a many-horned dilemma.

In the argument of which fragments B1 and B2 form a substantial part, Zeno is alleged by Owen to be meeting the view that the world can be divided indefinitely into parts and that a division of this kind could be completed. This would be an alternative to the theory that such a division of the world could never be completed, a theory, on Owen's interpretation, reduced to absurdity in turn by the Achilles. But all our reports of B1 and B2 come from Simplicius, and in Simplicius there is not a word to the effect that the argument is designed to meet only one alternative view of plurality. Simplicius[53] describes the first arm of the paradox in these words: "Having shown beforehand that each of the many has no size because it is the same as itself and one" (*or*, with the manuscripts' text, "Having shown beforehand that nothing has size because each of the many is the same as itself and one..."). There is no premiss mentioned here to which any supporter of any kind of plurality of existents could object. The premisses are, first, the existence of more than one thing and, secondly, the self-identity and consequent unity of each existent. There is no reason to suppose Zeno to have doubted that these properties belonged to all members of any plurality whatever. For the second part of this argument, Simplicius gives us, at least in part, Zeno's own words.[54] The thought may be outlined as follows. In order to exist, each member of our plurality must have size. Since each must have size, one part of each must be separate from another part. If we take the part in front, we find that it too must have size, and of it too one part will be in front of another; and this process (presumably one of division) can go on for ever. This outline of the argument should make clear Owen's error in stating that in this second arm Zeno "went on to specify the collection of parts in which he was interested, namely the collection produced by completing a division in which every step has a successor."[55] No such specification is visible to the naked eye. Zeno certainly does not here specify the collection of parts in which he is interested to the temporary exclusion of other collections. He appears on the surface to be analysing not the possible, but the necessary, consequences of the assumption that many things exist. In this phase of the argument Zeno starts very simply with the hypothesis that they exist; from their existence he deduces their possession of size. From this is deduced their possession of parts. Zeno does not, at least in Simplicius' version, mention the further obvious point that these parts must also exist. If they exist, they too must have size, and therefore have parts . . .

So all that is *specified* about the parts is that they are parts of the units that form a plurality. This much Owen seems to admit; for, despite his previous remarks about the specification of a collection of parts, he says after giving his outline of the argument: "In this there is no clear implication that such a division can have been completed."[56] He adds, however: "But Zeno does make that assumption in drawing his conclusions." This seems right as a statement about Zeno's logic but cannot alter the fact that Zeno does not mention this implication of the course of his argument. There is little difficulty in the assumption that Zeno did not see every premiss needed to render his arguments rigorous; but there is serious difficulty in the supposition that Zeno intended to drive an opponent from one position to another on the subject of an infinite division when he does not even mention the position concerned. To drive an opponent from a position, the normal and reasonable procedure is to specify the position concerned and then reduce it to absurdity; not to leave the position concerned almost the only important step in the argument that is not spelled out. Owen concludes his exposition of this argument with the words: "And both conclusions are absurd. They were presented as an antinomy; but as a dilemma they are equally lethal." This surely amounts to an admission that Owen, fascinating and revealing as is his philosophy, is writing dubious history. For he nowhere faces the problem why, if Zeno intended his argument to be taken as a dilemma, he should even think of casting it in the form of an antinomy. To do so would be at once to convert a brilliant argument into an evidently invalid one. Further, Zeno is supposed to perform this conversion with his eyes open. He is supposed to realize that as it stands his conclusion is faulty, to know that he has not introduced the premiss on which he knows it to be based, and to know that he is presenting as necessary a conclusion he knows is only possible. This he is supposed to do in order to reduce to absurdity a proposition he does not mention. It seems difficult to resist the conclusion that, if Zeno did this kind of thing, he was either knave, fool, or obscurantist.

The reply might be made here that, if Zeno intended his argument merely as an antinomy, there was little point in making each arm absurd. But we may at once retort that there is certainly no harm in so constructing an antinomy as to show not only your opponent's self-contradiction but also his position's absurdity. We have already seen that the Platonic Parmenides, in constructing a series of antinomies, stops at least once to point out an absurdity. We may therefore feel no reluctance to believe that Zeno from time to time did the same. Since Parmenides in Plato's dialogue says that his method is in the main Zeno's, this confirmation is doubly welcome. Our interpretations of Plato and of Zeno may here without circularity of argument be said to support each other.

After analysing Achilles and Racecourse as an attempt to block the alternative "that anything is infinitely divisible but that such divisions can never be completed,"[57] Owen stated a third possibility: that "any division terminates in some finite number of steps beyond which no further step is even logically possible." Possibly levelled at this, on his view, is the argument quoted by Simplicius and given as fragment B3. Zeno argues as follows: "If there exist many things, they must be as many as they are, and neither more nor fewer, but if they are as many as they are they will be limited. If many things exist, the things that exist are infinite; for there are always things between the things that exist, and again other things between them and the things that exist. And thus the existing things are infinite in number."

Owen characterizes this argument as follows: "This is the argument that a collection containing a finite number of parts must also contain an infinite number of them. It must contain just the number that it does, whatever that number is; but between any two members there must be another member, so that the collection is infinitely numerous."[58] To Simplicius' interpretation of this as concerned again with infinite division Owen prefers understanding it as a "foretaste of Bradley's paradox. Any two members of a collection must be separated by something if they are to be two things and not one; but by the same argument what separates them must itself be separated from each by something else; and so forth." Now, whatever the connection with Bradley's paradox, it is clear that Owen's account of the argument itself is not in accordance with the text translated above. Zeno simply does not argue that any collection with a finite number of parts (or units) must have an infinite number of them. He argues instead that any collection with more than one member must have both a finite and infinite number of members. The argument therefore is meant, in so far as it is valid at all, to be valid against *any* plurality. It is not an argument that to suppose a division logically terminated in a finite number of steps is absurd; it is an argument that a plurality of any kind is absurd, because from the assumption of a plurality there follow the conclusions that the plurality is both finite and infinite. In short, the argument does not begin "from the consideration of a finite collection";[59] it begins from the consideration simply of a collection with more than one member.

Nor can it be argued that in the second half of the argument a *particular* kind of collection is first defined and then discussed. Zeno does not say, for example, that he is about to consider a plurality in which each unit is spatially separate from its neighbour(s). What he says is that, if a plurality exists at all, each member must be separated by something from its neighbour(s). He deduces from the existence of a plurality the consequence that each member must be so separate; he utters no definition of any kind. It is true that his argument is, as it stands, unconvincing; but that does not absolve us from the duty to discover what Zeno meant by it, and this duty is not fulfilled by turning his deduction into a definition in plain defiance of the text. Nor is there anything in the text about boundaries, and Owen's argument from design that Zeno must have meant such a reference is hardly convincing, especially without an explanation why Zeno should not refer *openly* to boundaries.

The same kind of objection can be brought against the anti-Pythagorean interpretation of this argument, otherwise one of the most tempting of such interpretations. If Zeno was arguing here that the Pythagorean conception of a plurality was illogical, then clearly it behoved him, and was indeed natural, to say so. We have no evidence, after all, that every argument in his book *had* to begin with the words εἰ πολλὰ ἔστιν without further explanation. The Pythagoreans of a relevant period may indeed have held that the plurality constituting the world was formed by the "one" breathing in the void and so dividing itself into a plurality of units separated from each other by empty space; the theory is recorded in a Pythagorean context and looks primitive.[60] What is more, if one takes Zeno's hypothesis that "many things exist" to mean that "a Pythagorean plurality exists," then the first step of the argument, at least, is now logical. The first step is also logical, and the subsequent steps perhaps more so, if one takes the hypothesis on this occasion as meaning "if there are many things having the properties of points on a line."[61] But there is simply no intelligible reason why one should take the text to mean this when it says nothing of the sort. There is no apparent reason why Zeno should not both mean what he says and say what he means. There is indeed every reason why he should be exact if he knew that to be inexact was in this case to be illogical and to expose himself to ridicule by a large proportion of his hearers or readers. Nor can there be any question here of Pythagorean views being in some sense representative of common sense or of the general opinion. For it is precisely here that Pythagorean views are at their most distinct from normal common sense; the natural reaction of any person of common sense to Zeno's argument here is surely to reply that it is quite possible for one thing to be next to another and that there is a sense in which such contiguous objects are continuous; it is indeed precisely this which makes Zeno's argument surprising and has called forth so many different interpretations of it. There should really be no question of Pythagoreanism here standing as representative of popular views. If, despite the lack of evidence or a priori probability for them, there ever were any popular views of plurality resembling the Pythagorean theories at this point, then we may once again adduce the point that in that case there remains no evidence for any Pythagorean influence on the argument. But it may be reiterated that the evidence for such a popular view is non-existent.

An attempt to do without the Pythagorean interpretation was made by Hermann Fränkel.[62] "If we assume plurality, i.e., divisibility of any unit, some part of it is here and some other part is there. But even if Here and There are very close together, nothing can prevent us from making the Something here and the Something there small enough to allow for a third thing to be squeezed in between them. The operation can be repeated indefinitely without reaching a limit. The premise of plurality and divisibility does not admit the assumption of an ultimate indivisible unit, and strict logic does not allow a gradual transition from the very small to the unextended." Greatly as we are indebted to Fränkel for his philological contributions to the study of Zeno, there are several disquieting things about this particular interpretation. The first is the absence of any proof that the premiss of plurality applies to the unit at all. In strict logic it is not the case that the hypothesis of a plurality implies the divisibility (or any other internal property) of the units composing it. More disturbing still is the observation that the word "always" in Zeno's argument is apparently reduced in Fränkel's exposition to the much weaker "nothing can prevent us . . ." Zeno does not say that the operation *can* if one wishes be repeated indefinitely; he states firmly that in the case of any pair of objects the regress he wants *will always* follow. It is clear that this will not do; Fränkel has turned this very different argument into something too like a pale reflection of the argument in fragments B1 and B2.

Zeller asserted boldly, in the course of his rejection of the anti-Pythagorean interpretation of Zeno, that two things are only two if they are separated from one another.[63] But on this interpretation one has the choice, it seems, of two alternatives neither of which is readily acceptable. One can suppose that the word "separated" is used in so wide a sense that it does not follow from the separation of two things that there is anything spatially between them; or one can suppose that the word "two" or "many" has only one sense, namely "separated by a spatial interval." The first supposition will not help Zeno's argument; the second is contrary to fact, as witness the analysis of the different senses of "many" in Aristotle's lexicon of philosophical terminology.[64]

Yet another stab at this argument is made by Booth, who renders it as follows: "Zeno argues that each existing thing must be separated from its neighbour. This is necessary, because if two neighbouring things are not separated, they would be one. Such an argument implies that all the units were of a single homogeneous nature; presumably Zeno thought that because they were all equally existent, they were all made of the single substance of 'beings.'"[65] This interpretation also, though there are elements of truth in it, is not wholly satisfying. It makes Zeno argue from strictly Eleatic premisses which his opponents need not accept, whoever they were; if his opponents had already accepted the Eleatic denial of differentiation, there was little left for Zeno to reduce to absurdity, unless it be the alleged Pythagorean number-atomism. So Booth's interpretation boils down to the anti-Pythagorean view. But, on the other hand, in another article[66] Booth cuts out the Eleatic premiss that all being is homogeneous in quality and says simply "If they were not separated, they would be *together, and therefore one*" (my italics). But this reduces his interpretation this time to the same as Zeller's; so it cannot be said that Booth's attempt to find a via media is very successful.

What most of these interpretations have in common is not that they make Zeno argue either too illogically or (given the necessary knowledge) with a logic beyond his powers. It is not so much that they are philosophically altogether implausible for a thinker of Zeno's time and calibre; some indeed are carefully integrated into their authors' views on the development of fifth-century Greek philosophy. What all have in common is their failure to explain why Zeno should not make his reasoning explicit. The gaps in Zeno's reasoning here (as elsewhere) are plugged too effectively; one still wants to know why, if Zeno's thought was as clear as this, he could not or would not expound it; and in some cases one wonders why his contemporaries and successors, among them men themselves of proved philosophical ability, could not follow his exposition—if it was as clear as his thought should, on these interpretations, lead us most naturally to expect. What seems to be needed is an explanation of Zeno's logic (especially, but not only, in B3) which accounts for Zeno's faulty reasoning, not by improving upon it and reading the improvements into the text but by showing that the logical ignorance prevalent in Zeno's day allowed him to believe that the inferences, as they appear in the texts, and without embellishment of any kind, were correct inferences. At the very least, it should be shown that, even if the clever and logically imaginative Zeno could have seen what was wrong, or that something was wrong, his contemporaries were likely to be incapable of detecting the fallacies and repaying their author in his own coin of ridicule. At the same time, it must be explained why Plato could regard Zeno's work with the slightly patronizing air of the first part of the *Parmenides*. In order so to examine Zeno's logic and that of his contemporaries it seems advisable to return to Plato's account in the second part of the *Parmenides* of a method explicitly stated to be closely similar to Zeno's. That account has not so far led us astray from the narrow path of strict adherence to Zeno's text; and so, at the risk of committing an *ignotum per ignotius*, we should at all events persevere in the inquiry whether it has any more positive information to offer than has hitherto been extracted from it.

POSITIVE EVIDENCE FROM PLATO

In the introduction to his *Parmenides* (137b) Plato sets the scene for the dialectical part by having Parmenides choose as his interlocutor the young Aristoteles, for the avowed reason that he will give the least trouble of those present; that is to say because Aristoteles will raise the fewest awkward questions. This is perhaps a hint from Plato (hardly from the fictional Parmenides) that at least some of the arguments in the second half of the dialogue are in some respects fallacious. Aristoteles is made not to notice the illogicalities that are known to Plato, who used them to concoct, for whatever purpose, a set of contradictory conclusions. The hint would reasonably be meant to insinuate that a mature person would be able to spot the illogicalities, but at the same time, in the fictional context of Plato's second part, Parmenides' arguments are still depicted as having dialectical force.

It is no part of the task now before us to attempt to disentangle from the welter of faulty inferences in the *Parmenides* the single basic type (if there be such) which Plato wished his contemporaries to notice. But Parmenides' argument in the dialogue has certain prominent features which are, or may be, pertinent to the positive interpretation of Zeno, and to these the reader's attention is now drawn.

We may first observe that several times in the second part of the *Parmenides* the Eleatic's argument takes an abrupt about turn, a premiss (not necessarily the initial premiss) of one argument directly contradicting the conclusion reached by its immediate predecessor. This is particularly the case in the arguments forming those "Hypotheses" which establish not a set of negative conclusions but a series of antinomies (within the larger-scale antinomies formed by successive pairs of Hypotheses). Thus, for example, at 145b–e it is argued (a) that the One is in itself and (b) that the One will be in something else. Now (a) is argued as follows: (1) each of the One's parts will be in the whole, and none outside it; (2) all the parts are encompassed by the whole; (3) the One and all its parts (no more and no less) are equivalent; therefore (4) the One is the whole; therefore *if* (1) all the parts are in the whole and (3) all the parts together are the One and (4) the whole and (2) all the parts are encompassed by the whole, then (5) the One is encompassed by the One and (6) the One is in itself. So far (granted the premisses) the logic is not too bad. But then the argument (b) runs that, not being in any one part of itself nor in some parts (but not others) nor in all (for that would entail its being in one), the One must not be in itself and therefore (since it is not nowhere, which would make it non-existent, but is a whole) is in something else. Thus the negative of the first conclusion is used to establish the second. In this instance, it is true, a veneer of innocuousness is put upon the argument by Parmenides' saying at the end that the One is in something else in so far as it is whole, and is in itself only in so far as it is all its parts together. But this is indeed only a bogus veneer; for, if we cast our eyes back to argument (a), we see that it is implied there that all the parts together are the whole. Parmenides has only covered one volte-face by smartly executing another.

In a later argument, beginning at 146d, there is not even a bogus cover. Parmenides first proves that the One is at rest and then that it is not at rest, but in motion. Similarly at 146dff, Parmenides first argues (a) that the One is different from the Others and then, as the first step in the succeeding argument for (b) the sameness of One and Others, argues (down to 147a3) that they are not different after all. And yet at the end of the total antinomy (to wit, 147b) both (a) and (b) are true simultaneously —and Parmenides, unlike Plato's commentators, has said nothing about their being true in different senses.

Again, in the opening lines of Hypothesis III, at 157b, the Others are not the One, but they do partake of it. For, if they lacked parts, they would be absolutely one, and therefore they must have parts and be one whole of parts. But in the opening gambit of Hypothesis IV, at 159b, it is argued that the others are not one in any sense, since they must be quite separate from the One, in order to be "Others" at all. This, to all appearances, demolishes, according to Parmenides' lights, the premiss from which the later conclusions of Hypothesis III were drawn. Yet, at the beginning of Hypothesis IV, Plato represents Parmenides as supposing the arguments of Hypothesis IV as being *added* to those of Hypothesis III; ἆρα καὶ οὐχ οὕτως ἔχει τὰ ἄλλα τοῦ ἑνὸς ἢ οὕτω μόνον; Parmenides is adding one set of conclusions to another, not stating alternatives; this is made doubly clear in the summary of conclusions offered at 160b. The volte-face duly takes place but is ignored by its fictional author.

An argument disproves its immediate successor at 161c–e, in Hypothesis V. There it is said in one place that to attribute equality to the non-existent One would be to imply its existence. No more is heard of this when in the next paragraph the One is proved to partake in equality.

What is common to all these is the bland jettisoning of the content of one argument in an immediately succeeding or manifestly parallel piece of reasoning. The form of construction in which a succeeding argument disproves one of its predecessor's interim conclusions on the way to proving a contradiction of its predecessor's final conclusion is but one among many such about turns to be found in Parmenides' labyrinth of reasoning in the second part of Plato's *Parmenides*. It is as hard to believe that Plato did not see these strange twists as it is to believe that, having seen them, he chose to ignore them. But that Plato's philosophical purpose was presumably not to re-state such arguments as genuine proofs, but rather to achieve some other philosophical end, is not relevant to present purposes. The present aim is rather to elucidate certain characteristics of Parmenides' reasoning *as it stands* which may prove to be as relevant to Zeno as we should naturally be led to expect by Parmenides' original statement that he is going to follow Zeno's method. Not content with one such characteristic, we may now proceed to another two which are possibly relevant.

This is a pair of closely related types. Plato may have believed in his younger days that "a proposition ... can entail its own contradictory without the aid of extra premisses"[67]—even if not of the special class of propositions typified by Russell's notorious paradox. There are two obvious and closely related methods by which one can at least appear to elicit self-contradictions from a single proposition. The first is to take the proposition first in one sense and then in another, deducing contradictory consequences from the two senses while ignoring the equivocation involved in the process; the second is to emphasize first one concept employed in the proposition and then another, taking the emphasized concept in each case with absolute strictness while allowing the other a normal conversational looseness. Obviously, these two procedures are closely related: the second could indeed be regarded as a species of the first, which is evidently more general.

This description, though heavy-handed, may serve to bring out the similarities and differences between the two types. Examples may help. In Hypotheses VII and VIII Plato develops two arguments concerning the consequences for "the Others" if the "One" is not. The first starts at 164b–c with the deduction that, for the Others to be other, there must exist something for them to be other than, and this cannot be the One, for that is non-existent. The second starts from the deduction at 165e that the "others than one" cannot be many, for that would be to contain a one and, being other than one, they cannot even contain a one. Plato makes his Parmenides draw from these two beginnings conclusions which flatly contradict one another. Now, even apart from fallacies appearing later in these arguments, it is by no means a simple matter to pin down the equivocations in the opening deductions. In the first, one could argue, the word "others," in the sentence "If the one is not, what are the consequences for the others?," is taken to mean not "others than the one" but simply "others," and something existent is then demanded for these "others" to be other than. Stress is laid on the "relative" nature of the term "others." In the second argument the word "others" is taken to mean, as it normally would in this context, "others than the one" and an extreme notion of "otherness than" is then invoked; stress is laid on the exclusive force of the term "others." An alternative, but perhaps less persuasive, possibility is to suppose that in Hypothesis VII the phrase "is not" is taken more strictly than in Hypothesis VIII, where it is the non-being one than which the others are other. But at any rate it is fairly clear that Plato has made Parmenides use the same word or words in different senses within the same pair of arguments and that this is one important reason for the final contradiction between their results. Since Parmenides treats each deduction as necessary, his procedure may be tabulated as follows: (1) he takes one possible sense of a sentence and deduces consequences applicable only to that sense; (2) he takes another possible sense and deduces from it consequences deducible only from this sense; (3) he treats each sense as if it were the only and necessary sense, and deductions from each sense as the necessary analytical consequences of the original sentence. Again, in Hypotheses I and II Plato mounts a double argument with the premiss that one thing is, each series of deductions being represented by the fictional Parmenides as necessary. In Hypothesis I it is the unity of the existent one which is analysed to the virtual exclusion of its being; in Hypothesis II it is the being of the one thing which is analysed to the virtual exclusion of its unity. In one chain of deduction the word "one" is emphasized and isolated, and in the second the word "is" is treated in the same way. Both sets of conclusions are assumed by the fictional Parmenides to be true if his premiss is true, and both sets are for him simultaneously true on that condition. An alternative way of treating the whole argument is to say that in Hypothesis I the word "one" is taken in the strictest possible sense, excluding all plurality of any kind, but in Hypothesis II the word "one" is taken at its conversational face value while "being" is taken strictly, as implying οὐσίας μετέχειν, to "have being."

We see, therefore, that Plato depicts his Parmenides, who, he says, is following a method close to Zeno's, as arguing from one way of taking a proposition as if it were the only and necessary way of taking it, treating another sense of the proposition in the same way, and then adding together the conflicting results so obtained to produce an antinomy. We may note further that the assumption underlying this procedure is fundamentally simple. It is a necessary and sufficient condition for the validity of this manner of argument that no proposition or word be able, logically, to have more than one meaning; for on this assumption the otherwise obvious charge of equivocation is immediately void. It is also worthy of note that this is by no means the first time that a Presocratic thinker has been accused of arguing on that assumption. Plato's portrayal of Zeno's method is thus historically plausible; Zeno's text, we shall see, confirms it.

CONFIRMATION FROM ZENO'S TEXT

In the argument forming his B2 and B1, Zeno starts from the proposition that many things exist. From this he first deduces that each will be the same as itself and one. From this, if Simplicius' summary is accurate, he deduces further that the whole will have no magnitude.[68] Zeno then turns round and argues that things with no magnitude cannot exist, because when added to or subtracted from anything else they make no difference to it. Therefore, since ex hypothesi they exist, the plurality he postulated originally will after all have size. From this point is deduced (by an argument from dichotomy) their infinity of magnitude.

Two things need observing here about this line of thought. First, it certainly illustrates the very kind of volte-face exemplified in (especially) the second Hypothesis of the *Parmenides*. The kind of volte-face involved is precisely that in which a subsequent argument disproves its predecessor's conclusion on the way to its own. The existence of the many with no magnitude, the conclusion, so far as we can see, of the first part of Zeno's argument, is promptly annihilated by the proof which opens the second part, showing that existence and nil magnitude were incompatible. And yet the two conclusions are both accepted at the end of the day. Evidently one trick of Zeno's reasoning is faithfully portrayed in the *Parmenides*.[69] We are encouraged to look for more.

Our second observation is that a further trick of Plato's Parmenides *may* be discernible in this same argument of Zeno's. The second half of Zeno's argument does not depend on the plurality of the assumed existents. All that it visibly requires is that they should indeed exist. Zeno has taken one concept in the proposition "many things exist" and analysed it to the virtual exclusion of the other main concept contained in that proposition. It is possible, but not, I think, provable, that Zeno has done the same thing with the concept of plurality in the first part of this argument. The second half of this first part, from the unity of the individuals in the assumed plurality to their lack of magnitude, has rightly been illustrated from Melissus and need not be discussed here.[70] But what about the first steps? How did Zeno get from many existent things to the self-identity and unity of each? Vlastos recently suggested (unfortunately without space for supporting argument) that self-identity and unity were regarded as minimal conditions of being.[71] Presumably, on this hypothesis, being would imply self-identity and self-identity would imply unity. This is a very reasonable suggestion, and hardly could be disproved; but it is not the only possibility. The argument could here run something like this: many things exist; in order to be members of a plurality the things must each be distinct from the others and not from itself, and in consequence each must be one. In this context should be cited an argument from Plato's *Parmenides* 157e–158a. Parmenides has proved to his satisfaction that the Others must form one perfect whole with parts, and he next proceeds to argue that each part must also partake of unity. "For if (we say that) each of them is a part, by applying the word 'each' we surely mean 'one, distinct from the rest, but existing in itself,' if the word 'each' is to be rightly applied to them" (εἰ γὰρ ἕκαστον αὐτῶν μόριόν ἐστι, τό γε ἕκαστον εἶναι ἓν δήπου σημαίνει ἀφωρισμένον μὲν τῶν ἄλλων, καθ' αὑτὸ δὲ ὄν, εἴπερ ἕκαστον ἔσται).[72] Self-identity would naturally accompany difference from the other members of a set, as at Parmenides B8.57–58, ἑωυτῷ πάντοσε τωὐτόν, τῷ δ' ἑτέρῳ μὴ τωὐτόν. Zeno may after all have deduced the unity of each member of the hypothetical plurality from its status as a member of a plurality rather than from its existence. Nor would he have been alone in doing this. The Platonic Parmenides at 165e makes the direct deduction from "many" to a set of "ones"; Eudemus actually says that Zeno argued that a plurality of existents was impossible, since (a) there was no existent one and (b) a plurality is a collection of units.[73] The possibility cannot by any means be ruled out that self-identity and unity are for Zeno minimal conditions of membership of a *plurality*. If they were, and he said so in this argument, then what he has done here is simply to take the proposition "many things exist" and deduce, by analysis first of one and then of another concept in it, two conclusions which contradict each other. It should be noticed that during the deduction from the things' plurality their existence could not be taken in the same strict way as it is in the argument from their existence—and vice versa. A glance back at previous remarks on Parmenides' procedure in Plato's dialogue will suffice to show that Zeno would thus be doing in this argument of B2 and B1 one of the things that Plato makes his Parmenides do: he has taken his proposition and deduced contradictory conclusions from it by placing the emphasis in his analysis first on one concept and then on another. This is what we found Plato's Parmenides doing in Hypotheses I and II.

Thus fortified in our conclusions by one clear and one possible agreement between Plato's representation of Zeno's methods and our own observation of them in Zeno's writings, we may turn to B3, the other argument of which we have the bulk in Zeno's own words. To recapitulate, Zeno argues first that, if there are many things, then they will be as many as they are, and therefore limited. Apart from the paralogism, this is straightforward enough: the word "many" here is simply used numerically, and all that is needed is that the members of the assumed plurality should not be identified with one another; "non-identical" is one sense—indeed the minimum sense—of "many." The second half of the argument is more complex. The argument is that between any two of the members of the plurality mentioned in the hypothesis there must be a third, and so on. Now, it is evident at once that it is possible to have two members of a plurality in contact, and as Plato's Parmenides (at 149a) would have it, contact excludes a third object in between, so that this argument cannot, it seems, get under way at all. That is the reason for the recurring explanation of the argument as assuming that the many have the property of points on a line; no point has a next point but there is always another point between two points, however small one makes the distance between them. In default of direct or convincing indirect evidence for any such explanation, we are thrown back on the evidence that we have analysed already. This showed that Parmenides in Plato's dialogue, in an avowed imitation of the historical Zeno, from time to time treated one possible sense of the proposition under examination as if it were the only sense, and thus propounded as deductions, certain deductions, from the original hypothesis propositions which followed only if the propositions were taken in one particular sense. It must not, therefore, be considered strange, or in any way unexpected, if we find Zeno doing precisely the same thing in his extant writings. But this is exactly what we have now found; for the problem that has vexed scholars on this argument of B3 is why Zeno should treat as following from "many things exist" a proposition that follows only from one sense of that hypothesis, namely that in which the word "many" bears the meaning "spatially separate." The answer to the question is that Zeno was in the habit of doing this, saw nothing illogical in it, and was indeed represented by Plato as having done it. Not knowing much about equivocation, and making in this difficult case the common early assumption that an utterance has only one meaning, Zeno could argue without a qualm exactly as the text of B3 argues.

POSSIBLE OBJECTIONS

In conclusion it is advisable to forestall some possible objections to the foregoing interpretation. The first starts from the remark of Eudemus, mentioned above, reporting Zeno's saying that, if anybody could tell him what the one was, he would admit a plurality. I have suggested already that this does not imply an attack by Zeno on a particular view of the units in a plurality. But it remains to warn the reader that it fails also to imply that Zeno went looking for all available different notions of the unit in order, like Herod, to murder all he could find. Zeno's remark is compatible with a very different situation.

It seems to be almost generally assumed that Zeno's challenge was meant as a general statement about the whole range of arguments that he deploys. But this need not be true. Eudemus cites it and then says that its context seems to be a difficulty in finding anything "one" in sensible things. One of the two reasons given by Eudemus for this difficulty is "division"; clearly he means that (according to Zeno) any sensible object is divisible and hence many—and therefore not one after all. This is very like an Eleatic argument given by Aristotle, an argument concerned with division, one of whose steps is that there is no one thing and therefore no plurality of things.[74] So far as this argument goes, and as an introduction or epilogue to it, Zeno would be quite justified in remarking that, if his opponents could genuinely offer him a unit, he would accept a plurality. It is their inability to produce a unit unimpaired by plurality which hamstrings Zeno's opponents here. Of course the remark would be meant in some degree ironically; Zeno has other arguments ready in case his opponents do find a unit. But it is perfectly appropriate to the single argument in question, and we have no evidence whatever that it was meant as a general statement concerning the whole set of arguments.

A different and difficult problem is presented, and not only to one holding the view of Zeno advanced here, by a passage in the extant versions of Gorgias' "On Nature," or "What Is Not." The Pseudo-Aristotelian *MXG* is of little help, the text at 979b13ff being pretty hopelessly corrupt; but Sextus Empiricus at *Adversus mathematicos* 7.73 is very interesting. Gorgias is arguing either (1) that what is is neither one nor many or (2) that neither one thing nor many things exist. For present purposes the distinction between (1) and (2) is scarcely relevant. The argument takes the form of a reductio ad absurdum successively of "one" and "many" (whether as subject or predicate does not, I repeat, matter here). The reduction of "many" to absurdity depends, in good Zenonian fashion, on the impossibility of a plurality, given the already demonstrated impossibility of a "one." No unit, no plurality. The important portion of the argument from our present point of view lies in the disproof of "one." Here Sextus makes Gorgias set up a series of alternatives and demolish each in turn, in just the way Owen says Zeno did. εἰ γὰρ ἕν ἐστιν, ἤτοι ποσόν ἐστιν ἢ συνεχές ἐστιν ἢ μέγεθός ἐστιν ἢ σῶμά ἐστιν. ὅ τι δ' ἂν ᾖ τούτων, οὐχ ἕν ἐστιν... Now, as Diels pointed out, some of the language of this is unlikely to be anything but Peripatetic.[75] ποσόν looks very like an Aristotelian category; but that by no means precludes this general type of analysis from Gorgian authorship. The passage is not demonstrably alien in toto to the time when Gorgias may be supposed to have written it, probably the fifth century.[76]

Several points must accordingly be discussed concerning it. The first is that the passage would knock firmly on the head any argument to the effect that, because X says you cannot have a one which is also a many, therefore it *must* be true that X should not distinguish any different applications of "one" or "many." For Gorgias—if this be indeed he—uses Zeno's objection to a unity tainted with plurality but does nevertheless analyse out some kinds of unity, or at least applications of "one." But it leaves open the invitation, given by the argument relying on the impossibility of a tainted unity, to inspect other arguments by the same person for symptoms of the inability to distinguish different applications of "one" or "many." If Gorgias indeed combined the arguments against plurality and against unity offered by Sextus in this passage, then he represents an uneasy situation unlikely to be primitive and likely to be merely transitional. Since Gorgias probably wrote after Zeno and possibly late in the fifth century, his occupation of this transitional and uneasy resting-place is not good evidence against Zeno's having, as his text shows, argued in ignorance of the possibility or of the relevance of the homonymy of "many." It should at the same time be noted that (a) the analysis of different kinds of "one" in Sextus is crude[77] and (b) in the version given by Sextus the analysis into different applications is, as one would expect, explicit. Both these points are in sharp contrast to the procedure sometimes attributed to Zeno, whereby the analysis of different kinds of plurality (a) is subtle and (b) inexplicit. That Gorgias should (a) be doing something cruder than Zeno and (b) find it more necessary to say what he is doing, may be thought to consort ill with his later date of writing. But this is by no means the strongest argument in favour of the present interpretation of Zeno against plurality and is not to be pressed further than it will legitimately go.

Another objection is pertinent, though in the last analysis ill founded. The reader may be worried by the thought that, for one with no idea of the senses of "one" and "many," Zeno shows remarkable, indeed incredible, skill in persisting with one sense throughout the steps of the argument in the second half of B3. I can imagine a reader asking, "Surely Zeno could not do this without knowing what he was doing?" To this question the answer is quite simply that he could. Zeno set out in this argument, as in many others, to arrive at an infinite. The easiest way to do this is to repeat ad infinitum the same process. Zeno in B3 is not sticking to one sense of "many" because it is right to stick to one sense of "many" but because, having started putting things between other things, he has no choice but to go on. He is not being remarkably perceptive but is merely displaying his customary nose for the technique of argument according to the logical canons of his day.

CONCLUSION

The foregoing is designed to show that Zeno did not appreciate that the word "many" is more complicated than his logic demanded, that he failed to understand that it had more than one sense, and that he was not a sufficiently mature logician to see that such complexity was relevant to his argument. As a minimum position, even if Zeno himself appreciated these things, he could rely on the logical ignorance of his contemporary opponents. From these views it follows that any attempt to show Zeno analysing one kind of plurality after another, in order to drive opponents from one position to another, is doomed to failure: doomed because it substitutes the requirements of modern logic for those of the fifth century B.C. It would follow also that attempts to explain Zeno's mode of inference by reading into his text a reference to a contemporary Pythagorean theory are unnecessary and therefore unconvincing. Zeno is his own best expositor, and Plato is more to be relied on for understanding than any of the moderns.

The contention that Zeno and/or most of his contemporaries could not understand that common but difficult words had more than one meaning may in general be acceptable. But in the particular case now before us it could still be argued that Plato was misinterpreting Zeno. Plato could be supposed to have omitted to notice that Zeno's argument referred to Pythagorean theories, and could perhaps have hit on the type of fallacy illustrated above as a mere expedient for the understanding of Zeno. The expedient would also offer a chance of training the young in the detection of ambiguities and equivocations. This could be the point of Plato's *Parmenides*. But the case for this type of alternative view is not strong. Plato was sufficiently steeped in Pythagorean thought not to forget about it when he came to read Zeno and sufficiently acute to see its relevance if it became necessary. It cannot be claimed that the present reading of the second half of the *Parmenides* is such as to leave room for only a contemptuous judgement by Plato on Zeno; for the points here taken from the *Parmenides* are not intended as a complete reading of it, and no one need shrink from acknowledging that there is much serious argument embedded in the fallacies of the second half. What is more, we have found some independent evidence that early philosophers, and even some later than Zeno, found it difficult to distinguish the different senses of one and many.[78]

It is at least clear that we do not hear of any distinction between senses of "one" and "many" before Zeno. If the view be accepted that Zeno analysed out the various kinds of plurality and then demolished each in turn, we shall have to suppose that he performed a colossal task of analysis at one fell swoop. The history of philosophy is full of surprises, and one should never underestimate the great thinkers of the past; but it should surely be admitted that, in an age which had barely begun the task of analysing linguistic usage[79] and was still floundering in the most primitive stages of that analysis, this particular feat is hardly probable. The development of philosophy is normally more gradual than this. It is more reasonable to suppose that Zeno's mistaken logic led his successors, in their attempts to solve his paradoxes, gradually closer to understanding of the complexities inherent in the terms "one" and "many." On this view, Gorgias would represent a substantial advance, won perhaps almost unconsciously. The *Parmenides* of Plato could on this hypothesis represent (among other things) a further stage in the exploration of the numerous ambiguities of these terms and the many possible equivocations on them, and Aristotle's brilliant analysis in *Metaphysics Δ* would represent the crowning achievement of Greek thought in this line of development.

It may be admissible, if not too immodest, to close this chapter with a brief statement of the advantages to be gained by acceptance of my interpretation in its entirety. First, there is no single word of either Plato or

Aristotle which has to be glossed over, supposed other than trivially wrong, or otherwise cavalierly treated. Secondly, there is no word of Zeno's own written text as it is extant which has to be either wished away (as Fränkel virtually did ἀεί in B3) or embellished with a gloss (such as specification of a Pythagorean target) not to be found in the ancient sources. By placing Zeno's reasoning firmly in the context of the logical ignorance of his time, we may suppose at last that Zeno meant exactly what he said: no more, no less. We have not thus succeeded in making sense of Zeno's B3, and other arguments; but we have perhaps succeeded in showing that as they stand, and without embellishment of any sort, they are the kind of nonsense that Zeno might have believed to be sense.

VIII

ONE-MANY PROBLEMS IN ATOMISM

ZENO AND THE ATOMISTS

This is not the place to discuss details over the whole range of the remarkably comprehensive system excogitated by Leucippus and Democritus in order in some degree to save appearances from the Eleatic onslaught. Much of the work has already been done.[1] What I do wish to discuss is the origin and the place in the Atomists' philosophy of one particular argument especially germane to the present subject. Aristotle four times attributes to the Atomists the suggestion that what is one, or "truly one," cannot give rise to a plurality. At least one recent writer has chosen to connect this with the alleged argument of Parmenides that what is one cannot become many.[2] I believe the truth of the matter to be somewhat different. But, before we can plunge into that issue, the way must be prepared by summarizing the probable relations between Atomists and Eleatics in the light of the conclusions about Zeno reached in the previous chapter and in the light of arguments against plurality there omitted. Such a summary must start from Aristotle's account in the eighth chapter of the first book of *De generatione et corruptione*.[3]

ἐνίοις γὰρ τῶν ἀρχαίων ἔδοξε τὸ ὂν ἐξ ἀνάγκης ἓν εἶναι καὶ ἀκίνητον· τὸ μὲν γὰρ κενὸν οὐκ ὄν, κινηθῆναι δ' οὐκ ἂν δύνασθαι μὴ ὄντος κενοῦ κεχωρισμένου, οὐδ' αὖ πολλὰ εἶναι μὴ ὄντος τοῦ διείργοντος—τοῦτο δ' οὐδὲν διαφέρειν, εἴ τις οἴεται μὴ συνεχὲς εἶναι τὸ πᾶν ἀλλ' ἅπτεσθαι διῃρημένον, τοῦ φάναι πολλὰ καὶ μὴ ἓν εἶναι καὶ κενόν. εἰ μὲν γὰρ πάντῃ διαιρετόν, οὐθὲν εἶναι ἕν, ὥστε οὐδὲ πολλά, ἀλλὰ κενὸν τὸ ὅλον· εἰ δὲ τῇ μὲν τῇ δὲ μή, πεπλασμένῳ τινὶ τοῦτ' ἐοικέναι. μέχρι πόσου γάρ, καὶ διὰ τί τὸ μὲν οὕτως ἔχει τοῦ ὅλου καὶ πλῆρές ἐστι, τὸ δὲ διῃρημένον; ἔτι δ' ὁμοίως ἀναγκαῖον μὴ εἶναι κίνησιν. ἐκ μὲν οὖν τούτων τῶν λόγων ὑπερβάντες τὴν αἴσθησιν καὶ παριδόντες αὐτὴν ὡς τῷ λόγῳ δέον ἀκολουθεῖν, ἓν καὶ ἀκίνητον τὸ πᾶν εἶναί φασι καὶ ἄπειρον ἔνιοι· τὸ γὰρ πέρας περαίνειν ἂν πρὸς τὸ κενόν ... Λεύκιππος δ' ἔχειν ᾠήθη λόγους, οἵτινες πρὸς τὴν αἴσθησιν ὁμολογούμενα λέγοντες οὐκ ἀναιρήσουσιν οὔτε γένεσιν οὔτε φθορὰν οὔτε κίνησιν καὶ τὸ πλῆθος τῶν ὄντων. ὁμολογήσας δὲ ταῦτα μὲν τοῖς φαινομένοις, τοῖς δὲ τὸ ἓν κατασκευάζουσιν ὡς οὐκ ἂν κίνησιν οὖσαν ἄνευ κενοῦ, τό τε κενὸν μὴ ὂν καὶ τοῦ ὄντος οὐθὲν μὴ ὄν φησιν εἶναι· τὸ γὰρ κυρίως ὂν παμπλῆρες ὄν. ἀλλ' εἶναι τὸ τοιοῦτον οὐχ ἕν, ἀλλ' ἄπειρα τὸ πλῆθος καὶ ἀόρατα διὰ σμικρότητα τῶν ὄγκων. ταῦτα δ' ἐν τῷ κενῷ φέρεσθαι (κενὸν γὰρ εἶναι), καὶ συνιστάμενα μὲν γένεσιν ποιεῖν, διαλυόμενα δὲ φθοράν. ποιεῖν δὲ καὶ πάσχειν ᾗ τυγχάνουσιν ἁπτόμενα (ταύτῃ γὰρ οὐχ ἓν εἶναι), καὶ συντιθέμενα δὲ καὶ περιπλεκόμενα γεννᾶν. ἐκ δὲ τοῦ κατ' ἀλήθειαν ἑνὸς οὐκ ἂν γενέσθαι πλῆθος οὐδ' ἐκ τῶν ἀληθῶς πολλῶν ἕν, ἀλλ' εἶναι τοῦτ' ἀδύνατον· ἀλλ', ὥσπερ Ἐμπεδοκλῆς καὶ τῶν ἄλλων τινές φασι πάσχειν διὰ τῶν πόρων, οὕτω πᾶσαν ἀλλοίωσιν καὶ πᾶν τὸ πάσχειν τοῦτον γίνεσθαι τὸν τρόπον, διὰ τοῦ κενοῦ γινομένης τῆς διαλύσεως καὶ τῆς φθορᾶς, ὁμοίως δὲ καὶ τῆς αὐξήσεως, ὑπεισδυομένων στερεῶν ...

Aristotle does not state but, I think, implies Atomist acceptance of the doctrine that there was no plurality without something to keep its components asunder. Leucippus thought he had arguments which would preserve the motion, genesis and/or destruction, and plurality of things as revealed by the senses. Motion, he conceded to Melissus, could not occur without void,[4] and allowing that void was non-existence he replied simply that "not-Being does exist"—a classic example of a man reduced to paradox because unable to find the language in which to say "in a sense."[5] This ignores Parmenides' ontological argument against motion, but that subject can be postponed. Leucippus treats genesis and destruction as special cases of motion. The coming-together and entanglement of atoms constitutes genesis, and dissolution (the Atomist version of destruction) takes place through the void, which allows the relevant movement.

Little is said directly about the preservation of plurality. But Aristotle does not say that Leucippus thought that plurality could exist without gaps. The atoms act upon, and are acted upon by, each other as they chance to come into contact. Such contact does not make them one —which might appear to indicate Leucippus' insight that a plurality without gaps could exist. But it seems on close inspection that what he means (according to Aristotle) is that mere transitory contact does not constitute a proper closing of the gaps. For Aristotle goes on to say that from a true one no plurality could come to be, nor from a true plurality could a unity arise. All changes take place by dissolution (just as Empedocles uses pores) through the void. It is difficult here to separate dissolution from the process of a unity giving rise to a plurality. Aristotle contrasts coming-to-be (by entanglement) with the formation of a plurality from unity, and coming-to-be is most naturally contrasted in Greek philosophy with passing-away. The *impossibility* of a unity giving rise to a plurality or vice versa is then put in contrast (ἀλλ') with the process of dissolution by dissipation through the void. Clearly there must be something in the production either of a unity from a plurality or vice versa which introduces void and so dissipates and destroys. This can only mean that the formation of a plurality from a true unity introduces void where there was none before. So that a true unity has no void in it, and a plurality does. A true plurality does contain void, and such a plurality cannot become a unity—mere contact does not constitute the closing of the gap but allows the presence of void around the point or surfaces of contact. Leucippus in fact conserves plurality, like motion, by means of the void.

So, as D. J. Furley puts it, "There could be no plurality without something to separate the units."[6] Furley construes this as an acceptance of Parmenides' statement of the continuity of Being; but, though this statement was important to the Atomists elsewhere, the connection here seems to me a little thin. At his B8.22–25 Parmenides is arguing that only Being exists and therefore there can be no differences or separations within it. Parmenides is saying that there can be no plurality or distinctions of any kind; the question what kind of distinction (for example, separation by void) constitutes a true plurality does not arise in this context. If we have to connect Aristotle's "no plurality without a separator" with an extant Eleatic argument, a far better choice would be Zeno's B3. For Zeno there says precisely that, if there is a plurality, it must have something separating its components. It would be preferable to associate the reasoning declared by Aristotle to have influenced the Atomists with its exact counterpart in Zeno rather than with the only vaguely similar Parmenides. But this is one of the many places in Presocratic philosophy where certainty is unattainable; for Aristotle's context is Melissan, including as it does the argument from "no void" to "no motion," and the possibility remains that Melissus capped this argument with one against plurality, an argument running from "no void" to "no separator," and hence "no plurality." Even a lost Parmenidean origin for such an argument, though not very likely, cannot altogether be ruled out.

Whether the statement that plurality necessitates a separator was taken by Aristotle from Zeno's B3, or from another Eleatic source now lost, the attribution of it to a group of thinkers clearly Eleatic offers strong support to the interpretation of Zeno's B3 given in the previous chapter. For we have now the authority of Aristotle for supposing that an Eleatic could indeed argue, as simply and straightforwardly as the first sentence of B3 argues, that any plurality must have something between its members.

But this is not the end of the matter. It would be tempting for critics of this interpretation to make use of Aristotle's transition from οὐδ' αὖ πολλὰ εἶναι μὴ ὄντος τοῦ διείργοντος to the subsequent reasoning about divisibility. To a superficial glance, it looks as if Aristotle is making his Eleatic(s) say: "Either a plurality has its members separated by gaps or it does not. If you do not like the consequences of supposing that it does, then here is an argument which does not number such separation among its premisses. You have the choice." But I do not think this would be a fair deduction from Aristotle. Aristotle seems to me to make his Eleatics say something rather different; "There *is* no plurality without a separator. But in any case, whether this is true or not, divisibility with or without separation would have the following disastrous consequences." Aristotle does in fact firmly attribute to his unnamed Eleatics the belief that every plurality had a separator between its members. His unnamed Eleatics can conceive that somebody might not share this belief, but Aristotle says nothing to show that his Eleatics treated what he says they believed as a mere alternative analysis of plurality. If Zeno (or any Eleatic) could conceive of an opponent differing from him, then he perhaps had the faintest glimmer of suspicion that there might be something wrong with such a statement as begins B3, or as is reported by Aristotle here; but no more need be conceded than the faintest glimmer. Aristotle does after all confirm, and does not demolish, the straightforward interpretation of Zeno's B3.

Zeno has it, then, that the components of a plurality must be separated. If the separator in turn was to be an entity distinguishable from the components, it too must be separated from them by something, and so on. The first step in this regress the Atomists, according to Aristotle's plausible account, accepted. But, although, by accepting the first step and thus the univocality of πολλά (or at least its treatment in this argument as if it were univocal), they had denied themselves the most obvious reason for rejecting subsequent steps, they nevertheless did reject those subsequent steps. How they were able to do so is matter for conjecture only. But there is a way in which they could have dealt with this problem after their fashion, and I should like to suggest, with the utmost diffidence, that it may have been their way out. Zeno had argued, we remember, that a plurality of ὄντα, of "being things," had to have something to separate them. This Leucippus accepts. Then Zeno says that the separator also must be separated, and so on, until we have an infinity of ὄντα, of "being things." But Leucippus at this stage replies: "I have no such infinity of ὄντα, since the primary separator is itself not an ὄν—it is void, which we are agreed is μὴ ὄν." Thus the Atomists would have it both ways: the void does exist, when they are asked how they can either talk about it or explain motion; but it is not-Being when they are answering Zeno, and there is no argument of Zeno's that not-Being has to be separated from Being in order to be a distinguishable entity, for the simple reason that not-Being is not an entity. We shall find other places where having things both ways in this fashion would have been of the greatest assistance to Leucippus, but in the meantime whatever degree of neatness this answer has must remain its only recommendation. What needs emphasis here is that Aristotle is quite likely to have had in mind in this passage of the *De generatione et corruptione* an argument of Zeno's, or at least an argument based on the same striking premiss.

The argument given in the following lines (still from 325a8ff) is that, whether you have discretes in contact or spatially separate units, (a) it is arbitrary[7] to suppose any limit to the division of the whole thus set on foot and (b) if there is no such limit, then there is no unit to be found in things, presumably because any unit you take is divisible into many subunits, and so ad infinitum. If there is no unit, then there can be no plurality. The assumption behind the last step is that any plurality must be made up of units. The assumption behind the preceding step is the archaic supposition that a thing cannot be at the same time both one and many.

This argument has points of similarity with another expounded by Aristotle at *De generatione et corruptione* 316a14ff and is sometimes identified with it.[8] This second argument assumes the possibility of division at any and every point. But then, if the division is complete, the resulting parts either have magnitude or not; if they do, then the division is incomplete after all (the infinite divisibility of space is here assumed), and, if they do not, then spatial magnitudes either are composed of nil magnitudes, which was deemed impossible, or are nothing (and the "all" is nothing but a mere appearance). The final conclusion of the argument here is superficially like that of the argument at 325a, namely, that the "whole" is empty. But this does not settle the question whether they are the same argument. One argument appears in Aristotle to assume infinite divisibility, the other (at 325a9-10) appears to argue explicitly for it, or at least to refute the contradictory of it; but this, since Aristotle is at liberty to omit such a preliminary argument if he chooses, cannot be called decisive either. What seems to decide the issue is the difficulty of fitting the units of 325a, non-existent because divisible into pluralities, into the argument of 316a. Which, at 316a, are the ones which are always many, however far the division goes? The best place to put them in might seem to be where we arrive at an infinity of division products.

These products are with magnitude or without; supposing them to have magnitude, and suppose them "ones," then not only will the division be incomplete, but each "one" will not be one but many. But the words "not only . . . but" in this sentence of mine do not conceal that this is a wholly otiose addition to the argument: they lay bare the fact that the two arguments diverge at this point towards two quite different absurdities; one that the division, ex hypothesi complete, is not complete after all, and the other that no unit survives from which to build up a plurality. Nor can it be said that one of these absurdities represents a step in reasoning necessary on the way to the other. These are two distinct arguments and should no longer be confounded.

What evidence do we have to pin either argument on Zeno? First, the argument of 325a from the abolition of the unit to the death of plurality. This is assigned by Aristotle to "some of the ancients" in a conspicuously Eleatic context; it also fits in beautifully with the famous statement of Eudemus that Zeno was recorded to have said that, if anyone could tell him what the one was, he could allow them a plurality—a statement whose follow-up mentions the problem (among others) of division.[9] So far, so good; but there is also some evidence from Alexander, and this is more problematic. We have a statement of his cited (not necessarily verbally) by Simplicius on *Physics* 187a1 concerning what looks like this argument (*in Physica* p. 138.3ff). Alexander thought the "dichotomy" mentioned by Aristotle at *Physics* 187a1 as causing the adoption of atomic magnitudes was an argument of Zeno's, to wit ὡς εἰ μέγεθος ἔχοι τὸ ὂν καὶ διαιροῖτο, πολλὰ τὸ ὂν καὶ οὐχ ἓν ἔτι ἔσεσθαι καὶ διὰ τούτου δεικνύντος ὅτι μηδὲν τῶν ὄντων ἔστι τὸ ἕν. This is highly abbreviated, whether the faults are Alexander's or Simplicius'. The kind of division concerned, whether infinite, or "everywhere," or any other, is omitted, though the omission is supplied, I think, by Themistius.[10] But in any case the argument looks more like one containing the step οὐθὲν εἶναι ἕν, as at *De generatione et corruptione* 325a8–9, than like one (as at 316a) whose most nearly relevant portion argues that if a division is complete nothing with magnitude can be left. It looks as if Alexander attributed the argument of 325a to Zeno. On the other hand, Alexander is not likely to have been ignorant of the *De generatione et corruptione* and may have been reasoning from the context in 325a just like the moderns. He could conceivably be following Eudemus, and Eudemus not, perhaps, at his best. For Eudemus may have mixed up several arguments, since he alludes to the quite different puzzle about the one thing being many by virtue of having many predicates as if it were part and parcel of the same difficulty. Since Alexander follows Eudemus in thus associating divisibility problems with the θόρυβος τῶν ἀρχαίων concerning predication of Aristotle's *Physics* 185b25ff, he may have been following him in the attribution to Zeno of the argument at 325a. We are therefore left, in default of a surer foundation in the ancient authorities, to fall back on Aristotle's Eleatic context and the general nature of the argument, which may fairly be said to reek of Zeno.

Simplicius on *Physics* 187a1, after dealing with Alexander, retails Porphyry's version of the "dichotomy," evidently in the belief that this was indeed a version of the same argument as Alexander's, that is, the "dichotomy" of 325a (*in Physica* p. 139.24ff). This belief at least there is no need for us to share, since Porphyry's dichotomy is quite certainly a paraphrase of another dichotomy, the one at *De generatione et corruptione* 316a. Porphyry attributed this to Parmenides, but Alexander preferred to attribute it to Zeno, and Simplicius follows him, on the grounds that there is no evidence for it in Parmenides and that the bulk of the tradition attributes the "dichotomy" to Zeno.[11] The bulk of the tradition probably did indeed assign the "dichotomy" to Zeno, but it is not self-evident which dichotomy was meant or whether every dichotomy is Zeno's.

To those wishing to attribute the dichotomy of 316a to Zeno, it is a little worrying to find Simplicius offering as examples of Zenonian dichotomy, to clinch the attribution, none other than B3, and also B2-1, but not either of the two other dichotomy arguments, found in *De generatione et corruptione*. The implication which leaps—a trifle prematurely —to the mind is that Aristotle's dichotomy arguments in the *De generatione et corruptione* were not in Zeno's book for Simplicius to cite. But this implication is far from cast-iron. Simplicius has been proven careless in assimilating one dichotomy to another, and he may have reread only as far as the first dichotomy arguments he found, without persisting far enough to find the right one(s); or he may only have been using lengthy excerpts rather than the complete work(s) of Zeno. So this particular doubt of Zenonian authorship is hardly to be pressed.

But nevertheless some doubt persists. The possibility remains that (a) Aristotle at *De generatione et corruptione* 316a was expounding not an Eleatic argument but one erected on Eleatic bases by the Atomists themselves; (b) Alexander and Porphyry, in the absence of any Eleatic argument precisely corresponding to this one, were both guessing, Alexander more sensibly; (c) Simplicius followed Alexander's guess for the same sensible reasons. I cannot say I am wholly convinced by the attribution to Zeno of the argument of *De generatione et corruptione* 316a, or indeed by its attribution, as a whole in its present form, to any Eleatic; whereas that of 325a2ff is clearly meant by Aristotle to belong to an Eleatic, and we have no reason to disbelieve him. Here Zeno is on the whole the most likely candidate.

How could the Atomists counter these arguments? For both the argument of Zeno's B2-1 and that of the *De generatione et corruptione* 325a look like purporting to *demonstrate* that divisibility is infinite. It turns out that this is nevertheless a chink in Zeno's armour which the Atomists did well to exploit. In Zeno's B1 the argument for infinite divisibility is hardly more than a statement; the mere assertion that οὐδὲν γὰρ αὐτοῦ τοιοῦτον ἔσχατον ἔσται does not on examination carry conviction, despite its air of appeal to common sense. This at least Democritus could without any philosophical qualms simply deny. Slightly more serious is the argument of *De generatione et corruptione* 325a, to the effect that any plurality implies division and that to choose any stage at which to halt the division is arbitrary. There is no obvious direct answer to this one except "So what?"; but the Atomists could surely suggest that the salvation of the phenomena was cheap at the price. The hypothesis of infinite divisibility had to wait for respectability (apart from the mathematical interpretation of incommensurability) until Aristotle's examination of time and space in the second half of the *Physics*.

The argument against *motion* called "Dichotomy" is also in this respect a piece of hectoring rather than of persuasive argument. It is there merely asserted that every continuous length can be divided and has a mid-point. Democritus could simply have denied this also, and again it was left to Aristotle (apart from geometers who understood incommensurability) to argue in favour of infinite divisibility and find another way of blocking Zeno's arguments from dichotomy. Whichever side turns out in the end to be right, it is safe to draw attention to the Atomists' capacity for seizing on some of the weak spots in the arguments as Zeno expressed them.

NO PLURALITY FROM UNITY

ARISTOTLE'S INTENTIONS

It seems clear to me that Aristotle's defence of the sensible continuum against the Eleatics on one side and the Atomists on the other presupposes that the argument was about "theoretical indivisibles" and not about objects merely "physically unsplittable" (the phrases are borrowed from Furley).[12] There are certain difficulties in the way of this interpretation, and some pieces of evidence against it. But the evidence of Eleaticism itself, and of Aristotle's whole treatment of the subject, weighs heavily in favour of theoretically indivisible atoms in Leucippus and his followers.[13] I cannot myself escape the conclusion that such evidence as there is against this interpretation cannot stand against the whole picture of the debate between Eleatics, Atomists, Aristotle, and Epicurus.[14] On this subject I have nothing significant to add to what others have already argued with a force and elegance I could not hope to rival. I therefore refrain from further discussion of this issue and proceed to the question posed at the beginning of this chapter, namely, what the function is, in the context I have sketched, of the doctrine that from the truly one no plurality can be derived. The answer to this question may be obtained first by looking at the contexts in which Aristotle attributes the doctrine to his Atomist opponents, and ultimately by reopening another issue, the question why the atoms had to be not merely theoretically indivisible but *also*, and because of their hardness, physically unsplittable.

Let us first try to recover Aristotle's intentions in attributing the doctrine "no plurality from unity" to the Atomists.[15] Among the most informative passages, as one might expect, is one cited by Simplicius from Aristotle's essay on Democritus.[16]

"ἐκ τούτων (sc. from atoms and void) οὖν ᾔδει [sc. Democritus] καθάπερ ἐκ στοιχείων γεννᾶν καὶ συγκρίνειν τοὺς ὀφθαλμοφανεῖς καὶ τοὺς αἰσθητοὺς ὄγκους· στασιάζειν δὲ καὶ φέρεσθαι ἐν τῷ κενῷ διά τε τὴν ἀνομοιότητα καὶ τὰς ἄλλας εἰρημένας διαφοράς, φερομένας δὲ ἐμπίπτειν καὶ περιπλέκεσθαι περιπλοκὴν τοσαύτην, ἣ συμψαύειν μὲν αὐτὰ καὶ πλησίον ἀλλήλων εἶναι ποιεῖ, φύσιν μέντοι μίαν ἐξ ἐκείνων κατ' ἀλήθειαν οὐδ' ἡντιναοῦν γεννᾷ· κομιδῇ γὰρ εὔηθες εἶναι τὸ δύο ἢ τὰ πλείονα γενέσθαι ἄν ποτε ἕν. τοῦ δὲ συμμένειν τὰς οὐσίας μετ' ἀλλήλων μέχρι τινὸς αἰτιᾶται τὰς ἐπαλλαγὰς καὶ τὰς ἀντιλήψεις τῶν σωμάτων· τὰ μὲν γὰρ αὐτῶν εἶναι σκαληνά, τὰ δὲ ἀγκιστρώδη. τὰ δὲ κοῖλα, τὰ δὲ κυρτά, τὰ δὲ ἄλλας ἀναρίθμους ἔχοντα διαφοράς· ἐπὶ τοσοῦτον οὖν χρόνον σφῶν αὐτῶν ἀντέχεσθαι νομίζει καὶ συμμένειν, ἕως ἰσχυροτέρα τις ἐκ τοῦ περιέχοντος ἀνάγκη παραγενομένη διασείσῃ καὶ χωρὶς αὐτὰς διασπείρῃ." λέγει δὲ τὴν γένεσιν καὶ τὴν ἐναντίαν αὐτῇ διάκρισιν οὐ μόνον περὶ ζῴων, ἀλλὰ ... συλλήβδην περὶ τῶν αἰσθητῶν σωμάτων ἁπάντων. εἰ τοίνυν ἡ μὲν γένεσις σύγκρισις τῶν ἀτόμων ἐστίν, ἡ δὲ φθορὰ διάκρισις, καὶ κατὰ Δημόκριτον ἀλλοίωσις ἂν εἴη ἡ γένεσις.

The last of these sentences is Simplicius' own and shows his interest in proving that Democritus' worlds undergo not γένεσις but ἀλλοίωσις. This does not, however, cast any doubt on the report cited from Aristotle, to the effect that genesis and destruction of sensible objects are in Atomism aggregation and separation of atoms respectively. In the course of this citation Aristotle is reported to have explained that things discrete cannot become in truth one φύσις. Now, Aristotle remarks of the Atomists at *De caelo* 275b32 τὴν δὲ φύσιν εἶναί φασιν αὐτῶν (sc. τῶν ἀτόμων) μίαν, explaining this with the words ὥσπερ ἂν εἰ χρυσὸς ἕκαστος εἴη κεχωρισμένος. But this μία φύσις of the *De caelo* cannot be what is forbidden to come from a true unity in the essay on Democritus. It seems that the kind of unity which

Aristotle in that essay meant to report Democritus as excluding from aggregates was rather unity of continuity.[17] For the "true unity" of the reported veto is contrasted on the one hand with contact and proximity, and on the other with a mere temporary coexistence—συμμένειν . . . μέχρι τινός. This temporary adherence is caused by the interlocking of atoms of various shapes and sizes. Such contact and merely temporary contiguity is evidently to be contrasted with the complete absence of interstices of void in the atoms themselves. The point appears to be that only single atoms contain no void at all and only single atoms therefore are true unities. No amount of external pressure will convert a combination of atoms into one single atom with no void in it.

This duly confirms the relevant portion, perhaps not quoted as often as it should be,[18] of our old friend *De generatione et corruptione A* 8, where Aristotle perhaps drew on his own separate essay on Democritus. We found there that a true unity excluded void, and a plurality contained it. The doctrine against a unity giving rise to plurality was there also connected with the concatenation (but non-coalescence) of atoms. Only the individual atom is without void, is not therefore a plurality, and cannot therefore be dispersed.

Much the same point, with a possible but not demonstrable addition, is made briefly in the *De caelo* (303a5–6). φασὶ γὰρ (sc. the Atomists) εἶναι τὰ πρῶτα μεγέθη πλήθει μὲν ἄπειρα μεγέθει δὲ ἀδιαίρετα, καὶ οὔτ' ἐξ ἑνὸς πολλὰ γίγνεσθαι οὔτε ἐκ πολλῶν ἕν, ἀλλὰ τῇ τούτων συμπλοκῇ καὶ ἐπαλλάξει πάντα γεννᾶσθαι. The sense of the statement about the impossibility of unity giving rise to plurality is here at least partly elucidated by the proposition following it and contrasted with it. As in our other passages, temporary entanglement of atoms is possible, complete unity formed of two or more atoms is not; rejected also is the dislocation of any atom. But in this passage we may have something extra. The statement about unity and plurality follows immediately on the phrase indicating the atoms' indivisibility of extension. But there is no logical connection stated between the two; and, though it may have been indivisibility which led Aristotle here to think of writing next about unity, this passage would not be cast-iron evidence for an Atomist argument that the atoms were truly one (and therefore could not become many) *because* they were of theoretically indivisible extension.

The next passage which falls to be considered is indeed partly concerned with divisibility but is rather different in that Aristotle is less directly concerned with historical facts. This is a passing reference embedded in an abstruse ontological argument in the *Metaphysics*. Aristotle is engaged in a series of arguments against the finding of substance in universals. Moving on to a fresh member of this series (1039a3), he urges the impossibility of a substance consisting of substances in actuality: two actualities cannot be one actuality; only if the two ingredients are potential can the whole be one single actuality. Therefore, if the actual substance is one, it will not consist of actual substances. The impossibility, he says, is of that kind which Democritus rightly speaks of, saying that one thing cannot come to be from two, nor two from one. For Democritus' substances are the atomic magnitudes.

ἀδύνατον γὰρ οὐσίαν ἐξ οὐσιῶν εἶναι ἐνυπαρχουσῶν ὡς ἐντελεχείᾳ. τὰ γὰρ δύο οὕτως ἐντελεχείᾳ οὐδέποτε ἓν ἐντελεχείᾳ, ἀλλ' ἐὰν δυνάμει δύο ᾖ, ἔσται ἕν (οἷον ἡ διπλασία ἐκ δύο ἡμίσεων δυνάμει γε· ἡ γὰρ ἐντελεχεία χωρίζει), ὥστ' εἰ ἡ οὐσία ἕν, οὐκ ἔσται ἐξ οὐσιῶν ἐνυπαρχουσῶν καὶ κατὰ τοῦτον τὸν τρόπον, ὃν λέγει Δημόκριτος ὀρθῶς· ἀδύνατον γὰρ εἶναί φησιν ἐκ δύο ἓν ἢ ἐξ ἑνὸς δύο γενέσθαι· τὰ γὰρ μεγέθη τὰ ἄτομα τὰς οὐσίας ποιεῖ.

Ross on this passage speaks of the atom "from whose atomic nature it follows that one atom cannot contain two atoms." This is indeed a logical consequence of the nature of theoretically indivisible atoms, and it is apparently this particular consequence that Aristotle had in mind when he wrote these lines of the *Metaphysics*. But did Democritus have this kind of difficulty in mind when he wrote whatever it was that Aristotle thus reports? Was Democritus concerned partly or wholly with the theoretical distinguishability of parts within the atom, or rather with physical unsplittability? Or did Democritus use this doctrine in both types of context? It may be wondered whether this, and the *De caelo* passage if it too connects the unity-prohibition with theoretical indivisibility, are mistaken or whether they represent, if taken in detail at face value, a portion (however important or unimportant) of Democritus' meaning. It is certainly tempting to ignore this last passage altogether and regard its possible companion in the *De caelo* as inconclusive. It is tempting to suppose Aristotle to be merely illustrating his remarks in the *Metaphysics* by a use of Democritus' words with a lack of concern (legitimate in a philosopher by no means primarily a historian) for Democritus' original meaning. It may be that this is the wisest course. It may be recommended by Aristotle's substitution here, to fit his own context, of "two" for "many" or "two or more." But before following it we should explore further the kind of consideration which may reasonably be supposed to have led the Atomists to assert the impossibility of many becoming one or vice versa.

ATOMIST REASONS

Exploration is the more necessary because, though "one becoming many" could understandably be forbidden in the light of a philosophy based on the admission of indivisibles, there is one very plausible reason why the Atomists should have accepted combination. Given an infinity of shapes,[19] some atoms ought to dovetail exactly. At least, on the principle of sufficient reason (a weapon certainly in Atomist hands),[20] I see no good argument against the existence and occasional meeting of dovetailing pairs. Such a pair, when fitted, ought presumably to present the same solidity as a single atom. Atomist neglect of this by no means obscure point is likely to be a symptom of their concentration on other matters, notably the permanence and indivisibility of the atoms.

The denial of the power of any force to split or otherwise affect the nature of the atom is mentioned several times in the ancient sources, and the single discordant voice of Galen may safely be ignored.[21] Cicero calls the atoms *individua propter soliditatem* (*De finibus* 1.6.17, DK 68A56). Diogenes Laertius calls them ἀπαθῆ καὶ ἀναλλοίωτα διὰ τὴν στερρότητα,[22] and Plutarch makes the slightly different point that nothing can come to be from the things that are, τῷ μήτε πάσχειν μήτε μεταβάλλειν τὰς ἀτόμους ὑπὸ στερρότητος (*Adversus Coloten* 8 p. 1110F, DK 68A57). The converse of this, that interstices of void are what permits destruction, is stated by Aristotle himself in *A* 8 of the *De generatione et corruptione*; after remarking of atoms that τὸ κυρίως ὂν παμπλῆρες ὄν, Aristotle later says διὰ τοῦ κενοῦ γιγνομένης τῆς διαλύσεως καὶ τῆς φθορᾶς. This point is clearly taken up by Simplicius (*De caelo* 242.19ff, DK 67A14), referring to the atoms as ἀδιαιρέτους ... καὶ ἀπαθεῖς διὰ τὸ ναστὰς εἶναι καὶ ἀμοίρους τοῦ κενοῦ. τὴν γὰρ διαίρεσιν κατὰ τὸ κενὸν τὸ ἐν τοῖς σώμασιν ἔλεγον γίγνεσθαι ... Thus there is no doubt of the ascription of solidity to fifth-century atoms.

If we ask the question *why* the atoms had to be solid, two sets of answers suggest themselves. One of these is connected with Zeno, the other with Parmenides, and not all the answers are relevant to precisely the same formulation of the question. We may take Zeno first. The argument concerned is the dichotomy reported by Aristotle at *De generatione et corruptione* 325a. According to Zeno (and the Atomists) things plural are separated, and they would certainly have agreed that things separated are plural. The Atomists separate things by the void. Now, if the atoms could themselves, by the presence or introduction of void, be or become pluralities, then there would be no firm unit to be found which could not be or become a plurality by division. So the infinite regress of *De generatione et corruptione* 325a could not be stopped; the Atomists would then be unable to answer Zeno's challenge and produce a unit untainted with present or potential plurality. To avoid all such taint the atoms had to be and to remain wholly without void. They had to be unsplit, and also unsplittable, by the physical intrusion of void. At least, just as there had to be an end somewhere to theoretical divisibility, so there had to be reached at some stage in physical division a piece of "Being" wholly lacking in, and impenetrable by, void, and, in that respect at least, "truly one."

But the solidity of the atoms could also be relevant to Parmenides. The neatness of the Atomist theory depends partly on the apparent acceptance of the disjunction ἔστιν ἢ οὐκ ἔστιν, and the subsequent argument οὐδὲ διαιρετόν ἐστιν, ἐπεὶ πᾶν ἔστιν ὁμοῖον. As Aristotle puts it in *De generatione et corruptione A* 8, Leucippus says, as Parmenides would have said, "Of Being nothing is not-Being, for what *is* in the fullest sense is completely full of Being." The undivided state of the atom is doubtless related to Parmenides' denial of divisibility. This needs some elaboration. The Atomists cannot have appreciated the *full* force of Parmenides' taboo on divisibility, since they persistently produced divisions between the atoms, thus making Being divided and plural. But these divisions were composed of something different from the atoms, of not-Being, which the Atomists declared did exist. Given some single thing which was, all of it, Being in the full sense, they may well have felt that Parmenides' veto on dividing it applied. They could have had this both ways in the following fashion: "To divide Being proper, a piece of Being unadulterated, is impossible, as Parmenides says, and we admit that in the atom there is no not-Being; τοῦ ὄντος οὐθὲν μὴ ὂν ... εἶναι, as in Parmenides πᾶν ἔστιν ὁμοῖον. But at the same time these undivided homogeneous pieces of Being are divided from one another; in other words, Being as a whole is divided. This is possible because not all of the whole is Being, since some not-Being exists, τὸ μὴ ὂν ἔστιν." They could go further and defend themselves against the charge of contravening Parmenides' additional argument οὐδέ τι τῇ μᾶλλον, τό κεν εἴργοι μιν συνέχεσθαι, οὐδέ τι χειρότερον;[23] for they declared not merely τὸ μὴ ὂν εἶναι but (if Aristotle and other ancient sources may be trusted)[24] that οὐθὲν μᾶλλον τὸ ὂν τοῦ μὴ ὄντος εἶναι. On the subject of not-Being the Atomists appear determined both to have their cake and eat it. But in all this they are concerned with *Being*; there is no sign that in their manifold reactions to Parmenides they were accepting from him a suggestion specifically concerning *unity*, and no indication that they were accommodating an attack of Parmenides on unity giving rise to plurality.

So far we have accounted, twice over, for such remarks as Cicero's *individua propter soliditatem*. Solidity reinforced indivisibility, even if hardness was not indispensable to indivisibility. But we have not finished yet. Atomism accepted from Parmenides that the real could not come to be and pass away in the same way as sensible things. It declared that sensible things come to be by the aggregation, and pass away by the separation, of eternal atoms. As Aristotle in *De generatione et corruptione A* 8 puts it, συνιστάμενα μὲν (sc. τὰ ἄτομα) γένεσιν ποιεῖν, διαλυόμενα δὲ (sc. by void) τὴν φθοράν. But if coming-to-be is aggregation and destruction is separation, then, if the parts of the atom can be physically separated, the atom as such would be destroyed, just as sensible objects are destroyed by dissolution. So for the sake of their answer to Parmenides the Atomists had to deny that atoms could ever be split. To make sure that the point went home they had to lay considerable stress on the uncreated indestructibility of their atoms and show why atoms should be different in this respect from ordinary objects—the difference consisting of the atoms' total lack of the otherwise omnipresent void. In the realm of the senses many things might come together to make one thing, but on an atomic scale this kind of event could not take place; an atom could not be made, or come to be. In the world of sense perception, again, a single thing can be broken up, but this cannot happen to the imperishable atom; a true unity, an absolutely solid continuum, could not perish by being dispersed in a plurality. In short, what truly is (ἐτεῇ at 68B9) cannot come to be or pass away.

If not only physical but also theoretical divisibility was in Democritus' mind, when he prohibited a true unity from producing a plurality and vice versa, he need again have been using no more than the general Eleatic denial of coming-to-be. Given that denial, it is evident that you cannot allow a theoretically indivisible object to give rise to a plurality of parts (for it has none and none can come to be) or a plurality of any other kind (for no distinctions exist within it and none can come to be). But, though this could be the logic of the matter, it is not likely that it is the whole reason why the Atomists should bother to express a veto on this particular kind of becoming. Here, as in other contexts, the twin influences of Zeno and Parmenides are probably to be seen at work.

If we ask why the Atomists chose, in expressing their doctrine that an atom could not be split and so perish, a statement about unity and plurality, the question is not simple. Parmenides had spoken of his Being as being ἕν, συνεχές, and the Atomists may have taken their cue from this passage. But Parmenides probably meant two different things by the two words in this context, and there is no need to debit the Atomists with a mistaken interpretation. If Aristotle's whole context in *De generatione et corruptione A* 8 is not misleading, there seems to have been an Eleatic dogma that a plurality has to have a separator between its components, and that dogma would perhaps explain the terminology of the Atomist doctrine we are considering, a doctrine in which continuity is an important factor. The prominence of unity and plurality in the dichotomy of Zeno cited by Aristotle at *De generatione et corruptione A* 8.325a8ff also supplies a plausible antecedent. Zeno—or something very like Zeno—looks as if it may be responsible for the form of the Atomist doctrine that the truly one could not become many. But I should not now wish to emphasize Zeno's influence on the doctrine to the total exclusion of Parmenides.[25]

The ease of deduction, mentioned in the penultimate paragraph, from a belief in theoretically indivisible things to the impossibility of splitting them physically is what gives point to Furley's question[26] why the Atomists lay stress on both theoretical and physical indivisibility. Furley's own answer is that the Atomists need the hardness of the atoms as a reply to the Eleatic argument cited by Aristotle to the effect that it is arbitrary to postulate a universe divisible in one place and not in another. With all respect to a scholar from whom I have learnt much, I cannot follow this reasoning. To me it seems that the alleged Atomist reply is irrelevant to this particular argument. The Eleatics and Aristotle were clearly concerned with theoretical divisibility; to answer the question "Why should theoretical divisibility stop at the atoms?" with the reply "Because they are physically hard" makes no sort of sense to me. Indeed, its admission would undermine much, if not the whole, of Furley's own admirably constructed philosophical argument for Atomist belief in theoretical indivisibles. I should like to suggest that the reason why Leucippus and Democritus chose to accord separate and emphatic mention to the physical unsplittability of atoms was somewhat different: it was to answer Parmenides, as I have outlined, by denying atoms the power to come to be or pass away in the same physical way as physical aggregates of atoms. Atomist desire not only to evade this snare but actually to show that they had evaded it would account for the emphasis they placed on their escape—if indeed such emphasis is reflected in Aristotle's repeated mention of it among the prominent features of their thought.

In this context we may stress the uncertainty surrounding the Atomist *argument* (if any) for the proposition that what is truly one cannot give rise to a plurality or vice versa. Did they explicitly argue that it was impossible for a true continuum to be split because it had no weak spot? Did they argue directly the impossibility of splitting a thing with no parts to split into? Did they directly and explicitly answer Parmenides in the ways I have suggested? It is not immediately clear which of these questions can be answered in the affirmative; but, since the Atomists were philosophers, it seems probable that they argued, rather than merely asserted, that it was silly to have a unity give rise to a plurality.[27] What appears to lie behind Cicero's *propter soliditatem*, and the Greek διὰ στερρότητα in Diogenes' and Plutarch's accounts, is the denial of any weak spot in a continuum. To me at least, though I admit to subjectivity here, these phrases read as if derived from a summary of something much fuller. That the Atomists answered Parmenides directly in the way here suggested may also with plausibility be deduced from doxographical accounts. Not only Diogenes, but also Plutarch and Simplicius, associate the hardness of the atoms with the impossibility of change, which in Eleatic thought means also the inadmissibility of coming-to-be or passing-away. Furthermore, a version of such an explicit accommodation to Parmenides (though not mentioning him by name) is to be found in Epicurus;[28] and Epicurus is not likely to have been the inventor of an argument so appropriate to the late fifth century and so unnecessary (one would have thought) a hundred years later. (The point holds good, in my opinion, even though Epicurus does not in his extant works connect with this argument the rejection of the origin of plurality from unity and vice versa.) What we shall never know is whether the fifth-century Atomists argued directly from the theoretical indivisibility, the partlessness, of atoms to their physical unsplittability. No such argument appears in Epicurus, but that is doubtless because Epicurus assigned theoretical and physical indivisibility to different types of entity.[29] I can only say that I see no necessity for the postulation of such a direct argument in the earlier Atomists, granted that they could defend physical unsplittability on other grounds. Whether or not the Atomists argued directly from theoretical to physical indivisibility, the possibility remains, but not the certainty, that in the Democritean antecedent of Aristotle's ἐκ δὲ τοῦ κατ' ἀλήθειαν ἑνὸς οὐκ ἂν γενέσθαι πλῆθος οὐδ' ἐκ τῶν ἀληθῶς πολλῶν ἕν the words meaning "truly one" had the sense "partless."[30] There is reason to suppose that these words mean, or at least include the notion of, "that which has the highest theoretically possible degree of continuity."

Here we may pause in our positive account of Atomist thinking to emphasize the negative point foreshadowed in the first paragraph of this chapter. In so far as the Atomists were thus accommodating Parmenidean logic to the evidence of the senses, there is no reason whatever to imagine that they were accepting a hypothetical argument from Parmenides to the express effect that whatever was one could not become many. The general Parmenidean argument against sense perception, that the senses tell us that things pass away and come to be, whereas no real thing, no subject of discourse, can logically come to be or pass away—this whole line of argument suffices to explain the Atomists' need to prohibit the formation of a true unity from plurality or vice versa. If one is left seeking evidence in the Atomist philosophy for a specific Parmenidean attack on a "one" becoming "many," then one is left to seek in vain. There is no need to suppose the Atomists incapable of thinking out their prohibition for themselves in reaction to the general Parmenidean argument, and there is no need in this context to credit Parmenides with anything but a comprehensive blanket denial of coming-to-be and passing away. We may observe in passing that the sort of "one-becoming-many" being prohibited is very different from the kind often attributed to the Milesians and supposed to be forbidden by Parmenides to cosmogonists.

It is extremely interesting to the student of philosophical language to observe that not only in reporting the Atomist doctrine of Being does Aristotle use the expression τὸ κυρίως ὄν, but also in speaking of unity he has the term τὸ κατ' ἀλήθειαν ἕν, a "true" one. We may doubt if the expression κυρίως was used by the Atomists, but κατ' ἀλήθειαν (or perhaps ἀληθῶς) may have been. It looks as though the Atomists, though unable to say "in a sense X, in a sense not-X," were being driven by the exigencies of defence against Eleaticism into a position where such distinctions were almost inevitable. "One" normal object could be taken apart, but atoms were "one" in a different way. One recalls here Empedocles' statement that τῇ μέν ... things come to be, τῇ δέ ... they remain ἀκίνητοι κατὰ κύκλον.[31] Clearly, the second part of the fifth century B.C. was a period of dim groping for such fine distinctions of meaning, without (except perhaps for Socrates) the ability in philosophically interesting cases to detect them clearly or use them freely. It should be admitted that Proclus (*in Cratylum* p. 6.10ff, DK 68B26) credibly reports Democritus' ability not merely to indicate the existence of homonyms but to use their existence as an argument against the "natural" view of language. But it may be wondered how philosophically interesting these homonyms were; on the face of it it is likely that they were fairly obvious ones. It is one thing to distinguish fairly obvious homonyms and quite another to point out the ambiguities of words like "is" and "one."

If the Atomists did use the term κατ' ἀλήθειαν ἕν or anything like it, then notice should be taken of the following points. If, and in so far as, they applied the term in a context where total theoretical indivisibility was relevant, then indeed nothing more unified can be conceived; Aristotle himself would probably have had no qualms about speaking in such a context of "the truly one," meaning that in which no distinctions were to be observed or imagined, as opposed to that in which, despite the absence of some kinds of distinction, some plurality is inherent. In so far as they used the expression to denote the absence of void, they were distinguishing the truly continuous from the less so. In both of these two usages they would have been focussing attention on unity or continuity "in the highest degree," rather than "in the true sense of the term": on a matter of degree rather than a matter of "sense." Both the usages are consistent with their having failed to discern the senses of "one" and "many" with which we have been concerned. But, nevertheless, Leucippus and his followers are evidently beginning to move in the right direction and are pressing on to the frontiers of logic.

CAN THE "ONE" *BE* "MANY"?

How and why the Atomists were worried by the thought of a true unity becoming many, we have seen. It remains to inquire how far they were also troubled by the notion of one thing *being* many. Their prohibition of ἐξ ἑνὸς πολλά and ἐκ πολλῶν ἕν may in part have rested on the absence of plural parts to be extracted from a true unity. It was necessary, to be sure, in order to avoid the dissolution of an atom, to make it physically unsplittable; it was necessary, in order to escape what the Atomists thought were the implications of infinite divisibility, to make the atom theoretically indivisible. Now, theoretical indivisibility forbids not only the process, in thought or action, of taking something apart but also the existence of many parts into which the object may be divided. The prohibition of theoretical divisibility is a veto not only on what is one becoming many but also on what is one being many.

But there were senses in which what was one *could*, for the Atomists, be many. The "true" or "absolute" unity of the atom which in fifth-century Atomism excludes gaps and divisibility is not the only sort of unity. Since we have here a different kind of unity from that which is at issue in the oft-accepted Milesian unity of all things and the supposed assault on it by Parmenides, we may next look at homogeneity, the kind of unity involved in that supposed controversy, to see if there are, as we might expect, any echoes of the supposed battle to be heard in Atomism.

The Atomists indubitably believed that there was only one real stuff. This was "Being." Void did indeed exist, but could scarcely be described as a stuff and, in any case, had a peculiar and paradoxical form of existence. Between one piece of solid Being and another there were no differences of quality, but only differences of size, shape, perhaps weight,[32] position, and arrangement. No other properties could be said really to exist. The stuff thus excogitated is peculiar, and pieces of it may well be thought to bear closer resemblance to the subjects of geometry than to any readily imaginable physical matter.[33] But it was nevertheless hard, so hard that, though presumably (unlike geometrical shapes) in principle accessible to a knife, it was in principle uncuttable. The unity of this stuff is expressed with clarity by Aristotle in a passage already cited from the *De caelo*. He says that the atoms were composed of a single φύσις, as if each separate thing were to be (say) gold. The unity of the atoms' material comes out also in *De generatione et corruptione* A 7. There Aristotle states that agent and patient were "the same and similar" for the Atomists. There follows an argument from which this unity could be deduced: the Atomists apparently held, like Diogenes of Apollonia, that different things could not affect one another except in so far as they possessed something in common.

I see no reason to doubt the Atomist provenance of both this argument and its conclusion, the unity of the stuff of which things are made.

Granted that the Atomists are credibly reported to have held that there was no difference of basic material between one atom and another; granted that Aristotle saw fit to describe this state of affairs, quite legitimately, though not necessarily in Atomist terms, as the existence of one stuff: we see at once that here the Atomists reduce the element of difference to a minimum, and exile from the world of truth all qualitative difference. They do not, as would Parmenides, abolish *all* distinctions, and for them Being is as a whole divided, in a way intolerable to the Eleatic. This division is made possible by a straight contradiction of Parmenides which figures prominently in our sources, by saying that not-Being exists. It would appear that for the Atomists Being was both one (substance) and many (numerically and by discontinuity) at the same time. If Parmenides is believed to have settled the point, according to fifth-century lights, that what is one cannot be many, it has to be accepted that on this question also the Atomists contradicted him. It has also to be accepted that Peripatetic historians, keenly interested in the Atomist paradox of not-Being, showed a total lack of interest in this other paradoxical skirmish. It must be supposed that in Peripatetic analyses of the relation between Eleatics and Atomists the new paradox left not a hint behind. Surely this is a most improbable series of suppositions. If there *was* a battle between the Milesians and Parmenides over the question whether many things could be made of one stuff, it is pretty safe to say that no whisper of it reached the ears of Leucippus, Democritus, Aristotle, or Theophrastus. In fact, the making of many things from one stuff is best understood as forced in *acceptance* of a Parmenidean argument, namely, the argument against difference—apart from the fact that by having a single basic stuff the Greeks were able, even in the face of a veto on becoming, to retain the traditional type of cosmogony starting from a single stuff.[34] It may be thought that this part of the case against a specific argument by Parmenides rejecting any kind of plurality in a unity rests too heavily on an argument from silence to carry much weight. Perhaps it does; but not only does it, in my view, amount to a further important reduction in the amount of evidence for such a Parmenidean thesis; in the next chapter it will be seen to gather momentum.

IX

MISCELLANEOUS PRESOCRATIC CONTEXTS

ANAXAGORAS B8

None of the late fifth-century philosophers took Parmenides more seriously than Anaxagoras. In this context the eighth fragment of Anaxagoras presents an interesting use of the word "one": οὐ κεχώρισται ἀλλήλων τὰ ἐν τῷ ἑνὶ κόσμῳ οὐδὲ ἀποκέκοπται πελέκει οὔτε τὸ θερμὸν ἀπὸ τοῦ ψυχροῦ οὔτε τὸ ψυχρὸν ἀπὸ τοῦ θερμοῦ. But it is perhaps not immediately obvious what kind of unity Anaxagoras had particularly in mind in writing these words. More than one view of the matter can be exemplified from the scholarly literature. It is perhaps easier to say what Anaxagoras does not mean.

One thing he does not mean is that the world is homogeneous. Anaxagoras certainly believed in a multitude of different things each real and each unlike the others. He accepted the reality of every stuff he knew to be perceptible by the senses, and of every sensible quality to boot.[1] If at the same time he held that the world was homogeneous, he would not rank as a serious thinker at all. Another view which can be safely dismissed is that Anaxagoras was thinking primarily of continuity.[2] Admittedly, the denial of *separation* (οὐ κεχώρισται) might make us think of continuity, and admittedly Anaxagoras denied the void and could therefore accept no gaps of emptiness between one thing (or part of a thing) and another.[3] But, if we ask what could be the object of mentioning continuity in the context of B8, no answer is readily forthcoming. The opposites for Anaxagoras are indeed linked; but they are not linked simply by juxtaposition without a gap. The link consists rather in their being indissolubly mixed. When Anaxagoras says that in the beginning "all things were together," he means above all that they were mixed with complete thoroughness; mixture is explicitly named in this context in B4b (DK II p. 34, line 18).[4] So it is natural to take the word ἑνί in B8 to refer to this state of mixture, which still in a sense obtains.

A conceivable rival to this interpretation is the supposition that it is the orderly wholeness of the cosmos that is relevant here. The orderliness of the world is the result of Mind's action on the primeval mixture. That action is described by the verb διεκόσμησε in B12 (DK II p. 38, lines 11ff). If this is the point, then the general drift of the eighth fragment must be that the process of unifying the world in a single ordered whole has not progressed, and indeed cannot progress far enough to produce total separation of hot and cold and so forth. This makes the phrase ἐν τῷ ἑνὶ κόσμῳ adversative or concessive in tone. Although, in our ignorance of the surrounding sentences, this interpretation must remain a possibility, I own that it seems to me somewhat less plausible; it is something less in accord with the canons of clear writing to see in the phrase a reason against the impossibility of separating than to find in it a reason in favour of that impossibility. One is not, I think, expecting a concessive phrase at this point.[5]

Whatever the truth of this question, it may be observed that Anaxagoras' statement does nothing to support, and something to undermine, the hypothesis that Parmenides had specific arguments against "one" becoming or being "many." The world order here emphatically called "one" consists undeniably of a multitude of things. A multitude of different stuffs and an infinity of differing parts are contained in it. Obviously, in Anaxagoras' thought unity did not always exclude plurality. Once again we find that, if Parmenides did argue expressly the incompatibility of unity and plurality, then his successors paid no attention to this particular argument and show no signs of surprise at their own audacity.

It is relevant to add that, if Anaxagoras believed that things were one by mixture, he believed also that the original state of the world when all things were together was a unity by mixture. But evidently, though all things are now still mixed as in the beginning, they are certainly somehow less thoroughly mixed. The state of affairs, described in B4b, in which no colour is discernible, is certainly different from the present. The manifold world evolves from a unity but remains a unity. It is hard to imagine a more complete ignoring of Parmenides' alleged arguments concerning unity.

THE ECLECTICS

The unity of the manifold world was at least implicitly a tenet of the so-called Eclectics of the late fifth century, and especially of Diogenes of Apollonia, the best known of them. This should be taken more seriously than it usually is. It is commonly believed that Diogenes and the rest were purely eclectic: that, with the exception of a few minor improvements,[6] their principal doctrines were all taken over from others, some from outdated sources. This harsh view of their limitations is the natural accompaniment to the belief that the Milesians preceded them in finding the world's unity in a single stuff.[7] What may cause surprise is a similar attitude to Diogenes in those who reject the Aristotelian interpretation of Milesian thought.[8] It is clear that, if Thales and Anaximenes did not believe the world to be made of a single underlying perceptible substance, then the "Eclectics" were the first to name one of the "elements" as this kind of single underlying but perceptible substance—perhaps prompted by what Aristotle called the μία φύσις of the Atomists (to which the Atomists gave only such names as ὄν and δέν).[9] It is germane to the arguments of the preceding chapters to consider why they may have done this and what it meant to them. The nature of "Eclectic" reaction to the Eleatics stands in need of analysis.

The fragments show some evidence of concern with problems affecting the post-Parmenidean physical philosophers. Hans Diller long ago pointed out certain resemblances of vocabulary between Diogenes and Melissus.[10] The stem ἑτεροιο- and the verb μεταπίπτειν are especially interesting. Ἑτεροιοῦσθαι is of obvious relevance to post-Parmenidean problems, since it supplies a way of expressing change of nature or property without resort to the fatal γίγνεσθαι. Μεταπίπτειν conveys the notion of change of place while avoiding the equally fatal connotations of κινεῖσθαι.[11] Such words as these were almost bound to come into prominence in the aftermath of Parmenides' intransigence. Diogenes' use of them, whatever the chronology of the thinkers concerned, is evidence that he had not failed to observe the problems besetting the belief in change in the late fifth century. These words already have the appearance of placing Diogenes (and presumably the other "Eclectics") in the mainstream of post-Parmenidean philosophy.

If this were all, we should perhaps still be inclined to put Diogenes down as an outdated ignoramus who merely aped his betters by employing some of their jargon. But it is not only the use of anti-Eleatic vocabulary which suggests that Diogenes had an answer, however inadequate, to Parmenides.

The first passage deserving mention here comes from an intelligent, though historically inaccurate, source and does not even mention Diogenes. It is from the pseudo-Aristotelian *MXG*, 975b21ff:

ἔτι οὐδὲν κωλύει μίαν τινὰ οὖσαν τὸ πᾶν μορφήν, ὡς καὶ ὁ Ἀναξίμανδρος καὶ ὁ Ἀναξιμένης λέγουσιν, ὁ μὲν ὕδωρ εἶναι φάμενος τὸ πᾶν, ὁ δέ, ὁ Ἀναξιμένης, ἀέρα, καὶ ὅσοι ἄλλοι οὕτως εἶναι τὸ πᾶν ἓν ἠξιώκασιν, τοῦτο ἤδη σχήμασί τε καὶ πλήθει καὶ ὀλιγότητι, καὶ τῷ μανὸν ἢ πυκνὸν γίγνεσθαι, πολλὰ καὶ ἄπειρα ὄντα τε καὶ γιγνόμενα ἀπεργάζεσθαι, τὸ ὅλον. φησὶ δὲ καὶ ὁ Δημόκριτος τὸ ὕδωρ τε καὶ τὸν ἀέρα ἕκαστόν τε τῶν πολλῶν, ταὐτὸ ὄν, ῥυθμῷ διαφέρειν. τί δὴ κωλύει καὶ οὕτως τὰ πολλὰ γίγνεσθαί τε καὶ ἀπόλλυσθαι, ἐξ ὄντος ἀεὶ εἰς ὂν μεταβάλλοντος ταῖς εἰρημέναις διαφοραῖς τοῦ ἑνός, καὶ οὐδὲν οὔτε πλέονος οὔτε ἐλάττονος γιγνομένου τοῦ ὅλου;

From Eleatic arguments as presented to him Pseudo-Aristotle cannot see why the manifold world should not be made of one stuff, varying in shape, size, and density. The Atomists themselves probably said that the plurality of existing things are essentially the same, differing in "rhythm," form, or arrangement. The author continues,[12] "Why should not the many come to be and be destroyed even in this way, the One changing continually from Being to Being by the above-mentioned differences and the whole becoming not a whit either greater or less?" The particularly relevant phrase for us is "changing continually from Being to Being." Parmenides had argued against change that it involved the destruction of what is and the genesis of what is not. To this it is a half-reply, not unlike other fifth-century half-replies, to suggest that change need involve no such thing. Apparent changes take place, appearances come and go, but the real, what is, is neither brought to birth nor destroyed and undergoes neither addition nor subtraction. The one real substance, be it air, water, or fire, could persist in spite of changing appearances.

That this kind of "reply" to Parmenides was what Diogenes of Apollonia actually had in mind is strongly suggested by two passages. The first is from Diogenes Laertius (9.57, DK 64A1), who records the doctrine of his namesake that οὐδὲν ἐκ τοῦ μὴ ὄντος γίνεσθαι οὐδὲ εἰς τὸ μὴ ὂν φθείρεσθαι. On this titbit we must of course keep in mind the usual reservations for isolated doxographical pronouncements. But for a thinker of the generation or two after Parmenides this doctrine has such verisimilitude that it may provisionally be accepted. It has certainly been unduly neglected. It suggests that Diogenes' air was real and was not either created or destroyed. Then Diogenes of Apollonia himself implies clearly enough at B2 that he does not accept changes or differences τῇ ἰδίᾳ φύσει, though the senses report changes and differences of various kinds. It looks indeed as if Diogenes took the natural course for his time of accepting ἑτεροιώσιες but not γενέσεις, and this distinction can only have been forged in answer to Eleaticism. Finally and most explicitly, we have Diogenes' B7, quoted by Simplicius. The commentator expresses (*in Physica* p. 153.17ff) his surprise that Diogenes should declare air eternal at the same time as he envisages the formation of other things from it by alteration (κατὰ ἑτεροίωσιν). The words he quotes from Diogenes show that, however unjustified his surprise, his interpretation is correct: καὶ αὐτὸ μὲν τοῦτο καὶ ἀίδιον καὶ ἀθάνατον σῶμα, τῶν δὲ τὰ μὲν γίνεται, τὰ δὲ ἀπολείπει. The implications of this are clear. The air is eternal and immortal and never passes away, but sensible objects do come to be and pass away. Coupled with the statement that sensible things are air, this shows that Diogenes regarded air as a sole element remaining substantially unchanged while its guise continually altered. The difficulty of giving an account of Diogenes without lapsing into Aristotelian terminology shows how far we have here advanced. If we have not reached the Aristotelian clarity of definition of substance and quality, we are here well on the road to it, perhaps as far as it was possible to go without dissecting the use of "is." To change the metaphor, Greek thought can here be felt straining at the leash. It is charitable, and reasonable, to assume that other "Eclectics" than Diogenes thought along similar lines.

In taking up this kind of position, Diogenes is of course riding roughshod over many other Eleatic arguments. Parmenides' argument against motion he ignored, as also the argument against otherness or difference of any kind. Like the Atomists he declared for the existence of void,[13] perhaps (we have no information) to enable things, despite Melissus' argument, to move.[14] Motion he doubtless attributed to the living intelligence of his underlying air, deriving this conception partly from Anaxagoras, partly from the Milesian conception of a divine substance guiding the universe, partly perhaps from Heraclitus' intelligent Fire.[15] He possibly found here the answer to Parmenides' question τί δ' ἄν μιν καὶ χρέος ὦρσεν ὕστερον ἢ πρόσθεν τοῦ μηδενὸς ἀρξάμενον φῦν; or possibly in this instance he was merely derivative, since he agreed with Parmenides that nothing could come from nothing. His debts to other physical thinkers are indeed sufficiently obvious—one could add his assimilation of the Atomist assumption of an unlimited universe; but, in so far as he may have been the first to postulate a single substance changing qualitatively but not essentially, he may rank as an original metaphysician, with a not untypical fifth-century accommodation of Parmenides to offer.

In this connection it is worth while to recapitulate some of these fifth-century answers for comparative purposes. Empedocles accommodated Parmenides by accepting the denial of becoming and perishing while allowing motion, some difference, and much mixture. Anaxagoras travelled a similar road but went much further in the amount of difference he was prepared to allow. The Atomists also accepted the denial of genesis and destruction: they accounted for variety not by difference of material, like Empedocles and Anaxagoras, but by variations in quantitative and spatial properties, such as shape, size, and arrangement. Diogenes and probably his fellow "Eclectics" did away, like the Atomists, with material distinctions but substituted for the Atomists' geometrical differences various τρόποι or modes of the basic stuff, varying ἑτεροιώσιες or different forms of it. By this substitution they turned their backs, to be sure, on anything likely to develop into the quality-less prime matter of Aristotle but made some advance towards the Aristotelian notion of a material substratum of change between opposites. Diogenes' underlying stuff was a material actually found in the world and nameable; it admitted, so far as we know, of no further analysis and was not an entity distinguishable only in thought. But, if we detect in this a lack of subtlety, of boldness, and of philosophical maturity, we may retain some respect for its soundly empirical attitude. The difference between Diogenes and Leucippus is closely akin to that between Anaximenes and Anaximander. One failure must be admitted: there is not in Diogenes' extant thought the slightest inkling of any reply to Zeno, unless the adoption of void was for him (as probably for the Atomists) necessitated by Zeno as well as by the need for a medium for motion. It must be admitted also that Melissus' detailed exposition of the difficulties of any kind of difference or change of place, arrangement, and so forth was either unknown to, or ignored by, Diogenes. But, so far as their attempted answer to Parmenides is concerned, the "Eclectics" deserve a place alongside their contemporaries in the history of the concepts of substance and quality; they should not be treated merely as stragglers wandering up an intellectual cul-de-sac.

We shall accordingly do well to take Diogenes seriously. If we do so, we shall see that the case for Parmenides' having argued against a "one" being many is further weakened. Diogenes accepts the argument against becoming and perishing in general. He takes some account of Parmenides. But he not only believes that the manifold world is a homogeneous unity, "the same thing"; his whole attempt to answer Parmenides hinges on the proposition that the things of this world are fundamentally a unity. No concern at this is displayed by any of the ancient sources. Did Diogenes actually use the term ἕν to describe the world, or did he skate gingerly round it? We have no certain information on this point, but the absence of the term from the meagre extant fragments proves little. The Hippocratic *De natura hominis* (chapter 1) attributes to unnamed but probably near-contemporary thinkers, very probably including Diogenes himself, the view that what is, is one, either air, water, earth, or fire.[16] Unfortunately, "Hippocrates" appears to have read Melissus, so that his evidence is not above reproach.[17] It is clear, however, that "Hippocrates" saw a parallel between Eleatic unity and "Eclectic" single stuff, and this is of interest in itself. Whether or not Diogenes explicitly used the terms ἕν and πολλά to express the fact that the world was a unity in multiplicity, it is clear that he could have and that his theory was describable by a near contemporary in those terms. There is no shadow of evidence that he avoided them or that he did not see the clear implications of his doctrine that all things were τὸ αὐτό, the same, and yet changed in many ways, πολλαχῶς.

It remains to deal with the recent suggestion that, whereas Parmenides had argued that what was one could not become many, Diogenes set about showing how plurality could be produced from unity.[18] Allegedly Diogenes "had to meet the further consequence of Eleatic logic, which had made the theory of ultimate pluralism seem inevitable, namely that there was no means by which a world of change and motion could be produced from unity. But the stumbling-block here had been the denial of empty space, which the Eleatics equated with non-being." Diogenes is then rightly said to have adopted the void from Leucippus. "It is impossible," the historian continues, "that anyone in his day could fail to be aware that condensation and rarefaction (the process by which air took on its manifold disguises) demanded void as a precondition. The contemporary Eleatic Melissus drew this conclusion explicitly." Thus, what is here recounted is that Diogenes sought to reconcile (1) change and (2) motion with an underlying unity, by the postulation of void in order to facilitate (a) condensation-rarefaction and (b) motion. The idea that the denial of empty space was connected by the Eleatics with the denial that a one could give rise to a many is derived from a view of Parmenides B8.22ff which we have already rejected. If it was, as we are agreed, motion in general which Diogenes sought to explain by the void, there is no need to import into his theory, or the problems it was designed to solve, any reference to a one giving rise to a many. We may agree that the void probably also played a part in condensation-rarefaction; but that does not make it play a part in change as such.

We are apparently supposed to believe that the one, or at least the fundamental, process of change in Diogenes' world was condensation-rarefaction, which demands void. But this is not to be found, so far as I can see, in the ancient texts. Certainly Diogenes believed in condensation-rarefaction, and he may have followed Melissus in believing void indispensable for it. But that this was *the* process of change envisaged by Diogenes is not, I think, stated by the ancients or implied by Diogenes' own extant words. Theophrastus (apud Simplicium *in Physica* p. 25.5) speaks on Diogenes of the air ἐξ οὗ πυκνουμένου καὶ μανουμένου καὶ μεταβάλλοντος τοῖς πάθεσι τὴν τῶν ἄλλων γίνεσθαι μορφήν. Nothing here shows that the μεταβολή is exclusively—or indeed in any way—dependent on the process of condensation-rarefaction. We must admit that condensation-rarefaction is prominent in Diogenes' cosmogony as outlined by Pseudo-Plutarch (*Stromateis* 12, DK 64A6), but even here we have no proof of its causing all other changes. Other mentions of the rare and dense in the doxography of Diogenes are hardly here significant—unless Aëtius at A30 might be held to support the independence of some properties from the dense and the rare.[19] The fragments of Diogenes himself do not offer any better evidence for the special position of dense and rare in Diogenes' physics. Indeed, at B5 after describing air as πολύτροπος Diogenes offers a list of τρόποι which does not include density and rarity at all—unless they are included in the final etcetera καὶ ἄλλαι πολλαὶ ἑτεροιώσιες ... καὶ ἡδονῆς καὶ χροιῆς ἄπειροι. The pair of opposites most prominent here is hot-cold; and, even if A6 suggests that these were somehow related to rare and dense, there is no evidence for the subordination of one pair to the other.[20]

If there is no evidence that change was the result solely of condensation and rarefaction, it follows that there was no necessary connection in Diogenes' thought between change and void. I do not therefore see how he can have intended the void to assist in the reconciliation of change as such with the material unity of the world or of its original state. The void *may* perhaps have been thought necessary, after Zeno's B3, to separate distinct objects; but this, if Diogenes' mind stretched to this as well as to the post-Melissan problems of motion, would not be evidence of any concern with the problem of how what is one can be or become many. It would show rather an interest in the quite different problem how there can be a many at all. For Zeno's B3 does not, it will be recalled, speak of πολλά which are also ἕν, but of πολλά simpliciter.

In fact, there is no sign discernible to me in the ancient evidence that Diogenes was bothered about any problem of the one and the many. He believed that one thing could give rise to many appearances, but he does not appear to have been either hesitant or apologetic about this belief. His thought does not support, and his casualness in this regard tends to undermine, the hypothesis that Parmenides argued that what was one could not be or become many.

SOME PYTHAGOREAN VIEWS

The intention of this section is not exhaustiveness (or anything approaching it) either in modern references or in examination of the large corpus of ancient evidence for Pythagoreanism. The following disjointed remarks are intended solely to bring out certain points relevant to my central argument which are not always given the attention they deserve. It should be stressed that few of these remarks have any claim to originality.

It is often believed that Aristotle in *Metaphysics A* 5 distinguishes two views of unity, to be found in Classical Pythagoreanism. One of these equates the unit with "the active principle of limit itself," the other with "the first product of that principle imposing itself on the undifferentiated mass of the *apeiron*."[21] In keeping with the position of the relevant opposites in Aristotle's Pythagorean Table of Opposites is the suggestion that the unit equated with limit was regarded as odd, the other unit being both even and odd, ἀρτιοπέριττον. It is sometimes argued that this is a difference between periods, that the belief in an odd unit was earlier than the belief in an even-odd one; it is occasionally urged that this difference between early and late fifth-century Pythagoreans was due to Parmenides' having shown that an original unity cannot give rise to a plurality.

The principal champion of this view is J. E. Raven.[22] In his first book, *Pythagoreans and Eleatics*, two reasons are offered for the claimed abandonment by late fifth-century Pythagoreans of the equation of unity with Limit. The first, repeated later in *The Presocratic Philosophers*, was that the Pythagorean definition of the odd numbers excluded the unit, which nevertheless was shown to be odd because it was not even. The resulting discrepancy was resolved by the creation for the unit of a special category, the even-odd. A second reason from the earlier book concerns Eleatic logic: "So long as the principle of unity was regarded as ultimate, then there could neither exist nor come into existence anything else beside it. This point [the Pythagoreans] countered by retaining their traditional dualism between Limit and the Unlimited or Odd and Even, but making Unity—or to be more precise, the unit—no longer interchangeable with the principle of Limit, but rather the first product of the imposition of Limit upon the Unlimited."[23] In *The Presocratic Philosophers* the same change in the Pythagorean unit is said to have occurred, and Parmenides is still said to have seemed to establish that plurality cannot come from an original unity.[24] But the cause-effect relationship between these two alleged events is not mentioned either for assertion or denial. The critic can only flog the horse without knowing whether it is alive or dead. What *is* asserted in *The Presocratic Philosophers* is that Parmenides caused the abandonment of the odd unit by criticizing the inhalation of one principle (Unlimited) by the other (Limit).[25]

There is no need to doubt that there were at any rate some fifth-century Pythagoreans who did believe in the even-odd unit.[26] It is more doubtful whether there was any school of thought among earlier Pythagoreans who believed in an odd unit. The evidence for such a belief in the early period of Pythagoreanism is far from cast-iron.[27] But let that pass; for, even if the two views were both to be found in the Classical period of the school, there is still no good reason to put them down as chronologically successive,[28] and, even if they are so successive, there is no good reason to put the postulated change down to an argument of Parmenides to the effect that a unity could not give rise to plurality.

The chapter of Aristotle's *Metaphysics* already referred to contains two sentences which have been used to establish a chronology for this kind of development. The first is the statement at the beginning of the chapter, with reference to the Atomists, that the so-called Pythagoreans were active "among and before these thinkers." This is rightly described by Walter Burkert as "quite vague";[29] it certainly does not suggest that the Pythagoreans whose philosophy is next expounded are a later school of thought than some others. The sentence is designed to bring these Pythagoreans into a relationship with the Atomists and thus serve as a transitional chronological remark. This purpose would be served perfectly well by the sentence as it stands, on the assumption that the Pythagoreans concerned included the first generation of the Master's followers. It is not said how long before Leucippus they began work. This piece of chronology is on a par with other pieces in *Metaphysics A*. Aristotle starts (983b6) with "the first philosophers" (or rather "most" of them), then (984b8ff) remarks that their kind of philosophy was finished before the necessary turn to other causes was made, (though the two periods overlap in the person of Anaxagoras and perhaps of Hermotimus); this second period includes the Atomists. Then (985b23ff) we are told that the Pythagoreans were active both during the second period and earlier; and finally we find at the beginning of the next chapter the statement that Plato came after the Pythagoreans (987a29ff). In all this there is good reason to suppose the initial placing of the Pythagoreans in chapter 5 designed to fix them in relation to other thinkers or schools, and no reason whatever to believe Aristotle's intention to be the distinction of two groups of Pythagoreans.

In any case, Aristotle does not say or imply that the group mentioned at the start of chapter 5 was later than any other. After his initial placing of Pythagoreans in general he talks about a particular group of them who formulated a Table of Opposites, noting their views' similarity to Alcmaeon's and refusing to commit himself to a decision as to who borrowed from whom. This is sometimes supposed to mean that Aristotle thought they were active about the same time as Alcmaeon;[30] but it could simply mean, as Burkert has again rightly said,[31] that Aristotle did not know the chronology of this group and/or the date of Alcmaeon. Even if, as I do not myself believe,[32] the dating of Alcmaeon in the generation directly after Pythagoras is Aristotelian, the possibility is still open that Aristotle refuses to commit himself here from caution, in sheer ignorance of the stage at which the Table of Opposites was first forthcoming.

It is doubtful, then, whether the Table of Opposites implies a different view of "one" from the usual even-odd designation; and, if there was such a different view, there is no good reason to believe that Aristotle—or indeed anybody else—dated it after the usual view. But we may pile on the agony. Even if one admits that such a different theory was held and was a successor to the even-odd interpretation, there is good ground for refusing to attribute the change to an argument of Parmenides that a one could not give rise to a many. This ground is that we have not the slightest reason to suppose that the Pythagoreans ever abandoned the idea of a unit giving rise to plurality. Platonizing Pythagoreanism certainly put the unit at the head of things, making the One the ἀρχὴ πάντων, as "Philolaus" has it (DK 44B8). If, as Aristotle says (*Metaphysics* 986a19), there was a school of Pythagorean thought holding the unit to be a compound of Limit and Unlimited, then at least these same thinkers believed that number came from the unit, τὸν δ' ἀριθμὸν ἐκ τοῦ ἑνός. In so believing they were obviously ignoring the veto—if there ever was a veto—on a "one" producing a "many." A clearer case of derivation of a plurality from a unity it would be hard to find.

If one asks, as in the case of Empedocles, how this Pythagorean school are related to the supposed argument that an *original* unity could not produce a plurality, the answer is more complex. It seems on the face of it that it is not necessary in logic to make the compounded unit later in time than its ingredients Limited and Unlimited. But probably these Pythagoreans did, in fact, believe their unit derived from, and not merely analysable into, these ingredients.[33] How, then, is the change from an original unit to a derived unit to be accounted for? It is not possible entirely to shirk this question, even if we retain some scepticism in the face of confident assertions that this was indeed a change, rather than a difference. Nor is it possible to rule out the influence of Parmenides as a factor in this difference of Pythagorean opinion. If the early Pythagoreans treated the initial unit as homogeneous, made up solely of Limit, Parmenides' argument against becoming in general would, once again, prove devastating. Such a homogeneity cannot give rise to variety without a process of becoming. If it was on this ground that some Pythagoreans decided to make the unit a compound, they would then tend naturally—whatever the logical necessities—to put the ingredients chronologically before the compound. Genealogy is the primitive way of stating analysis,[34] and there is much that is primitive in Pythagoreanism even as we see it in the time of Philolaus. It follows that it is not necessary to postulate an explicit argument from Parmenides to the effect that an original unity could not give rise to a plurality in order to explain the adoption by some Pythagoreans of a derived unit.

It remains to discuss Raven's suggestion in *Pythagoreans and Eleatics* that his supposed Parmenidean criticisms had validity "only if cosmogony consists in the inspiration of void into a true unity, such as a compound of two principles could not be."[35] The notion that the unit's unity was infringed by its composition from two principles is without foundation. If Philolaus and Archytas held the unit to be even-odd, they did not therefore have to deny its unity, or say that the One was not one. The very idea would have seemed absurd. A unit is, in Greek at least, inescapably a unity; the "one" is inevitably one and can hardly be regarded as an inferior, or not-"true," one. There is no reason why late fifth-century Pythagoreans should not have presupposed innocently in their practice, like the Atomists and others, that it was possible to call a thing "one" when it was in some senses "many." Nor is it necessary to suppose this innocent presupposition of linguistic practice to have been accompanied by any conscious awareness of different senses of "one."

X

CONCLUSION

The foregoing pages present two main lines of argument. The first is concerned with the theory that Parmenides argued directly that what was one could not be or become many. The second is designed to show that the terms "one" and "many" are ambiguous and incomplete, in ways not analysed and hardly suspected by the Presocratics, though some of them were known to Aristotle.

The first line of argument begins with the Milesians. These thinkers probably did not, after all, believe in one single stuff of which the many things of the world were made. Nor did Xenophanes certainly believe in one god coextensive with the world's plurality. Heraclitus did indeed believe in the unity of all things, in a somewhat different sense; but he cannot be proved to have been available for Parmenides to attack. A Parmenidean assault on the notion that many things could be one cannot therefore be shown to have any relevance to the philosophical or scientific issues confronting him. It should not, accordingly, come as a surprise that investigation of Parmenides' text has failed to reveal any passage arguing from unity to the exclusion of plurality. It was only after Parmenides, and probably in acceptance, so far as possible, of his argument against differentiation, that the doctrine arose of the world's unity in one stuff. This doctrine was at least implicit in Atomism, and most probably explicit in the philosophies of the so-called Eclectics, being mentioned explicitly by the "Hippocratic" *De natura hominis*. In Anaxagoras also the post-Parmenidean period produced a theory of the world's unity, but this is a theory of a kind less immediately connected with Parmenides. In some respects the Sphere of Empedocles is connected with Parmenides; it is described as "one" but nevertheless contains within itself the four roots. If Parmenides placed any veto on a unity being at the same time a plurality of any sort, then his successors blatantly ignored it in important parts of their physics. Certainly Zeno's argument reported by Aristotle at *De generatione et corruptione A* 8 presupposes that unity excludes all plurality; this presupposition, however, need not have been derived directly from an explicit Parmenidean veto but could have resulted from the impulse to dialectic, and the blow to any apparent contradiction, given by the general nature of Parmenides' argument.

There is again no justification in Parmenides' extant text for supposing him to have argued specifically that a unity could not give rise to a plurality. Of course Parmenides would have denied that any "giving rise" was possible, but there is nothing in his extant text which constrains us to believe that he directed attention to this particular kind of "giving rise." Once again, the theory that he did so direct attention finds no support in the extant writings of his predecessors or successors. The Milesians, and perhaps Xenophanes, believed that the manifold world arose from one thing or stuff but are not known to have emphasized the unity or the plurality concerned, or even to have used in this kind of context the words "one" and "many." Heraclitus' ἐξ ἑνὸς πάντα is probably not a statement about a process in which a plurality is produced. The Pythagoreans, if their primitive-sounding arithmetical cosmogony does indeed go back before Parmenides, would supply a target for an argument against a unity producing a plurality; but the history of Pythagoreanism nevertheless offers no good historical reason for assuming the existence of such an argument, since some, if not all, Pythagoreans continued to believe in the "one" as an early stage of cosmogony, prior to plurality. Indeed, post-Parmenidean thought in general offers no evidence for this supposed argument in Parmenides. The Empedoclean oscillation from unity to plurality and back tells strongly against it. So does the belief of the "Eclectics" that one substance gave rise to the manifold world—without ceasing to be the same substance, and so without violating too extravagantly the Parmenidean prohibition on coming-to-be. And the "Eclectics" are not to be dismissed as mere Rips Van Winkle. At first sight, the Atomist denial that a "true one" can turn out a plurality seems a refuge for defenders of a similar argument in Parmenides; but it happens that there are plausible explanations of this denial other than the presumption of a Parmenidean argument of which there is no trace elsewhere.

But to discount these two supposed Parmenidean arguments is not to deny all place in Eleatic writings to the one-many antithesis. It is not for nothing that Melissus calls the Eleatic subject "the one." Yet the antithesis is clearer in Zeno than in the two positive Eleatics. For Zeno, the destruction of plurality was equivalent to the establishment of the Eleatic One. One of his arguments, at least, clearly presupposes that a thing cannot be one and many at the same time, and another may well have ended in the antinomy of one and many. For Parmenides and Melissus, the abolition of distinctions, an abolition which resulted in the doctrine that Being was one, was a step, and indeed a vital step, on the way to the denial of process, whether of absolute becoming or perishing, of qualitative change, or of motion in space. Two things about this are significant. First, the unity of Being was not, for Parmenides, any more than for his predecessors—or, for that matter, Heraclitus—the *initial* premiss for argument or discussion. It represents the conclusion of a major argument, even if it served in turn as the premiss from which the further properties of Being could be deduced. Second, the fact that Parmenides deduces several distinct things about Being from the proposition that it alone exists, that it is single, does not show that Parmenides was in any position to distinguish clearly between several kinds of unity, any more than the denial of what amounts to qualitative change shows that he could have enunciated with Aristotelian crispness the distinction between quality and substratum.

The words "one" and "many" (or "all") attain some prominence also in Heraclitus and Empedocles, but here there is some difficulty in deciding what precisely they mean. In speaking of the unity and identity of opposites, Heraclitus seems to have had in mind a number of different relationships; it is not clear how far he was able to distinguish these, but it looks as if he thought he was arguing for identity when he was in fact tending to establish mutual validation, mutual succession, or some kind of connection. The resulting paradoxes he seems to have accepted, without being unaware of their paradoxicality. Here we have, in my opinion, a confusion, but a confusion likely to prove usefully thought-provoking. For what it is worth, there is also the possibility that Empedocles, who uses "one" in more than one sense, was not clear in his mind about these senses. Zeno himself was, as we have seen, satisfied that one could not escape the *choice* between a thing—be it all existence or something more trivial—being either one or many. To suppose this is to neglect the incompleteness and polysemy of the words "one" and "many." In this context it seems legitimate to try and interpret Zeno's main surviving arguments against the plurality of things as based on such neglect. The attempt is the more successful since it enables one to read the texts straightforwardly whereas older interpretations seem to read into the text ideas which are not there, but which could have been put there if Zeno had understood them. The discussion of Zeno's arguments against plurality was in all probability one of the formative influences in the development of Atomism. But the Atomists, though not incapable of subtlety, did not take Zeno apart in such a way as to expose his basic neglect of the polysemy of "many." They certainly believed, like normal people before and since, that they could refer, for example, to many things as being made of one stuff; but they were quite incapable of seeing that Zeno's argument at *De generatione et corruptione A* 8 depended on the assumption that "many" is univocal, and there is some reason to believe that they would have accepted the doctrine, strange as it seems to us, that any plurality must have gaps, or at least potential gaps only temporarily bridged, to separate its members. The distinction they draw between a "true one" and other ones is not necessarily a distinction between what Aristotle would have recognized as different senses of "one." Not much more subtle is the analysis attributed to Gorgias by Sextus, though, if genuine, it does represent an important advance in the generation or two after Zeno: it is at least an analysis of a sort.

This state of affairs, if this be indeed how matters stood in Plato's early manhood, may throw light indirectly on a number of questions far too complex for discussion here. The inadequacy of available analyses of "one" and related words should be a factor in the assessment of what Plato thought he was saying when he discussed the unity of virtue, or the unity of a Form. It is also to be borne in mind in trying to sort out how much of the second part of the *Parmenides* is serious argument and what Plato meant by it. This should in turn lead on to the question how original were Aristotle's various accounts of unity. These problems, however, must here only be mentioned; others may judge how far the results of this work may help in their solution.

APPENDIX / PARMENIDES B8.7-12

Another explanation is here propounded of the corruption that I presuppose of B8.12. It is not necessarily exclusive, and is in any case, as an explanation, somewhat hypothetical. I print it here in the belief that the philosophical questions raised are important enough to warrant discussion, but too far from my main theme to form an integral part of the chapter concerned.

Against the possibility of saying that Being comes to be out of not-Being Parmenides argues (a) that you cannot talk about not-Being, οὐ γὰρ φατὸν οὐδὲ νοητόν ἐστιν ὅπως οὐκ ἔστιν: one would then expect him to argue (b) that, even if one could talk about it, it could never give rise to anything existent. This horn of the dilemma despatched, Parmenides could then turn to the other, to Being coming from Being. But he does not after all produce argument (b) at B8.9–10, if the usual interpretation be followed. Instead of asking "What could have caused it to grow from nothing?" Parmenides is made to ask what is clearly a posterior question, namely "What could have caused it to come into being from nothing at one time rather than another?" Such, whatever the detail, was the interpretation of antiquity, if Simplicius' unquestioning statement of it (*in Physica* 78.26–27) be a sound guide. Interpreting thus, it was not unnatural that someone should supply the missing, more obvious, question/argument by inserting a negative in the next horn. This is in fact what results from the manuscripts' negative at line 12: the sentence thus constituted, οὐδὲ ποτ' ἐκ μὴ ἐόντος κτλ., does state the impossibility of something arising from nothing. The trouble is that it states it *after* the question "How could something arise out of nothing at one time rather than another?" So with the manuscripts' reading of line 12 we still do not have the natural philosophical rhetoric of (a) there is no not-Being, (b) if there were nothing could come from it, and (c) if something were to come from it, why should it come at one time rather than another? What we do have, on the usual interpretation of lines 9–10, is the less effective and less logical order (a), (c), (b), and a conclusion stuck between (c) and (b) in the shape of line 11, οὕτως ἢ πάμπαν πελέναι χρεών ἐστιν ἢ οὐχί. So that the attempt to introduce the missing argument by insertion of a negative in line 12 fails and should not mislead us. Where, then, is the missing argument?

I venture to suggest that it is to be found after all in lines 9–10, τί δ' ἄν μιν καὶ χρέος ὦρσεν ὕστερον ἢ πρόσθεν, τοῦ μηδενὸς ἀρξάμενον, φῦν; If, instead of taking ὕστερον ἢ πρόσθεν to mean either "later rather than sooner"[1] or "at one particular moment, either later or sooner,"[2] we take the expression as truly *polar*, we are left with the question "What necessity would ever have caused it to grow, starting from nothing?"—which is, precisely, the argument which the natural flow of philosophic rhetoric leads us to expect. Polar opposites nowadays hardly need either illustration or explanation. On this interpretation we are now able, for the first time, to attribute to Parmenides the explicit statement (albeit in the form of a rhetorical question) that nothing can come from nothing, without, by the retention of the negative at line 12, destroying the natural sequence of his argument. For the only place in the extant fragments to which one can assign this famous dogma, so important in the history of Greek philosophy,[3] is in this opening paragraph of B8.

Some further explanation may be deemed necessary before we let go from the poem of Parmenides the equally famous argument, with perhaps an even longer history, which Simplicius (*in Physica* 78.26–27) expresses in the middle of his (admittedly) free paraphrase in the words καὶ διὰ τί δὴ τότε ἀλλὰ μὴ καὶ πρότερον ἢ ὕστερον ἐγένετο; It is very often held that it was this argument that Anaxagoras and Empedocles were answering when they postulated moving causes such as Νοῦς or Love and Strife. And yet Anaxagoras evidently did not say *why* Νοῦς should decide to act at one time rather than another, a point he might have been expected at least to raise; for Aristotle uses against him in *Physics* Θ (252a4ff) essentially the same argument as this alleged one of Parmenides, "Why at one time rather than another?"[4] Empedocles (B30.3) has at best a dusty answer to the argument, an oath sworn by Love and Strife[5]—and even this need not be an answer to an argument already produced, but could easily be an answer to the question arising directly out of Empedocles' own system, namely, Why and when should the reign of one cause give way to the power of the other? And Plato—who certainly knew his Parmenides—may also have fallen a victim in the *Timaeus* to this same argument and (if he did) has no answer ready. On the usual interpretation of Parmenides there is something amiss in the dialogue which many see as the story of Greek philosophy; but if we interpret Parmenides' meaning as I have suggested, then we not only restore to him one famous argument of which later philosophy offers many traces, we also remove another famous argument of which the history of pre-Aristotelian philosophy shows no unambiguous traces.

The dialogue now becomes more intelligible. Parmenides objects to "something from nothing," asking what can have caused it. Anaxagoras and Empedocles in an attempted answer[6] introduce the notion of a moving cause, to give a reason for the creation of a cosmos which was not there before. The Atomists, postulating a universe infinite in duration as well as extent and containing infinite κόσμοι, do not need a cause of movement of the same type. Plato in the *Timaeus* (whether literally or metaphorically I cannot here discuss) implicitly rejects the Atomist way out and replaces Νοῦς and Love/Strife with his Demiurge. Aristotle then asks the deeper and more probing question why these alleged causes should act at one time rather than another. This more coherent picture need not be the right one just because it is more coherent. But, since this greater coherence in the history of philosophy is matched by an increased coherence in the writing of Parmenides, it gains in respectability. And certainly, it seems to me, the onus of proof should rest on those who would differ.[7]

ABBREVIATIONS / BIBLIOGRAPHY
NOTES / INDICES

ABBREVIATIONS

(See also Bibliography)

AGP	Archiv für Geschichte der Philosophie
AJP	American Journal of Philology
CP	Classical Philology
CQ	Classical Quarterly
CR	Classical Review
GCFI	Giornale critico della filosofía italiana
HSCP	Harvard Studies in Classical Philology
JHI	Journal of the History of Ideas
JHS	Journal of Hellenic Studies
MusHelv	Museum Helveticum
MXG	De Melisso Xenophane Gorgia
PQ	Philosophical Quarterly
RE	Real-Encyclopädie der Klassischen Altertumswissenschaft, hrsg. von Pauly–Wissowa–Kroll–Ziegler
REA	Revue des études anciennes
REG	Revue des études grecques
RhM	Rheinisches Museum
SVF	Stoicorum Veterum Fragmenta, vols. 1–3, ed. von Arnim
TAPA	Transactions and Proceedings of the American Philological Association
WS	Wiener Studien

BIBLIOGRAPHY

Albertelli, P., *Gli Eleati, testimonianze e frammenti*, a cura di P.A., Bari 1939.
Archiloque, *Fragments* . . . F. Lasserre . . . A. Bonnard. Paris 1958.
Aristotle and Plato in Mid-Fourth Century . . . ed. I. Düring and G. E. L. Owen, Gothenburg 1960.
Aristotle's Categories and De interpretatione, tr. J. L. Ackrill, Oxford 1963.
Aristotelis *De caelo* . . . D. J. Allan, Oxford 1936.
Aristotle, *De generatione et corruptione*, tr. H. H. Joachim (Oxf. Trans.), Oxford 1930.
Aristotle, *On Coming-to-Be and Passing-Away*, ed. H. H. Joachim, Oxford 1922.
[Aristotle], *De Melisso Xenophane Gorgia*, tr. T. Loveday and E. S. Forster, Oxford 1913.
Aristotle, *De partibus animalium*, ed. and tr. A. L. Peck (Loeb), rev. and repr. London 1961.
Aristotle, *Metaphysica* Volumen II . . . H. Bonitz, Bonn, 1849, repr. Hildesheim 1960. Cited in the notes as Bonitz, *Comm.*
Aristotle, *Metaphysics*, tr. W. D. Ross, Oxford 1908.
Aristotle's *Metaphysics*, ed. W. D. Ross, Oxford 1924, 2nd impression.
Aristotle, *Metaphysics*, ed. and tr. H. Tredennick (Loeb), Cambridge 1947.
Aristotle, *Metaphysica*, recog. W. Jaeger, Oxford 1957.
Aristotle, *Physics*, tr. R. P. Hardie and R. K. Gaye, Oxford 1930.
Aristotle's Physics . . . by W. D. Ross, Oxford 1936.
Aristotle, *The Physics* . . . by Philip H. Wicksteed and Francis M. Cornford (Loeb), Cambridge, Mass., vol. 1, 1929; vol. 2, 1934.
Arndt and Gingrich, see W. Bauer.
von Arnim, H., "Die Weltperioden bei Empedokles," *Festschrift T. Gomperz* . . . Wien 1902.
ASPW, see Solmsen.
Austin, J. L., *Sense and Sensibilia*, reconstructed from the manuscript notes by G. J. Warnock, Oxford, 1962.
Bailey, C., *The Greek Atomists and Epicurus: A Study*, Oxford 1928.
Bambrough, R., "Socratic Paradox," *PQ* 10 (1960) 289–300.
——— "Universals and Family Resemblances," *Proceedings of the Aristotelian Society* 61 (1960–1961) 207–222.
Bauer, J. B., "*MONIH*: Empedocles B27,4 und 28,3," *Hermes* 89 (1961) 367–369.
Bauer, W., *Greek–English Lexicon of the New Testament* . . . tr. and adapt. . . . 4th ed. rev. by W. F. Arndt and F. W. Gingrich, Cambridge 1952.
Bernays, J., *Die Heraklitischen Briefe* . . . Berlin 1869.
Bicknell, P. J., "Parmenides' Refutation of Motion and an Implication," *Phronesis* 12 (1967) 1–5.

Bignone, E., *Empedocle: Studio critico* ... E.B. (i.e., *Pensiero Greco* vol. 2), Torino 1916.
Black, M., *Problems of Analysis: Philosophical Essays*, London 1954.
Bonitz, H., *Comm*. See Aristotle, *Metaphysica*.
—— *Index Aristotelicus*, Berlin 1870.
Booth, N. B., "Zeno's Paradoxes," *JHS* 77 (1957) 187–201.
—— "Were Zeno's Arguments a Reply to Attacks upon Parmenides?" *Phronesis* 2 (1957) 1–9.
Bowra, C. M., "The Fox and the Hedgehog," *CQ* 34 (1940) 26–29.
Brochard, V., *Études de philosophie ancienne et de philosophie moderne*, recueillies ... par V. Delbos, nouv. éd., Paris 1954.
Burkert, W., *Weisheit und Wissenschaft: Studien zu Pythagoras, Philolaus und Platon* (Erlanger Beitr. zur Sprach- und Kuntswiss. Bd. 10), Nürnberg 1962.
Burn, A. R., *The Lyric Age of Greece*, London 1960.
Burnet, J., *Early Greek Philosophy*, 4th ed., London 1930. Cited in the notes as *EGP*[4].
Bury, J. B., Πινδάρου Ἐπίνικοι Νεμεονίκαις .. ed. J.B.B., London 1890.
Calogero, G., *Studi sull' Eleatismo*, Rome 1932.
—— "Eraclito," *GCFI* 1936, pp. 195–224.
—— "Senofane e Eschilo," *Studi di filosofia greca* ... R. Mondolfo, (Bari 1950), pp. 31–55.
Campbell, D. A., *Greek Lyric Poetry: A Selection* ... London 1967.
Campbell, L., *The* Sophistes *and* Politicus *of Plato* ... by L.C., Oxford 1867.
Chappell, V. C., "Time and Zeno's Arrow," *Journal of Philosophy* 59 (1962) 197–213.
Cherniss, H., *Aristotle's Criticism of Presocratic Philosophy*, Baltimore 1935. Cited in the notes as *ACPP*.
—— Review of Gigon, *Untersuchungen zu Heraklit*, *AJP* 56 (1935) 414–416.
—— "The Characteristics and Effects of Presocratic Philosophy," *JHI* 12 (1951) 319–345.
Cicero, *Academica*, text revised and explained by J. S. Reid, London 1885.
Classen, C. J., "Bemerkungen zu zwei griechischen 'Philosophiehistorikern,'" *Philologus* 109 (1965) 175–181.
Clement of Alexandria, ed. O. Stählin, 3 Aufl. neu hrsg. von L. Früchtel, Bd. 2, Berlin 1960.
Corbato, C., *Studi Senofanei*, Estratto dagli Annali Triestini, Trieste 1952.
Cornford, F. M., "Parmenides' Two Ways," *CQ* 27 (1933) 97–111.
—— *Plato's Theory of Knowledge*, London 1935.
—— *Plato's Cosmology*, London 1937.
—— *Plato and Parmenides*, London 1939.
—— *Principium Sapientiae*, Cambridge 1952.
Corpus paroemiographorum Graecorum, ed. E. F. von Leutsch und F. W. Schneidewin, Göttingen 1829 (repr. Hildesheim 1968).
Covotti, Aurelio, *I Presocratici*, Coll. di studi fil., ser. stor., monogr. 3, Napoli 1934.
Coxon, A. H., "The Philosophy of Parmenides," *CQ* 28 (1934) 134–144.

Crombie, I. M., *An Examination of Plato's Doctrines*, London, vol. 1, 1962; vol. 2, 1963.
Denniston, J. D., *Greek Particles*, 2nd ed., ed. K. J. Dover, Oxford 1954.
Diels, H., *Doxographi Graeci*, 3rd ed., Berlin, 1958. Cited in the notes as Diels, *Dox*.
——— *Parmenides' Lehrgedicht*, Gr. und Deutsch von H.D., 1st ed., Berlin 1897.
——— *Aristotelis qui fertur de Melisso Xenophane Gorgia libellus*, Philosophische und historische Abhandlungen der königlichen Akademie der Wissenschaften zu Berlin 1900. Cited in the notes as Diels, *MXG*.
——— *Poetarum philosophorum fragmenta*, ed. H.D., Berlin, 1901. Cited in the notes as *PPF*.
——— *Fragmente der Vorsokratiker*, 4th ed., Berlin 1922. Cited in the notes as *VS*.
Diels, H.–Kranz, W., *Fragmente der Vorsokratiker*, 6th ed., Berlin 1951–1952. Cited in the notes as DK.
Diès, A., "Le problème de l'un et du multiple avant Platon," *Revue de l'histoire de la philosophie* 1 (1927) 5–22.
Diller, H., "Die philosophiegeschichtliche Stellung des Diogenes von Apollonia," *Hermes* 76 (1941) 359–381.
Diogenes Laertius, *Vitae philosophorum*, recog. . . . H. S. Long, Script. class. bibl. Oxon., Oxford 1964.
DK, see Diels–Kranz.
DuP, see Fränkel.
Encyclopedia of Philosophy, ed. Paul Edwards, New York, 1967.
Epicuro, *Opere* . . . G. Arrighetti, Torino 1960.
Euripides, *Herakles*, erklärt von U. von Wilamowitz-Moellendorff, Berlin 1889.
——— *Hippolytus*, ed. . . . W. S. Barrett, Oxford 1964.
Farnell, L. R., *The Works of Pindar*, tr. with . . . commentaries L.R.F., London 1932.
Farrington, B., *Greek Science: Its Meaning for Us*, vols. 1–2, Pelican books, Harmondsworth etc., 1944, repr. with revisions 1963.
FGrHist, see Jacoby.
Fondation Hardt, *Entretiens sur l'antiquité classique*, Tome I: *La notion du divin depuis Homère à Platon*, Vandœuvres-Genève 1954.
Fränkel, H., *Wege und Formen: Frühgriechischen Denkens* . . . 2te . . . Aufl., Munich 1960. Cited in the notes as *WuF*.
——— *Dichtung und Philosophie des frühen Griechentums* . . . 2te . . . Aufl., Munich 1962. Cited in the notes as *DuP*.
Freudenthal, J., *Über die Theologie des Xenophanes*, Breslau 1886.
Fritz, K. Von, *Philosophie und sprachlicher Ausdruck bei Demokrit Plato und Aristoteles*, New York [1940].
Furley, D. J., *Two Studies in the Greek Atomists*. Study I: *Indivisible Magnitudes*. Study II: *Aristotle and Epicurus on Voluntary Action*. Princeton, N.J., 1967.
Gigon, O., *Untersuchungen zu Heraklit*, Leipzig 1935.
——— *Der Ursprung der griechischen Philosophie von Hesiod bis Parmenides*, Basel 1945.
Gladigow, B., *Sophia und Kosmos: Untersuchungen zur Frühgeschichte von σοφός und σοφίη* (Spudasmata Bd. 1), Hildesheim 1965.

Gomperz, H., *Psychologische Beobachtungen an griechischen Philosophen*, Leipzig 1924.

——— "ΑΣΩΜΑΤΟΣ," *Hermes* 67 (1932) 155–167.

Gomperz, T., *The Greek Thinkers*, English translation of *Griechische Denker*, tr. L. Magnus and G. G. Berry, London 1901–1912.

Goodwin, W. W., *Greek Moods and Tenses*, 3rd ed., London 1912.

Gottschalk, H. B., "Anaximander's Apeiron," *Phronesis* 10 (1965) 37–53.

Guthrie, W. K. C., *A History of Greek Philosophy*, Cambridge, vol. 1, 1962; vol. 2, 1965. Cited in the notes as *HGP* I and II.

——— *The Greek Philosophers from Thales to Aristotle*, London repr. 1956.

——— "Aristotle as a Historian of Philosophy: Some Preliminaries," *JHS* 77 (1957) 35–41.

HCF, see Kirk.

Heath, Sir T., *A History of Greek Mathematics*, vol. 1, Oxford 1921.

Heidel, W. A., "Qualitative Change in Presocratic Philosophy," *AGP* 19 (1906) 333–379.

——— "The Pythagoreans and Greek Mathematics," *AJP* 61 (1940) 1–33.

——— "Hecataeus and Xenophanes," *AJP* 64 (1943) 257–277.

Heinemann, s.v. Herakleitos, Briefe des, *RE* Suppl. 5, Stuttgart 1931, cols. 228–232.

Heinimann, F., *Nomos und Physis*, Basel 1945.

Herodotos, erklärt von H. Stein, Berlin: my copy 1893–1908.

HGP, see Guthrie.

Hippocrates, *Œuvres complètes* ... par E. Littré, Paris 1839–1861.

Hölscher, U., "Weltzeiten und Lebenszyklus: Eine Nachprüfung der Empedokles-Doxographie," *Hermes* 93 (1965) 7–33.

Jacoby, F., *Apollodors Chronik*, Berlin 1902.

——— *Fragmente der griechischen Historiker*, Berlin 1923–1958. Cited in the notes as *FGrHist*.

Jaeger, W., *The Theology of the Early Greek Philosophers*, Oxford 1947. Cited in the notes as *TEGP*.

Joel, K., *Geschichte der antiken Philosophie*, Tübingen 1921.

Jouanna, J., "Rapports entre Mélissos de Samos et Diogène d'Apollonie, à la lumière du traité Hippocratique *De natura hominis*," *REA* 67 (1965) 306–323.

Kahn, C. H., "Anaximander and the Arguments Concerning the ἄπειρον at *Physics* 203b4–15," *Festschrift Ernst Kapp* (Hamburg 1958) 19–29.

——— *Anaximander and the Origins of Greek Cosmology*, New York, 1960.

Karsten, S., *Philosophorum Graecorum ... reliquiae*, vols. 1 and 2, Amsterdam 1830–1838.

Kaufmann, W., *Philosophic Classics*, vol. 1, Englewood Cliffs, N.J., 1963.

Kerferd, G. B., "Gorgias on Nature or That Which Is Not," *Phronesis* 1 (1955–1956) 3–25.

Kerschensteiner, J., "Der Bericht des Theophrast über Heraklit," *Hermes* 83 (1955) 385–411.

——— *Kosmos*, Munich 1962.

Kirk, G. S., "Natural Change in Heraclitus," *Mind* 60 (1951) 35–42.

——— *Heraclitus, The Cosmic Fragments*, Cambridge 1954. Cited in the notes as *HCF*.

BIBLIOGRAPHY

——— "Some Problems in Anaximander," *CQ* n.s. 5 (1955) 21–38.
——— "Logos, harmonie, lutte, dieu et feu dans Héraclite," *Revue Philosophique* 147 (1957) 289–299.
Kirk, G. S., and Raven, J. E., *The Presocratic Philosophers*, 2nd impression, Cambridge 1960. Cited in the notes as KR.
Kirk, G. S., and Stokes, M. C., "Parmenides' Refutation of Motion," *Phronesis* 5 (1960) 1–4.
KR, see Kirk and Raven.
Kranz, W., "Empedokles und die Atomistik," *Hermes* 47 (1912) 18–42.
——— "Vorsokratisches I, II," *Hermes* 69 (1934) 114–119 and 226–228.
——— *Empedocles, antike Gestalt und romantische Neuschöpfung*, Zürich 1949.
——— "ΠΑΛΙΝΤΡΟΠΟΣ ΑΡΜΟΝΙΗ," *RhM* 101 (1958) 250–254.
Kühner, R., *Ausführliche Grammatik der griechischen Sprache*, Teil 2 *Satzlehre*... besorgt von B. Gerth, Hannover 1897–1904. Cited in the notes as Kühner–Gerth.
Lasserre, F., *Les Épodes d'Archiloque*, Paris 1950.
Leaf, W., *The Iliad*, 2nd ed., London 1900–1902.
Lee, H. D. P., *Zeno of Elea*, text... by H.D.P.L., Cambridge 1936.
Liddell, H., and Scott, R., *Greek Lexicon*, 9th ed. revised... by H. Stuart Jones... Oxford 1925–1940. Cited in the notes as LSJ.
Lloyd, G. E. R., *Polarity and Analogy: Two Types of Argumentation in Early Greek Thought*, Cambridge 1966.
Long, A., "The Principles of Parmenides' Cosmogony," *Phronesis* 8 (1963) 90–107.
LSJ, see Liddell.
Lumpe, A., *Die Philosophie des Xenophanes von Kolophon*, Munich 1952.
Lyons, J., *Structural Semantics: An Analysis of Part of the Vocabulary of Plato*, Philol. Soc. of Lond. Publ. 20, Oxford 1963.
McDiarmid, J. B., "Theophrastus and the Presocratic Causes," *HSCP* 61 (1953) 85–156.
McGibbon, D., "The Atomists and Melissus," *Mnemosyne* 4 ser. 17 (1964) 248–255.
Mansfeld, J., *Die Offenbarung des Parmenides und die menschliche Welt*, Assen 1964.
Marcovich, M., s.v. Herakleitos, *RE* Suppl. 10, Stuttgart 1965, cols. 246–320.
——— *Heraclitus*, Merida 1967.
Mathewson, I. R., "Aristotle and Anaxagoras: An Examination of F. M. Cornford's Interpretation," *CQ* n.s. 8 (1958) 67–81.
Matson, W. I., "Democritus, Fragment 126," *CQ* n.s. 13 (1963) 26–29.
Mau, J., *Zum Problem des Infinitesimalen bei den antiken Atomisten*, Deutsche Akad. d. Wiss. zu Berl., Inst. für Hellenistisch-römische Phil., Veröffentl. 4, Berlin 1954.
Mélanges Desrousseaux, Mélanges offerts à A. M. Desr. par ses amis et ses élèves, Paris 1937.
Millerd, C. E., *On the Interpretation of Empedocles*, Chicago 1908.
Minar, E. L., "Cosmic Periods in the Philosophy of Empedocles," *Phronesis* 8 (1963) 127–145.

Mondolfo, R., *L'infinito nel pensiero dell' antichità classica*, Florence 1956.
Müller, C. W., *Gleiches zu Gleichem, ein Prinzip frühgriechischen Denkens*, Klass.-philol. Studien 31, Wiesbaden 1965.
Mugler, C., "Le problème d'Anaxagore," *REG* 69 (1956) 314–376.
Munding, H., "Zur Beweisführung des Empedokles," *Hermes* 82 (1954) 129–145.
Natorp, P., s.v. Diogenes (44) von Sinope, *RE* Suppl. 5, Stuttgart 1905, cols. 765–773.
New Essays on Plato and Aristotle, ed. R. Bambrough, London 1965.
Norden, E., *Die antike Kunstprosa*, Leipzig 1898.
O'Brien, D., "Empedocles' Cosmic Cycle," *CQ* n.s. 17 (1967) 29–40.
Owen, G. E. L., "Eleatic Questions," *CQ* n.s. 10 (1960) 84–102.
——— "Zeno and the Mathematicians," *Proceedings of the Aristotelian Society* 58 (1957–1958) 199–222.
——— *New Essays* = "Aristotle on the Snares of Ontology," pp. 69–95 of *New Essays on Plato and Aristotle* (see above).
——— "Plato and Parmenides on the Timeless Present," *Monist* 50 (1966) 317–340.
Patin, A., "Parmenides im Kampfe gegen Heraklit," *Jahrbb. für klassische Philologie*, Suppl. 25 (1899) 489–660.
Pfeiffer, R., *A History of Classical Scholarship*, vol. 1, Oxford 1968.
Philippson, R., review of Bailey's *Greek Atomists and Epicurus*, *Gnomon* 6 (1930) 460–473.
Pindars Siegeslieder, erklärt von F. Mezger, Leipzig 1880.
Platon, *Parménide*, ed. A. Diès, Assoc. G. Budé, Paris 1923.
Platon, *Sophiste* . . . par A. Diès, Assoc. G. Budé, Paris 1925.
Pötscher, W., "Zu Xenophanes frgm. 23," *Emerita* 32 (1964) 1–13.
Powell, J. E., *Lexicon to Herodotus*, Cambridge 1938.
PPF, see Diels.
Preisigke, F., *Wörterbuch der griechischen Papyrusurkunden* . . . Bearb. . . . von E. Kiessling, Berlin/Marburg 1924–1958.
Ramnoux, C., *Héraclite ou L'homme entre les choses et les mots*, Paris 1959.
Raven, J. E., *Pythagoreans and Eleatics*, Cambridge 1948. See also Kirk, G. S.
Reinhardt, K., *Parmenides und die Geschichte der griechischen Philosophie*, Bonn 1916.
——— "Heraklits Lehre vom Feuer," *Hermes* 77 (1942) 1–27.
——— "Heraclitea," *ibid.*, pp. 225–248.
——— "Empedokles, Orphiker und Physiker," *CP* 45 (1950) 170–179.
Rivier, A., "L'homme et l'expérience humaine dans les fragments d'Héraclite," *MusHelv* 13 (1956) 144–164.
Robinson, R., *Plato's Earlier Dialectic*, 2nd ed., Oxford 1953.
Rudberg, G., "Empedokles und Evolution," *Eranos* 50 (1952) 23–30.
Rose, V., *Aristotelis . . . fragmenta*, 3rd ed., Leipzig 1886.
Schwabl, H., "Sein und Doxa bei Parmenides," *WS* 66 (1953) 50–75.
——— "Parmenides" (Forschungsbericht 1939–1955), *Anzeiger für die Altertumswissenschaft* 9 (1956), cols. 129–156.
Schwyzer, E., *Griechische Grammatik*, Bd. 2 . . . A. Debrunner, Munich 1953. Cited in the notes as Schwyzer–Debrunner.

Sccck, G. A., "Empedokles B17, 9-13 (=2.8-12), B8, B100 bei Aristoteles," *Hermes* 95 (1967) 28-53.
Shakespeare, *Macbeth*, ed. Kenneth Muir (Arden Shakespeare), 8th ed. repr. Cambridge, Mass., 1957.
Shorey, P., review of Patin's *Parmenides im Kampfe gegen Heraklit, AJP* 21 (1900) 200-216.
Sikes, E., and Wynne Willson, St. J. B., *The Prometheus Vinctus of Aeschylus*, London 1898.
Snell, B., "Die Sprache Heraklits," *Hermes* 61 (1926) 353-381.
───── "Heraklits Fragment 10," *Hermes* 76 (1941) 84-87.
───── "Die Nachrichten über die Lehren des Thales und die Anfänge der griechischen Philosophie und Literaturgeschichte," *Philologus* 96 (N. F. 50) (1944) 170-182.
Solmsen, F., *Aristotle's System of the Physical World*, Ithaca, N.Y., 1960. Cited in the notes as *ASPW*.
───── "Nature as Craftsman in Greek Thought," *JHI* 24 (1963) 473-496.
───── "Love and Strife in Empedocles' Cosmology," *Phronesis* 10 (1965) 109-148.
Sophocles, *Ajax*, commentary by J. C. Kamerbeek, Leiden 1953.
Sprague, R. K., "Parmenides: A Suggested Rearrangement of Fragments in the Way of Truth," *CP* 50 (1955) 124-126.
Stanford, W. B., Sophocles, *Ajax*, ed. W.B.S., London 1963.
Stebbing, L. S., *A Modern Introduction to Logic*, 7th ed. repr. London 1958.
Stokes, M. C., "Parmenides fr. 6," *CR* 10 (1960) 193-194.
───── "Hesiodic and Milesian Cosmogonies," *Phronesis* 7 (1962) 1-37, and 8 (1963) 1-34.
───── Review of R. S. Brumbaugh's *Plato on the One, AGP* 46 (1964) 121-125.
───── "On Anaxagoras," *AGP* 47 (1965) 1-19 and 217-250.
───── Review of Guthrie's *HGP* I, *PQ* 15 (1965) 65-67, and of Guthrie's *HGP* II, *ibid.*, 17 (1967) 164-166.
───── s.v. *Heraclitus* in *Encyclopedia of Philosophy*, New York 1967.
Strang, C., "The Physical Theory of Anaxagoras," *AGP* 45 (1963) 101-118.
Tannery, P., *Pour l'histoire de la science hellène*, 2ᵉ éd., Paris 1930.
Tarán, L., "El significado de νοεῖν en Parménides," *Anales de filología clásica* 7 (1959) 122-130.
───── *Parmenides: A Text with Translation, Commentary, and Critical Essays*, Princeton, N.J., 1965.
Taylor, A. E., *Elements of Metaphysics*, London 1903.
───── *Aristotle on his Predecessors, Being the First Book of His Metaphysics*, tr. A.E.T., Chicago 1907.
TEGP, see Jaeger.
Teichmüller, G., *Neue Studien zur Geschichte der Begriffe*, I Heft: *Herakleitos*, Gotha 1876.
Thesleff, H., "On Dating Xenophanes," *Societas scientiarum Fennica, Commentationes humanarum litterarum*, vol. 23 (1958), no. 3, pp. 1-22.
Trevaskis, J. R., "The Sophistry of Noble Lineage (Plato, *Sophistes* 230a5-232b9)," *Phronesis* 1 (1955-1956) 36-49.

Tugwell, S., "The Way of Truth," *CQ* n.s. 14 (1964), 36–41.
Überweg, F., *Die Philosophie des Altertums*, hrsg. von K. Praechter, Berlin 1926. Cited in the notes as Überweg–Praechter.
Untersteiner, M., *Senofane: Testimonianze e frammenti*, Florence 1955.
――― *Parmenide: Testimonianze e frammenti*, Florence 1958.
――― *Zenone: Testimonianze e frammenti*, Florence 1963.
Van der Waerden, B. L., "Zeno und die Grundlagenkrise der griechischen Mathematik," *Mathematische Annalen* 117 (1939–1941) 141–161.
Van Groningen, B. A., "Trois notes sur Empédocle," *Mnemosyne* 4 ser. 9 (1956) 221–224.
Varia Variorum (Festgabe für Karl Reinhardt), Münster etc. 1952.
Verdenius, W. J., *Parmenides: Some Comments on His Poem*, Groningen 1942 (repr. Amsterdam 1964).
Vlastos, G., "Parmenides' Theory of Knowledge," *TAPA* 77 (1946) 66–77.
――― "The Physical Theory of Anaxagoras," *Philosophical Review* 59 (1950) 31–57.
――― Review of Kirk's *Heraclitus: The Cosmic Fragments*, *AJP* 76 (1955) 310–313.
――― "On Heraclitus," *ibid.*, pp. 337–368.
――― Review of H. Fränkel's *Wege und Formen*, *Gnomon* 31 (1959) 193–204.
――― "Minimal Parts in Epicurean Atomism," *Isis* 56 (1965) 121–147.
――― "A Note on Zeno's Arrow," *Phronesis* 11 (1966) 3–18.
VS, see Diels.
Wilamowitz-Moellendorff, U. von, "Lesefrüchte" CXCVI, *Hermes* 60 (1925) 300–303.
Windelband, W., *Geschichte der abendländischen Philosophie im Altertum*, 4te Aufl. ... von A. Goedeckemeyer, Munich, 1923. Cited in the notes as Windelband–Goedeckemeyer.
WuF, see Fränkel.
Zeller, E., *La filosofía dei Greci nel suo sviluppo storico*, tr. R. Mondolfo, 1st part, Rome, vol. 1^3, 1951; vol. 2^2, 1950; vol. 3, 1961; vol. 4, 1963. Cited in the notes as ZM.
――― *Die Philosophie der Griechen in ihrer geschichtlichen Entwicklung*, I Teil, 6te Aufl. ... W. Nestle, Leipzig, 1919–1920. Cited in the notes as ZN (other parts are referred to by ZN and a volume number).
ZM, see Zeller.
ZN, see Zeller.

The Greek commentators are cited from the Berlin Academy text; the early Peripatetics from F. Wehrli's edition; the lyric poets from D. L. Page, *Poetae Melici Graeci*, E. Lobel and D. L. Page, *Poetarum Lesbiorum Fragmenta*, or E. Diehl, *Anthologia Lyrica Graeca*,[3] or B. Snell's text of Pindar, as appropriate; fragments of Greek tragedy from Nauck, except those of Sophocles cited from Jebb–Pearson.

NOTES

CHAPTER 1: ARISTOTLE AND THE ANALYSIS OF UNITY AND PLURALITY

1. 185b25. I have adapted the Oxford translation.
2. The general case is made by G. E. R. Lloyd, *Polarity and Analogy*, esp. pp. 111ff, the particular (see below) by Gregory Vlastos at *Encyclopedia of Philosophy* s.v. Zeno, vol. 8 p. 369. I owe a great deal to these stimulating works, and should have owed more if they had not reached me when my own was already far advanced.
3. Especially not to G. E. L. Owen: see *Proceedings of the Aristotelian Society* 58 (1957) 201ff.
4. B3.73–74, discussed below, pp. 213–215.
5. John Lyons, *Structural Semantics*, esp. (on polysemy) p. 90.
6. Similar doctrine at Aristotle *Topics* 106a12ff, esp. 19f πολλαχῶς τὸ βαρὺ λέγεται, ἐπειδὴ καὶ τὸ ἐναντίον.
7. See on this I. M. Crombie, *An Examination of Plato's Doctrines*, vol. 1, pp. 83f.
8. See esp. *Metaphys Γ* 1–2.
9. 1236a16ff, cf. *Metaphys.* 1060b36ff on "medical" and "healthy."
10. This whole discussion omits the question of metaphor. It is probably true that the more "dead" a metaphor, the more appropriate the description "sense," but the question is difficult and does not require discussion here.
11. Aristotle makes the point himself at *Topics* 148b16–22, but with a closing reservation (which J. L. Austin for one would probably have accepted). See Owen, *New Essays*, pp. 91f.
12. See A. E. Taylor, *Elements of Metaphysics*, pp. 123–128 (unfortunately failing to distinguish adequately between necessary and sufficient conditions of unity), and esp. J. L. Austin, *Sense and Sensibilia*, pp. 69ff. Much history is to be learnt from pursuing the references under "Unity" in the index to the *Encyclopedia of Philosophy*.
13. *Soph. El.* 182b13ff with Owen, *Aristotle and Plato in Mid-Fourth Century*, pp. 164f.
14. The title of this work is less certain than its subject. Aristotle himself refers to it as the "division of the opposites" (*Metaphys.* 1054a29f) and as the "selection of the opposites" (*Metaphys.* 1004a2). Simplicius several times refers to it as Περὶ ἀντικειμένων, once as Περὶ ἐναντιοτήτων (*in Categ.* 288.14). It is possible that Alexander's references to *De bono* (*in Metaphys.* 250.17ff and elsewhere: see Rose[3] frag. 30) are a confusion; but there is no obvious reason why Aristotle should not have treated this theme twice in works no longer extant.
15. Cf. Lloyd, *Polarity and Analogy*, p. 64 n. 2.

16. *New Essays*, p. 94.
17. *Ibid.*, p. 77.
18. *Sense and Sensibilia*, p. 69.
19. Admittedly at *Metaphys.* 1016a7ff Aristotle glimpses this substantive-hunger. He argues there that two pieces of wood in contact are not called one piece of wood, one body, or one continuous *anything*, to show that "one" is inapplicable. To do this is to assume that there is no use of "one" (or indeed of "continuous") except with a substantive present or implied. But we cannot be sure that Aristotle properly appreciated this whole point.
20. *Sense and Sensibilia*, p. 70; cf. Aristotle *Metaphys.* 1016b6ff, and note esp. καὶ γάρ, emphasizing the reasoning from pluralities to unities.
21. Owen, *New Essays*, p. 78 on "being."
22. For this paragraph see Owen, at *Aristotle and Plato in the Mid-Fourth Century*, pp. 163–190 passim.
23. On this see Lyons, *Structural Semantics*, pp. 51ff.
24. Though Aristotle is not always clear on the point, it is difficult not to suppose that this expression indicates an interest in the senses of "being" at least as important as his interest in classifying the elements of the real. But one should not be exclusive on this: see Ross, *Aristotle's Metaphysics*, vol. 1 p. xc and n. 5.
25. At 1016b17ff, the essence of "one" is ἀρχῇ τινὶ τοῦ ἀριθμοῦ εἶναι, the first measure of number. But this need not be rooted in a "central meaning" analysis of "one," despite 1016b23 πανταχοῦ δὲ τὸ ἓν ἢ τῷ ποσῷ ἢ τῷ εἴδει ἀδιαίρετον: it is consistent with Aristotle's believing that other uses of "one" are best understood with reference to its use in respect of quantity. In this passage we are not told whether τὸ ποσῷ ἀδιαίρετον and τὸ εἴδει ἀδιαίρετον are on the same level or not.
26. Ross's translation (Oxf. trans.) of ἰδίᾳ χωριστῷ (the now usual text, from the MS A[b]) as "capable of existing apart" seems to overtranslate. Tredennick in the Loeb is better, with "distinct and separate."
27. It is not clear how far the references back to Δ in *I* (1055a2, 1055b7, 1056b34) are Aristotelian; and, even if they are from Aristotle's hand, only that at 1056b35 (to Δ 15) is deeply embedded in the syntax, let alone the argument. Ross (*Metaphysics*, p. xxv) argues that the *Physics* and *De generatione* refer to Δ and that they precede the main body of the *Metaphysics*, which according to Ross includes *I*. Finding this something less than conclusive, I prefer to depend on the intrinsic improbability of Aristotle's composing so badly ordered an analysis of continuity and wholeness as that of Δ 6 after the beautifully compact discussion of *I*. But others may find this also inconclusive, and I do not make a major issue of the matter.
28. The books, like the Aristotelian pieces of wood, form one pair, and the pair has some unity (in the sense of uniformity), but they are not one continuous book, even if the binding of each is removed for closer contact. See Chap. VIII below on the Atomist refusal to allow unity to the juxtaposition of two atoms.
29. Aristotle mentions contact at *Metaphys.* 1045a7ff, where he discusses what causes the unity of a definition. There must be a reason for the existence of a

whole over and above the parts, he says, ἐπεὶ καὶ ἐν τοῖς σώμασι τοῖς μὲν ἁφὴ αἰτία τοῦ ἓν εἶναι τοῖς δὲ γλισχρότης ἤ τι πάθος ἕτερον τοιοῦτον. Here it appears that either contact or "stickiness" can cause unity in bodies. The next sentence, ὁ δ' ὁρισμὸς λόγος ἐστὶν εἷς οὐ συνδέσμῳ καθάπερ ἡ 'Ιλιὰς ἀλλὰ τῷ ἑνὸς εἶναι, adds "binding together" to the list. We are here in the laxer world of *Metaphys. I*, as also, apparently, at 1082a15ff, esp. 20f.

30. Shakespeare, *Macbeth* II ii 62, where see, e.g., Kenneth Muir's note in the Arden Shakespeare: "i.e. changing the green sea into total red." On reflection I am not sure whether Shakespeare's Macbeth means by "one" here "continuous" or "uniform"; but I console myself with the reflections that, where qualities are concerned, "continuous" and "uniform" amount to very nearly the same thing, and that "continuous" can be used in such a context to replace "one" no less easily than "uniform" can.

31. Aristotle speaks at *Metaphys.* 1023b36 ὡς οὔσης τῆς ὁλότητος ἑνότητός τινος. Aristotle makes in that same chapter some useful distinctions concerning "whole"; he separates "that of which no part is *missing* of those of which it is said naturally to be a whole" from "that which contains the things it contains with the effect that they are a unity" ("a unity" here is the Oxford translator's English for ἕν τι). This second category includes for Aristotle universals, but also (1023b32ff) τὸ συνεχὲς καὶ πεπερασμένον, ὅταν ἕν τι ἐκ πλειόνων ᾖ, ἐνυπαρχόντων μάλιστα μὲν δυνάμει, εἰ δὲ μή, ἐνεργείᾳ· τούτων δ' αὐτῶν μᾶλλον τὰ φύσει ἢ τέχνῃ τοιαῦτα, ὥσπερ καὶ ἐπὶ τοῦ ἑνὸς ἐλέγομεν ... This is the type of whole we are concerned with here; it is interesting that Aristotle, perhaps wrongly, regards continuity as a necessary condition of it. The phrase εἰ δὲ μή, ἐνεργείᾳ presumably alludes to the possibility of a cake's total ingredients being regarded as a whole even before cooking—but, as Aristotle hints, this is stretching a point.

32. This kind of oneness is virtually identifiable with the unity by position (θέσει) listed together with unities by contact and by mixture at *Metaphys.* 1082a15ff, esp. 20f.

33. See *Metaphys.* 1044a2ff.

34. As indicated at *Metaphys.* 1040b5ff.

35. *Elements of Metaphysics*, p. 124.

36. Cf. Δ 26.1023b34f, where Aristotle refers back to Δ 6.

37. *Elements of Metaphysics*, p. 125.

38. For this fault see Bonitz ad loc.; for unity by analogy see Zeller, ZN II 2 p. 257 n. 2 and passages there cited.

39. *Metaphysics* 1016a24ff, esp. 28–32. Aristotle suggests also that horse, man, and dog (as, presumably, scalene, isosceles, and equilateral triangle) are one thing (ἕν τι) or a unity because all are animals (as all triangles are shapes). But I do not think there are many contexts in which "one" is used in English with this kind of force, and wonder how conversational Greek behaved in the matter. We should be inclined rather to say "horse, man, and dog are *the same* (sort of) thing" than to use "one."

40. *Metaphys.* 1018a15ff and 1014b26. See also 1021a11f, where ὁμοῖα ὧν ἡ ποιότης μία.

41. A good example of "unity" as uniformity at D. A. Campbell, *Greek Lyric*

Poetry: A Selection, p. xi: "Such unity as the poems have may be found in two circumstances: they belong, roughly speaking, to the two centuries from 650 to 450; and they are short in comparison with epic poetry and drama."

42. Cf. ἓν καὶ ὁμοῖον at Hippocrates *VM* 7, vol. 1 p. 584 Littré, and at 14 fin., p. 604 Littré, οὔτε ἄκρητον οὔτε ἰσχυρόν, ἀλλ' ὅλον τε γέγονε καὶ ἁπλοῦν: the latter associates wholeness with well-mixed homogeneity.

43. I have adapted Joachim's (Oxford) translation of 328b22.

44. I prefer Bonitz' text (followed by Jaeger) to Ross's, at 1015b19.

45. *Metaphysics* 1016b30ff, cited above.

46. One is tempted to call things springing from the same origin "one in genus"; but the genus as springing from the same source is different from the genus as a stage in classification (see *Metaphysics Δ* 28 passim), and the latter is meant in the phrase "one in genus." When Pindar writes (*Nem.* 6.1–2) "Ἓν ἀνδρῶν, ἓν θεῶν γένος· ἐκ μιᾶς δὲ πνέομεν ματρὸς ἀμφότεροι, he is drawing not on a sense of "one" but on a normal unphilosophical use of γένος: to belong to a family (as a kinship group) is to be sprung ultimately from the same personage as the other members. What Pindar is emphasizing is that the family of men and the family of gods are parts of one and the same family. Being sprung from the same mother is a function of γένος rather than of ἕν; it is the result of being one *family* rather than of being *one*. (There is at least one other possible interpretation of this Pindaric passage; but see J. B. Bury ad loc.)

47. 1052b18: see other passages in Bonitz, *Index Aristotelicus*, p. 223a54ff.

48. See n. 20 above.

49. *Metaphys.* 1017a3: see Bonitz, *Comm.*, p. 239.

50. E.g., *Metaphys.* 1041b11ff.

51. In some cases, as D. B. Robinson points out to me, the incompatibility is clear. If Ἰατρικός is given a focal meaning, focussed on the art of medicine, ἰατρική (τέχνη), it cannot at the same time have a central meaning: if one takes ἰατρικός to mean centrally "related to medicine," then ἰατρική itself is not iatric, which is difficult to swallow. I am a little worried concerning another more immediately germane example. Suppose we take the word εἷς to mean ἀδιαίρετος, centrally. Suppose we then define ἀδιαίρετος by focal meaning with reference to quantity: have we then succeeded in making consistent the possession of focal and central meanings?

CHAPTER II: THE MILESIANS

1. For the history of this work see still Diels, *Dox.*, pp. 1–263.

2. Especially in *Aristotle's Criticism of Presocratic Philosophy*, summarized by Cherniss himself at *JHI* 12 (1951) 319–345.

3. Not all of the same kind or equally convincing; see W. K. C. Guthrie at *JHS* 77 (1957) 35ff. But, e.g., on Empedocles contrast *De gen. et corr.* 333b20–22 with *De gen. et corr.* 315a19–25: see Cherniss, *ACPP* p. 196 n. 211, where Cherniss' point seems to me to be missed by Guthrie at *JHS* 77 (1957) 38 n. 7. See also

Cherniss, *ACPP* p. 171 and n. 119 contrasting *Metaphys.* 1071b27f with passages distinguishing Anaxagoras from the other physicists.

4. Notably the making of Empedocles' sphere into a substrate, and similar errors with respect to the Milesians and Anaxagoras.

5. *ACPP* pref. p. ix.

6. One might cite *De caelo* 305b2ff as an instance of Aristotle's being captious and misleading.

7. Guthrie, *HGP* I p. 230, citing K. Joel, *Geschichte der antiken Philosophie*, p. 364. I am by no means sure that this is the correct solution; Cherniss makes the point (*ACPP* p. 392) that things are only said once to imitate numbers, at *Metaphys.* 987b11f, where Aristotle is tendentiously trying to assimilate Platonism and Pythagoreanism as closely as possible without actually equating them. I confess I cannot see the relevance here of Guthrie's remarks (*HGP* I pp. 230f) on acting and Dionysiac religion; numbers surely do not "act" in the required sense. W. D. Ross ad loc. notes that Pythagorean things are like numbers at *Metaphys.* 985b32f also, and that Aristoxenus (frag. 23 Wehrli) has a similar report. But the earlier passage of *Metaphys. A* may already be preparing the way for the interpretation to follow (unless Burnet was right at *EGP*[4] p. 307 n. 2), and Aristoxenus' malicious gossip may be the source of the whole conception (see Cherniss, *ACPP* p. 392). Aristotle elsewhere (see Cherniss, *ACPP* pp. 36ff and n. 137, citing *Metaphys.* 1080b14ff) makes Pythagorean numbers unseparated from things, a hard doctrine for "imitated" numbers.

8. Mixture in an aside at *Metaphys.* 1069b22, and clearly implied by ἐνούσας at *Phys.* 187a20. Zeller, ZN I p. 279 n. 1, speaks of a light zeugma in the *Metaphysics* passage, but despite the brevity of the passage it is hard to believe that at the time of writing it Aristotle did not believe that the ἄπειρον was a mixture. The *Physics* passage reads οἱ δ' ἐκ τοῦ ἑνὸς ἐνούσας τὰς ἐναντιότητας ἐκκρίνεσθαι, ὥσπερ Ἀναξίμανδρός φησι, καὶ ὅσοι δ' ἓν καὶ πολλά ὥσπερ Ἐμπεδοκλῆς καὶ Ἀναξαγόρας· ἐκ τοῦ μίγματος γὰρ καὶ οὗτοι ἐκκρίνουσι τἆλλα. H. B. Gottschalk (*Phronesis* 10 [1965] 46) wants ἐνούσας to come from Anaxagoras, but this is not likely in a passage where (according to Gottschalk) Aristotle is carefully distinguishing Anaxagoras and Empedocles from Anaximander and where in any case such an assimilation of vocabulary is quite unnecessary. The word itself is not necessarily Anaximander's; but it suggests unmistakably that when Aristotle wrote the sentence he thought of the ἄπειρον as a mixture of opposites. The distinction of Anaximander from those like Empedocles and Anaxagoras who say that one and many exist appears on this interpretation tenuous. Such I believe it to have been; καὶ ὅσοι δ' ἓν καὶ πολλά φασιν may mean here "and indeed all who say being is one and many," adding others to Anaximander rather than distinguishing them from him. Zeller's argument against this (ZN p. 278 n. 1) that the καὶ οὗτοι can only have been meant to contrast the ὅσοι ... φασιν with Anaximander is not conclusive, since the καὶ οὗτοι could refer simply and solely to the distinction between, on the one hand, the individual men Anaxagoras and Empedocles and, on the other, the different individual Anaximander. Aristotle does not make Anaximander any the less a physicist by writing Ἀναξίμανδρος καὶ οἱ πλεῖστοι τῶν φυσιολόγων (*Phys.* 203b15), and surely Aristotle could even there have

written πάντες for πλεῖστοι without making him a non-physicist. That the ἄπειρον is a single substance is presumably implied by Aristotle at *Phys.* 203b10ff, where he speaks of it as divine (Gottschalk, *Phronesis* 10 [1965] 39 and 45), as also at *Phys.* 204b22ff (without naming Anaximander, but see Simplicius ad loc.). For the reconciliation mentioned in my text cf. Guthrie at *JHS* 77 (1957) 38 n. 7.

9. See Cherniss, *ACPP* p. 57; also Chap. VIII below on Empedocles' Sphere.

10. Aristotle seems to me guilty of misinterpreting Xenophanes in the light of Plato *Sophist* 242d–e; see below. But we need not accept the suggestion that Aristotle necessarily took seriously Plato's jests at *Cratylus* 402d and *Theaetetus* 152e (if they were jests). See Guthrie at *JHS* 77 (1957) 40 n. 11, and my remarks on the *Sophist* passage later in this chapter.

11. *ACPP* p. 354.

12. At, e.g., *Phys.* 205a25ff Aristotle talks of the physicists' refusal to admit fire or earth as the element of things, as these elements have a definite place at top or bottom; they selected air and water, which are placed ambiguously in the middle. It is a moot point whether this attributes to the Ionians the doctrine of "natural place" or refers rather to the usual world view of the Presocratics, which did place earth at the centre and fire or aether at the periphery of the universe. In any case, the Ionian doctrine is directly ancestor to Aristotle's. (Of course, Aristotle here contradicts other accounts of Heraclitus; but this is not the point I wish to make here.)

13. See especially Guthrie at *JHS* 77 (1957) 39 for Aristotle on Thales.

14. See, e.g., *De gen. et corr.* 315a3ff: "Empedocles *seems* (ἔοικε) to contradict himself... for he says (φησί) that none of the elements can change into one another, but everything else comes from them... but at the same time that... *so that, obviously,* (ὥστε ... δῆλον ὅτι) one thing came to be fire and another water when things were separated by some differences and qualities.... If then we take away these qualities ... it obviously follows that (δῆλον ὡς ἀνάγκη)..." How else could one set about demonstrating a hidden self-contradiction in an earlier thinker?

15. Guthrie (*JHS* 77 [1957] 36) ascribes to McDiarmid the imputation to Aristotle of dishonesty; I confess I am not sure that either McDiarmid or Cherniss would be willing to accept this as an implication of their statements.

16. *ACPP* p. 357.

17. I should include Aristotle's assimilation of Empedocles' process of disrupting the Sphere to condensation-rarefaction (*De caelo* 305b2ff). I should also include Aristotle's ascription of "fire and earth" to Parmenides' "way" of seeming: from the equation of fire and light (Alex. ap. Simpl. *in Phys.* 38.23f) it is a far cry to the equation of night (or darkness) and earth. I suspect that Alexander was doing his best for Aristotle here; Guthrie, *HGP* II p. 58 n. 2, cites Simpl. *in Phys.* 25.16 with the remark that it "seems to throw some doubt" on the equation of earth with darkness in Parmenides: but we know that Simplicius possessed the work of Parmenides, and his self-correcting remark πῦρ καὶ γῆν (ἢ μᾶλλον φῶς καὶ σκότος) seems not so much to throw doubt as to make it virtually certain that such Peripatetic accounts were wrong. Be it noted that Aristotle at *Metaphys.* 986b34 (also cited by Guthrie) says οἷον πῦρ καὶ γῆν λέγων but is less cautious

elsewhere (*De gen. et corr.* 330b14), and it is the less circumspect formulation that has found its way into our extant versions of Theophrastus, whether or not Theophrastus himself was less cautious.

18. KR p. 109 n. 1 compare what is presumably Theophrastus' ἑτέραν τινὰ φύσιν ἄπειρον (ap. Simpl. *in Phys.* 24.17) with Aristotle's "radically different" ἑτέραν τινὰ φύσιν τῷ ἀπείρῳ at *Phys.* 203a17. Further, the language of Anaximander's "fragment" as it appears in Theophrastus' excerptors *may* have been influenced in some respects by that of Aristotle's generalization at *Metaphys.* 983b6ff, but this is hardly susceptible of proof. See C. H. Kahn, *Anaximander*, pp. 168ff; but it seems to me curious that γένεσις and φθορά are not to be found in extant literature as a pair before Plato's middle age (*Phaedo* 95e), and Kahn (*Anaximander*, p. 174) hardly proves that Plato is citing earlier language in this particular phrase. Certainty here is unattainable, and it would be a pity if the current reaction against overscepticism were carried too far.

19. So Kahn, *Anaximander*, p. 18.

20. See ibid., p. 20; but I should find it hard to accept the remark (italics mine), "It would in short be a mistake to suppose that Theophrastus was *ever* stupidly bound by the obiter dicta of his master." Neither Guthrie nor Kahn has, so far as I know, adequately replied to J. B. McDiarmid, *HSCP* 61 (1953) 128, who shows that Theophrastus in the *De sensibus* alone recognizes that atoms differ in size, whereas in the *Phys. Op.* he believes that only shape, order, and position differ. Clearly in the *Phys. Op.* Theophrastus was following Aristotle in error—unless the *De sensibus* is wrong in company with other passages from Aristotle.

21. Kahn justly cites Diels, *Dox.*, p. 219, in this connection.

22. Kahn cites (a) the probable preservation of ἀποκρίνεσθαι from Anaximander—a point of mainly linguistic interest; (b) the correction of Aristotle's doctrine at *Phys.* 187a20f (cited above, n. 8), where Kahn says Aristotle "seems to identify the primeval unity of Anaximander (and Empedocles) with the μῖγμα of Anaxagoras." But, if Theophrastus offers an un-Aristotelian condition in cautious language for the assimilation of the pluralists to Anaximander (ap. Simpl. *in Phys.* 27.19ff), that does not correct Aristotle's assimilation of Anaximander to the pluralists. This last assimilation I now believe was not mentioned in our extant excerpts from Theophrastus, since I was overhasty at *AGP* 47 (1965) 250 n. 50 in rejecting the arguments of Kahn, *Anaximander*, pp. 41f, and my previously published arguments should be amended accordingly. (I confess that Gottschalk's arguments at *Phronesis* 10 [1965] 41ff strike me as less convincing.) Assimilation of pluralists to Anaximander is indeed found in Aristotle at *Metaphys.* 1069b20ff, as Gottschalk (*Phronesis* 10 [1965] 39) reminds us; but it is couched in such language as to make clear that Aristotle no less than Theophrastus was perfectly aware of, and not desirous of concealing, the violence thus done to the text and meaning of the pluralists. Kahn cites (c) the restriction of condensation-rarefaction to Anaximenes at Simpl. *in Phys.* 149.32f. Kahn and Guthrie (*HGP* I pp. 120f) both imply that Theophrastus somewhere remarked that only Anaximenes used condensation and rarefaction, or that only Anaximenes actually worked out the theory of monism in these terms. But this is surely not what Simplicius' words indicate. Simplicius *says* ἐπὶ γὰρ τούτου μόνου Θεόφραστος

ἐν τῇ Ἱστορίᾳ τὴν μάνωσιν εἴρηκε καὶ πύκνωσιν· δῆλον δὲ ὡς καὶ οἱ ἄλλοι τῇ μανότητι καὶ πυκνότητι ἐχρῶντο. καὶ γὰρ Ἀριστοτέλης περὶ πάντων τούτων εἶπε κοινῶς ὅτι τὰ ἄλλα γεννῶσι πυκνότητι καὶ μανότητι πολλὰ ποιοῦντες ἐκ τῆς μιᾶς ὕλης; this means, I take it, that Theophrastus spoke of condensation and rarefaction only in the case of Anaximenes. This is clearly untrue, since Theophrastus mentions the process in connection with Heraclitus also. If we are to take Simplicius to mean what he says, without improving arbitrarily upon it, it is clear that Simplicius was making a faulty generalization from memory without checking it. From this we can deduce nothing about Theophrastus at all, and certainly nothing about details of his presentation. (Another way of embellishing Simplicius is found in a cautiously expressed observation by Kirk at *HCF* p. 22; the suggestion is that Anaximenes *explained* change by condensation and rarefaction, whereas others merely described it in those terms. This is equally arbitrary.)

23. Simpl. *in Phys.* 150.18ff: καὶ οὗτος μὲν εἷς τρόπος τῶν ἓν τὸ ὂν ὑποτιθεμένων τὸ μανότητι καὶ πυκνότητι τὸ πλῆθος τῶν ὄντων ὑφιστάνειν. ἕτερος δὲ τρόπος καθ᾽ ὃν οὐκέτι τὴν μεταβολὴν τῆς ὕλης αἰτιῶνται οὐδὲ κατὰ ἀλλοίωσιν τοῦ ὑποκειμένου τὰς γενέσεις ἀποδιδόασιν, ἀλλὰ κατὰ ἔκκρισιν· ἐνούσας γὰρ τὰς ἐναντιότητας ἐν τῷ ὑποκειμένῳ ἀπείρῳ ὄντι σώματι ἐκκρίνεσθαί φησιν Ἀναξίμανδρος, πρῶτος αὐτὸς ἀρχὴν ὀνομάσας τὸ ὑποκείμενον. ἐναντιότητες δέ εἰσι θερμὸν ψυχρὸν ξηρὸν ὑγρὸν καὶ τὰ ἄλλα. The clear and natural sense of the words underlined is that Anaximander was the first to call the substrate by the name ἀρχή. This I believe to be indeed what they mean. Burnet (*EGP*⁴ p. 54 n. 2) thought the context showed that Simplicius meant "the first to name the substratum of the opposites as the material cause." In reply W. Jaeger (*TEGP* p. 201 n. 28) pointed out that ὀνομάζω means "give the name of" here as at Simpl. *in Phys.* 7.13, and does not mean simply "identify as." In retort to this, Kirk (at *CQ* n.s. 5 [1955] 23 n. 1) cited Plato *Rep.* 428e; but inspection of this passage shows that ὀνομάζονταί τινες εἶναι can there mean (and no doubt does mean) "are given some name (like 'smiths')." Burnet's plea on context does not help him; the passage quoted in full above reveals that Simplicius is distinguishing two types of monist, namely (1) those who produce the world by alteration (condensation-rarefaction) of their "principle" and substrate, and (2) those who separate out the opposites that are in the "principle" or substrate. Simplicius uses the word "substrate" in describing each kind of theory and cannot therefore have wished to emphasize, in order to distinguish Anaximander from the other class of monists, that he first made the *substrate* the ἀρχή. The clause underlined in my citation above must be a mere incidental note by Simplicius even on Burnet's rendering, which is otherwise unlikely. McDiarmid (*HSCP* 61 [1953] 139) tries to avoid this problem by emending αὐτός to οὕτως—a prime case of emendation of correct and idiomatic Greek to fit one's own preconceptions: there is nothing against the insertion by Simplicius of such an incidental note. In any case Anaximenes' air was also unlimited, so that even with McDiarmid's emendation Simplicius' remark is irrelevant to the distinction he is drawing here.

24. Derivation of this clause from Theophrastus is constant in the literature but has never, I believe, been argued. It seems unfounded; Eudemus is at least as likely a source for such information and for such a passing remark.

25. Simpl. *in Phys.* 24.13ff: Ἀναξίμανδρος ... ἀρχήν τε καὶ στοιχεῖον εἴρηκε τῶν ὄντων τὸ ἄπειρον, πρῶτος τοῦτο τοὔνομα κομίσας τῆς ἀρχῆς. The natural rendering of this is "Anaximander... named as principle and element of things the Unlimited, being the first to introduce this name (i.e., 'Unlimited') of the ἀρχή," and this I believe to be what Theophrastus said and meant. But some recent writers suppose these words to mean that Anaximander was the first to introduce the term ἀρχή. Against this is the genitive τῆς ἀρχῆς, but Kahn, *Anaximander*, pp. 30f, attempted to show that this genitive "may represent a mere stylistic variant for apposition." Kahn cited periphrases from the poets such as ὄνομα τῆς σωτηρίας, in which the genitive is certainly not appositional in the required sense (Euripides did not mean "the name 'Salvation'"); Kahn further referred to Schwyzer–Debrunner II pp. 121f, where the *relevant* passages cited are but few, under the heading "vereinzelt" (and from these few Kahn rightly removes *Cratylus* 402c). On the basis of these few isolated passages ("Suid." s.v. Thales πρῶτος δὲ Θαλῆς τὸ τοῦ σοφοῦ ἔσχεν ὄνομα is, incidentally, more relevant than any cited by Kahn) Kahn declares Simplicius' sentence "ambiguous" and attempts to "resolve" the ambiguity by reference to other passages on the same subject. It is, however, surely an error in method to seize on a remotely possible, linguistically only just bearable, rendering of a Greek sentence and then support that rendering against the natural meaning by reference to other passages on similar topics. The "remotely possible alternative" should cease to bedevil classical scholarship. In any case, Kahn's other passages are hardly cogent; Simpl. *in Phys.* 150.23 is not demonstrably quoted from, or interpreted out of, Theophrastus, and Hippolytus *Ref.* 1.6.2 (πρῶτος τοὔνομα καλέσας τῆς ἀρχῆς) is clearly an inferior text of Theophrastus. Whether the bishop or his copyist was responsible, the word καλέσας after ὄνομα came more easily to the mind and thence to the pen than κομίσας, and τοῦτο was omitted by haplography; the genitive τῆς ἀρχῆς was copied correctly but bereft of its proper context. To see an interpretation behind this is to outrun both evidence and antecedent probability, and Hippolytus may safely be ignored. Guthrie, *HGP* I p. 77, is sensible about this but unfortunately adds an old chestnut, that "Theophrastus deemed it necessary to explain the archaic word ἀρχή by adding the Aristotelian term στοιχεῖον (element)." Guthrie admits truly that McDiarmid (see Guthrie, *HGP* I p. 77 n. 4) has "cast legitimate doubt on this," which leaves one wondering why Guthrie left it in his text. Against it may be urged that (1) the suggestion that ἀρχή in the sense "principle" was specifically archaic, and would need glossing in Peripatetic circles, would be fantastic, and (2) Guthrie is in an awkward position, as he holds that Anaximander used the word ἀρχή in a sense ("permanent ground of being") nearer to the Peripatetic "principle" than many scholars believe. The point of the insertion of καὶ στοιχεῖον is surely that ἀρχή is a word (in Peripatetic circles) of many meanings and must therefore be delimited in this case as in some others; for the ambiguity of ἀρχή see *Metaphys.* 1012b34ff.

26. *CQ* n.s. 5 (1955) 24. Kirk admits that Anaximander could have used ἀρχή to mean "source," cf., e.g., the Homeric νείκεος ἀρχή. Kirk is not open to the argument from doxographical attention, since he does not believe that any doxographical passage ascribes to Anaximander the term ἀρχή. He argues

from silence, from the fact that no Presocratic fragment contains the word ἀρχή in the nominative, of a primary substance. The argument is admittedly inconclusive and can hardly stand against the evidence from Anaximander's argument (for which see below). The reason why the post-Parmenideans did not, so far as we know, use the word ἀρχή for their "elements" may have been precisely that ἀρχή had too narrow a meaning. Their "elements" were more than a mere beginning or source; and, if that were the only philosophical sense of ἀρχή known to them, they might have hesitated to use the word for an element. (Be it noted that this is not intended as an argument in favour of the hypothesis that ἀρχή had indeed only the sense "beginning" or "source" in sixth- and fifth-century Greek.)

27. Guthrie, *HGP* I pp. 83f.

28. See *Festschrift Ernst Kapp* (Hamburg 1958) pp. 19–29, justly described as "illuminating" by Guthrie, *HGP* I p. 352 n. 2. I should believe the unity of Aristotle's argument even closer than Kahn and would fain strengthen the case for the ascription to Anaximander; but I hope to discuss this matter more at leisure elsewhere; be it noted meanwhile that Gottschalk (*Phronesis* 10 [1965] 39f), in refusing to accept a dilemma, or series of dilemmas, before Eleaticism, outruns the evidence.

29. The argument here is that the "unlimited" must either be an ἀρχή, or come from an ἀρχή: if it has an ἀρχή, it has a πέρας or limit. From this one may conclude that the author of the argument thought that an ἀρχή was a πέρας, but not that for him a πέρας was necessarily an ἀρχή.

30. I have not written "all the Milesians," since Aristotle nowhere, I think, ascribes this view to Anaximander by name. See further below.

31. See Kahn at *Festschrift Kapp*, pp. 20f and nn.

32. So, e.g., Kahn, *Anaximander*, p. 44, and Gottschalk at *Phronesis* 10 (1965) 39.

33. For Anaximander's cosmogony see Stokes at *Phronesis* 8 (1963) 5ff and Guthrie, *HGP* I pp. 89ff.

34. See esp. Aristotle *Phys.* 204b22–29 and Kahn, *Anaximander*, pp. 36ff and 186ff.

35. In Anaximander's fragment the relation between the "unlimited" and the "ordinance of time" is not gone into.

36. See, e.g., Guthrie, *HGP* I p. 56.

37. Cherniss, *ACPP* pp. 364 ff, esp. pp. 366f; McDiarmid at *HSCP* 61 (1953) 92 (if I have rightly understood him).

38. *ACPP* p. 368.

39. *AGP* 19 (1906) 333ff.

40. E.g., Burnet *EGP*[4] p. 180: "So much the worse for the senses, says Parmenides. That is the inevitable outcome of a corporeal monism..." followed by more in the same vein; Bailey, *Greek Atomists*, p. 24; Cornford, *Plato and Parmenides*, p. 28: "Parmenides...held to the notion of one substantial being with all the consequences deduced by his logic"; Raven, *Pythagoreans and Eleatics*, p. 37: "The Way of Truth has demonstrated that, if you postulate a basic principle one aspect of which is Unity, it follows that this principle is one and unique, motionless and changeless..."; Guthrie, *HGP* II p. 16: "Of course if it had been

said to them [sc. the Milesians] 'What is, *is*, is it not?', they must have agreed at once. In refuting their contentions Parmenides is not so much *proving* the tautology as showing that earlier thinkers, as well as the ordinary run of mankind, had never formulated it explicitly, and so had evaded its implications."

41. Cherniss, *ACPP* pp. 220f, makes the point that Aristotle has different accounts of the rise of Eleaticism, and claims that they contradict each other; I believe rather that Aristotle deals in the relevant passages with different aspects of Eleaticism and therefore do not feel bound to scepticism on this ground.

42. I confess I am not sure what Cherniss means by Aristotle's assumption of the early Ionians' knowledge of "the logical implications of identity." But if this is supposed to mean that Aristotle assumes their knowledge of the *argument* of Parmenides to the effect that Being logically excludes genesis and destruction, it is surely false. Aristotle does appear to assume the Ionians' supposition that the element was in fact uncreated and indestructible but does not say how they arrived at this belief (except in the case of Anaximander, where "being" and "identity" have nothing to do with it).

43. None of the post-Parmenidean Presocratics answers the argument that change of place infringes the "law of identity" just as much, and for the same reasons, as change of quality. There are, however, evasions (notably the Atomist) of the argument (whenever produced) that the impossibility of void rules out movement.

44. Cherniss at *JHI* 12 (1951) 344. Guthrie, *HGP* II p. 368, is right in saying that "(Diogenes' theory) was a serious attempt to rival the fashionable pluralistic worlds as a defence of phenomena from Parmenides." See below, Chap. IX.

45. See D. L. 9.57 (DK 64A1), especially the words οὐδὲν ἐκ τοῦ μὴ ὄντος γίνεσθαι οὐδὲ εἰς τὸ μὴ ὂν φθείρεσθαι, and B2 πάντα ... τὸ αὐτὸ εἶναι.

46. See Diogenes B5. This fragment incidentally disproves decisively the thesis that nobody before Plato's *Theaetetus* could talk about one substance (in this case air) remaining the same through changes of quality, even though Diogenes, like his contemporaries, had no general word for substance or quality.

47. We have a specimen of such arguments in Diogenes B2.

48. This irony was apparently noticed by the author of the *MXG*; see 975b21ff (DK I, p. 263).

49. See Kahn, *Anaximander*, pp. 36 ff.

50. *Metaphys.* 983b22ff (note ἴσως).

51. Conveniently outlined by Guthrie, *HGP* I, p. 54 n. 1.

52. E.g., Hippon; so ("possibly") Cherniss at *JHI* 12 (1951) 321.

53. Burnet, *EGP*[4] p. 48, followed by McDiarmid at *HSCP* 61 (1953) 93, answered by Guthrie at *JHS* 77 (1957) 39.

54. See, e.g., KR pp. 15ff. If the analogy with wood and other floating substances belongs to Thales at all (see Aristotle *De caelo* 294a28ff), it may have been invented by him.

55. The actual expression at Simpl. *in Phys.* 23.25, νεκρούμενα ξηραίνεται is unlikely to belong to Theophrastus, unless LSJ are wrong in citing no example of νεκρόω before the Christian era, but the thought is most unlikely to come from anyone but Theophrastus.

56. T. Gomperz, *Greek Thinkers* (Eng. trans.) I pp. 44f, suggested that observations of plant and animal nourishment and decay would stimulate the question whether the variety of stuffs involved were "really of alien nature." But I doubt if this question need have arisen until somebody rejected the obvious notion of change from one stuff to another—until Parmenides in fact.

A. R. Burn (*Lyric Age of Greece*, pp. 330f) suggests that acquaintance with Near Eastern metallurgy induced "the conception of matter as something which changes its form." I cannot, however, see why such knowledge, wherever obtained, should lead to anything more than the observation that certain things change under certain circumstances into certain other things. No generalized conception of matter as a single entity seems to be called for.

57. L. S. Stebbing, *A Modern Introduction to Logic*, p. 404, applied with approval to the Milesians by Guthrie, *HGP* I p. 56.

58. Such, at least, seem to be the implications of B. Farrington's remarks at *Greek Science*, pp. 35ff, contrasting the Ionian "mercantile aristocracy" and "comparatively simple political structure" with the older empires' "necessity of governing by superstition."

59. The comparative abstractness of Hesiod's initial stages of cosmogony has often been noted. See *Theogony* 116ff.

60. For Heraclitus' leap from the unity (as he saw it) of opposites to the unity of all things, see below, Chap. IV.

61. Professor Vlastos, in generously giving permission for this letter to be made public, wished me to make it clear that it did not necessarily represent his final views but was tentative.

62. I owe this reference to *Iliad* 7.99 to Guthrie, *HGP* I pp. 386f. It grieves me the more to dissent in some respects from what he says there. It seems to me arbitrary to suppose that Xenophanes had this particular passage in mind. But it seems equally so to doubt if the Homeric bard was very conscious of the old myth of earth and water as the materials of living creatures. Guthrie suggests that earth and water in the Homeric passage are paradigms of the inanimate, but he cites no parallel for this. It seems unlikely to be sound to refuse to connect what is crying out for connection, and to imagine that the myth was not either in the bard's head or in the head of whoever coined the phrase that Menelaus uses.

63. See Stokes at *Phronesis* 8 (1963) 17ff, and Gottschalk in *Phronesis* 10 (1965) on Anaximander.

64. The defence will be found in the curious argument at Diogenes B2, on which see Guthrie, *HGP* II p. 367. It is easy to see the logic in the dependence of ὠφέλησις and βλάβη on the possession by opposites of the same fundamental nature: if the hot can absorb the cold, it could well be argued, once the possibility of simple change of substance had been denied, that the two must be fundamentally the same stuff, appearing doubtless in different forms. Such absorption, once change had been denied, could well replace the Anaximandrean encroachment of one opposite on the other and could well be expressed by the metaphor of "help" and "harm" in place of Anaximander's moral and legal metaphor. It is not so immediately obvious why *mixture* should be possible only

on Diogenes' postulate of a single fundamental stuff. Perhaps Diogenes had in mind what we should call solutions rather than mixtures in general; solution of (say) salt in water would appear to constitute an encroachment of wet upon dry.

65. See Stokes at *AGP* 47 (1965), esp. pp. 244ff.

66. Theophrastus ap. Simpl. *in Phys.* 24.26ff thought that Anaximenes believed air to be condensed or rarefied into fire, wind, cloud, water, earth, and rocks, and other things to have come from these. But, even if the phrase τὰ δ' ἄλλα ἐκ τούτων is Theophrastean, the truth of it is not above suspicion; see KR pp. 147f.

67. Perhaps this is why distinguished scholars disagree. KR p. 93 read: "Certainly [Thales'] near successor Anaximenes believed that all things were made of air (but he had thought of a way in which this could be so: air takes on different forms when compressed or rarefied), and it is invariably assumed that he was extending and refining a line of thought initiated by Thales. It would be imprudent entirely to reject this assumption, which goes back to Theophrastus and Aristotle." Cherniss, on the other hand, though describing condensation-rarefaction as a quantitative and mechanical change, remarks (*ACPP* p. 371): "In the case of the 'air' of Anaximenes we are not justified in assuming with Aristotle a persistence in his sense which implies logical and physical homogeneity." See further Cherniss, *ACPP* p. 379. (It is worth noting that, as an argument about Thales, Kirk's reasoning is circular: it defends the Aristotelian remark that Thales was the τῆς τοιαύτης ἀρχηγὸς φιλοσοφίας on the basis of the remark itself.)

68. After completing my own collection of material (as far as it goes) I found that Friedrich Solmsen (*ASPW* pp. 138–140) had collected most of it: I owe a good deal to Solmsen's discussion.

69. "Hippocrates" at *Anc. Med.* 22 (vol. 1 p. 626 Littré) numbers πυκνὰ καὶ μανά among σχήματα as opposed to δυνάμεις—so he also understood.

70. 28B9.1ff. The dispute over the meaning of the last line of this fragment seems irrelevant to present issues.

71. See DK 28B8.56–59. I doubt if Parmenides used the word ἀραιόν at 8.57, but Preller's conjecture (see app. crit. in DK) *could* be right.

72. Aristotle *De respiratione* 470b30ff (DK 59A115); cf. *MXG* 976b20ff and others.

73. I. R. Mathewson, at *CQ* n.s. 8 (1958) 71, does indeed withhold belief in rarity and density as "material substances capable of mixture"; but Solmsen is, I think, nearer the truth at *ASPW* p. 345 n. 37 in insisting that for "Anaxagoras the dense and the rare (or 'the thin') are powers of the same order as the cold and the warm, the dark and the bright etc." Certainly no distinction is apparent at, e.g., B12 (DK II p. 38.15f), cited in this connection by Solmsen.

74. There is, I suppose, a position of last resort for those who maintain Anaxagoras' clear-headedness on the subject of condensation and rarefaction. It could be alleged that when water boils it is mixed with sufficient air, containing enough "rare" to counterbalance the dense in the water; an object (49B12 fin.) is those things of which it has most in it. It is evident that Anaxagoras did not openly express this view in a sentence surviving in late antiquity, or Simplicius' question would be uncharacteristically foolish, but is it nevertheless what Anaxagoras

meant? It may be, but this view would not in any case solve my immediate problem: on this view also, rare and dense would be different stuffs, just as are the hot and the cold; the giving of the name "air" to what is rare makes no difference to this central point, and it would only be by admixture of "the rare" that things became rarefied.

75. Solmsen, *ASPW* p. 140 n. 91, in an especially illuminating note, suggests that for some Presocratics, and for Empedocles in particular, dense and rare appear not to have been "being things" ($\dot{\epsilon}\acute{o}\nu\tau\alpha$) but rather a mode of organization of these being things, and he cites 31B104 and "perhaps also B75." At B104 he would regard $\dot{\alpha}\rho\alpha\iota\acute{o}\tau\alpha\tau\alpha$ as an adverb, not, like Kranz, as an adjective. The lack of context makes it virtually impossible, in my opinion, to decide the grammatical function of $\dot{\alpha}\rho\alpha\iota\acute{o}\tau\alpha\tau\alpha$ at 31B104. B75 is admittedly tenuous evidence. Solmsen calls in aid A86.11, as representing (1) the probable context of B104 and (2) an example of $\pi\upsilon\kappa\nu\acute{\alpha}$ and $\mu\alpha\nu\acute{\alpha}$ as "modes of organization." But "probable" in (1) seems an overstatement, and (2) depends too much for my liking on the acceptance of Theophrastus' phraseology as Empedoclean, or similar in the relevant respect to Empedocles'. I doubt if much can be deduced in this respect from Aristotle *De gen. animal.* 747a34ff, ap. DK 31B92.

76. 10a16ff, cited in this connection by Cherniss, *ACPP* p. 55 n. 223. On the dubiety of Aristotle's actual distinction here see J. L. Ackrill ad loc. (his p. 107).

77. It attracted attention from Theophrastus; see Simpl. *in Phys.* 27.2f, where Anaxagoras is described in an obviously Theophrastean context as $\kappa o\iota\nu\omega\nu\acute{\eta}\sigma\alpha\varsigma$ $\tau\hat{\eta}\varsigma$ $\mathring{A}\nu\alpha\xi\iota\mu\acute{\epsilon}\nu o\upsilon\varsigma$ $\phi\iota\lambda o\sigma o\phi\acute{\iota}\alpha\varsigma$.

78. *EGP*[4] p. 9 n. 2, *HCF* p. 71 (where I think the context shows that the Milesians are in Kirk's mind, but cannot be sure).

79. Guthrie, *HGP* I p. 58, n. 2.

80. Allowing for Aristotle's tendency to make a material cause from originative and/or terminative substances.

81. See DK II p. 51, citing Sextus Empiricus *Adv. math.* 9.360.

82. See esp. Simpl. *in Phys.* 23.23 (DK 38A4).

83. See D.L. 6.19 (DK 66A1).

84. Scholars have tended to play down the seriousness and importance of *Sophist* 242d–e. Thus Corbato, *Studi Senofanei*, pp. 15–17, is highly critical, and the words "ironical," "playful," and "half-fanciful" appear in the literature. See, e.g., Jaeger, *TEGP* p. 215 n. 65; Cherniss, *ACPP* p. 353 and p. 201 n. 228; Burnet *EGP*[4] p. 127 (all cited, but not with great exactitude, by Corbato).

85. E.g., Kirk, *HCF* pp. 336f, and Guthrie, *HGP* I p. 456 n. 1.

86. On Plato's version of Eleaticism see Leonardo Tarán, *Parmenides*, pp. 269ff.

87. See below, Chap. III.

88. On Heraclitus B49a see below.

89. Page 104.

90. The question whether $\mathring{\upsilon}\sigma\tau\epsilon\rho o\nu$ should be taken with both Ionian and Sicilian Muses or with the Sicilian alone—that is, whether both Muses are said to be later than Xenophanes, or the Sicilian later than the Ionian—has been the subject of much disagreement but little debate. Lewis Campbell in his rendering

of the whole passage (his p. 102) has "later" with the Sicilians alone; Zeller (ZN 827 n. 1) agreed that this was possible. F. M. Cornford, on the other hand, translated with the word "later" first in the sentence (*Plato's Theory of Knowledge*, p. 217) and was followed by A. Diès in the "Budé" translation. Holger Thesleff ("On Dating Xenophanes," p. 8) urged that Plato cannot have meant the whole Eleatic school to come before the Ionian Muses of Heraclitus; but no one, I think, has ever supposed that he did. What Plato means is that the enunciation of Eleatic doctrine came before Heraclitus. I doubt if word-order is helpful here. We should be guided by the structure of the passage, which requires the compromise doctrines to come after the monists; if ὕστερον was meant to draw attention to the fulfilment of this requirement, it has a good deal more point than there would be to the quite gratuitous statement that Heraclitus preceded Empedocles.

91. For Ion's threefold being see DK 36A6; Philoponus' list of fire, earth, and air is shown to be at least an oversimplification by Harpocration's citation from Ion (DK 36A1 and B1). At A6 Kranz refers (with due hesitation) to Plato *Sophist* 242d–e.

92. See Aristotle *Metaphys.* 986a29f with Ross's note and Jaeger's app. crit. Guthrie, *HGP* I pp. 341ff, following Wachtler, undermined some of Ross's arguments, but see Stokes at *PQ* 15 (1965) 66 n. 3. Guthrie further argues (p. 343) that the suspect sentence "gains point" from the next sentence, in which Aristotle "expresses uncertainty whether Alcmaeon or the Pythagoreans can claim priority for the particular doctrine in question." But this is not conclusive: first because the question is whether the sentence under dispute gives point to its surroundings, and not whether they give point to it; and secondly because Aristotle's uncertainty could equally well be based on ignorance of the precise date of the Pythagoreans in question. Even if Alcmaeon were born as early as 510 B.C. (suggested by Guthrie, p. 357) he would be a contemporary of Parmenides according to the dates deduced from Plato *Parmenides* 127b–c and, coming as late in the Presocratic period as this, could well be later in Aristotle's eyes than some Pythagoreans (but earlier than others); and we do not know the extent of Aristotle's ability to distinguish different generations of Pythagoreans.

93. The passage of Aëtius (Diels, *Dox.*, p. 442) cited by DK as Alcmaeon's B4 has some probably Alcmaeonic words in it, but the primacy accorded to hot/cold and wet/dry contrasts with Aristotle's omission of them at *Metaphys.* 986a33f; and, since hot/cold and wet/dry were a centre of Peripatetic interest, it would be well to suspect Aëtius or his source of Peripateticizing Alcmaeon.

94. Cornford earlier (*CQ* 27 [1933] 102 n. 2) wrote: "The Milesians are treated not as monists, but as dualists, who have two ὄντα 'the hot and the cold.'" This Cornford believed to be in accordance with Parmenides' own view of his predecessors (a more doubtful point).

95. Cornford, *Plato's Theory of Knowledge*, p. 218.

96. See J. R. Trevaskis at *Phronesis* 1 (1955–1956) 39f.

97. Guthrie, *HGP* I p. 115.

98. Guthrie, *HGP* I pp. 362ff (cf. Hermann Fränkel, *Dichtung und Philosophie*[2] p. 371). I am unable, like Thesleff ("On Dating Xenophanes," pp. 4ff), to see any clear "Parallelität" (Fränkel, *DuP* p. 372 n. 2) between Xenophanes B8 and

B22, such as would allow us to place the beginning of Xenophanes' wanderings with any certainty in the year of the Mede's coming. There is no trace of evidence that the questions of B22 are imagined as addressed in particular to Xenophanes himself. Fränkel wishes us (*Hermes* 60 [1925] 176 n. 1) to accept that Xenophanes mentioned the Persian invasion of Ionia as an epoch in his life, but this also is conjecture. He guesses that Xenophanes' exile from Colophon began with the Persian invasion, and uses the figures of B8 to give, in accord with his guess, dates for Xenophanes' birth and the composition of B8. He also suggests that 14A8.33ff, from the *Theologumena arithmeticae*, associates Xenophanes with the coming of the Medes under Harpagus. But this passage could be based itself on the same interpretation of Xenophanes' words as the modern one; it could also be based in part on the association of Xenophanes with Pythagoras (see D.L. 9.18), Pythagoras with Polycrates of Samos (e.g., Strabo 638), and of Polycrates either directly or through Anacreon (see J. P. Barron, "The Sixth-Century Tyranny at Samos," *CQ* n.s. 14 [1964] 218ff) with the Medes' arrival. This last hypothesis is complicated, but not, given the ramifications of Greek chronology, to be excluded on that ground.

It results that Xenophanes' dates are more fluid than many like to suppose. But I find Thesleff's late dating equally unproved. In any case, as Guthrie remarks (p. 363), "Since we do not know at what age he wrote his various poems, his exceptionally long life makes it impossible to place him within any narrow limits." It will be observed that the later Xenophanes is placed (within certain limits) the better for my argument. But I do not pretend to know the answer to this dating problem.

99. Cited by Campbell, *Sophistes*, p. 104.

100. See Campbell's remark, cited above, assimilating this passage to *Theaet*. 179e: περὶ τούτων τῶν Ἡρακλειτείων ἢ ὥσπερ σὺ λέγεις Ὁμηρείων, καὶ ἔτι παλαιοτέρων.

101. E.g., *Theaet*. 174a.

102. *Philologus* 93 (1944) 170ff.

103. Ibid., p. 172.

104. Snell cited H. Tredennick in the Loeb Aristotle's *Metaphys*. He could have added H. Bonitz, *Comm.*, pp. 63ff, and Ross ad loc.

105. Ross notes that Plato in the *Theaetetus* (181b), like Aristotle at *Metaphys*. 983b28, uses the word παμπάλαιος (a rare word, in classical Greek elsewhere only, I believe, at *Metaphys*. 1074b1). Ross observes that Aristotle (frag. 7) did not accept the authenticity of the Orphic verses—but, for all that, Aristotle may have had them in mind here and merely refrained from naming Orpheus as the author. I do not find Bonitz' objections to Orpheus convincing either: his objection vanishes as soon as we remark that it was not Aristotle, but an earlier writer with uncertain habits of work, who supplied in the first instance the Orphic illustration.

106. Snell thinks Hippias probable but seems to me to attribute more to him than is prudent; see, however, C. J. Classen, *Philologus* 109 (1965) 175ff, esp. 177, and now Rudolf Pfeiffer, *History of Classical Scholarship*, p. 52 (with literature cited n. 1).

107. E.g., Ross, *Metaphys.* ad loc. Guthrie at *JHS* 77 (1957) 40 n. 11 is more cautious. Guthrie further suggests that Aristotle may be joking too: he well points out the "expressive dryness" of εἰ μὲν οὖν ἀρχαῖα ... ταχ' ἂν ἄδηλον εἴη. But, though Aristotle may be allowed to steal a joke from Plato, did the τινές do the same? And, if so, is not Aristotle's irony at their expense a little misplaced?

108. Cherniss at *JHI* 12 (1951) 321.

109. Cf. Diès, *Revue de l'histoire de la philosophie* 1 (1927) 11.

110. See n. 108 above.

111. *JHS* 77 (1957) 38f. Cherniss does in fact contrast Plato's picture of Thales with Aristotle's, noting Thales' absence from Plato's flux theorists; but this is not probative. Plato knew of water in connection with Thales but refrained from citing him for reasons unknown: conceivably because he was not ancient enough and/or because he could not be cited verbatim.

112. *Philologus* 93 (1944) 179.

113. Aristotle (*De caelo* 294a29ff) develops the analogy between the floating earth and pieces of wood and similar substances which float on water but not in air. But this (if it *is* Thales) may be an explanation of how it is possible for the earth to rest on water, rather than an argument to show that it does. If it is an argument, it does not conflict with, but might reinforce, the argument derived in my text from *Metaphys. A*.

114. See above, n. 23.

115. See pp. 29–30 above and Kahn at *Festschrift Kapp* p. 21 on Aristotle's *Phys.* 203b4ff.

116. It is noticeable indeed that Plato's citations also, so far as we can check them, had the effect of anticipating *not* the doctrine that water was the material of all things (a doctrine as helpful potentially in Plato's context as in Aristotle's) but the theory that water was the origin of all things. The Homeric quotation on Ocean is shared by Plato with Aristotle, and the Orphic verses also contain a reference to a beginning; Ὠκεανὸς πρῶτος καλλίρροος ἦρξε γάμοιο ....

117. Actually, Aristotle distinguishes between this (the proximate) and the ultimate material, but I have not thought it necessary to encumber my analysis of usage with this Aristotelian baggage.

118. In *Phys. B*, see *Metaphys.* 983a24–b3. Ross well remarks (*Aristotle's Physics*, p. 37) that, where we find the doctrine of four causes in Aristotle, it is "not argued for but presented as self-evident: ... reflection was aided by the work of his predecessors." But there is no need to assume that the complete analysis of all his predecessors preceded *Phys. B*.

119. For an explanation of Aristotle's account of Anaximander's "unlimited" in particular, see by all means Gottschalk at *Phronesis* 10 (1965) 49. The resemblance of a substance from which everything came to a substance potentially everything is sufficiently close to have misled Aristotle in other cases than that of Anaximander's "unlimited."

120. It is worth mentioning that I wish I could be as sure as some (most recently Gottschalk, *Phronesis* 10 [1965] 38 and n. 6) that the phrase ἐν ὕλης εἴδει at *Metaphys.* 983b7 was a deliberately cautious expression due to Aristotle's recognition of the difference between early theories and his own. But this is not

necessarily the case, since at *De caelo* 268b5 the phrase τῶν ... ἐν μορίου εἴδει σωμάτων means simply, as Guthrie has it in the Loeb, "Bodies which are parts of a whole..." (Moraux's "Budé" version, "... qui joue le rôle des parties," if it implies caution, is in the context an overtranslation. Stocks's Oxf. trans. has "bodies which are classed as parts of the whole.") The phrase ἐν ... εἴδει is in that passage nothing more than a periphrasis and therefore could be such at *Metaphys.* 983b7.

121. See pp. 25–26 above with nn. 3 and 17.

122. *ACPP* p. 220. It is perhaps worth recording that A. E. Taylor (*Aristotle on his Predecessors*, p. 33), cited by Cherniss n. 13, remarked indeed that "Aristotle ignores (Anaximander) as completely as he can throughout this sketch" but prudently refrained from attributing any motive for the omission.

123. *Metaphys.* 983b6, τῶν δὴ πρώτων φιλοσοφησάντων οἱ πλεῖστοι ...

124. *Metaphys.* 1069b22, a note inserted in the dense argument of *Metaphys.* Λ, and *Phys.* 207b34ff. On these passages see Gottschalk at *Phronesis* 10 (1965) 37f, with literature there cited. But in his paraphrase (his p. 38) of the second, Gottschalk makes it seem more cautious than it is by rendering φαίνονται ... χρώμενοι as "appear to treat" rather than the correct "evidently treat" (see the Oxf. trans.). There is perhaps more doubt than Gottschalk believes about the reference to Anaximander of Aristotle's closing criticism of the notion of the infinite "encompassing"—for Anaxagoras B2 has τό γε περιέχον ἄπειρόν ἐστι τὸ πλῆθος, and the early Pythagoreans are other conceivable victims of the argument. Aristotle certainly ought to have had Anaximander in mind in generalizing about believers in the "unlimited" (especially after writing 203b10ff), but there is no conclusive proof that he did; Aristotelian generalizations are unsafe bases for argument.

125. *Phys. Op.* frag. 2, ap. Simpl. *in Phys.* 24.13ff. No Theophrastean source attributes condensation and rarefaction to Anaximander, and Theophrastus uses ἀποκρίνεσθαι of Anaximander's original cosmic separation.

126. Theophrastus may have gone further than Aristotle also in interpreting Anaximander's "unlimited" as a mixture. But see n. 8 above.

127. See Chap. I above.

128. Frag. 484: KR pp. 32f cite two similar tales with similar phraseology at Diodorus Siculus 1.7.1 and Ap. Rhod. 1.496. Both these could have been written in the knowledge not only of Eleatic thought but also of Euripides' text. Diodorus admittedly speaks of a *mixture* of earth and heaven; but this is pretty clearly not a primitive mode of thought. Euripides, Diodorus, and Apollonius all speak of "one form" (μορφή or ἰδέα), and this surely meant in the first instance one person, and secondarily one continuous mass without gap.

CHAPTER III: XENOPHANES

1. C. Corbato, *Studi Senofanei*, Trieste 1952; M. Untersteiner, *Senofane: Testimonianze e frammenti*, Florence 1955.

2. See Diels, *Dox.*, pp. 112f, and n. 15 below.

3. Where references are given in this table, author's name and (where necessary) title will suffice for citations below in this chapter.

4. See Diels, *Dox.*, pp. 45 and 284n.

5. Perhaps sharing Ps.-Galen's source here as elsewhere, cf. Diels, *Dox.*, pp. 248ff. His plural συμφυῆ τοῖς πᾶσιν may indeed be a mere inexact substitute (Karl Reinhardt, *Parmenides*, p. 101) for the "generally" ("allgemein") transmitted καὶ τοῦτο ὑπάρχειν (εἶναι) τὸν θεόν (though "generally" is an exaggeration).

6. The singular is used of Parmenides by Theophrastus (*Phys. op.* frag. 6) and accordingly by Hippolytus *Ref.* 1.11.1, but see on the Eleatics in general Plato *Sophist* 242d ὡς ἑνὸς ὄντος τῶν πάντων καλουμένων.

7. Diels, *Dox.*, pp. 120f, citing J. Krische. But the evidence is far from cogent.

8. Diels (*Dox.*, p. 120) has for Cicero's Greek original ... καὶ θεὸν εἶναι τοῦτο ... but thus to change Cicero's order of words is neither necessary nor, in view of Ps.-Galen, even plausible. A rare slip by Diels.

9. Either this is a mistake by Ps.-Galen's copyists, in which case it is no doubt coincidence, or the slip stems from Ps.-Galen himself, in which case it could well be a "Freudian" error.

10. Diels, *Dox.*, p. 120.

11. The possibility that Theophrastus wrote the singular ἓν τὸ ὂν καὶ πᾶν cannot, however, be disregarded. It is to be found in Simplicius and may lie behind Cicero's (in the *De nat. deor.*) *omne ... quod esset*. But Cicero's Greek original is not easy to determine here. The possible guess that Theophrastus talked about an ἀρχή here is not proved by Simplicius, to whose context the word is suspiciously appropriate.

12. The *MXG* wavers on this point: θεός is subject at, e.g., 3.3 and 3.4 but predicate at 3.9, in a passage somewhat resembling Simplicius. But too much faith cannot be placed in the wording of *MXG*.

13. So McDiarmid (*HSCP* 61 [1953] 119) says Theophrastus asserts that the One is God.

14. Diels, *Dox.*, pp. 109ff.

15. Simplicius purports to be quoting Theophrastus with the words καὶ οὔτε πεπερασμένον οὔτε ἄπειρον ... Ξενοφάνην ... ὑποτίθεσθαί φησιν ὁ Θεόφραστος ... at *in Phys.* 22.26ff. Zeller (ZN I p. 625 n. 3) took the vital words to mean *in context as they stand in Simplicius* that Theophrastus said that Xenophanes stated neither that the One was limited nor that the One was unlimited. He may have been followed by Jaeger (*TEGP* pp. 214f n. 64), who, however, did not specify that Simplicius was quoting the words in their correct context. McDiarmid (*HSCP* 61 [1953] 151 n. 154) says that this rests on a mistaken translation; and, if the words are taken in Simplicius' context, he is obviously right. But it is possible that Simplicius has transferred a sound, if ambiguous, Theophrastean sentence from another context to this one. The kind of ambiguity involved may be paralleled from Aristotle *De caelo* 269b19f, φανερὸν ὅτι οὔτε κουφότητα οὔτε βάρος ἔχει σῶμα ἅπαν, where only the whole preceding argument renders

impossible the sense "every body has neither weight nor lightness." If Theophrastus wrote some such sentence as Simplicius attributes to him, but in another context, then we can acquit Theophrastus of misunderstanding Aristotle while at the same time attributing a less heinous type of error to Simplicius than has hitherto been necessary. It is also possible to account for the chaos in the doxographical tradition at large on this point by reference to Theophrastus' hypothetical ambiguity. But we are here in the realm of the possible rather than the provable.

16. For McDiarmid (*HSCP* 61 [1953] 117) it showed that "almost certainly" these writers correctly reproduced Theophrastus. But McDiarmid ignores here the contrary evidence, also from different lines of tradition.

17. See n. 15 above.

18. ZN I pp. 661ff; Heidel at *AJP* 64 (1943) 270; KR p. 175; Cornford, *Principium Sapientiae*, p. 147 n. 1; Guthrie, *HGP* I p. 381 n. 1, to cite only a few. Heidel followed Burnet (*EGP*⁴ p. 125) in supposing the point to be the elimination of Tartarus, Reinhardt (*Parmenides*, p. 147) and others have detected a polemic against Anaximenes. On the sun(s) in Xenophanes see below, n. 22.

19. The passage strongly suggests that to the Greeks themselves the word ἄπειρος was indeed the privative of πεῖραρ or πέρας, meaning "without boundary." I see no reason whatever to believe either Olof Gigon's implied suggestion (*Ursprung der griechischen Philosophie*, p. 162) that Xenophanes could mean that the earth descended to an unknown or unknowable distance, or Kahn's (*Anaximander*, p. 232) that he meant an impassable distance. The roots of earth (cf. passages at DK A47, but bracket with D. J. Allan the phrase ἐπ' ἄπειρον ... λέγοντες at *De caelo* 294a22f) might be found objectionable on the hypothesis of earth's infinite downward extent; but I find no reason why the roots should not themselves extend downwards infinitely. I doubt if the different preposition ἐπ' ἄπειρον in those MSS of Aristotle which have the phrase is of any significance (*pace* Corbato, *Stud. Senof.*, p. 40).

20. Why the fragment should be found obscure (Kahn, *Anaximander*, p. 234) I do not know; I find myself here in agreement with J. Kerschensteiner, *Kosmos*, p. 86 n. 2.

21. Guthrie, *HGP* I p. 381 n. 1, suggests that Ps.-Plutarch's addition to frag. 28 is "a doxographer's gloss," seeming to overlook the parallel passage in Hippolytus, unless the doxographer meant is Theophrastus! (Cf. Reinhardt, *Parmenides*, p. 147.)

22. I have not made use in the text of the doctrine that the sun's path across the sky proceeds to infinity, because we have not Xenophanes' own words for it and because the doxographical tradition for his astronomy is of unusual obscurity. The doctrine seems to me as to Reinhardt (*Parmenides*, p. 147) fully in keeping with the empirical attitude characteristic of Xenophanes' physical statements. It is possible that Ettore Bignone (*Empedocle*, p. 434) was right in seeing Empedoclean polemic against this doctrine also, in Aëtius 2.23.3 (DK 31A58). The only direct evidence is Aëtius 2.24.9 (Xenophanes A41a) ὁ δ' αὐτὸς τὸν ἥλιον εἰς ἄπειρον μὲν προϊέναι, δοκεῖν δὲ κυκλεῖσθαι διὰ τὴν ἀπόστασιν. It is hard to see why this strange belief should be invented by a doxographer, unless to account

for the need for a new sun every day (Hippolytus *Ref.* 1.14.3, A33); and it is not used for this purpose by our only authority. The evidence is not of the most secure, but cannot be ruled out of court. Guthrie, *HGP* I p. 393 n. 4, denies that εἰς ἄπειρον here can mean "to infinity," on the ground that the sun burns out each night. But the possible evidence concerning the sun burning out consists of A38 and A41; A38 refers to the stars only, not to the sun (note ἀναζωπυρεῖν νύκτωρ; if the subject of the last sentence quoted here by Diels–Kranz is the sun, the change is extremely sudden); and A41 is hopelessly confused (see Reinhardt, *Parmenides*, p. 147), and the extinction there mentioned, if not transferred from the stars, may have to do with eclipses, which need not be wholly accounted for by the sun's withdrawal to other parts of the earth and its "treading on emptiness" (A41a); cf. Reinhardt, *Hermes* 77 (1942) 236 and n. 1. If the sun *is* burnt out every night, which there is at best doubtful reason to believe, it could still proceed in the form of cold ashes to infinity (as Gigon, I think, says at *Ursprung*, p. 169). We are moving here in realms of the cloudiest uncertainty and should move accordingly with the greatest caution. *If* Xenophanes held the earth to extend infinitely in all directions not above the plane of its surface, this would, as Paul Tannery saw (*Science hellène*[2] p. 137), account for his alleged (A33 and 41a) large number of suns; but my trust in the doxographers is none the greater for that. Some irony may well have crept in to obscure Xenophanes' real beliefs on the heavenly bodies (cf., e.g., Burnet, *EGP*[4] p. 123).

23. *Metaphysics* A 986b21ff. Diels's objections to the text (*Dox.*, pp. 110f), though followed by Tannery (*Science hellène*[2] p. 140), are unconvincing. If διεσαφήνισεν be unique in Aristotle, that is reason (not *good* reason) for emending to διεσάφησεν, not for deleting the whole characteristic sentence, and the unique ἐνίσας is deliberately vague (see below): for a different explanation see Burnet, *EGP*[4] pp. 126f and 126 n. 2).

24. With the rendering "nor does he seem to have grasped either of these two kinds of unity." Cherniss (*ACPP* p. 201 n. 228) makes the same point. I regret that I find far-fetched the doctrine of KR pp. 171f, that the presence of both corporeal and apparently non-corporeal elements in Xenophanes' description (δέμας and the shaking of all things by mind) is the explanation of Aristotle's implication that Xenophanes' god is neither immaterial nor material. Indeed, a formal unity need not be immaterial.

25. Contra, Mondolfo, *L'infinito nel Pensiero dell' antichità classica*, pp. 351ff.

26. See the table above and Corbato, *Stud. Senof.*, p. 57. Reid in comment on Cicero's *Academica* seems to think Cicero's *conglobata figura* represents ὅμοιον πάντῃ, but it is surely more likely to mean simply "spherical."

27. E.g., Guthrie, *HGP* I p. 382, citing with approval Cornford, *Principium Sapientiae*, p. 147.

28. See Lumpe, *Xenophanes*, p. 23, and also KR p. 172. But I doubt, *pace* KR, if Aristotle's (or his elaborators') failure to recognize Xenophanes' anticipation of the Prime Mover proves anything, for such failures are merely human.

29. *EGP*[4] p. 129 n. 1, followed by KR, p. 170.

30. Guthrie, *HGP* I p. 375 n. 2.

31. On Euripides *Heracles* 1106, cited by Burnet: for further literature see

Corbato, *Stud. Senof.*, p. 59 n. 56, and W. S. Barrett on Euripides *Hippolytus* 441–442.

32. *Über die Theologie des Xenophanes* pp. 7f, against Zeller.

33. E.g., Überweg–Praechter, *Philosophie des Altertums*, p. 76 (in their translation), and Guthrie, *HGP* I p. 374 with n. 1. P. Albertelli, *Gli Eleati*, p. 30, punctuates εἷς, θεός, ..., understanding οὐρανός as subject; admittedly, one cannot be quite sure that the subject did not precede εἷς, but the sentence is complete as a sentence, and Albertelli's hypothesis is quite arbitrary.

34. Guthrie, *HGP* I p. 374 n. 1, is possibly misleading when he says that the couplet is *certainly* a complete sentence (my italics).

35. See Kühner–Gerth I p. 28 for examples, and add Hdt. 1.93.2. and 8.113.3 (whether or not the relevant sentence is genuine). Stein on Hdt. 7.113 adds examples from Thucydides. See further Corbato, *Stud. Senof.*, p. 63 n. 65.

36. Lumpe, *Die Philosophie des Xenophanes*, p. 28, Pötscher at *Emerita* 32 (1964) 6 n. 1; Pötscher's further reference to E. Peterson I have been unable to locate.

37. Such, if I have not misunderstood it, is the purport of Guthrie's note at *HGP* I p. 374 n. 1. Homer's εἷς οἰωνὸς ἄριστος *could* mean "there is one best omen, ...," and was so punctuated by Walter Leaf, but could also mean "the one best omen is to ...," and was so punctuated by T. W. Allen in the Oxford text.

38. *AJP* 64 (1943) 275.

39. *Geschichte der antiken Philosophie* I p. 413.

40. We may note that at Entretiens Fondation Hardt I (*La notion du divin*) pp. 162ff there are a number of interesting remarks by various scholars on monotheism and polytheism in Greece. Gigon cites Heraclitus B67 as an example of attempted monotheism followed by the Stoa. Yet ὁ θεός in Greek need not imply belief in a single god, and Heraclitus B53 (a positive statement of Heraclitus' own) indicates unambiguously a belief in more than one god. Philosophical attacks on the traditional religion were for the most part directed, as O. Reverdin remarks, not against cults but against the moral content of the tradition; and the cults imply a plurality of gods. Gigon's remarks about atheists do not unsettle this point. Better on the resemblances between Xenophanes and Heraclitus is Kahn, *Anaximander*, p. 156 n. 3.

41. "Senofane e Eschilo," p. 35.

42. See Corbato, *Stud. Senof.*, p. 60, with literature.

43. Ibid.

44. *Pace* Untersteiner, *Senof.* p. 95 ad loc., the plural gods of Cic. *De div.* 1.3.5 (DK A52) are quite likely to be derived from such concessional uses.

45. Cf. Burnet, *EGP*[4] p. 128.

46. DK A32; cf. Corbato, *Stud. Senof.*, pp. 59ff, and Untersteiner, *Senof.*, pp. 64f.

47. Reinhardt, *Parmenides*, p. 95.

48. Reading θεῖον at 977a27 for the first θεόν of the MSS, of which I make no sense.

49. Matters are not helped by the bland assertion (Kahn, *Anaximander*, p. 156 n. 3), ignoring the difficulties, that Xenophanes' plural gods are the "elements" and the heavenly bodies. I see no reason to place this religious pioneer

so deeply in the Milesian tradition, and doubt the relevance of Empedocles' Sphere.

50. See above, Chap. II.

51. For discussion of Parmenides' text here see below, Chap. V.

52. But it should not be forgotten that mortal men too have a νόος, which is indeed πλακτός (Parmenides B6) and directed by ἀμηχανίη.

53. If Ps.-Plutarch is right in attributing to Xenophanes the argument that of the gods ἐπιδεῖσθαι μηδενὸς μηδένα, this may be compared with Parmenides B8.33 οὐκ ἐπιδεές. Diels in *PPF* on Timon (Xenophanes A35) compared Timon's ἀσκηθῆ with Parmenides' οὖλον.

54. The parallel is sometimes quoted of Aristotle's having taken seriously Plato's joking allusion to a Homeric theory of flux (so most recently Tarán, *Parmenides*, p. 288 n. 21). But see Guthrie at *JHS* 77 (1957) 39f and n. 11, and see the discussion above of the antecedents of this interpretation.

55. Überweg–Praechter p. 81 say (without citing examples) that λέγεται is used here "in a not uncommon fashion" not indicating doubt, but rather merely stating a known historical fact. It need not be so used here, and in any case there is an odd *conglomeration* of cautious phraseology at this point in Aristotle.

56. Burnet, *EGP*[4] p. 127 n. 4, claimed that ἀποβλέψας was colourless, and it is usually translated here "with reference to"; but Bonitz in his commentary (p. 84) has *contemplatus*, and the instances of the word in his *Index Aristotelicus* s.v. do not entirely bear out Burnet's unqualified assertion. See, e.g., *Politics* 1334b33, where ἀποβλέποντα means not "with reference to" but "with an eye to." KR p. 172 rightly describe Aristotle here as cryptic, and offer a correct translation, but strangely go on to say that Aristotle "clearly" implies that god is identical with the world. The words seem indeed designed to give that impression but at the same time to avoid clarity. But the views taken in my text owe most and bear most resemblance to those of Kirk and Raven.

57. See Tarán, *Parmenides*, pp. 269ff and esp. p. 288.

58. One can hardly agree with Jaeger, *TEGP* p. 215 n. 65, that in Aristotle "we find Plato's combination laid down as historical fact."

59. Cf. McDiarmid at *HSCP* 61 (1953) 85–156 passim and Guthrie at *JHS* 77 (1957) 36.

60. See the excellent discussion by Guthrie, *HGP* I pp. 383ff, and Kahn's valuable remarks, *Anaximander*, pp. 110f, 115f, and 180.

CHAPTER IV: HERACLITUS

1. Copious modern bibliography and ancient references are to be found in Zeller–Mondolfo IV, and in M. Marcovich's article s.v. Herakleitos at *RE* Suppl. 10, cols. 246–320; a brief summary of my own views is contained in the article s.v. Heraclitus in *Encyclopedia of Philosophy* (New York 1967). On questions of text see especially Kirk *HCF* passim and Marcovich cols. 260ff, not forgetting the views of Cherniss enshrined in Clémence Ramnoux, *Héraclite*. Marcovich's *Heraclitus* (Merida 1967) came into my hands too late for more than incidental reference.

2. Reinhardt, *Parmenides*, esp. pp. 201ff, rejected by nearly all subsequent scholars, and not argued again even by Reinhardt himself.
3. J. Kerschensteiner, *Kosmos*, p. 97.
4. For the interpretation see Marcovich, *Heraclitus*, pp. 507f.
5. Taken politically by Marcovich, *Heraclitus*, p. 520, and many others, perhaps rightly; epistemologically by H. Fränkel, *DuP* p. 448.
6. Cf., e.g., Pindar *Nem.* 7.23f for this motif. I do not include B89D, which I still regard as suspect, despite Vlastos at *AJP* 76 (1955) 344 and Marcovich s.v. Herakleitos, col. 265. The argument that, far from being a mere combination of parts of B2 and B1, B89D adds the notion of a separate world for the sleeper seems to me inconclusive. Those who believe that the phrase in B30 τὸν κόσμον τόνδε τὸν αὐτὸν ἁπάντων is wholly by Heraclitus should not find it difficult to see in B89D a reminiscence of that fragment in addition to B2 and B1. But I do not so believe (cf. KR p. 199 n. 1) and can therefore use this argument only *ad homines*. But, in any case, the notion thus added seems at least as likely to be Plutarch's as Heraclitus', and the fragment remains under suspicion. Marcovich's interpretation of the fragment as a "*Simile* or metaphor" (sic), *Heraclitus*, p. 99, apart from being mere conjecture, does not cause me to alter this opinion.
7. F. Jacoby, *FGrHist* 1F1.
8. *HCF* p. 387.
9. See, e.g., Kirk, *HCF* p. 231.
10. *CQ* 34 (1940) 26ff, denied by Lasserre, *Épodes d'Archiloque*, p. 62, on insubstantial grounds. See Bowra, p. 28, for some passages pointing to the superiority of the ἕν.
11. Archilochus is alleged by Zenobius (*Cent.* 5.68, *Corpus paroemiographorum Graecorum* I p. 147) to have borrowed the line from Homer, and is said elsewhere to have taken it (perhaps he *cited* it; "Budé" *Archiloque*, pp. 54f) from the *Margites*. Ion Tragicus mentioned the hedgehog's οἰζυραὶ τέχναι (again according to Zenobius), and the expression was more than possibly proverbial in Aristophanes' time (see *Knights* 1065ff with scholion on 1068). Cf. also the scolion attributed to Thales by Lobon: Οὔτι τὰ πολλὰ ἔπη φρονίμην ἀπεφήνατο δόξαν· / ἕν τι μάτευε σοφόν, ἕν τι κεδνὸν αἱροῦ ... which Wilamowitz attributed to the fifth century, *Hermes* 60 (1925) 300f, but which is not included in Page's *Poetae Melici Graeci*. There is no need to suppose Heraclitus influenced by the *Margites* or by Archilochus. All may have been reacting, some in different ways, against the prevalent view of the early Greeks that knowledge of many things is virtually equatable with σοφία. The virtue in knowing many things (the more the better) is brought out at four passages in the *Iliad* (N 355, T 219, Φ 440, Ψ 311f, cf. perhaps *Od.* μ 188) and in other poets, e.g., Soph. *Antig.* 710f: ἀλλ' ἄνδρα κεἴ τις ᾖ σοφός, τὸ μανθάνειν πόλλ' αἰσχρὸν οὐδέν ... and Solon's declaration at frag. 22.5 (Diehl), hardly to be dissociated from this view, ἀεὶ γηράσκω πολλὰ διδασκόμενος. Stemming from the same common point of view is Euripides *Medea* 285, σοφὴ πέφυκας, καὶ κακῶν πολλῶν ἴδρις. An epic verse sharing the same assumption is cited by Diogenianus (*Cent.* 7.78, *Corp. paroem. Gr.* I p. 300), πολλά κεν εἰδείης, οἷς τὸν θεὸν ἐξαπατήσεις. The same is perhaps accepted by Antiphon Trag. frag. 3 (Nauck) σοφόν γέ τοί τι πρὸς τὸ βουλεύειν ἔχει τὸ γῆρας, ὡς δὴ πόλλ'

ἰδόν τε καὶ παθόν—though the literary ancestry of this includes *Od.* α 3–4 as well as the *Iliad* passages cited above. Aristarchus Trag. frag. 1.3f (Nauck) has πλέον γὰρ οὐδὲν οἱ σοφοὶ τῶν μὴ σοφῶν εἰς ταῦτα γιγνώσκουσιν, where the emphasis is heavily on εἰς ταῦτα, and the implication that normally the wise man knows more is plain. Mr. Gordon Howie suggests to me (orally) that Pindar *Pyth.* 9.48–54 is another example of the same general attitude on the subject of wisdom. Apart from Democritus B64 and B65, clearly direct imitations of Heraclitus, and attacks elsewhere on the same notion, we have a possible philosophical sequel to this quarrel in Aristotle *Metaphys. A* 1–2, where πολλαὶ μνῆμαι are a necessary, but not a sufficient, condition of τέχνη. For further references on πολυμαθίη see B. Gladigow, *Sophia und Kosmos* (Hildesheim 1965) p. 22 n. 4. I do not find it "erstaunlich" with Gladigow (p. 107 n. 3) that Diogenes of Apollonia should speak the language of his time in calling his ἀήρ "πολλὰ εἰδός" (64B8).

12. *Quis rer. div. heres* 214 (p. 503 M.) ap. DK I p. 491. What source Philo could have designated by Ἕλληνες I have no idea: "many in the ancient world" (Vlastos at *AJP* 76 [1955] 367) is perhaps overoptimistic. Did Philo share a source with Hippolytus? The allusion at *Qu. in Gen.* 3.5 (p. 178 Aucher) does not prove the point.

13. I do not believe (for example) with Marcovich that B12 is among the examples Heraclitus gives of the coincidence of opposites. Marcovich's version of the genesis of our extant river-statements is tidy but (in my view) misleading. In B12, ποταμοῖσι τοῖσιν αὐτοῖσιν ἐμβαίνουσιν ἕτερα καὶ ἕτερα ὕδατα ἐπιρρεῖ, Marcovich (s.v. Herakleitos, cols. 289f) wants the present participle ἐμβαίνουσιν to be "cursive" and supposes that Cratylus, misinterpreting it as "iterative," only thus produced from Heraclitus' words the garbled version saying that "one cannot step into the same river twice." But this theory of Marcovich's rests itself, I believe, on a mistaken interpretation of the present participle concerned. If the word "the same" is to have any meaning, it must mean "the same as something," whether that something be an object other than that to which "the same" is applied, or the object to which "the same" is applied at a different time, in a different place, or in different circumstances. I cannot normally talk of "the same river" unless I am saying (for example) either that River X is the same as (say) River Y which I struck fifty miles north, or that River X is the same river as (say) Y which I struck yesterday, or that River X is the same river which somebody described to me as clear, though in fact it is muddy. Without some such point of reference one cannot talk meaningfully about "the same river." But in Heraclitus B12 we are told that people step into the same rivers, and this "same" must have some reference of the kind I have exemplified. But this point of reference can only be contained in the participle ἐμβαίνουσιν, and the only way in which this can be done is to have ἐμβαίνουσιν iterative. "The same rivers" means the same rivers as they step into on more than one occasion. That is to say the present participle ἐμβαίνουσιν *is* iterative, and Cratylus, if he took it thus, did not misunderstand it. If ἐμβαίνουσιν is cursive, "the same" is forced, in a way unique among Heraclitus' extant statements of unity in opposition. A further point against Marcovich is that Heraclitus' unified opposites do not themselves include any terms which are involved in the predication to an opposite pair of

unity or divergence; Marcovich would doubtless cite as an example B10, but I believe he would be mistaken; see n. 54 below. (But I entirely agree with Marcovich that there is no idea of regularity of flow contained in B12, and that it should not be interpreted as an image of *regular* change; in view of Kirk's interpretation of Heraclitean flux, the point is important.)

14. Notably by Reinhardt at *Hermes* 77 (1942) 242f; KR pp. 189ff; Guthrie, *HGP* I pp. 445f; and Marcovich s.v. Herakleitos cols. 287ff.

15. Gigon, *Untersuchungen zu Heraklit*, p. 100. Marcovich (s.v. Herakleitos, col. 273, and *Heraclitus*, p. 175), I think unwarrantably, renders ξυνόν as equivalent to ἓν καὶ ταὐτό.

16. Cf. Kirk, *HCF* p. 115.

17. B60, ὁδὸς ἄνω κάτω μία καὶ ὡυτή. I do not know whether Theophrastus was right or wrong in giving this fragment a physical interpretation but have little doubt that its primary purpose was to exemplify the unity of opposites. Such is its plain meaning, and such the sense put upon it by the normally fairly reliable Hippolytus. See Kirk, *HCF* pp. 105ff. A different view is taken by Vlastos at *AJP* 76 (1955) 349 n. 26, who seems to me to play down unduly the temptation which this fragment, even if originally not physical in import, would have offered to Theophrastus, imbued as he was with the Peripatetic theory of natural motion. (See J. Kerschensteiner at *Hermes* 83 [1955] 401 on how Diogenes Laertius' interpretation fits in with Peripatetic theory.) Vlastos' point about the banality of the fragment seems satisfactorily answered by Kirk (KR p. 190 n. 1 on p. 191). R. Mondolfo (ZM pp. 193ff) also argues against Kirk here (1) that the context of citation in Lucian *Vit. auct.* 14 adds the notions of circular motion and exchanges for all the opposites (but these need not in context be based on this fragment alone) and (2) that Marcus Aurelius 6.17 has ἄνω κάτω κύκλῳ φοραὶ τῶν στοιχείων (which, however, is quite likely to depend at least partly, though probably indirectly, on Theophrastus). But Mondolfo himself does not make the mistake of denying a logical sense to the fragment altogether, though I confess I do not understand why he follows Göbel in believing that the fragment exemplifies the *mutual implication* of the opposites (ZM p. 196). See on this passage, and Parmenides' παλίντροπος κέλευθος, Chap. V n. 33 below.

18. I am convinced by Marcovich's note on the text, *Heraclitus* pp. 163f, against Kirk, *HCF* pp. 97f.

19. I accept the last clause of the fragment as Heraclitus', with Guthrie (*HGP* I p. 445 n. 1), Kirk (*HCF* pp. 139ff), and Marcovich (*Heraclitus*, pp. 218f). Even if this clause does not go back verbally to Heraclitus, there need be no doubt whatever that Heraclitus thought on these lines. On the beginning of the fragment see Kirk (*HCF* pp. 135ff); like him I see no need for emendation as by Bernays (ταὐτῷ for ταὐτό) or by Wilamowitz (ταὐτό γένει). See also Marcovich, *Heraclitus*, pp. 216ff.

20. See *Encyclopedia of Philosophy* s.v. Heraclitus, and Kirk, *HCF* pp. 144ff.

21. *Theogony* 748ff. I do not here discuss the problem where exactly they meet.

22. See Kirk, *HCF* p. 64 on B89.

23. I do not believe with W. Bröcker that this fragment is a quotation from Anaximander; see ZM p. 28.

24. See Snell at *Hermes* 61 (1926) 356ff; Kirk, *HCF* pp. 150ff.

25. See Kirk, *HCF* pp. 152ff.

26. Compare Melissus B8.3 (plausibly conjectured by Kirk, *HCF* pp. 139ff, to be influenced by Heraclitus): if Melissus was in fact independent, Kirk's comparison is more interesting still, as indicating fifth-century "common sense."

27. *O.T.* 374, μιᾶς τρέφει πρὸς νυκτός (to the blind Teiresias).

28. In Anaximander's fragment the succession of opposites is an injustice, for which recompense is made. For Heraclitus, Strife is Justice (B80), and everything takes place in accordance with it (... κατ' ἔριν ...). The process of which half was for Anaximander unjust is for Heraclitus wholly just. The importance of the succession of opposites in early Greek philosophy needs no new emphasis, and the connection between this and Heraclitus' central doctrine of the unity of things is not therefore unexpected.

29. Marcovich has a separate class (s.v. Herakleitos, col. 287) of those in which the opposites "bilden ein Ganzes... dank der Interaktion (gegenseitigen Wirkung) zwischen ihnen..." The fragments concerned (B51, 125) are, however, rather statements about the opposites than examples of kinds of opposites. No specific opposite is mentioned in the simile of B51 or in the statement of B125 about the κυκεών. The latter is doubtless an image of the necessity of continuous motion to keep the world from falling apart (contra Marcovich, *Heraclitus*, p. 157).

30. See Kirk, *HCF* pp. 124ff; Marcovich, *Heraclitus*, pp. 227f.

31. Parmenides B6, discussed below.

32. *AJP* 76 (1955) 350; I am no more convinced by Marcovich, *Heraclitus*, pp. 125f.

33. KR pp. 193f n. 1.

34. See LSJ s.v. Ia and b.

35. See Powell, *Lexicon to Herodotus* s.v.

36. See Farnell and Mezger ad loc.

37. See Sikes and Wynne Willson ad loc.

38. LSJ s.v. ἁρμονία I 3.

39. "Appartenant à un seul tout," as Kirk says at *Revue Philosophique* 147 (1957) 289.

40. *HCF* pp. 203ff, esp. 216.

41. *Untersuchungen zu Heraklit*, pp. 95f (cf. Guthrie, *HGP* I p. 477 n. 3).

42. See *Varia Variorum* (Festgabe Karl Reinhardt) 77.

43. What seems to make it more probable (I do not say "certain") that Hölscher is right in deleting the whole phrase ἑαυτῷ ἀποθανών is not that ἑαυτῷ is un-Ionic (for inconsistency in transcribing Ionic is common enough), nor that there are Christian parallels, dubious according to Marcovich *Heraclitus* p. 244, for the collocation ἑαυτῷ ἀποθανεῖν—but the combination of these with the fact that, if the fragment had specified that the light was lit by man for himself, that would have made it useless for Clement, who is referring to the light of Christ. I have accordingly preferred deletion of the whole phrase to deleting the word ἀποθανών alone, with Wilamowitz (ap. DK), Kranz, Kirk (KR p. 207), and

Marcovich, tempting though it is to adduce the references to ἰδίαν φρόνησιν and so forth at B2 and elsewhere (cf. Gigon, *Untersuchungen zu Heraklit*, pp. 95f; and Mondolfo, ZM IV p. 285). The text of the second clause is also disputable. Cherniss (ap. Ramnoux, *Héraclite*, p. 394) prefers to delete εὕδων and retain both occurrences of ἀποσβεσθεὶς ὄψεις.. If this be right, then the drift of the fragment is that life is a sleep ending in death. From the present point of view the effect of this would be that the contact between sleep/death and life/waking is one of temporal succession (not necessarily thought of here as reciprocal succession) rather than closeness of resemblance. Hölscher's argument in favour of εὕδων that the simple verb is unknown to the *Κοινή* is hardly worthy of him, since the hypothetical glossator would have had the word εὕδοντος in front of him. Nevertheless εὕδων seems perfectly possible for Heraclitus, and if ἀποσβεσθεὶς ὄψεις or εὕδων has to go, then we should presumably regard ἀποσβεσθεὶς ὄψεις as a dittograph. But I part company with Hölscher when he makes εὕδων give not the "condition" (*Bedingung*) of the connection between life and death, but the mean between life and death. One cannot object to the giving of such a condition for the unity of opposites in Heraclitus; there is a similar condition implied (though not stated with a participle) at B59 with γναφέων (or γραφέων) and at B103 with the phrase ἐπὶ κύκλου (see Kirk, *HCF* p. 113, on the text). In the logical structure of the two first clauses, ζῶν is contrasted with τεθνεῶτος, and φάος in parallel fashion with εὐφρόνη; εὕδων corresponds indeed to ἀποσβεσθεὶς ὄψεις, but not necessarily exactly—it is not necessary for εὕδων not to mark a condition just because ἀποσβεσθεὶς ὄψεις does not.

I do not know whether, with the text of the first clause thus established as far as the evidence permits, it is right to read into it (as is traditional) an epistemological reference, such as seems inescapable for the last clause of the fragment. The first clause in Hölscher's version could be a perfectly straightforward statement that men light lamps in the dark when they cannot see; if I have adopted the normal interpretation in the text, it is because of a purely subjective feeling that ἀποσβεσθεὶς ὄψεις would be superfluous unless Heraclitus meant more than this.

44. *Parmenides*, p. 192.
45. See Chap. I above.
46. If Cherniss' text and interpretation be adopted (see n. 4 above), this fragment rather repeats the point from B88 that these opposites stand in temporal succession. But this makes very little difference to the general trend of my argument, since what is most important for that is the term ἅπτεται used to connect opposites, and nothing in Cherniss' interpretation invalidates this point.
47. B57 says that night and day are "one"—ἕν. This may *say* only that night and day form a continuous whole, but in view of B59 and B60 is more likely to have been intended to mean that they were also identical.
48. On paradox in general and Heraclitus in particular see Renford Bambrough at *PQ* 10 (1960) 289ff.
49. This is true whether Strife is interpreted simply as opposition (Marcovich s.v. Herakleitos, col. 285) or as deeply involved in change (for literature see Marcovich) or as both; Marcovich's view is perhaps supported by the point that

change between two opposites is in Heraclitus a sign of their unity, not of their difference.

50. Such seems to be the drift of Kirk, *HCF* pp. 69f.

51. It is hardly possible to agree with Kirk when he says (*HCF* p. 93): "Heraclitus was concerned to demonstrate an underlying connexion or identity, and ... identity for him did not have the rigid connotation of oneness and inseparability which it has had since Aristotle. Certainly Heraclitus recognised a practical difference..." A glance at *Metaphys. Δ* is surely enough to show that Aristotle did not think of words like "one" and "same" as rigid, but allowed them several senses which he appears to have been the first to analyse out. It is much more probable, on the other hand, that Heraclitus did not distinguish between different senses of "one" and was treating the word in the rigid way in which Archaic Greeks tended to treat words. When he asserts that two things are one and the same, it is hard to believe that he would not be understood by his contemporaries, and intend to be understood, as asserting their identity. Marcovich s.v. Herakleitos, cols. 286f, does not convince me to the contrary (though he at least avoids there the error of supposing Aristotle rigid in his use of the terms "one" and "same"): his words "trotz der Terminologie" are more than a trifle cavalier.

52. For the text see Kirk, *HCF* pp. 167ff.

53. *Hermes* 76 (1941) 84ff, followed by Kirk. (Marcovich's bibliography, *Heraclitus* p. 106 init., is topsy-turvy.) Marcovich (s.v. Herakleitos, cols. 280f, and *Heraclitus*, pp. 105ff) disagrees, taking συλλάψιες as a heading followed by examples subsumed under it; συλλάψιες is thus effectively a predicate. But his arguments are inconclusive, and he does not deal, in my opinion, with the difficulties brought out by Kirk (*HCF* pp. 175f). Neither of the first two pairs of words ὅλα καὶ οὐχ ὅλα, συμφερόμενον διαφερόμενον are opposites in the normal Heraclitean modes; positive and contradictory are not elsewhere opposites in Heraclitus, but appear side by side in statements about subjects dear to Heraclitus (e.g., B32): and words used of the relationships holding between opposites are not themselves elsewhere, at least in sayings, treated as opposites (I do not accept Marcovich on B12; see n. 14 above): if συμφερόμενον and διαφερόμενον *were* "opposites," they can, as Kirk says, "themselves only be described as 'connected' in a very unusual sense, and certainly not that which scholars have attached to the word in this context." Marcovich's parallels (in Hippocratic paradoxes) for "whole" and "part" as opposites are hardly persuasive, since the minor Hippocratics doubtless went far beyond Heraclitus in their playing with paradox.

54. For Aristotelian thought on this topic see Chap. I above.

55. See Kirk, *HCF* p. 67, on the pun enshrined in the word ὁμολογεῖν.

56. Cherniss, *ACPP* pp. 380f, and esp. McDiarmid at *HSCP* 61 (1953) 93ff. Theophrastus' evidence was apparently B90, which proves nothing of the kind. See n. 64 below.

57. Mondolfo argues at *ZM* p. 180 in favour of the cosmogonical interpretation but not convincingly. He advances, in addition to a fantastic interpretation of Plato *Sophist* 242d–e and a fruitless appeal to Peripatetic authority, three particular arguments: (1) that the primacy of Fire in Heraclitus must be temporal and cosmogonical; (2) that B30 only affirms the eternity of the world if it be punctuated

after ἔσται, and that this is impossible; and (3) that present tenses can refer to cyclical as well as to constant change. (3) is obviously inconclusive, and (1) and (2) are simply false. On p. 181 Mondolfo urges that the language of B31 refers to cosmic masses, not to mere bits of them, and that the fragment must refer to a cosmic cycle; so it may, but the cycle need not be one of cosmogony and cosmic destruction. Mondolfo underestimates the freedom of use of words in the Archaic period of science. Equally unconvincing are the general arguments in favour of a periodic conflagration at ZM pp. 257ff.

58. The text of this fragment, B31b, is disputed, and needs to be disputed more. The basic problem is how to interpret the fragment as meaning anything like what Clement appears to have thought it said. Clement cites B31a as saying that fire turns completely to water (via air!), which is the seed of the world, and that this gives rise to earth, sky, and τὰ ἐμπεριφερόμενα. This proves (for Clement) the first half of what he set out to prove, namely that Heraclitus' world is created and destroyed. He now, in citing B31b, seeks to show that all the things of this world are changed back into fire, and the world is thus destroyed. Now, with the text as printed by Kranz and Kirk (*HCF* p. 325), it is very difficult to see how this is to be squared with Heraclitus' words: ⟨γῆ⟩ θάλασσα διαχέεται, καὶ μετρέεται εἰς τὸν αὐτὸν λόγον ὁκοῖος πρόσθεν ἦν ἢ γενέσθαι γῆ, can only refer to the change from earth to sea. To meet this objection Kranz suggested that another sentence has been lost which mentioned the final change to fire; but this will not do, since Clement's further statement, ὁμοίως καὶ περὶ τῶν ἄλλων στοιχείων τὰ αὐτά, then has little meaning, for practically all the elements are already accounted for. Kirk, on the other hand, has to suppose that Clement (a) had probably a text which omitted γῆ before θάλασσα, (b) failed completely to notice the phrase ἢ γενέσθαι γῆ at the end of the fragment, and in consequence (c) misinterpreted the word διαχέεται to mean "dispersed" of the sea. This is surely a desperately complicated series of hypotheses, especially in handling an author as intelligent as Clement, whose citations normally at least make sense. Kirk and Marcovich s.v. Herakleitos, col. 261, adduce in support of their theory the statement of Diogenes Laertius 9.9 πάλιν τε αὖ τὴν γῆν χεῖσθαι, and Marcovich (*Heraclitus*, p. 280) adds Chrysippus, *SVF* II no. 413; but Diogenes' support is worth nothing, since (a) we have not the slightest reason to suppose the statement itself based on this fragment, and χεῖσθαι in the context of physical change of state under the influence of heat is ordinary Stoic terminology (cf. Diels, *Dox.*, Index s.v. χεῖν); (b) Chrysippus' variant διαχεομένης is stylistically motivated. Admittedly, the omission by the scribes of γῆ could (Marcovich) be syntactically motivated; but what would be philosophically motivated by the presence in the context of B31a is an *addition* by the scribes of an initial reference to earth.

It is not necessary to suppose with Vlastos (at *AJP* 76 [1955] 360 n. 47) and Marcovich (*Heraclitus*, p. 285) that the words ἢ γενέσθαι γῆ presuppose a γῆ at the beginning of B31b. The scribe may well have been motivated by B31a. For, if only half sea becomes fire, then clearly the proportion of fire will not be the same as before, supposing that *all* fire turned (B31a) into sea. The scribe may then have wanted to make the part of sea which had turned to earth to turn back into sea again so that the whole could turn back to fire. He would achieve the equivalent of this (he might suppose) by making the sea turn into fire in the same proportion as it existed before half of sea became earth; i.e., after the change from sea to earth had been balanced by a change from earth to sea. It is not likely therefore to be coincidence that the MSS of Eusebius, who copied out this passage (and much else) of Clement, omit the initial word γῆ. The MSS of Clement himself are the only group of authorities to have the strongly motivated final addition.

Much of this was doubtless seen by Cherniss, who accordingly proposed (ap. Ramnoux, *Héraclite*, pp. 85 and 403) the suppresssion of ἢ γενέσθαι γῆ and the acceptance of πρῶτον from Clement's MSS against the πρόσθεν of Eusebius. This solution has the merit of keeping the original statement θάλασσα διαχέεται in the form, and with the sense, in which Clement understood it and of not saddling Clement with a total neglect of the end of the fragment. Without this suggestion, which may indeed be right, this note would not have been written. But it is not, I think, the most plausible solution palaeographically. It presupposes that a scribe substituted for a word common in his day a word uncommon at that epoch (see Arndt and Gingrich s.v., who cite for πρόσθεν only the *Epistle to Diognetus*, and Preisigke, *Wörterbuch der griechischen Papyrusurkunden*, who cites only two examples). Further, it assumes two glosses where one (as we shall see) will do; it assumes that one glossator added ἢ γενέσθαι and another added γῆ (unless part of a single gloss was accidentally, without special motivation, omitted by one set of scribes, namely those of Eusebius). Further, though in certain respects the text given by Eusebius is inferior to that of Clement's own scribes, there are only a very small number of omissions by the MSS of Eusebius which are not visually easy to understand, which the omission of γῆ here is not. There are also a substantial number of points at which Stählin at least accepted against the MSS of Clement the text offered by those of Eusebius. If we suppose that the MSS of Eusebius are right throughout this passage we have the following excellent sense: θάλασσα διαχέεται, καὶ μετρέεται εἰς τὸν αὐτὸν λόγον ὁκοῖος πρόσθεν ἦν ἢ γενέσθαι (sc. θάλασσαν) to be translated as in my text. On this supposition the scribes of Clement's MSS have been guilty (1) of substituting πρῶτον for the rarer πρόσθεν, and (2) of inserting under philosophical motivation the word γῆ, to link the fragment with the immediately preceding B31a. (1) would have been further facilitated by the facts that πρῶτον and πρόσθεν share three letters and that a normal scribe might well grasp the sense of the whole before reaching the end of the sentence in copying and be led thus to write down a word which in fact completes the sense. Neither πρῶτον ἢ nor πρόσθεν ἢ is known to me from elsewhere followed (like πρίν) with an infinitive, but the construction is readily intelligible and would result from a simple "transformation" of better known constructions. But, whatever the precise reading, the general sense extracted by Cherniss from B31b seems to be right: water changes to fire, in the same ratio as it had previously, before it came to be (obviously out of fire). Clement's addition that all the other elements did the same is then seen to make from his point of view reasonable sense, though we do not know how far it was based on fragments we do not possess. We can in fact scarcely do more than guess what this "etc." of Clement's represents in Heraclitus; the earth may have been mentioned in this kind of context, and indeed D.L. 9.9 and Chrysippus, *SVF* II no. 413, make it quite likely.

59. Ap. Ramnoux, *Héraclite*, p. 403.

60. *Neue Studien zur Geschichte der Begriffe* I pp. 54f, cited by Zeller, ZN p. 848 n. 1.

61. The text of B31a is not normally disputed; but there seems to be a possibility of disagreement over its meaning. It is commonly assumed that the genitive θαλάσσης is partitive, to be taken with τὸ μὲν ἥμισυ ... τὸ δὲ ἥμισυ ... But the resulting statement that sea *is* half earth and half πρηστήρ is treated nevertheless in some published paraphrases as if it referred to the *turnings* of sea; thus, though Kirk (*HCF* p. 325) translates "of sea the half is earth, the half lightning-flash," and he states (*HCF* p. 329) that "Earth, like sea, is described as a 'turning' of fire, and *not of its own immediate origin*, sea," he can also write (*HCF* p. 331), "Half sea is thought of as *reverting to* fire, half as *turning to* earth," and (*Mind* 66 [1957] 39) "first into sea, and half sea is *turning to* earth" (italics all mine). Having dismissed the suggestion that the sea is, at present, a mixture of earth and fire, it is obviously relevant to explore the possibility that Heraclitus not only did not mean this but did not say it either. In normal Greek, it must be admitted, one would scarcely have to think twice; the genitive would most naturally be taken with the expression of quantity (cf. Stokes at *AGP* 47 [1965] 18 n. 55). But we are not now dealing with normal Greek, but with a highly compressed and at times awkward style, to which normal rules do not always apply. The following points should be observed, in view of the alternative possibility that θαλάσσης should be taken as parallel with πυρός, and that τροπαί should be "understood" with it from the immediately preceding phrase. (1) Clement probably took θαλάσσης as parallel with πυρός, since he says, evidently in paraphrasing from θαλάσσης onwards, ἐκ δὲ τούτων αὖθις γίνεται γῆ καὶ οὐρανὸς καὶ τὰ ἐμπεριεχόμενα: αὖθις marks the symmetry of the two halves of the fragment. But Clement is not by himself conclusive evidence, since Stoic doctrine would naturally favour such an interpretation. His paraphrase does, however, suggest that my way of taking θαλάσσης is not impossible Greek. (2) The symmetry alluded to under (1) is itself in favour of my suggested interpretation; following practically immediately on πυρός, θαλάσσης would perhaps be more easily taken as the same kind of genitive. (3) If, as many have supposed without absolute proof, B30 and B31a are indeed closely connected, then it is worthy of note that the accusatives μέτρα in B30 are adverbial, and then symmetry would help a reader to discern the adverbial function of the accusatives τὸ ... ἥμισυ in B31a. At least, if one were to adopt this rendering of B31a, one would avoid the Hobson's choice between (a) taking θαλάσσης κτλ. with Cherniss as saying only that sea is made up of two opposites and (b) supposing with Zeller (ZN p. 848 n. 1) and, implicitly, many others that Heraclitus declares the sea to contain half *potential* earth and half *potential* fire. The alternative (a) here seems to produce an implausible doctrine in a context in which it is a pure irrelevance and (b) at worst is anachronistic and at best makes Heraclitus talk with needless inexactitude (as also does Marcovich's tentative solution, *Heraclitus*, p. 288). I cannot, and do not, lay any claim to

certainty here, but would suggest that the possibility of understanding τροπαί after θαλάσσης is far from remote and should by no means be overlooked.

62. Some examples of such phrases in the literature: "Dieser Stoff erscheint in verschiedenen Formen" (Kerschensteiner, *Kosmos*, p. 104; at p. 105 n. 3 Kerschensteiner makes this and B90 the basis for the assertion of unity in B10); "The total amount of fire in all its forms remains the same" (Kirk at *Mind* 60 [1951] 40; but Kirk does not believe fire to be a substrate); Fränkel, *DuP* p. 439, mentions higher and lower forms of Fire; even Hölscher's more cautious remarks (*Varia Variorum*, p. 74), to the effect that Fire is the unity of all things "als Substanz gedacht" and that "was auf eine geheimnisvolle Weise alle Dinge sind" is fire, seem hard to justify from the texts.

63. *HCF* pp. 307ff, and KR p. 199 n. 1. I remain unconvinced that τὸν αὐτὸν ἁπάντων is Heraclitean; contra, e.g., Marcovich, *Heraclitus*, pp. 268ff.

64. See Kirk, *HCF* pp. 345ff. Mondolfo (ZM pp. 259ff) seems, on the other hand, to take the fragment too literally when he argues that only important business would be done in gold, that *all* the client's gold was exchanged for the totality of goods, and hence that an ecpyrosis is implied in this fragment. Clearly, alliteration (χρυσοῦ χρήματα) played a part in Heraclitus' choice of words here; cf. Marcovich s.v. Herakleitos, col. 275.

65. *AJP* 56 (1935) 415. Nor have I found any text to support Cherniss' other view (at *ACPP* p. 380) that "all things are both one and many *because* all things are in a constant flux" (italics mine).

66. *HCF* p. 348 (italics Kirk's).

67. Are earth and πρηστήρ turnings of fire, as πρῶτον might imply, or only of sea? cf. n. 61 above.

68. Kirk, *HCF* p. 165, and see Marcovich, *Heraclitus*, pp. 324ff.

69. *HCF* p. 348 (italics mine).

70. Kirk, *HCF* p. 185. Mondolfo (at ZM p. 129) tries to show τἀναντία Heraclitean, citing Philodemus *De pietate* p. 70 G., but the word τἀναντία there, even if we read with Mondolfo θε[ὸν ε]ἶναι, need not have been intended as part of a quotation from Heraclitus; as an interpretation it is sufficiently obvious to occur to more than one writer independently. (I am also unconvinced by Mondolfo's defence of Nestle's ⟨οἶνος⟩, cf. Marcovich, *Heraclitus*, pp. 415f, on the text.) Cherniss (cited by Ramnoux, *Héraclite*, p. 482) unfortunately has not published his reasons for doubting the authenticity of the whole comparison. As an example of the kind of loose importation of the one-many antithesis into texts lacking it which this book is designed to put an end to, it would be hard to beat ZM p. 128. "Esso (B 67) determina infatti il rapporto fra l'uno (Dio) e la molteplicita (serie degli opposti) ..."—but at least Mondolfo's importation is explicit. Would that the same could always be said.

71. I have condensed here Kirk, *HCF* p. 183.

72. Ibid., p. 189.

73. Not refuted by ZM pp. 130ff; Marcovich's purely theological interpretation, *Heraclitus*, p. 417, seems to me also to have much truth in it but to be unnecessarily one-sided.

74. See Gigon, *Entretiens Fondation Hardt* I (*La notion du divin*) pp. 162ff, discussed at Chap. III n. 40 above.

75. I cannot bring myself to believe with Kirk (*HCF* pp. 393f) that ἓν τὸ σοφὸν μοῦνον can mean "one thing, the only wise." For neither Kirk nor Kühner–Gerth (I p. 621) offers any exception to the rule that μόνος has attributive position when it is an attribute. Kirk's description of his rendering as "syntactically harder" is therefore a serious understatement. To the translation implied by my text Kirk would doubtless object that μοῦνον is thus weakened. He finds no reason why Heraclitus should stress with the addition of μοῦνον that this bizarre description is exclusive, given no likely candidate for inclusion or exclusion. But Heraclitus may have wanted to stress that wisdom alone is predicable of the supreme power of the universe; no other (and especially no anthropomorphic) attributes are to be assigned to it. That is precisely why, though willing to be called Zeus (as being the supreme power), it is at the same time unwilling (because not possessed of Zeus's anthropomorphic paraphernalia). The influence of Xenophanes may here be at work.

76. *Rhetoric* 1368b7, cited by Kirk, *HCF* p. 53 n. 1. In general see Kirk's discussion of the fragment at *HCF* pp. 48ff.

77. Heinimann, *Nomos und Physis*, p. 66, is somewhat rash in actually equating them; Kirk, *HCF* p. 57, more cautiously speaks of the "common to all" as "analogous to the single divine law." Cf. Marcovich, *Heraclitus*, p. 95.

78. I follow Marcovich s.v. Herakleitos, col. 298, in the belief that Aristotle did attribute a conflagration to Heraclitus in consequence of associating him with the supposed general doctrine of the early physicists that everything comes from, and returns to, a single stuff. Marcovich admits the possibility that Heraclitus did contradict himself by propounding the theory of the general conflagration—but the contradiction seems so fundamental and so little backed by Heraclitus' own extant words that for practical purposes the possibility is best ignored.

79. See Marcovich, *Heraclitus*, pp. 434ff.

80. Marcovich s.v. Herakleitos, col. 298.

81. *Untersuchungen zu Heraklit*, p. 43.

82. *HCF* p. 177.

83. See, for instance, Rivier (*Mus Helv* 13 [1956] 149 n. 20) referring the paradox of the second half of B10 not to the judgement of the person taking the συλλάψιες together but to reality itself; and Marcovich s.v. Herakleitos, col. 281, who paraphrases thus: In this way one can make a unity of any pair of opposites one chooses, and this unity "liegt im Grunde aller bestehender Dinge." Marcovich's paraphrase, however, seems to make the πάντων opposites, and the πάντα things (explicitly at *Heraclitus*, p. 106), and one must surely be reluctant to take them as thus representing different sets of objects.

CHAPTER V: PARMENIDES AND MELISSUS

1. Marcovich s.v. Herakleitos, cols. 247ff.

2. D. L. 9.1, *Suda* s.v. Ἡράκλειτος, Euseb. *Chron.* s. Ol. 70.1 (for variants see Jacoby, *Apollodors Chronik*, p. 229 n. 4).

3. Clem. Al., *Strom.* 1.65.4 (p. 41 Stählin–Früchtel), see Jacoby, *Apollodors Chronik*, p. 228 n. 3. Jacoby himself demolishes Bernays' contentions that Epictetus referred to Heraclitus' connection with Darius at *Ench.* 21 W., that Eudemus referred to it also, and that it was probably in any case historical. Most of what Bernays said on this topic (*Die Heraklitischen Briefe*, pp. 13f) is uncharacteristically in the air. Zeller (ZN p. 914 n. 2), admitting that Bernays' remarks did not make the Persian invitation to Heraclitus more than a possibility, suggested that the forged letters proved the story known beforehand to their author. A clear non sequitur, surprisingly accepted by Kirk, *HCF* p. 1. Heinemann at *RE* Suppl. 5 col. 229 plausibly suggested that the tale of Darius' invitation to Heraclitus was an imitation of the late story concerning Diogenes and Alexander the Great, for which the first extant source is Cicero (see Natorp at *RE* 5 col. 767).

4. Cf. Sotion ap. D. L. 9.5. and *Suda* s.v. Ἡράκλειτος (cited by Jacoby).

5. To take only English examples, see Burnet, *EGP*[4] pp. 169f; KR (much more cautiously) pp. 263 f; Guthrie, *HGP* II pp. 1f.

6. See last note; Jacoby was prepared (*Apollodors Chronik*, p. 233) to stretch the limit for Parmenides' birth as far back as 520; I know nothing solid against this.

7. Marcovich (s.v. Herakleitos, cols. 248f) remarks with justice that Ion of Chios and the *vaticinium post eventum* of Letter 4 supply termini ante quem to place Heraclitus at any rate in the first half of the fifth century. But whether Heraclitus' interest in Pythagoras and Hecataeus is sufficient to place his activity around 490 is doubtful: both these thinkers were the object of much interest later in the century, and we are in no position on this account to rule out a date for Heraclitus' writing as late as (say) 480.

8. The suggestion (e.g., KR p. 268) that the goddess' address to Parmenides as κοῦρε dates the poem in Parmenides' youth is rash; see Tarán, *Parmenides*, p. 16.

9. For bibliography see Marcovich s.v. Herakleitos, col. 249.

10. This procedure is in effect followed by Calogero at *GCFI* 4 (1936) 195, who accepts that Heraclitus and Parmenides were contemporaries, if not coevals.

11. See esp. Vlastos at *AJP* 76 (1955) 341 n. 11, and Tarán, *Parmenides*, pp. 61ff. Guthrie (*HGP* II p. 24) more cautiously suggests: "Where no single phrase brings conviction, the cumulative effect may be considerable. There are, then, strong hints in his language that for Parmenides Heraclitus was the archoffender..."

12. Brief bibliography at Owen, *CQ* n.s. 10 (1960) 84 n. 1, more extensive at ZM IV pp. 392ff.

13. *Jahrbücher für klassische Philologie* Suppl. 25 (1899) 489–660.

14. For various selections see Nestle at ZN p. 684 n. 1, Kranz at *Hermes* 69 (1934) 117f, Vlastos at *AJP* 76 (1955) 341 n. 11.

15. *AJP* 21 (1900) 200–216.

16. Regrettable is F. Heinimann's strange notion (*Nomos und Physis*, p. 93 n. 8) that Parmenides B8.22 οὐδὲ διαιρετόν ἐστιν is aimed at Heraclitus B1 διαιρέων...

17. For the Heracliteans see Guthrie, *HGP* II p. 23 n. 2, who admirably disposes of them in this connection.

18. *Parmenides*, pp. 59f.

19. I do not find conclusive Tarán's point that τά, being plural, ought to include more than one statement: more than one word might suffice. But that μηδὲν δ' οὐκ ἔστιν does not *describe* the way of not-Being seems to me clear.

20. This is Guthrie's way out at *HGP* II p. 22; but Guthrie had evidently seen the difficulty.

21. Denniston, *Greek Particles*, p. 55, cites no examples in a different position; contrast his treatment of ἀτάρ on p. 54.

22. *CP* 50 (1955) 124ff, rejected, e.g., by Schwabl at *Anzeiger für Altertumswissenschaft* 9 (1956) 148.

23. See Tarán, *Parmenides*, pp. 75f. (But again not all Tarán's arguments convince; thus, Simplicius may have been simply wrong in distinguishing the views attacked at B6.4–9 from those denounced at B7.1ff at *in Phys.* 78.2. It is perfectly reasonable to accept Simplicius' statements on the order of lines preserved, without trusting always in his interpretation of them. Simplicius' faults as an interpreter should not nowadays need illustration.)

24. It is perhaps worth mentioning that Diels's supplement ἐπάγει was not introduced simply because of the parallel at *in Phys.* 78.6, as Tarán (*Parmenides*, p. 61) might seem to imply, but was obviously devised in the first instance to meet the need for a main verb in Simplicius' sentence.

25. The difficulty of the γάρ on the old interpretation may be illustrated by the fact that Burnet and KR, eminent Hellenists all and literally though they normally translate, here omit γάρ altogether. Tarán does translate it; but on his interpretation there are other difficulties. The postponement (alleged by Tarán) of discussion of the first way, and the rejection of the way of ignorant mortals, are both relevant indeed to the instruction to "keep in mind" the argument of B6.1f, but the sort of "keeping in mind" that gives them relevance differs from one half of the sentence B6.3ff to the other; the first half of that sentence presupposes on Taran's interpretation that the "keeping in mind" is for the purpose of later discussion, the second surely that the "keeping in mind" involves the firm belief in the soundness of the argument (for only acceptance of the argument of B6.1f could motivate the emphatic rejection of mortal views, in the lines following B6.4). Mrs. Sprague removes the difficulty of the γάρ either by removing B6.3 or by putting B7.2 before it; but this, as we have seen, is an unsuccessful remedy.

26. It is highly unlikely that Simplicius anticipated Tarán's improbable interpretation.

27. Kühner–Gerth I pp. 646f cite a number of examples; see esp. Hdt. I.125. The grammarians say: "Während ὅδε den folgenden Gedanken als eben erst an den Redenden herantretend hinstellt, lässt ihn οὗτος (wie zuweilen *illud*) als vorher schon in der Seele schlummernd erscheinen." I am not sure that this distinction is universally true, and it is not repeated by Schwyzer–Debrunner II p. 209. But, whether true or not, it does not rule out the forward reference of ταύτης in Parmenides B6, for there the following thought would actually have

been expressed by the goddess in a previous passage and is certainly not presented as occurring to her for the first time.

28. Thus KR p. 272 n. 1, and Guthrie, *HGP* II p. 21. On the other hand, Gigon, *Ursprung*, p. 258, and Owen, at *CQ* n.s. 10 (1960) 91, apparently assume without argument that πάντων is masculine.

29. *CR* n.s. 10 (1960) 193–194.

30. Tarán, *Parmenides*, pp. 66ff, produces several arguments against my thesis of 1960 to which I reply in turn: (1) "To answer why Parmenides, if he intended the second clause to be considered as parallel to the first, did not put παλίντροπός ἐστι κέλευθος in indirect discourse dependent on νενόμισται is simple; he did not do so because παλίντροπον εἶναι κέλευθον would not scan and neither would any arrangement of them (or substitutes like πέλειν, ἔμμεναι—ὁδός, πόρος, πάτος); this by itself indicates that the term παλίντροπος has a significance such that Parmenides could not sacrifice it." But, even if we insist on keeping παλίντροπος, then we could use Parmenides' own word ἄταρπος: παλίντροπον εἶναι ἄταρπον. Tarán's last sentence implies a special point in the actual word παλίντροπος that would not be present in a semantic equivalent—a clear reference to the common view that the παλίντροπος κέλευθος alludes to the παλίντροπος ἁρμονίη of Heraclitus B51. But Tarán's interest in this verbal allusion is merely ad hoc; for on his p. 69 we find "The allusions to Heraclitus need not be to any particular expressions or words in the latter's fragments. Whether in Heraclitus B51 we read παλίντροπος or παλίντονος makes no difference, for with παλίντροπος ἐστι κέλευθος Parmenides almost certainly did not refer to a παλίντροπος ἁρμονίη." If we abandon παλίντροπος, we could, for example, have had a Parmenidean... πάλιν τὰ κέλευθα τρέπεσθαι—the plural makes little if any difference. My dexterity in Greek being certainly far beneath a native speaker's, I content myself with these illustrations. (2) I am told that my distinction of questions of fact and questions of value is an illusory one, and referred to the first example given by Kühner–Gerth I p. 421, namely, *Iliad* 23.595 καὶ δαίμοσιν εἶναι ἀλιτρός. Tarán alleges that this is represented as a matter of fact from the point of view of the gods, not merely a matter of opinion. This doctrine is not to the point; the distinction between fact and opinion is not identical with the distinction between fact and value. The gods are undoubtedly supposed to believe it true that the speaker is an ἀλιτρός—but this will be for them as much as for anyone else a judgement of value, and certainly not only of fact. (3) I am supposed to go too far in considering that πάντων ... κέλευθος is for Parmenides a question of fact, "because for Parmenides the doctrines of mortals are not a question of fact but a matter of convention, of custom, empty names which have nothing to do with true reality; the only question of fact is for Parmenides the sole reality of Being." With most of this I agree; but again it does not touch on my argument. Parmenides thinks that all human opinions are false; but that need not prevent him from distinguishing in his syntactical usage (of course he could not so distinguish in abstract terms) between a statement of approval or disapproval and an intended statement of fact. Further, Tarán did not, in his criticism of the Homer passage, consider what Homer would have thought, but only what the people in the dative would have thought; he has here shifted his ground.

More important, to my way of thinking, is a note by F. Heinimann at *Nomos und Physis*, p. 75, published in 1945, which I had overlooked when I wrote my note in *CR*. "Vielmehr zeigt der sogennannte dativus auctoris (nicht ὑπό!) hier noch deutlich seinen ursprunglichen Charakter als Dativ des Interesses, der die Person nicht als Subjekt einer Handlung, sondern nur als geistig an einen Zustand oder Vorgang beteiligt darstellt." This suggestion, which is extremely plausible, admittedly makes the zeugma between οἷς νενόμισται and οἷς ἐστιν a good deal easier to understand. But I submit that there is still a difference between the two implied datives; the first points to people actively interested in the situation concerned, the second ("understood") dative would indicate mere spectators of the process, people who merely thought it was going on. Thus Heinimann's exposition does not fully convince me that the zeugma is not still awkward. I should not now say that it was impossible, especially if no other way of taking the Greek were open to us, that such a zeugma were right; and I have stressed elsewhere that the grammatically unexampled is not to be equated with the impossible. But I should be disinclined to adopt such a harsh construction if there were an easier way to read the sentence concerned.

31. *AJP* 21 (1900) 215.

32. I do not find proof that Heraclitus B51 originally spoke of a παλίντροπος ἁρμονίη. KR pp. 193f show the difficulty in finding an appropriate sense in Heraclitus' context for παλίντροπος, and this argument is answered neither by Tarán, *Parmenides*, p. 69, nor by the writers to whom he refers. Kranz also strikes me as arguing unconvincingly at *RhM* 101 (1958) 250–254. Admitting that Hippolytus' text of Heraclitus may have contained variants, he does nothing therefore to diminish the probability that the variant παλίντονος was at least as old as the variant παλίντροπος. His further appeal to the "parallel" at Euripides *Hippolytus* 161ff falls flat; we do not nowadays regard the Attic tragedians as writing, nor their audience as listening, with copies of obscure Ionian philosophers at their elbow. Furthermore, even if παλίντροπος has finally to be accepted as the correct reading in Heraclitus B51 (which I do not believe), it can only be as a bold metaphor, which would presuppose previous more literal usage. Since Parmenides' use of the word is literal (even if κέλευθος is a metaphor, παλίντροπος is a literal enough epithet for a path), we are absolved from the necessity of associating the two earliest *extant* occurrences of παλίντροπος by the consideration that, if Heraclitus wrote before Parmenides, then others than Heraclitus had used the word literally before either Heraclitus or Parmenides used it. The earliest extant occurrences would not then be the earliest occurrences, and the survival of two around the same period would be coincidental after all.

33. Vlastos (*AJP* 76 [1955] 349 n. 26) does not convince me that Theophrastus was necessarily right in interpreting the "road up and down" of the path of the cosmic masses. See Chap. IV n. 18 above. Cornford at *CQ* 27 (1933) 101 n. 2 described πάντων παλίντροπος κέλευθος as "specially suitable" for a description of the ὁδὸς ἄνω κάτω which according to him figures in all the Ionian systems, not only in Heraclitus. But we know nothing of any use of the word ὁδός in such a context apart from the bare possibility of its use thus by Heraclitus; and, though suitable, the πάντων παλίντροπος κέλευθος is certainly not specially so, and

certainly not unintelligible without an allusion to Heraclitus. I see no reason to limit the sense of παλίντροπος (with Mansfeld, *Offenbarung*, p. 28) to "in cyclic movement identical."

34. KR p. 272 n. 1.
35. Tarán, *Parmenides*, p. 66.
36. *HGP* II pp. 23f.
37. This appears to be assumed by Vlastos' question (*AJP* 76 [1955] 341 n. 11) why "Parmenides should (a) impute to *anyone* the belief in the identity of being and not-being (rather than merely the belief in not-being, which is bad enough from his point of view and would have given his critical dialectic all the scope it needs . . ." To believe in the existence of non-existence is tantamount in Parmenidean terms to believing that what exists and what does not are the same; and ordinary men are constantly asserting the existence of what for Parmenides is non-existent (since it is other than Being). Tarán is equally unconvincing in his dogmatic pronouncement (*Parmenides*, p. 65) that the lines cannot be a construction by Parmenides "since to be such it would have to assert that both Being and non-Being exist, whereas it states only that they are considered to be the same and not the same." Such trammelling of Parmenides' imagination to suit the logic of twentieth-century critics is out of place. In Parmenides' eyes, to say that what does not exist exists is to identify existence and non-existence, whereas to use the terms "existence" and "non-existence" at all is to distinguish them. As a construction of Parmenides', designed to reduce common sense to as many simultaneous self-contradictions as possible, these lines make perfect sense.

As for verbal references, on B6.8–9 and Heraclitus B32 see n. 145 below; the alleged reference to Heraclitus B91 at Parmenides B4 now falls to the ground with Marcovich's indication (s.v. Herakleitos col. 265, cf. *Heraclitus*, pp. 206ff) that the vocabulary of Heraclitus B91D is in all probability derived from Aenesideman Scepticism. Nor do I find it necessary (*pace* Vlastos at *TAPA* 77 [1946] 69 n. 21, followed by Kirk, *HCF* p. 2) to see an allusion to Heraclitus at B8.57–58; see Tarán ad loc.

38. Tarán, *Parmenides*, pp. 70f.
39. The expression "tantamount to" in this sentence makes it apparent that even on this theory Parmenides is supposed to be "interpreting" Heraclitus to some degree by a construction of his own.
40. Sextus' record in the transmission of Parmenides' order is not impeccable, but see Tarán, *Parmenides*, pp. 76f on B7.3–6.
41. Cf. Cornford at *CQ* 27 (1933) 100 n. 3: contra Simplicius *in Phys.* 143.29f.
42. See against Owen especially Tarán, *Parmenides*, pp. 33ff and particularly 35f, and Guthrie, *HGP* II pp. 13ff. In reply to Guthrie see my review of *HGP* II at *PQ* 17 (1967) 164ff. Tarán p. 36 follows Owen in arguing that Fränkel's impersonal interpretation is unintelligible in the light of the demonstration of the characteristics of Being in B8, but on the same page Tarán asserts that "ἔστιν and οὐκ ἔστιν in lines 3 and 5 of B2 are used as impersonals and no subject has to be understood with them." What the difference is between his impersonal interpretation and Fränkel's I am unable now to discover from his book.
43. Guthrie, *HGP* II p. 16.

44. No example (1) is quoted for τὸ ἐόν with infinitive meaning "that which it is possible to..." (though a *possible* one is to be found at Epicurus *Epist.* 1, ap. D. L. 10.60, where H. S. Long and G. Arrighetti are perhaps right to leave ἄγειν ὄν in their texts); nor (2) is anything quoted like the articular infinitive with χρή required by Covotti's "è necessario il dire e il pensare che l'essere è" (*I Presocratici*, p. 102 n. 3). But, if I had to bet, purely as a grammarian, on one of them, I would choose the former on the grounds that τὸ νοεῖν ἐόν is more likely as a "transformation" of ἔστι νοεῖν (for which see B2.2 ἔστι νοῆσαι) than is an extension of the usage of the aricular infinitive, still relatively unfamiliar to the Greeks of Parmenides' day. Tarán usefully refutes some other interpretations, but his own, literally "It is necessary to be to say and to think being," remains wholly obscure to me, since I can find no subject in his sentence for his "copula" to copulate with the alleged predicate.

Tarán also criticizes Burnet's rendering, holding that the construction it implies should properly be rendered "that which exists for speaking and thinking must exist," which he calls a tautology. S. Tugwell at *CQ* n.s. 14 (1964) 36 would go even further and holds that it is unfair to translate ἔστι νοεῖν as "it is possible for it to be thought about," because to translate thus is to separate off the potential εἶναι from the existential εἶναι "to an anachronistic extent." Tugwell accordingly prefers ἔστι in B3, and the indicative implied at B6.1, to be rendered "it is there for thought." Far from agreeing with Tarán that this gives an impossible tautology at B6, Tugwell suggests that Parmenides was vexed by the ambiguity of ἔστι between potential and existential senses and was led partly by this ambiguity to believe that, if a thing is thinkable, it must exist. But this, it seems, goes too far in the direction of thinking away our own presuppositions in the interpretation of Parmenides. If Parmenides were even partly misled by the question "How can it be there for thought (or speech) when it is not there?" then it becomes difficult to see how he could say of Being that "it is not there for X," where X is any infinitive. But at B2.3 we find the path of Persuasion stated as follows: ὡς ἔστιν τε καὶ ὡς οὐκ ἔστι μὴ εἶναι. This surely indicates that Parmenides could indeed imagine a thing as being there but not being a possible subject for a particular infinitive. Existence is therefore not incompatible with being attached to οὐκ ἔστιν in the "potential" sense. From the same passage may be drawn a positive argument in favour of Parmenides' ability to distinguish in usage between existential and potential εἶναι. In the statement of the false way (B2.5) Parmenides has ὅπως οὐκ ἔστι, καὶ ὡς χρεών ἐστι μὴ εἶναι. It is obvious that each half of this statement is designed to contrast as starkly as possible with the corresponding half of B.2.3. I submit that the natural contrast with line 5 "It is necessary for the subject to be-not" would be at line 3 "It is impossible for the subject to be-not." Neither Tugwell with his implied "The subject is not there for not-being," nor for that matter Kranz with his "Nothing is not," seems to extract so good a contrast from ὡς οὐκ ἔστι μὴ εἶναι. The upshot is that Parmenides could distinguish in use, if not in the abstract, between ἔστι "it is possible" and ἔστι "it exists." I cannot in any case recall any other example of confusion between these two meanings of ἔστι.

45. *CQ* n.s. 10 (1960) 94.

46. I doubt whether many scholars would agree with Owen (ibid., p. 99) that Parmenides was a wholly explicit reasoner, though certainly he was wholly honest; Owen himself is more cautious at *Monist* 50 (1966) 318.

47. Cf. KR p. 269: "At this early stage in his poem Parmenides' premise ἔστι has no definite subject at all: if it is necessary to translate the sentence ἔστιν ἢ οὐκ ἔστιν, then perhaps the least misleading rendering is 'Either a thing is or it is not.'" Windelband–Goedeckemeyer p. 40 paraphrase with "etwas" as the subject: Calogero, *Studi sull' Eleatismo*, pp. 17f, thinks that, having no determined subject, Parmenides' ἔστι is the copula; but Parmenides often uses the negatived copula and cannot have meant to exclude the use of it. See further bibliography in Mansfeld, *Offenbarung*, pp. 45ff.

48. Tarán, *Parmenides*, p. 59.

49. See J. R. Bambrough at *Proc. Arist. Soc.* 1960–1961, p. 215, cited by Guthrie, *HGP* II p. 16 n. 1.

50. Mansfeld, *Offenbarung*, p. 90, is surely right to connect B6.1–2 with the disjunctive syllogism of B2.

51. Guthrie, *HGP* II p. 16, says: "Even here in fr. 2 it seems too much to say that 'It is' is proved or argued for. It is stated, and said to be true. For the sake of completeness Parmenides then mentions its contrary..., and briefly dismisses it as inconceivable." Having argued against Guthrie's interpretation before (*PQ* 17 [1967] 164) on other grounds, I may now be permitted to suggest that this appears to assume without warrant that Parmenides was interested in completeness for its own sake and fails to appreciate that an argument by elimination is an *argument*: Mansfeld, *Offenbarung*, p. 58, is right in analysing it as *modus tollendo ponens*. (Tugwell's analysis at *CQ* n.s. 14 [1964] 36 is rather far from Parmenides' Greek.) After arguing, with normal use of γάρ, that you would not conceive or speak of not-being, Parmenides continues the argument by saying "*For* it is impossible." If anyone is disposed to ask why, Parmenides then continues the argument further: *for* it is the same thing that can be thought and that can be. Surely Parmenides here thought himself that he was arguing, advancing reasons for what he believed. This is why he refers back at B7.5–6 to the πολύδηριν ἔλεγχον which the goddess has already given (I owe this point to Professor Owen). The alleged brief dismissal is in fact part of a crucial argument, further elaborated in B6. We may add that, even if it were right to describe these lines as merely a brief dismissal of a contrary point of view, it would still be true to say that Parmenides does not start from ἔστι, but from the possibility of thought and discourse.

52. The clearest statement of this line of argument is by Tarán, *Parmenides*, pp. 65f.

53. I adopt in the main Tarán's interpretation of Parmenides B8.61; that is, of its wider bearing. The syntax is not, however, as Tarán (conventionally) believes, appropriate to a final clause, but rather to a strong denial with οὐ μή; see A. Long at *Phronesis* 8 (1963) 105 n. 3, and (more hesitant) Goodwin, *Greek Moods and Tenses*² p. 393 (Burnet's translation, *EGP*⁴ p. 176, is correct). Naturally, if a strong denial is meant, and ὡς acts as a connective, then the preceding line should end with a colon, rather than with a comma as Long still prints it.

54. This, at least, may without disquiet be deduced from Parmenides' general

line of argument. It is, however, far from certain that it was this particular point which Parmenides was making at B8.53f. See below.

55. *Pace* Calogero, *Studi sull' Eleatismo*, p. 37; Croissant, *Mélanges Desrousseaux*, p. 100 fin.; Tarán, *Parmenides*, p. 65.

56. Vlastos at *AJP* 76 (1955) 341 n. 11.

57. The form "X and not-X", common to τὸ πέλειν τε καὶ οὐκ εἶναι ... ταὐτὸν κοὐ ταὐτόν and Heraclitus' οὐκ ἐθέλει καὶ ἐθέλει (B32), certainly did not originate with the philosophers: there is a good example at Anacreon frag. 83 (Page), but I see no reason to believe that Anacreon was the inventor of it.

58. *CQ* n.s. 10 (1960) 91 n. 3.

59. *Psychologische Beobachtungen*, p. 8 n. 25.

60. *TEGP* p. 100. Zeller may have held similar views; see ZN pp. 687ff and also p. 929 n. 1, though here he is less clear in this respect than one would have wished. KR p. 272 are also a trifle indefinite at the point which interests me now; I am not sure that I understand their sentence "To be and not to be are the same in that they are both found in any event", but they do not mention any variation in space at this point in their exposition.

61. *Parmenides*, p. 51.

62. Reinhardt, *Parmenides*, pp. 69ff, and 87 n. 1. On this see Tarán, *Parmenides*, pp. 64f.

63. This is not meant to imply acceptance of Owen's thesis that B8.22-25 constitute a rejection of temporal discontinuity. Rejection of movement in space follows from the rejection of change according to Parmenides B8.26ff (contra P. J. Bicknell at *Phronesis* 12 [1967] 1ff); the same ontology is at work in the argument for continuity at B8.22f; it is likely that "continuity" here includes homogeneity of quality/substance). On Guthrie's interpretation of this passage see my review at *PQ* 17 (1967) 164–166.

64. *CQ* n.s. 10 (1960) 91.

65. Untersteiner's thesis (*Parmenide*, passim) eliminating the One altogether from Parmenides is adequately dealt with by Schwabl, *Anzeiger für Altertumswissenschaft* 9 (1956) 150f. F. Solmsen's important analysis, reducing the significance of unity in Eleatic thought perhaps too drastically, came into my hands as this book was going to press, too late for detailed criticism: see "The 'Eleatic One' in Melissus," *Mededelingen der koninklijke Nederlandse Akademie van Wetenschappen*, Afd. Letterkunde, Nieuwe Reeks, Deel 32, No. 8 (1969) 221–233.

66. See Proclus *in Tim.* 1.345.12f (Diehl) and Simpl. *in Phys.*, e.g., 7.1ff, 21.16ff.

67. See Owen at *CQ* n.s. 10 (1960) 102, Tarán pp. 93ff.

68. Owen objected to ἀτέλεστον that it simply repeats ἀνώλεθρον, and Guthrie (*HGP* II p. 27) replied that on Owen's own interpretation οὖλον μουνογενές in 8.4 is the exact equivalent of ἕν, συνεχές in 8.6. I agree with Owen that οὖλον μουνογενές is exactly equivalent to ἕν, συνεχές, but it is used in a very different context, when the argument has already begun, and is not therefore redundant. I do not believe Parmenides guilty of redundancy in the programme.

69. Guthrie (*HGP* II p. 44) says that at B8.48 (ἐπεὶ πᾶν ἐστιν ἄσυλον) the dependent clause "expresses the conclusion in a religious or metaphorical form ...

in v. 48 it hardly adds a cogent reason for the uniformity of being to say 'Since it is all inviolate.'" It does not indeed; Tugwell's defence (*CQ* n.s. 14 [1964] 40) that the argument is that you cannot pull bits off (which would destroy the symmetry), is inappropriate since the passage as a whole does not deal with any process such as "pulling off," but with a state of affairs which might detract from Being. It does not help this point to treat ἄσυλον with Mansfeld (*Offenbarung*, p. 103) as a consequence of the bond in which δίκη has surrounded the subject, sound though Mansfeld's remark is in itself. Scholars have been too ready to fob off on Parmenides a feeble argument, like the one Mansfeld suggests, when his words could offer a strong one. Here, as ὁμοῖον at B8.22 is proved adverbial by the surrounding adverbs, so ἄσυλον must be adverbial to make good sense. If ὁμοῖον can be an adverbial accusative, so can ἄσυλον. The sense required by the argument, supported by symmetry, and not forbidden by grammar, is "since it all inviolably *is*." This does not remove the metaphor or its religious overtones, but it leaves the argument sharp; there cannot be degrees of being, since that would violate the being of part of the subject (by introducing something different from Being, even if only in degree, i.e., not-Being). Of course Parmenides leaves the reference to not-Being inexplicit, as he does at 22ff, but that does not spoil the argument for the reader who knows what is going on; and in the later passage Parmenides has just condemned not-Being. Once this is granted, it cannot be argued that ἐπεί anywhere in Parmenides fails to introduce an argument. I do not believe that even γάρ fails to do this in Parmenides.

70. See Denniston, *Greek Particles*, p. 193 with n. 1.

71. Fränkel, *WuF* p. 191 n. See Owen at *CQ* n.s. 10 (1960) 100 with n. 2, and *Monist* 50 (1966) 320–325; Guthrie, *HGP* II p. 30 n. 1.

72. *Monist* 50 (1966) 317ff.

73. Ibid., p. 333. I do not find anything in Plato which necessitates the assumption that his "timeless present" was even partially anticipated by Parmenides. Nor do I find wholly convincing Owen's subtle argument from Anaxagoras' ἦν ὁμοῦ πάντα (ibid., p. 323 and n. 10). True, Anaxagoras must here be dealing directly with our passage of Parmenides. True, also, that Anaxagoras cannot have meant to introduce a past tense in the sense "was, but is no longer," because for Anaxagoras things are still together. But I see at present no objection to supposing Anaxagoras to say that, though Parmenides was right in denying ἦν in that sense, it can be used of eternal existents or states of affairs. Which would explain why Anaxagoras states so firmly that the initial state of affairs in some sense still holds.

74. Tarán, *Parmenides*, p. 178. Tarán (p. 177 n. 7) makes very firmly the right point about νῦν. Owen (*Monist* 50 [1966] 332f) draws an argument from Augustine's (and other Christians') conception of God's ever-present but timeless eternity. But Owen's non-theological parallel (p. 333) does not seem apt; we do not seek another example of "leaving some expression its familiar use while cutting it off from its family connections in the language," but another example of this particular use of νῦν which is not theologically conditioned. Augustine and his fellows were, as W. M. Kneale (cited by Owen) pointed out, constrained to find some link between God's timeless eternity and his personality; there is no trace of such a

problem in Parmenides to excuse what therefore remains, on Owen's interpretation, a blunder.

75. Tarán argues further that τίνα γὰρ γένναν should explain what immediately precedes, but this is a less cogent argument. For, supposing the whole programme to end, after all, at συνεχές, the question τίνα γὰρ γένναν could without strain constitute or begin an argument for the first item in the programme. But there is no *need* to produce this state of affairs by imagining Parmenides so incapable of organizing his argument as to include a demonstration in his demonstrand.

76. There have been a number of misunderstandings of this argument, from which I select two for comment here, not only because they tend to destroy the arrangement of Parmenides' paragraph, but also because the scholarly prestige of their authors may give these particular ideas wide currency. (1) K. von Fritz, *Sprachlicher Ausdruck* p. 14, makes Parmenides' argument run: Either Being from Being (which is not becoming) or Being from not-Being, which does not exist. I regret that I find nothing in the text whatever to support the phrase I have bracketed and see nothing in logic to support it either. There is no reason why Parmenides should not have seen the alternative possibility of some Being other than the first arising from Being: this would indeed be becoming, it is what he speaks of at B8.12–13 (reading ἐκ τοῦ ἐόντος), and he does not say it would not be becoming. (2) Guthrie, *HGP* II p. 99 appears to say that B8.12–13 contains the proof that nothing *exists* (my italics) besides what is. But the lines surely are a denial of any *coming-to-be* of anything besides what is (out of what is). The argument here *assumes* that there can be nothing besides what is, but these two lines do not contain any *proof* of the proposition so assumed.

77. See Tarán ad loc.

78. E.g., B omits οὐ at Plato *Euthydemus* 286e8 (before πάνυ cf. BTWf at *Meno* 98b2), as does Y at *Politicus* 264d10; Plato *Laches* 179e1 ὅτι]οὐ B. At *Laches* 197d1 BTW have probably inserted μή. At *Meno* 73a7 οὐ om. F (cf. 84d1); *Meno* 87e6 οὐχί om. P; *Meno* 89e5 οὐ inseruit W. *Meno* 93e8 οὐδὲν BTWf: μηδέ F; *Meno* 99c7 μὴ om. F; *Meno* 100a1 οὐκ (before ἄνευ) inseruit Clem. Al. At Aristotle *Metaphys.* 983a17, E has οὐκ with Asc^c against the other sources, at 984b12 William of Moerbeke inserts a negative.

79. For which see Appendix.

80. The latest support for Karsten's reading πῶς δ' ἂν ἔπειτ' ἀπόλοιτο ἐόν; for the MSS πῶς δ' ἂν ἔπειτα πέλοι τὸ ἐόν; comes from Guthrie, *HGP* II p. 27, on the grounds that, representing an alteration of but one letter, "a reference to perishing, balancing that to coming-into-being in the second half of the line, seems the more probable." It is not, however, just this line which has to be balanced. The next, connected with this by γάρ, reasons first against becoming and then against future being. The chiasmus (noted in my text) is obvious, the structure is clear, the argument beautifully presented: not even a single letter need or should be changed. (There is naturally no need to manufacture a reference to destruction in 8.19 for 8.21 to refer back to, since there is similarly no direct mention of destruction in the argument immediately preceding its denunciation at 8.14.)

81. *Parmenides*, pp. 104f.

82. Objection could be taken to the change of subject from τὸ ἐόν (in all the

other verbs of lines 19–20) to "the subject of discourse" (in the case of οὐκ ἔστιν). But the objection is not cogent; there is a parallel at B8.9, where the subject of οὐκ ἔστι is "the subject," not the expected "not-Being," nor Being (as could also be expected, since it is represented by μιν as the subject of φῦν and is the topic discussed in the whole passage, lines 5–15 ἀλλ' ἔχει). The change of grammatical subject might appear more abrupt and striking in line 20 than at line 9, but appearances would deceive; for at 15–16, preceding 20, the question is (as at 20) not whether "what is" is or is not (which would scarcely have needed decision) but whether "the subject of discourse" is or is not (which was decided at B2 and B6).

83. Cf. Tugwell at *CQ* n.s. 14 (1964) 37.

84. This is another reason why it is essential to read οὐδέ ποτ' ἐκ τοῦ ἐόντος at B8.12.

85. It is surprising to find that (unless I am mistaken) Owen does not discuss this second passage at all in either of his papers on Parmenides, and that Guthrie does not discuss it in this connection.

86. A. H. Coxon at *CQ* 28 (1934) 136 n. 1 points out that Parmenides often starts with a statement of his demonstrand and then passes backwards through the stages of demonstrating it; cf. also Verdenius, *Parmenides: Some Comments*, p. 33. Of course, Parmenides repeats the demonstrand at or near the end of each such argument.

87. Tarán's denial that Parmenides *identified* not-Being and void (*Parmenides*, pp. 99f) may be accepted, but there is no reason to deny that Parmenides' not-Being may have *included* void (which after all differs from Being), perhaps in an ill-defined sense.

88. Cf. *PQ* 17 (1967) 165.

89. For the adverbial interpretation of ὁμοῖον I gratefully follow Owen, *CQ* n.s. 10 (1960) 92 and n. 4.

90. I see no reason whatever to suppose with Guthrie, *HGP* II pp. 32f, that degrees of being in Parmenides have to be understood as degrees of density, and do not see why this should be supposed to make Parmenides' language more intelligible.

91. See Owen at *CQ* n.s. 10 (1960) 96 n. 4.

92. Ibid., 97 n. 2.

93. Ibid., 97.

94. Guthrie, *HGP* II p. 34 n. 1, admits that πᾶν ἔστιν ὁμοῖον rests on line 11, οὕτως ἢ πάμπαν πελέναι χρεών ἐστιν ἢ οὐχί, which excluded a bit-by-bit process of temporal generation. It is not clear to me how this could have as a consequence that Being cannot exist *in varying degrees* in different places; by this admission Guthrie, though denying Owen's conclusion that 22ff are temporal, has in effect surrendered to Owen. Furley (*Two Studies*, p. 61 n. 3) also accepts Owen's derivation of 8.22 from 8.11 but refuses to believe 8.22ff spatial. He cites the parallel of Melissus on the infinite. But Parmenides could not move from the temporal to the spatial without vitiating the whole chain of argument, which leads from the denial of difference to the denial of process.

95. Fränkel, *WuF* p. 211 n. 2, points out that it was differentiation against

which the Eleatic thesis was directed and which stood to be defended by common sense. Also sound on this passage is Tugwell at *CQ* n.s. 14 (1964) 37ff.

96. See Guthrie, *HGP* II p. 36 with refs., and Stokes at *PQ* 17 (1967) 165. The present text is only an adumbration of the argument, which I have given below more fully. The limits are to be taken metaphorically, as by Owen (*CQ* n.s. 10 [1960] 99) and Tarán (*Parmenides*, pp. 115ff); D. J. Furley (*Two Studies*, p. 58) finds then a problem in Empedocles' having taken Parmenides' simile literally. How much of a problem one finds here depends on how high is one's opinion of Empedocles' ability to appreciate a profound philosophical subtlety; I cannot say the problem worries me very much. Parmenides' limits are probably those of invariancy, and the completeness of Being excludes alteration alike of quality or of place. Parmenides surely cannot have argued that Being is complete and therefore limited and therefore unmoved and unchanging. Such an argument is too absurd to tolerate for a moment in a thinker of this calibre.

P. Bicknell, at *Phronesis* 12 (1967) 1ff, wants ἀκίνητον to refer only to change, and a new argument against motion to begin at 8.29; but there is denial of change in the statement ταὐτόν ... [μένει] at 8.29f, then of motion in ταὐτῷ ... [μένει], and then of difference in καθ' ἑαυτό τε κεῖται in the same line. The themes are here inextricably mixed. See further on this passage below, and observe that since I do not regard the πείρας of 8.31 as physical, I at least am not committed to a physical argument against motion even if 29–33 are a separate argument.

97. *CQ* n.s. 10 (1960) 94 n. 1.

98. Guthrie's suggestion (*HGP* II p. 36) that "the banishment of becoming and perishing substantiates only the impossibility of beginning or ceasing" is thus wrong in Parmenidean logic; change of place is excluded by the banishment of γένεσις (which includes not only "changelessness" of quality) in the same way as any other change.

99. I avoid using διά τε χρόα φανὸν ἀμείβειν as an example of κίνησις in case this be a subordinate species rather of γένεσις. I doubt if Tarán (*Parmenides*, p. 110) is right in supposing that for Parmenides change and motion imply *one another*, though certainly motion implies change. Both, however, could be described by the word κίνησις; this seems to me to be clear from Plato *Parmenides* 138b–c and *Theaetetus* 181d5–6. I doubt if κίνησις covered every type of change (surely not total destruction?) but believe normal Greek usage to have included among κινήσεις both change of quality and locomotion.

100. I am conscious of owing much at this point to conversation with Mr. A. H. Coxon but hesitate to commit him to any views of mine.

101. Fränkel (*WuF* p. 191) wanted to read μίμνει and then in 8.30 μενεῖ. To this Kranz objected that a positive future was dubious for Parmenides. The objection is not cogent: it is possible that μενεῖ is merely a manner of speaking, a way of saying that Being will not move: in any case, there is no conflict between the "remaining" of Being and the denial of future (without present) being at 8.5 and 8.19f. I do not believe that Parmenides wanted to deny that future verbs in general could apply to his subject; provided they are verbs of standing still and not of change. Admittedly, on Parmenidean principles there ought to be no moment other than that occupied by his subject any more than there ought to be

another place than the one it occupies. But I fail to find any trace of this point in the Way of Truth; one recalls Melissus' troubles with spatial extension, for which see below.

Tarán (*Parmenides*, p. 114) adopts a strange combination of views. He wants Parmenides' Being not to be atemporal, but he excludes the future on the grounds that "Being is eternal, so that it can be expressed at any moment by ἔστιν; because it is always the same it is impossible to distinguish in it the difference that past or future imply." But Tarán denies that 8.5 and 8.19f argue for the total exclusion of past and future, leaving no ground left on which to rest such a total exclusion.

102. See Aristotle *Phys.* 239b6 with the commentators.

103. Tarán's interpretation of καθ' ἑαυτό as "self-sufficient" (*Parmenides*, p. 159) is inadequately supported.

104. Guthrie, *HGP* II pp. 37ff takes Parmenides' πείρατα literally here (for which view see nn. 96 above and 139 below) and makes B8.26ff prove that Being is not only unmoved but limited. This is difficult to reconcile with the γάρ at 8.30, which presumably indicates that, whatever the statement about limits here means, it is not an additional point but explains (I should say "argues for") either the statement about Being remaining, or the whole set of statements beginning at 8.29 ταὐτόν. In either case, the logic would be childish beyond at least one reader's belief if Guthrie's interpretation of the limits were sound. At *HGP* II p. 44 Guthrie argued (see n. 69 above): "Sometimes a clause made dependent on another through a 'for' ... is little more than a repetition in different words; sometimes it expresses the conclusion in a religious or metaphorical form." But, even if the γάρ at 8.30 has this force, the sentence can hardly constitute a new and supposedly important point in Parmenides' conception of Being; if the limits represent the absence of motion and change in a religious or metaphorical form, then the assertion of them is no novelty. And why does the epithet "limited" find no place in the programme?

105. A large number of interpretations of ἐν ᾧ πεφατισμένον ἐστιν are discussed and adequately criticized by Tarán, *Parmenides*, pp. 123ff. It is distressing to see how few of them pay any attention to the perfect tense; e.g., Burnet at *EGP*[4] p. 176 has "as to which it is uttered" (and I am unable to understand Burnet's n. 1). Von Fritz's explanation (*CP* 40 [1945] 238, taking φατίζω to mean "unfold" or something similar rather than merely "express") is open to this criticism, though not, I think, to Tarán's argument that φατίζω only means "unfold" in the sense "express"—see 8.60, where "express" would surely be a mistranslation. Tarán himself follows Albertelli (*Gli Eleati*, p. 147) in translating the relative clause "in what has been expressed," glossed by Tarán (p. 128) as "i.e. in the thought." But this gloss too makes little of the perfect tense, and the syntax implied by this rendering is (*pace* Albertelli and Tarán) hardly "assai frequente" or "normal Greek." It makes ἐν ᾧ ... stand for ἐν τούτῳ ὅ ...; the attraction of the relative pronoun out of the *nominative* into another case is comparatively infrequent, and I have yet to find an instance in which there is in the relative clause a periphrastic tense with a nominative participle agreeing with a subject nominative now no longer visible (or audible). More plausible Greek

syntax is given by interpreting ἐν ᾧ ... as ἐν τούτῳ ἐν ᾧ ... The clause then means "in the [conditions and circumstances] in which it has been revealed." The goddess would then be saying "without Being, in the state in which I have described it, you will not find thought." The effect of her remark would be that only Being, exactly as the goddess has up to now described it, can be the object of thought. The goddess has by now applied to Being all the necessary attributes; her revelation is virtually complete; and what follows is summary, repetition, and clarificatory metaphor. On this interpretation, though it is put forward with the greatest diffidence, at least the perfect tense is appropriate, and φατίζω here can now (for what the point is worth) bear the same meaning as at 8.60.

106. This alone would suffice to prove that differentiations not arising in the course of time are indeed discussed in the part of the poem ending at 8.40.

107. See Tarán, e.g., *Parmenides*, p. 108.

108. Mansfeld, *Offenbarung*, pp. 78ff, denies the direct attachment of B3 to B2. His main grounds are: (1) Plotinus ignored B2 in interpreting B3; Aristotle, on the other hand, took B3 as the axiom on which the argument of B2 rested: from this discrepancy Mansfeld deduces a certain independence between B2 and B3. (2) B2 and B3 are referred to in B8 at separate places, viz. at 8.15ff and 8.34ff; and, though if B2 and 3 are consecutive, B3 is the basis of B2, in B8 the relation is reversed, and B8.15ff, corresponding to B2, is the basis of 8.34ff, corresponding to B3. Against (1) it should surely not need stressing that late (or even classical) philosophers were scarcely incapable of taking a line out of context to suit their own book. Plotinus' difference from Aristotle proves little, even if he did read Parmenides at first hand. Against (2), there is already implicit in Parmenides a circle of argument: B8.34ff argues that the object of thought and what is are inseparable because there *is* nothing other than Being; if we look for the reason why there is nothing other than Being, we are given answers that depend directly on the assumption that nothing except Being is thinkable.

B3 fits quite well immediately after B2; to the sheer stonewalling of οὐ γὰρ ἀνυστόν it adds another block, namely, that all that can be the object of thought is what can be. (This Mansfeld seems to agree is the meaning of B3, though he takes the syntax in accordance with the literal translation "thinking and Being are the same.")

109. This is presumably what Parmenides means when denying the coexistence of Being and not-Being (see Guthrie, *HGP* II p. 40).

110. Most recently Guthrie, *HGP* II pp. 43ff.

111. The point is made by Tarán, *Parmenides*, p. 158, that 8.44–48 "show the point of comparison with a sphere to be that Being is undifferentiated." Strictly true of 47–48, Tarán's point is valid and important.

112. This makes against Tugwell's view (*CQ* n.s. 14 [1964] 40) that the lines are designed to prove the new predicate of Being's regularity and balance.

113. Tarán, *Parmenides*, pp. 151ff, esp. 159.

114. *CQ* 27 (1933) 103.

115. E.g., *Plato and Parmenides*, p. 35.

116. It is worth noting that he nowhere even reduces mortals to the statement that Being is both one and many in order to point to the obvious contradiction.

I am unable to see anything in the text to correspond to K. von Fritz's words (*Sprachlicher Ausdruck*, p. 15): "Nähme man den Gegenteil an, so wäre das Seiende Einheit und Vielheit zugleich. Das ist ein Widerspruch."

117. Not even the confusions in Parmenides' argument are based on ignorance of the ambiguities of "one" or of "many." Simplicius (*in Phys.* 118.20) was wrong in accusing Parmenides of confusing τὰ τῷ λόγῳ ἕν and τῷ ἀριθμῷ ἕν. Parmenides confuses "other than Being" with "not-Being"; this leads to the abandonment alike of τὰ τῷ λόγῳ πολλά and τὰ τῷ ἀριθμῷ πολλά.

118. Tarán, *Parmenides*, pp. 216ff; Guthrie, *HGP* II pp. 50 and 54; Mansfeld, *Offenbarung*, pp. 123–131 and elsewhere (following in some respects Schwabl, *WS* 66 [1953] 50ff).

119. Tarán, *Parmenides*, p. 220; Schwabl at *WS* 66 (1953) 53ff; and Mansfeld, Schwabl's citation of Aesch. *P.V.* 209f I do not understand; the relation between Themis' many names and one μορφή is different from that between Parmenides' two forms and their alleged unity.

120. Cornford, *Plato and Parmenides*, p. 46; Untersteiner, *Parmenide*, pp. CLXXf; perhaps H. Gomperz, *Pyschologische Beobachtungen*, p. 16.

121. Diels in *VS*, Kranz, etc.

122. E.g., A. Diès, *Platon, Parménide*, p. 14.

123. Neither Croissant (*Mélanges Desrousseaux*, pp. 99ff) nor Tarán *argues* for the belief that the first half of 8.54 is part of mortal belief, and Fränkel, *WuF* p. 180 n. 1, has a powerful argument against it.

124. See Tarán ad loc.

125. *Parmenides*, p. 219, and *HGP* II p. 50; see also Shorey at *AJP* 21 (1900) 204f.

126. See Croissant, *Mélanges Desrousseaux*, p. 103; Tarán, *Parmenides*, p. 218; Mansfeld, *Offenbarung*, p. 124.

127. *HGP* II p. 50.

128. See further Tarán, *Parmenides*, p. 220 n. 49 (on p. 221).

129. *Pythagoreans and Eleatics*, p. 39.

130. II p. 181.

131. *Offenbarung*, p. 124.

132. *WuF* p. 180.

133. Croissant, *Mélanges Desrousseaux*, pp. 102f; Raven, *Pythagoreans and Eleatics*, pp. 39f; KR p. 281 n. 1.

134. Cornford, *Plato and Parmenides*, p. 46.

135. So KR p. 281.

136. Croissant, *Mélanges Desrousseaux*, pp. 102ff, followed by Cherniss (*JHI* 12 [1951] p. 338 and n. 101, citing for some reason unknown to me Plato *Sophist* 243d–244b) and Tarán, *Parmenides*, p. 220 n. 49. Verdenius (*Parmenides: Some Comments*, p. 62) rejects their view, but on somewhat insubstantial grounds.

137. Cf., e.g., Hdt. 7.52.2, contrasting it with Hdt. 9.55.4, where Amompharetus' intended action is clearly not so much unnecessary as wrong. At Thuc. 3.40.4 οὐ χρεών means "wrongly."

138. Guthrie, *HGP* II p. 53, cf. pp. 48f.

139. Apart from the point that Parmenides' πείρατα, heavily insisted on by

Guthrie, *HGP* II pp. 48f, are more probably metaphorical, symbolizing the exigencies of logic enjoining invariancy; see Owen at *CQ* n.s. 10 (1960) 99, Tarán, *Parmenides*, pp. 115ff. (Coxon interpreted the πείρατα rightly in connection with the sphere passage at *CQ* 28 [1934] 140.)

140. KR p. 300, rejected rightly by Furley, *Two Studies*, p. 59.

141. Cf. B8 fin.

142. Guthrie, *HGP* II p. 104, suggests that this was "motivated by the thought that, if change is admitted at all, then Heraclitus had *shown* [italics mine] that it must be continuous even if imperceptible." I believe with Guthrie that Heraclitus held change to be continuous, but Heraclitus surely asserted this, rather than proved or argued for it. There is no need to invoke Heraclitus to explain an argument eminently reasonable in itself.

143. J. Jouanna at *REA* 67 (1965) 316 well compares with this passage the sentence from [Hippocrates] *De nat. hom.* 2: εἰ ἓν ἦν ὤνθρωπος, οὐδέποτ' ἂν ἤλγεεν· οὐδὲ γὰρ ἂν ἦν ὑφ' οὗ ἀλγήσειεν ἓν ἐών· εἰ δ' οὖν καὶ ἀλγήσειεν, ἀνάγκη καὶ τὸ ἰώμενον ἓν εἶναι· νῦν δὲ πολλά. Precisely what Polybus meant by this ἕν is not easy to say. He is busily combating the theory that man is made of one single stuff, and the words ἓν ἐών ought to refer to that theory. But it is difficult to see why constitution from one homogeneous stuff should prevent man from being hurt. It may be suggested, most tentatively, that the Hippocratic has confused the argument; Melissus saw that pain was inconsistent with the unique exclusiveness of Being, and the doctor has applied the argument to something ἕν in another sense. The slip was perhaps facilitated by Melissus' use of ὅμοιον.

144. Here also (see n. 142 above and Chap. IX n. 14 below) I find no reason to suppose Melissus tilting at his fellow philosophers rather than at common sense, which does, after all, speak of things as πυκνά or ἀραιά (especially in medical writers).

145. Against the view that this argument represents a foreshadowing of Atomism, see Calogero, *Studi sull' Eleatismo*, p. 83 n. 1, and Guthrie, *HGP* II pp. 117f.

146. Many have followed Zeller in doubting Simplicius' two explicit statements to the effect that this argument was a positive contribution to Melissus' account of Being and have supposed it rather a part of reduction to absurdity of common sense (somewhat on the lines of B8). For this rejection of Simplicius only one argument (as opposed to nebulous and general suspicion) has been produced: this is that the possession of no parts is inconsistent with the spatial infinity of Being in Melissus' B2 and B3. We may reasonably find H. Gomperz' parallels (*Hermes* 67 [1932] 155ff) unconvincing and should reject with Guthrie (*HGP* II p. 110 n. 2) Vlastos' suggestion that B2 and 3 imply only temporal infinity. But that is not the end of the matter. Owen wrote (*CQ* n.s. 10 [1960] pp. 100f) of the ladder of ordinary language, to be thrown away at the summit of the argument. This, it seems to me, is the heart of the matter. Melissus could not but argue that, being one, his Being could have no parts. He also could not but reject a limited Being; a beginning in time or in space was impossible. What he did not see clearly enough was that he could abolish limit without making Being unlimited. He did not perceive the way followed by Plato's "Parmenides" (137d, rightly expounded by Cornford, *Plato and Parmenides*, p. 118). In this he was fettered by the bonds of

ordinary language: wishing to say something negative, he found in ἄπειρον, the only word available to him, a positive meaning. The resulting contradiction was made all the more inevitable by the parallelism between time and space in Eleatic reasoning; Melissus saw no reason why he should not make his Being extended in time, and extension in space followed. The contradiction, due to the inadequacy of ordinary language, could only be left unreconciled. It is relevant to observe that Plato's "Parmenides" also leaves inexplicit the reconciliation between "partless" and ἄπειρον. I cannot find here a reason to reject the two definite statements of Simplicius; see further KR pp. 303f, whose arguments, though not absolutely conclusive, seem to me to establish a fair probability. Two points may be added: (1) Zeno had argued that what was of null extension was non-existent, thus closing an avenue to Melissus; and (2) the problem could hardly be solved by giving Being a mysterious non–bodily extension, since parts would still be *logically* distinguishable in such an extension.

147. Fränkel, *WuF* p. 212 n. 3, appositely cites *Parm.* 137c–d (see esp. d1); at *Parm.* 159c5 only *true* unity is excluded by the possession of parts. For Zeno the case is more doubtful; and, since I have interpreted Zeno from Melissus at p. 211 below, it is dangerous now to interpret Melissus from Zeno. But observe the statement of Simpl. *in Phys.* 138.4ff: Ζήνωνος ... λέγοντος ὡς, εἰ μέγεθος ἔχοι τὸ ὂν καὶ διαιροῖτο, πολλὰ τὸ ὂν καὶ οὐχ ἓν ἔτι ἔσεσθαι (?leg. ἔσται). This seems to be independent evidence for Zeno's meaning.

148. Similarly, it is not clear precisely what Melissus meant by B5, εἰ μὴ ἓν εἴη περανεῖ πρὸς ἄλλο. He may have meant to include internal boundaries, making ἕν mean not merely "unique" but also (because there was nothing other than Being) "homogeneous"; or he may have had in mind only external boundaries.

149. I confess I cannot attribute to Melissus the argument against mixture at *MXG* 974a23ff, despite persuasive advocacy from Guthrie (*HGP* II pp. 103f and 115f). The argument given by the *MXG* is as follows: mixture is to be ruled out as implying that the One is many (this much *could* be Melissan), that not-Being is born, and Being destroyed, which are all impossible. If the One is a mixture of many things, and things are plural and move into one another, and mixture is either a unified synthesis or an overlapping superposition of one thing on another: in the first kind of mixture the ingredients could be distinguished on separation, and in the case of superposition the lower layers could be distinguished on removal of the other. Neither of these two things in fact (according to Melissus as reported) happens. Much depends on the exact meaning attached to the last clause, ὧν οὐδέτερον συμβαίνειν. Apelt (cited by Guthrie, *HGP* II p. 116 n. 3) wanted this to mean that neither was compatible with unity. But this is an unlikely rendering of an evident appeal not to logic (to be compatible is not one of the senses of συμβαίνειν given by Bonitz, *Index Aristotelicus*, 713a10ff), but to fact. If Melissan, such an appeal to fact could only occur in a reductio ad absurdum of common-sense as in B8. But against such an interpretation two points should be urged: (1) the *MXG* itself represents the argument as being about Melissus' Being, and as on a plane with the arguments against change of "cosmos" or quality; (2) if the argument is a reductio ad absurdum of common-sense or of Empedoclean ideas, then the final ὧν οὐδέτερον συμβαίνειν is a plain

misstatement of fact: in both the common-sense and Empedoclean world such things do habitually occur. I conclude that at least from 974a23 καὶ γάρ ... the argument is not even Eleatic, let alone Melissan. I do not find this conclusion any the less plausible for the fact that the *MXG* paraphrases many Melissan arguments more or less exactly, since I cannot see that a gift for more or less exact paraphrase is incompatible with a penchant for unsubtle invention.

CHAPTER VI: EMPEDOCLES

1. See esp. Guthrie's chapter on Empedocles in *HGP* II; U. Hölscher, "Weltzeiten und Lebenszyklus," *Hermes* 93 (1965) 7–33; F. Solmsen, "Love and Strife in Empedocles' Cosmology," *Phronesis* 10 (1965) 109–148; D. O'Brien, "Empedocles' Cosmic Cycle," *CQ* n.s. 17 (1967) 29–40.
2. O'Brien, "Cosmic Cycle," pp. 34f, on the subjunctive γένηται at B35.4.
3. See Van Groningen cited by Solmsen, "Love and Strife," p. 111 n. 5.
4. See Burnet, *EGP*[4] p. 207, who renders γένεσις apparently as "generation." Guthrie, *HGP* II p. 153, seems to think Burnet's rendering "generation" merely a translator's expedient not meant to be taken literally; if he is right, I owe an apology to the shades of Burnet. Hölscher, "Weltzeiten und Lebenszyklus," p. 30 n. 3, distinguishes Zeller's "Entstehung der Dinge" from Bignone's "un mondo organico"; the reference to Zeller should presumably be to ZN p. 947 n., but I have located neither the cited German nor the cited Italian phrase in their respective works, though closely similar phrases do occur. Whether there is any distinction between Zeller and Bignone in this matter is doubtful; a careful rereading leaves Zeller's precise intentions in some doubt, but I incline to the belief that his conception is something like Bignone's (rash though it may seem to challenge Hölscher on his native language).
5. Hölscher, "Weltzeiten und Lebenszyklus," pp. 30ff.
6. *HGP* II p. 153.
7. See, e.g., Solmsen, "Love and Strife," p. 138 n. 79. Hölscher, "Weltzeiten und Lebenszyklus," p. 31, objects that θρυφθεῖσα is a less simple word than θρεφθεῖσα, but it is not so uncommon as to rule out such a mistake of a scribe. The particle theory of matter on which Hölscher further relies is problematic. See further n. 42 below.
8. Apart from Hölscher, Zeller (ZN p. 946 n. 2, on p. 947) mentions older adherents of this view.
9. See Heinz Munding at *Hermes* 82 (1954) 136f. (I accept Munding's demonstration at his pp. 133f that this fragment opens Empedocles' main exposition but do not believe that ἀκίνητοι refers to θνητοί. Panzerbieter's conjecture ἀκινητί has perhaps received less attention than it deserves.)
10. *Hermes* 47 (1912) 37 n. 2 on p. 38.
11. Solmsen, "Love and Strife," pp. 129f and 136f.
12. As it is by E. L. Minar, *Phronesis* 8 (1963) 143 n. 2, following Cherniss, *ACPP* pp. 194f, who ignores (with most scholars before Solmsen and Hölscher) the distinction between cosmos and living creatures.

13. Solmsen, "Love and Strife," pp. 124f.
14. Most recently O'Brien, "Cosmic Cycle," pp. 38ff, and Guthrie, *HGP* II pp. 200ff.
15. Aëtius 5.19.5 (DK 31A72), Aristotle *Physics* B8, Simpl. *in Phys.* 371f and 380–382.
16. E.g., Guthrie, *HGP* II p. 205; Hölscher, "Weltzeiten und Lebenszyklus," p. 24.
17. E.g., Guthrie, *HGP* II p. 206, and very explicitly O'Brien, "Cosmic Cycle," p. 38. See for the view taken here especially Solmsen, "Love and Strife," pp. 133f (but I cannot altogether accept his remark that "Empedocles' words suggest that fire by itself had the impulse"; see B35.6, quoted in my text).
18. Guthrie, *HGP* II p. 207 and n. 1; O'Brien, "Cosmic Cycle," p. 38.
19. See for one view Minar at *Phronesis* 8 (1963) 143, following Zeller; for the other see previous note. Guthrie's criticism of Minar rests on a failure to see that the process of differentiation is not Strife's only function, nor is the production of similars the only kind of unifying performed by Love. But Guthrie is right (or at least consistent) at p. 200 n. 2 against Minar. Minar argues from the silence about sexual intercourse in the world of Love which has to be attributed to Aëtius if we divide the cosmogony; Guthrie, once having divided Aëtius' account, rightly does not hesitate to accuse him further of such an omission.

Guthrie p. 207 n. 1 draws attention to the absence of sexuality in the god, at frags. B29 and 134; but this does not, I think, invalidate the point that sexless human beings are imperfect human beings. The point of removing μήδεα γεννήεντα from the god at B29 is to make his shape perfectly spherical (whence the emphasis on the absence of other excrescences as well) and at frag. 134 is to make him as non-bodily as possible (whence the absence of other members). I see no reason to believe that in either case the main point is to make him sexless.

20. Simpl. *in Phys.* 382.20 is used to prove the division of the οὐλοφυεῖς τύποι by Bignone, *Empedocle*, pp. 580f (introducing the unprobative parallel of Anaximander), Guthrie, *HGP* II p. 211 n. 1f, and O'Brien, "Cosmic Cycle," p. 38. But grave doubts remain. Simplicius (382.5ff) suggests two possible meanings for the Aristotelian phrase (*Phys.* 199b9) καὶ τὸ "οὐλοφυές (sic) μὲν πρῶτα" σπέρμα ἦν. The first version is that Empedocles is under attack for having himself undermined the view that a seed was unnecessary by having a seed, namely, the οὐλοφυές. The οὐλοφυές Simplicius describes as ὕδωρ ἐνεργείᾳ but δυνάμει ἄνθρωποι. This is clearly based on a combination of B62.5 (Simplicius has just quoted B62) with the notion of a seed derived from Aristotle. Alternatively (μήποτε δέ, 382.8) Simplicius supposes that neither hen nor egg (animal nor seed) can come before the other; the point is, as the next sentence shows, that each must come after the others. Aristotle's attack on this basis (οὖν) would be (ἐφιστάνοι ἄν) that Empedocles fails to have seed *always* before the animal (Simplicius adds that it is obvious that animal comes before seed). Aristotle is then supposed to correct his own attack with the words καὶ "τὸ οὐλοφυὲς μὲν πρῶτα" σπέρμα ἦν, since Empedocles would have seen after all that a seed must come before an animal. Having reached the end of this exposition, Simplicius remarks on his own initiative (382.15) how appropriate the word οὐλοφυές is to a seed. "For an οὐλοφυές in

the proper sense (κυρίως) is that which all over itself (καθ' ὅλον ἑαυτό) is the whole of (πᾶν ἐστιν) that thing precisely, whatever it is (ὅπερ ἄν ἐστι with doubtful syntax), since the division has not yet taken place." Still in the same generalizing vein, Simplicius goes on to point out that seeds correspond well with this sense of οὐλοφυές, since every part of a seed is all the parts of the body. The parts of the body, on the other hand (this is what distinguishes body from seed), are not each of them the other parts as well as itself, since in the body the necessary distinction has taken place and the οὐλοφυές has been divided. It is important to notice that Simplicius is not here talking about what happens in Empedocles' poem at all. He is talking about Aristotle's comparison of the "whole-natured" to a seed. He deduces, from a (quite mistaken, or at least unique) notion of what οὐλοφυής ought to mean, its similarity to a seed. He then expounds how, given this sense, an οὐλοφυής would differ from a body: it would have to be divided to make a body. But we who do not accept Simplicius' unnecessarily elaborate definition of οὐλοφυής are under no obligation to accept all the details of his comparison with a seed or to believe them to have any but the remotest connection with Empedocles' text.

21. Aristotle does not say at 199a33ff that limbs came together to form man; he implies only that they cannot have come together to form the monsters, saying that monsters arise from the corruption of some ἀρχή such as the seed—you cannot have animals formed without seed. This, as Ross says ad loc., is probably a subsidiary argument against Empedocles' account of the monsters. Empedocles himself does sometimes admit the priority of a seed—or so Aristotle thinks, making the οὐλοφυές of his faulty memory into a seed. It is only Simplicius, in the effort to interpret Aristotle's difficult argument, who says that men are formed direct from limbs, and Simplicius, as O'Brien obligingly admits ("Cosmic Cycle," pp. 38f), is under suspicion "that he has himself produced men and women from separate limbs in order to illustrate a passage from Aristotle." (I may remark that Kranz's account at *Empedokles*, p. 54, seems to me fantastic; he imagines fully and rightly formed men and women unable to reproduce themselves!)

O'Brien further cites Aristotle *De gen. animalium* 722b11; but this passage does not say, as O'Brien makes it say, that man and woman are a σύμβολον of each other, but rather that each *contributes* a σύμβολον (to be precise, "as it were" a σύμβολον) to the seed—a wholly different doctrine by no means to be confused with Aristophanes' story in the *Symposium* of Plato. (But it is not inconceivable that Plato's Aristophanes has influenced the *language* in which Empedocles' theory is expounded in the *De gen. animalium*.)

O'Brien's further citation of Simplicius' πρὸ τῆς τῶν ἀνδρείων καὶ γυναικείων σωμάτων διαρθρώσεως (*in Phys.* 381.29f) proves little, since he wrongly ignores the probability that Simplicius' wording is a reminiscence of Aristotle *Phys.* 199b10 διήρθρωται (only one line below the passage on which Simplicius is here commenting).

22. O'Brien adds the further argument that the limbs and the whole-natured creatures both sprang from the earth and so were the first to be born in their respective worlds. He does not refer even in a footnote (this being an abridged version of a longer work, see "Cosmic Cycle," p. 29, n. 1) to Aëtius' remarks at

5.7.1 (Diels, *Dox.*, p. 419). This, quoted by DK at A81, says it ἱστορεῖται that the first males were born from the earth in the south and the first females in the north. Solmsen, "Love and Strife," p. 135 n. 74, is perhaps wise to be cautious about the phrase ἐκ τῆς γῆς in this account. Yet we are hardly in a position to prove it mistaken. Varro, cited at A72, is perhaps too vague in support, declaring that Empedocles *natos homines ex terra ait ut blitum*, which could conceivably be attached to the arrival of the limbs on the scene. Censorinus, it must be admitted, actually says (also at A72) that the separate limbs were born from the earth and then subsequently *coisse et effecisse solidi hominis materiam igni simul et umori permixtam*. But I should be reluctant to take Censorinus' word against Aëtius', and in any case Censorinus says that the *material* for men, not the actual men, came from the limbs, and it is difficult to be sure what exactly he means by this. The material is *igni simul et umori permixta*, which recalls the οὐλοφυεῖς τύποι at B62.4–5, ἀμφοτέρων ὕδατός τε καὶ εἴδεος αἶσαν ἔχοντες. It would be very difficult indeed to prove that the "whole-natured" forms and the limbs were the *only* living creatures to be born afresh from the earth. I wish we knew what lay behind D. L. 9.29, where Zeno is confused with Empedocles and said to have believed γένεσίν τε ἀνθρώπων ἐκ γῆς εἶναι. In any case, it seems to me that to argue from terrestrial origin to primacy in the relevant worlds would be inconclusive and dangerously a priori reasoning.

There is the further point that B62 occurs in Empedocles' Second Book, and the formation of bones (B96) in the First Book (see Simplicius quoted by Diels with the fragments concerned). This could be taken to imply that Love's formation of bones and the zoogony of B62 cannot form part of a single sequence; but it does not in fact imply it necessarily, since it is not known how arbitrary was the division between the Books of Empedocles, nor to whom it was ultimately due.

23. Cf. Minar at *Phronesis* 8 (1963) 142 with his valuable note.

24. I have quoted A. L. Peck's Loeb translation.

25. There is not the slightest reason to believe the οὐλοφυεῖς τύποι to have been bisexual. For some strong arguments against associating Empedocles' "whole-natured forms" with Aristophanes' hermaphrodites in Plato's *Symposium* see Guthrie, *HGP* II p. 205 n. 2, and Solmsen's warning, "Love and Strife," p. 135 n. 76. The point that bisexual creatures appear among the monsters at B61 surely rules out the bisexual interpretation of the "whole-natured forms." That interpretation is not reinforced by the argument (O'Brien, "Cosmic Cycle," p. 38) that the οὐλοφυεῖς have (presumably equal) shares of fire and water and that these are the male and female elements respectively. This equality could, evidently, as plausibly imply asexuality as bisexuality. The rest of O'Brien's arguments—no more substantial than this—have been dealt with already. (Guthrie appears, I think, at *HGP* II p. 209 to imply that trees are like the "whole-natured forms" in being bisexual; but this I take to be a slip of the pen.)

26. Only one piece of evidence exists to my knowledge which *might* indicate a combination of cosmogony and zoogony in the same period, and that is the statement of Aëtius (5.26.4, A70) that trees were the first living things to grow out of the earth, πρὶν τὸν ἥλιον περιαπλωθῆναι and before the distinction of night and day. This statement obviously links zoogony with cosmogony. But it

does not tell us that there was anything more than a single incidental remark, perhaps in the middle of the account of our world, to this effect. It does not show that there was a complete zoogony attached to a solid and complete cosmogony. No connected cosmogony would be necessary to account for Aëtius' remark here. It is not certain from the texts concerning them whether trees were formed early in the rise of Strife or of Love; the MSS of Aëtius have in connection with their mixture the word συμμετρίαν, but Galen (Diels, *Dox.*, p. 647.5) had apparently ἀμετρίαν, from which Diels proposed to read ἀσυμμετρίαν. Since trees are evidently bisexual, and bisexual creatures appear among the (doubtless early) monsters, it would be plausible to accept the meaning given by Galen.

The continuing lack of a sun is, according to Guthrie, *HGP* II p. 206 n. 3, the reason why the ἐννυχίους ὄρπηκας of men and women are called ἐννυχίους at B62.2. I incline, however, to doubt this, believing Karsten right in thinking the ὄρπηκες to be ἐννύχιοι for the same reason that in Hesiod (*Theogony* 224) Philotes is included among the progeny of Night. Bignone ad loc. (*Empedocle*, p. 450) argues against this that these first creatures were not born of sexual intercourse but from the earth. What gave Bignone the impression that the ἐννύχιοι ὄρπηκες are the same as the οὐλοφυεῖς τύποι I am unable to say; the former could quite naturally be taken to refer to the final development towards which the "whole-natured forms" are only the first step (πρῶτα!).

27. *De gen. et corr.* 334a5, Simpl. *in Phys.* 1123.28ff, etc.

28. This distinction between cosmogony and zoogony is owed to Solmsen, "Love and Strife," esp. p. 120.

29. Both points are rightly made by Hölscher, "Weltzeiten und Lebenszyklus," p. 24.

30. Less easy to explain, admittedly, is the statement by Simplicius at *in Phys.* 1124.2f that Strife makes a world ὅταν ἐπικρατῇ μὴ τελέως. Indeed, this is less easy to account for than Hölscher, "Weltzeiten und Lebenszyklus," p. 22, appears to think. On the theory here adopted we have either to explain this clause as referring to the time when Strife was still making a world (which would constitute a bad parallel with the preceding statement about Love) or to have Simplicius make Empedocles more logical in his construction than he really was. (Or did Simplicius include living creatures made by Love's increase in the world made by Strife and hence have the total cosmos, including creatures, when Strife was not at his peak?)

31. See esp. von Arnim at *Festschrift T. Gomperz*, pp. 17ff; Hölscher, "Weltzeiten und Lebenszyklus," pp. 9ff; O'Brien, "Cosmic Cycle," pp. 31ff; and G. A. Seeck, *Hermes* 95 (1967) 28ff.

32. See bibliography at O'Brien, "Cosmic Cycle," p. 31 n. 11; contra O'Brien himself and Seeck, *Hermes* 95 (1967) 32ff (the latter on very different grounds from the former).

33. We do not know in what respects Aristotle (see Chap. I above) "reduced" all other oppositions to that between one and many, but direct general equivalence is hardly a likely guess even for Aristotle's inexperienced youth. Associations in the Presocratics do not prove anything relevant either; for a list see O'Brien, "Cosmic Cycle," p. 32—a list which, particularly with the inclusion of Anaxagoras,

scrapes the bottom of the barrel. One reason for the frequent *association* of movement with plurality is that movement implies at least two positions; it was therefore natural for those denying plurality also to deny movement. But this has nothing to do with Empedocles' system, and less still (if possible) to do with Aristotle's exposition of it.

34. See Hölscher, "Weltzeiten und Lebenszyklus," pp. 11ff. O'Brien wants us, rightly disregarding Aristotle's use of χρόνος and χρόνῳ, to interpret this passage from what Aristotle says in other works about Empedocles. But he offers no reason for not interpreting the opening of *Physics* Θ from other passages in the *Physics*, with Simplicius, Hölscher, and now Seeck. Aristotle's statements about Empedocles and his Strife *need* not have been consistent. There is no reason to believe that he had before him any detailed description of Empedocles' reign of Strife. See, e.g., Solmsen, "Love and Strife," pp. 122f, and n. 35 below. Further, *De caelo* 295a30, if we take it at face value, implies that under Strife (1) there was no vortex and (2) the earth at least was stable. This would seem to rule out a universal disorderly motion such as seems inevitable if, taking *De caelo* 300b25-31 at its face value, one postulates accordingly an unordered motion in the materials that lay ready to Love's hand. Something has to go.

35. Plutarch's quotation of B27 as a description of the reign of Strife is clearly wrong; see Hölscher, "Weltzeiten und Lebenszyklus," p. 21. Plutarch's faulty memory may also explain his different text. ἀγλαὸν εἶδος, read by Plutarch, is clearly more commonplace than ὠκέα γυῖα in this context. Some have suggested that ὠκέα γυῖα is unsuitable for the element Fire, even when represented by the Sun, and even that "Earth's shaggy might" (or "kind," for which see Van Groningen at *Mnemosyne* 9 [1956] 221f) is unsuitable for the element and ought to refer to the cosmic mass. So Solmsen, "Love and Strife," p. 132 n. 65, and Minar at *Phronesis* 8 (1963) 131. But this suggestion seems again to underestimate Empedocles' poetic imagination; the coincidence alleged by Solmsen I find unimpressive.

36. So, e.g., Burnet, *EGP*⁴ p. 210 n. 3; C. E. Millerd, *On the Interpretation of Empedocles*, p. 34; and esp. Bignone, *Empedocle*, p. 422. J. B. Bauer (*Hermes* 89 [1961] 367ff) is right in slightly modifying the usual version of this interpretation. It is not the Sphere's solitude or numerical unity which is relevant, but rather other kinds of unity, for which Bauer's "Einssein" seems to an Englishman a better rendering than "Einsamkeit." Jaeger's arguments against this whole line of thought at *TEGP* pp. 141f are not convincing. Eudemus (ap. Simpl. *in Phys.* 1183.28ff) probably thought ἐστήρικται a literal statement, took the indiscernibility of the sun's ὠκέα γυῖα to be appropriately followed by a denial of motion, and his interpretation of μονίη was then a foregone conclusion. B31 he overhastily interpreted in the same sense, unless Simplicius (*in Phys.* 1183.28ff) has supplied these quotations for himself, which in context does not seem likely. The existence of καμμονίη from μένω in Homer proves nothing—homonyms are not unknown to Greek. Jaeger's parallel with Parmenides is inconclusive. The prime property of the Sphere, in which we should expect it to rejoice, is its unity.

37. I believe with Hölscher, "Weltzeiten und Lebenszyklus," pp. 15ff, that Aristotle's δι' ἴσων χρόνων need go back to no more than Empedocles' ἐν μέρει

and need therefore imply no statements on Empedocles' part that we do not possess.

38. It remains to mention one of O'Brien's remarks à propos of the Aristotelian passage (*Phys.* 251a4f) explaining his extraction of the "rest" theory from Empedocles B26. O'Brien urges that the reading ἐνθένδε (not ἐνθένδε ἐκεῖσε) has the stronger MSS support (E, K, and Simpl.) as against FHIJ, which he supposes to have derived their readings from Simplicius' paraphrase. But this does not close the discussion. We have here two quite different recensions, both of which may be ancient; the tradition of Aristotle's *Physics* is contaminated. The omission of ἐκεῖσε, moreover, would be a simple homoeoteleuton. If Aristotle wrote ἐνθένδε alone, meaning "from here on," i.e., "from this world of increasing Strife on," he was surely guilty of *obscurum per obscurius*.

39. The reader may like to compare and contrast my approach with Guthrie's at *HGP* II p. 170.

40. Solmsen at *JHI* 24 (1963) 478 n. 27 points out that Aristotle has employed Empedocles' terms in his analysis of unity.

41. For the exact meaning of this simile see Reinhardt at *CP* 45 (1950) 178.

42. I do not subscribe to such a view, despite Kranz at *Hermes* 47 (1912) 18ff and elsewhere and Guthrie, *HGP* II pp. 149ff. It is doubtful whether Empedocles had any theory of matter at all, in the sense of the atomic theory or the continuum theory. The Empedoclean vocabulary cited by Kranz (*Hermes* 47 [1912] 24f) and endorsed by Guthrie, *HGP* II p. 149 n. 2, is perfectly consistent with an unthinking notion of pieces of matter—some of them no doubt too small to be seen with the naked eye, but so what? Theophr. *De sensu* 11 would imply that these pieces can be very fine—and again so what? *Aristotle* said that it was *a necessary consequence* of Empedocles' views that the elements must lie side by side in small particles in the mixture (*De gen. et corr.* 334a26ff) and again (*De gen. et corr.* 325b5) that Empedocles "almost has to" talk like Leucippus, to explain the doctrine of pores. Aristotle does not say that Empedocles explicitly drew this inference himself; and, if he had so drawn it, it would be difficult to explain the contrast between the confident tone adopted by Aristotle in speaking of Leucippus' atoms with the diffidence of his remark concerning Empedocles, that the Sicilian did not himself carry analysis beyond his elements and that it is therefore impossible to give an account of how masses of them come to be and pass away. If the doxographers chose to turn an Aristotelian inference into an Empedoclean statement, so much the worse for them. It is not in the least probable that problems of infinite divisibility or of indivisibles ever occurred to Empedocles; and, if they did, no contribution of his to their solution is reliably recorded. Reinhardt's arguments at *CP* 45 (1950) 178, if incomplete, are substantially correct.

43. See Solmsen, *ASPW* p. 346, and Stokes at *AGP* 47 (1965) 18f.

44. It was precisely this sense of homogeneity, the absence of perceptible difference, that Aristotle seemed to recognize at *Metaphysics* Δ 1016a17ff, though not in connection with mixture.

45. See B28 and B31: admittedly, "geordnete Fügung" is not, as Jula Kerschensteiner points out (*Kosmos*, p. 128), quite the expression we should be tempted to use of the Sphere. But that Empedocles regarded it as a single organic whole of

parts (note the γυῖα θεοῖο of B31) seems to me certain. Its shape is also perhaps a point in its wholeness; according to Aëtius 2.31.4 (A50) his κόσμος is egg-shaped, and Aristotle (here perhaps not analysing usage) takes the circle as the most "whole" of plane figures and might so regard the Sphere in three-dimensional figures.

46. See passages quoted under B53 by Diels in *PPF*.

47. Contra Minar at *Phronesis* 8 (1963) 139f. Minar seems to me to underrate Empedocles' debt to Pythagoreanism: the importance of numerical ratio in his system is great, despite the deliberate inexactitude of B98 (designed to allow room for improvement in mortal thinking).

48. I am unable to accept Guthrie's interpretation, who (*HGP* II p. 157) refers to "thoughts of peace and loving-kindness" and on his p. 153 translates B17.23 "whereby they think kindly thoughts and do peaceful works"; I doubt if Empedocles' Greek readers would so understand him in such a context. In the "Purifications," however, Love evidently sometimes meant what Guthrie takes it to mean here, and on B110 Guthrie, *HGP* II pp. 230f, has an attractive theory that Empedocles' teachings are to be at least closely associated with Love—obviously not here sexual. But I doubt if this proves very much for B17.

49. Sex brings opposites together and does not in English "mix" or make a single whole of them ("one flesh" is something rather different). But Empedocles cannot for that reason be accused, any more than any other Greek who used μίγνυσθαι in such contexts, of confusing bringing together and mixing, or unities θέσει and μίξει.

50. For some bibliography see Guthrie, *HGP* II p. 202 n. 1.

51. Hölscher, "Weltzeiten und Lebenszyklus," p. 32, aparently takes τοῦτο as referring to some general statement concerning the organic world, to be illustrated from the human organism. But this is not a necessary inference from ὡς δ' αὔτως θάμνοισι etc.; ὡς δ' αὔτως need not in Empedocles introduce the thing illustrated but can add a new point, as it clearly does at B22.4.

52. O'Brien's variant ("Cosmic Cycle," p. 39) on Diels's interpretation suffers from the same defects, as does G. Rudberg's view (unelaborated, at *Eranos* 50 [1952] 27) that B20 presents examples from different world-periods.

53. I dismiss thus the views of Bignone (*Empedocle*, p. 410; but Bignone's reference to death is surely on the right lines) and of Kranz (*Empedokles*, p. 361 n. 9). But one must be grateful for Bignone's point that ἀριδείκετον implies a treatment in the fragment "della vicenda ... consueta ... del corpo umano."

54. O'Brien, "Cosmic Cycle," p. 39. An unworthy suspicion occurs to me that O'Brien's italics for "*again*" in his translation imply that (in his opinion) αὖτε must mean "for a second (or subsequent) time." This would be false; see LSJ s.v.

55. O'Brien, "Cosmic Cycle," p. 39 n. 2, compares B57 and Simpl. *De caelo* 587.19.

56. Hölscher, "Weltzeiten und Lebenszyklus," p. 13. Wilamowitz "solved" the difficulty by excision without explanation; see Solmsen, "Love and Strife," p. 126 n. 48.

57. *Hermes* 82 (1954) 141f, distinguishing between "absoluten ἕν" at B17.7, ἕνα κόσμον at B26.6, and ἕν of mortal body at B20.2. Munding's view of B26.7

is accepted by Kerschensteiner, *Kosmos*, p. 127 n. 1, and "almost" by Solmsen, "Love and Strife," p. 126 n. 47.

58. See Solmsen at *JHI* 24 (1963) 476ff.

59. B22, to be discussed below.

60. C. W. Müller, *Gleiches zu Gleichem*, p. 36 n. 35, has a useful analysis of the problem whether to take together (1) ἀλλήλοις ἔστερκται and ὁμοιωθέντ' Ἀφροδίτῃ or (2) ἀλλήλοις ὁμοιωθέντα and ἔστερκται Ἀφροδίτῃ, rejecting (1) for reasons of logic and (2) for reasons of style and language. His rejection of (2) I find wholly convincing, but his objections to (1) rather less so. Principally, he objects that it is impossible for the elements to be made ὅμοια, but I doubt (a) if it is impossible in every sense (Love can make a kind of homogeneity out of the elements) and (b) whether it is necessarily implied by what Empedocles says at B22. Müller's own solution is to take both datives with ἔστερκται as datives of agent and instrument, leaving ὁμοιωθέντα to stand by itself and mean "infolge seiner Ähnlichkeit." Examples quoted (outside the lyrics of tragedy) are simpler than this (e.g., at Homer *Od.* 14.205f line-end helps to clarify the syntax), and we have here an artificial and ingenious way of understanding a straightforward Greek sentence, only to be adopted in dire necessity. I cannot see that we have any such necessity here.

61. But I doubt Müller's notion (*Gleiches zu Gleichem*, pp. 16ff) that like-to-like is a principle of *Parmenides'* physics. The conventional epithet στυγεροῖο applied to τόκου at Parmenides B12.4 is no more evidence of the elements' natural reluctance to mix than it is of Orphism; and the knowing of like by like is to be distinguished clearly from the principle of like to like. The like-to-like principle was connected by the ancients especially with Empedocles (see Müller, *Gleiches zu Gleichem*, p. 27 and nn.), and with good reason; the suggestion of Müller (pp. 64f) that Empedocles was encouraged in the like-to-like theory by the Orphic/Pythagorean view that the soul eventually rejoined the gods is possible, but one wonders whether Empedocles would have abstracted a physical generality from so particular a point of psychology. Like-to-like was a principle of several post-Parmenidean cosmogonies, starting as they did almost necessarily from a mixture. Homer's generalization at *Od.* 17.218 may have influenced Empedocles' expressions, if not his way of thinking.

62. Bignone's rejection (*Empedocle*, pp. 524ff) of the view that Love can ever be responsible for like to like is based on the statement that B22.4f deal with mixtures. In view of the close connection between the first three lines of the fragment and the next pair, this seems to me an irrelevance. See further n. 69 below.

63. *Empedocle*, pp. 415f.

64. *HGP* II p. 158.

65. *Hermes* 82 (1954) 138f.

66. *Gleiches zu Gleichem*, pp. 29ff.

67. Ibid., p. 31 (Müller's italics).

68. Bignone ad loc. p. 416 claims (cf. his p. 537) that it is the structures which are united, that the phrase ὁμοιωθέντ' Ἀφροδίτῃ corresponds to, and means the same as, συναρμοσθέντ' Ἀφροδίτῃ at B71.4. The correspondence is well noted, but the word ὁμοιωθέντα does not mean "united" in quite the same sense as συναρ-

μοσθέντ'. "Fitted together" and "made alike" or "having something all alike produced from them" are not the same thing. The process of fitting together may necessitate some degree of ὁμοίωσις, but that is a different matter.

69. Cornford, *Plato and Parmenides*, p. 35; Guthrie, *HGP* II pp. 170ff and elsewhere (as in *The Greek Philosophers from Thales to Aristotle*, pp. 48–51).

70. KR pp. 319 and 324.

71. See KR p. 389, omitting the word "original" as applied to "unity," and contrast in this respect their p. 388.

72. See Stokes at *AGP* 47 (1965) 217–250 on Anaxagoras' cosmogony and its debt to traditional cosmogonical ideas.

CHAPTER VII: ZENO OF ELEA

1. *Aristotle's Physics*, p. 72; cf. Guthrie, *HGP* II p. 97 n. 2.
2. Particularly at *Phys. Z* 9.
3. Particularly at *in Phys.* pp. 138ff.
4. Particularly at 127a–130a.
5. Lee (*Zeno of Elea*, p. 8) and Guthrie (*HGP* II p. 81) are perhaps not pessimistic enough; see Owen ("Zeno and the Mathematicians," *Proc. Arist. Soc.* n.s. 58 [1957–1958] 201 n. 5), and Vlastos ap. Kaufmann, *Philosophic Classics*, vol. 1, p. 27 n. 2. For a fairly clear case of confusion between the two Zenos, see D.L. 9.29, where, however, some confusion with Empedocles is also present. See on this Bignone, *Empedocle*, p. 539 n. 1, and Diels, *Dox.*, p. 167 and n. 1. Bignone denies confusion with Zeno the Stoic here because the same notice about Zeno of Elea is found in Stobaeus (no reference given) in terms applicable to Empedocles. If this refers to Diels, *Dox.*, p. 303.22ff, it does not cause me to waver; Aëtius (represented by Stobaeus) is indeed guilty there of confusing Zeno of Elea with Empedocles, but there are crucial differences between his version and Diogenes Laertius'.

6. It is interesting that Aristotle calls the Flying Arrow "third" and expounds it in that position, though he has occasion to mention it first. This might lead one to suppose that Aristotle knew and followed Zeno's order; but this is not conclusive, since Aristotle's order could be an order of exposition familiar in the Academy and/or the Lyceum.

7. Some bibliography by Vlastos ap. Kaufmann, *Philosophic Classics*, p. 27 n. 1; and, more recently, Guthrie, *HGP* II pp. 85–87, and Vlastos at *Phronesis* 11 (1966) 17f. I would select G. Calogero, *Studi sull' Eleatismo*, pp. 115ff; W. A. Heidel at *AJP* 61 (1940) 1ff; B. L. Van der Waerden at *Mathematische Annalen* 117 (1939–1941) 141ff; H. Fränkel, *WuF* p. 234 n. 1; and D. J. Furley, *Two Studies*, pp. 63–78.

8. Burnet, *EGP*[4] p. 315.

9. Eudemus only *says* καὶ Ζήνωνά φασι λέγειν, but see Calogero, *Studi sull' Eleatismo*, pp. 144f. Even if Eudemus' story be actually false, it will still represent a reputable fourth-century interpretation of Zeno. For its application see below.

10. E.g., Mondolfo, *L'infinito nel pensiero dell' antichità classica*, p. 246 n. 3; Guthrie, *HGP* II, esp. p. 100.

11. KR p. 291.

12. Ibid.

13. This analysis was stimulated by V. C. Chappell's at *Journal of Philosophy* 59 (1962) 207.

14. See the works cited by Mondolfo, *L'infinito*, p. 248 n. 1.

15. E.g., V. Brochard, *Études de philosophie ancienne et moderne*, pp. 18f.

16. A useful collection of evidence on the Flying Arrow in Lee, *Zeno*, nos. 28–34. See, on this argument especially, N. B. Booth at *JHS* 77 (1957) 188f; Owen, "Zeno and the Mathematicians," pp. 216ff; Vlastos, *Phronesis* 11 (1966) 3ff.

I should like to be able to believe Vlastos' theory that the argument preserved by Diogenes Laertius, Epiphanius, and Sextus Empiricus, and printed in part by DK as B4, is part of the genuine Zenonian Flying Arrow but regret that I do not feel compelled to do so. Vlastos has two main arguments: (1) the fact that the neighbouring citations in D.L. are all verbatim, (2) the suggestion that the argument as put by D.L. is useless by itself, in that "to be told out of the blue that a thing cannot move 'in the place in which it is' would only provoke the retort, 'And why not? Why cannot the dog move in the kennel, the man in the courtyard, the ship in the bay?'"; whereas the first step given by Aristotle, namely "everything is always at rest when it is at a place equal to itself," fills the gap and answers the retort. The second point is clearly the most far-reaching.

Let us look at the Flying Arrow as it finally stands on Vlastos' p. 8:

The arrow could not move in the place in which it is not.
But neither could it move in the place in which it is.
For this is a place equal to itself.
And everything is always at rest when it is in a place equal to itself. Etc.

Now, if a reader would object to the arrow's being forbidden to move in the place where it is, then surely this same sharp reader would retort after the third step in Vlastos' version, "But why should the place where it is be equal to the arrow? Why cannot the arrow move, and be, in the cloud, the ship in the bay etc., although the cloud is greater than the arrow, the bay than the ship, etc.?" In a word, I do not find that this helps to solve Vlastos' original problem. But the solution to that problem is, it seems to me, not far to seek. By talking about the place where the moving thing is not, the version of D.L. and his fellows automatically narrows down the place where it is. For, if asked where the ship (for instance) was not, the reader would have to list (among other places) all the sites in the bay other than the actual position of the ship. If contrasted with "where X is not," "where X is" can only have the narrow sense. This once granted, D.L.'s argument is seen to be self-contained.

We are left to fall back on Vlastos' (1). But this in turn is not as cogent as one could wish. There are two possible reasons why D.L.'s Sceptic source should quote Zeno in summary while quoting verbatim from other authors. The first is that Zeno's book might not have been available so readily, and he might therefore have had to rely on a mere paraphrase. The second is that the complete Arrow might have been longer when set out in full than this author was prepared to quote; no passage in D.L.'s context is longer than three iambic trimeters, and most are shorter.

I conclude that there is no necessity to suppose B4 anything but a summary of the Flying Arrow.

17. In my text there follows a translation of part of a sentence in Tannery's account (*Pour l'histoire de la science hellène*, p. 266) of another paradox. I hope and believe that this procedure results in no distortion of Tannery's view.

18. *Problems of Analysis*, pp. 127ff, esp. p. 128. See his p. 133 n. 9 for the parallel with the Stadium.

19. *JHS* 77 (1957) 191.

20. *Problems of Analysis*, pp. 129f and pages following.

21. *Phronesis* 11 (1966) 9 n. 20a.

22. *Two Studies*, p. 72.

23. *Problems of Analysis*, p. 129.

24. Booth at *JHS* 77 (1957) 193 even remarks with some justice that "Zeno's problem seems to treat Achilles and the Tortoise with mathematical exactitude, as though they were unchanging points." The Racecourse more probably deals with an attempt to complete the course rather than a failure to start it; see below.

25. By Aristotle at *Phys.* 239a35ff, more exactly by Owen, "Zeno and the Mathematicians," pp. 216ff, esp. 221.

26. Plato *Theaetetus* 181b–d (cf. *Parmenides* 138b) is still occupied with the more elementary distinction between "movement" of space and of quality.

27. See, e.g., versions cited by Black, *Problems of Analysis*, p. 135.

28. *Science hellène*, pp. 264ff.

29. See Aristotle *Phys.* Z 9.239a33ff and esp. Ross ad loc. and Cornford's note on p. 188 of the Loeb *Physics*, vol. 2.

30. *Two Studies*, pp. 72–75.

31. I am less sure even than Furley that the second half proves $t = 2t$ to the first half's $t = t/2$. It could be argued that in the first statement Aristotle has the leading C pass 4 B's in (say) 4m, while the leading B passes 2 A's in 2m. Result, $4m = 2m$. In the second statement the B's again pass the C's in 4m, while at the same time (presumably) the leading C passes but 2 A's. So again the result is $4m = 2m$. Furley seems to mean two different things by t in his two equations. Zeno may have done so too, but I see no need for this assumption. But I admit to little confidence on this point.

32. Furley prints here with the MSS ἅμα γὰρ ἔσται τὸ πρῶτον Γ καὶ τὸ πρῶτον Β ἐπὶ τοῖς ἐναντίοις ἐσχάτοις, ἴσον χρόνον παρ' ἕκαστον γινόμενον τῶν Β ὅσον περ τῶν Α, ὥς φησι, διὰ τὸ ἀμφότερα ἴσον χρόνον παρὰ τὰ Α γίγνεσθαι. But this makes the leading B pass the B's and, if it is what Aristotle wrote, is accordingly inexact. Ross's deletion of ἴσον χρόνον παρ' ἕκαστον ... φησιν is no answer; it leaves the argument διὰ ... γίγνεσθαι in the air, with no properly logical consequence. The point ought to be that each C is opposite a B for the same time as

a B or C is opposite an A. The nearest emendation to making this point is Lachelier's, τῶν Γ, ὅσον περ ⟨τὸ Γ⟩ ... But conceivably Aristotle did not write the phrase τῶν ... A at all; the sentence is, if anything, clearer without this attempted clarification. Be that as it may, Furley seems to me to have cleared up the point of the argument and made of it a much better puzzle than it used to be. But, on the other hand, it still seems to me that the fallacy consists in ignoring the fact that the A's are stationary, and the B's and C's moving. Zeno's ingenious little trap is still, after Furley's exposition of it, open to this attack.

33. *Science hellène*, p. 266. Contra. e.g., Booth at *JHS* 77 (1957) 193–194.

34. Aristotle in several passages, e.g., *De gen. et corr.* 325a2ff; and see Chap. VIII below.

35. Vlastos ap. Kaufmann, *Philosophic Classics*, p. 43 n. 31; cf. Furley, *Two Studies*, pp. 73f.

36. Owen, "Zeno and the Mathematicians," pp. 208f.

37. *JHS* 77 (1957) 194, citing another possible blunder by Zeno.

38. "Zeno and the Mathematicians," pp. 221f.

39. Owen, "Zeno and the Mathematicians."

40. Ibid., p. 207.

41. Ap. Kaufmann, *Philosophic Classics*, p. 35.

42. The words διελθεῖν or διιέναι or διεξελθεῖν occur, to express the action allegedly impossible, at *Topics* 160b9, *Phys.* 233a22, *Phys.* 263a6. The word ἀφικνεῖσθαι appears at *Phys.* 239b22. At 239b11 the argument is called "the one about there being no movement because..." but this (in context) need be no more than a general statement that the argument refutes motion; the same goes for the words οὔτε ἐνδέχεται κινεῖσθαι at *Topics* 160b9. I see no reason to doubt Aristotle's assimilation of Racecourse to Achilles.

43. It is, I think, probable that the Atomists believed in indivisible lines and magnitudes; the degree of separation in Atomism of geometry and physics will be discussed below, in Chap. VIII.

44. Cf. Plato *Parmenides* 145a1?

45. Proclus and Elias, cited at DK 29A15, both mention the figure forty. See further M. Untersteiner, *Zenone*, pp. 66ff. Plato (*Parm.* 127e and *Phaedrus* 261d) mentions an argument on likeness and unlikeness whose exact course is unknown to us. Whether the other arguments mentioned in the *Phaedrus* are among extant arguments or not I do not claim to know; in particular, we do not have any evidence to connect the antinomy of one and many certainly with any extant argument—though both the argument at *De gen. et corr.* 325a (see next chapter and especially Philoponus' version of that argument at Lee, *Zeno* no. 8, *in Phys.* 42.27f and 43.3) and the argument from predication (on which see Lee, *Zeno*, pp. 27–29, though Lee there omits reference to Eudemus frag. 37a, Simpl. *in Phys.* p. 97, esp. 12–14, and pp. 138.32–139.1) are possible candidates.

46. For rebuttal of an attempt to make a philosophical point of it see *Archiv für Geschichte der Philosophie* 46 (1964) 123.

47. I owe this convenient phrase to Professor J. P. Sullivan both through conversation and from his paper "The Hedonism in Plato's *Protagoras*" at *Phronesis* 6 (1961) 10ff. It is not used to imply that Plato's dialogues are purely

fictitious. It may be observed that we have, strictly, only Plato's portrayal of what *Parmenides* would have made of Zeno; but there would surely be no motive for putting a distortion into Parmenides' mouth here.

48. *Plato and Parmenides*, p. 114; "Each Hypothesis begins with a definition, sometimes disguised as a series of inferences"; cf. p. 111: "...these opening paragraphs, though usually cast into the form of a deduction, really define..." What exceptions Cornford intended by his use of "sometimes" and "usually" I am not sure.

49. Ibid., p. 114.

50. *Parmenides* 142a6f. The translation here and in the next citation is Cornford's.

51. At 137b Parmenides refers to the whole proceeding in advance as a πραγματειώδης παιδία. But, whatever the significance of this much discussed phrase, it can hardly have been meant to differentiate between the seriousness of individual propositions or types of proposition in the second half of the dialogue. It does not suggest that some deductions were meant as definitions nor that the final conclusion should be taken with a larger pinch of salt than the preceding arguments.

52. Note the ἄρα at 160c7.

53. *In Phys.* 139.18f; I translate first the text as emended by Fränkel, *WuF* p. 214 with n. 5.

54. See DK 29B2 and B1. The exact sense of the Greek is best discussed by Vlastos at *Gnomon* 31 (1959) 195ff.

55. Owen, "Zeno and the Mathematicians," p. 202.

56. Ibid., p. 203.

57. Ibid.

58. Ibid., p. 210.

59. Ibid., p. 211.

60. See Guthrie, *HGP* I pp. 276ff, and passages translated there.

61. For this interpretation see Lee, *Zeno*, p. 31 on his no. 11 (=B3).

62. See Fränkel, *WuF* p. 202. This citation is actually taken from the earlier English version of the paper (*AJP* 63 [1942] 5); the German clarifies, I think, an ambiguity in the first phrase.

63. ZN p. 752.

64. *Metaphysics Δ* 6, esp. ad fin., on which see Chapter I above, passim.

65. *JHS* 77 (1957) 199.

66. Booth at *Phronesis* 2 (1957) 5 n. 3.

67. R. Robinson, *Plato's Earlier Dialectic*[2] p. 28.

68. See n. 53 above, and the text referring to it.

69. Be it noted in passing that it is above all in the second Hypothesis that Plato's Parmenides appears on the surface to be attempting the establishment of antinomies like that which results from this argument of Zeno's against plurality.

70. See, e.g., Vlastos, *Encyclopedia of Philosophy*, vol. 8 p. 369. Magnitude implies the possession of parts, which implies plurality, which for Zeno excludes all unity.

71. Ibid.; but I observe with pleasure that my general interpretation of Zeno, though differing on some major points, bears a closer resemblance to Vlastos' than to any other known to me.

72. One may endorse Cornford's observation (*Plato and Parmenides*, p. 207 n. 1) on the difficulty of translating this sentence; but the general drift of it is reasonably clear. I doubt if the Budé translation was right in taking the emphasis in the final clause to be on ἔσται, rather than on ἕκαστον.

73. Frag. 37a Wehrli (ad fin.), Lee no. 6. See chap. VIII below.

74. Compare Eudemus frag. 37a with Aristotle *De gen. et corr.* 325a8f, discussed more fully in the next chapter.

75. Diels, *Dox.*, p. 113; this particular part of Diels's argument he did not withdraw at *Aristotelis qui fertur de MXG libellus*, pp. 7f.

76. The volte-face in Sextus' version at *Adv. math.* 7.67, noted by G. B. Kerferd at *Phronesis* 1 (1955–1956) 15, is characteristically Zenonian; it can hardly be denied to a fifth-century sophist, as Kerferd thinks, and makes indeed against any extensive remodelling of the argument by our late sources.

77. "A quantity, a continuum, a magnitude or a body" is hardly a clear-cut series of alternatives. A body is often continuous, and a magnitude, at least in early Greek (in so far as that is relevant to Sextus' text), can be either a continuum or a body. It looks as if Gorgias was preparing for the later part of his argument, to the effect that each of the different "one"s is divisible, by setting up a set of divisibles. No harm need have resulted from this; but only three elementary senses of διαιρεῖν are implicitly invoked: the arithmetical, the geometrical, and the physical (with a knife).

78. See Chapter I above.

79. Guthrie does well to point out the beginnings of such analysis in Empedocles B17.9ff (on which see *HGP* II p. 156); but this, if one can dignify it with the name of analysis, is a tremendous distance from the sort of thing attributed to Zeno by Owen—even further, in fact, than the analysis attributed to Gorgias by Sextus (see n. 77).

CHAPTER VIII: ONE-MANY PROBLEMS IN ATOMISM

1. Apart from the older standard works, a notable contribution is D. J. Furley's *Two Studies in the Greek Atomists*, to the first of which this chapter is particularly indebted.

2. Guthrie, *HGP* II pp. 390f.

3. I cite 325a2–16, and 325a23–325b5. I succumb to the temptation to offer an observation on the text. The intervening passage consists of a transitional formula, οἱ μὲν οὖν οὕτως καὶ διὰ ταύτας τὰς αἰτίας ἀπεφήναντο περὶ τῆς ἀληθείας together with a note of an argument against the Eleatics which seems to most students out of context. Joachim puts a lacuna after the transitional formula; but a more economical hypothesis is that (a) the transitional formula was originally meant to run on directly (as it naturally does) with Λεύκιππος δ' ἔχειν ᾠήθη λόγους ... and that (b) the intervening lines are a separate note on the Eleatics and sense perception, inserted here by Aristotle's original editors in order to place it before Aristotle's comment on the Atomist attitude to sense perception.

4. For the Melissan origin of this argument see Kirk and Stokes at *Phronesis* 5 (1960) 1–4. The point of this paper seems to be misunderstood by Furley, *Two Studies*, p. 80 and n. 2, who cites it in favour of *Parmenides*' probably having produced this argument. P. J. Bicknell (*Phronesis* 12 [1967] 2) also misunderstands: he wrongly dissociates me from the main point of the paper, that Parmenides did not employ the argument that the abolition of void precluded motion. I hope to deal more fully elsewhere with Bicknell's further arguments concerning Parmenides.

5. Bailey, *Greek Atomists and Epicurus*, p. 75: "In the old sense empty space is not real ... but it none the less exists."

6. Furley, *Two Studies*, p. 80.

7. Literally, πεπλασμένον is indeed "a piece of fiction"; but, as Bonitz remarks (*Index Aristotelicus* s.v. πεπλασμένως), its adverb is contrasted with πεφυκότως at *Rhet.* Γ 2.1404b19. The general sense of the whole objection is that finite divisibility is a hypothesis with an air of being made up as the author(s) went along.

8. Most recently by Vlastos, *Encyclopedia of Philosophy*, vol. 8 pp. 371f; but Vlastos is surely right in separating the *De gen. et corr.* arguments as a whole from those in Zeno's fragments. Cherniss distinguished the argument of 316a from that of 325a at *ACPP* p. 113; on the other hand, Furley (*Two Studies*, p. 84) declares the argument of 316a "unmistakably reminiscent" of Zeno's B2–1, which he believes to be the argument meant at 325a.

9. Eudemus frag. 37a (Wehrli), ap. Simpl. *in Phys.* p. 97.11ff and p.138.31ff.

10. Themistius *in Phys.* p. 12.1ff, cited in part by Simpl. *in Phys.* 139.19ff; I think the comma in Schenkl's text before διά should be placed rather after σωμάτων: the whole of Themistius' sentence is about the dichotomy, and so Simplicius clearly took it.

11. Porphyry has applied the argument (Simpl. *in Phys.* p. 139.26f) to Being rather than to the members of a plurality, and has made of it a reductio ad absurdum of the supposition that τὸ ὄν is διαιρετόν. Then he explains this (καὶ γὰρ δή at p. 140.1) by a very similar reductio ad absurdum. One is tempted a priori to suppose that this represents an attempt at direct paraphrase of Parmenides, by way of justifying his earlier ascription. The feature of the argument beginning at καὶ γὰρ δή is that it starts with the assumption that Being is everywhere alike πάντῃ ὁμοῖον, and concludes (of course) that Being is ἀδιαίρετον. One is struck by the coincidence that Parmenides at B8.22 announces οὐδὲ διαιρετόν ἐστιν, ἐπεὶ πᾶν ἐστιν ὁμοῖον (how Porphyry accented the second ἐστιν we do not know). The coincidence does not stop here: Parmenides continues οὐδέ τι τῇ μᾶλλον, τό κεν εἴργοι μιν συνέχεσθαι, / οὐδέ τι χειρότερον, πᾶν δ' ἔμπλεόν ἐστιν ἐόντος. Porphyry also has the word τῇ: καὶ γὰρ δή ἐπεὶ πάντῃ ὁμοῖόν ἐστιν, εἴπερ διαιρετὸν ὑπάρχει, πάντῃ ὁμοίως ἔσται διαιρετόν, ἀλλ' οὐ τῇ μέν, τῇ δὲ οὔ. Suppose Porphyry's eye to have lit, in the middle of thinking about the dichotomy, on Parmenides B8.22–24, suppose him in haste to have taken μᾶλλον with διαιρετόν instead of with ἔστιν, and we have an explanation of his assignment to Parmenides of an argument that, since Being is πάντῃ ὁμοῖον, it is all alike (and nowhere more than anywhere else) divisible. *If* Porphyry recollected *De gen. et corr.* 325a, he will also have found in Parmenides' πᾶν δ' ἔμπλεον ... a

firm rejection of the conclusion of Aristotle's version there of "the dichotomy," namely that κενὸν τὸ ὅλον. This series of suppositions may seem to the reader (as it sometimes does to me) fantastic; but it is unlikely that Parmenides dealt with "divisibility" elsewhere, and the only alternative I can see is that Porphyry was inventing on no basis whatever. Belief in such invention would leave the following combination of facts unaccounted for: that Porphyry is the *only* authority who thinks fit to give two versions, the second explaining the first; and these differ in that the second (*alone* among the versions of "the dichotomy" known to me) starts from the "Parmenidean" assumption that Being is πάντῃ ὁμοῖον.

12. See esp. Furley's elucidation of them at *Two Studies*, pp. 3ff.

13 See J. Mau, *Zum Problem des Infinitesimalen*, esp. pp. 23ff; Furley, *Two Studies*, pp. 79ff. A somewhat different, but convergent, approach is Guthrie's at *HGP* II pp. 503ff.

14. Such explicit evidence as we find against it is well analysed by Furley. On the question whether Democritus was too good a mathematician to believe in theoretically indivisible magnitudes, Furley remarks that we know of other authors of the classical period who combined a knowledge of mathematics (and presumably of the rudiments of incommensurability) with a belief in theoretical indivisibles. It is perhaps necessary to add that we simply do not know how good a mathematician Democritus was; the few extant mathematical titles of works are uninformative about the quality of their contents, and the very few concrete examples of Democritus' mathematics are very hard to interpret. On the cone in particular see Furley, *Two Studies*, p. 100.

15. I have lumped Leucippus and Democritus together here as elsewhere in this chapter. Cherniss, *ACPP* p. 96 n. 402, points out that this reasoning is attributed to Leucippus at *De gen. et corr.* 325a–b, but to Democritus in Aristotle's essay on Democritus (frag. 208). The odd passage (see below) *Metaphys. Z* 13.1039a9f mentions Democritus alone. I cannot see any reason to suppose the peculiarity of that passage due to a difference between Leucippus and Democritus; no radical distinction between the two men's opinions has come down to us. (For Cyril Bailey's attempts to separate the two see R. Philippson at *Gnomon* 6 [1930] 463 and Furley, *Two Studies*, pp. 94f).

16. See Simpl. *De caelo* p. 294.33ff (DK 68A37, Aristotle frag. 208 Rose); my citation begins at Simpl. p. 295.8.

17. Bailey, *Greek Atomists*, p. 88, has the not unimportant point that atomic motions have to continue in juxtaposition. This is due to the atomic motion's being accounted for by its eternity. It means, since void is necessary for motion, that there must always be void even in the closest juxtaposition of atoms. This is an apparent example of the combined influence of Melissus and Parmenides on the Atomists: Parmenides' question τί δ' ἄν μιν καὶ χρέος ὦρσεν / ὕστερον ἢ πρόσθεν τοῦ μηδενὸς ἀρξάμενον φῦν; would here be combined with Melissus' B7 §7 on the impossibility of motion without void.

18. KR omit it, though quoting some other relevant passages, interpreted (KR p. 419) as here, but without considering reasons. Furley surprisingly omits it from consideration, perhaps because of a suspected ambiguity so far as his main theme is concerned.

19. See Aristotle *De gen. et corr.* 315b9f, with KR p. 409 n. 2; also Aristotle frag. 208 (cited above), for "numberless" shapes.

20. It is attributed to Leucippus by Theophrastus ap. Simpl. *in Phys.* 28.9f and apparently to both Leucippus and Democritus at Simpl. *in Phys.* 28.25f. (Bailey's conjecture that the argument here is Democritus' alone is ill grounded on the "relative sophistication" of this compared with the argument from the infinite variety of the sensible world. The argument is similar in structure to, though less cogent than, the argument from equilibrium attributed to Anaximander [Aristotle *De caelo* 295b11ff]. Here also there is no valid reason that I can see for distinguishing Leucippus from Democritus.)

21. Galen *De elem. sec. Hippoc.* 1.2 (DK 68A49) distinguishes the Epicurean doctrine of atoms unbreakable from hardness and the Leucippan of atoms indivisible from smallness. Clearly, in view of the other passages, a confusion.

22. D. L. 9.44 (DK 68A1), in Diogenes' syntax perhaps referring to ἀτόμων συστήματα, but, if so, this is doubtless a slip of the pen.

23. On Parmenides 8.22ff, see pp. 134–137 above.

24. 67A6 (Aristotle *Metaphys.* 985b8), cf. 68B156 (Plutarch *Adv. Colot.* 1108f), 67A8 (Theophrastus ap. Simpl. *in Phys.* 28.11f). The belief of W. I. Matson, *CQ* n.s. 13 (1963) 26ff, that B156 is deliberate nonsense in quasi-parody of Melissus, is well refuted by D. McGibbon at *Mnemosyne* 4 ser. 17 (1964) 248ff.

25. In my review of Guthrie's HGP II, *PQ* 17 (1967) 164–166, esp. 165, written before I had fully worked out the ideas of this chapter, I fell a victim myself to the tendency to overestimate in this connection the importance of Zeno at the expense of Parmenides. Though my continued disagreement with Professor Guthrie's thesis will be evident, I owe him an apology for the overdogmatic tone of parts of the review. I still believe that Parmenides did not argue or assert that a "one" could not become "many," but now accept some indirect connection between Parmenides B8.22–25 and the Atomist one-many prohibition.

26. *Two Studies*, p. 99.

27. It may be observed that Socrates at Plato *Phaedo* 76e rejects out of hand the notion that one can become two; but he is not rejecting what is one becoming many, but rather the *number* one becoming a different plural number.

28. Whence the point made at *Ep. ad Hdt.* 41 that the atoms are both indivisible and unchanging (ἀμετάβλητα) to avoid destruction εἰς τὸ μὴ ὄν. The same is spelled out in greater detail at *Ep. ad Hdt.* 54 (in contrast with the destructible qualities).

29. On this question I refer the reader to Furley's book and my review, *CR* n.s. 19 (1969) 286ff. I believe against Vlastos (*Isis* 56 [1965] 121ff) that "parts" in the general sense, not the specialized mathematical "submultiples," are at issue in Epicurus *ad Hdt.* 58–59. This is, I think, proved by the phrase οὐδὲ μέρεσι μερῶν ἁπτόμενα, where the parts must be normal parts: one does not touch someone with a submultiple of one's body. Lucretius was surely talking of theoretical indivisibles at 2.599ff.

30. Philoponus *in Phys.* 80.23ff twice mentions τὸ κυρίως ἕν in referring to an argument resembling that of *De gen. et corr.* 325a, but this does not prove that Zeno mentioned it in this connection, still less that the Atomists did.

31. See Guthrie, *HGP* II p. 156.

32. On this vexed question see Guthrie's excellent summary of the evidence and the proper conclusions at *HGP* II pp. 400ff.

33. This alone surely makes it impossible to believe that Democritus even believed in atoms large enough to be visible. See Philippson at *Gnomon* 6 (1930) 463f and Furley, *Two Studies*, pp. 95f. Vlastos at *Isis* 56 (1965) 139 n. 88 cites Aristotle ap. Simpl. *De caelo* 295.7–8 for infinite variety of shapes *and sizes* of fifth-century atoms. But this is not cogent evidence; Aristotle does not repeat the epithet "infinite" (if παντοῖα means "infinite") with the difference of size, and it is wholly gratuitous to assume that he meant his reader to "understand" it. Democritus could easily, I think, have failed to see Epicurus' point that infinite variety of atomic shape, for an Atomist, implies infinite size in the largest atoms. I prefer, at least, to accuse him of this oversight rather than of making atoms too small to be visible (Simpl. *De caelo* 295 lines 5 and 9) at the same time as they are large enough to be seen.

34. See *AGP* 47 (1965) 217ff for argument that Anaxagoras maintained as far as possible the traditional cosmogony.

CHAPTER IX: MISCELLANEOUS PRESOCRATIC CONTEXTS

1. See *AGP* 47 (1965) 4ff and 16ff, and Guthrie, *HGP* II pp. 281ff.

2. This view, at least, has received scholarly support, namely from O. Gigon, *Ursprung der griechischen Philosophie*, p. 255. Gigon sees in Anaxagoras' B8 a reference to Parmenides' B4, an unnecessary conjecture. (Equally unnecessary is Mugler's guess at *REG* 69 [1956] 325 that the axe metaphor is a comic motif aimed at Leucippus' τομή).

3. See Aristotle *De respiratione* 471a2.

4. For my numbering see H. Fränkel, *WuF* p. 287 n. 1.

5. What does not seem to be a possibility is the rendering "the things in an individual world"; I am not sure whether this is how Bailey (*Greek Atomists and Epicurus*, p. 539) meant to take it, but, if he took the fragment this way, he was wrong. I accept plural worlds in Anaxagoras (see Colin Strang, *AGP* 45 [1963] 114 n. 28) but do not believe that "in *an* individual world" is a possible rendering of the Greek; Bailey's translation in *The Greek Atomists* omits the definite article.

I cannot agree with Fränkel (*WuF* p. 288), if he is there wishing to imply that B8 is a good basis for argument against plural worlds in Anaxagoras, for two reasons: (1) to be conclusive against plural worlds, the word εἷς here would *have* to mean "unique," "one and only"—and I cannot see why the meaning of "one" should be so restricted; (2) the assertion of a unique world would have no point in the context of B8 itself.

It is not quite clear to me what Vlastos means at *Philosophical Review* 59 (1950) 38, where he writes: "When he asserts that 'the contents of the one world'—whose unity had been shattered by the cosmological dualism of Parmenides and Empedocles—'are not sundered from each other, the hot from the cold, or the cold from the hot' (B8), the butt of his attack is clear and has been noticed often enough." In Vlastos' context the "dualism" of Parmenides and Empedocles appears to mean the distinction between "two classes of things, the one original and everlasting, the other derivative and temporary"—but I do not see what the unity mentioned in Anaxagoras' B8 has to do with this.

6. The improvement most often noted is the explicit attribution of intelligence to the fundamental stuff. So Zeller, ZN p. 339.

7. As in Zeller, ZN p. 339, and Burnet, *EGP*[4] pp. 350f and 352ff. KR pp. 429ff stress at least that Diogenes' thought, though eclectic, was not without value; but they strangely do not mention Parmenides in their chapter on Diogenes. Guthrie, *HGP* II pp. 367ff, believes, I think, that Diogenes' theory was both a return to older modes of thought and an answer to Parmenides. The former point sits somewhat uneasily beside the latter; and, since in any case I am not wholly satisfied with Guthrie's account of Eleatic influence, I have allowed myself space for a fresh analysis. But Guthrie well recognizes that Diogenes was fighting on two fronts: against pluralists (as in the atomist argument of B2 in favour of a single substance) and against the Eleatics. Contrast KR p. 430 n. 1, where attention is focussed on the pluralists.

8. Notably Cherniss at *JHI* 12 (1951) 344, referring to Diogenes as talking "as if Parmenides had never lived."

9. Guthrie, *HGP* II p. 368: "Diogenes was not an atomist, but he had read Leucippus and agreed with him on two fundamental points: the material uniformmity of all body and the existence of empty space."

10. *Hermes* 76 (1941) esp. 361ff, where references are given for the passages concerned: the argument is strengthened by J. Jouanna at *REA* 67 (1965) 320f, with a much more plausible chronology than Diller's (on which see n. 14 below).

11. Cf. KR p. 430 n. 1: "Words like $\mu\epsilon\tau\alpha\kappa\sigma\sigma\mu\epsilon\hat{\iota}\sigma\theta\alpha\iota$ were liable to be used in any philosophical writing of the latter half of the fifth century B.C."

12. I have used Loveday and Forster's Oxford translation here; the most accessible text is probably at DK I p. 263.

13. See Guthrie, *HGP* II pp. 367f, in contrast with the lukewarm remarks of KR p. 432 (fin.) n. 1, where, however, the second impression of the book is at least more correct than the first.

14. Diller in *Hermes* 76 (1941) tries to prove Melissus subsequent to Diogenes and the Atomists. The verbal arguments are rightly dismissed by KR p. 430 n. 1, and the others are not cogent. The coincidence of the order in Diogenes' and Melissus' list of the Empedoclean "elements" is insignificant for relative chronology and shows merely a shared dependence on Empedocles, who uses the selfsame order twice in extant fragments (compare Melissus B8.2 and Diogenes B2 with Empedocles B38.3–4 and B.109.1–2). Melissus' argument in his B7 against the possibility of hurting or paining Being is indeed not inappropriate as an attack on Diogenes; but it is not unlikely that Melissus invented the idea himself to give added breadth and force to his negative characterization of Being; this kind of possibility is too often ignored.

The arguments for the priority of Melissus over the Atomists are not so strong as many have believed. But, on the whole, it seems most likely that Melissus' explicit denial of the possibility of motion without void preceded the Atomist connection of void with motion and helped to effect the change from Empedocles' and Anaxagoras' denial of void to the Atomists' and Diogenes' acceptance of it. That Diogenes as well as the Atomists connected the void with motion is suggested, but not proved, by Aristotle's account of Diogenes on the breathing of fish (*De respiratione* 471a2ff), where the expression ἕλκειν τῷ κενῷ seems to imply (though it could conceivably be a mere looseness of writing) that a void was for Diogenes a sufficient condition of motion.

15. See Diller at *Hermes* 76 (1941) 370ff.
16. See Chap I above. A strong case for Diogenes as the particular target of *De nat. hom.* is made out by J. Jouanna at *REA* 67 (1965) 307ff.
17. See esp. Jouanna at *REA* 67 (1965) 314ff.
18. Guthrie, *HGP* II pp. 367f.
19. What Aëtius says here (Diels, *Dox.*, pp. 432f) is that animals partake of the intelligent air but are prevented from full intelligence, some by density, others by excess moisture. This implies at least that dense and rare were not directly associated with wet and dry respectively.
20. This result (cf. the well-founded emphasis by Jouanna on hot and cold in Diogenes, *REA* 67 [1965] 311 and n. 2) is in agreement with the view of Kirk, KR p. 437, that Diogenes "does not appear to be interested in explaining all changes of air as being due solely to rarefaction and condensation." It is, I think, a pity that Kirk goes on to remark with a touch of superciliousness that "Diogenes has clearly overlooked, or at least failed to stress, the elegant consistency of Anaximenes." It is hard on a thinker whose greater sophistication prevents him from adopting a simple solution to a complex problem to be accused by implication of a lack of elegance. It is the more surprising to find this judgement when we are assured at KR p. 430 that Diogenes' theory of the world was, among other things, less complicated than its monistic forebears. The prejudice against Diogenes of Apollonia dies hard.
21. Guthrie, *HGP* I p. 247, a notably cautious statement of the theory.
22. *Pythagoreans and Eleatics*, pp. 114ff, and (more circumspectly) KR pp. 239ff.
23. *Pyth. and El.*, p. 178.
24. See KR pp. 317f, and (e.g.) p. 319 respectively.
25. KR p. 318. On the "parallel" between this inhaling process and human conception/birth see Burkert, *Weisheit und Wissenschaft*, pp. 250f.
26. It hardly matters in this connection whether Philolaus 44B5 is genuine or not, or whether or not the mention of Archytas at 47A21 (from Theo of Smyrna) is justified. Aristotle treats the unit as a compound of Limit and Unlimited and also of Odd and Even (frag. 199 Rose^3, from the same passage of Theo, and *Metaphys.* 986a17–20).
27. At *Metaphys.* 987a13ff and 987b22ff, Aristotle might seem to imply an equation of Limit with One. But it is difficult to say how far this is due to confusion with Academic doctrine and how deeply the Academy may have transformed the Pythagorean number theory. It is not easy to see how the Table of Opposites at *Metaphys.* 986a22 can be persuaded to tell us that Unity was not merely a manifestation of Limit, but synonymous with it in the field of arithmetic (KR p. 241). If the unit is forbidden, because it appears wholly on the Limit side of the Table

together with Odd, to be a mixture of odd and even, then plurality must also suffer a veto on the inclusion of both odd and even—which is absurd. See further Burkert, *Weisheit und Wissenschaft*, p. 34 n. 110.

28. Raven (e.g., KR 317f) has an elegant account of the development within arithmetical theory based on Theo Smyrnaeus p. 21.20ff (Hiller). Theo first divides numbers into odd and even on the basis of their divisibility into equal parts or unequal. Clearly (though Theo does not say so) this would exclude the unit for either class, and place it in a special category. Quite possibly, those who reasoned in this way held that the unit was not a number at all, but the principle of number; (see Heath, *Greek Mathematics*, p. 69, and esp. on p. 71 the comment that "the explanation of this strange view (that the one is both even and odd) might apparently be that the unit, being the principle of all number, even as well as odd, cannot itself be odd and must therefore be called even-odd." Theo mentions another school believing the unit to be odd: these argue that the one must be odd or even and cannot (being not divisible at all, let alone into equal parts) be even. This argument obviously assumes that "one" is a number on the same footing as other numbers. Theo's other argument (on the same basic assumption) for an odd "one" is that, when added to an even number, it produces an odd sum; this characteristic it shares with odd numbers and it is therefore not even but odd. Finally, Theo cites from Aristotle (frag. 199 Rose) a notoriously feeble argument for the even-odd unit, namely, that, added to an odd number, it gives an even sum, and vice versa. (It seems no less feeble as an illustration than as a proof.)

On this basis Raven supposes that in historical succession there are two phases: in the first are combined (a) the postulation of only two classes of number, so defined that the unit will fit into neither and (b) the suggestion that the unit was odd because not even; in the second the obvious discrepancy is smoothed out by creating the special even-odd category for the unit. But I do not find this conclusion from Theo as "hard to resist" as Raven does. There are other possibilities. For instance, if we can talk of historical succession at all, rather than of rival schools of thought, the following would do: (1) some relatively early Pythagoreans believe the unit not a number, but the principle of number, and therefore in a class by itself as both even and odd (cf. my quotation from Heath above), even and odd being *for numbers* incompatible properties; (2) some others, after realizing that the unit was a true number, made it therefore odd, because it was not even, choosing (as they would obviously have to) a different definition of odd numbers, conceivably a definition based on their property of not giving an even sum when added to an even number. In this context it is worth observing that the exclusion of the unit from number has a primitive air. But the gaps in our knowledge of early Greek number theory are far too great for this or any other such theory to be propounded otherwise than exempli gratia.

29. *Weisheit und Wissenschaft*, p. 43 n. 171: "sehr unscharf."
30. E.g., Raven, *Pyth. and El.*, pp. 11 and 114: Guthrie, *HGP* I p. 247.
31. *Weisheit und Wissenschaft*, p. 43 n. 171.
32. See *PQ* 15 (1965) 66 n. 3; the sum of the arguments against the Aristotelian origin of this sentence seems to me stronger than any of the individual arguments.

33. I accept Raven's arguments (*Pythagoreans and Eleatics*, pp. 11ff) against Cornford's old view that Aristotle is here making the unit prior to the opposites.

34. Cf. Burkert, *Weisheit und Wissenschaft*, p. 35 n. 123.

35. Pages 120f. It should by now be clear that Parmenides' πῇ πόθεν αὐξηθέν; and οὐδὲ διαιρετόν ἐστιν ἐπεὶ πᾶν ἔστιν ὁμοῖον were not aimed specifically at Pythagoreanism but take a natural, unforced place in Parmenides' argument.

APPENDIX

1. E.g., Burnet, *EGP*⁴ p. 175. For caution on the use of ἤ as equivalent to μᾶλλον ἤ see W. B. Stanford on Sophocles *Ajax* 966f. (Kamerbeek on the same passage is hardly convincing.) I have found no clear examples except after verbs of wishing etc. (for which see Kühner–Gerth II p. 303 n. 19). In any case, the construction must be extremely rare.

2. E.g., DK, who however regard Burnet's translation as possible.

3. Its Eleatic origin is clear: see Melissus B1.

4. Aristotle's argument is that no movement which begins at some moment after infinite rest can be natural, for nature acts in orderly fashion; there is no ratio between infinite and infinite (and hence no order).

5. Aristotle did not think much of this: *Phys.* Θ 252a23ff.

6. Anticipated by Parmenides himself in his Δόξα. Cf. Simpl. *in Phys.* 34.14ff.

7. I do not find this burden discharged by G. E. L. Owen at *Monist* 50 (1966) 317ff. The following observations seem to be called for. (a) If Aristotle *Metaphys.* 984a29–984b1 does refer to this argument of Parmenides, as I think it must, then it supports my interpretation rather than Owen's; Aristotle says the Eleatics asked simply "What started movement?" not "What started it at one time rather than another?" (b) Owen (p. 326) distinguishes with useful clarity between the world starting (i) "whenever it did (whether later or earlier)" and (ii) "at a given time t rather than some earlier time $t - n$)." But *pace* Owen (p. 327), Melissus at B1 (and in the paraphrase of *MXG*) shows no sign of concern with either sense (i) or sense (ii) but simply propounds that nothing can come from nothing. Melissus says that there is no way in which something can come from nothing, not that there is no reason why at one time rather than another. There is no reason to suppose that Owen's corollary (p. 327), "if any event occurs uniquely at t there is a sufficient reason for its not occurring at $t - n$," had ever entered Melissus' head. (c) Owen admits that Anaxagoras and Parmenides' other near successors took no care to meet the query why the first event should have happened when it did. He suggests "instinct" or "logic" as reasons, but the absence of any such query is no less simple an explanation. (d) Democritus on the non-commencement of time (see Owen p. 331) need not have been stimulated by our passage of Parmenides but could easily have been an independent argument. It bears no outward sign of the question "Why at one time rather than another?" Owen's fascinating paper begs (understandably) the question I have raised in this Appendix.

INDEX OF PASSAGES

Aeschylus, *Eum.*, 456: 96;
P.V., 551: 96;
fr. 390: 89
Aëtius, 1.7.28: 327; 2.4.11: 68–70, 84; 2.13.14: 287; 2.23.3: 286; 2.24.4: 287; 2.24.9: 286, 287; 2.31.4: 325; 5.7.1: 321; 5.19.5: 157–158; 5.20.5: 244, 338; 5.26.4: 321–322
Alcmaeon, B4: 281; fr. 95b: 96
Alexander, *In Metaphys*, 250.17ff: 267; *Quaestiones*, 2.23: 44
Anacreon, fr. 83: 308
Anaxagoras, B2: 284; B4b: 237–238; B8: 237–238, 336; B12: 45, 238, 279–280; B15: 45
Anaximander, B1: 93n28, 293
Antiphon, *Tetralogies*, 2B6: 76
Antiphon Trag., fr. 3: 290
Apollonius Rhodius, 1.496: 286
Archilochus, fr. 103: 88, 89, 290
Aristarchus Trag., fr. 1.3f: 291
Aristophanes, *Equites*, 1065ff: 290; 1236: 96;
Thesmophoriazusae, 569: 145
Aristotle, *Categories*, 10a16ff: 47;
Concerning Opposites, 8;
De caelo, 268b5: 284; 269b19f: 285–286; 275b32: 226, 235, 239; 294a21ff: 73; 294a22f: 286; 294a28ff: 277; 294a29ff: 283; 295a30: 323; 295b11ff: 335; 298b29: 102; 300b25–31: 323; 301a15: 156; 303a5–6: 227–228; 305b2ff: 271, 272;
De gen. animalium, 722b11: 320; 747a34ff: 280;
De gen. et corr., A7: 235; A8: 249, 251; A10: 19, 162; 315a3ff: 272; 315a19–25: 270; 315b9f: 335; 316a14ff: 222–224, 333; 325a2–325b5: 186n34, 218–225, 229–231, 330, 332, 335; 325a2–9: 333; 325a28–325b4: 229; 325a34–325b5: 227, 334; 325a34–36: 233–234; 328b22: 19, 270; 330b14: 273; 333b20–22: 270; 334a5: 159; 334a26ff: 324;
De part. animalium, 693a23–25: 158;
De respirat, 470b30ff: 45n72; 471a2: 237n3; 471a2ff: 338;
Eud. Eth., 1236a16ff: 6;
Metaphysics, A1–2: 291; A5: 244–246; Δ5: 8; I10: 13; 983a17: 310; 983a24–983b3: 283; 983a33ff: 32; 983b6ff: 32–38; 983b6ff: 273; 983b6: 62n123; 983b7: 283–284; 983b18ff: 37; 983b20–22: 57; 983b22ff: 36n50; 983b27ff: 54, 59; 983b28: 282; 984a29–984b1: 340; 984a2: 57; 984a7: 102; 984b12: 310; 985b8: 230n24; 985b32f: 271; 986a17–20: 338; 986a19: 247; 986a22: 338; 986a29f: 281; 986a33f: 281; 986b2: 83–84, 289; 986b18ff: 68–69, 71–74, 78, 82, 83; 986b21ff: 74, 287; 986b27–987a2: 144; 986b34: 272; 987a13ff: 338; 987b11f: 271; 987b22ff: 338; 999b33ff: 19; 1003b35ff: 8; 1004a2: 267; 1004b27ff: 8; 1005b19ff: 2; 1012b34ff: 275; 1014b26: 18n40; 1015b19: 19n44; 1015b23f: 20; 1015b36ff: 14; 1016a17: 18; 1016a7ff: 268; 1016a17ff: 324; 1016a24–32: 17, 269; 1016b6–11: 22, 268; 1016b6: 20; 1016b11: 15; 1016b17ff: 12n25, 268; 1016b17: 13; 1016b30ff: 21n45; 1016b32ff: 19; 1017a3: 22n49; 1018a15ff: 18n40; 1021a11ff: 269;

341

Aristotle—Continued
   1023a26ff: 60; 1023b32ff: 269;
   1030b7: 22; 1039a3: 227–228;
   1039a9f: 334; 1040b5ff: 269;
   1041b11ff: 22n50; 1044a2ff: 269;
   1045a7ff: 268; 1052a19: 13; 1052a22:
   15; 1052a34: 11; 1052b18: 21n47;
   1054a29ff: 8, 267; 1055a2: 268;
   1055b7: 268; 1056b34–35: 268;
   1060b36ff: 267; 1061a10ff: 8;
   1069b20ff: 273; 1069b22: 62n124,
   271, 284; 1071b27f: 271; 1074b1:
   282; 1080b14ff: 271; 1082a15ff: 269;
   Physics, 185b5ff: 1; 185b25ff: 223;
   185b32ff: 2, 22; 187a12ff: 62;
   187a20f: 273; 187a20: 271; 199a33ff:
   320; 199b9: 319; 199b10: 320;
   203a17: 273; 203b3–15: 29n29–31;
   203b10ff: 272; 203b15: 271; 204b22–
   29: 276; 204b22ff: 272; 205a25ff:
   272; 207b34ff: 284; 209a23: 190;
   216b22–26: 44; 216b30: 46; 216b33–
   217a3: 46; 217a8–10: 46; 227a14:
   14; 233a22: 330; 239a33ff: 184n29;
   239a35ff: 184n25; 239a35–239b9:
   181; 239b1–4: 181; 239b6: 313;
   239b8–9: 181; 239b10–11: 187;
   239b11: 330; 239b22: 330; 239b30–
   33: 181; 250a19–25: 190; 250b23–
   251a5: 159; 251a4f: 324; 252a4ff: 254,
   340n4; 252a23ff: 340; 257a33ff: 61;
   263a4–263b9: 192; 263a6: 330;
   Politics, 1334b33: 289;
   Rhetoric, 1368b7: 107; 1404b19: 333;
   Soph. el., 182b13ff: 267;
   Topics, 103a6: 18; 103a14: 21; 103a19:
   18; 103a23: 18, 19; 106a12ff: 267;
   148b16–22: 267; 160b9: 330; fr. 7:
   282; fr. 199: 338, 339; fr. 208: 334
Aristoxenus, fr. 23: 271

Censorinus, 4.7: 321
Chrysippus, *ap. Stobaeum* I. 1281ff (W): 296
Cicero, *Academica*, 2.118: 67–70, 287;
   De div., 1.3.5: 288;
   De finibus, 1.6.17: 229, 232;
   De natura deorum, 1.28: 68–69, 72, 285
Clement of Alexandria, *Stomateis*, 1.65.4: 110

Democritus, 68B9: 231; B64: 291; B65: 291; B156: 335
Demosthenes, 30.23: 145
Diodorus Siculus, 1.7.1: 284
Diogenes Laertius, 6.19: 280; 9.1: 109;
   9.5: 301; 9.9: 296; 9.18: 282; 9.19:
   68–69, 71, 72; 9.29: 321, 327; 9.44:
   229, 232, 335; 9.57: 240, 277; 1.60:
   306
Diogenes of Apollonia, B2: 240, 277,
   278–279, 337; B5: 244, 277; B7: 240;
   B8: 291
Diogenianus, *Cent.*, 7.78: 290

Elias, *In Categorias*, 109.6ff: 330
Empedocles, B7: 163; B8: 163; B9:
   163; B11: 163; B12: 163; B13–14:
   163; B17.1–6: 154–156, 318; B17.1–5:
   168; B17.2: 161; B17.4: 161; B17.5:
   161; B17.7: 161, 325; B17.9ff: 332;
   B17.10: 161; B17.11–13: 234; B17.23:
   164–165, 325; B17.33: 163; B20:
   165, 325; B20.2: 325; B20.4: 161;
   B20.4–5: 168; B21.7: 161; B21.8:
   161; B22: 168–173; B22.4f: 326;
   B22.5: 25–26, 161; B22.8–9: 161;
   B23: 162, 167; B26.3–7: 166–167;
   B26.5: 167; B26.7: 168, 325; B26.8–
   12: 159–160; B26.10: 135; B27: 160,
   161, 323; B28: 160, 164n45, 324–325;
   B29: 319; B30.3: 254; B31: 160,
   164n45, 323, 324–325; B32: 161;
   B33: 161; B34: 161, 167; B35.4: 318;
   B35.5: 161; B35.6: 161, 319; B38.3–4:
   337; B53: 164n46; B57: 157, 325;
   B58: 157; B59.2: 161; B60: 157; B61:
   157; B62: 157, 158, 321; B62.2: 322;
   B62.4–5: 321; B62.5: 319; B71.3:
   162; B71.4: 161, 326–327; B73: 167;
   B75: 167, 280; B86: 167; B87: 161;
   B91: 170; B95: 161; B96: 321;
   B96.4: 161; B98: 325; B104: 280;
   B109.1–2: 337; B110: 325; B134: 319
Epictetus, *Ench.*, 21(W): 301
Epicurus, *Ad Hdt.*, 41: 335; 54: 335;
   58–59: 335
Eudemus, fr. 37a: 176, 211n73, 223n9,
   327, 330
Euripides, *Heracles*, 1106: 76; 1341ff:
   80–81;
   Hippolytus, 161ff: 303; 441–442: 288;
   Medea, 285: 290;
   Troades, 763: 95;
   fr. 484: 64n128, 284
Eusebius, Chron. S. Ol., 70.1: 109

Galen, *De elem. sec. Hippoc.*, 1.2: 335

Harpocration, s.v. Ἴων: 281
Hecataeus, 1: 87
Heraclitus, B1: 290, 301; B2: 87, 290; B5:

INDEX OF PASSAGES

106; B10: 100–102, 108, 292, 295n53, 299, 300; B12: 291, 295; B17: 87; B22: 88; B23: 93; B26: 97, 293–294n43, 294; B29: 87; B30: 40–41, 76, 104, 108, 295–296, 299n63; B31: 40, 41, 103, 105, 108, 295–299; B32: 88, 106, 295, 300n75, 308; B40: 88; B41: 88; B49: 87; B50: 89, 102; B51: 94–97, 101, 293, 303n4; B53: 288; B57: 87–88, 92–93, 294; B59: 91, 99, 294; B60: 90, 99, 292, 294; B61: 91; B66: 108; B67: 105–106, 108, 288, 299n70; B80: 293; B88: 92, 99, 292, 294; B89: 290, 292; B90: 40, 105, 295, 299n64; B91: 305; B99: 105; B102: 105–106; B103: 90, 99, 294; B104: 87, 88; B111: 93; B114: 107; B125: 293; B126: 92–93, 99, 108, 293

Herodotus, 1.93.2: 288; 1.125: 115n27, 302; 2.96.2: 96; 2.124.5: 96; 2.148.7: 96; 3.6: 145; 5.86.1: 144; 5.89: 145; 7.52.2: 315; 7.113: 288; 8.73.1: 145; 8.113.3: 288; 8.119: 145; 9.55.4: 315

Hesiod, *Erga*, 25: 171;
Theogony, 27–28: 41; 116ff: 39, 278; 224: 322; 748ff: 92, 292; 937: 96

Hippocrates, *Anc. Med.*, 14 fin. p. 604(L): 270; p. 584: 270; pp. 607–608: 162; p. 626: 279;
Nature of Man, 1: 48–50, 242, 249; 2: 316

Hippolytus, *Ref.*, 1.6.2: 275; 1.11.1: 285; 1.14.3: 287; 6.14.2ff: 67–69, 71–73, 75, 286

Homer, Γ 333: 95; H 99: 278; M 243: 77, 78, 288; N 355: 290; P 210: 95; T 219: 290; Φ 440: 290; X 255: 96; Ψ 311f: 290; Ψ 595: 303; α 3–4: 291; ε 162: 95; ε 247: 95; ε 248: 96; ε 361: 96; μ 188: 290; ξ 205f: 326; ρ 218: 171, 326

Ion, A1: 281; A6: 281; B1: 281

Lucretius, 2.599ff: 335
Lucian, *Vit. auct.*, 14: 292

Marcus Aurelius, 6.17: 292
Melissus, B1: 340; B2: 150, 316–317; B3: 150, 316–317; B5: 148, 317; B6: 148; B7: 148, 157, 316, 337; B7.2: 150; B7.7: 334; B7.8: 44; B8: 71, 149, 316–317; B8.2: 337; B8.3: 293; B9: 149–150; B10: 157

Nicolaus Damascenus Περὶ Θεῶν ap. Simplicius *In Physica*, 23.14ff: 68–69, 71, 72

Parmenides, B2–3: 139; B2: 112, 116, 119, 120, 125, 131, 132, 140, 147, 307, 311, 314; B2.2: 306; B2.3: 113, 121, 306; B2.3–5: 306; B2.5: 121, 122, 306; B2.6–8: 120; B2.7: 140; B3: 140, 306, 314; B4: 305, 336; B6: 94, 112–126, 131–132, 289, 302–305, 307, 311; B6.1f: 302; B6.1–3: 112–115, 120, 121; B6.1–2: 122, 307; B6.1: 306; B6.3ff: 302; B6.4–9: 113, 302; B6.5: 120; B6.8–9: 115, 116–120, 122–126, 308; B7: 115, 116, 120, 124; B7.1ff: 302; B7.1–2: 113, 119–120, 122; B7.2: 302; B7.5–6: 307; B8: 305, 314, 340; B8.1–14: 128; B8.3–4: 127, 141; B8.4: 83, 141, 308; B8.5–6: 128–131, 132, 133, 310; B8.5–21: 132; B8.5: 312–313; B8.6–15: 132–134; B8.6: 308; B8.7–12: 253–255; B8.7–8: 132; B8.7: 131, 340n35; B8.9–10: 131, 241, 253; B8.9: 311; B8.11: 135, 136, 143, 311; B8.12–13: 310; B8.12: 131, 253, 311; B8.13–14: 133; B8.14: 310; B8.14–15: 133; B8.15ff: 124, 314; B8.15–18: 133; B8.15–16: 136, 311; B8.15: 140; B8.16: 131; B8.19f: 312–313; B8.19–22: 132, 310, 311; B8.19–21: 133; B8.21: 137; B8.22ff: 243, 309, 311; B8.22–26: 140; B8.22–25: 134–137, 142, 220, 308; B8.22–24: 333; B8.22–23: 142; B8.22: 301, 333, 340; B8.26ff: 137, 308, 313; B8.26–33: 138–140; B8.29–33: 312; B8.29: 82; B8.33: 289; B8.34–41: 136–137; B8.34–38: 139–140, 141, 314; B8.34: 82, 139–140; B8.36–38: 83, 138, 142; B8.36–37: 121; B8.39: 117; B8.40: 314; B8.41: 312n99; B8.43–49: 140–141; B8.44–48: 316; B8.46: 121–122; B8.48: 308–309; B8.52–54: 122–123; B8.53ff: 122, 315n119; B8.53–54: 146–148, 308; B8.54: 315; B8.56–59: 279; B8.57–58: 147, 211, 305; B8.60: 313–314; B8.61: 147, 307; B9.1ff: 45n70; B12.4: 326; B16: 144

Pherecydes, B1: 52
Philo, *Qu. in Gen.*, 3.5: 291;
Quis rer. div. heres, 214 (503M): 89n12, 291
Philodemus, *De pietate*, 70G: 299
Philolaus, B5: 338; B8: 247

Philoponus, *De gen. et corr.*, 207.18ff: 281;
  In phys., 42.27f: 330; 80.23ff: 335
Pindar, *Olympian*, 2.86: 89;
  Pythian, 3.114: 95; 4.80: 95; 8.68: 96;
    9.13: 95; 9.48–54: 291; 9.117: 95;
  Nem., 6.1–2: 270; 7.23f: 290; 7.98: 95;
    8.11: 96;
  Isthmian, 6(7) 139: 95
Plato, *Cratylus*, 402b: 54; 402c: 275; 402d: 272;
  Euthydemus, 283d: 4; 286e8: 310;
  Laches, 179e1: 310; 197d1: 310;
  Meno, 73a7: 310; 84d1: 310; 87e6: 310; 89e5: 310; 93e8: 310; 98b2: 310; 99c7: 310; 100a1: 310;
  Parmenides, 127a–130a: 175; 127b–c: 281; 127e: 330; 128c–d: 179; 135d–136a: 194; 137b: 206, 331; 137c–d: 196–197, 317; 137d: 316; 138b–c: 312; 142a: 197; 142a6ff: 197n50; 145a1: 330; 146d–147b: 207; 149a: 212; 157b: 207; 157b6: 197; 157e–158a: 211; 159b: 198; 159c5: 317; 160b: 208; 160b2: 198; 160b5: 198–199; 160c7: 199n52, 331; 160d3: 199; 161c–e: 208; 163c1: 199; 164b–c: 209; 165e: 197, 209, 211; 166c: 199;
  Phaedo, 76e: 335; 95e: 273;
  Phaedrus, 261d: 330;
  Politicus, 266d10: 310;
  Republic, 352dff: 5; 428e: 274;
  Sophist, 242d–e: 50–57, 59–60, 63, 272, 280, 281, 295; 242c–d: 68–70, 82–84; 242d: 285; 243d–244b: 315;
  Theaetetus, 152e: 54, 272; 179e: 51, 282; 180c–d: 54; 181b: 282; 181d5–6: 312;
  Timaeus, 59b: 44–45
Plutarch, *Adversus Colotem*, 1108ff: 230n24; 1110F: 229, 232
Proclus, *In Parmenidem*, 694.23: 330;
  In Cratylum, 6.10ff: 234;
  In Tim., 1.345.12ff (D): 308
Pseudo-Aristotle, *De Melisso Xenophane Gorgia*, 3–4: 67–72, 79, 81, 285; 3.1–2: 70; 3.3: 80; 974a12ff: 157; 974a23ff: 317–318; 975b21ff: 239–240, 277; 976b2off: 279; 977a27: 288; 979b13ff: 214
Pseudo-Galen, *Hist. Philos.*, 7: 67–70, 72, 285; 130 (p. 647.5 Diels): 322
Pseudo-Plutarch, *Strom.*, 4: 67–69, 73, 80, 81, 286, 289; 12: 243, 244

Sappho, fr. 16: 87

Sextus Empiricus, *Adv. Math.*, 7.67: 332; 7.73: 214–215; 9.1: 70; 9.360: 280;
  Pyrrh. Hyp., 1.224: 67–71, 84
Simplicius, *In Categ.*, 288.14: 267;
  De caelo, 242.19ff: 229; 294.33ff: 334; 295.5–9: 336; 295.8: 226; 587.19: 325;
  In Phys., 7.1ff: 308; 7.13: 274; 21.16ff: 308; 22.22ff: 67–72, 285; 22.26ff: 66, 285–286; 23.4: 70; 23.16ff: 68–70, 72; 23.21ff: 36; 23.23: 280; 23.25: 277; 24.13ff: 28n25, 62n125, 275, 284; 24.17: 273; 24.26ff: 279; 25.5: 243; 25.16: 272; 27.2f: 280; 27.19ff: 273; 28.9f: 335; 28.11f: 230n24; 28.25f: 335; 34.14ff: 340; 38.23f: 272; 78.2: 115, 302; 78.5ff: 128; 78.6: 302; 78.26–27: 253–255; 97.12–14: 330; 99.12: 177; 103.31ff: 151; 117.2: 115; 118.20: 315; 138ff: 175n3; 138.3ff: 223; 138.4ff: 317; 138.32–139.1: 330; 139.18f: 200n53; 139.24ff: 224; 139.26f: 224n11, 333; 143.29f: 305; 149.32f: 273–274; 150.18ff: 28n23, 274; 150.23: 275; 153.17ff: 240–241; 174.30ff: 45; 371f: 157–158; 380–382: 157–158, 319–320; 381.29f: 320; 382.5ff: 319; 1123.28ff: 159; 1124.2f: 322; 1183.28ff: 323
Solon, fr. 22.5: 290; 24.19: 95
Sophocles, *Ajax*, 966f: 340;
  Antigone, 570: 96; 710f: 290; 1109: 76;
  Oedipus Coloneus, 198: 95; 908: 96;
  Oedipus Tyrannus, 374: 93, 293;
  Thamyras, fr. 244: 96
Strabo, 638: 282
Suda, s.v. Ἡράκλειτος: 109, 301; s.v. Θαλῆς: 275
Syrianos, *In Metaphysica*, 61.12ff: 8

Theo of Smyrna, 21.20ff: 339; 22.5–8: 338
Theodoretus, 4.5: 67–69, 71–72
Theognis, 253: 145
Theologoumena. Arithmetica 40 (Ast) (= Pythagoras A8): 282
Theophrastus, *De Sensu*, 11: 280, 324;
  Phys. Op., fr. 1: 36;
  fr. 5: 67–76, 84;
  fr. 6: 285
Thucydides, 3.40.4: 315
Timon, fr. 59: 289
Tyrtaeus, fr. 9: 87

Varro, *Eumenid. Sat.*, fr. 27 (Büch.): 321

Xenophanes, B1: 79; B8: 281–282; B11: 79, 80; B12: 79, 80; B14: 79, 81; B15.4: 79; B18: 79; B22: 282; B23: 76–78, 80, 81, 82, 83; B24: 77, 78, 82; B25: 75, 82; B26: 75, 82; B27: 84–85; B29: 40–41; B34: 80; B38: 80

Xenophon, *Anabasis*, 5.6.12: 145

Zeno, B1–2: 200–202, 205, 210–212, 224–225, 333; B3: 190, 202–206, 212–213, 215, 217, 220, 221, 224, 244; B4: 328–329

Zenobius, *Cent.*, 5.68: 290

GENERAL INDEX

Absolute/relative, 91, 185, 187, 192, 330
Academy, 8, 10, 55, 84, 194, 327, 338
Addition/subtraction, 149, 210
Aenesidemus, 305
Aer, see Air
Aeschylus, 89, 96
Aesop, 88
Aether, 37, 73
Aëtius: on Alcmaeon, 281; on Diogenes, 244, 338; on Empedocles, 157–158, 319–322, 325–327; on Xenophanes, 67–70, 84, 286; on Zeno, 327
Air: in Anaxagoras, 279–280; in Anaximenes, 43–44, 48; in Diogenes, 35, 42, 291, 338; in Empedocles, 163; in Heraclitus, 296; in Ion of Chios, 281; mentioned, 24, 40, 49, 73, 171, 272
Alcmaeon, 52–53, 246, 281
Alexander of Aphrodisias, 8, 44, 70, 72, 177, 223, 267, 272
Ambiguity, 97, 100, 195, 275. See also Equivocation; Meaning
Anacreon, 282
Anaxagoras: answers Parmenides, 35, 241, 254–255, 309; one/many in, 237–238, 249, 271, 335–337; cosmogony of, 238, 327; infinite in, 284; mixture in, 35, 174, 237–238; dense/rare in, 45–48, 279–280; mentioned, 65, 246, 322
Anaximander: monism of, 43, 62, 274; opposites in, 53, 99, 271, 274, 293; Unlimited, 24, 25, 28, 30–31, 61–62, 271–277, 284; use of ἀρχή, 28, 30–31, 58, 274–276; mentioned, 36, 59, 242, 319, 335
Anaximenes: monism of, 273–274; on air, 24, 36, 43–44, 48, 274, 279; condensation/rarefaction, 43–48, 53, 273–274, 279; opposites in, 53; mentioned, 103, 239, 242, 286, 338
Anthropogony, 157, 320–321
Anthropomorphism, 78
Antinomy, 198–202, 206–207, 210, 330–331
Antisthenes (Heraclitean), 49
Aphrodite, 96, 165, 168–169, 172, 326
Apollodorus, 109–111
Apollonius Rhodius, 284
Application, types of, 4–7, 9, 12, 22–23
Arche, see Principle
Archilochus, 89, 290
Archytas, 248, 338
Aristophanes, 290; in Plato, 320–321
Aristotle: as historian, 24–28, 29–30, 32, 49, 63, 280; on Alcmaeon, 281; on Anaximander, 25, 29–31, 271–273, 276; on Anaximenes, 279; on Atomism, 218–222, 225–230, 232–233, 236, 239, 334, 336; on the Eleatics, 1–2, 213, 218–224, 231, 277; on Empedocles, 25–26, 156–161, 271–272, 319–320, 323; on Heraclitus, 102, 300; on the Milesians, 28–35, 40, 43, 49, 60–62, 102, 277; on Parmenides, 144, 272–273, 314; on the Pythagoreans, 244–247, 271, 281, 338–340; on Thales, 36–38, 54–60, 277, 279, 282, 283–284; on Xenophanes, 66, 68–69, 71–74, 78, 83, 84, 287, 289; on Xuthus, 44; on Zeno, 175–176, 180–193, 216–217, 249, 327, 329, 330; influence on Theophrastus, 27–28, 62, 84; on "one," 1–2, 7–23, 63, 161–163, 171, 216, 234, 267–270, 295, 322, 325; on "many," 21–23, 164, 205, 216, 322; on condensation/rarefaction, 46–48; on divisibility,

Aristotle—*Continued*
225, 332; on motion/rest, 255, 340; on "principles," 29–30; on substrate and quality, 32, 46, 59, 61, 242; mentioned, 44, 45, 53, 98, 100, 107, 143, 158, 167, 216, 241, 249, 280, 283, 285, 291, 324, 332

Aristoxenus, 271

Atomists: in relation to Anaximander, 242, 273; in relation to Diogenes, 239, 241–243, 337–338; in relation to Zeno, 186, 191, 218–225, 251, 332–336; one/many in, 225–236, 248, 249, 250, 251–252, 332–336; on atomic shapes, 44, 229, 335, 336; on dense/rare, 44; on the infinite, 73, 255; on void, 44, 243, 277, 334; mentioned, 31, 49, 174, 186, 240, 246, 268, 324, 330

Attribute/subject, 33

Augustine, 309

Austin, J. L., 9, 10, 22

Backward-turning path, 116, 124, 303–305

Becoming, *see* Coming-to-be; One

Being: in Aristotle, 1–2, 9–11, 16, 268; in Empedocles, 163; in the Eleatics, 1–2; in Lycophron, 1–2; in Melissus, 148–152, 316, 317; in Parmenides, 117–148, 251, 253–255, 276–277, 305–315, 333; in Plato's *Parmenides*, 196–200, 208–210; in Plato's history of thought, 50–56; in Zeno's arguments, 200–203, 205, 211–213, 333–334; mentioned, 174, 337

Bignone, E., 169

Black, M., 180–183

Blood, 41

Body, 149–150, 214; human, 38, 41, 166–167

Bonitz, H., 22

Booth, N. B., 180, 187

Boundaries, *see* Limit

Boundless, *see* Unlimited

Bowra, C. M., 88

Bradley, F., 202

Brandis, C., 127

Burkert, W., 246

Burnet, J., 36, 59, 76, 154

Callimachus, 98

Calogero, G., 79

Campbell, L., 51

Cantor, M., 178

Categories, 6–11, 15, 22–23

Causes, 60–63, 74

Censorinus, 321

Change: in Aristotle, 46–47, 61; in Atomism, 219; in Diogenes, 277–279; in Heraclitus, 41, 92–93, 103, 294–295; in Melissus, 148–152; in Parmenides, 124–126, 136–140, 142, 147, 308, 312; in Xenophanes, 41, 70; between opposites, 46–47, 61, 92–93, 294–295; between substances, 41, 43, 103, 178; denied, 70, 124–126, 136–140, 142, 147, 148, 150, 219, 251, 278, 308, 312; in cosmogony, 42, 143–144, 147; of arrangement, 149, 151, 152, 317; of quality, 31–35, 44, 45–46, 61, 138, 140, 149, 219, 251, 277; of place, 138, 140, 150, 277. *See also* Motion

Chaos, 52

Cherniss, H. F., 24–27, 33, 57, 62, 102–104

Chrysippus, 296

Cicero, 67–72, 229, 230, 232, 285, 287, 288, 301

Circle, 90; of argument, 140, 314

Clement of Alexandria, 77, 82, 103, 110, 293, 296, 297, 298

Clitomachus, 67, 70

Coming-to-be: the term, 273; in Atomism, 219–220, 230–233; in Empedocles, 154–156, 163, 168; in the Milesians, 31–36; in Parmenides, 34–35, 124, 130–133, 135–140, 142, 143–144, 147–149, 250–251, 253–255, 310–312; in Parmenides' successors, 35, 63, 163, 174; in Xenophanes, 40–41, 70; as coming-together, 168, 219; mentioned, 48, 127

Coming-together, 154–157, 161. *See also* Coming-to-be

Common sense: opposed to Eleaticism, 35, 117–126, 174, 176–178, 183, 204, 293, 305, 312, 316, 317–318; opposed to other ancient philosophies, 39–40, 43–44, 90, 102, 163

Condensation-rarefaction, 43–48, 62, 272–274, 279, 284, 338. *See also* Dense/rare

Connection, 91, 97, 101, 102, 284, 295. *See also* Harmonia

Contact, 13–15, 64, 94–98, 212, 218, 268–269, 294

Continuity: in Aristotle, 12–17, 22, 268–269; in Empedocles, 161–164, 172; in Gorgias, 214; in Heraclitus, 92–93, 95, 97–102, 294; in Parmenides, 124, 128, 130–131, 134–136, 140, 142, 308; related to homogeneity, 164; related to wholeness, 15–17, 97, 101, 124, 128, 130, 134, 140, 158, 172; in time,

GENERAL INDEX

92–93, 98–99; mentioned, 143, 150, 158, 179, 183, 192, 204, 284
Copula, 77
Corbato, C., 66, 79
Cornford, F. M., 53, 123, 127, 141, 145, 196
Cosmogony: in Anaxagoras, 327; in Diogenes, 243; in Empedocles, 156–159, 319, 321–322; in Hesiod, 52; in the Milesians, 29, 40, 42, 43, 55, 58–59, 64–65, 276; in Pherecydes, 52; supposed in Heraclitus, 103, 107, 295–296; demolished by Parmenides, 42, 143–144; one/many in, 64–65, 84–85, 143–144, 147, 174, 284; like-to-like in, 326; separation in, 42, 64–65, 284
Cosmos: in *De Melisso Xenophane Gorgia*, 317; in Empedocles, 160, 164, 167–168, 318, 322, 325; in Heraclitus, 104, 290
Cratylus, 291
Curved/straight, 91

Dark/bright, 272, 279
Day/night, 61, 92, 93, 98, 105, 106. *See also* Night
Definition: in Plato's Parmenides, 195–197, 200, 331; in Zeno, 195–197, 200, 203; in relation to meaning, 5–6, 9, 12; unity of, 11
Democritus, 225–228, 231–236, 291, 334–336, 340. *See also* Atomists
Dense/rare, 33, 44–47, 53, 149, 279–280, 311, 316. *See also* Condensation-rarefaction
Diels, H., 70, 71, 114, 115, 144, 168, 169, 214
Difference: in Aristotle, 8; in Heraclitus, 101, 119; in Melissus, 150, 152; in Parmenides, 118–120, 123–126, 130–132, 134–142, 311–312, 314; in Plato's *Parmenides* (the Others), 207–209, 211; in Zeno, 175, 205; in cosmogony, 174; in sense-distinctions, 5–7; mentioned, 45, 199
Differentiation: in Empedocles, 157, 163–164, 169–172, 174. *See also* Difference
Diller, H., 239
Diodorus Siculus, 284
Diogenes Laertius: on Atomism, 229, 232–233, 240, 335; on Diogenes of Apollonia, 35; on Heraclitus, 88, 109, 292; on Xenophanes, 70–72, 282; on Zeno, 328–329
Diogenes of Apollonia: in relation to Parmenides, 35, 42, 238–244; in relation to Melissus, 243–244, 337; debts to other physicists, 42, 235, 238–239, 241–242, 338; one/many in, 238, 242–244; on Air, 35, 49, 240–244, 277, 291; opposites in, 35, 243–244, 278–279, 338; mentioned, 235
Division/divisibility: in general, 178–179; in Atomism, 218–225; ignored by Empedocles, 163–164; in Heraclitus, 301; in Melissus, 150–152; in Zeno, 150, 179, 183–186, 191, 200–204, 220–225. *See also* Indivisibles
Doxographers: on Anaximander, 275; on Empedocles, 153–154, 158; on Xenophanes, 66–74, 285–287; relation to Aristotle and Theophrastus, 24, 84, 285–286, 324; one/many in, 86
Dualists, 52–53, 281

Earth (the stuff): in Empedocles, 163, 171, 323; in Heraclitus, 103, 105, 296, 298, 299; in Parmenides, 144, 272; in Xenophanes, 40–41, 49; mentioned, 33, 48
Earth (the body): in Empedocles, 320–321, 323; in Hesiod, 52; in Thales, 36–37, 57, 283; in Xenophanes, 73–74, 84–85, 286–287; separated from sky, 42, 64
Eclectics, 238–244, 249, 250. *See also* Diogenes of Apollonia; Hippo; Idaeus
Ecpyrosis, 50, 104, 107–108, 296, 299, 300
Eleaticizing, 75, 81, 84
Eleatics: in general, 312, 317, 340; in relation to Atomists, 218–225, 231–234; in relation to the Milesians, 33–36, 43, 64, 240, 250, 276; in relation to other physicists, 35–36, 240–244, 337; in Plato's history of Being, 51–53, 280, 285; mentioned, 83, 86, 332
Element(s): in Empedocles, 25–26, 154–159, 161–174, 324; in Heraclitus, 92, 296–297; in Aristotle on the Milesians, 32, 62, 272; in Theophrastus on the Milesians, 275; lists of, 337; mentioned, 11, 26, 288, 326. *See also* Air; Earth; Fire; Water
Elias, 330
Elimination, argument by, 115, 122, 307
Empedocles: in general, 153–174, 318–332; in Aristotle, 25–26, 156–160, 219, 270–273, 319–320, 323–324; in Simplicius, 157, 319–320; in Plato's history of Being, 50, 52, 82, 280–281; confused with Zeno of Elea, 321; in relation to Melissus, 337–338; in relation to Parmenides, 35, 173–174, 241, 247, 249, 254, 312, 337; in relation to

349

Empodocles—*Continued*
Xenophanes, 73, 289; in relation to Pythagoras, 164, 325; one/many in, 153–154, 159–165, 166–168, 171–174, 249, 251, 319, 322–325; on condensation-rarefaction, 46–48; distinguishes senses of "becoming," 234, 332; opposites, 163; on the cycle, 153–161, 318–325; on cosmogony, 157–159, 321–322; on zoogony, 154, 156–169, 165, 168, 170, 171, 319–322; on motion/rest, 159–161, 322–323; on the functions of Love and Strife, 161–172, 319, 322, 325–327; on mixture, 154–157, 161–163, 165, 168–173, 321–322, 324–325; style, 154, 155, 156, 162, 165, 166, 170, 172, 323, 326. *See also* Glue
Epicharmus, 111
Epictetus, 301
Epicurus, 225, 233, 335, 336
Epiphanius, 328
Equality, 208
Equivocation, 4, 5, 12, 99, 208–210, 216
Eristics, 70
Eros, 52
Eudemus: on Anaximander, 28, 274; on Empedocles, 161, 323; on Heraclitus, 301; on Zeno, 211, 213, 223–224, 327
Euripides, 64–65, 275, 284, 290, 304
Eusebius, 109, 297
Existence, *see* Being

Fire: in Empedocles, 157, 163, 319, 321; in Heraclitus, 40–41, 89, 102–108, 295–300; in Parmenides, 122, 144, 146, 272; mentioned, 33, 38, 48–49, 171, 272, 279, 281
Flux, 54–55, 83, 283, 289, 291–292
Form, 8, 16, 17–19, 144–146, 167–171, 315. *See also* One
Forms (Platonic), 139, 194
Fränkel, H., 128–129, 145–146, 204–205, 217
Freudenthal, J., 76
Furley, D. J., 181, 185, 220, 225, 232

Galen, 229, 335. *See also* Pseudo-Galen
Gerth, B., 145
Gigon, O., 90, 97, 108
Glue, 14, 160, 161, 164, 166
God(s): in Empedocles, 160; in Heraclitus, 76, 105–107, 288, 299; in the Milesians, 39, 42; in Xenophanes, 66–84, 285, 287–289. *See also* Monotheism; Polytheism
Gomperz, H., 123–124

Good/bad, 9, 87
Gorgias, 2, 214–216, 252, 332
Guthrie, W. K. C., 29, 49, 57, 76, 117, 128–129, 144–145, 154, 170

Harmonia, 94–97, 164, 167, 204, 326–327
Harpocration, 281
Heaps, 16, 22, 164–166
Heavenly bodies, 37, 286–287. *See also* Sun
Heavy/light, 45
Hecataeus, 87, 88, 301
Heidel, W. A., 33, 78
Heraclides Ponticus, 186
Heracliteans, 282, 302
Heraclitus: in Aristotle, 102, 107, 272, 300; in Clement of Alexandria, 103, 296–299; in Plato, 50–52, 55, 82, 83, 107–108, 280–281; in relation to Parmenides, 109–127, 300–305, 316; imitated by Democritus, 291; influenced Diogenes, 241; influenced by Xenophanes, 106, 110, 288, 300; one/many in, 86–89, 100–108, 250–251, 295–299; unity of all things, 100–107; unity of opposites, 9–10, 89–102, 105–106, 118–119, 291–295; on the Logos, 89, 105–107; on the god(s), 76, 105–107, 288, 299; on wisdom, 88–89, 106; paradoxes in, 41, 93, 99–100, 123, 294, 295; style of, 92; chronology, 89, 109–127, 249, 300–305; mentioned, 76, 244, 278. *See also* Ecpyrosis; Flux
Herodotus, 96
Hermotimus, 246
Hesiod: attacked by Heraclitus, 88, 92–93; attacked by Xenophanes, 79–80; supposed anticipation of flux, 54–55, 59; on cosmogony, 39, 52, 278; on Harmonia, 96; on the Muses, 41
Hippias, 282
Hippo, 49, 56, 277
Hippocrates, 47–50, 242, 249, 270, 279, 295, 316
Hippolytus: on Anaximander, 30, 275; on Heraclitus, 105, 291, 292, 304; on Parmenides, 285; on Xenophanes, 67–75, 286; reliable, 30, 292
Hölscher, U., 97, 154, 156, 166–167
Homer: anticipation of Thales, 51, 54, 56, 59; supposed anticipation of Heraclitus, 57, 282, 283, 289; on the gods, 39, 75, 79–80; linguistic usages of, 73, 77, 95–96, 278, 288, 323, 326; cited, 41, 278, 303
Homogeneity: in Aristotle, 12, 18–19,

GENERAL INDEX

23, 268, 269; in Atomists, 337; in Empedocles, 163–164, 167–68, 172, 326; in Melissus, 148–150, 316, 317; in the Milesians, 63–64; in Parmenides, 82, 131, 139–141, 143–144, 308; in Xenophanes, 82; related to continuity, 131, 308; related to mixture, 139, 162, 167–168, 316, 324, 326; related to wholeness, 172; related to uniqueness, 148–150; in cosmogony, 143–144; mentioned, 205

Hot/cold: in Alcmaeon, 52, 281; in Anaxagoras, 45, 47, 237, 279–280, 336; in Diogenes, 35, 278, 338; in Heraclitus, 92–93, 99, 108; in the Milesians, 33, 37, 50–53, 278

Idaeus, 49
Identity, *see* Indistinguishables; Same; Self-identity
Incorporeality, 77, 100, 150, 317
Indistinguishables, 12, 18, 90, 99
Indivisible: the term, 11–13; applied to unit, 21; applied to Parmenides' subject, 134–135, 142–143, 333. *See also* Indivisibles
Indivisibles: in general, 178; in Aristotle, 186, 188, 192; in Atomism, 330, 335; in the Pythagoreans, 178, 180, 186; in Zeno, 178–189, 192. *See also* Atomists
Infinite: in Atomism, 222, 229, 255, 336; in Empedocles, 73; in Melissus, 148–150, 316; in Xenophanes, 72–74; in Zeno, 190, 192–193, 202–203, 210, 215, 222, 225, 229. *See also* Unlimited
Infinitesimals, 180–191
Inherence, 47, 91
Instants, 180–184
Ion of Chios, 52, 281, 301
Ion Tragicus, 290
Ionians: in general, 26, 39, 47–48, 278, 304; in Plato, 53; on cosmogony, 143–144; on the elements, 272, 277; on religion, 78–79, 107; mentioned, 1

Jacoby, F., 109–110
Joel, K., 78
Just/unjust, 105
Justice, 95

Kahn, C. H., 29
Kirk, G. S., 29, 49, 88, 94, 97, 104–110, 117, 173
Kranz, W., 156, 168
Kühner, R., 145

Leucippus, *see* Atomists

Like(s), 8, 19, 169–173, 330
Like-to-like, 157, 169–171, 326
Limbs: human, 165; divine, 160, 325; monstrous, 157, 158, 170, 320, 321; acted on by Love, 170–171
Limit: in Anaximander, 29, 276; in Heraclitus, 90; in Melissus, 316–317; in Parmenides, 74, 312–313, 315–316; in Pythagoreanism, 245, 247, 338; in Xenophanes, 72–74; in Zeno's B3, 212; in division, 178, 203; of a moment, 182; on a par with things, 190
Living/dead, 38, 97–99
Logos, 89, 102–107
Love, 153, 156–174, 254–255, 319–326
Lumpe, A., 78
Lycophron, 1, 32
Lyons, J., 305

Macrocosm, 163, 165, 168. *See also* Cosmos
Male/female, 157–158, 321
Mansfeld, J., 144–145
Many: senses of, 2, 3, 21–22, 143, 189–193, 200, 251; the people, 87–88, 107; popular conception of, 177–178; Pythagorean conception of, 176–180, 203–205. *See also* Heaps; One; Separation
Marcovich, M., 108, 109
Mathematics, 85, 147, 334
Matter, 318, 324. *See also* Substrate
Meaning, 3–7, 11–12, 22–23, 270. *See also* Many; One; Senses (of words)
Melanippe, 64
Melissus: in general, 148–152; in relation to Diogenes, 239, 241–244, 337; one/many in, 148–152, 211; "the one" in, 71, 127, 150; on condensation-rarefaction, 44, 47–48, 149; on mixture, 317–318; on opposites, 293; on pain, 316; on "nothing from nothing," 340; on one, 316; on the Unlimited extension of Being, 148–150, 313, 316–317; on void and motion, 44, 49, 219, 241, 244, 333, 337–338; mentioned, 70, 311, 335
Microcosm, 155, 156, 163, 164, 168, 174
Milesians: in general, 24–65, 270–283; in Aristotle, 24–38, 40–43, 48–49, 50, 54–64, 271, 276; in Hippocrates, 48–50; in Plato, 50–56, 60; in relation to the Eclectics, 239, 241; in relation to Heraclitus, 89, 90, 100, 102, 108; in relation to Parmenides, 144, 234, 236, 249–250, 276–277; on the opposites, 52–53, 100, 281. *See also* Anaximander; Anaximenes; Thales

351

GENERAL INDEX

Mixture: in Anaxagoras, 241, 271; in Anaximander, 271; in Aristotle, 19, 162–163, 269, 270, 324; in Diogenes of Apollonia, 278–279; in Empedocles, 154, 155, 157, 161–163, 168–172, 241, 271, 325, 326; in Hippocrates, 162–163; in Melissus, 317–318; in Parmenides, 326
Moments, 180–184
Mondolfo, R., 107, 179
Monism: in the Eclectics, 238–244, 338; in the Eleatics, 51–56; in the Milesians, 36–44, 49–56, 239, 273–274, 276; in Plato's history of Being, 49–56, 280–281; in Simplicius, 273–274; in Xenophanes, 51–56, 83
Monotheism, 66, 76–84, 106–107, 288
Monsters, 157–159, 168, 170, 320–322
Motion: connected with plurality, 160, 175, 189, 322–323; connected with void, 44, 149, 152, 218; paradoxes in, 175–193, 328–338; denied on other grounds, 35, 71–72, 75, 137–140, 149–152, 251, 308, 312; asserted against the Eleatics, 35, 159–161, 219, 225, 241–242. *See also* Rest
Müller, C. W., 170–171
Munding, H., 167, 170
Musaeus, 54
Muses, 41, 50, 280–281
Myth, 39, 42, 54, 58, 77, 81, 107, 157, 159

Nicolaus of Damascus, 71, 72
Night, 45, 61, 122, 146, 272, 322
Not-Being: in Heraclitus, 118–119; in Melissus, 148–152, 317; in Parmenides, 112–127, 130–144, 163, 253–255, 302, 305–307, 309–311, 314; in Plato's *Parmenides*, 198–199, 209, 211; in Zeno, 317
Nothing from nothing, 253–255
Nous, 82, 88–89, 238, 254
Now, 129–130, 180–182, 188, 192
Null magnitudes, 200, 210–211
Number(s), 21, 247, 271, 338–339. *See also* One; Unit

O'Brien, D., 153, 160
Oceanus, 54, 56, 59, 283
Odd/even, 245–248, 338–339
One, the, 50, 71, 74, 83–84, 107, 127, 176, 197, 203, 207–209, 213, 285, 308; senses of, 1–4, 7–23, 100, 102, 149–151, 161–164, 168, 172–173, 194–195, 214, 215, 216, 251–252, 267, 268, 287, 295, 315, 325–326, 332; in number, 13, 17, 19, 89, 130, 131; in kind (species, form, genus, definition), 12–19, 98, 106, 163, 270; by analogy, 17–18, 269; strictly (truly), 23, 51, 210, 219, 252, 317, 335. *See also* Contact; Continuity; Glue; Homogeneity; Indivisibles; Like(s); Mixture; Same; Substrate. Convertible with Being, 8–11; a superfluous predicate, 23; substantive-hungry, 9, 16, 23, 150, 268; opposed to many, 1, 64, 65, 79, 85, 86, 107, 127, 143, 159, 160, 166, 271, 299, 314, 315, 322, 330, 331, and see below; being many, 1, 2, 63–64, 84, 101, 127, 143–144, 152, 174, 222, 235–236, 238, 242–243, 249–251; becoming many, 1, 42, 64–65, 84–86, 107–108, 127, 142–147, 151–155, 160–161, 173–174, 218, 225–234, 335; idiomatic uses of, in Greek, 77–78, 83, 144–146, 288. *See also* Opposites; Unit; Unity
Opposites: in Alcmaeon, 52; in Anaxagoras, 45–46; in Anaximander, 271, 278; in Aristotle, 8, 45–47, 60–61, 267, 322; in Diogenes, 278–279; in Empedocles, 163; in Heraclitus, 89–102, 105–108, 118–119, 251, 291–295, 298–299; in Hippocrates, 162–163; in the Milesians, 52–53; in Parmenides, 45, 122–123; in Philistion, 163; in the Pythagoreans, 52–53, 338; polar, 76, 254; mentioned, 274
Originative stuff, 40–48, 54, 58–61, 64, 276, 283. *See also* Element(s); Principle
Orpheus, 53–55, 282, 283, 326
Owen, G. E. L., 9, 120–129, 187–194, 200–202, 214

Pain, 149, 151, 316, 337
Panzerbieter, 155
Paradox: in Heraclitus, 41, 93, 99–100, 123, 251, 294, 295; in Parmenides, 122–123. *See also* Zeno
Parmenides, 48, 50–51, 64, 65, 67, 70, 71, 74, 75, 82–86, 94, 102, 109–148, 163, 218, 220, 224, 249–251, 253–255, 276–277, 278, 279, 285, 289, 301–316, 323, 333–337, 340; chronology, 109–127, 281, 301; proem, 144; programme, 127–131, 141, 308, 313; Way of Truth, 112, 113, 115, 124, 127, 131–144, 146, 147, 308–316; Seeming, 34, 45, 112, 119, 122–125, 144–148, 174, 272, 302, 314–315; answers to, 35–36, 42–43, 63, 174, 179, 219, 229–236, 237–238, 239–244, 245–247, 249–250, 277, 309, 312, 334,

335, 340; originality of, 42–43, 66; in Plato's *Parmenides*, 110, 150, 175, 179, 194–200, 202, 206–210, 281, 316, 317, 331

Parts: in Epicurus, 335; in Melissus, 150, 316–317; in Parmenides, 134–135; in Plato's *Parmenides*, 150, 196–197, 207–208, 211; in Zeno, 150, 178–182, 200–203. *See also* Division/divisibility

Passing-away: the term, 273; in Anaximenes, 48; in Atomism, 219–220, 230–233; in Diogenes, 42, 240–242; in Empedocles, 154–156, 167–168; denied by Empedocles to elements, 163; denied by Melissus, 148–151, 251; denied by Parmenides, 63, 124, 127, 130–144, 240, 251, 277

Patin, A., 111
Pherecydes, 52
Philistion, 163
Philo, 89
Philolaus, 244, 248, 338
Philoponus, 281, 330, 335
Pindar, 89, 95, 96, 270, 291
Place, 138–139, 190, 328
Plato: as historian, on Heraclitus, 50–52, 54–56, 107–108, 281, 283, 295; on the Milesians, 50–57, 59–60; on Parmenides, 84, 110, 113; on Xenophanes, 50–54, 66, 68–69, 70, 82–84, 289; on Zeno, 175, 179, 192, 193–200, 202, 206–213, 215–217, 330, 331; on theories of Being, 50–57, 280–281; as a philosopher, on unity, 10, 22; on "Being," 4, 10; on cosmogony, 254–255; on dense/rare, 44–45; on infinitesimals, 190; on kinesis, 187; on "living well," 5; on the timeless present, 309; Forms in, 139, 252; in relation to Empedocles, 320–321; in relation to Pythagoreanism, 246–247. *See also* Parmenides

Plotinus, 314
Pluralists, 47, 51–52, 177–178, 277, 337
Plutarch, 229, 232, 233, 290, 323
Pötscher, W., 78
Point(s), 178–184, 203, 212
Polybus, 316
Polycrates of Samos, 282
Polysemy, *see* Senses (of words)
Polytheism, 76–81, 106–107
Pores, 170, 219, 324
Porphyry, 224, 282, 333, 334
Potential/actual, 2, 19, 47, 163, 191, 192, 298
Powers, 45, 162. *See also* Opposites
Prester, 40, 41, 103, 298, 299

Priamel, 87
Principle: Anaximander's use of the term, 24, 28–30, 274–276; Aristotle's equivocation on the term, 29–30, 58–59, 60; function of, in the Milesians, 31, 33, 37–41, 57–62, 64; in the Eclectics, 49; in Xenophanes, 71, 285; mentioned, 90
Proclus, 138, 234, 330
Pseudo-Aristotle (author of MXG): on Gorgias, 214; on Melissus, 151, 317–318; on Xenophanes, 68–72, 79–81, 285; on physical replies to the Eleatics 239–240, 277
Pseudo-Galen: on Empedocles, 322; on Xenophanes, 67–70, 72, 285
Pseudo-Plutarch: on Diogenes, 243; on Empedocles, 157–158; on Xenophanes, 67, 70, 73, 80–81, 286, 289
Pythagoras, 88, 164, 282, 301
Pythagoreans: in relation to Alcmaeon, 246, 281, 339; in relation to Empedocles, 325, 326; in relation to Parmenides, 245–248, 250, 340; in relation to Plato, 216, 246, 247, 338; in relation to Zeno, 176–180, 186, 203–205, 215–217; theories of the unit, 244–248, 338–340; on numbers, 271, 338–339; on opposites, 52–53, 90, 245–246, 338; supposed atomism of, 186

Qualities, 6, 32, 47, 90, 91, 277. *See also* Attribute/subject

Raven, J. E., 110, 117, 145, 177–178, 245, 247
Reality, *see* Being
Reinhardt, K., 50, 80, 86, 98, 124
Repetition, 113, 156
Rest, 8, 71, 159–161, 324. *See also* Unmoved
Ross, Sir W. D., 12, 175, 228
Rough/smooth, 47
Russell, B., 208

Same: in Aristotle, 8–9, 17–19, 21, 269; in Heraclitus, 90–91, 93, 100, 102, 292, 294, 295; in Parmenides, 118–120, 124–126, 138, 143
Satiety/hunger, 106
Sceptics, 305, 328
Sea, 37, 40, 41, 91, 103, 105, 296–299. *See also* Oceanus; Water
Seeck, G. A., 160
Self-identity, 123, 141, 200, 211–212
Senses (bodily), 119, 122, 123, 144, 147, 149, 213. *See also* Common sense

Senses (of words), 2, 3, 23, 207–209, 212–213, 267. *See also* Many; Meaning; One

Separation: as discontinuity, 22, 202–205, 212–213, 218–222, 229–231, 236, 252; of earth and sky, 42, 64; of the elements, 154–155, 157, 161, 163, 166–170; of the opposites, 237, 271, 273, 274; of parts of an atom, 227, 229–233. *See also* Continuity

Sextus Empiricus, 67–71, 119, 252, 305, 328, 332

Sexuality, 95, 157, 164–166, 171, 319–322, 325. *See also* Aphrodite

Shorey, P., 112, 116

Similar(s), *see* Like(s)

Simplicius: on Anaxagoras, 45, 279, 280; on Anaximander, 28, 272–275; on Anaximenes, 273–274; on Atomism, 229, 233; on Diogenes, 240–241; on Empedocles, 157, 159, 164, 319–320, 322–324; on Melissus, 316–317; on Parmenides, 113–115, 127, 138, 253, 254, 272, 302, 315; on Thales, 36, 277; on Xenophanes, 66–72, 285–286; on Zeno, 175, 177, 191, 200, 202, 210, 223–224, 317, 333; sources of, 28, 36, 66, 70–72, 191, 273–274, 277, 280, 285–286, 323; cited, 226, 243, 267, 277

Sky, 42, 64, 73, 83, 84

Sleeping/waking, 92, 97–99

Snell, B., 54–57, 101

Socrates: Platonic, 4, 45, 175, 335; historical, 234

Solmsen, F., 256

Solon, 95, 290

Sphere: in Empedocles, 155–156, 160–164, 166–168, 171–172, 174, 271, 319, 323–325; in Parmenides, 140–141; in Xenophanes, 74–76, 81, 287

Sprague, Mrs. R. Kent, 113

Stein, H., 136

Steinhart, 53

Stobaeus, 70, 327

Stoics, 108, 288, 296, 298

Straight/crooked, 95

Strife: in Empedocles' cosmos, 153, 156–164, 167–172, 254–255, 319, 322–323; in Empedocles' living creatures, 156–157, 166, 167–168, 322; in Heraclitus, 100, 102, 108, 293–294; in the Milesians, 100, 293

Styx, 59

Substrate: in Anaxagoras, 271; in Aristotle, 46, 280; in Empedocles, 271; in Heraclitus, 102–106, 299; in the Milesians, 34–35, 38–42, 58–63, 239, 271, 274, 283; unity of, 18, 63–64, 102, 106, 251

Suda, 109, 110

Sun, 105, 286–287, 321–322

Syrianos, 8

Tannery, P., 180, 184–186

Tarán, L., 112, 113, 118–121, 128, 130, 132, 141, 144

Tartarus, 286

Tautology, 121–122, 277

Taylor, A. E., 16

Teichmüller, G., 103

Thales: in the Peripatetics, 37–38, 40, 43, 54–61, 272, 279, 283; in Plato, 51–52, 54–57, 59–60, 283; in relation to Anaximander, 28–29; in relation to Eclecticism, 239; in relation to Homer, 51, 54, 56, 59; in relation to the myths, 24, 39–40, 42, 58; on floating earth, 36–37, 57–58, 277; reasons for postulating a principle, 38–42; reasons for choice of water, 37–38; mentioned, 275, 290

Themis, 315

Themistius, 223, 333

Theo of Smyrna, 338, 339

Theodoret, 67–72

Theophrastus: on Anaximander, 28, 30, 61–62, 273–275; on Anaximenes, 273–274, 279; on Atomism, 236, 273, 335; on Diogenes, 243; on Empedocles, 158, 280, 324; on Heraclitus, 116, 274, 292, 295, 304; on the Milesians, 43, 61, 63; on Thales, 36–40, 277, 279; on Xenophanes, 66–76, 84, 285–287; as historian, 24–25, 27–28, 60–63, 273–275; depends on Aristotle, 24–25, 27, 273

Thinking and speaking, 120–122, 132, 134, 140, 142, 143, 253–254, 306–307

Thrasymachus, 5

Timelessness, 128–130, 309, 310, 312–313

Timon, 289

Uniformity, *see* Homogeneity

Unique(ness), 130–136, 142–143, 148–149, 152, 316, 317, 336

Unit, 12, 21, 22, 176–179, 201–204, 213, 338–340. *See also* One; Unity

Unity of the world (*or* of all things): in Atomism, 235–236; in Diogenes, 242–243; in the Eclectics, 48–50; in Heraclitus, 100–107, 293, 299; in the Milesians, 24–65, 99; in Xenophanes, 66–71, 76–84, 106, 249, 285–289

Unlimited, Anaximander's: in Aristotle's scheme of causes, 61–62, 283–284; in cosmogony, 42; as mixture, 25, 271; as principle, 28, 30–31, 274–276; mentioned, 24. *See also* Infinite; Melissus; Xenophanes

Unmoved: in Parmenides, 34, 123, 136–139, 142, 312; in Xenophanes, 68, 71–72, 75–76; includes "unchanged," 34, 136, 138, 142, 312; mentioned, 218. *See also* Rest

Untersteiner, M., 66

Van Leeuwen, J., 145
Varro, 321
Vlastos, G., 40, 94, 180, 186, 190, 211
Void: in Atomism, 218–222, 226–227, 229–231, 234, 235, 333–334, 337–338; in Diogenes, 241, 337; in Empedocles, 163; in Melissus, 44, 149, 152, 219, 337–338; in Parmenides, 45, 128, 130, 134–136, 311; in the Pythagoreans, 203; in condensation-rarefaction, 44–48. *See also* Motion

War/peace, 106, 108
Water: in Anaximenes, 279; in Empedocles, 163, 171, 321; in Heraclitus, 91, 103, 296–299; in Hippo, 49; in Hippocrates' attack on monism, 48–50; in Ionian physics, 272; in Thales, 24, 33, 36–38, 40, 42, 54–60, 61, 283; in Xenophanes, 40–41, 278
Wet/dry: in Alcmaeon, 52, 281; in Anaximander, 53; in Diogenes, 35, 279, 338; in Heraclitus, 92–93, 99; in the Milesians, 52–53; in the Pythagoreans, 52; in Thales, 37–38
Whole(ness): in Aristotle, 13, 15–17, 20, 268–269; in Empedocles, 161, 164–168, 171–172, 174, 324–325; in Heraclitus, 97, 101, 294–295; in Hippocrates, 162, 270; in Melissus, 150; in Parmenides, 82–83, 124, 127–128, 130, 134, 136, 138–140, 142–143, 289, 308, 312; in Plato's *Parmenides*, 196, 207–208, 211; related to continuity, 15–17, 20, 22, 97, 101, 124, 128, 130, 134, 136, 158, 172, 269, 294, 308; related to uniformity, 82, 171–172, 270; opposed to heap, 16, 164; natural or organic, 16, 164, 168. *See also* Continuity
Whole-natured: in Empedocles, 157–158, 319–322; in Aristotle, 158

Wilamowitz-Moellendorf, U. von, 76
Winter/summer, 106
Wisdom, 87–89, 290–291

Xenocrates, 186
Xenophanes: in Aristotle, 66, 71, 74, 78, 82–84, 272, 286–287, 289; in Clement of Alexandria, 77, 82, 288; in Plato, 50–54, 56, 66, 70, 82–83, 280, 289; in Simplicius, 66–72, 285–286; in Theophrastus, 66–76, 84, 285–287; assimilated to the Eleatics, 67, 70, 71, 74, 75, 79, 285; influence on Euripides, 80–81; in relation to Heraclitus, 106, 110, 288, 300; compared to the Milesians, 40–41, 278; one/many in, 84–85, 250; use of "one" in, 76–78, 83–84, 288; on unity of world or god, 67–71, 76–84, 106, 249, 285–289; on equation of world and god, 71, 74–75, 83–84, 288–289; on limit/unlimited, 72–74, 285–287; on motion/rest, 71–72, 75–76; on sphericity of the god, 74–76, 81, 287; on meteorology, 73–74, 286–287, 288–289; chronology of, 281–282
Xuthus, 44

Young/old, 92, 99

Zeller, E., 176, 205
Zeno of Citium, 327
Zeno of Elea, 2, 150, 163, 175–217, 218–225, 229, 231, 242, 244, 249–252, 267, 317, 321, 327–335; confused with Empedocles, 321, 327; confused with Zeno of Citium, 327; hypothetical anti-Pythagorean intent, 176–189; arguments against plurality, 200–217, 218–225; arguments against motion, 180–189; Achilles, 180, 183, 184, 189–190, 192, 200, 202, 329, 330; Dichotomy (Racecourse), 175, 180, 183, 184, 189–190, 192, 202, 210, 329, 330, 333–334; Flying Arrow, 139, 180–183, 188, 327, 328–329; Stadium, 180, 183, 184–189, 190, 192, 327, 328–329; Millet-seed, 190–191; Place, 190; book(s) of, 175–176, 179, 194, 329, 330; number of arguments, 191; order of arguments, 327
Zeus, 77, 78, 95, 96, 106, 107, 300
Zoogony, 154, 156–159, 165, 167, 170, 278, 321–322

355

THE CENTER FOR HELLENIC STUDIES

The Center
for Hellenic Studies, located
at 3100 Whitehaven Street, Washington, D.C.,
is a residential center for research in the
fields of ancient Greek history, literature, and
philosophy. The land upon which the Center
stands was devised to the Old Dominion
Foundation by Marie Beale and the Center
was established and endowed in 1961 by a
grant from the Old Dominion Foundation
to the Trustees for Harvard University.
Eight resident fellows are appointed each
year, from America and from abroad; the
publications of the Center present work begun
or completed by them during their tenure
of the fellowship.

PUBLICATIONS OF THE CENTER FOR HELLENIC STUDIES

Theocritus' Coan Pastorals: A Poetry Book, by Gilbert Lawall, 1967
Theopompus and Fifth-Century Athens, by W. Robert Connor, 1968
Formula, Character, and Context: Studies in Homeric, Old English, and Old Testament Poetry, by William Whallon, 1969
One and Many in Presocratic Philosophy, by Michael C. Stokes, 1971